FIFTH EDITION

CRITICAL ENCOUNTERS WITH TEXTS
— FINDING A PLACE TO STAND —

MARGARET HIMLEY
ANNE FITZSIMMONS

Custom Publishing

New York   Boston   San Francisco
London   Toronto   Sydney   Tokyo   Singapore   Madrid
Mexico City   Munich   Paris   Cape Town   Hong Kong   Montreal

Cover Art: 1970, *Gay Liberation Poster*. Photograph by Peter Hujar. Courtesy of the Matthew Marks Gallery, NY and the Estate of Peter Hujar.

Printed in the United States of America

10 9 8 7 6 5 4 3 2 1

2009240061

LR/MC

**Pearson
Custom Publishing**
is a division of

www.pearsonhighered.com

ISBN 10: 0-558-22649-3
ISBN 13: 978-0-558-22649-7

Copyright Acknowledgments

"The Politics of Staring: Visual Rhetorics of Disability in Popular Photography," by Rosemarie Garland-Thomson, reprinted from *Disability Studies: Enabling the Humanities,* edited by Sharon L. Snyder, Brenda Jo Brueggemann, and Rosemarie Garland-Thomson (2002), Modern Language Association of America.

Photo of Judith E. Heumann, courtesy of the United States Department of Education.

"Changing the Face of Poverty: Nonprofits and the Problem of Representation," by Diana George, reprinted from *Popular Literacy* (2001), by permission of University of Pittsburgh Press.

"Attacks on the Homeless Rise, With Youths Mostly to Blame," by Amy Green, reprinted from the *New York Times,* February 15, 2008, by permission of PARS International Corporation.

"Priorities," by Jose Marcial Guerrero, reprinted from *Xispas Magazine* (2005), Tia Chucha Press.

"A Story About the Body," by Robert Hass, reprinted from *Human Wishes* (1989), by permission of HarperCollins Publishers, Inc.

"A Dumped Car," by Gay Hawkins, reprinted from *The Ethics of Waste,* by permission of Rowman & Littlefield Publishers, Inc.

"From Poster Child to Protester," by Laura Hershey, reprinted from *Spectacle* (spring/summer 1997), by permission of the author.

"Seeing and Making Culture: Representing the Poor," by bell hooks, reprinted from *Outlaw Culture: Resisting Representations* (1994), by permission of Taylor & Francis.

"Selling Hot Pussy: Representations of Black Female Sexuality in the Cultural Marketplace," by bell hooks, reprinted from *Black Looks: Race and Representation* (1992), by permission of South End Press.

"I, Too," by Langston Hughes, reprinted from *Selected Poems of Langston Hughes,* by permission of Random House, Inc.

"Nobody Mean More to Me Than You and the Future Life of Willie Jordan," by June Jordan (1995), by permission of The June Jordan Estate.

"Helping Students Use Textual Sources Persuasively," by Margaret Kantz, reprinted from *College English* 52, no. 1 (January 1990), by permission of National Council of Teachers of English.

"Girl," by Jamaica Kincaid, reprinted from *At the Bottom of the River* (2000), by permission of Farrar, Straus & Giroux.

"When Girls Will Be Boys," by Alissa Quart, reprinted from the *New York Times Magazine* (March 16, 2008), by permission of The New York Times Magazine.

"Maps of the Everyday: Habitual Pathways and Contested Places," by Nedra Reynolds, reprinted from *Geographies of Writing: Inhabiting Places and Encountering Differences* (2007), by permission of Southern Illinois University Press.

"Ordnance Survey Map of Leeds Proper," reprinted from *Geographies of Writing: Inhabiting Places and Encountering Differences* (2007), Her Majesty's Stationery Office.

Photo: "Hyde Park Cinema," by Randy Blackburn, reprinted from *Geographies of Writing: Inhabiting Places and Encountering Differences* (2007).

Photo: "A Small Section of Brudnell Road, Hyde Park," by Randy Blackburn, reprinted from *Geographies of Writing: Inhabiting Places and Encountering Differences* (2007).

Photo: "A Part of Little London," by Randy Blackburn, reprinted from *Geographies of Writing: Inhabiting Places and Encountering Differences* (2007).

"The 1963 Hip-Hop Machine: Hip-Hop Pedagogy as Composition," by Jeff Rice, reprinted from *College Composition and Communication* 54, no. 3 (February 2003), by permission of College Composition and Communication.

"The Veil," by Marjane Satrapi, reprinted from *Persepolis: The Story of a Childhood* (2003), by permission of Pantheon Books, a division of Random House, Inc.

Excerpt from *Geographies of Exclusion* by David Sibley (1995), by permission of Taylor & Francis.

"Broken Sentences: Women in Prison Tell Their Stories Straight," by Anna Deavere Smith, reprinted from *The New Yorker*, February 26 and March 4, 1996, by permission of Watkins/Loomis Agency.

"Black English/Ebonics: What It Be Like?" by Geneva Smitherman, reprinted from *The Real Ebonics Debate: Power, Language, and the Education of African American Children* (1998), by permission of the author.

"The Photographs ARE Us," by Susan Sontag, reprinted from *New York Times Magazine*, May 23, 2004, The Wiley Agency.

Photo of an Iraqi detainee, reprinted from "The Photographs ARE Us", Polaris Images Corporation.

Photo of sadomasochism, reprinted from "The Photographs ARE Us", New York Times Magazine.

"Running in Ordinary Time," by Kathleen Stewart, reprinted from *Ordinary Affects* (2007), by permission of Duke University Press.

"Politics of the Ordinary," by Kathleen Stewart, reprinted from *Ordinary Affects* (2007), by permission of Duke University Press.

"Home Is Where the Heart Is," by Kathleen Stewart, reprinted from *Ordinary Affects* (2007), by permission of Duke University Press.

"Odd Moments," by Kathleen Stewart, reprinted from *Ordinary Affects* (2007), by permission of Duke University Press.

"My Five-Paragraph-Theme Theme," by Ed White, reprinted from *College Composition and Communication* 59, no. 3 (February 2008), by permission of College Composition and Communication.

"Trash and Treasure: The Gleaners and I," by Jake Wilson, reprinted from *Senses of Cinema,* no. 23 (NovemberDecember 2002), Senses of Cinema, Inc.

"A Boy's Life: For Matthew Shepard's Killers, What Does it Mean to Pass as a Man?," by JoAnn Wypijewski, reprinted from *Harper's Magazine* (September 1999), by permission of Harper's Magazine.

Contents

Contents

Finding a Place to Stand
Writing, Reading, and Researching
in a Transnational World

Margaret Himley & Anne Fitzsimmons

The Scene of Writing

> *And in this scene, writing favors immediacy, quickness, associative leaps, and a fluid and flexible sense of correctness (Lunsford 8).*

On May 1, 2008, in Syracuse, NY, Margaret opens up the daily paper, called *The Post-Standard,* and reads the front page. The lead story is the second in an occasional series looking at childcare in Central New York, and reports on a family no longer able to pay for child care when, ironically, both parents began to earn more money. The additional $4000 to their annual income meant they no longer qualified for the childcare assistance they previously received (A-1). Alongside of this story are other stories about stagnation in the economy and fear of recession.

There are also the inevitable articles and editorials about the Presidential election, specifically Hillary Rodham Clinton and Barack Obama continuing to do battle for the Democratic nomination. Obama is shifting his stump speech to speak more about the American dream (A-6), as he approaches the primaries in Indiana and North Carolina, and columnist Thomas L. Friedman takes Clinton and McCain to task for what he deems a "ridiculous" idea to suspend the federal excise tax on gasoline over the summer (A-10).

New York State's new Governor David Paterson calls for reducing the number of local government entities (A-8), and Penguin Group announces a new book "about the rise and stunning decline" of former Governor Elliot Spitzer, who resigned recently over allegations about his connections to a call girl ring (A-8).

And there is of course news about the war in Iraq. The death toll of US soldiers hits a seven-month high as the Iraqi civilian death toll remains high. The number of US military personnel who have died since the US-led invasion in 2003 is at 4,061 (A-9).

This is the beginning of a typical reading day, as Margaret works to stay aware of local, national, and global events; to follow up on interests of her own; to gather the information she needs to analyze events and reach decisions about what she might want to do in response, if anything. She may seek more information online, or from other sources of news, and she's likely to talk about these events with friends and colleagues to get their take on things. Whether in Indiana or Iraq, these events matter to her, connect to her life, require some research, and are entangled with one another in urgent and complicated ways.

Margaret will save articles electronically, take notes for future writing, use online resources to follow up on other references, order a book from Amazon, and write more on a book project she has initiated. She toys again with the idea of starting a blog as a way to communicate early versions of her ideas and to get feedback from folks interested in similar topics and questions. This is the contemporary scene of writing—transnational, interactive, complex, and mediated by information technologies and mass communication.

Entangled with History

> *. . . never before have individual histories (because of their necessary relations with space, image and consumption) been so deeply entangled with general history (Augé 119).*

We are living in a world that French sociologist Marc Augé has called the "supermodern" (29) and other scholars have labeled the "transnational." We live within a density of present events with fewer and fewer traditional frameworks to hold them all together. We have nearly instant access to stories and images and events from around the globe, relayed by satellites or transmitted by digital technologies. We grow familiar with references to places and figures from Moscow to Mumbai, beamed daily into our living rooms or our iPhones, even if we don't really know all that much about them. And we ourselves are often on the move— in transit, out of place—as students abroad, as tourists, as immigrants, as refugees and asylum seekers, as transnational business people, as global nomads or citizens of the world.

Just to get through the day we may have to grasp the interconnected and complex systems that organize the ordinary actions of our lives. Steve Tarpin, the owner of Steve's Authentic Key Lime Pies in Brooklyn, NY, for example, has had to explain to his customers why the price of his pies has gone from $20 to $25 through an analysis of global economics: the increase, he explains, is caused by "dairy prices driven higher by conglomerates buying up military supplies, heat waves in Europe and California, demand from emerging markets and the weak dollar" (Simon, A-1).

As Robert Samuels points out in an article about higher education and social change, colleges and universities now have a big job to do, as they teach students about these complex interconnections and about how to explore them on their own. How many people know, he illustrates with just one such example, "that one of the leading causes of poverty in Africa is the high level of subsidies that American and European governments pay domestic farmers to produce crops at an artificially cheap rate" (p. 239)? Or, at the beginning of the Iraq War in March 2003, why did so many of us in the U.S. know little more about Iraq than phrases about Saddam Hussein as a madman and despot and a vague sense of wars between Iraq and Iran and a slight awareness that the country has rich oil deposits? We have had to get up to speed quickly, if we want to understand the effects and the implications of this new war on ourselves, on friends or family, especially those called up to fight in the war, and on our own economic and political future.

It is, of course, remarkably challenging to make sense of this superabundance of information, to determine the values and beliefs and investments that inform it, to assess the credibility of sites and sources, and most importantly to locate ourselves in this endlessly expanding network of information. As Marc Augé notes above, our lives are deeply entangled with others across the globe, and we have to work hard to make sense of it and to find a place to stand, even temporarily.

We argue in this book that writers succeed best when they approach topics of inquiry from this idea of multiple perspectives and when they recognize the complexity, history, and entanglement of information, ideas, images, and texts. Postcolonial writer Amitava Kumar illustrates what it means to put multiple perspectives into dialogue:

> When Charles Barkley defends his aggressiveness against Angolan players at an Olympic game by saying, 'It's a ghetto thing, you won't understand,' he needs to be heard. At the same time, Barkley needs to understand too that there are ways of broaching historical links with the Angolans that would help explain what put him in the ghetto in the first place. Or, dammit, just help explain why the folks King Charles grew up with remain in the ghetto while he is a star selling his powerful body and a brand of cologne on TV (p. 145).

From one perspective, anyone not from a U.S. ghetto may not understand Barkley's aggressiveness against the Angolan players, because people's particular experiences are in many ways so different. From another perspective, however, black U.S. ghettos have been produced by the same historical forces, such as slavery and colonization, that have shaped the African country of Angola. That's also true, and produces some common ground. But yet from a third perspective, what requires explaining is why we in the U.S. reward athletes in the regal way that we do. Thus, this one statement from Charles Barkley opens up larger, interconnected topics and perspectives and calls forth different experiences and histories.

Transformed by Technology

. . . a new rhetoric and writing as epistemic, performative, multivocal, multimodal, and multimediated (Lunsford 8).

If we are to become actively and critically informed, we may choose to listen not only to CNN but also to NPR, to read editorials not only in the local paper but also in *The Independent* from Britain online, and to study not only traditional history books but also contemporary websites and blogs and databases. We talk with friends and family in person and through Skype. We watch films and TV and log on to the Internet, and consume with interest and often pleasure images and ideas from across the globe that provoke us to re-think and re-imagine our own lives and the communities we are a part of, such as various environmental groups or LGBT political organizations or religious groups. As Arjun Appadurai claims, this interconnected and highly mediated world offers "new resources and new disciplines for the construction of imagined selves and imagined worlds" (3) as part of our everyday life, opening up new horizons of possibility. From US students watching soap operas and reality TV, to Muslim families gathering around tape recorders and listening to the speeches of Islamic leaders, we turn to these new and ever present media to stir our imaginations and produce new sodalities (Appadurai 7).

No longer alone in a garret, drafting with paper and pen, creating text out of her own knowledge or experience, the writer now faces a networked computer screen and has access to text-making possibilities and information-accessing potential and communication possibilities undreamed of in the not very distant past. Search engines have dramatically expanded our ability to read widely, as we have thorough and systemic access to what often seems like unlimited information on endless topics. We can raid a nearly infinite number and variety of texts as we construct our own. It's remarkably easy to import an image of the Iraq War, or pull up the exact date of Michael Jordan's retirement from the Bulls, or determine which countries have legalized same-sex marriage, or locate a working definition of human cloning, or find out what editorials in Malaysia are saying about the US's role in the global economy. We find old friends and make new ones on social networking sites, and we are aware of events happening simultaneously through newsbreaks on our computer screens and Blackberries.

In this new transnational and highly mediated world, how do writers identify purposes, analyze audiences, and achieve power and authority?

We must learn to read, write, talk, and research broadly and actively to know what is going on and to know how to communicate to others—to prepare to post a blog entry, to decide how to vote in the next election, to develop plans to expand a business across the globe, to design curriculum for high school students, to search for a cure for HIV/AIDS, to pitch a new television show, to decide to enlist in the military or not, or to initiate a fundraiser for a non-profit organization that matters to us.

This is the world in which we live and work and act. This is the scene in which we write for all kinds of reasons: to express ourselves; to explore ideas and possibilities; to produce a wider and wider range of texts, from formal academic essays to power point presentations to i-movies; to engage with others, those we know and those we don't; and to communicate to potentially far flung audiences in the most effective and persuasive ways possible.

It's an exciting new scene of writing—and this book is designed to give you a jumpstart on these challenges and possibilities, for your success in college and in the world beyond.

Reading

> *The individual production of meaning is thus more necessary than ever (Augé 37).*

This book offers essays, poems, newspaper articles, scholarly articles, images, and visual essays as texts to encounter. Unlike other readers, where the texts have been organized for you under predetermined topics, we present these texts as starting points for your own and your class's further reading and exploration—and of course for writing—based on the ways you put these texts to use. The book is loosely structured around a number of themes: language and identity, academic writing, gender and sexuality, the body, popular culture, publics and counter-publics, resistance and dissent, raced encounters, representation, and nature and the environment. But the themes are fluid, and a number of texts can be slotted in multiple thematic categories.

Just like in the real world, your job—and your opportunity—is to jump in, perhaps do a little quick and dirty research about the author or the topic, read the texts closely and critically and inventively, make connections with other readings and with your own experience and expertise, and trace out a line of inquiry across the readings that leads to an interesting, perhaps even an important analysis and argument of your own. This is what we mean by finding, even temporarily, a place to stand as a writer, reader, and researcher.

We hope that the readings toss you a *curveball,* and make you think, get angry, fret, wonder, and want to read further. You may need to do some background reading, you may need to pursue references in the bibliography, you may want to look at different perspectives in the library or online, you may want to interview someone on campus or test these ideas out on your housemates or friends, or you may want to do some research of your own by observing a site or constructing a classroom survey or asking your family about their history. Your teacher is likely to provide suggestions and insight and response to help you shape your project. Your classmates are likely to have other perspectives and responses.

We encourage you not to worry too much if you don't understand something or if the reference is outside of your experience in some way or you feel overwhelmed at times. That's all part of critical encounters and critical learning. One scholar, realizing she had neglected to include some important research in her first book, referred to her shame as "fruitful embarrassment" (Cohn and Enloe 1194). We agree. Think of those moments of surprise ("I *never* thought of trash that way before!") or suspicion ("I don't believe it's possible to live as an entirely separate gender.") or startling realization ("Who knew that art could be so subversive?!") as the chance to think twice about something, to learn from others, to reconsider a decision or claim or belief, even to re-examine ideas you have taken for granted all your life.

Of course it is risky to draw attention to what you don't know, especially in an academic environment where passing the test, getting it right, knowing the answer become the markers of success. But if we don't allow for questioning and inquiring, if the answers are always worth more than the questions, then we quickly limit the range of ideas we can work with.

Think about it: the more you read, the more you come in contact with views, language, experiences, and claims that take you beyond what you already know and that compel you outside of yourself. Soon, the embarrassment of not knowing will be replaced by the confidence of having filled in gaps and understanding something in a new or more complex way. The willingness to address what you don't know can be a most generative and empowering trait, and it is bound to impact your ability to engage with topics in writing more confidently and more complexly.

Framed as Encounter

> At one level, we can think about encounters as face-to-face meetings.
> . . . More generally, a meeting suggests a coming together of at least
> two elements. For example, we can think of reading as a meeting
> between reader and text (Ahmed 7).

In this book we frame writing, reading, and researching as an *encounter*. We have borrowed this trope from theorist Sara Ahmed, who defines an encounter as "a meeting, but a meeting which involves surprise and conflict" (6). Very often these encounters happen face-to-face, but reading is also an encounter between the reader and the text.

Think about meeting someone new for the first time. We make quick judgments about who they are, where they are from, whether we will like them or not, based on their clothes, their age, their (apparent) ethnicity or sexuality, their way of speaking, their stance and gestures. Sometimes these decisions are conscious, and sometimes they are what cognitive psychologists call "fast and frugal" (cited in Gladwell, p. 11)—that is, they happen in the blink of an eye. Sometimes those judgments prove accurate, and sometimes they reveal to us how wrong we are, how limited our knowledge and perspective can be. Sometimes we feel attracted to this new person, eager to get to know them better; sometimes we feel threatened or indifferent.

Produced at a particular moment, these encounters are framed by history and geography. If we grew up in a middle class suburban home in the 1950's in the US, we may have learned a *Donna Reed-Father Knows Best* idea about what families should look like, and if we visit a family from a different class or country, we may be quite startled by and perhaps judgmental about other versions of family. If we grew up in a part of the country where there were no open lesbian or gay men or transgender folks, when we meet one for the first time, we may be quite startled by and judgmental about these other versions of sexuality. If we grew up in a Christian religious tradition, that first encounter with Islam or Judaism may startle and provoke in similar ways. Of course we always hope to assert our openness to difference and our eagerness to learn about others, but it takes real effort and real time to be open and eager, because we also have to be willing to be unsettled.

By framing reading as an encounter, we are interested in exploring what happens when we meet someone from a different country or different class, or when we walk into a neighborhood where we suddenly feel out of place, or when we read about a history of struggle against oppression that has been unknown to us, or when we work to cross lines of racial difference, or when we want to learn about different sexual orientations or gender identities.

Meeting a text for the first time is this encounter with the familiar and the unfamiliar, the known and the unknown, the certain and the uncertain. Sometimes we know exactly what a writer means. At other times, we may not understand a word, or we can't seem to get the argument, or we fail to recognize a reference, or we just can't discern the perspective of the authors. We hit the limits of our knowledge and our experience. We find ourselves a bit lost as we follow the links in a web page or hunt up sources referenced in a bibliography or try to map the history of an idea or claim.

Living in a transnational world—as student, as scholar, as professional, as citizen—is full of these encounters with other people, other perspectives, other histories, other geographies, and finally other visions of ourselves. So in this book we propose starting the writing process from the moment of encounter—from that moment that unsettles us, that brings us up against what we don't know or don't know well, that challenges our sense of place in the world, but that motivates us to respond, to encounter others with generosity and humility, to learn more, and to have our say.

We believe this is the kind of person and the kind of writer, reader, and researcher that you want to be—one open to the challenges, resources, possibilities, and surprises of an increasingly transnational, mediated, and interconnected world.

Sometimes the readings are challenging because they are academic, and you will encounter disciplinary knowledges and discourses that you, perhaps as a class, will have to take some time to understand. As a complex theoretical text, Sara Ahmed's "Recognising Strangers" requires and rewards more than one reading. Geraldine Pratt's "Abandoned Women and Spaces of the Exception" drops you into a disciplinary conversation in Geography that makes you feel like a party crasher who doesn't know what's going on or who's who, but who decides to stick around because it looks like fun.

Sometimes the readings are challenging because they present unconventional perspectives or uncommon topics, which may unsettle your assumptions about the body, about language, about sexuality and gender, about representation. Anna Deavere Smith finds beauty in the "Broken Sentences" of woman in prison. Gay Hawkins challenges our easy conversion of objects into waste—the short life of the plastic cup chucked on the way out of the football stadium—in "A Dumped Car." And Kathleen Stewart's short pieces from *Ordinary Affects* make big anthropological claims out of the little moments of everyday life. You may find yourself agreeing or disagreeing, and in both cases you'll learn more by looking at the assumptions that drive the argument and claims.

Sometimes the readings are challenging because, at first, they don't seem interesting or relevant to you. If you are not intersexed, for example, you might question why you should have to read Cheryl Chase's essay "Hermaphrodites with Attitude."

We'll ask you to find points of entry by analyzing assumptions in the text: what does it say about being male or female or about a binary gender system supposedly grounded in the body? What does it claim about the role of doctors in our society, or the possibilities for medical-scientific interventions that might revolutionize the body? How might this topic relate to cosmetic surgery or designer babies?

We also encourage you to compare and contrast readings, and to look for connections across them. Say you read Hawkins' "A Dumped Car," a chapter in which she advocates for a new way of looking at and "imagining" waste. In the course of the text she does a close reading of Agnes Varda's documentary *The Gleaners and I*, which is reviewed by Jake Wilson in "Trash and Treasure: *The Gleaners and I*" in this book. If you're really adventurous or curious, you might rent the movie and develop ideas and perspectives of your own about Varda's approach to the topic, or about waste and our relationship to it. You might work closely with the two articles, juxtaposing Hawkins' claims about Varda's film with Wilson's, and ask yourself, "Where do the two writers' ideas overlap?" You might also attend to the key words and concepts that characterize Hawkins' analysis of the film, and compare them with Wilson's. And finally, you might read Anna McCarthy's short, powerful piece "Rodents," and place it in the context of the other texts: is McCarthy's argument about the "pestilence" of electronic waste persuasive after reading Hawkins and after screening Varda? Lots of questions, lots of connections, lots of concepts that you can carry with you into new projects of your own.

Thus we present the readings in this book as encounters that are meant to provoke thought, to provide key concepts and ideas, and to initiate work. We do not expect you to master or memorize these readings, but to engage energetically with them, muck around in them, learn something new, take up concepts and lines of argument, and then put them to use them in your own writing projects. We are leaving the work and the excitement of the journey—getting lost, finding new connections, making decisions about what it is important to know and to say—up to you and to your class, though we will provide guideposts along the way.

Reading inventively—reading widely, reading critically, reading passionately, reading for perspective and purpose, reading as a researcher—is fundamental to effective and exciting writing in the supermodern and transnational world you inhabit.

Five Reading Practices

[1] Close Reading

Sometimes you have to read *closely* in order to understand, perhaps even memorize the content, as when preparing for the CPA exam or mastering the intricacies of stem cell biology.

For example, an essay early in the reader is a chapter entitled "Recognising Strangers" from *Strange Encounters: Embodied Others in Post-Coloniality* by Sara Ahmed—and it is definitely challenging. A close reading of the first paragraph will get you off to a strong start:

> *How do you recognise a stranger? To ask such a question, is to challenge the assumption that the stranger is the one we simply fail to recognise, that the stranger is simply* any-body *whom we do not*

> *know. It is to suggest that the stranger is* some-body *whom we have* already recognised *in the very moment in which they are 'seen' or 'faced' as a stranger. The figure of the stranger is far from simply being strange; it is a figure that is painfully familiar in that very strange/r/ness. The stranger has already come too close; the stranger is 'in my face.' The stranger then is not simply the one whom we have not yet encountered, but the one whom we have already encountered, or already faced. The stranger comes to be faced as a form of recognition: we recognise somebody* as a stranger, *rather than simply failing to recognise them.*

What a strange text, you might reasonably assert! Ahmed starts with a question that seems almost silly, because it challenges our commonsensical idea that the world is divided into people we know and people we do not know, or 'strangers.' And then she writes a number of variations on this question. She is developing a theoretical or conceptual argument around the key phrase 'strange encounters.' Here are some close reading strategies you might use to trace out this argument:

- **Look up key words in the dictionary.**

  For example, "recognize" (the U.S. spelling) means "1. To know to be something that has been perceived before: *recognize a face.* 2. To know or identify from past experience or knowledge: *recognize hostility*.

  That helps. If I 'recognize' you as a friend, or a stranger, or an enemy, or an ally, it is because I already know something about friends and strangers and enemies and allies, and I can put you in one of those categories. We recognize by dress, skin color, body posture that which is not of 'us'—but which is still known as 'strange.' So instead of hitting the limits of my knowledge in this encounter, I'm actually using the knowledge I already have.

- **Invent an example.**

  For example, I might hear a knock at my door, open the door, and worry because the person is a stranger. If I open the door and begin to worry, it might be because the person is not only unknown to me individually, but seems somehow out of place. A woman in an apron who could be a new neighbor is less likely to be recognized as a stranger, perhaps, than a woman poorly dressed and carrying lots of old grocery bags. One seems to belong; one seems to threaten, to be out place, to not belong. Why? Because I have a sense of who belongs in my neighborhood and who doesn't, based on class, maybe, or race, or nationality.

- **Look at words in italics or otherwise emphasized.**

  Ahmed marks a distinction between '*any-body*' and '*some-body*.' Ask yourself why she has hyphenated the two words? What does that accomplish? She takes two ordinary, everyday pronouns and alters their meaning by separating 'any' and 'some' from 'body.' Hmmm, 'body'—this kind of body versus that kind of body. 'Anybody' as undifferentiated—it could be 'anybody.' 'Somebody' becomes differentiated from all those anybodies.

That seems important because it takes us back to the idea of recognizing, of seeing patterns or hierarchies in masses.

- **Analyze the structure of the paragraph.**

   In this case, Ahmed starts with a question and provides an answer in the last sentence.

- **Paraphrase.**

   Select a sentence or a phrase and try to put it in your own words. For example, "The stranger then is not simply the one whom we have not yet encountered, but the one whom we have already encountered, or already faced" might be paraphrased as "We only label someone a stranger if we already know who strangers are likely to be."

- **Summarize.**

   Here's one way to summarize this paragraph: Ahmed takes a common-sense understanding of who becomes figured as 'the stranger' and asks questions about it in several ways. In this way she comes to argue that 'strangers' are people for whom we already have a recognizable category system. The figure of the stranger does not take us to the end of our knowledge, but rather makes visible how our knowledge works.

[2] Critical Reading

Sometimes we have to read *critically* in order to evaluate a methodology or argument, as when we are analyzing the effects of a national tax cut on the poor or arguing for or against Spike Lee as a talented filmmaker.

For example, in the essay "Changing the Face of Poverty: Nonprofits and the Problem of Representation," Diana George begins with a description of the types of images—most often of people in despair—nonprofit organizations use to persuade Americans to contribute money to those in need. George goes on to argue why such images and appeals are problematic, and then offers suggestions for alternative and ultimately more effective ways of representing poverty. Here are some critical reading strategies you might use to trace out and evaluate the claims:

- **Map out the essay.**

   Notice that the essay is divided into four sections (with a space separating each section). The essay opens in section one with George contextualizing what she sees as a "problem" of representation and then outlining her project for the rest of the essay. In the second section George provides historical background for representations of the poor as well as advocacy efforts. In the third section George refines and focuses her argument through a close analysis of one nonprofit organization. And in the concluding section George points to efforts of nonprofits to break away from the stereotyped representations of the needy in order to depict a broader, more complex picture of poverty.

- **Ask questions.**

  Mark places in the essay that raise questions for you—for example, what *are* the causes of poverty and homelessness in the US? What are the goals of nonprofits in addressing people's needs? What exactly constitutes "poverty" or the poverty line in the US?

- **Raise challenges.**

  Mark places in the essay that you think are or might be wrong. Is George's claim that representations of the poor that elicit sympathy are ultimately ineffective valid and adequately supported? Does the historical background strengthen her argument? Does George paint a broad or full enough picture of poverty and representation in the US? And in what ways is her argument, now over ten years old, still timely—or not?

- **Draw examples or counter-examples.**

  Think back to images of poverty or actual impoverishment you have witnessed or heard about—and test the theories and claims in George's essay against your own experiences and knowledges.

- **Talk with others.**

  Ask your roommate or your friends or your parents or your classmates what they think about poverty in the US. Tell them about George's essay and listen to their responses. Figure out what that teaches you.

- **Reread the essay.**

  Come back to the essay with greater awareness, more knowledge, fuller context, and some questions and ideas of your own.

- **Take a stand.**

  Imagine that you have been asked to write a review of this essay: How would you summarize it? How would you assess it? What is strong? What is weak or missing? What is your final evaluation of the essay and its argument?

[3] Inventive Reading

Sometimes you have to read *inventively,* looking for the larger frameworks or debates or conversations that a text is embedded in and responding to. An article in the newspaper about the cholera epidemic in Zimbabwe in the southern part of the continent of Africa, for example, may raise questions for you about this country's history as a British colony, its role in African nationalism and struggles for independence, the contested leadership of Robert Mugabe, and current humanitarian crises. What, you might reasonably ask, has been the role of the US and the United Kingdom? What are the political debates? What is our government doing and saying—and why? You need to put that newspaper article into its historical and political context—and it's about time you learned more about Zimbabwe and Africa anyway.

Here's another example. The first chapter from Marjane Satrapi's graphic auto-biography *Persepolis: The Story of a Childhood* is called "The Veil." Satrapi is writing about growing up in Iran, and she starts with an account of the veil in Iranian culture. How does a U.S. reader approach this topic? Don't let the cartoon style fool you into thinking this is going to be easy. Here are some inventive reading strategies you might use to understand an idea or reference or history that you know little about:

- **Inventory.**

   Jot down quickly all that you know about the veil in Islamic culture—from watching the news, seeing images, people you have talked with. This is your starting point—what you know, what you don't know, why you have a particular way of knowing and not knowing.

- **A Quick Internet Search.**

   Go to a search engine or another source of information, and type in *veil* and read around in the first couple of websites that turn up.

- **Re-reading.**

   Since this is a short chapter, read and reread it several times. Write out the questions it poses for you, such as, Do women still wear the veil? Is it always a sign of oppression? What is the Western view? What do Islamic women themselves say? What does the veil symbolize to various groups of people? Why?

- **Authorial Purpose.**

   Based on this close reading and perhaps discussion with others, explain as best you can (and you can't ever fully know this) what you think Satrapi is trying to accomplish by writing her life as a cartoon and by starting with the veil.

- **Intended Audience(s).**

   Based on the text itself, who do you think is her intended audiences? Westerners? Why? What assumptions of Westerners might she be trying to unsettle or challenge or confirm? What in the text suggests that to you?

- **Develop a project.**

   Decide what you'd like to know about and how you are going to find information so that you can write a 'good enough' essay on this graphic autobiography and on this topic.

- **Draft.**

   Begin to put your ideas into words or, in this case, drawings.

[4] Reading Researched Texts

As you read in your courses, you have probably noticed that often writers draw on the ideas, arguments, and words of other writers. They quote, use statistics or anecdotes, and apply the theories developed by other writers. This happens all the time in the university: one writer builds on the work of other writers in responsible and respectful ways. It's not easy to follow and comprehend this kind of sourced writing, and you have to deploy a particular set of reading strategies to attend to it well.

A number of the readings in this collection are sourced—some quite extensively, and some minimally. Amy Best's chapter "Race-ing Men" from her book *fast cars, cool rides: The Accelerating World of Youth and their Cars* arises out of years of primary and secondary research and reflects Best's new thinking about race and gender in the car-cruising scene in San Jose, California. The chapter rewards close attention to the ways Best negotiates a range of sources, from interviews with teen cruisers, to blog entries from online chat rooms, to the ideas and arguments of scholars in a range of fields from sociology, to subcultural studies, to cultural geography, to Asian American studies, and so on. Here are some reading strategies you might deploy to gain a better appreciation for Best's analysis, and to re-imagine your own relationships to sources.

- **Signals**

  Look carefully at the ways Best signals that she is working with the voices and ideas of other writers.

  —Where and how she uses quotation marks and italics.

  —The brief summaries she provides of another writer's background as well as that writer's general argument, when introducing a theorist or scholar for the first time.

  —How she varies how much she uses her sources: for example, the 16th page of "Race-ing Men" is 100% devoted to transcription of a conversation between three subjects; but the next page is approximately 85% Best interpreting that conversation, 5% continued citing of the conversation, and 10% reference to three other scholars—Freire, Goffman, and Patricia Hill Collins.

- **Chapter Notes**

  Make the effort to move back and forth between the chapter and the accompanying notes, and think about how your reading experience changes as a result.

  —What did Best deepen, complicate, explicate in the notes?

  —What did the notes help you understand about a particular scholar or idea?

  —Why is the material in the notes not woven into the main text?

- **Evidence**

  Analyze how and where Best's ideas arise.

  —From direct observation of a pattern or trend?

  —From a connection to another scholar's claim/argument?

  —From application of a particular concept or key term?

  —From an intuitive leap?

- **Evaluation**

  Rank Best's ideas on a plausibility scale: which ones seem the most persuasive, or interesting, or substantial, and why? What sorts of evidence accompanies the most plausible claims? Think critically about whose voices are represented in the article.

  —Who is granted expertise, and what sort of expertise is evident?

  —Who is writing and speaking about this subject?

  —What urgencies and agendas do the cited voices bring to the wider conversation?

[5] Reading Visual Images

Images, in isolation or surrounded by text, are mobilized to persuade viewers to think and to act differently—to be shocked, or moved, or encouraged to buy, or informed, or rethink their sense of the world. Examples include political cartoons, advertisements, posters, propaganda, photojournalism, and websites. Even the clothes you wear promote a particular brand and all that that brand means, even if you decide to refuse those fashion statements and meanings. We live in an iconographic world that influences not only what we see but also how we see.

Take the image below: At first glance it appears pretty self explanatory—joyous young men and women, likely from a different era based on their clothing and hair styles, and not so different from the pictures we might see today of young men and women gathering, celebrating, forming community.

But your understanding of the photo will strengthen and deepen if you practice some critical reading strategies specific to visual images:

- *Observations:* Jot down all the initial things you notice from this photograph—from the figures in the photograph, their expressions, their bodies, their clothes, and especially their fists. What do these expressions and gestures signify to you? What do you think these people are doing? Why are they on the street?

- *Audience:* Consider what the photographer is trying to capture here and who the photographer imagines as the potential audience. What does the photographer want the audience to feel or do?

- *Narrative:* What story does this photograph seem to be telling? Where is this photograph likely to have been taken—and at what point in history?

- *Research:* How might you go about finding out more about this photograph? A quick trip to Google images will tell you that it is a poster from the Gay Liberation Front in 1970, and in the original version it says COME OUT!! on the top and JOIN THE SISTERS AND BROTHERS OF THE GAY LIBERATION FRONT on the bottom. What do you know about the GLF? Where can you find out more?

- *Context:* Where did the image originally appear, and what was its original purpose? What was going on in the culture at the moment the image first arose? With what other images is it consistent? With what other images is it in conflict?

- *Claim:* How do you assess the purpose and the effect of this photograph? What would it have meant in 1970—and why? What does it mean in 2009—and why?

Even though these five reading practices may appear discrete, they actually overlap, and all are what writing teachers call *recursive*. Readers often read closely, critically, inventively, and with an eye on sourcing at the same time. That is, they note details, as they assess rhetorical effect. They evaluate writers and their arguments, as they make connections to the larger issues. They move ahead in the text, drawing their own conclusions, and then circle back to see how a second, third or fourth reading might affect that conclusion. They pay attention to the visual aspects of the text—what they add, or what they obscure.

Reading recursively does not necessarily happen automatically, though. It requires practice, training, and sometimes even permission. If you have been asked to read mostly for content through most your schooling, then it will take guidance and reinforcement for you to engage the different kinds of critical encounters with texts we are promoting in this book.

Writing

> *We shall not cease from/exploring/And the end of all our/exploring/ Will be to arrive where we/started/And know the place for the/first time (TS Eliot* Four Quartets).

Of all the types of writing you might be asked to produce in college, analysis and argument are likely two of the most common. For our purposes here we're going to talk about analysis and argument as *genre* and as *practice*. College teachers routinely assign analysis and argument essays in their courses—genres that have distinct characteristics and purposes, even as they share some qualities in common. Both analysis and argument, for example, are built upon claims and evidence, and they require writers to closely examine a subject or situation in order to develop a deeper understanding of it. The end results are texts that persuade readers. In the case of analysis, the text persuades a reader to *see* what the writer sees—an interesting connection, for example, or a meaningful trend, or a causal relationship; in the case of argument, the text attempts to persuade the reader to hold the same position as the writer, or to act in some manner, or to switch alliances.

The practices of analysis and argument precede and often transcend the writing of academic essays, however. You analyze when you think carefully enough to recommend a course to a friend, or prepare an acquisitions memo for the local library, or decide who you will vote for in the Presidential election, or come to understand better the geopolitical situation produced by the US presence in Afghanistan. Argument involves analysis—and goes beyond pro/con debates on abortion or gun control and extends into situated social practices such as when you are working together as a sorority to plan the next event, or persuading your parents that body piercing makes social statements, or taking a stand in an education class on the value of anti-racist pedagogy, or advocating for more funds for the local public schools. Evidence for your arguments comes from analysis, from discussion with others, from your personal experience, and eventually from research in the library and on the web.

Recognizing the features of analysis and argument is an important step in developing your own skills as a writer. The essays in this reader showcase a wide range of approaches to interpretation and argument, and also illustrate the necessary relationships between the two.

Analysis

Analysis often follows from an observation or a question; analysis is what we do when we attempt to make sense of something. Take, for example, Margaret Price's "Artificial Assimilation: Representational Politics of the Gayby Boom." Price was motivated to write her piece after noticing a trend in the visibility of gay parents and gay parenting—a shift from virtually no representation to an overabundance of representation. But, "be careful what you wish for," she writes. The super- or hyper-visibility of gay parenting on the web, in newspapers and magazines, in television programs and movies, and in advertisements results, claims Price, in a sanitizing of queer folk and their efforts to raise families. Gay parents are represented as "just like" straight parents, that is "normal." And the end result, according to Price, is that the complexity of queer parenting—its specific challenges and struggles and compromises, its successes and failures—is glossed over and denied. Price builds her analysis through a close examination of a range of cultural artifacts, specifically cable television programs devoted to gay characters and gay parenting. She notices certain trends in the representations of gay parents and draws conclusions based on her new understanding of the trends. She also notices what is missing in the representations—no attention to transgender parents, for example—and makes claims about that as well.

So, analysis starts with a question or an observation, it moves into close attention to a subject or subjects and, at its most successful, it results in creative leaps, insights, and new awarenesses. The *practices* of asking good questions, noticing details and recognizing trends, making connections, and developing interpretive claims increase the potential for composing a persuasive analysis essay that satisfies the conventions of the *genre*: plausible interpretation, claims well supported by evidence, and an overarching point to it all—what might be called a thesis, or an umbrella claim, or even a statement of purpose.

Price's essay is a generative starting point for doing an analysis of your own. Let's go back to her concept of hypervisibility: *visibility* is a concept currently in vogue in theater, psychology, sociology, cultural studies, queer studies, political science and many other disciplines. The concept is especially interesting to scholars because of the sheer volume of images, texts and ideas people are exposed to each day through television, radio, advertising, newspapers, magazines, and other forms of communication.

And inextricably linked with visibility is the concept of *hypervisibility* (or surplus visibility)—that is, the images or identities or figures in heavy rotation in US culture. Certain images—e.g. the person in the wheelchair, the flamboyant gay man, the dying person with AIDS, the starving African child—stand in for larger, more diverse, more complex groups of people. An analysis of a hypervisible representation might start with questions: what do these images and representations achieve? who benefits? who—and what—gets sacrificed?

You might select a hypervisible representation of your own, and explore what the image is doing. An example: On Wednesday, July 7th 2004 the Syracuse *Post Standard* ran an article on the advances in prosthetics that are helping American soldiers injured in Iraq return to more "normal" lives. The article was accompanied by photos of a soldier amputee walking confidently, comfortably, and proudly on an artificial leg. That depiction (text and photos) of soldiers is hypervisible—that is, it comes to stand in for all soldiers injured in Iraq, and it relieves the public of the strain of bearing witness to (and thinking about) the emotional, physical, and economic devastation that is much more the "norm" for those wounded in battle. It is the devastation, for the most part, that remains invisible. Soldier deaths also remain invisible—as until just recently Americans were not allowed to see pictures of the flag-draped coffins coming into Dover Air Force Base on a regular basis.

Analysis gets us to a place we hadn't been aware of in advance; it surprises us, gets our attention, and forces us to rethink our assumptions. As you engage in analysis you learn to discipline yourself 'back into the text,' to slow down and let yourself notice and see what is there *before* deciding what you think about it. You work on seeing, noticing, and exploring an object of study.

Argument

Ideally, the practices of analysis impact your approach to argument, particularly your ability to suspend judgment and seek out rather than suppress tensions.

Whether talking in class or in the hallway, selecting books for a course, or publishing academic articles, those of us in the academy are always saying, 'this is how I see the world and I'd like you to see it that way too.' This is not the Jerry Springer version of argument, where everyone yells and screams and calls each other names in order to win at all costs (well, typically the academy is not like that, and it's certainly not supposed to be). Argument, instead, is a way of making claims about a topic of inquiry in the hopes of creating knowledge, testing the waters, persuading others, solving problems, and acting in the world. Academic argument, ideally, is not afraid of contradictory evidence—even when it threatens the whole structure of the argument—because it is those very tensions that make research worthwhile.

Academic argument assumes multiple perspectives on 'truth,' and starts from the premise that we have only partial knowledge. It also assumes that there are significant differences among us that need to be taken into account, that some 'facts' are more significant than others, that some 'experts' carry more weight than others, that some claims are more likely to be true or right or more feasible than others—and overall, that we want to reach fair and equitable decisions about how the world is and should be.

Academic argument also assumes we'll make an initial claim, do more research and thinking and reading, and alter or reject that claim as part of the process of thinking and acting in the world. Argument that is most closely connected to analysis is argument to *inquire*—to learn more about the world, about others' ideas, about our own ideas—and, ultimately, to construct writings that will persuade others to see those ideas the same way(s) we do.

Let's look at a specific argument to inquire in the reader—June Jordan's "Nobody Mean More To Me Than You and the Future Life of Willie Jordan." The title itself is provocative, with its (absolutely intentional) ungrammatical pronouncement, and it suggests the stance Jordan intends to take on the issue of Black English. Jordan's argumentative thesis is explicit and it arrives early in the essay: Black English is an "endangered species," she writes, and if it disappears so will much of what constitutes Black culture and identity. What is most compelling about her opening paragraphs is the urgency of the argument: this issue *matters*; something enormous is at stake.

The evidence for her argument arises mostly from personal experience and anecdote—stories about her efforts to design a course on Black English, about her students' collective response to a fellow student's tragedy. Throughout the essay Jordan carefully, even painstakingly examines her evidence—the raw data that informs her argument—and carefully interprets it. Her purpose in the essay is clear—to change readers' perceptions of the legitimacy of Black English—but it's equally important that readers *see* what she and her students have come to see and appreciate about the beauty and complexity and sophistication of Black English. Ultimately Jordan's argument is all the more powerful because of the recursive relationship between argument and analysis.

The essays in this reader encourage you to read, research, and write arguments through exploring a topic of inquiry together from multiple points of view. Doing some shared reading and discussing in order to complicate easy answers or cultural commonplaces creates a rich intellectual context in the classroom, and generates new questions that the readings don't address or answer or don't answer well. For example, bell hooks' essay "Selling Hot Pussy: Representations of Black Female Sexuality in the Cultural Marketplace" may prove to be dated or limited in its theoretical explanations for how and why the African American female body is eroticized and objectified in popular culture. The essay initiates, but does not complete a line of research and argument. You might consider updating or extending hooks' argument by analyzing more contemporary trends in representations of women of color; you might shift the focus of your argument to representations of black *male* sexuality. Ultimately each essay in the reader is a starting point for inquiry and discussion, not the final word on any issue.

It's important that you take up the readings not as 'answers' or 'content' per se, but as prompts to further questions. You want to develop the ability to read as writers with a critical eye toward the moves that writers make within texts, so that you can broaden your own writerly choices. And it is also very important that you find a way (as June Jordan does, for example) to intersect with your topic from your own perspectives and experiences, so you can claim ownership of your claims, projects, and final papers.

Use these readings to generate a rich discussion and debate—and to analyze and assess the argument stances, practices, and skills the authors are using. Don't get bogged down in the readings, but use them to get things stirred up, so that you feel motivated and knowledgeable enough to develop your individual argument within this topic of inquiry.

The following are thematic possibilities for argument topics and essays, drawing on the selections in the reader.

[1] Language and Identity:

  Jordan's "Nobody Mean More to Me than You and the Future Life of Willie Jordan"

  Kumar's "Language" from *Passport Photos*

  McHugh's "I Knew I'd Sing"

  Smith's "Broken Sentences: Women in prison tell their stories straight"

  Smitherman's "Black English/Ebonics: What It Be Like?"

[2] Academic Writing: Skills and Standards, Resistances and Refusals

  Jordan's "Nobody Mean More to Me than You and the Future Life of Willie Jordan"

  Kantz's "Helping Students Use Textual Sources Persuasively"

  Rice's "The 1963 Hip-Hop Machine: Hip-Hop Pedagogy as Composition"

  Smitherman's "Black English/Ebonics: What It Be Like?"

  White's "My Five-Paragraph-Theme Theme"

[3] Gender and Sexuality:

  Addonizio's "What Do women Want?"

  Chase's "Hermaphrodites with Attitude"

hooks' "Selling Hot Pussy: Representations of Black Female Sexuality in the Cultural Marketplace"

Kincaid's "Girl"

McDowell's "In Public: The Street and Spaces of Pleasure"

McHugh's "I Knew I'd Sing"

Pavese's "Ancestors"

Pratt's "Abandoned Women and the Spaces of the Exception

Quart's "When Girls Will Be Boys"

Wjpijewski's "A Boy's Life: For Matthew Shepard's Killers—what does it take to pass as a man?

[4] The Body:

Ahmed's "Recognising Strangers"

Chase's "Hermaphrodites with Attitude: Mapping the Emergence of Intersex Political Activism"

Eye's "Negative, 1996"

Garland-Thomson's "The Politics of Staring: Visual Rhetorics of Disability in Popular Photography"

Hass's "A Story About the Body"

Hershey's "From Poster Child to Protestor"

Quart's "When Girls Will Be Boys"

Sontag's "Regarding the Torture of Others"

[5] Popular Culture:

Best's "Race-ing Men: Boys, Risk and the Politics of Race"

Cosgrove's "The Zoot-Suit and Style Warfare"

Crimp's "No More Business as Usual"

Duncombe's "Introduction" to *The Cultural Resistance Reader*

Hawkins' "A Dumped Car"

hooks' "Selling Hot Pussy: Representations of Black Female Sexuality in the Cultural Marketplace"

Macek's "The Cinema of Suburban Paranoia"

McCarthy's "Rodents"

Price's "Artificial Assimilation: Representational Politics of the Gayby Boom"

[6] Publics and Counter Publics:

Ahmed's "Recognising Strangers"

Anderson's "Among Elms and Maples, Morgantown, West Virginia, August 1935"

Duncombe's "Introduction" to *The Cultural Resistance Reader*

Flusty's "Building Paranoia"

Green's "Attacks on the Homeless Rise, With Youths Mostly to Blame"

Lippard's "Marking the Spot"

Martone's "Country Roads Lined with Running Fences: A Dozen Story Problems About the Place of Place"

McDowell's "In Public: The Street and Spaces of Pleasure"

Geraldine Pratt's "Abandoned Women and the Spaces of the Exception"

Reynolds' "Maps of the Everyday: Habitual Pathways and Contested Spaces"

Sibley's "Introduction" from *Geographies of Exclusion*

[7] Resistance and Dissent:

Brodine's "June 78"

Chase's "Hermaphrodites with Attitude"

Crimp's "No More Business as Usual"

Eye's "Negative, 1996"

Faiz's "You Tell Us What To Do"

Guerrero's "Priorities"

Hughes' "I, Too, Sing America"

Jordan's "Nobody Mean More to Me than You and the Future Life of Willie Jordan"

Marable's "What We Talk About When We Talk about Race"

Smitherman's "Black English/Ebonics: What It Be Like?

Wilson's "Trash and Treasure: *The Gleaners and I*"

[8] Raced Encounters:

Ahmed's "Recognizing Strangers"

Best's "Race-ing Men: Boys, Risk and the Politics of Race"

Cosgrove's "The Zoot-Suit and Style Warfare"

Flusty's "Building Paranoia"

Guerrero's "Priorities"

hooks' "Selling Hot Pussy: Representations of Black Female Sexuality in the Cultural Marketplace

Hughes' "I, Too, Sing America"

Jordan's "Nobody Mean More to Me than You and the Future Life of Willie Jordan"

Kumar's "Language"

Macek's "The Cinema of Suburban Paranoia"

Marable's "What We Talk About When We Talk about Race"

Satrapi's "The Veil"

[9] Representation:

Anderson's "Among Elms and Maples, Morgantown, West Virginia, August 1935"

Cosgrove's "The Zoot-Suit and Style Warfare"

Crimp's "No More Business as Usual"

Garland-Thomson's "The Politics of Staring: Visual Rhetorics of Disability in Popular Photography"

George's "Hermaphrodites with Attitude: Mapping the Emergence of Intersex Political Activism"

Green's "Attacks on the Homeless Rise, With Youths Mostly to Blame"

Levi Strauss's "Epiphany of the Other"

Macek's "The Cinema of Suburban Paranoia"

Satrapi's "The Veil"

Sontag's "Regarding the Torture of Others"

Wilson's "Trash and Treasure: *The Gleaners and I*"

[10] Nature and the Environment:

Hawkins' "A Dumped Car"

Lippard's "Marking the Spot"

McCarthy's "Rodents"

Wilson's "Trash and Treasure: *The Gleaners and I*"

[11] Poverty and Class Difference

George's "Changing the Face of Poverty: Nonprofits and the Problem of Representation"

Green's "Attacks on the Homeless Rise, With Youths Mostly to Blame"

Guerrero's "Priorities"

Hawkins' "A Dumped Car"

hooks' "Seeing and Making Culture: Representing the Poor"

Kincaid's "Girl"

Levi Strauss' "Epiphany of the Other"

Macek's "The Cinema of Suburban Paranoia"

Pratt's "Abandoned Women and the Spaces of the Exception"

Reynolds' "Maps of the Everyday: Habitual Pathways and Contested Spaces"

Smith's "Broken Sentences: Women in Prison Tell their Stories Straight"

Researching

Research is woven into our daily lives—from checking out the time for the college basketball team's next game, to grabbing an initial definition of stem cell research from the Wikipedia, to checking in with a knowledgeable friend on email about the best movie to see or best candidate to vote for or best professor to take next semester. We check out how our friends are doing on Facebook. We catch up on celebrity gossip on Perez Hilton, and international news on the online version of the *New York Times*. And at times we do more extended research, like when we need to understand the causes and symptoms of diabetes or when we want to know everything we can about forensic anthropology as a possible career choice—or when, of course, we have to do researched essays for college classes.

Research deepens what we know, and research takes us out of our comfort zone and into new territory, compelling us beyond ourselves and our worlds into new selves and new worlds—all with a click of the mouse.

Invention and Desire

> *The mobilization of passions . . . is a task for rhetoric (Crowley,* Toward a Civil Discourse *22).*

Invention is a term from classical rhetoric, where it refers to the discovery of resources for making a persuasive argument. In ancient Greece that meant speaking before the assembled citizens to make the case for going to war, or to honor a fallen leader, and engage in other such public deliberations. The speaker would not only have to gather facts, but also make the case in terms of the values, beliefs, desires, and commonplaces of the audience being addressed. The speaker would have to make decisions about style, length, focus, and he (always 'he' in this case) would have to anticipate the possible responses from the audience, both positive and negative. A good rhetor was able to invent—to discover the resources—for any speaking occasion.

But you are not in ancient Greece, where the audience was known, the values and beliefs shared, and the commonplaces . . . well, commonplace. You are in the supermodern and transnational world Augé and others have described, full of competing perspectives, a bombardment of information and image, an explosion of knowledge, and a compression of time/space. Within all of that you have to find a place to stand. You have to figure out what you think, you have to consider the limits of your thinking, you have to seek out further information and ideas by trekking through the sources available to you online and in libraries and through your own research, you have to imagine audience reactions, and you have to design and write a text that gets the attention of readers and that makes your case in persuasive ways. This is the dance of invention and desire.

For a number of years Anne has been testing the limits of her writing students' desires by 'imposing' topics on them and watching what happens. Her students often claim that, "I can't write about something unless I already relate to it," or "I do my best writing if I'm personally involved in my topic." Is that necessarily true, though? Could 'involvement' in a topic be re-imagined—not necessarily or exclusively as 'personal,' but characterized by other important affects like curiosity, shock, confusion, or even a little embarrassment? Can desire to know more, to engage the world, to be compelled outside of yourself arise out of encounters with the unknown, the unfamiliar, the strange? And, Anne wondered, what sorts of engagement, what types of thinking and writing, might that kind of desire motivate?

In her research writing course Anne put five topics on slips of paper into a hat—each one an historical event in 20th century America when encounters with others or conflicts over space turned confrontational and/or violent. Her students formed small groups, and each group picked one of the topics and embarked upon quick and dirty research to situate themselves. None of the topics were already familiar; no one recognized any of the references; and the preliminary research, though helpful in contextualizing the event, did not bring with it a jolt of recognition. So how could her students possibly write about their assigned topics? What would it take for them to find a place to stand?

Philadelphia Daily News, August 1978

Let's see how the project unfolded, looking closely at one of the events—the firebombing of MOVE in Philadelphia in 1985. The students who picked that topic went right to Google and immediately found a host of artifacts from a variety of media, including newspaper articles (current and historical), radio clips, YouTube videos, interviews with MOVE members, legal documents, photographs, and websites galore. The students quickly discovered that MOVE was a radical (mostly) black group that formed in the early 1970s and was led by a white man who took the name John Africa and who encouraged all members to adopt the surname Africa. They also learned that MOVE is not an acronym, but a shortened version of a core belief of the group that life is all about "movement." And finally, they began to understand that MOVE members had a history of conflict as far back as the 1970s both with Philadelphia law enforcement as well as with residents of their neighborhood in the western edge of the city that reached a crisis point in May of 1985 when police officers arrived at the MOVE residence with arrest warrants for four members.

The first burst of web research got the group's attention: within minutes they were surrounded by documents and images and narratives and arguments that rendered MOVE and the attack on MOVE twenty-three years ago urgent and compelling and worth further investigation, even though they had no previous knowledge to draw on, and no personal experience with which to relate to the event. Anne's students were certainly motivated by curiosity. They had a ton of questions they wanted answers to: How did MOVE originate? Why were MOVE members so combative? What beliefs motivated the organization? How did MOVE's neighbors feel about them? What has happened in Philadelphia in the years since the firebombing? How come no one in class had ever heard about the event?

In the course of satisfying their initial curiosities, Anne's students also became attuned to the voices and experiences of others whose marginal position in culture and history, whose provocative philosophies and life choices, made it easy to dismiss or ignore or respond violently toward them. And they were shocked by what they discovered—that, for example, the Philadelphia police set fire to an entire residential neighborhood in the process of arresting MOVE members. That MOVE members intentionally provoked their neighbors by, among other things, lecturing them night and day through electric bullhorns. That five children died in the fire.

By George Widman, AP

But the goal of the project wasn't just to find and report random facts about MOVE, or to offer a cohesive narrative of the events that led up to the firebombing, or to talk about what a "weird" organization MOVE was. Anne's students ultimately had to analyze *why* the event occurred, specifically addressing what issues of space and power and difference contributed to tensions. They needed to develop a sophisticated enough understanding of the event to make claims about it, and persuade their audience of a specific interpretation. The project didn't necessarily require the students to master the subject, but it did put pressure on them, for example, to sift through conflictisng reports, to evaluate their sources of information, and to contextualize and historicize the event—that is, to learn more about what was happening in the US in 1985. The students also had to apply to the event the arguments of two theorists in this reader, Sara Ahmed and David Sibley, who write about space, power, exclusion, and otherness.

In their final projects—an i-movie as well as a lengthy collaborative essay—Anne's students juxtaposed cultural artifacts specific to 1985, like the Billy Joel anthem "We Didn't Start the Fire" and the Michael Jackson-inspired famine relief fundraising ballad "We Are the World," with actual news coverage and analysis of the MOVE fire bombing. They also worked closely with Ahmed and Sibley, selecting quotes that helped illuminate the tensions surrounding public space and the ways that space defines who does and doesn't belong. The topic ultimately mattered to them, not because it reinforced their assumptions about history or difference or violence or conflict, or because they connected with it personally, but because it positioned them to explore something *new*—to ask questions, to make connections, to experience the pleasure of being surprised by what they discovered. It produced new desires—as well as linked to old ones. It also allowed them the pleasure of sharing new knowledge with their audience, of imagining all the possibilities for making the event meaningful to their readers and viewers as well.

From Invention and Desire to a Final Researched Essay

The trajectory from knowing nothing about a topic like MOVE to producing i-movies and essays that speak with authority and that provoke interest and response from readers and viewers includes a lot of strategies for inventing, arranging, and delivering texts. We have developed a list of skills that you might turn to heuristically to generate ideas, to explore connections, to move from an emerging claim to a final thesis, and to craft the most effective written and visual text that you can. You don't have to use these skills each time, nor do you have to go through them linearly. They offer backup—for when you have no place to start, for when you don't know how to locate sources, for when you struggle with organization, for when you put the polished text together.

Let's imagine that you have decided you want to know about poverty within the US and transnationally. You have been watching the economic news, as people have been losing their homes and as the holiday retail sales have been disappointingly low. You have also watched the PSAs asking viewers to send money to the Rescue Mission and the local food bank. You yourself are worried about meeting next semester's tuition increases and about what kind of career will give you a chance at a good income for the rest of your life. These are immediate and urgent questions—and they may emerge too out of course assignments about representations of poverty or about global economic trends or about public schooling in economically depressed cities. Poverty claims your attention.

Skill #1: Starting from Your Own Experience, Knowledge, Claims

- Free writes: Take ten minutes and write as quickly as possible whatever comes to mind on the topic of poverty. If you blank, write 'nothing comes to mind' until something else does.

- Questions: Take ten minutes and write as quickly as possible every thing you ever wanted to know about poverty but were afraid to ask. Don't judge your questions; just get them down on paper.

- Memory Lane: Think back to your first experience with the topic poverty, and recreate it as fully as possible. Where were you? Who else was there? What were you doing and thinking? What surprises you in retrospect?

- Warrants: List all the basic assumptions or beliefs or values or hopes you have about the topic—who are 'the poor'? when does someone count as 'poor'? how do the poor get represented on TV or in the press or in political campaigns? why?

- Historicize: Delve into where you think these basic assumptions or beliefs or values or hopes come from in terms of your family, community, culture.

- Texts: List movies or books or songs or plays that represent the topic of poverty to you. Then annotate the list: what did each text mean to you and why?

- Counter-argue: what ideas or arguments do you really, really disagree with—and why? What phrases or images make you furious?

Skill #2: Quick and Dirty Research (Online and Library)

- Google: Type in poverty and study the first ten entries that come up. What is the Institute for Research on Poverty (http://www.irp.wisc.edu/)? What does it mean that Global Issues (http://www.globalissues.org/article/26/poverty-facts-and-stats) claims that almost half the world—over three billion people—live on less than $2.50 a day? What are Barack Obama and Joe Biden proposing to do about poverty in both rural and urban areas (http://www.barackobama.com/issues/poverty/)—and why?

- Library Databases: Type in a keyword or phrases (note instructions on your library webpage) and study the first ten entries that come up. You could pursue research on poverty and children, on poverty and education, on poverty and political systems, and poverty and the risk of armed conflict. You can read in anthropology, sociology, economics, social work, education, and public health, just for a start.

- Possible questions to assess sites and sources:
  —What is the perspective of the site or text?
  —What disciplines emerge as important?
  —What questions are being asked?
  —What answers are being proposed?
  —What seems most important to you?
  —What seems right? Wrong? Why?

Skill #3: Locating Credible Sources (Online and Library)

Your library has a very useful page, no doubt, for you to use in order to master the basics of library and online research at your college. Use the online library help site for specific questions, or go to the library and talk with a reference librarian to get started.

Skill #4: Getting Started

- Go the library home page and click on databases. For example, click on W and find Wilson Full Text. This is a good place to start because it's easier to work with a full text database. Type in poverty, and note all the entries that come up. Select one, notice the discipline and type of text, read the abstract, determine if the full text is available online or through the library, and note the list of keywords for further searching and for further organizing of your research and argument.

- Ask yourself: What do I make of this article? What new ideas does it suggest for me? Why might this be a good place to start my scholarly research?

Sample Wilson Full Text article:

Title: Will the Poor Be With Us Always?

Other Titles: Review Article

Personal Author: Goddard, Terry D.

Journal Name: *Journal of Urban History*

Source: *Journal of Urban History* v. 34 no. 4 (May 2008) p. 704–11

Publication Year: 2008

Abstract: The eradication of poverty has become a hot topic not only among scholars but also among rock stars, Hollywood actors, philanthropists and so on. These four recently published volumes all assert that the causes of poverty can be solved with a united, concentrated effort. They look for views other than the one that understands poverty through the inadequacies of the poor. They argue that some of the causes of poverty are inherent in capitalism. Simply working hard, they show, will not change things for the better. Rather, they advocate forming some form of community empowerment program that will enable people to work together to solve problems of poverty.

Subject(s): *Poverty*

Peer Reviewed Journal:

Physical Description: Bibliographic footnotes

ISSN: 0096-1442

Language of Document: English

Book(s) Reviewed:

Title: One nation underprivileged [2004; Rank, Mark Robert]

Title: The end of poverty [Sachs, Jeffrey]

Title: The working poor [2004; Shipler, David K.; Knopf]

Title: Ending global poverty [2005; Smith, Stephen C.]

Document Type: Review Article

This looks like a good article to read because it is a review of current books on the big questions of poverty, so you will get a quick overview of the terms of discussion, the questions up for debate, the suggestions people are proposing, and the names of key theorists and researchers on the topic of poverty. The article also has a bibliography, which makes it easier to find other relevant sources, and it offers a framework or argument about capitalism as the cause of poverty that will help you assess the further reading you will do. Book reviews are also short, and written to a more general audience. It's a good starting place.

Skill #5: Reading Actively and Critically (Double Entry Research Journal)

- From this initial entry point, you begin to develop a list of significant, relevant, helpful, accessible, and useful sources for your researched essay on poverty. As you read these sources, consider some kind of structured way to record your responses and ideas to help you develop your line of argument and to provide the bibliographic information you will need later as your prepare your References or Works Cited pages. This saves you a lot of time later.

- Left column
  —Enter full bibliographic information in MLA or APA style:
    - Book (edited collection): *Family Poverty in Diverse Contexts.* Edited by C. Anne Broussard and Alfred L. Joseph. New York: Routledge, 2009.
    - Book (single author): *Traveling Light: On the Road with America's Poor.* By Kate Weston. Boston: Beacon Press, 2008.
    - Article in journal: "Multidimensional Poverty: An Alternative Measurement Approach for the United States" by Udaya R. Wagle in *Social Science Research* v. 37, no. 2 (June 2008), pp. 559–80.
    - Article in alternative press: "Who Should Take Care of the Poor?" by Tony Campolo in *Tikkun* 23, no. 4 (July 2008), pp. 56–57.
    - Article in alternative press: "The Irresponsibility of the Rich" by Ruth Lister in *Red Pepper* No. 161 (August 20, 2008), pp. 25–27.
    - Film: *The End of Poverty? Think Again.* Director: Phillippe Diaz. Cinema Libre Studio. 2008.
    - Website: The End of Poverty: In a world with so much wealth, why is there still so much poverty? Cinema Libre Studio. 27 December 200 < http://endpoverty.ning.com/>.
    - Website: Poverty New York (State) Statistics: 2007 County Level Poverty Rates for NY. United States Department of Agriculture Economic Research Service. 27 December 2008 <http://www.ers.usda.gov/data/povertyrates/PovListpct.asp?st=NY&view=Percent>.
  —Type in key quotations in full (include page numbers)—no more than one per page or you will be recopying the essay.
  —Mark for yourself key sections with a quick notation so you can find it easily later if you need it.
- Right column
  —Agree or disagree or qualify or critique the quotations and claims.
    - What do I think of this idea?
    - How true is it?
    - How important is it to me?
    - Does it challenge anything I already know or believe?
    - Does it raise or answer questions?
  —Jot down notes for how you might use this quotation or claim in your paper.
  —Note further sources to pursue.

— Raise questions—how does this quotation or claim make you think differently about your topic? How does it challenge your thinking or give you a new line of thought to pursue?

— Emote!

Skill #6: Crafting an Emerging Thesis

As you do your research and develop your argument, your ideas are likely to change and become more focused.

- Every few days, write down in 25 words or less what you want the reader to know or think or do differently after reading your essay.
- Ask yourself, "So what?" What is the significance of this thesis or its real point?
- See how this emerging thesis matches or does not match the evidence or ideas or conclusions you are discovering in your research.
- Think of this as your emerging thesis statement (which may or may not appear in your final essay).
- Use this strategy to move from having a topic, to making a general claim, to crafting a specific argument.

Skill #7: Annotating

To annotate is to note main argument, types of evidence, style, tone, and rhetorical devices to persuade the reader, and the main strengths/ weaknesses.

Skill #8: Summarizing

- To summarize is to put in your own words the main argument of the text or a section of a text.
- Summarizing others' ideas requires that you document the source.

Skill #9: Paraphrasing

- To paraphrase is recast the specific language of a text in a mixture of the author's and your own words.
- Paraphrasing others' words requires that you document the source.

Skill #10: Interviewing and Informal Surveying

- Find expert sources by noting who is quoted often in your sources, by checking the phone book or faculty directory (e.g., the head of the Economics or Social Work Department), and by asking teachers and students.
- Consider too 'nonexpert' sources such as your roommate who had had personal experience with your topic, or your family, or . . .
- Make contact by calling or emailing the interviewee and explaining briefly what your research project is about and asking when it would be convenient, if he or she is willing, to talk or to respond to emailed questions.

- Decide what kinds of questions you want to pose in your interviews or surveys:
  — Open-ended so interviewees have plenty of room to invent their own answers ("What do you think the main causes of poverty are in the US and across the globe?")
  — Directed so you get answers focused on your research ("Do you think that community empowerment programs will work?")
  — Avoid loaded questions ("Do you think poor people are morally lax?").
  — Avoid vague questions ("What do you know about poverty?").

Skill #11: Working with Quotations

- Reasons for selecting and incorporating exact quotations in your final essay:
  — Offers definitions of technical knowledge
  — Conveys ideas eloquently and persuasively
  — Tells a story needed for the essay
  — Grants authority to the claims and arguments
  — Provides data or illustration
- Introducing quotations with tag lines—"As President Obama says," or "As Kate Weston claims in *Traveling Light*," or "As research has proven."
- Blocking quotations—When a quotation is more than four lines long, set it off from the text by indenting one inch (or ten spaces) from the left margin and double space the quotation.
- Cutting quotations—When you want to use only a part of the quotation, use an ellipsis (three periods separated by a space) to indicate that you have removed text.
- Don't over-quote—your essay should not be a string of quoted and paraphrased material. Use sources to authorize and support and develop and highlight your argument.

Skill #12: Crafting a Final Thesis

- Narrow your focus: decide how much ground you can realistically cover, with the intent of going as deep as possible over limited territory versus going for broad but surface coverage of wide territory.
- Identify tension: what competing or conflicting forces or ideas do you see at work in your topic? Why does this issue matter now, at this particular moment in time? What is at stake in the issue?
- Specify and subordinate: do not generalize, do not offer a cliché, do not merely identify a topic and make no claim, and do not overstate
- Rephrase the thesis: specify and subordinate
  — "The economic situation is bad" → "The tax policies of the current administration threaten to reduce the tax burden on the middle class by sacrificing education and healthcare programs for everyone."

Skill #13: Arrangement

- Let your thesis guide you: as you draft your essay, keep checking back to your thesis, and ask yourself, am I remaining consistent with my stated focus? And, does each new idea somehow build on my thesis—extending and deepening the thesis and not just repeating it?

- Map your essay: once you've drafted, write a quick summary of each paragraph in the margins to see where you've gone and if the organization makes logical sense.

- Ask yourself, what do I have to say first, and then second, and then next?

- Locate key arguments: block out the most important ideas and claims of the essay, and determine if they are situated in the appropriate places.

Skill #14: Citing Sources—MLA or APA—and Preparing "Works Cited" or "References" Pages

Use the documentation sections of your handbook. You will see an example of a References page below.

References

Ahmed, Sara. *Strange Encounters: Embodied Others in Post-Coloniality* (NY: Routledge, 2000).

Appadurai, Arjun. *Modernity at Large: Cultural Dimensions of Globalization* (Minneapolis: University of Minnesota Press, 1996).

Augé, Marc. *Non-Places: Introduction to an Anthropology of Supermodernity.* Trans. By John Howe (London: Verso, 1995).

Cohn, Carol and Cynthia Enloe. "A Conversation with Cynthia Enloe: Feminists Look at Masculinity and the Men Who Wage War." *Signs: Journal of Women in Culture and Society,* Vol. 28, No. 4, 2003, 1187–1207.

Crowley, Sharon. *Toward a Civil Discourse: Rhetoric and Fundamentalism* (Pittsburgh: University of Pittsburgh Press, 2006).

Eliot, T.S. *Four Quartets* (San Diego, CA & New York, NY: Harcourt, Inc., 1968).

Gladwell, Malcolm. *Blink: The Power of Thinking without Thinking* (New York: Little, Brown and Company, 2005).

Kumar, Amitava. *Passport Photos* (Berkeley: University of California Press, 2000).

Lunsford, Andrea A. *Writing Matters: Rhetoric in Public and Private Lives* (Athens: University of Georgia Press, 2007).

Samuels, Robert. "Promoting Social Change through Higher Education." *JAC* 27.1–2, 2007, pp. 234–242.

Simon, Ellen. "Food Takes Bigger Bite of Budgets." *The Post-Standard,* April 15, 2008, A-1.

1

"What Do Women Want?"

KIM ADDONIZIO

In this poem from a collection called Tell Me, *Kim Addonizio addresses the age-old question raised by Freud and others about women's sexual desire, and she answers it directly, with touching bravado, without apology, as a direct challenge to the pressures that mute women's desires.*

I want a red dress.
I want it flimsy and cheap,
I want it too tight, I want to wear it
until someone tears it off me.
I want it sleeveless and backless,
this dress, so no one has to guess
what's underneath. I want to walk down
the street past Thrifty's and the hardware store
with all those keys glittering in the window,
past Mr. and Mrs. Wong selling day-old
donuts in their café, past the Guerra brothers
slinging pigs from the truck and onto the dolly,
hoisting the slick snouts over their shoulders.
I want to walk like I'm the only
woman on earth and I can have my pick.

I want that red dress bad.
I want it to confirm
your worst fears about me,
to show you how little I care about you
or anything except what
I want. When I find it, I'll pull that garment
from its hanger like I'm choosing a body
to carry me into this world, through
the birth-cries and the love-cries too,
and I'll wear it like bones, like skin,
it'll be the goddamned
dress they bury me in.

2

Among Elms and Maples, Morgantown, West Virginia, August, 1935

MAGGIE ANDERSON

In this poem from her book called Cold Comfort, *Maggie Anderson presents an unassuming complication to pictures by acclaimed photographer Walker Evans that do not portray Great Depression era subjects in their everyday, haphazard lives. The poem provides a snapshot of a moment in the life of a family in Morgantown, West Virginia. Anderson, Professor of English at Kent State University, demonstrates how creative works might comment on or extend pre-existing representations of a community or group.*

Houses were wedged between the tall stacks
of Seneca Glass beside the Monongahela
and waffle up steep hills. Here, the terrain
allows photographers to appear acrobatic.
Walker Evans liked standing on a hill, focusing
down so it seemed he was poised on a branch.
He liked the single telephone pole against

the flat sky, crossed off-center like a crucifix.
Beneath it, among elms and maples, is the house
my mother lived in with her sister and their mother
nearly fifty years ago. In this shot, Evans
only wanted the rough surfaces of clapboard
houses, their meshed roofs and slanted gables.
He didn't want my mother peeling the thin skin
from tomatoes with a sharp knife, my clumsy
Aunt Grace chasing the ones she'd dropped
around the linoleum floor. That would be another
picture, not this one. I look back from the future,
past the undulating, unremitting line of hills
Evans framed my family in, through the shaggy fronds
of summer ferns he used as foreground and as border.

3

Recognising Strangers

SARA AHMED

In this chapter from Strange Encounters: Embodied Others in Post-Coloniality, *Prof. Sara Ahmed analyzes Neighbourhood Watch pamphlets that instruct the good citizen to be on the alert for those who are deemed suspicious, and she provides a powerful way for thinking about how 'we' decide who belongs and who doesn't. She talks about those encounters where this figure of the stranger is produced—the figure we want to expel, or perhaps kill, as the source of danger, or that figure we are asked to embrace as the sign of difference. As a Professor in Race and Cultural Studies at Goldsmiths-University of London, Ahmed is interested in how bodies and worlds take shape and how power is secured and challenged in the everyday world.*

> *I turn around as you pass me. You are a stranger. I have not seen you before. No, perhaps I have. You are very familiar. You shuffle along the foot path, head down, a grey mac shimmering around your feet. You look dirty. There are scars and marks on your hands. You don't return my stare. I think I can smell you as you pass. I think I can hear you muttering. I know you already. And I hold myself together and breathe a sigh of relief as you turn the corner. I want you not to be in my face. I cast you aside with a triumph of one who knows this street. It is not the street where you live.*

How do you recognise a stranger? To ask such a question, is to challenge the assumption that the stranger is the one we simply fail to recognise, that the stranger is simply *any-body* whom we do not know. It is to suggest that the stranger is *some-body* whom we have *already recognised* in the very moment in which they are 'seen' or 'faced' as a stranger. The figure of the stranger is far from simply being strange; it is a figure that is painfully familiar in that very strange(r)ness.[1] The stranger has already come too close; the stranger is 'in my face'. The stranger then is not simply the one whom we have not yet encountered, but the one whom we have already encountered, or already faced. The stranger comes to be faced as a form of recognition: we recognise somebody *as a stranger,* rather than simply failing to recognise them.

How does this recognition take place? How can we tell the difference between strangers and other others? In this chapter, I will argue that there are techniques that allow us to differentiate between those who are strangers and those who belong in a given space (such as neighbours or fellow inhabitants). Such techniques involve ways of reading the bodies of others we come to face. Strangers are not simply those who are not known in this dwelling, but those who are, in their very proximity, *already recognised as not belonging,* as being out of place. Such a recognition of those who are out of place allows both the demarcation and enforcement of the boundaries of 'this place', as where 'we' dwell. The enforcement of boundaries requires that some-body—here locatable in the dirty figure of the stranger—has already crossed the line, has already come too close: in Alfred Schutz's terms, the stranger is always approaching (1944: 499). The recognition of strangers is a means by which inhabitable or bounded spaces are produced ('this street'), not simply as the place or locality of residence, but as the very living form of a community.

In this chapter, I analyse how the discourse of stranger danger produces the stranger as a figure—a shape that appears to have linguistic and bodily integrity—which comes then to embody that which must be expelled from the purified space of the community, the purified life of the good citizen, and the purified body of 'the child'. Such an approach to 'the stranger' considers how encounters between others involve the production and over-representation of the stranger as a figure of the unknowable. That is, such encounters allow the stranger to appear, to take form, *by recuperating all that is unknowable into a figure that we imagine we might face here, now, in the street.*

On Recognition

To recognise means: to know again, to acknowledge and to admit. How do we know the stranger *again*? The recognisability of strangers is determinate in the social demarcation of spaces of belonging: the stranger is 'known again' as that which has already contaminated such spaces as a threat to both property and person: 'many residents are concerned about the strangers with whom they must share the public space, including wandering homeless people, aggressive beggars, muggers, anonymous black youths, and drug addicts' (Anderson 1990: 238). Recognising strangers is here embedded in a discourse of survival: it is a question of how to survive the proximity of strangers who are already figurable, *who have already taken shape,* in the everyday encounters we have with others.

A consideration of the production of the stranger's figure through modes of recognition requires that we begin with an analysis of the function of local encounters in public life. As Erving Goffman suggests, 'public life' refers to the realm of activity generated by face-to-face interactions that are organised by norms of co-mingling (1972: ix). Such an approach does not take for granted the realm of the public as a physical space that is already determined, but considers how 'the public' comes to be lived through local encounters, through the very gestures and habits of meeting up with others. How do such meetings, such face-to-face encounters, involve modes of recognition that produce the stranger as a figure?

Louis Althusser's thesis of subjectivity as determined through acts of misrecognition evokes the function of public life. Althusser writes:

> *ideology 'acts' or 'functions' in such a way that it 'recruits' subjects among the individuals (it recruits them all), or 'transforms' the individuals into subjects (it transforms them all) by that very precise operation which I have called* interpellation *or hailing, and which can be imagined along the lines of the most commonplace everyday police (or other) hailing: 'Hey, you there!'*
>
> *(1971: 162–163)*

All individuals are transformed into subjects through the ideological function of interpellation, which is imagined as a commonplace everyday police (or other) hailing. The recognition of the other as 'you there' is a misrecognition which produces the 'you' as a subject, and as subject to the very law implicated in recognition (the subject is suspect in such encounters). Althusser's thesis is clearly to be understood as a universal theory of how subjects come into being as such. However, we might note the following. First, the constitution of the subject through hailing implies that subjectivity is predicated upon an elided 'inter-subjectivity' (see Ahmed 1998a: 143). Second, the function of the act of hailing an-other, 'hey you', opens out the possibility *that subjects become differentiated at the very same moment that they are constituted as such*. If we think of the constitution of subjects as implicated in the uncertainties of public life, then we could imagine how such differentiation might work: the address of the policeman shifts according to whether individuals are already recognisable as, 'wandering homeless people, aggressive beggars, muggers, anonymous black youths, and drug addicts' (Anderson 1990: 238). Hailing as a form of recognition which constitutes the subject it recognises (= misrecognition) might function to differentiate *between* subjects, for example, by hailing differently those who seem to belong and those who might already be assigned a place—out of place—as 'suspect'.

Such an over-reading of Althusser's dramatisation of interpellation through commonplace hailing suggests that the subject is not simply constituted in the present as such. Rather, inter-subjective encounters in public life continually reinterpellate subjects into differentiated economies of names and signs, where they are assigned different value in social spaces. Noticeably, the use of the narrative of the police hailing associates the constitution of subjects with their subjection to a discourse of criminality, which defines the one who is hailed as a threat to property ('Hey, you there'). If we consider how hailing constitutes the subject, then we can also think about how hailing constitutes the stranger in a relationship precisely to the Law of the subject (the stranger is constituted as the unlawful entry into the nation space, the stranger hence allows Law to mark out its terrain). To this extent, the act of hailing or recognising some-body as a stranger serves to constitute the lawful subject, the one who has the right to dwell, and the stranger at the very same time. It is not that the 'you' is or can be simply a stranger, but that to address some-body as a stranger constitutes the 'you' as the stranger in relation to the one who dwells (the friend and neighbour). In this sense, the (mis)recognition of strangers serves to differentiate between the familiar and the strange, a differentiation that allows the figure of the stranger to appear. The failure embedded in such misrecognition—rather than the failure of recognition—determines the impossibility of reducing the other to the figure of the stranger: as I will argue in Chapter 2, the singularity of the figure conceals the different histories of lived embodiment which mark some bodies as stranger than others.

By analysing recognition in this way, I am suggesting that the (lawful) subject is not simply constituted by being recognised by the other, which is the primary post-Hegelian model of recognition (see Taylor 1994). Rather, I am suggesting that it is the recognition of others that is central to the constitution of the subject. The very act through which the subject differentiates between others is the moment that the subject comes to inhabit or dwell in the world. The subject is not, then, simply differentiated from the (its) other, but comes into being by learning how to differentiate between others. This recognition operates as *a visual economy*: it involves ways of *seeing the difference* between familiar and strange others as they are (re)presented to the subject. As a mode of subject constitution, recognition involves differentiating between others on the basis of how they 'appear'.[2]

Given the way in which the recognition of strangers operates to produce who 'we' are, we can see that strangers already 'fit' within the 'cognitive, moral or aesthetic map of the world', rather than being, as Zygmunt Bauman argues, 'the people who do not fit' (1997: 46). There are established ways of dealing with 'the strangers' who are already encountered and recognised in public life. The recognisability of strangers involves, not only techniques for differentiating strange from familiar (ways of seeing), but also ways of living: there are, in Alfred Schutz's terms, 'standardized situations' in which we might encounter strangers and which allow us to negotiate our way past them (1944: 499). Goffman's work on bodily stigma, for example, attends to how the bodies of others that are marked as different, such as disabled bodies, are read in ways which allow the subject to keep their distance (1984: 12). Social encounters involve rules and procedures for 'dealing with' the bodies that are read as strange (Morris 1996: 72–74).

Encounters between embodied others hence involve *spatial negotiations* with those who are already recognised as either familiar or strange. For Schutz, the stranger is always approaching—coming closer to those who are at home (1944: 499). In the sociological analysis of strangers offered by Simmel, the stranger is understood, paradoxically, as both near and far (1991: 146). In the next section, I consider how the determination of social space and imagined forms of belonging takes place through the differentiation between strangers and neighbours in relationships of proximity and distance.

Neighbourhoods and dwelling

How do you recognise who is a stranger in your neighbourhood? To rephrase my original question in this way is to point to the relation between the recognition of strangers and one's habitat or dwelling: others are recognised as strangers by those who inhabit a given space, who 'make it' their own. As Michael Dillon argues, 'with the delimitation of any place of dwelling, the constitution of a people, a nation, a state, or a democracy necessarily specifies who is *estranged from* that identity, place or regime' (1999: 119; emphasis added). At one level, this seems to suggest the relativisability of the condition of strangers: any-one can be a stranger if they leave home (the house, the neighbourhood, the region, the nation).[3] However, in this section I want to argue that forms of dwelling cannot be equated in order to allow such a relativisation. Some homes and neighbourhoods are privileged such that they define the terrain of the inhabitable world. The recognition of strangers brings into play relations of social and political antagonism that *mark some others as stranger than other others.*

How do neighbourhoods become imagined? In the work of Howard Hallman, neighbourhoods are understood as arising from the 'natural human trait' of being neighbourly, which combines a concern with others and a concern for self (1984: 11). According to Hallman, the neighbourhood is an organic community that grows, 'naturally wherever people live close to one another' (1984: 11). It is both a limited territory—a physical space with clear boundaries—and a social community where 'residents do things together' (1984: 13).The simple fact of living nearby gives neighbours a common social bond. However, according to Hallman, some neighbourhoods are closer and hence better than others. He argues that neighbourhoods are more likely to be successful as communities when people live near 'like people': 'people with similarities tend to achieve closer neighbour relationships' (1984: 24). Hallman defines a close neighbourhood through an analogy with a healthy body, 'with wounds healed, illness cured, and wellness maintained' (1984: 256).

The analogy between the ideal neighbourhood and a healthy body serves to define the ideal neighbourhood as fully integrated, homogeneous, and sealed: it is like a body that is fully contained by the skin (see Chapter 2). This implies that a good or healthy neighbourhood does not leak outside itself, and hence does not let outsiders (or foreign agents/viruses) in. The model of the neighbourhood as an organic community—where a sense of community arises from the simple fact of shared residence—defines social health in terms of the production of purified spaces and the expulsion of difference through ways of living together. Matthew Crenson's consideration of neighbourhood politics hence concludes, 'social homogeneity and solidarity . . . may contribute to the defensive capabilities of neighbourhoods, and in fact it may take an external attack upon some of these homogenous neighbourhoods to activate the latent sense of fellow feeling along local residents' (1983: 257). Likewise, David Morris and Karl Hess describe neighbourhoods as protective and defensive, like 'tiny underdeveloped nations' (1975: 16).

Neighbourhoods become imagined as organic and pure spaces through the social perception of the danger posed by outsiders to moral and social health or well-being. So although neighbourhoods have been represented as organic and pure communities, there is also an assumption that those communities will fail (to be). A failed community is hence one which has weak or negative connections: where neighbours appear as if they are strangers to each other. The neighbour who is also a stranger—who only passes as a neighbour—is hence the danger that may always threaten the community from within. As David Sibley argues, 'the resistance to a different sort of person moving into a neighbourhood stems from feelings of anxiety, nervousness or fear. Who is felt to belong and not to belong contributes to an important way of shaping social space' (1995: 3). However, the failure of the community should not just be understood in terms of failed communities. *It is the very potential of the community to fail which is required for the constitution of the community*. It is the enforcement of the boundaries between those who are already recognised as out of place (even other fellow residents) that allows those boundaries to be established. The 'ideal' community has to be worked towards and that labour requires failure as its moment of constitution (to this extent, then, the organic community is a fantasy that *requires* its own negation).

It is symptomatic then of the very nature of neighbourhood that it enters public discourse as a site of *crisis*: it is only by attending to the trauma of neighbourhoods which fail that the ideal of the healthy neighbourhood can be maintained as a possibility (which is then, endlessly deferred as 'the real', as well as endlessly kept in place as 'the ideal', by that very language of crisis). Such failed communities are the source of fascination: they demonstrate the need to regulate social spaces. On British television in 1998, there were a number of programmes dedicated to 'neighbours from hell', neighbours who are dirty, who make too much noise, who steal, and who are 'at war' with each other. On *Panorama*'s 'Neighbours from Hell' (30 March 1998), urinating in the street becomes the ultimate expression of the antisociability of stranger neighbours. The passing of bodily fluids in public spaces becomes symptomatic of the failure to pass as neighbours. In the United Kingdom, new powers of eviction for local councils give further power to the community to reassert itself against these stranger neighbours. The imaginary community of the neighbourhood hence requires enforcement through Law.

The enforcement of the boundaries which allow neighbourhoods to be imagined as pure and organic spaces can be understood as central to neighbourhood watch schemes. Such schemes began in the United States in the 1970s, and in the United Kingdom in 1982. The National Neighbourhood Watch Association in the United Kingdom (NNWA) describes it as, 'the best known and most effective example of the police and community working together in partnership to prevent crime, build safer communities and improve quality of life'. In the United Kingdom, there are currently over 161,000 schemes and over 10 million people involved. Neighbourhood Watch brings together the creation of an ideal community as one 'which cares' and the production of safer spaces through the discourse of 'crime prevention'. Its main motto is, 'Crime cannot survive in a community that cares—Neighbourhood Watch works'. In other words, crime only exists when communities fail, when communities do not care. Marginalised or under-valued spaces where there is a high rate of crime against property are hence immediately understood in terms of *a failure to care*.

Neighbourhood Watch schemes are more common in middle-class areas, where residents are more likely to want to co-operate with the police, and where there is more 'property' with value to protect (Hill 1994: 150). The value attached to certain spaces of belonging is enforced or 'watched' through schemes that allow middle-class spaces to become valued: the subject who watches out for crime, is also *maintaining the value of her or his neighbourhood*. The link here between value of spaces, the protection of property, and the maintenance of social privilege helps us to theorise how the defence of social boundaries against unwelcome intrusions and intruders produces certain categories of strangers—those who don't belong in the leafy suburbs—that are socially legitimated and enforced. In Elijah Anderson's work, there is a discussion of how the concern with safety amongst residents means that, 'they join their diverse counterparts in local struggles to fight crime and otherwise preserve the ideal character for the neighbourhood, forming town watches and shoring up municipal codes that might discourage undesirables and encourage others more to their liking' (1990: 4). The production of safe spaces that have value or 'ideal character' involves the expulsion of unlike and undesirable 'characters'. In Anderson's work, these characters have *already* materialised or taken the form of, 'wandering homeless people, aggressive beggars, muggers, anonymous black youths, and drug addicts' (1990: 238).

How does neighbourhood watch work to produce such safe spaces? The literature produced on the Neighbourhood Watch schemes by the Home Office in the United Kingdom certainly links the designation of value to social spaces with the detection of strange events, and the expulsion of strangers. There is a double emphasis on the improvement of community living and on security and crime prevention. So Neighbourhood Watch schemes are described as both providing 'the eyes and ears of the police' and as providing, 'the soul and heart of the community' (Home Office 1997). The NWS link the production of safe spaces with the organic growth of a healthy social body: 'Neighbourhood Watch is not just about reducing burglary figures—it's about creating communities who care. It brings local people together and can make a real contribution to improving their lives. The activity of Watch members can foster a new community spirit and a belief in the community's ability to tackle problems. At the same time, you feel secure, knowing your neighbours are keeping an eye on your property' (1997). There is a constant shift between an emphasis on a caring community and a safe one: a safe community moreover is one in which you feel safe as your property is being 'watched' by your neighbours. A link is established here between safety (in which safety is associated with property), a discourse on good neighbourliness (looking out for each other) and the production of community as purified space ('a new community spirit'). Hence, 'it is widely accepted that within every community, there is the potential for crime prevention. Neighbourhood Watch is a way of tapping into this and of drawing a community together'. Neighbourhood Watch hence constitutes the neighbourhood as a community through the protection of the property of nearby others from the threat posed by the very proximity of distant others.

In an earlier Neighbourhood Watch pamphlet (Home Office 1992), the reader is addressed more directly, 'Deciding to join your local group means you have made a positive commitment to act against crime in your community. You have also become one of the largest and most successful grass-roots movements in the country.' Here, the reader is praised for her or his community spirit: not only are you a good neighbour—willing to look out for your neighbours—but you are also a good citizen, who has displayed a positive commitment to 'act against crime in the community'. Neighbourhood watch purifies the space of the community *through purifying the life of the good citizen,* whose life becomes heroic, dedicated to fighting against crime and disorder. Significantly, then, the praise given to the reader/citizen involves a form of reward/recognition: 'You can also get lower insurance premiums from some Insurance companies' (1992). The reward demonstrates the value given to social spaces where subjects watch out for the extraordinary sounds and signs of crime, or the sounds and signs of that which is suspect and suspicious.

But how does Neighbourhood Watch involve techniques of differentiating between the ordinary life of the purified neighbourhood and the extraordinary events that threaten to contaminate that space? The Home Office pamphlet is cautious, 'Sometimes it is hard to tell if you are witnessing a crime or not. You must rely on common sense. . . . You may also become suspicious if you notice something out of the ordinary. Don't be afraid to call your local police station to report the incident' (1992). Here, common sense should tell the good citizen what they are witnessing. Whatever happens, the good citizen must be a witness: a witness to an event that might or might not be a crime, an *event that unfolds before the patient eye and ear*. The last sentence moves from the importance of differentiating between extraordinary events through common sense (is it a crime?), to the differentiation between ordinary and extraordinary. Here, you might be made suspicious by *some-thing* out of the ordinary. The good citizen is a citizen who *suspects rather than is suspect,* who watches out for departures from ordinary life in the imagined space of the neighbourhood. The good citizen hence watches out for the one who loiters, acts suspiciously, looks out of place. As a Chief Inspector explains in a letter to *The Independent,* 'Neighbourhood Watch is about looking after your property and that of your neighbours, taking sensible crime prevention action *and reporting suspicious persons to the police*' (Scougal 1996, emphasis added). According to the leaflet given by the Divisional Commander to Neighbourhood Watch coordinators, Neighbourhood Watch 'rests on the concept of good neighbourliness', which means that, 'Neighbours are encouraged to report suspicious persons and unusual events to the police'. With such an exercise in good neighbourliness and good citizenship, the neighbourhood comes to police itself: not only is it 'the heart and soul of the community', but in being the 'heart and soul of the community', it is also '*the ears and eyes of the police*'.

The signifier 'suspicious' does an enormous amount of work in Neighbourhood Watch discourse precisely insofar as it is *empty*. The good citizen is not given any information about how to tell what or who is suspicious in the first place. It is my argument that the very failure to provide us with techniques for telling the difference is itself a technique of knowledge. It is the technique of *common sense* that is produced through Neighbourhood Watch discourse. Common sense not only defines what 'we' should take for granted (that is, what is normalised and already known as 'the given'), but it also involves the normalisation of ways of 'sensing' the difference between common and uncommon. That is, information is not given about how to tell the difference between normal and suspicious, because that difference is already 'sensed' through a prior history of making sense *as* the making of 'the common'. The good citizen knows what they are looking for, because they know what is common, and so what departs from the common: 'You must rely on common sense' (1992). Neighbourhood watch is hence about *making* the common: it makes the community ('the heart and soul of the community') insofar as it looks out for and hears the threat to the common posed by those who are uncommon, or those who are 'out of place' in 'this place' ('the eyes and ears of the police').

In this way, the 'suspicious person' and 'the stranger' are intimately linked: they are both emptied of any content, or any direct relationship to a referent, precisely as they are tied to a (missing) history of seeing and hearing others: *they are both already seen and heard as 'the uncommon' which allows 'the common' to take its shape.* The failure to name those who inhabit the signifier 'suspicious' hence produces the figure of the unspecified stranger, a figure that is required by the making or sensing of 'the common', of what 'we' are, as a form of distinction or value (property). Neighbourhood Watch can be characterised as a form of humanism. Such a humanism—Neighbourhood Watch is 'about creating communities who care' (1992)—conceals the exclusions that operate to allow the definition and policing of the 'we' of the good neighbourhood. The definition and enforcement of the good 'we' operates through the recognition of others as strangers: by seeing those who do not belong simply as 'strangers' (that is, by not naming *who* are the ones who do not belong in the community), forms of social exclusion are both concealed and revealed (what is concealed is the brute fact of the matter—only some others are recognisable as 'the stranger', the one who is out of place). In this sense, the policing of valued spaces allows the legitimation of social exclusion by being tied to a heroic 'we' who takes shape against the figure of the unspecified stranger. The production of the stranger as a figure that has linguistic and bodily integrity conceals how strangers are always already specified or differentiated. Neighbourhood Watch becomes definable as a mechanism for ensuring, not only that certain spaces maintain their (property) value, but that *certain lives become valued over other lives.* The recognition of strangers within the neighbourhood does not mean that anybody can be a stranger, depending on her or his location in the world: rather, some-bodies are more recognisable as strangers than other-bodies precisely because they are already read and valued in the demarcation of social spaces.

What is also significant about the Neighbourhood Watch concern with seeing and hearing the difference (becoming the eyes and ears of the police), is that it involves the production of a model of 'good citizenship'. The discourse on good citizenship involves an individualising of responsibility for crime (Stanko 1997). This model of the good citizen, which Stanko's work suggests is very much gendered as masculine, takes such responsibility in part through a form of self-policing by, in some sense, *becoming the police.* Certainly in post-Foucauldian work on surveillance, the emphasis is on the shift from public forms of monitoring—where the subject is watched by an anonymous and partially unseen and partially seen Other—to self-monitoring, when *the subject adopts the gaze of the other* (Foucault 1975). My analysis of Neighbourhood Watch might complicate this model of displacement from the gaze of the other to the gaze of the self. The 'eye' of the good citizen is certainly the site of labour—it is this 'eye' that is doing the work. However, that 'eye' does not simply return to the body, as that which must be transformed and regulated as 'the seen', but looks elsewhere, to and at others. In other words, 'the good citizen' is one who watches (out for) suspicious persons and strangers, and who in that very act, becomes aligned, not only with the police (and hence the Law), but with the imagined community itself whose boundaries are protected *in the very labour of his look.*

45

Furthermore, self-policing communities are inscribed as moral communities, those that care. Caring evokes a figure of who must be cared for, who must be protected from the risks of crime and the danger of strangers. So Neighbourhood Watch 'reassures vulnerable members of the community that you are keeping a neighbourly eye on them' (1992). The construction of the figure of the vulnerable member/body alongside the heroic good citizen provides the moral justification for the injunction to watch; it detaches 'watching out for' from 'busybodying' (1992) by redefining it as 'watching out on behalf of'. The discourse of vulnerability allows self-policing to be readable as the protection of others: the risk posed by suspects and strangers is a risk posed to the vulnerable bodies of children, the elderly and women. The figuring of the good citizen is built on the image of the strong citizen: in this sense, the good citizen is figurable primarily as white, masculine and middle-class, the heroic subject who can protect the vulnerable bodies of 'weaker others': 'crime cannot survive in a community that cares—Neighbourhood Watch Works' (NNWA).

The 1997 pamphlet also describes the newer scheme 'Street Watch' (there are currently over 20,000 in operation in the United Kingdom) which, 'covers many different activities, ranging from providing transport or escort services for elderly people, to walking a specific route regularly, keeping an eye out for trouble and reporting it to the police'. Here, the good citizen is valued not only for his heart, eyes and ears, but also his feet.[4] He takes specific routes, but most importantly, according to the Home Secretary responsible for the introduction of the scheme, Michael Howard, he is 'walking with purpose' (Bennetto 1995). Street Watch is described as 'patrolling with a purpose'.

We can consider here Hallman's definition of who and what must be watched in his work on neighbourhoods: 'people who seem to have no purpose in the neighbourhood' (Hallman 1984: 159). Strangers are suspicious because they 'have no purpose', that is, they have no legitimate function within the space which could justify their existence or intrusion. Strangers are hence recognisable precisely insofar as they *do not enter into the exchanges of capital that transforms spaces into places*. Strangers are constructed as an illegitimate presence in the neighbourhood: they have no purpose, and hence they must be suspect. You can recognise the stranger through their loitering gait: strangers loiter, they do not enter the legitimate exchanges of capital that might justify their presence. In contrast, the street watcher is constructed as a heroic figure whose purpose is the very detection of those who are without a legitimate purpose, of those whose purpose can hence only be explained as suspicious, as criminal, as a crime (Young 1996: 5). The stranger's presence on the street is a crime (waiting to happen). The proximity of such loitering strangers in the purified space of the good neighbourhood hence requires that the heroic citizen take a specific route: those who are recognisable as strangers, *whose lack of purpose conceals the purpose of crime,* need to be expelled through purposeful patrolling in order that the value of property can be protected.

Such a construction of the good citizen through the figure of the loitering stranger is clearly subject to forms of social differentiation: in one reading, the good citizen is structured around the body of the dominant (white, middle-class) man, who protects the vulnerable bodies of women and children from the threat of marginalised (black, working-class) men. However, these differences are concealed by the very modes of recognition: the figure of the stranger appears as 'the stranger' precisely by being cut off from these histories of determination (= stranger fetishism). That is, the recognition of strangers involves the differentiation between some others and other others at the same time as it conceals that very act of differentiation. What is significant about Neighbourhood Watch is precisely the way in which it links the formation of community with safety and the detection of crime: such links produce the figure of the stranger as a *visible danger* to the 'we' of the community, and hence as the necessary condition for making what 'we' have in common.

Stranger danger

If the construction and enforcement of purified spaces of belonging takes place through the production of the figures of the good citizen, the vulnerable body and the loitering stranger, then how is this linked to the social perception of danger? In this section, I examine the discourse of stranger danger as a way of analysing how strangers are already recognised as posing danger to property and person, not just in particular valued dwellings and neighbourhoods, but also in public life as such. I want to consider, not only how the construction of stranger danger is tied to valued and devalued spaces, but also how strangers are read as posing danger *wherever* they are: the projection of danger onto the figure of the stranger allows the definition of the subject-at-home, and home as inhabitable space, as inherently safe and valuable. One *knows again* those whom one does not know by assuming they are the *origin* of danger.

Partly, this concern with public life involves a consideration of urban space and cities as 'a world of strangers' (Lofland 1973). Lofland suggests that cities, in particular public spaces within cities (such as streets and leisure spaces), involve perpetual encounters between people who are not personally known to each other, although they may be known through forms of visual identification and recognition (1973: 15–16). As a result, he argues that cities involve particular kinds of social and spatial encounters. I would not want to refute the premise that there are different kinds of spaces that involve different kinds of encounters between others (such as urban and rural spaces, or such as different forms of the public within urban spaces). However, Lofland's account does involve a form of spatial determinism— these spaces determine these encounters between others—which shifts quickly into a form of cultural determinism—cultures have different spaces and therefore involve different encounters between others.[5] What I am interested in is how the very encounters that take place between others involve the forming of both cultural and spatial boundaries: that is, how the (mis)recognition of others as strangers is what allows the demarcation of given spaces within 'the public domain', but also the legitimation of certain forms of mobility or movement within the public, and the delegitimation of others.

I am positing here a relationship between dwelling and movement:[6] spaces' are claimed, or 'owned' not so much by inhabiting what is already there, but by moving within, or passing through, different spaces which are only given value as places (with boundaries) through the movement or 'passing through' itself. The relationship between movement, occupation and ownership is well documented in feminist work: for example, women's restricted movement within public spaces is a result, not only of the fear of crime, but of the regulation of femininity, in which 'being seen' in certain spaces becomes a sign of irresponsibility (Stanko 1997: 489). Women's movements are regulated by a desire for 'safe-keeping': respectability becomes measured by the visible signs of a desire to 'stay safe'. In this sense, movement becomes a form of subject constitution: *where* 'one' goes or does not go determines *what* one 'is', or where one is seen to be, determines what one is seen to be.

Elijah Anderson's work on how communities are established through the concern with safety examines how the fear of crime becomes a fear of strangers. Such a fear produces a way of inhabiting the world, as well as moving through it. He writes, 'Many worry about a figure lurking in the shadows, hiding in a doorway or behind a clump of bushes, ready to pounce on the unsuspecting victim' (Anderson 1990: 5). The danger posed by the stranger is imagined as partly concealed: the stranger always lurks in dark spaces. While the victim is unsuspecting, the safe subject must be suspecting: the safe subject suspects that the suspect is around the corner, always hidden to the gaze, to the watchful eye. The danger of the stranger is hence always there in the imagined future of the subject who is safely at home, the stranger is always lurking as the threat of that-which-might-yet-be. Safety hence requires that the subject must become familiar with the terrain: the safe subject must become 'street wise' and 'alive to dangerous situations' (Anderson 1990: 6). Certain lives become liveable as both safe and valuable insofar as they are *alive to* the danger of strangers.

The discourse of personal safety is not about the production of safe and purified spaces from which strangers are expelled (such as 'the home'), but also defines ways of moving through spaces that are already dangerous given the possibility that strangers are close by, waiting in the shadows of the streets (where good citizens walk only with purpose, living their legitimated lives). The possibility of personal safety for mobile subjects hence requires 'collective definitions' of that which is 'safe, harmless, trustworthy' and that which is 'bad, dangerous and hostile' (Anderson 1990: 216). Such collective definitions provide the subject with the knowledge required to move within the world, allowing the subject to differentiate between familiar and strange, safe and dangerous, as well as to differentiate between different kinds of strangers ('characters').

Clearly, discourses of personal safety involve forms of self-governance that differentiate between subjects. As much feminist research has suggested, safety for women is often constructed in terms of not entering public spaces, or staying within the home (see Stanko 1990). Safety for men also involves forms of self-governance, not in terms of refusing to enter the public space, but in terms of *how* one enters that space. So at one level, the discoruse of personal safety presumes a vulnerable citizen who is gendered as feminine, at another level, it legislates for a form of mobile and masculine subjectivity that is not only a safe form of subjectivity, but also one that is heroic. Such a mobile subject, who can 'avoid' the danger of strangers in public spaces is constructed as 'street wise'. This subject's mobility is legitimated as a form of dwelling: first, in relation to the vulnerable bodies that stay within the home; and second, in relation to the strangers whose passing though public spaces is delegitimated as the 'origin' of danger (the movement of strangers is hence not a form of dwelling: it does not lead to the legitimated occupation of space).

The knowledges embedded in street wisdom are linked by Anderson to a kind of 'field research' (Anderson 1990: 216). The wise subject, the one who knows where and where not to walk, how and how not to move, who and who not to talk to, has an expertise that can be understood as both *bodily and cultural capital*. It is such wise subjects who will prevail in a world of strangers and dangers: 'To prevail means simply to get safely to one's destination, and the ones who are most successful are those who are "streetwise" ' (Anderson 1990: 231). In this sense, the discourse of stranger danger involves techniques of knowledge that allow wise subjects to prevail: to arrive at their destination, to leave and return home and still maintain a safe distance between themselves and dangerous strangers. Community is not just established through the designation of pure and safe spaces, but becomes established *as a way of moving through space*. Becoming street wise defines the subject in terms of the collective: the wise subject has collective knowledge about what is, 'safe, harmless, trustworthy' and what is 'bad, dangerous and hostile' that gives that subject the ability to move safely in a world of strangers and dangers. The stranger is here produced as a figure of danger that grants the wise subject and community, those who already claim both knowledge and capital, the ability to prevail.

The discourse of stranger danger also involves the figuring, not only of the wiser subject who can move through dangerous places (a mobile subject who is racialised, classed and gendered), but also the vulnerable body, the one who is most at risk. Here, 'the child' becomes a figure of vulnerability, the purified body that is most endangered by the contaminating desires of strangers. Indeed, it is the literature on child protection that has familiarised 'stranger danger' as the mechanism for ensuring personal safety. One double page of the Home Office leaflet on crime prevention in the United Kingdom is hence dedicated to 'your family' and, 'to keeping your children safe' (the ideal reader/subject/citizen is always a parent, bound to Law and duty through the demands of parenthood). The pamphlet advises, 'Do not talk to strangers. Most well-meaning adults will not approach a child who is on his own, unless he is obviously distressed or in need. Tell your children never to talk to strangers, and to politely ignore any approach from a stranger. Get them to tell you if a stranger tries to talk to them.' Immediately, strangers are differentiated from 'well-meaning' adults, who would not approach children. Indeed, the child itself must become 'street wise': one colouring-in book produced by the Lancashire Constabulary in the United Kingdom is entitled, 'Operation Streetwise workbook' and aims 'to provide children with an exciting opportunity to learn and practice personal safety skills'. Here, growing up is narrated in terms of acquiring the wisdom to deal with danger that already stalks in the figure of the stranger.[7]

The figure of the child comes to perform a certain role within the narrative of crime prevention and stranger danger: the innocence of the child is what is most at risk from the proximity of strangers. The child comes to embody, in a narrative that is both nostalgic (returning to an imagined past) and fearful (projecting an unimaginable future), all that could be stolen or lost by the proximity of strangers. The child's innocence and purity becomes a matter of social and national responsibility: through figuring the stranger as too close to the child, the stranger becomes recognisable as an attack on the moral purity of nation space itself. It is over the bodies of children that the moral campaign against strangers is waged.

In recent debates in the press, the paedophile is hence represented as the ultimate stranger that communities must have the power to evict. A change in the law in 1997 allowed the British police force to inform members of the community when a paedophile is in their midst, on a 'need to know' basis. Community action groups, as well as some local councils, have redefined the need to know as *a right to know*: arguing that paedophiles should not be allowed into communities as they pose a risk to children, 'Recent moves include attempts by some councils to ban paedophiles from their communities altogether, and campaigns to keep them in prison longer' (Hilpern 1997). The construction of sex offenders against children as monsters who do not belong in a community is clear in the following statement from John O'Sullivan, from the pressure group, *Parents Against Child Abuse*: 'If there is a wild lion loose in the street, the police would tell us. A paedophile in the neighbourhood is the same. They might not rip the flesh, but they are just as damaging to the mind of a child. We need to know who they are.' The number of vigilante attacks on suspected paedophiles in Britain in the 1990s suggests what this knowledge will be used for.

Significantly, then, the paedophile comes to embody the most dangerous stranger as he poses the greatest risk to the vulnerable and pure body of the child. The community comes together through the recognition of such dangerous strangers: they must expel him, he who is the wild animal, the lion, at loose in the street. The monstrosity of such recognisable strangers is figured through the tearing of the skin of the child. The monsters who must be excluded to keep children safe, prey on children: they require the heroic action of the moral community that cares. The imaginary community is constructed as a safe community where children's bodies are not vulnerable: the moral community itself becomes the child, pure, innocent and free. The recognition of dangerous strangers allows the enforcement of the boundaries of such communities: a definition of the purity of the 'we' against the monstrous 'it'.

Sally Engle Merry's *Urban Danger: Life in a Neighbourhood of Strangers,* discusses how the fear of crime 'focuses on the threat of the violent attack by a stranger' (Merry 1981: 6). Such a fear means that the familiar is already designated as safe: one is safe at home, unless there is an intrusion from a stranger. One could comment here how such a reduction of danger to the stranger conceals the danger that may be embedded in the familiar: much feminist work, for example, demonstrates how the perception of the rapist as a stranger conceals how most sexual attacks are committed by friends or family. As Elizabeth Stanko argues, 'Danger many of us believe arises from the random action of strangers who are, we further assume, usually men of colour. Yet according to most people's experiences . . . danger and violence arise within our interpersonal relationships' (1990: 3). The projection of danger onto the figure of the stranger allows violence to be figured as exceptional and extraordinary—as coming from outside the protective walls of the home, family, community or nation. As a result, the discourse of stranger danger involves *a refusal to recognise how violence is structured by, and legitimated through, the formation of home and community as such*.

The stranger is here figured as the violent monster whose elimination would mean safety for women and children. Such a figuration allows the home to be imagined as a safe haven: an imagining that cannot deal with the violence that is instituted through the social relations within the home. As Merry argues, 'Violence at the hand of the stranger is usually perceived as dangerous, but an assault in the context of a fight with a known enemy or neighbour is rarely viewed in this way' (Merry 1981: 14). The notion of violence as domestic, while now recognised through Law as a result of years of feminist campaigning, remains a difficult one for the social imaginary: the violent husband is then read as a monster underneath, as a stranger passing as husband, rather than as a husband exercising the power that is already legitimated through hegemonic forms of masculinity. According to stranger danger discourse, the stranger husband has intruded into the ideal home: he is not understood as an element *in the ordinary production of domestic space*, and in the formation of relations of power and exchange within that space.

The ultimate violent strangers are hence figured as immigrants: they are the outsiders in the nation space whose 'behaviour seems unpredictable and beyond control' (Merry 1981: 125). Cultural difference becomes the text upon which the fear of crime is written: 'cultural difference exacerbates feelings of danger. Encounters with culturally alien people are defined by anxiety and uncertainty, which inhibits social interaction and reinforces social boundaries' (Merry 1981: 125). The projection of danger onto that which is already recognisable as different—as different from the familiar space of home and homeland—hence allows violence to take place: it becomes a mechanism for the enforcement of boundary lines that almost secure the home-nation as safe haven. On the one hand, the fear of crime embedded in the discourse of stranger danger allows the protection of domestic, social and national space from the outsider inside, the stranger neighbour, by projecting danger onto the outsider. On the other hand, the stranger only appears as a figure of danger by coming too close to home: the boundary line is always crossed, both 'justifying' the fear and legitimating the enforcement. In doing so, the discourse of stranger danger, not only allows the abdication of any social and political responsibility for the violence that takes place within legitimated spaces, and which is sanctioned through Law, but also becomes a mechanism for the justification of acts of violence against those who are already recognised as strangers.

In this chapter, I have examined how 'the stranger' is produced as a figure precisely by being associated with a danger to the purified space of the community, the purified life of the good citizen, and the purified body of 'the child'. Rather than assuming that the stranger is any-body we don't recognise, I have argued that strangers are those that are already recognised through techniques for differentiating between the familiar and strange in discourses such as Neighbourhood Watch and crime prevention. The 'knowing again' of strangers defines the stranger as a danger to both moral health and well-being. The knowing again of strangers as the danger of the unknown is a means by which the 'we' of the community is established, enforced and legitimated.

Endnotes

1 To the extent that I am challenging the assumed opposition between strange and familiar (and also in Chapter 4, between home and away), I am following Freud, whose model of the uncanny emphasises how the strange leads back to the

familiar. He also suggests that homely (*das Heimliche*) and unhomely (*das Unheimliche*) are intimately linked (Freud 1964: 225–226). However, Freud explains this intimacy of apparent opposites through a model of repression: 'this uncanny is in reality nothing new or alien, but something which is familiar and old established in the mind and which has become alienated from it only through a process of repression' (1964: 241). In contrast, I am seeking to explain the familiarity of the stranger by considering the *production* rather than repression of that which is strange: the stranger is produced as an effect of recognition and as a category of knowledge (see Chapter 2), and is henceforth familiar in its very strangeness. When we look out 'for strangers' we already know what we are looking for.

2   In Chapter 2, I consider how the recognition of strangers involves an economy of touch, as well as a visual economy. We can also note here that recognition has become an important part of political struggle—marginalised groups struggle to be recognised, or *to be seen,* by mainstream politics, which is also a struggle against forms of misrecognition (Taylor 1994; Fraser 1997). A key debate has emerged within feminism on the limits of the politics of recognition (see also Brown 1995; Skeggs 1999). Although I can't enter these debates here, my analysis of how recognition operates as a visual economy in everyday life and social encounters between others might suggest some limits to a politics of recognition, although it might also suggest the difficulties of simply overcoming recognition. In Chapter 6, I complicate this model of recognition as 'seeing the difference' by considering the implications of the structural possibility that the difference might not be seeable as the subject may be passing as it 'passes through' the community.

3   For a discussion of the relationship between migration and strangers see Chapter 4. Here, I argue that migration does not allow us to relativise the condition of strangerness.

4   Alene Branton, secretary to the steering committee of the National Neighbourhood Watch Association in the UK, is reported to have said, 'We were set up to be the eyes and ears of the police. We never expected to be the feet as well' (Bennetto 1995).

5   He contrasts the modern proximity of strangers with 'primitive cultures' where strangers are more at a distance.

6   I also consider the relationship between dwelling and movement in chapters 4 and 8 where I develop the notion of 'global nomadic citizenship'.

7   Importantly, stranger danger discourse attempts to define the stranger as anybody we don't know; it seeks to contest what I have called the recognisability of strangers, and the assumption that 'strangers' only look a certain way. As James Brewer puts it, 'Who are the bad guys? How can you recognise them before its too late? . . . What do the bad guys look like? They look like *YOU*' (1994: 15, 17). What this reveals, despite itself, is precisely the ways in which strangers are already recognised as looking unlike 'YOU': the discourse of stranger danger seeks to contest the very familiarity of strangers, but can only do so, by first confirming that familiarity, and the 'common-sense' assumption that danger is posed only by certain bodies, who are marked by their difference from the everyday of the neighbourhood.

4

Race-ing Men: Boys, Risk, and the Politics of Race

AMY L. BEST

As an ethnographer, Amy Best studies youth, culture, and social inequalities, by analyzing how gender, sexuality, race and class, and nationality inform how youth produce identities for themselves and how they travel in and between different social spaces. Best has studied the rules and rituals governing proms, and in this 2006 book called fast cars, cool rides: the accelerating world of youth and their cars, *she explores the significance of cars for youth today—as transportation, as freedom, as status, as identity. This chapter draws on over 100 interviews with young men and women in order to analyze the intersections of race and masculinity. Best is an Associate Professor of Sociology and Anthropology at George Mason University.*

On a warm Tuesday morning at Freedom High School, I find myself at "auto shop" class. The room is cavernous and full of the sort of clutter one would expect to find at an actual mechanic's garage: soiled rags blackened by oil and grease strewn throughout the room, a small mountain of safety glasses in one corner, a dust-covered wind-shield in another, rows of tires stacked like doughnuts, metal cabinets spilling over with an assortment of tools. I spend much of my morning moving between the groups of boys who are scattered throughout the room before making my way over to a small huddle of boys working on a Honda CRX, a beat-up car that officially belongs to the auto shop. Right now they are working on recharging the car's battery, since it won't start. Moments before, two of the boys, Justin and David, had pushed the CRX over beside a much newer Honda Civic parked in the car lot a few feet from the car bays. The Civic is painted a purplish-blue and is equipped with a sleek body kit and shiny chrome rims. Its frame rests much lower to the ground than any stock Honda, but just enough above the shiny rims to still be "street legal." I ask the group whose car it is and a tall South Asian boy whom I come to know as Shrini offers up, "Mine." Don, who is sitting in the driver's seat of the CRX, his hands firmly placed on the steering wheel, sticks his head out the car's window to ask if I like it, which causes the group to erupt into laughter. "You can buy it if you want," Shrini tells me with a more serious tone. I ask him why he's selling it. He explains he wants to get a Subaru STi, which is much faster. Tim, a classmate, has a Subaru, the very one Shrini hopes to get after he unloads this car. Nearly all agree Tim's is the fastest car in school. And they should know. These boys and a string of others are "racers," a tag they use to distinguish themselves from the "cruisers," "lowriders," "gang-bangers,"[1] and the endless variety of other "subcultural" groups of boys at their school.[2]

Shrini's car is an automatic, a point he reluctantly offers only after I ask. Though his car has undergone some changes to the body, there have been no performance upgrades. Right now, the car doesn't run fast enough, and since it is automatic, it is unlikely it ever will. A slow car confers little status to its owner among the street racers, especially if its exterior has been customized to look fast. Such a look eventually discredits racers, attaching to them what is arguably the worst sort of shame. Speed, driver skill, and a willingness to take risks behind the wheel are what matter most in the world of street and organized racing. A slow car, no matter its appearance, provides little opportunity to demonstrate any of these virtues.

This band of boys race imports: Honda Civics and Accords, Nissans and Acura Integras, all cars imported from Japan, where a vibrant and parallel racing scene has also emerged.[3] They are part of what has been called "the Import Car Scene," which originated in southern California in the early 1990s but has spread north to San Jose and San Francisco and east beyond California. The import scene in southern California and in San Jose is dominated by Asian and Asian American young men in their teens and twenties.[4]

These young men are all Asian, first-and second-generation Chinese, Indian, and Vietnamese mostly, with exceptions like Daniel, who is Mexican. And they are students at Freedom High School, one of a handful of "low-income schools" in San Jose that has an overrepresentation of immigrants and kids of color and is also underserved in terms of both academic resources and avenues of upward mobility. The kids make up a loosely organized group of small crews that know each other mostly by the cars they drive.

Most in this group at Freedom High School own used cars, almost all purchased for less than $5,000 and almost all having anywhere between 100,000 and 150,000 miles already logged before the new owners get behind the wheel. Justin, who drives an emerald green Acura, bought his car for a clean $3,500 almost four months ago and currently has 127,000 miles logged on the odometer. For most in the group, these low-priced cars serve as templates for a series of costly modifications that in the end can more than double the initial cost of the car. Body kits, lowered suspensions, engine upgrades, multimedia systems, and altered exhaust systems make up a multibillion-dollar industry of after-market car parts, an industry largely supported by these young men and others like them who on weekend nights gather in the early hours of the morning in abandoned industrial zones and business parks to see whose car will outdrive all the others.

How do they afford these expensive car modifications? For a small number of young men tied to the import car scene, parents finance these indulgences, but not for these boys. Long hours stocking shelves, slinging burgers, punching cash register keys, and mopping floors provide just enough disposable income for them to gain access to this dizzying world of pulleys and bbk's, h-pipes, adjustable struts, sway bars, inter-cooler kits, and injectors called alternately "moding" or "tuning." They spend hours surfing the Web in search of a deal, special struts for $100 each on eBay, for example, and are proud of their ability to know a good deal when they see one. Few in the group drive new cars because they can not afford them, but others in the import car scene do. The middle- and upper-middle-class Asian American young men from Orange County, California in Victoria Namkung's 2004 study of Asian American youth culture and the import car scene all appeared to drive new cars, spending upwards of $25,000 when including the initial cost of the car and the upgrades. Many of the young men in Namkung's study came from far more affluent families than the boys at Freedom High School and were already in college, with a lot more of their own disposable income than these high schoolers. Within the broader import scene in San Jose, this is also the case.

For this group of high school boys, life revolves around their cars and racing. Economic constraint keeps them from funneling the same kind of cash into their cars that upper-income and older kids do, but it doesn't prevent them from putting whatever money they do have into "tuning" their cars. Thuy Vo, who drives a customized Honda Civic hatchback, works at Great America, a local theme park where many youth work the rides in exchange for baseline wages.[5] *All* his money, he tells me, goes to transforming his car's engine and exterior. So far he has installed a sway bar, which enables him to better handle turns at high speeds, and a new exhaust. He has shaved his door handles and removed the windshield wipers. In their place he has sprayed "Rain Off" on the windshield, a commercial product which is supposed to repel the rain. The car has been lowered several inches, the "H" that normally resides on the car's hood has been removed, and the back lights have been replaced. These exterior changes enable Thuy Vo to achieve what he considers "a cleaner look." I heard many of these import racers describe a "clean look" as a car's ideal. In many ways, this clean look achieves "an aesthetic of speed." With its sleek streamlining, its center of gravity hugging the road, the car visually appears to look fast and not "frumpy" and "rumpled" like the standard stock Civic hatchback or, worse, a lumbering American giant like a Dodge or Chevy. Beyond these changes, his car has been painted "egg-shell white," a custom color, and he has installed red car seats, new "racing" seat belts, a new steering wheel, a red racing stripe, and red and gold rims, which he painted himself to resemble from a distance a very expensive set of rims he admits he can not afford. Thuy Vo, like a number of these boys, uses auto shop to make as many of these modifications to his car as is possible given the limited resources of the school (sometimes at the expense of completing the official class projects assigned by Mr. O'Malley, the auto shop teacher). On the weekends, Thuy Vo, along with the others in his crew, travels to meeting spots to race against other imports. During the week, he spends his time outside work and school driving around malls, local streets in the neighborhood and sometimes Santa Clara Street in the hope that his car will be recognized, especially now that he has all but finished customizing it.[6] Thuy Vo's car, which was always parked just outside the car bays despite a school policy that restricts students from parking in that specific school lot, was the subject of much discussion among the students, racers and nonracers alike, in the three other classes I observed. On one occasion, two boys came by to take digital pictures of the car. When I asked Don, one of the students, about the picture taking, he explained, "See, we see cars as artistic, like artwork. . . . Taking pictures is a way to show appreciation for the car and the work that has gone into it." On another occasion, I overheard one of the boys from a class remark to another, "Daammmn, I see that car everywhere." Thuy Vo has gained what he had hoped to achieve, a much-sought-after visibility for his individual style and a collectively recognized one through his car.

Imports versus American Muscle

Thuy Vo, Don, Shrini, Vicrum, and Justin, along with other boys who participate in the import car scene, distinguish themselves from another groups of racers, those who have declared a devout allegiance to American Muscle, Ford and Chevy drivers who at Freedom High School represent at best a handful of boys. (Among the four auto shop classes I observed only one boy, Jeff, identified himself with American Muscle. He drove a 1966 Chevelle that he was restoring with his father).[7] Since the 1950s, American Muscle has stood at the center of the "illegal" street and "legal" organized car racing and hot-rodding scenes. However, in the past decade, the flourishing import scene has given hot rodders a run for their money. Writing on the cultural relevance of the import car scene in southern California, Victoria Namkung has argued that "the growing import racing scene has unquestionably changed the automotive industry and altered the dynamics of the vibrant car culture. . . . Import racing has propelled a historically invisible ethnic group onto center stage of the previously Anglo-dominated consumer market and culture."[8] Many would agree that the ascendance of import racing and import racers in the commercial world and the world of car enthusiasts has subverted the longstanding rivalry between Chevy and Ford, replacing it with a new one—a rivalry between domestics and imports. Two different value systems organize the domestic and import scenes. Within the world of American Muscle, having a car that is either "fast," "loud," or "big," a car with "hog power," that is, translates into what the late French scholar Pierre Bourdieu, writing on the social practices that produce social distinctions and symbolic boundaries, called "symbolic capital."[9]

A car's muscle is not celebrated among participants in the import scene, where far less emphasis is placed on horsepower or having a large engine. Quick, lightweight cars reign over the import scene. Acuras and Hondas are regarded as superior to Mustangs, the reigning modern American muscle car. They are low cost and lightweight, and their more powerful Honda engines (like the Prelude's) can be dropped easily into the car. The more powerful engine in a lightweight car can make the car very fast, particularly if it also has a nitrous oxide boost (usually called NOS by insiders to this world). The boys from Freedom High School swear to me that such a Honda could outrun a 4.6- or 5.0-liter Mustang in a second. This claim, of course, is met by howling protestations by those who align themselves with American Muscle, like Kenny and Tom, who both currently drive modified Mustangs and are part of the same crew. When I ask if they ever race against the imports, they are sure to let me know theirs is the superior car, working hard to convince me that it could barely be considered a "fair" race. "It's not worth it," Tom says with a firm shake of his head. "If you call it racing," Kenny, smirking, adds. "Their car's really slow; my car's really fast."

By all accounts, the car racing scene, made up of these so-called street racers, is "big" in San Jose. This despite increasing efforts by Bay Area police to dampen these underground activities. In June 2001, fifty officers from a South Bay task force discovered 247 cars at one of the business parks during a bust of an illegal street race, which led to nineteen cars being seized and fourteen arrests, according to the *San Francisco Chronicle*.[10] San Jose is not distinct in this regard. Street racing is popular in a lot of places where the boundaries between urban and suburban life are blurry, where cars can traverse long stretches of empty (and not-so-empty) road. Imports and American muscle serve as the two pivotal points around which this scene, fluid in its form, membership, rituals and rules, codes and conduct coalesces. These two groups regularly gather in the same meeting places, but import racers and domestics race primarily against cars of the same kind; every once in a while, they go head to head. The groups are largely ethnically split. "You got your Asian rice rockets. Honda Civics that are souped up, got their Na's, their flo masters and stuff. So, you have that and Latinos, Mexicans, with their old-school muscle cars," JP, an Anglo kid and self-described racer who drives a Chevy, explains. Melissa, who as a young woman resides at the periphery of these overlapping scenes, echoes JP's remarks: "Trust me, if you go out there and look, you'll see a complete difference between a Vietnamese car and a white person's car. I feel like I'm being racist, but I'm not. . . . Asian cars, they'll always do a body kit. And that's why they call them Rice Rockets. Because their cars sound a lot different than . . . they do something different with their mufflers and their intakes." These groups have become increasingly antagonistic as loyalists to American Muscle have attempted to reassert their dominance over the car-racing scene.

Formally and informally, the racing scene operates as a space of competition and antagonism, where racers regularly challenge other racers. Respect and recognition are extended to those who can "step up" and "hold their own" against those already recognized as the most skilled drivers with the fastest cars. Impromptu street racing is also common among those whose cars can compete, and a shared code of communication, the revving of an engine at a stop light or a quick nod to the rival driver, signals a willingness to race. Suffice it say, not to engage is to lose face. "You'll be at a stop light and guys pull up and you know they antagonize, you race. If a guy comes up and challenges you, then you race him," explains Trevor, who also drives a modified Mustang. "Even if I don't race him, you have to respond in some type of way. If you're not going to race, then you bark at him and how you bark at him is by revving your engine, just to let him know, you know, I'm not scared but at a different time."

Street racing and car customizing are activities shared among men—a set of social practices and relations from which young men work to construct and articulate coherent narratives that solidify a sense of being men. It is this heightened sense of competition that fortifies the enduring link between cars and masculinity. Perhaps this helps to explain why high-level risk-taking assumes such significance for these young men; the level of risk one is willing to take becomes the means to set oneself apart from other men.

Risky Business: Boys Who Race

AB: Um, what's the fastest you've ever driven?

KENNY: One hundred forty-two miles an hour.

AB: Really, on a highway?

KENNY: Uh-huh, on the freeway.

AB: Um, what, was it, like late at night, or?

KENNY: Yeah, it was coming home from those races you were talking about.

AB: Oh, my gosh. Did you have people in the car?

KENNY: Four people.

AB: Were you scared?

KENNY: Yeah.

AB: Well, describe what it's like. I mean, I've never driven that fast.

KENNY: It's a rush, it's like crazy, like.

AB: Well, how do you feel?

KENNY: Calm, I feel really calm when I do it, like I don't know, it just feels like you're flying or something. Yeah, it feels like you're floating across the road.

Daring, danger, and peril reside at the center of this competitive world of racing.[11] These boys travel to forbidden territories, abandoned industrial zones, in search of a profound "experience" that will enable them to transcend the shackles of time and place, to step outside the self as they step into the flow, to engage risk and defeat it. They race to *feel* the intense sensation, difficult to describe in words, that provides the means to anchor themselves within a physical world where one's existence is known because it is felt.[12] Their desire to do so at times almost overwhelms them. These boys talk incessantly about the rush they gain from racing, of being in the flow, the "high" they get from being at the edge, almost losing control and somehow finding their way back. "It is all about the rush," I hear over and over from this group of boys and others who race. The source of the rush? Testing themselves against themselves and against others, since displays of danger and daring are the principal means to gain respect and recognition. Perhaps that is why, when not racing, they spend hours with others in their crew reliving stories of near-peril, sharing what the adolescent psychologist Cynthia Lightfoot regards as "risk narratives."[13] These narratives make up these boys' "storyworlds," where their reality is constructed as much as it is expressed, through which they gain recognition and visibility. The auto shop is a particularly strategic space in this regard, since it provides opportunity to talk about cars, risk, danger, and peril of all sorts, and talk they do. The boys spend much of their time rehashing details of past races, whose car outdrove whose. Talk about speed, how fast they drive, and the fastest they have ever driven is regularly interjected into conversation as they debate what counts as "sick" driving, celebrating those who are willing to do "crazy shit." Their stories serve to signify a life lived at the edge. I hear countless stories of driving that seem to provide opportunity for these young men to flaunt, above all else, their own driving skill, since they did, after all, live to tell the tale. "I used to race people on the freeway 'cause this car it always attracts people that want to race me so I always end up racing," Olie, a young man, explains. "Sundays are really good days for when guys are out like older, like little thirty-years-olds in their Corvettes or whatever who want to race. I'm down, I'm okay. 'Cause I'm really good at maneuvering through traffic, and I make really crazy moves and stuff." On another morning, boys trickle into class, settling into their seats as they talk about the events of the past weekend. I overhear two of the boys rehash the race that occurred between two other boys in the class. This is interrupted by John, another student, also a racer, who begins to recount to Mr. O'Malley his race at Sacramento raceway over the weekend with a friend. He flips through an auto parts magazines, describing how the rear axle and the drive shaft broke on his friend's Camaro SS as a large number of the students now listen in. I am suddenly reminded of Daniel telling me last week how he had blown up the engine of his Civic in a race the weekend before. Beyond this, I hear countless stories of driving on bald tires, stripped struts, and ever-thinning break pads that seemed to be a way to affirm their participation in a world of risk.[14]

I hear several stories of tickets, like the story George, who drives a Jetta, told me one morning during class, as the two of us watched Rich sand down one of the side panels on his white pickup truck. Last month, George was racing down the road neck and neck with Rich. As the two lanes of the road merged into one, George pulled ahead of Rich. Neither noticed the cop car parked in the side street. The race resulted in a $400 fine for George, since his car was in the lead; Rich barely escaped. Speeding tickets, especially tickets issued for "exhibition speed" and "reckless driving," which carry hefty fines, are badges of courage and bravery, since such violations provide evidence of a life lived on the edge. I talk to David as he measures the tire pressure of one the cars as several hover around passing the time. "I have a Civic at home," he tells me, but he is not allowed to drive it since he has a suspended license, he says as he chuckles to himself. When I ask why, he responds, "Reckless driving." He and another guy were "just fooling around" in a parking lot. He says earnestly, "We weren't even racing," but the cops stopped them and checked their car "because they think we do drugs." This resulted in a $1,500 ticket and a suspended license, which won't be returned until some ten months hence. Strangely, he seems only slightly upset by this turn of events. Perhaps it is because he has simply resigned himself to the fact. Or perhaps it is because this has become a good story to tell, a story that secures his rightful place as a man among men.

Cops are important to the storyworlds these boys construct, since their presence helps to define racing as a risk activity that involves more than just the obvious physical risks taken for driving at breakneck speeds. Cops serve as reminders of the boys' willingness to put their life at risk in other ways. These young men risk arrest, tickets, fines, possible jail time, and the disruption of their futures. In short, they are willing to risk it all. I can't help wondering if taking such significant risks is a way to remain in control of their lives. This is a group whose lives are largely defined by a set of circumstances that are beyond their control. As low-income kids with few secure or promising avenues available to them, their futures beyond high school remain largely uncertain.[15] These risk narratives, which construct their reality as much as express it, seem to be a way to manage, if not control, the uncertainty of their future. Within their storyworlds, what lies ahead rests squarely within their own hands. They are the narrators of their own lives, and if they mess up they have only themselves to hold responsible. This is after all the model of the autonomous, self-determining individual to which many Americans aspire and upon which masculine status rests.

The Need for Speed: Masculinity and Performance Vehicles

Cars have long served as objects for men to position themselves in terms of masculinity, enabling an elaborated performance of the masculine. But the relationship these young men forge between cars and being masculine is far from uncomplicated; rather, it is fraught with messy contradictions and struggle. To understand the nature of this struggle, which is the subject of the rest of this chapter, requires an understanding of the world in which boys are becoming men. The sociologist Michael Kimmel, among other scholars, has argued that modern masculinity is in crisis, its foundation rapidly crumbling as the traditional anchors of manhood recede in importance or become all but impossible to obtain.[16] Financial independence is increasingly an empty pursuit, since most young men will be unable to provide for themselves, let alone for others, if they are to continue to reside in communities like San Jose. Outside the realm of sports, physical competence, a traditional marker of masculinity, carries little occupational prestige in a world organized around the exchange of information, not displays of muscle.[17] In an increasingly posttraditional world, where social roles (e.g., being the breadwinner) are less likely to serve as guides for action and identity formation, young men inevitably will face an existential crisis.[18] Their participation in the world of cars and car racing provides a space to manage the existential dilemmas of masculinity, where these young men work to construct and sometimes repair a set of boundaries through which masculine power is reasserted.

These boys invest in fast cars and this fast scene as they traverse a changing world in search of recognition, visibility, and respect when the traditional ways to gain respect as men is unavailable. They also confront other problems because their struggle to become men occurs in a context where masculinity is increasingly transparent as a social construct. (Consider, for example, the ways masculinity is increasingly parodied and satirized in the popular media.) In a so-called postmodern world of hyperreality, where there is no original, no "real," behind the imitation but only other imitations, as Baudrillard has argued, the struggle to gain recognition as masculine requires a far more nuanced and subtle performance to be believable.[19] Against a masculinity that reveals itself to others as a fake, as a performance, these boys struggle to be "authentically men."

Perhaps this explains why boys are increasingly called upon to monitor their own masculinity, to demonstrate a self-awareness that the performance of the masculine self is after all a performance. "I think, um, there's always some internalized pressures to drive a certain way in terms of my gender. There seems to be some expectation to drive fast and live and do everything fast," Richard, one particularly insightful twenty-year-old, remarked. "Like every time I see my little rearview mirror and I see people trailing behind me and I think oh maybe I should go faster. . . I feel those pressures."

These young men must be convincing as men not only for an ever-increasing group of skeptics and ironists but also to themselves.[20] Identity formation today occurs in a context where "the self is seen as a reflexive project for which the individual is responsible."[21] In a media-saturated culture where images and parodies of men are profuse, men are increasingly expected to be reflective about their manhood. Hypermasculine men are ones who are "unreflective about manhood." They are seen as not self-actualized and thus not in control of themselves.[22]

The shifting ground on which these "reflective masculinities" are mapped has consequences for understanding the struggle for masculinity of these young men who participate in the car-racing scene. Racers walk a thin line because the car-racing scene is often regarded as a hypermasculine space to outsiders (this given its ties to white working-class masculine culture).[23] This point is clearly illustrated in the following conversation with two young men who stand outside the car-racing scene. Here they link cars and "macho" as they attempt to present themselves as authentically masculine against macho men, men who are largely regarded as imposters.

ROBERT: I think it's kind of a macho thing to like, I don't know, I've heard people like, I can drive when I'm drunk and like, oh you can't do it? So it's just. . .

AB: What do you think about that, the whole macho thing?

ROBERT: Stupid.

MITCH: I don't know, I'm not a macho person, so I'm not going to try and play it off.

AB: So what defines like a macho person?

MITCH: Someone with flows and big subwoofers in the cars and—

ROBERT: Yeah.

AB: Well, I was going to ask actually because you had said earlier that you were not the type to do all that stuff to your car and um, and. . .

ROBERT: A sound system might be different because I really like music, but I'm not going to, like, put a lift on my car, get big twenty-inch wheels or whatever. What some people do to their car, like what they put into it, is so amazing.

MITCH: That's what the parking lot's [at school] like. It's like a battle between who has the loudest bass on their car or. . .

AB: Really?

MITCH: Yeah.

ROBERT: Or, who. . .

MITCH: The loudest engine.

AB: What do you think about that?

ROBERT: I think it's silly, yeah. I like to watch people, like while you're spinning out your tires, so you'll have to be like, you know, spending three hundred dollars on new tires like, you know, five months earlier than I am.

Young men today parody others and themselves for performances of masculinity that are too obviously fakes. This is perhaps especially apparent around cars because they have long been associated with masculinity and also provide ground for competition. A number of these boys sought to expose the ways some men use their cars as a status means to "get" women, lest they be accused of doing precisely that themselves. Trying to explain why he has such disdain for car cruising, Aldo offers, "I don't know, like, guys being dogged, you know trying to say, 'What's up baby?' you know, 'What's your number?'" Scott explains why he was not into "one of those big macho cars." "Why bother? I have nothing to show off." This young man saw having a "big macho car" as a feeble attempt "to get into somebody's pants." For Olie, talk about cars becomes a space to parody himself, perhaps before someone else does. "I was just pulling into the movie theater like I thought I was really cool 'cause I was with a girl and stuff. Yeah, you know what I'm saying and I didn't see one of those cement blocks and I was like, oh shit."[24]

Many young men today, whether racers or not, distance themselves from "macho"—the hypermasculine "straw man" as they solidify their own identities as authentic men. But their reflections and parodies fall short of actually subverting the privilege accorded to them by the mere fact that they are men. To the contrary, this kind of talk is central to reaffirming the power of masculinity that ultimately establishes, regulates, and sometimes rewards these young men.

Trevor, an African American young man who did not get his license until he was twenty-one, reveals, "I was ashamed of it [not having a license]. Ah man, you know, my girl drives me around. My friends kind of let me hear about it a lot. It's something you have to swallow and get on with life." Trevor now has a black Ford Mustang GT, a car with considerable power, especially following various engine modifications. Explaining why he chose to modify the engine, he remarked with a surprising frankness, "It makes it louder, meaner and tougher. . . . Like I said, some guys they pull up and they want to show off and they rev their cars, you know, and if you can't, you know, you feel embarrassed, stupid, so you got to get that." This sense of struggle to achieve masculinity by debasing and discrediting other men is well illustrated in the following example drawn from one of the countless electronic bulletin boards organized around street racing. The following posts represent an ongoing conversation, occurring over several days, about the meaning of a "real" racer.[25]

Malachi #1:

I've been in the game since '94. Not that duration is important, but for the last 9 years I've eaten, slept, dreamed and worked for going faster. My driving is always being examined, and my mechanical skills are always improving. The name racer always sounded stupid to me, but it's what I am. Who here is a real racer? Post up and tell me why. *Do not post if your just gonna list the parts you bought, and why your euro style tailights were a performance upgrade.*[26]

Green Goblin #2 is the first to respond, offering the following:

A racer is a one who races. I drive a Ford Explorer, but I've raced other SUVs. I know it isn't the fastest vehicle on the road, and I don't act like it is, but it IS at least faster than a lot of other SUVs. I don't go around places saying "I am a racer" but I have raced others in the past and I still do, so therefore, I am a racer.

This is followed by a series of messages. The conversation rapidly becomes hostile, with repeated attempts by these men to distance themselves from and to debase other young men as they talk about their own relationship to cars.[27] They position themselves against a particular group of racers who are recognized as "all show and no go," the aforementioned "ricers."

Abcd123 #3:

I see what you're getting at. I have a few friends like that. Some keep at it for more power, some keep at it, but for more speed. I don't consider myself a real racer. Maybe back in the day, I would drag anything that moved. Cars weren't as powerful, and the police was not an issue. There was more emphasis on being able to cut through traffic than actual horsepower, since mods were unheard off.

SL porn series #4:

I've been racing since 94 also back in high school. I guess I caught the bug from when pops was a kid. He raced anything from lola's old chevy station wagon, his triple deuce, GTO, Sting ray, Vet, his Suburban. We always BS about comparing apples vs oranges as no replacement to displacement. etc. . . . He's a strong vette follower and a supervisor mechanic for PG&E. He's a real racer from drag to autoX, to go carts, to road courses. He's pretty impressed with imports and he also likes driving my turbo hatch I do it for fun and not to be trendy. I've dragged charged buicks, Pop's C5, and a lot of Hondas. I respect anybody that races and works on their cars. I do it for sport. *Unlike most ricers these days who drive to be trendy and be "noticed". Peace!*

Sleeper #5:

Street . . . well that's just full of posers . . . it would be so easy for me to claim something that my car obviously does do . . . but it happens at the scene all the time (we usually call them ricers or idiots). I do push my car to the limits on the way back roads . . . if I have to drive 2 hours to find a remote spot, I will . . . with minimal risk to me, my car and more importantly others who wish not to be involved. I also, usually don't take anyone with me . . . the main reason is that most of the people in my town are all talk and I don't trust the abilities of other drivers. I do accept the risks and have no problem taking tickets if I'm doing something wrong . . . cops usually respect that too. I accept responsibility for my mistakes.

Lt. What? #6:

Fake racer. I pretend to drive my cars. They really drive themselves, they're the real racer.

Another thing, you ignorant prick, if you're going to talk shit in your sig, you might want to spell check. I'm sure you'll respond saying I don't know anything about the english language, much the same as engines, and 'your are' is proper english.

Lastly, did you really need to include a setup for your little rib at Nick? I'm sure only one with your intellect could put together that the comment in YOUR sig was FROM you. Thank you for labeling it for us mere mortals. *Eat a dick, bitch.*

333racer #7:

however i need to bring up another point, for all those people who proclaim they are "real" street racers. i find that term to be absolute BS. true you may be racing on the streets, but i noticed that all those who were from back in the day they don't admit to racing on the streets and many more are actually ashamed to say they do. i think that the term street racer has turned into a trendy little label to make people feel like they are important. real racers know the importance of keeping the racing secret.

Runner #8:

Let's not get into what is racing and what is not. I really don't like to drag now. I road race exclusively. I will drag once in a while though, I haven't for few years though.

I wrench, I don't really like to. But when it's my ass on the line, I gotta know my car will be there for me. I don't trust anyone. I've been screwed. No one will care like I do. I've only bought one aftermarket body panel in my life, a Spoon CF lip for my old EG. I drive a WRX now. It's ugly and fast as fock. Not done yet, it's being built as a well rounded car. Suspension/Brakes/Power-Driving skill. That's all that matters to me. No euro tails, no Z3 gills, no supra headlights, no lighted washer nozels and no 15 year old on my hood! But the WRX will have some nicer panels in the end.

I remember when the scene was pure. When all we wanted to do was go faster. I sold my civic because I was tired of being associated with scum. Too harsh? Stop doing ghetto shit to the car, get rid of the euro tail lights.

These young men draw on the language of purity and pollution, what the anthropologist Mary Douglas regards as central to the hierarchical distinctions groups invoke as they draw distinct moral boundaries between us and them. In the words of Runner #8, "I remember when the scene was pure."[28] These writers/racers define the boundaries clearly: "real" racers modify the performance of their cars, and "fakers" make modifications for aesthetic appeal.[29] In this sense, gender tropes are clearly in play as examples of display are linked to feminine activity. In their struggle to be recognized as real racers, these young men distance themselves from feminine practices of paying too much attention to the body (car body or otherwise), since the car body can be seen as a metaphor for the physical body. Spending too much time "primping" is decidedly unmasculine; recall from chapter 2 the time girls spent getting ready for their night out cruising. This can be seen primarily in the recurring challenge to needless and gratuitous display that emerges beginning in the first instance with Malachi: "*Do not post if your just gonna list the parts you bought, and why your euro style tailights were a performance upgrade.*" At several points, driving skill is privileged over aesthetic changes as they draw lines between those who are rightful insiders and those who are outsiders—those who are men and those who are not.

I also witnessed attempts to draw distinctions between real racers and fakers in the auto shop class. On one occasion, a group of import racers, Ping, Brad, and

Vicrum, are at work on Ping's Civic hatchback. They are planning to attach a black lip to the bottom. Other kids hover around watching them as they work to figure how precisely they are to attach this lip. As I look on, I ask why they want to attach the lip to the car, and one of the guys, the only nonimport racer in the group, responds with noted sarcasm, "To make it *look* lower," as he chuckles to himself before walking off. A few moments later, another nonimport racer approaches, asking the group at work sarcastically, "Does it make it faster?" Interestingly, though these young men are questioned about the types of modifications they are doing, because they are doing the work themselves, they are not discredited as "half men." As SL porn series #4 remarked in his post, "I respect anybody that races and works on their cars."

In this competitive context, having knowledge about car parts and how cars work serves as a key cultural resource affirming one's status within the group, solidifying a hierarchy of respect, and serving as a basis of exclusivity.[30] Boys who pay someone else to customize or modify their cars accrue less status than those boys who are able to work on their cars themselves, because they are seen as imposters.[31] This explains why a car that is fast but has only limited visual appeal is often regarded as a "work in progress," which enables its owner to claim respect. A primed hood, for example, becomes a way to announce that this car is being worked on by oneself. As a useful point of comparison, consider my earlier comments about Shrini's car, which had significant visual appeal but no speed. Shrini was actively trying to sell this car, lest he be discredited as "all show and no go."[32] Having to pay someone to fix and modify one's car can also serve to discredit a racer. It is in this sense that knowledge of car parts and cars themselves communicates what Sarah Thornton has termed "subcultural capital," a type of capital that structures an alternative hierarchy by which people vie for status—a social good that can be bestowed only by others and not awarded by oneself.[33]

American Muscle and Talking Trash

The comments posted on the bulletin boards that defined racers who focus on exterior changes rather than performance upgrades as "ricers" is quite telling.[34] As SL porn series #4 remarked in his post, "most ricers these days who drive to be trendy and be noticed." Runner #8 comments, "I remember when the scene was pure. When all we wanted to do was go faster. I sold my Civic because I was tired of being associated with scum. Too harsh? Stop doing ghetto shit to the car, get rid of the euro tail lights." Sleep #5 writes, "Street . . . well that's just full of posers . . . it would be so easy for me to claim something that my car obviously does do . . . but it happens at the scene all the time (we usually call them ricers or idiots)." Within the world of car racing, the term *ricer* or *rice rocket* is used interchangeable with the term "import." Ricers and rice rockets are Hondas, Nissan, and Acuras. Fords and Chevys are never called rice rockets.

The condemnation of "ricers" was widespread on these message boards and elsewhere. The following rap, entitled "The Ricer Anthem," appeared on one of the message boards where import and domestic racers routinely post messages, debate the merits of different cars, and constitute the moral and cultural perimeters of the racing world.

The Ricer Anthem

*Hi! My name is (who?) . . . my name is (what) . . . my name is
(scratches) . . . Rice Burner!*
Hi Kids, do you like 5 inch tips?
Wanna see me stick chrome fender flares over each of my Konigs?
Wanna follow me and do exactly as I did?
Try NAWS and get your motor fucked up worse than my life is?
My brains' dead weight, I'm trying to get my head on straight
But I can't figure out which sticker to put on my license plate.
And the mechanic says "Rice burner you's a crack head "Nu-uh"
  "Then why's your car dead man its wasted"
*Well since age 9 I've wanted an SI so I could put chrome 18s on it and
make it run 16.9's.*
Got pissed off and ripped all my Honda emblems off,
And replaced them with "R" badges so people know I'm not soft.
I smoke a big bowl of chronic, and lay in my lawn,
For longer then it took me to put my altezzas on.
"Come here bastard" "Dude, wait a minute that a viper dawg!!"
I don't give a fuck, I'll just fly by and put my hazards on!!!

After this anthem was posted on the message board, a number of writers posted replies, including jdanger, who wrote, "This rice burner anthem, it says exactly what needs to be said. Ricer burners want to look performance but can't perform. I would rather have performance than looks." Another wrote, "all show and no go, that's rice."

The distinction between an authentic racer, somebody who is focused on power, speed, and skill, and a "poser" is presented through racialized metaphors that align cars and aesthetics with particular ethnic or racial groups. This rivalry might be explained by the fact that these car scenes are ethnically organized. American Muscle continues to be dominated largely by Anglos, while the import scene is predominantly Asian. Recall also my earlier comments that American Muscle's hegemony in the racing world has been challenged in recent years as imports have posed a legitimate threat that must be taken seriously. American Muscle racers have managed this threat through attempts to discredit imports and import racers and by physically and discursively distancing themselves from this group. I repeatedly listened to young Anglo, Mexican, and African American men aligned with domestics denounce any association with the import car scene, the cars, rice rockets, and the drivers, known as "ricers." "Yeah, I'm not into the car scene where they all like rice rockets," seventeen-year-old Cesar explains. Jorge echoes Cesar: "Rice rockets the small, you know, Hondas, I don't like 'em. Honda Civics souped up, stereotypically Asian. . . . I have no respect for imports . . . they give them too much credit . . . for what they've done and if it wasn't for I guess the American cars you've got bigger muscle cars . . . they wouldn't be around. And they still have to give respect to those cars 'cause you know who you're messing with and who you're not messing with [laughing]." Even within the group of import racers, the distinction between ricer and racer was clearly drawn. Brad tells me, "To hot rodders and cruisers we're all ricers in the [import] racer community." But to Brad and his friends, there is a difference between an import racer and a ricer. In the words of the sociologist Erving Goffman, they "stratify their own," a common enough strategy among those who must routinely manage a stigmatized identity.[35] Brad and his friends distance themselves from those racers who make "excessive" exterior changes (pointing out some of the cars in the lot that are "ricers" or "border-on-ricers") as they struggle to maintain legitimacy within this world of risk and competition.

This condemning talk directed at import racers and the racial logic upon which it rests is also visible in a conversation that occurred during one of the focus group interviews at Weston High School. While this was a racially mixed group of kids, importantly, no Asian kids were present in this group. As was the case in other focus groups, the young men dominated the conversation. In this particular focus group, one of the boys, JP, an Anglo kid and the oldest in the group, initiated much of the dialogue.

JP: I don't like imports.

AB: You don't like imports, how come?

JP: I just don't.

AB: So what do you like then, like what's kind of . . .

JP: Oh no, I have, I respect them, I don't say anything about them at all, I just . . .

AB: It's just not your style?

JP: Like them, they don't like muscle cars, and then they actually do go and talk crap about muscle cars.

AB: Who's they?

ADAM: I know.

JP: Imports.

ADAM: Asian people.

JP: If you think about it, you go buy a $20,000 car okay, it might have some advantages like air conditioning, CD player, and all that, but then you get a car for half the price, an American one, and it ends up out running all those cars, for half that price, and you put, you work that other half of the money into your car, and then you have a machine . . . it's crazy.

ADAM: What you call them is you call them imports and domestics, me and him both drive domestics, so that's Chevy, Ford, all those, those are domestics.

JP: And then you got your imports, which is like Honda, your Integra.

ADAM: Your Acuras.

TOM: Integra.

JP: All that crap is imports and that's the ones you hear nnneeeennneeeee goin' down the street, and stuff like . . . See, I just like domestic cars a lot better, and like lowriders, they're cool, but I hate, why are you going to do that to an American car? I hate that, because when you see all them lowriders doing all their hydraulics.

JP starts out talking about cars but ends up talking about the drivers, too. Ricers are no longer cars but people, Asians, as he attempts to denounce imports and import racers. Racial tropes are mobilized as JP defines the values of this cultural scene. Asians are constructed as the outsiders—the others against which he and other hot rodders solidify their identities as men. This is further illustrated by additional comments he makes in the course of the focus group. He draws specifically on the emergent stereotype of Asians as "bad drivers" as he again attempts to discredit not simply the import scene but an entire racial group.

JP: I think Chinese shouldn't really drive because they don't even really know how to drive.

CYNTHIA: Oh my God.

AB: Who?

ADAM: Asian people.

JP: No actually a lot of Asians.

AB: So why do you think that?

JP: [imitating a Chinese accent] Ohhhh, oh, you son of bitch, you wreck my car.

          [laughter from the group]

AB: Well, what about American-born Asians?

JP: Then they get out and they start yelling at you for parking your car.

AB: What do other folks think? So, is this like all Asian folks, like Asian born folks or . . .

JP: They can't see.

          [Laughter again from the group]

AB: [referring to a comment by AS] Well, okay, well, he just said that your comment was racist.

TOM: No, actually Asian people are very good at racing, like I know lots of guys . . .

AB: [referring to DH] You just said it's because they are rich?

DH: 'Cause they always have nice cars.

AB: So are there any Asian kids that go to this school?

TH: A lot.

AB: So, well, what do you think about that? So what if there was an Asian person sitting here right now, would you be saying the same thing, or . . .

CJ: Maybe.

AM: I don't think so.

AB: You don't think so.

CC: I don't think so.

CJ: But, I mean they can't drive, seriously, they can't drive, they drive piece of shit cars, sounds like a goddamn mouse running through your house. It's like come on now, get a real car. I don't like the ones that make so damn, so much noise, like the, the ones they call "rice rockets."

The idea that Asians can't drive also emerged in auto shop class. On one occasion, a group of us are gathered around Brad's red Civic hatchback. He is balancing what are horribly bald tires. The group of young Asian men around the car is talking about another car on the lot whose fender has a deep and sizable scratch, and Sean, one of the Asian boys, remarks, as he explains the scrape, "He can't drive. He's Asian." Incredulous, Daniel, the only Mexican boy who hangs around with the import racers, responds, "Daaaammmnnn, and you're Asian." To this Sean retorts, "Yeah, I can't drive, I can admit it," as the groups collapses in laughter.

Interpreted one way, this comment reflects the psychosocial dynamics of racial dominance, revealing a pattern of internalized oppression, what Paulo Friere has called "horizontal violence." After all, this statement is articulated by a young Asian man and is met with laughter by other young Asian men and in this sense reflects what Goffman called "identity ambivalence." But, interpreted another way, this comment about Asian drivers in the context of this largely Asian, all-male group is a way to manage the enduring stereotypes, what Patricia Hill Collins refers to as "controlling images," used to discredit them as less than men and thus to justify their subordination. These boys know that JP is not alone in his condemnation of the import car scene or of Asians. By preemptively making the charge, they can control the joke themselves. In various ways, these young men are engaged in what Goffman regarded as interactional strategies to manage the stigma of race as they attempt to preserve a sense of being men in a context of an intense competition over the symbolic resources that define masculinity.

This point is also illustrated in another instance. One early evening I am driving across town to a restaurant for dinner, and I pull up behind a Honda Civic at a stop light; it is an older model of the very car I have, but, unlike mine, its suspension has been lowered, and while my muffler is barely audible, its exhaust buzzes each time the driver, a young Asian guy with short black hair shaped into small spikes, taps his foot on the accelerator. As I sit waiting for the light to turn green, I inspect this car, curious about its driver, who he is and where he's going. I notice that just above the car's back bumper is written in white script "*Got Rice?*" Within moments the light turns green, and the small vehicle idling in front of me is gone; its rear lights fade as the distance between us grows. I am left in its wake. I imagine a scenario where this car is racing against another on a highway or empty street; it pulls ahead, leaving its rival behind, with a derisive *Got Rice? Got Rice?*, all the more powerful as the last word, is loaded with intention and mocking, a means to invert and convert the pejorative meaning of *ricer*.[36] It is a call to war, an attempt to inflame the animosity that inspired the term in the first place and to subvert the hegemony of American Muscle.

The sociologist Paul Connolly argues that young men express deep racial animus in situations of tense competition, though they might not in other situations. Certainly car racing is a space of hypercompetition, since the activity is not only organized around winners and losers but emerges as a terrain of claims to dominance and superiority. Imports and domestics are locked in a battle over not simply whose cars are faster but also what constitutes the basis of legitimate masculinity for these young men coming of age in a posttraditional society. Because many import drivers are Asian, this struggle over dominance is largely directed toward Asian men and reflects the historical legacy of anti-Asian, nativist rhetoric.

Racial constructions are routinely used to work out deep anxieties about masculinity, to define who is authentically masculine and who is not. The sociologist R. W. Connell's understanding of race and what he calls "hegemonic masculinity," defined in part by invisible whiteness and reliance on the hypermasculinization of black men and the hyperfeminization of Asian men, is useful for making sense of these exchanges among young men who participate in the car-racing scene.[37] Asian import racers as a group, who have historically been feminized, get discredited in this car world as others actively (re)feminize them. The sociologist Yen Le Espiritu has argued, "Asian American men have been excluded from white-based cultural notions of the masculine," noting that Asian American men are regularly depicted in the media as "impotent eunuchs" and emasculated "model minorities."[38]

The feminization of Asian men is achieved in two specific ways. First, by arguing Asians can't drive, detractors position Asian men outside a masculine world of skill, risk, and competence. Similar arguments made about women drivers also once served as justification to keep women off the road.[39] Second, the cars of Asian import drivers are feminized as "rice rockets," cars with gratuitous display. Consider the comments of jdanger: "I hope you guys see where I am coming from. These little jap cars are nothing but the nastiest, dumbest girl in school with plastic surgery."

One might also consider the possibility that attempts to discredit import racers as ricers through a critique of gratuitous display is also part of an intense backlash against Asians and Asian immigrants in post-1965 America. Changes in immigrant policy in the mid-1960s led to an influx of immigrant groups in the 1980s and 1990s, a time of eroding economic opportunity as hundreds of thousands of manufacturing jobs were lost in the United States. A number of scholars and activists have identified a heightened anti-Asian, anti-immigrant sentiment in California and nationally in the context of economic uncertainty.[40] The charge of gratuitous display against "ricers" appears to be tied to nativist critiques of conspicuous consumption directed at Asians and Asian Americans that grows from the perception that they are claiming too large of a piece of the proverbial pie, thereby displacing other groups competing for employment and housing opportunities.[41] A deep racial animus against upwardly mobile Asians is present in JP's focus group where all Asians are defined as "being rich." Indeed, this has served as the very basis of the model-minority myth that continues to target Asians as interlopers.[42]

A larger narrative is at work here that reflects deepening inequalities and conflict in an increasingly global world marked by ever-growing economic and social polarization. The rise of distinct ethnically based car scenes and the emerging rivalry between domestics and (Asian) imports are consequences of a changing, competitive global world order where the perception that "Americans" must continually reassert their supremacy in the face of unwarranted attacks by outsiders and foreigners is intense and pervasive. Consider these comments, posted on another message board by jdanger:

> *You guys that LOVE imports can say all you want about how they're cool and stuff, but they still will be little jap cars. You can say NOS this and turbo that, but nothing is gonna beat American Muscle. I know maybe some American companies are manufacturing in other countries but they still make better cars than Honda, acura and all the other jap brands. I do want to ask you one question . . . why fix up*

> *little crappy 4 bangers, when you can fix up a muscle car and get at least twice the power?*

Posted comments of this kind often become the source of disagreement but seem to reflect longstanding anti-Asian ideas that led to a century of reactionary policies, panics, and sentiments against Asians and Asian countries, from the Immigration Exclusion Acts of the 1800s and 1900s, directed at Chinese immigrants and others, to the Japanese interment camps during World War II, to the "Buy American" movements that emerged in the 1970s and 1980s as U.S. multinationals halted production in the United States and relocated to other countries with cheaper labor and fewer environmental restrictions while U.S. laborers (many of whom were white union men) lost their jobs. Even some of the racers, though failing to see the broader historical context that has given rise to the anti-Asian sentiments that lurk beneath the anti-import rhetoric, recognize the narrow Americanism that is operating. Consider the following post, written by "Nissan Fan":

> *If you were a true car fan you would see past all the "American Pride in Our Cars" shit who the fuck cares what country it came from look at the car not at the country . . . just because you hopped on the bandwagon of biased Yankee car lovers does not mean that Japanese cars suck . . . P.S. jdanger what your saying is very stereotypical.*

LancasterWannaBE wrote, "I don't understand why there's always so much fuss about tuning Japanese cars. Last time I looked there were also many Jettas on the road—and guess what, they're imports too. I never hear anyone complaining about someone else tuning an Audi." The sociologist Lillian Rubin (2004) has argued that anti-immigrant sentiments are often articulated by white working-class men because they are the ones who have lost the most and who are increasingly vulnerable in a postindustrial America.[43]

Brave Men in a Brave New World: Global Masculinities

At the center of this competitive and antagonist world, where what you know serves to define where you are and where the level of risk you're willing to take is the measure of a man, is an ongoing and often heated rivalry between domestics and imports: Hondas against Mustangs, "Ricers" against "American Muscle." A quick car versus a powerful one. Asian versus Anglo. Who are the better drivers? Who has the fastest cars? Who can beat whom? Young men who participate in this world spend hours debating these points as clear and distinct lines are firmly etched. I have argued that this struggle, because it is organized to position Anglos and Asian at odds, is racialized. By this I mean that racist ideologies that have long suppressed and oppressed Asian men are used as a way to reaffirm white masculinities.

Phrases like *rice rockets, ricers,* and *riced out* operate as code words, allowing kids to talk about race, to participate in racial discourses, to express a deep racial animus, and to uphold a veiled racism that is taken as something else. All the kids I interviewed were familiar with these phrases and could use them easily. What stands behind these racial repertoires are young men's struggle for masculinity in a context where the traditional measures of being a man are increasingly out of their reach. For young men of color perhaps this has always been so. But for young white men who align themselves with American Muscle, many of whom are working class and have experienced a loss of status as they confront eroding job opportunities and as those jobs that remain open to them in the service economy are defined as women's work, they struggle to reassert their dominance in other ways. In this instance, it is through the symbolic work of distinction. As Sarah Thornton has argued in her writing about the social logic of subcultural capital, "Distinctions are never just assertions of equal distance; they usually entail some claim to authority and presume the inferiority of others."[44] Masculine identity construction for these young men occurs within a play of global and racial forces. Cars reveal some of the complexities that surround the process of becoming men and the role of symbolic boundaries.

An interesting parallel can be drawn between the work young men do on their cars and the work young women do on their bodies as both prepare to participate in spaces where the car rules. Boys work on their cars as a way to work on their masculinity, just as girls work on their bodies as a way to work on their femininity. Both converge in these car spaces, where boys' cars are presented for display much in the same way as girls' bodies are, that is, for boys to see. One might conclude that in these spaces, boys rule as much as cars do. Yet, one also wonders whether girls realize the time and energy boys direct towards fashioning their cars. Certainly, there are times when it exceeds the work young women do in fashioning their bodies.

In these spaces where boys and girls cruise "together but apart"[45] and where boys race against themselves and each other, young people search for recognition and visibility, for connection and belonging. They travel into these spaces where cars rule, where pleasure, desire, power, and struggle converge, to experience an intensity of emotion as they construct, play with, puzzle over, and defend who they are.

Endnotes

1. These are terms used widely by youth in San Jose. Concern about "gangs" in San Jose, specifically the Nortenos and Surenos, are frequently articulated in the context of school, youth, and community life. Additionally, there are several "gang prevention" programs in the wider county. However, what actually constitutes a gang has been the subject of much popular and academic debate. I do not address this debate here, but I do resist reifying this contentious term.

2. I hesitate to use the term *subcultural* given the increasing questioning over the value of this term in understanding the social practices that define the experiences of youth in an increasingly global context. The term *subcultural* originates with the "Birmingham School" of cultural studies and signifies youth groups formed in and against the "host" culture. *Subculture* was used to signify oppositional class-based groups (usually working-class young men) who engage in a sort of cultural and class warfare through style politics. In the past several decades, scholars studying youth culture have identified three problematic points arising from "subcultural studies": class reductionism; the romantic construction of these youth groups; and the limits of aesthetic forms of resistance in a con-

text of rapid market appropriation and cooptation that have led to a re-evaluation of this term. For a more comprehensive discussion see Muggleton and Weinzierl (2003).

3. In this sense, the import car scene has a transnational dimension.

4. Namkung (2004).

5. Mike, a bicultural Filipino whom we will meet in chapter 4, also worked at Great America while in high school. And while he travels within the same loosely extended group of import racers, he is an upper-income kid. He attended a prestigious private high school in the area, and his parents, both professional workers, own several homes in northern California. The import car-racing scene appears to be a scene where young men develop loosely formed ties across economic groups. In this instance, being Asian as much as having an interest in imports seems to serve as the basis of their social ties. Victoria Namkung (2004) has argued that the import scene reflects attempts to construct a pan-Asian identity among Vietnamese, Filipinos, Japanese, Chinese, and South Asian youth largely on the basis of their exclusion from "mainstream" or the dominant Anglo youth culture broadly and the hot-rodding car culture specifically. Signs of a pan-Asian identity are clearly visible in this research.

6. Some car racers cruise in the absence of a race. But there are fairly distinct lines between the racers and the cruisers. If there is nothing else to do, racers sometimes cruise, though they generally talk about this activity with some disdain. Cruisers attend races every once in a while but not routinely and usually do so as spectators, not racers. Tino told me that he did not race because he enjoyed the collective experience of cruising. In his words, you get to spend time with "your homies," but when you race, "you're alone." Most of the time racers in these semi-organized races in business parks do not have passengers in their cars when they actually race. While the boundaries between these two groups are sometimes fluid and allow some level of boundary crossing, when it comes to "identity talk," cruisers and racers draw distinct lines between their groups.

7. This has much do with the racial-ethnic composition of the school itself. A majority of the students are Asian or Latino. Hot rodding continues to have a predominately Anglo membership.

8. Namkung (2004): 160.

9. For example, twenty-year-old Melissa explains that her boyfriend, Jake, who aligns himself with American Muscle, "will park next to the lowest car to make his truck look bigger. . . . Jake will not park next to [trails off] he'll park next to a truck that he knows will make it look stupid. Like he'll park next to the truck that's smaller than his. He'll park next to like a '87 Blazer that's got a 3-inch lift and big tires and he'll park where his car looks bigger."

10. *San Francisco Chronicle,* June 12, 2001, available at www.sfgate.com.

11. The car-racing scene shares particular sensibilities with the underground graffiti world that MacDonald (2001) depicted as "an illegal confine where danger, opposition and the exclusion of women is used to nourish, amplify, and salvage notions of masculinity" (149).

12. McDonald (1999) sees the search for intensity and visibility as central to the project of self-creation in the context of what Zygmunt Bauman (2000) calls "liquid modernity," a period of late modernity that emerged in the late 1970s and was defined by flow and movement, rather than the stability and stasis that are associated with "solid modernity." Drawing from their insights, I see racing as an attempt to disassociate from the self on the one hand and an attempt to know the self through intense sensation on the other. It is as if the racer steps outside himself in order to step back in at some other point of entry. In some ways, I conceptualize the structure of the self along the lines of how George Herbert Mead conceptualized the self as made up of its component parts, the "I," the part of the self in action, and the "Me," the reflective self that allows for an awareness of self and also social control.

13. See Lightfoot (1977).

14. Bearing witness to dangerous scenarios and crazy situations is also central to constructing their world as a world of danger, daring, and peril. One morning I learned that Jason, who now drives a green Jetta, had originally had a Mustang until it was stolen, right out of the parking lot at school during fourth period. I responded with visible shock, since I was amazed that a car could be stolen from a high school parking lot. I could tell he still found the whole thing slightly bewildering. His was not the last nor the first story I heard about stolen cars. The boys seemed able to easily recall stories of theft in the neighborhoods where they live around the school, which is partly a function of their living in low-income neighborhoods. Thuy Vo, on another morning, showed me where someone tried to jimmy the lock on his Civic. His car had been parked outside his house in the driveway when this had happened (during the day, no less).

15. In talking with these boys and others in the class, I consciously directed the conversations toward future plans. I had the opportunity to speak with almost all of the 125 or so students in the four classes I observed. Only a handful (fewer than five) intended to move on to four-year colleges. Among this handful, all were in advanced placement classes and had decided to take this class to be either more "well-rounded" or because they saw the class as an easy "A." A much larger group planned to move on to community colleges or technical schools, where they hoped to gain career skills in graphic design or as auto technicians. About half of the racers with whom I spent the majority of my time planned to move on to community colleges because they weren't quite sure what else there was to do. A few talked about moving on to community college because it was a more affordable alternative to a four-year school. None (among this group of racers) talked about plans to move on to a four-year college after community college. All assumed they would continue with the jobs they currently held. It is likely that some in this group will move on to four-year colleges eventually, but this clearly was not on their immediate horizon.

16. Blackshaw (2003); Kimmel (1997); Horrocks (1994).

17. The declining significance of physical strength to masculine dominance in the Western world might also help to explain the proliferation of images of "ass-kicking" women in popular culture, from *Buffy, the Vampire Slayer,*

to the new *Charlie's Angels,* to the Quentin Tarantino film *Kill Bill I* and *II,* in which the female protagonist wreaks utter havoc (against a large group of Asian men in one instance) in her search for revenge.

18. See Anthony Giddens's (1991) discussion in "Ontological Security and Existential Anxiety."

19. See Baudrillard (2000) for a discussion of hyperreality and simulacra.

20. Vered Vinitzky-Seroussi (1998) makes a related point in her investigation of high school reunions. She examines how people manage the discrepancy between their biographical self and their social self, their past self and their present self, arguing that ultimately the most important audience for the performance of self is the self. This is a key point that Goffman (1959, 1963), in his investigations of impression management and the performance and presentation of the self, overlooked. I also argue that convincing the self of one's performance of self is especially important in the context of late modernity, given Anthony Giddens's arguments about the increased pressure to generate identity in a "reflexive" mode. In the posttraditional, demodernized period that characterizes late modernity, people are disengaged from social roles. Social roles have been replaced by a new individualism marked by the rise of anxiety and uncertainty as traditional anchors of identity become less secure. This has given rise to the idea of the self as a project for improvement, according to Giddens. See Giddens's (1991) discussion in "The Trajectory of the Self."

21. Giddens (1991): 75. Perhaps this explains why the feminist movements and the men's movement of the 1970s were able to publicly scrutinize masculinity in ways that were impossible at other historical moments.

22. The hypermasculine is increasingly antithetical to celebrated forms of masculinity, what R. W. Connell (1987, 1995) would regard as hegemonic masculinity because it is seen as inauthentic and unreflective.

23. The ultimate hypermasculine social type is almost always in the image of a white working-class guy. He can usually be seen drinking cans of domestic beer, wearing flannel, his belly spilling over his jeans, espousing reactionary racist rhetoric. His wife, worn and beaten, is relegated to the kitchen, lest she be the subject of his wrath.

24. One might regard these acts and actions as "gender strategies," a term sociologist Arlie Hochschild uses to talk about the ways men attempt to solve the problem of achieving masculinity. See Hochschild (1984).

25. These passages posted to the bulletin boards appear as they appeared on the bulletin boards. I did not change typographical or grammatical errors.

26. I have placed in italics those portions of the text that I identify as particularly important to this masculine struggle.

27. See Goffman's (1963) classic examination of the interactional work involved in managing discredited and discreditable identities.

28. There is also a logic operating here about cultural boundaries and status hierarchies that is similar to the logic elites use to prevent the popularizing and massification of cultural practices. Presumably the scene was pure when it was restricted to those in the know. The opening or broadening

of racer culture is seen to have spoiled or polluted the activity. See for example Lamont and Fournier (1992).

29. I draw here on boundary theory, which has explored the production and reproduction of social inequalities through the use of symbolic boundaries and status distinctions. Boundary theory often emphasizes the informal practices that constitute cultural boundaries, seeing these as central to the formation of cultural hierarchies. A particular emphasis has been placed on the connection between what Bourdieu first called "cultural capital," referring to types of "high-status" knowledge, and the reproduction of social and economic inequality. See Bourdieu (1977, 1984), Lamont (1992, 1995), Lamont and Fournier (1992). See DiMaggio (1982) for an examination of boundary distinctions and cultural capital in schooling. See Lareau (2003) for an examination of the distinctive class-based parenting logics that produce different kinds of cultural capital. See Carter (2003) for a discussion of dominant and nondominant forms of cultural capital (specifically black cultural capital) in educational contexts. See Vallas (2000) for an application of boundary theory to work organizations. Vallas explores the distinction between mental and manual labor and its role in creating new forms of social inequality at work as new technologies increasingly organize the workplace.

30. Boundary theory is particularly applicable to understanding the complex and subtle distinctions these young men draw between posers and fakes. "Symbolic capital" and "cultural capital" are both useful concepts here. See Bourdieu (1977, 1984); Vallas (2000). The refined knowledge about cars, car parts, and car engines held by many of these young men operates as a type of "cultural capital" that confers status on the knower, just as "symbolic capital," having a particular kind of cars with particular kinds of modifications, confers prestige or status on or discredits the car owner.

31. Somewhere along the way, I realized that my ability to pass in this world as a woman who looks more like their teachers than like them is entirely dependent on the fact that my questions became an occasion for them to demonstrate their knowledge about cars. I found myself in situation after situation listening attentively to the breadth and depth of their knowledge about cars and car parts, which these boys were eager to share. Many of these young men relished the opportunity to teach me about this world of which they are so thoroughly a part.

32. These young men are engaged in a struggle over the relevance of what R. W. Connell has referred to as hegemonic masculinity. In a traditional Gramscian sense of hegemony, allegiance to this masculine construct is achieved largely through the consent of men, many of whom gain very little from this social arrangement, since it depends upon various subordinated forms of masculinity. For Connell (1987, 1995), the production of masculinity exists within a hierarchical order, so that some forms of masculinity are deployed to debase and discredit men. As Connell reminds us, it is the interplay among varying modes of masculinity that helps sustain a patriarchal social order, and thus active attempts at debasing and discrediting others are critical to masculine dominance. Relating to my points earlier, I argue that a hypermasculine type is one example of a sub-

ordinated masculinity that is used to gain men's allegiance to a hierarchy of masculinities and to a dominant type. For Connell, there is no hegemonic femininity that corresponds to a hegemonic masculinity, although a hierarchy of femininities is in operation. Forms of femininity, although always defined by their relation to hegemonic masculinity, uphold dominant masculine forms in varying degrees. He identifies "emphasized femininity" as a dominant form of femininity that works to secure masculine power, but he also recognizes that other forms of femininity subordinate to emphasized femininity threaten masculine dominance. See also Diaz (2002); Horowitz (2001); Mac An Ghaill (1994); Messner (1992); Meyer (2001); Shackleford (2001) for discussion of masculine identity construction in the context of social struggle.

33. There is a very large body of sociological literature that examines the social mechanics of status arising from Weber's work on status as a social good, but I see little reason to rehearse that here.

34. Thuy Vo's car discussed earlier in the chapter, though admired by many as "artwork" was also referred to as a "ricer" by some of the racers.

35. Goffman (1963): 107.

36. There is also a clear play on the meaning that circulates in commodity culture. I am reminded of the cleverly conceived and wildly successful marketing campaign "Got Milk?" launched by the American Dairy Association, specifically targeting would-be young milk drinkers, that has appeared in a host of magazines for young readers, from *Rolling Stone* to *Seventeen*. The inscription *Got Rice?* as much as it reveals something about the racial order young people occupy, also provides clues about youths' immersion in a consumer world.

37. The import car culture emerged as a distinctly Asian American male youth culture within a broader context of hyperfeminization of Asian men. Cars became central to constructing masculine identity for young Asian men who had otherwise been excluded from the muscle car culture of the 1970s and 1980s, since cars are codified as masculine. Yet many of these Asian young men, as they forged alternative masculinities through the import car-racing scene, came to reject a "brutish" mode of masculinity epitomized in the muscle car of the 1970s and 1980s, distancing themselves from a masculinity rooted in white working-class culture, a form traditionally defined by one's physical strength and skill in working with one's hands (e.g., mechanics).

38. See Espiritu (1997): 90. See also Kondo (1998) and David Henry Hwang's *M. Butterfly.*

39. See O'Connell (1998).

40. During the conversation, as Brad talked, one of the guys, joking, said, "I am ricer." I was struck by how he embraced this. I raised the point of *ricer* being an anti-Asian slur, and the group fell silent. No one challenged me. While I cannot be sure if they too saw all this hubbub as expressing the anti-Asian and anti-immigrant nativist attacks that have intensified in post-9/11 America, they didn't attempt to teach me or correct me as they had at other times.

41. See Espiritu (1997); Rubin (2004); Wu (2002).
42. Within the context of Silicon Valley's economy, where Asian professionals play active roles in the tech sectors, the perception that Asian men on H1B visas are stealing jobs from skilled professional "American" workers (i.e., computer programmers and engineers) is widespread, fueled especially by the economic downturn that began in 2000. Thousands of professional workers were laid off as the tech bubble burst, among them were many South and Central Asians and Asian Americans. See also for historical discussions of this Anti-Asian pattern Takaki (1989); Nomura et al. (1989); Wu (2002).
43. Rubin (2004) argues that, although upper-middle-class whites have benefited from the influx of documented and undocumented immigrants because they provide a cheap source of domestic labor for the upper classes, the willingness of immigrants to work for cheap wages undercuts the demands for solid wages made by working-class unions. This point is also made by Fine and Weis (1998) in their examination of the eroding opportunities for young white working-class men who are part of the much maligned Generation X and in Weis's (1990) investigation of white working-class high-schoolers in deindustrialized Buffalo.
44. Thornton (1997): 201.
45. "Together but apart" is a statement Thorne (1993) used to describe the gender realities of elementary school playgrounds.

Works Cited

Collins, P.H. 1990: *Black Feminist Thought: Knowledge, Consciousness, and the Politics of Empowerment.* New York: Routledge.

Connell, R.W. 1995: *Masculinities.* Berkeley: University of California Press.

Connelly, P. 1998: *Racism, Gender Identities and Young Children: Social Relations in a Multi-Ethnic, Inner-City Primary School.* London: Routledge.

Espirtu, Y.L. 1997: *Asian American Women and Men: Labor, Laws and Love.* Thousand Oaks, CA: Sage.

Goffman, E. 1963: *Stigma: Notes on the Management of Spoiled Identity.* New York: Simon and Schuster.

Kimmel, M. 1997: "The Contemporary 'Crisis' of Masculinity in Historical Perspective." *The Making of Masculinities: The New Men's Studies,* ed. H. Brod. Boston: Allen and Unwin.

Lightfoot, C. 1997: *The Culture of Adolescent Risk-Taking.* New York: Guilford Press.

Namkung, V. 2004: "Reinventing the Wheel: Import Car Racing in Southern California." *Asian American Youth: Culture, Identity and Ethnicity,* ed. Jennifer Lee and Min Zhou. New York: Routledge.

Rubin, L. 2004: *Families on the Fault line: America's Working Class Speaks about the Family, the Economy and Race and Ethnicity.* New York: HarperCollins.

Thornton, S. 1997: "The Social Logic of Subcultural Capital." *The Subcultures Reader,* ed. Ken Gelder and Sarah Thornton. London: Routledge.

5

June '78

KAREN BRODINE

Karen Brodine, an MFA in Creative Writing, worked relentlessly for social-ist, feminist, labor, and multi-racial causes. Brodine's "June '78" from her second book of poetry Illegal Assembly *criticizes the deadening effects of working and living conditions as well as questions what a different social order might cause its inhabitants to produce and feel and think. The poem urges consideration of the imagination as a resource that both shapes and is shaped by political and social realities.*

it's like being sick all the time, I think, coming home from work,
sick in that low-grade continuous way that makes you forget
what it's like to be well. we have never in our lives known
what it is to be well. what if I were coming home, I think,
from doing work that I loved and that was for us all, what
if I looked at the houses and the air and the streets, knowing
they were in accord, not set against us, what if we knew the powers
of this country moved to provide for us and for all people—
how would that be—how would we feel and think
and what would we create?

6

Hermaphrodites with Attitude: Mapping the Emergence of Intersex Political Activism

CHERYL CHASE

Cheryl Chase (now known as Bo Laurent), founder of the Intersex Society of North America (see too Accord Alliance), presents an account of the development and increasing visibility of intersex communities and organizations in this article from a 1998 issue of GLQ: A Journal of Lesbian and Gay Studies. *Chase points to the multiplicities of sex and gender variations as well as to the personal and social stakes involved with political activism around intersex issues and identities.*

The insistence on two clearly distinguished sexes has calamitous personal consequences for the many individuals who arrive in the world with sexual anatomy that fails to be easily distinguished as male or female. Such individuals are labeled "intersexuals" or "hermaphrodites" by modern medical discourse.[1] About one in a hundred births exhibits some anomaly in sex differentiation,[2] and about one in two thousand is different enough to render problematic the question "Is it a boy or a girl?"[3] Since the early 1960s, nearly every major city in the United States has had a hospital with a standing team of medical experts who intervene in these cases to assign—through drastic surgical means—a male or female status to intersex infants. The fact that this system for preserving the boundaries of the categories male and female has existed for so long without drawing criticism or scrutiny from any quarter indicates the extreme discomfort that sexual ambiguity excites in our culture. Pediatric genital surgeries literalize what might otherwise be considered a theoretical operation: the attempted production of normatively sexed bodies and gendered subjects through constitutive acts of violence. Over the last few years, however, intersex people have begun to politicize intersex identities, thus transforming intensely personal experiences of violation into collective opposition to the medical regulation of bodies that queer the foundations of heteronormative identification and desires.

Hermaphrodites: Medical Authority and Cultural Invisibility

Many people familiar with the ideas that gender is a phenomenon not adequately described by male/female dimorphism and that the interpretation of physical sex differences is culturally constructed remain surprised to learn just how variable sexual anatomy is.[4] Though the male/female binary is constructed as natural and presumed to be immutable, the phenomenon of intersexuality offers clear evidence to the contrary and furnishes an opportunity to deploy "nature" strategically to disrupt heteronormative systems of sex, gender, and sexuality. The concept of bodily sex, in popular usage, refers to multiple components including karyotype (organization of sex chromosomes), gonadal differentiation (e.g., ovarian or testicular), genital morphology, configuration of internal reproductive organs, and pubertal sex characteristics such as breasts and facial hair. Because these characteristics are expected to be concordant in each individual—either all male or all female—an observer, once having attributed male or female sex to a particular individual, assumes the values of other unobserved characteristics.[5]

Because medicine intervenes quickly in intersex births to change the infant's body, the phenomenon of intersexuality is today largely unknown outside specialized medical practices. General public awareness of intersex bodies slowly van-

---

[1]Claude J. Migeon, Gary D. Berkovitz, and Terry R. Brown, "Sexual Differentiation and Ambiguity," in *Wilkins: The Diagnosis and Treatment of Endocrine Disorders in Childhood and Adolescence*, ed. Michael S. Kappy, Robert M. Blizzard, and Claude J. Migeon (Springfield, Ill.: Charles C. Thomas, 1994), 573–715.
[2]Lalitha Raman-Wilms et al., "Fetal Genital Effects of First-Trimester Sex Hormone Exposure: A Meta-Analysis," *Obstetrics and Gynecology* 85 (1995): 141–48.
[3]Anne Fausto-Sterling, *Body Building: How Biologists Construct Sexuality* (New York: Basic Books, forthcoming).
[4]Judith Butler, *Gender Trouble: Feminism and the Subversion of Identity* (New York: Routledge, 1990); Thomas Laqueur, *Making Sex: Body and Gender from the Greeks to Freud* (Cambridge, Mass.: Harvard University Press, 1990).
[5]Suzanne Kessler and Wendy McKenna, *Gender: An Ethnomethodological Approach* (New York: John Wiley and Sons, 1978).

ished in modern Western European societies as medicine gradually appropriated to itself the authority to interpret—and eventually manage—the category which had previously been widely known as "hermaphroditism." Victorian medical taxonomy began to efface hermaphroditism as a legitimated status by establishing mixed gonadal histology as a necessary criterion for "true" hermaphroditism. By this criterion, both ovarian and testicular tissue types had to be present. Given the limitations of Victorian surgery and anesthesia, such confirmation was impossible in a living patient. All other anomalies were reclassified as "pseudohermaphroditisms" masking a "true sex" determined by the gonads.[6]

With advances in anesthesia, surgery, embryology, and endocrinology, however, twentieth-century medicine moved from merely labeling intersexed bodies to the far more invasive practice of "fixing" them to conform with a diagnosed true sex. The techniques and protocols for physically transforming intersexed bodies were developed primarily at Johns Hopkins University in Baltimore during the 1920s and 1930s under the guidance of urologist Hugh Hampton Young. "Only during the last few years," Young enthused in the preface to his pioneering textbook, *Genital Abnormalities*, "have we begun to get somewhere near the explanation of the marvels of anatomic abnormality that may be portrayed by these amazing individuals. But the surgery of the hermaphrodite has remained a terra incognita." The "sad state of these unfortunates" prompted Young to devise "a great variety of surgical procedures" by which he attempted to normalize their bodily appearances to the greatest extents possible.[7]

Quite a few of Young's patients resisted his efforts. One, a "'snappy' young negro woman with a good figure" and a large clitoris, had married a man but found her passion only with women. She refused "to be made into a man" because removal of her vagina would mean the loss of her "meal ticket," namely, her husband.[8] By the 1950s, the principle of rapid postnatal detection and intervention for intersex infants had been developed at John Hopkins with the stated goal of completing surgery early enough so that the child would have no memory of it.[9] One wonders whether the insistence on early intervention was not at least partly motivated by the resistance offered by adult intersexuals to normalization through surgery. Frightened parents of ambiguously sexed infants were much more open to suggestions of normalizing surgery, while the infants themselves could of course offer no resistance whatever. Most of the theoretical foundations justifying these interventions are attributable to psychologist John Money, a sex researcher invited to Johns Hopkins by Lawson Wilkins, the founder of

---

[6]Alice Domurat Dreger, "Doubtful Sex: Cases and Concepts of Hermaphroditism in France and Britain, 1868–1915," (Ph.D. diss., Indiana University, 1995); Alice Domurat Dreger, "Doubtful Sex: The Fate of the Hermaphrodite in Victorian Medicine," *Victorian Studies* (spring 1995): 336–70; Alice Domurat Dreger, "Hermaphrodites in Love: The Truth of the Gonads," *Science and Homosexualities*, ed. Vernon Rosario (New York: Routledge, 1997), 46–66; Alice Domurat Dreger, "Doctors Containing Hermaphrodites: The Victorian Legacy," *Chrysalis: The Journal of Transgressive Gender Identities* (fall 1997): 15–22.

[7]Hugh Hampton Young, *Genital Abnormalities, Hermaphroditism, and Related Adrenal Diseases* (Baltimore: Williams and Wilkins, 1937), xxxix–xl.

[8]Ibid., 139–42.

[9]Howard W. Jones: Jr. and William Wallace Scott, *Hermaphroditism, Genital Anomalies, and Related Endocrine Disorders* (Baltimore: Williams and Wilkins, 1958), 269.

pediatric endocrinology.[10] Wilkins's numerous students subsequently carried these protocols to hospitals throughout the United States and abroad.[11] Suzanne Kessler notes that today Wilkins and Money's protocols enjoy a "consensus of approval rarely encountered in science."[12]

In keeping with the Johns Hopkins model, the birth of an intersex infant today is deemed a "psychosocial emergency" that propels a multidisciplinary team of intersex specialists into action. Significantly, they are surgeons and endocrinologists rather than psychologists, bioethicists, representatives from intersex peer support organizations, or parents of intersex children. The team examines the infant and chooses either male or female as a "sex of assignment," then informs the parents that this is the child's "true sex." Medical technology, including surgery and hormones, is then used to make the child's body conform as closely as possible to that sex.

The sort of deviation from sex norms exhibited by intersexuals is so highly stigmatized that the likely prospect of emotional harm due to social rejection of the intersexual provides physicians with their most compelling argument to justify medically unnecessary surgical interventions. Intersex status is considered to be so incompatible with emotional health that misrepresentation, concealment of facts, and outright lying (both to parents and later to the intersex person) are unabashedly advocated in professional medical literature.[13] Rather, the systematic hushing up of the fact of intersex births and the use of violent techniques to normalize intersex bodies have caused profound emotional and physical harm to intersexuals and their families. The harm begins when the birth is treated as a medical crisis, and the consequences of that initial treatment ripple out ever afterward. The impact of this treatment is so devastating that until just a few years ago, people whose lives have been touched by intersexuality maintained silence about their ordeal. As recently as 1993, no one publicly disputed surgeon Milton Edgerton when he wrote that in forty years of clitoral surgery on intersexuals, "not one has complained of loss of sensation, *even when the entire clitoris was removed.*"[14]

The tragic irony is that, while intersexual anatomy occasionally indicates an underlying medical problem such as adrenal malfunction, ambiguous genitals are in and of themselves neither painful nor harmful to health. Surgery is essentially a destructive process. It can remove and to a limited extent relocate tissue,

---

[10]John Money, Joan G. Hampson, and John L. Hampson, "An Examination of Some Basic Sexual Concepts: The Evidence of Human Hermaphroditism," *Bulletin of the Johns Hopkins Hospital* 97 (1955): 301–19; John Money, Joan G. Hampson, and John L. Hampson, "Hermaphroditism: Recommendations Concerning Assignment of Sex, Change of Sex, and Psychologic Management," *Bulletin of Johns Hopkins Hospital* 97 (1955): 284–300; John Money, *Venuses Penuses* (Buffalo: Prometheus, 1986).

[11]Robert M. Blizzard, "Lawson Wilkins," in Kappy et al. *Wilkins*, xi–xiv.

[12]Suzanne Kessler. "The Medical Construction of Gender: Case Management of Intersexual Infants," *Signs: Journal of Women in Culture and Society* 16 (1990): 3–26.

[13]J. Dewhurst and D. B. Grant. "Intersex Problems," *Archives of Disease in Childhood* 59 (1984): 1191–94: Anita Natarajan, "Medical Ethics and Truth-Telling in the Case of Androgen Insensitivity Syndrome," *Canadian Medical Association Journal* 154 (1996): 568–70; Tom Mazur, "Ambiguous Genitalia: Detection and Counseling." *Pediatric Nursing* (1983): 417–22; E. M. E. Slijper et al., "Neonates with Abnormal Genital Development Assigned the Female Sex: Parent Counseling," *Journal of Sex Education and Therapy* 20 (1994): 9–17.

[14]Milton T. Edgerton. "Discussion: Clitoroplasty for Clitoromegaly due to Adrenogenital Syndrome without Loss of Sensitivity (by Nobuyuki Sagehashi)," *Plastic and Reconstructive Surgery* 91 (1993): 956.

but it cannot create new structures. This technical limitation, taken together with the framing of the feminine as a condition of lack, leads physicians to assign 90 percent of anatomically ambiguous infants as female by excising genital tissue. Members of the Johns Hopkins intersex team have justified female assignment by saying, "You can make a hole, but you can't build a pole."[15] Positively heroic efforts shore up a tenuous masculine status for the remaining 10 percent assigned male, who are subjected to multiple operations—twenty-two in one case[16]—with the goal of straightening the penis and constructing a urethra to enable standing urinary posture. For some, the surgeries end only when the child grows old enough to resist.[17]

Children assigned to the female sex are subjected to surgery that removes the troubling hypertrophic clitoris (the same tissue that would have been a troubling micropenis if the child had been assigned male). Through the 1960s, feminizing pediatric genital surgery was openly labeled "clitorectomy" and was compared favorably to the African practices that have been the recent focus of such intense scrutiny. As three Harvard surgeons noted, "Evidence that the clitoris is not essential for normal coitus may be gained from certain sociological data. For instance, it is the custom of a number of African tribes to excise the clitoris and other parts of the external genitals. Yet normal sexual function is observed in these females."[18] A modified operation that removes most of the clitoris and relocates a bit of the tip is variously (and euphemistically) called clitoroplasty, clitoral reduction, or clitoral recession and is described as a "simple cosmetic procedure" to differentiate it from the now infamous clitorectomy. However, the operation is far from benign. Here is a slightly simplified summary (in my own words) of the surgical technique—recommended by Johns Hopkins Surgeons Oesterling, Gearhart, and Jeffs—that is representative of the operation:

> They make an incision around the phallus, at the corona, then dissect the skin away from its underside. Next they dissect the skin away from the dorsal side and remove as much of the corpora, or erectile bodies, as necessary to create an "appropriate size clitoris." Next, stitches are placed from the pubic area along both sides of the entire length of what remains of the phallus; when these stitches are tightened, it folds up like pleats in a skirt, and recesses into a concealed position behind the mons pubis. If the result is still "too large," the glans is further reduced by cutting away a pie-shaped wedge.[19]

For most intersexuals, this sort of arcane, dehumanized medical description, illustrated with close-ups of genital surgery and naked children with blacked-out

[15]Melissa Hendricks, "Is It a Boy or a Girl?" *Johns Hopkins Magazine*, November, 1993, 10–16.

[16]John E Stecker et al., "Hypospadias Cripples," *Urologic Clinics of North America: Symposium on Hypospadias* 8 (1981): 539–44.

[17]Jeff McClintock, "Growing Up in the Surgical Maelstrom," *Chrysalis: The Journal of Transgressive Gender Identities* (fall 1997): 53–54.

[18]Robert E. Gross, Judson Randolph, and John F. Crigler, "Clitorectomy for Sexual Abnormalities: Indications and Technique," *Surgery* 59 (1966): 300–308.

[19]Joseph E. Oesterling, John P. Gearhart, and Robert D. Jeffs, "A Unified Approach to Early Reconstructive Surgery of the Child with Ambiguous Genitalia," *Journal of Urology* 138 (1987): 1079–84.

eyes, is the only available version of *Our Bodies, Ourselves*. We as a culture have relinquished to medicine the authority to police the boundaries of male and female, leaving intersexuals to recover as best they can, alone and silent, from violent normalization.

My Career as a Hermaphrodite: Renegotiating Cultural Meanings

I was born with ambiguous genitals. A doctor specializing in intersexuality deliberated for three days—sedating my mother each time she asked what was wrong with her baby—before concluding that I was male, with a micropenis, complete hypospadias, undescended testes, and a strange extra opening behind the urethra. A male birth certificate was completed for me, and my parents began raising me as a boy. When I was a year and a half old my parents consulted a different set of experts, who admitted me to a hospital for "sex determination." "Determine" is a remarkably apt word in this context, meaning both "to ascertain by investigation" and "to cause to come to a resolution." It perfectly describes the two-stage process whereby science produces through a series of masked operations what it claims merely to observe. Doctors told my parents that a thorough medical investigation would be necessary to determine (in the first sense of that word) what my "true sex" was. They judged my genital appendage to be inadequate as a penis, too short to mark masculine status effectively or to penetrate females. As a female, however, I would be penetrable and potentially fertile. My anatomy having been relabeled as vagina, urethra, labia, and outsized clitoris, my sex was determined (in the second sense) by amputating my genital appendage. Following doctors' orders, my parents then changed my name, combed their house to eliminate all traces of my existence as a boy (photographs, birthday cards, etc.), changed my birth certificate, moved to a different town, instructed extended family members no longer to refer to me as a boy, and never told anyone else—including me—just what had happened. My intersexuality and change of sex were the family's dirty little secrets.

At age eight, I was returned to the hospital for abdominal surgery that trimmed away the testicular portion of my gonads, each of which was partly ovarian and partly testicular in character. No explanation was given to me then for the long hospital stay or the abdominal surgery, nor for the regular hospital visits afterward, in which doctors photographed my genitals and inserted fingers and instruments into my vagina and anus. These visits ceased as soon as I began to menstruate. At the time of the sex change, doctors had assured my parents that their once son/now daughter would grow into a woman who could have a normal sex life and babies. With the confirmation of menstruation, my parents apparently concluded that that prediction had been borne out and their ordeal was behind them. For me, the worst part of the nightmare was just beginning.

As an adolescent, I became aware that I had no clitoris or inner labia and was unable to orgasm. By the end of my teens, I began to do research in medical libraries, trying to discover what might have happened to me. When I finally determined to obtain my medical records, it took me three years to overcome the obstruction of the doctors whom I asked for help. When I did obtain them, a scant three pages, I first learned that I was a "true hermaphrodite" who had been my parents' son for a year and a half and who bore a name unfamiliar to me. The records also documented my clitorectomy. This was the middle 1970s, when I was in my early twenties. I had come to identify myself as lesbian, at a time when lesbianism and a biologically based gender essentialism were virtually synonymous: men were rapists who caused war and environmental destruction; women were good and would heal the earth; lesbians were a superior form of being uncontaminated by "men's energy." In such a world, how could I tell anyone that I had actually possessed the dreaded "phallus"? I was no longer a woman in my own eyes but rather a monstrous and mythical creature. Because my hermaphroditism and long-buried boyhood were the history behind the clitorectomy, I could never speak openly about that or my consequent inability to orgasm. I was so traumatized by discovering the circumstances that produced my embodiment that I could not speak of these matters with anyone.

Nearly fifteen years later, I suffered an emotional meltdown. In the eyes of the world, I was a highly successful businesswoman, a principal in an international high tech company. To myself, I was a freak, incapable of loving or being loved, filled with shame about my status as a hermaphrodite and about my sexual dysfunction. Unable to make peace with myself, I finally sought help from a psychotherapist, who reacted to each revelation about my history and predicament with some version of "no, it's not" or "so what?" I would say, "I'm not really a woman," and she would say, "Of course you are. You look female." I would say, "My complete withdrawal from sexuality has destroyed every relationship I've ever entered." She would say, "Everybody has their ups and downs," I tried another therapist and met with a similar response. Increasingly desperate, I confided my story to several friends, who shrank away in embarrassed silence. I was in emotional agony, feeling utterly alone, seeing no possible way out. I decided to kill myself.

Confronting suicide as a real possibility proved to be my personal epiphany. I fantasized killing myself quite messily and dramatically in the office of the surgeon who had cut off my clitoris, forcibly confronting him with the horror he had imposed on my life. But in acknowledging the desire to put my pain to some use, not to utterly waste my life, I turned a crucial corner, finding a way to direct my rage productively out into the world rather than destructively at myself. I had no conceptual framework for developing a more positive self-consciousness. I knew only that I felt mutilated, not fully human, but that I was determined to heal. I struggled for weeks in emotional chaos, unable to eat or sleep or work. I could not accept my image of a hermaphroditic body any more than I could accept the butchered one the surgeons left me with. Thoughts of myself as a Frankenstein's monster patchwork alternated with longings for escape by death, only to be followed by outrage, anger, and a determination to survive. I could not accept that it was just or right or good to treat any person as I had been treated—my sex changed, my genitals cut up, my experience silenced and rendered invisible. I bore a private hell within me, wretchedly alone in my condition without even my tormentors for company. Finally, I began to envision myself standing in a driving storm but with clear skies and a rainbow visible in the distance. I was still in agony, but I was beginning to see the painful process in which I was caught up in terms of revitalization and re-birth, a means of investing my life with a new sense of authenticity that possessed vast potentials for further transformation. Since then,

I have seen this experience of movement through pain to personal empowerment described by other intersex and transsexual activists.[20]

I slowly developed a newly politicized and critically aware form of self-understanding. I had been the kind of lesbian who at times had a girlfriend but who had never really participated in the life of a lesbian community. I felt almost completely isolated from gay politics, feminism, and queer and gender theory. I did possess the rudimentary knowledge that the gay rights movement had gathered momentum only when it could effectively deny that homosexuality was sick or inferior and assert to the contrary that "gay is good." As impossible as it then seemed, I pledged similarly to affirm that "intersex is good," that the body I was born with was not diseased, only different. I vowed to embrace the sense of being "not a woman" that I initially had been so terrified to discover.

I began searching for community and consequently moved to San Francisco in the fall of 1992, based entirely on my vague notion that people living in the "queer mecca" would have the most conceptually sophisticated, socially tolerant, and politically astute analysis of sexed and gendered embodiment. I found what I was looking for in part because my arrival in the Bay Area corresponded with the rather sudden emergence of an energetic transgender political movement. Transgender Nation (TN) had developed out of Queer Nation, a post-gay/lesbian group that sought to transcend identity politics. TN's actions garnered media attention—especially when members were arrested during a "zap" of the American Psychiatric Association's annual convention when they protested the psychiatric labeling of transsexuality as mental illness. Transsexual performance artist Kate Bornstein was introducing transgender issues in an entertaining way to the San Francisco gay/lesbian community and beyond. Female-to-male issues had achieved a new level of visibility due in large part to efforts made by Lou Sullivan, a gay FTM activist who had died an untimely death from HIV-related illnesses in 1991. And in the wake of her underground best-selling novel, *Stone Butch Blues,* Leslie Feinberg's manifesto *Transgender Liberation: A Movement Whose Time Has Come* was finding a substantial audience, linking transgender social justice to a broader progressive political agenda for the first time.[21] At the same time, a vigorous new wave of gender scholarship had emerged in the academy.[22] In this context; intersex activist and theoretician Morgan Holmes could analyze her own clitorectomy for her master's thesis and have it taken seriously as academic work.[23] Openly transsexual scholars, including Susan Stryker and Sandy Stone, were visible in responsible academic positions at major universities. Stone's "*Empire* Strikes Back: A Posttranssexual Manifesto" refigured open, visible transsexuals not as gender conformists propping up a system of

---

[20]Kira Triea, "The Awakening," *Hermaphrodites with Attitude* (winter 1994): 1; Susan Stryker, "My Words to Victor Frankenstein above the Village of Chamounix: Performing Transgender Rage," *GLQ* I (1994): 237–54.

[21]Leslie Feinberg, *Stone Butch Blues* (Ithaca, N.Y.: Firebrand, 1993); Leslie Feinberg, *Transgender Liberation: A Movement Whose Time Has Come* (New York: World View Forum, 1992).

[22]See, for example, Judith Butler, *Bodies That Matter: On the Discursive Limits of "Sex"* (New York: Routledge, 1993); Butler, *Gender Trouble*; Laqueur, *Making Sex*; and Julia Epstein and Kristina Straub, eds., *Body Guards: The Cultural Politics of Gender Ambiguity* (New York: Routledge, 1991).

[23]Morgan Holmes, "Medical Politics and Cultural Imperatives: Intersexuality Beyond Pathology and Erasure" (master's thesis, York University, Toronto, 1994).

rigid, binary sex but as "a set of embodied texts whose potential for productive disruption of structured sexualities and spectra of desire has yet to be explored."[24]

Into this heady atmosphere, I brought my own experience. Introduced by Bornstein to other gender activists, I explored with them the cultural politics of intersexuality, which to me represented yet another new configuration of bodies, identities, desires, and sexualities from which to confront the violently normativizing aspects of the dominant sex/gender system. In the fall of 1993, TN pioneer Anne Ogborn invited me to participate in a weekend retreat called the New Woman Conference, where postoperative transsexual women shared their stories, their griefs and joys, and enjoyed the freedom to swim or sunbathe in the nude with others who had surgically changed genitals. I saw that participants returned home in a state of euphoria, and I determined to bring that same sort of healing experience to intersex people.

Birth of an Intersex Movement: Opposition and Allies

Upon moving to San Francisco, I started telling my story indiscriminately to everyone I met. Over the course of a year, simply by speaking openly within my own social circles, I learned of six other intersexuals—including two who had been fortunate enough to escape medical attention. I realized that intersexuality, rather than being extremely rare, must be relatively common. I decided to create a support network. In the summer of 1993, I produced some pamphlets, obtained a post office box, and began to publicize the Intersex Society of North America (ISNA) through small notices in the media. Before long, I was receiving several letters per week from intersexuals throughout the United States and Canada and occasionally some from Europe. While the details varied, the letters gave a remarkably coherent picture of the emotional consequences of medical intervention. Morgan Holmes: "All the things my body might have grown to do, all the possibilities, went down the hall with my amputated clitoris to the pathology department. The rest of me went to the recovery room—I'm still recovering." Angela Moreno: "I am horrified by what has been done to me and by the conspiracy of silence and lies. I am filled with grief and rage, but also relief finally to believe that maybe I am not the only one." Thomas: "I pray that I will have the means to repay, in some measure, the American Urological Association for all that it has done for my benefit. I am having some trouble, though, in connecting the timing mechanism to the fuse."

ISNA's most immediate goal has been to create community of intersex people who could provide peer support to deal with shame, stigma, grief, and rage as well as with practical issues such as how to obtain old medical records or locate a sympathetic psychotherapist or endocrinologist. To that end, I cooperated with journalists whom I judged capable of reporting widely and responsibly on our efforts, listed ISNA with self-help and referral clearinghouses, and established a presence on the Internet (http://www.isna.org). ISNA now connects hundreds of intersexuals across North America, Europe, Australia, and New Zealand. It has also begun

---

[24]Sandy Stone, "The *Empire* Strikes Back: A Posttranssexual Manifesto," in Epstein and Straub, *Body Guards*, 280-304, quotation on 296.

sponsoring an annual intersex retreat, the first of which took place in 1996 and which moved participants every bit as profoundly as the New Woman Conference had moved me in 1993.

ISNA's longer-term and more fundamental goal, however, is to change the way intersex infants are treated. We advocate that surgery not be performed on ambiguous genitals unless there is medical reason (such as blocked or painful urination), and that parents be given the conceptual tools and emotional support to accept their children's physical differences. While it is fascinating to think about the potential development of new genders or subject positions grounded in forms of embodiment that fall outside the familiar male/female dichotomy, we recognize that the two-sex/gender model is currently hegemonic and therefore advocate that children be raised either as boys or girls, according to which designation seems most likely to offer the child the greatest future sense of comfort. Advocating gender assignment without resorting to normalizing surgery is a radical position given that it requires the willful disruption of the assumed concordance between body shape and gender category. However, this is the only position that prevents irreversible physical damage to the intersex person's body, that respects the intersex person's agency regarding his/her own flesh, and that recognizes genital sensation and erotic functioning to be at least as important as reproductive capacity. If an intersex child or adult decides to change gender or to undergo surgical or hormonal alteration of his/her body, that decision should also be fully respected and facilitated. The key point is that intersex subjects should not be violated for the comfort and convenience of others.

One part of reaching ISNA's long-term goal has been to document the emotional and physical carnage resulting from medical interventions. As a rapidly growing literature makes abundantly clear (see the bibliography on our website, http://www.isna.org/bigbib.html), the medical management of intersexuality has changed little in the forty years since my first surgery. Kessler expresses surprise that "in spite of the thousands of genital operations performed every year, there are no meta-analyses from within the medical community on levels of success."[25] They do not know whether postsurgical intersexuals are "silent and happy or silent and unhappy."[26] There is no research effort to improve erotic functioning for adult intersexuals whose genitals have been altered, nor are there psychotherapists specializing in working with adult intersex clients trying to heal from the trauma of medical intervention. To provide a counterpoint to the mountains of medical literature that neglect intersex experience and to begin compiling an ethnographic account of that experience, *ISNA's Hermaphrodites with Attitude* newsletter has developed into a forum for intersexuals to tell their own stories. We have sent complimentary copies of the newsletter filled with searing personal narratives to academics, writers, journalists, minority rights organizations, and medical practitioners—to anybody we thought might make a difference in our campaign to change the way intersex bodies are managed.

---

[25]Suzanne Kessler, *Lessons from the Intersexed* (New Brunswick, N.J.: Rutgers University Press, forthcoming).

[26]Robert Jeffs, quoted in Ellen Barry, "United States of Ambiguity," Boston *Phoenix*, 22 November 1996, 6–8, quotation on 6.

ISNA's presence has begun to generate effects. It has helped politicize the growing number of intersex organizations, as well as intersex identities themselves. When I first began organizing ISNA, I met leaders of the Turner's Syndrome Society, the oldest known support group focusing on atypical sexual differentiation, founded in 1987. Turner's Syndrome is defined by an XO genetic karyotype that results in a female body morphology with nonfunctioning ovaries, extremely short stature, and a variety of other physical differences described in the medical literature with such stigmatizing labels as "web-necked" and "fish-mouthed." Each of these women told me what a profound, life-changing experience it had been simply to meet another person like herself. I was inspired by their accomplishments (they are a national organization serving thousands of members), but I wanted ISNA to have a different focus. I was less willing to think of intersexuality as a pathology or disability, more interested in challenging its medicalization entirely, and more interested still in politicizing a pan-intersexual identity across the divisions of particular etiologies in order to destabilize more effectively the heteronormative assumptions underlying the violence directed at our bodies.

When I established ISNA in 1993, no such politicized groups existed. In the United Kingdom in 1988, the mother of a girl with androgen-insensitivity syndrome (AIS, which produces genetic males with female genital morphologies) formed the AIS Support Group. The group, which initially lobbied for increased medical attention (better surgical techniques for producing greater vaginal depth, more research into the osteoporosis that often attends AIS), now has chapters in five countries. Another group, K. S. and Associates, was formed in 1989 by the mother of a boy with Klinefelter's Syndrome and today serves over one thousand families. Klinefelter's is characterized by the presence of one or more additional X chromosomes, which produce bodies with fairly masculine external genitals. Above-average height, and somewhat gangly limbs. At puberty, people with K. S. often experience pelvic broadening and the development of breasts. K. S. and Associates continues to be dominated by parents, is highly medical in orientation, and has resisted attempts by adult Klinefelter's Syndrome men to discuss gender identity or sexual orientation issues related to their intersex condition.

Since ISNA has been on the scene, other groups with a more resistant stance vis-à-vis the medical establishment have begun to appear. In 1995, a mother who refused medical pressure for female assignment for her intersex child formed the Ambiguous Genitalia Support Network, which introduces parents of intersexuals to each other and encourages the development of pen-pal support relationships. In 1996, another mother who had rejected medical pressure to assign her intersex infant as a female by removing his penis formed the Hermaphrodite Education and Listening Post (HELP) to provide peer support and medical information. Neither of these parent-oriented groups, however, frames its work in overtly political terms. Still, political analysis and action of the sort advocated by ISNA has not been without effect on the more narrowly defined service-oriented or parent-dominated groups. The AIS Support Group, now more representative of both adults and parents, noted in a recent newsletter,

> *Our first impression of ISNA was that they were perhaps a bit too angry and militant to gain the support of the medical profession.*

> *However, we have to say that, having read [political analyses of inter-*
> *sexuality by ISNA, Kessler, Fausto-Sterling, and Holmes], we feel*
> *that the feminist concepts relating to the patriarchal treatment of*
> *intersexuality are extremely interesting and do make a lot of sense.*
> *After all, the lives of intersexed people are stigmatized by the cul-*
> *tural disapproval of their genital appearance, [which need not] affect*
> *their experience as sexual human beings.*[27]

Other more militant groups have now begun to pop up. In 1994, German intersexuals formed both the Workgroup on Violence in Pediatrics and Gynecology
and the Genital Mutilation Survivors' Support Network, and Hijra Nippon now
represents activist intersexuals in Japan.

Outside the rather small community of intersex organizations, ISNA's work
has generated a complex patchwork of alliances and oppositions. Queer activists,
especially transgender activists, have provided encouragement, advice, and logis-
tical support to the intersex movement. The direct action group Transsexual
Menace helped an ad hoc group of militant intersexuals calling themselves
Hermaphrodites with Attitude plan and carry out a picket of the 1996 annual
meeting of the American Academy of Pediatrics in Boston—the first recorded
instance of intersex public protest in modern history.[28] ISNA was also invited to
join GenderPAC, a recently formed national consortium of transgender organizations that lobbies against discrimination based on atypical expressions of gender
or embodiment. More mainstream gay and lesbian political organizations such as
the National Gay and Lesbian Task Force have also been willing to include intersex concerns as part of their political agendas. Transgender and lesbian/gay groups
have been supportive of intersex political activism largely because they see similarities in the medicalization of these various identities as a form of social control
and (especially for transsexuals) empathize with our struggle to assert agency within
a medical discourse that works to efface the ability to exercise informed consent
about what happens to one's own body.

Gay/lesbian caucuses and special interest groups within professional medical
associations have been especially receptive to ISNA's agenda. One physician on
the Internet discussion group glb-medical wrote:

> *The effect of Cheryl Chase's postings—admittedly, after the shock*
> *wore off—was to make me realize that THOSE WHO HAVE BEEN*
> *TREATED might very well think [they had not been well served by*
> *medical intervention]. This matters a lot. As a gay man, and simply*
> *as a person, I have struggled for much of my adult life to find my own*
> *natural self, to disentangle the confusions caused by others' pre-*
> *sumptions about how I am/should be. But, thankfully, their decisions*
> *were not surgically imposed on me!*

Queer psychiatrists, starting with Bill Byne at New York's Mount Sinai Hospital,
have been quick to support ISNA, in part because the psychological principles

---

[27]AIS Support Group, "Letter to America," *ALIAS* (spring 1996): 3–4.
[28]Barry, "United States of Ambiguity," 7.

underlying the current intersex treatment protocols are manifestly unsound. They seem almost willfully designed to exacerbate rather than ameliorate already difficult emotional issues arising from sexual difference. Some of these psychiatrists see the surgical and endocrinological domination of a problem that even surgeons and endocrinologists acknowledge to be psychosocial rather than biomedical as an unjustified invasion of their area of professional competence.

ISNA has deliberately cultivated a network of nonintersexed advocates who command a measure of social legitimacy and can speak in contexts where uninterpreted intersex voices will not be heard. Because there is a strong impulse to discount what intersexuals have to say about intersexuality, sympathetic representation has been welcome—especially in helping intersexuals reframe intersexuality in nonmedical terms. Some gender theory scholars, feminist critics of science, medical historians, and anthropologists have been quick to understand and support intersex activism. Years before ISNA came into existence, feminist biologist and science studies scholar Anne Fausto-Sterling had written about intersexuality in relation to intellectually suspect scientific practices that perpetuate masculinist constructs of gender, and she became an early ISNA ally.[29] Likewise, social psychologist Suzanne Kessler had written a brilliant ethnography of surgeons who specialize in treating intersexuals. After speaking with several "products" of their practice, she, too, became a strong supporter of intersex activism.[30] Historian of science Alice Dreger, whose work focuses not only on hermaphroditism but on other forms of potentially benign atypical embodiment that become subject to destructively normalizing medical interventions (conjoined twins. for example), has been especially supportive. Fausto-Sterling, Kessler, and Dreger will each shortly publish works that analyze the medical treatment of intersexuality as being culturally motivated and criticize it as harmful to its ostensible patients.[31]

Allies who help contest the medicalization of intersexuality are especially important because ISNA has found it almost entirely fruitless to attempt direct, nonconfrontational interactions with the medical specialists who themselves determine policy on the treatment of intersex infants and who actually carry out the surgeries. Joycelyn Elders, the Clinton administration's first surgeon general, is a pediatric endocrinologist with many years of experience managing intersex infants but, in spite of a generally feminist approach to health care and frequent overtures from ISNA, she has been dismissive of the concerns of intersexuals themselves.[32] Another pediatrician remarked in an Internet discussion on intersexuality: "I think this whole issue

---

[29]Anne Fausto-Sterling, "The Five Sexes: Why Male and Female Are Not Enough," *The Sciences* 33, no. 2 (March/April 1993): 20–25; Anne Fausto-Sterling, *Myths of Gender: Biological Theories about Women and Men*, 2d ed. (New York: Basic Books, 1985), 134–41.

[30]Kessler, "The Medical Construction of Gender"; Suzanne Kessler, "Meanings of Genital Variability," *Chrysalis: The Journal of Transgressive Gender Identities* (fall 1997): 33–38.

[31]Anne Fausto-Sterling, *Building Bodies: Biology and the Social Construction of Sexuality* (New York: Basic Books, forthcoming); Kessler, "Meanings of Genital Variability"; Alice Domurat Dreger, *Hermaphrodites and the Medical Invention of Sex* (Cambridge, Mass.: Harvard University Press, forthcoming).

[32]"Dr. Elders' Medical History," *New Yorker*, 26 September 1994: 45–46; Joycelyn Elders and David Chanoff, *From Sharecropper's Daughter to Surgeon General of the United States of America* (New York: William Morrow, 1996).

is preposterous. . . . To suggest that [medical decisions about the treatment of intersex conditions] are somehow cruel or arbitrary is insulting, ignorant and misguided. . . . To spread the claims that [ISNA] is making is just plain wrong, and I hope that this [on-line group of doctors and scientists] will not blindly accept them." Yet another participant in that same chat asked what was for him obviously a rhetorical question: "Who is the enemy? I really don't think it's the medical establishment. Since when did we establish the male/female hegemony?" While a surgeon quoted in a *New York Times* article on ISNA summarily dismissed us as "zealots,"[33] there is considerable anecdotal information supplied by ISNA sympathizers that professional meetings in the fields of pediatrics, urology, genital plastic surgery, and endocrinology are buzzing with anxious and defensive discussions of intersex activism. In response to the Hermaphrodites with Attitude protests at the American Academy of Pediatrics meeting, that organization felt compelled to issue the following statement to the press: "The Academy is deeply concerned about the emotional, cognitive, and body image development of intersexuals, and believes that successful early genital surgery minimizes these issues." Further protests were planned for 1997.

The roots of resistance to the truth claims of intersexuals run deep in the medical establishment. Not only does ISNA critique the normativist biases couched within most scientific practice, it advocates a treatment protocol for intersex infants that disrupts conventional understandings of the relationship between bodies and genders. But on a level more personally threatening to medical practitioners, ISNA's position implies that they have—unwittingly at best, through willful denial at worst—spent their careers inflicting a profound harm from which their patients will never fully recover. ISNA's position threatens to destroy the assumptions motivating an entire medical subspecialty, thus jeopardizing the ability to perform what many surgeons find to be technically difficult and fascinating work. Melissa Hendricks notes that Dr. Gearhart is known to colleagues as a surgical "artist" who can "carve a large phallus down into a clitoris" with consummate skill.[34] More than one ISNA member has discovered that surgeons actually operated on their genitals at no charge. The medical establishment's fascination with its own power to change sex and its drive to rescue parents from their intersex children are so strong that heroic interventions are delivered without regard to the capitalist model that ordinarily governs medical services.

Given such deep and mutually reinforcing reasons for opposing ISNA's position, it is hardly surprising that medical intersex specialists have, for the most part, turned a deaf ear toward us. The lone exception as of April 1997 is urologist Justine Schober. After watching a videotape of the 1996 ISNA retreat and receiving other input from HELP and the AIS Support Group, she suggests in a new textbook on pediatric surgery that while technology has advanced to the point that "our needs [as surgeons] and the needs of parents to have a presentable child can be satisfied," it is time to acknowledge that problems exist that "we as surgeons . . . cannot address. Success in psychosocial adjustment is the true goal of sexual assignment

---

[33]Natalie Angier, "Intersexual Healing: An Anomaly Finds a Group," *New York Times*, 4 February 1996, E14.
[34]Hendricks, "Is It a Boy or a Girl?" 10.

and genitoplasty. . . . Surgery makes parents and doctors comfortable, but counseling makes people comfortable too, and is not irreversible.[35]

While ISNA will continue to approach the medical establishment for dialogue (and continue supporting protests outside the closed doors when doctors refuse to talk), perhaps the most important aspect of our current activities is the struggle to change public perceptions. By using the mass media, the Internet, and our growing network of allies and sympathizers to make the general public aware of the frequency of intersexuality and of the intense suffering that medical treatment has caused, we seek to create an environment in which many parents of intersex children will have already heard about the intersex movement when their child is born. Such informed parents we hope will be better able to resist medical pressure for unnecessary genital surgery and secrecy and to find their way to a peer-support group and counseling rather than to a surgical theater.

---

[35]Justine M. Schober, "Long Term Outcomes of Feminizing Genitoplasty for Intersex," in *Pediatric Surgery and Urology: Long Term Outcomes*, ed. Pierre Mouriquant (Philadelphia: W B. Saunders, forthcoming)

7

The Zoot-Suit and Style Warfare

Stuart Cosgrove

In this article Stuart Cosgrove examines the origins and consequences of the 1943 zoot-suit riots. Originally published in a 1984 issue of History Workshop Journal, *this article focuses on a specific historical moment, highlighting the intimate relationship between cultural expression, social location, and the political work of identity and style. Cosgrove serves as Head of Programmes for the United Kingdom's Channel 4, a public service television network.*

Introduction: *The Silent Noise of Sinister Clowns*

What about those fellows waiting still and silent there on the platform, so still and silent they clash with the crowd in their very immobility, standing noisy in their very silence; harsh as a cry of terror in their quietness? What about these three boys, coming now along the platform, tall and slender, walking with swinging shoulders in their well-pressed, too-hot-for-summer suits, their collars high and tight about their necks, their identical hats of black cheap felt set upon the crowns of their heads with a severe formality above their conked hair? It was as though I'd never seen their like before: walking slowly, their shoulders swaying, their legs swinging from their hips in trousers that ballooned upward from cuffs fitting snug about their ankles; their coats long and hip-tight with shoulders far too broad to be those of natural western men. These fellows whose bodies seemed - what had one of my teachers said of me? - 'You're like one of those African sculptures, distorted in the interest of design.' Well, what design and whose?[1]

The zoot-suit is more than an exaggerated costume, more than a sartorial statement, it is the bearer of a complex and contradictory history. When the nameless narrator of Ellison's Invisible Man confronted the subversive sight of three young and extravagantly dressed blacks, his reaction was one of fascination, not of fear. These youths were not simply grotesque dandies parading the city's secret underworld, they were "the stewards of something uncomfortable"[2], a spectacular reminder that the social order had failed to contain their energy and difference. The zoot-suit was more than the drape-shape of 1940s fashion, more than a colourful stage-prop hanging from the shoulders of Cab Calloway, it was, in the most direct and obvious ways, an emblem of ethnicity and a way of negotiating an identiy. The zoot-suit was a refusal: a subcultural gesture that refused to concede to the manners of subservience. By the late 1930s, the term "zoot" was in common circulation within urban jazz culture. Zoot meant something worn or performed in an extravagant style, and since many young blacks wore suits with outrageously padded shoulders and trousers that were fiercely tapered at the ankles, the term zoot-suit passed into everyday usage. In the sub-cultural world of Harlem's nightlife, the language of rhyming slang succinctly described the zoot-suit's unmistakable style: 'a killer-diller coat with a drapeshape, real-pleats and shoulders padded like a lunatic's cell'. The study of the relationship between fashion and social action is notoriously underdeveloped, but there is every indication that the zoot-suit riots that erupted in the United States in the summer of 1943 had a profound effect on a whole generation of socially disadvantaged youths. It was during his period as a young zoot-suiter that the Chicano union activist César Chávez first came into contact with community politics, and it was through the experiences of participating in zoot-suit riots in Harlem that the young pimp 'Detroit Red' began a political education that transformed him into the Black radical leader Malcolm X. Although the zoot-suit occupies an almost mythical place within the history of jazz music, its social and political importance has been virtually ignored. There can be no certainty about when, where or why the zoot-suit came into existence, but what is certain is that during the summer months of 1943 "the killer-diller coat" was the uniform of young rioters and the symbol of a moral panic about juvenile delinquency that was to intensify in the post-war period.

At the height of the Los Angeles riots of June 1943, the New York Times carried a front page article which claimed without reservation that the first zoot-suit had been purchased by a black bus worker, Clyde Duncan, from a tailor's shop in Gainesville, Georgia.[3] Allegedly, Duncan had been inspired by the film "Gone with the Wind" and had set out to look like Rhett Butler. This explanation clearly found favour throughout the USA. The national press forwarded countless others. Some reports claimed that the zoot-suit was an invention of Harlem nigh' life, others suggested it grew out of jazz culture and the exhibitionist stage costumes of the band leaders, and some argued that the zoot-suit was derived from military uniforms and imported from Britain. The alternative and independent press, particularly Crisis and Negro Quarterly, more convincingly argued that the zoot-suit was the product of a particular social context.[4] They emphasized the importance of Mexican-American youths, or pachucos, in the emergence of zoot-suit style and, in tentative ways, tried to relate their appearance on the streets to the concept of pachuquismo.

In his pioneering book, *The Labyrinth of Solitude,* the Mexican poet and social commentator Octavio Paz throws imaginative light on pachuco style and indirectly establishes a framework within which the zoot-suit can be understood. Paz's study of the Mexican national consciousness examines the changes brought about by the movement of labour, particularly the generations of Mexicans who migrated northwards to the USA. This movement, and the new economic and social patterns it implies, has, according to Paz, forced young Mexican-Americans into an ambivalent experience between two cultures.

> *What distinguishes them, I think, is their furtive, restless air: they act like persons who are wearing disguises, who are afraid of a stranger's look because it could strip them and leave them stark naked.... This spiritual condition or lack of a spirit, has given birth to a type known as the pachuco. The pachucos are youths, for the most part of Mexican origin, who form gangs in southern cities; they can be identified by their language and behaviour as well as by the clothing they affect. They are instinctive rebels, and North American racism has vented its wrath on them more than once. But the pachucos do not attempt to vindicate their race or the nationality of their forebears. Their attitude reveals an obstinate, almost fanatical will-to-be, but this will affirms nothing specific except their determination . . . not to be like those around them.*[5]

Pachuco youth embodied all the characteristics of second generation working-class immigrants. In the most obvious ways they had been stripped of their customs, beliefs and language. The pachucos were a disinherited generation within a disadvantaged sector of North American society; and predictably their experiences in education, welfare and employment alienated them from the aspirations of their parents and the dominant assumptions of the society in which they lived. The pachuco subculture was defined not only by ostentatious fashion, but by petty crime, delinquency and drug-taking. Rather than disguise their alienation or efface their hostility to the dominant society, the pachucos adopted an arrogant posture. They flaunted their difference, and the zoot-suit became the means by which that difference was announced. Those 'impassive and sinister clowns' whose purpose was 'to cause terror instead of laughter,'[6] invited the kind of attention that led to both prestige and persecution. For Octavio Paz the pachuco's appropriation of the zoot-suit was an admission of the ambivalent place he occupied. 'It is the only way he can establish a more vital relationship with the society he is antagonizing. As a victim he can occupy a place in the world that previously ignored him; as a delinquent, he can become one of its wicked heroes.'[7] The Zoot-Suit Riots of 1943 encapsulated this paradox. They emerged out of the dialectics of delinquency and persecution, during a period in which American society was undergoing profound structural change.

The major social change brought about by the United States' involvement in the war was the recruitment to the armed forces of over four million civilians and the entrance of over five million women into the war-time labour force. The rapid increase in military recruitment and the radical shift in the composition of the labour force led in turn to changes in family life, particularly the erosion of parental control and authority. The large scale and prolonged separation of millions of families precipitated an unprecedented increase in the rate of juvenile crime and delinquency. By the summer of 1943 it was commonplace for teenagers to be left to their own initiatives whilst their parents were either on active military service or involved in war work. The increase in night work compounded the problem. With their parents or guardians working unsocial hours, it became possible for many more young people to gather late into the night at major urban centers or simply on the street corners. The rate of social mobility intensified during the period of the Zoot-Suit Riots. With over 15 million civilians and 12 million military personnel on the move throughout the country, there was a corresponding increase in vagrancy. Petty crimes became more difficult to detect and control, itinerants became increasingly common, and social transience put unforeseen pressure on housing and welfare. The new patterns of social mobility also led to congestion in military and industrial areas. Significantly, it was the overcrowded military towns along the Pacific coast and the industrial towns of Detroit, Pittsburgh and Los Angeles that witnessed the most violent outbreaks of Zoot-Suit Rioting.[8]

"Delinquency" emerged from the dictionary of new sociology to become an everyday term, as wartime statistics revealed these new patterns of adolescent behaviour. The pachucos of the Los Angeles area were particularly vulnerable to the effects of war. Being neither Mexican nor American, the pachucos, like the black youths with whom they shared the zoot-suit style, simply did not fit. In their own terms they were "24-hour orphans", having rejected the ideologies of their migrant parents. As the war furthered the dislocation of family relationships, the pachucos gravitated away from the home to the only place where their status was visible, the streets and bars of the towns and cities. But if the pachucos laid themselves open to a life of delinquency and detention, they also asserted their distinct identity, with their own style of dress, their own way of life and a shared set of experiences.

The Zoot-Suit Riots: Liberty, Disorder, and the Forbidden

The Zoot-Suit Riots sharply revealed a polarization between two youth groups within wartime society: the gangs of predominantly black and Mexican youths who were at the forefront of the zoot-suit subculture, and the predominantly white American servicemen stationed along the Pacific coast. The riots invariably had racial and social resonances but the primary issue seems to have been patriotism and attitudes to the war. With the entry of the United States into the war in December 1941, the nation had to come to terms with the restrictions of rationing and the prospects of conscription. In March 1942, the War Production Board's first rationing act had a direct effect on the manufacture of suits and all clothing containing wool. In an attempt to institute a 26% cut-back in the use of fabrics. the War Production Board drew up regulations for the wartime manufacture of what Esquire magazine called, "streamlined suits by Uncle Sam."[9] The regulations effectively forbade the manufacture of zoot-suits and most legitimate tailoring companies ceased to manufacture or advertise any suits that fell outside the War Production Board's guide lines. However, the demand for zoot-suits did not decline and a network of bootleg tailors based in Los Angeles and New York continued to manufacture the garments. Thus the polarization between servicemen and pachucos was immediately visible: the chino shirt and battledress were evidently uniforms of patriotism, whereas wearing a zoot-suit was a deliberate and public way of flouting the regulations of rationing. The zoot-suit was a moral and social scandal in the eyes of the authorities, not simply because it was associated with petty crime and violence, but because it openly snubbed the laws of rationing. In the fragile harmony of wartime society, the zoo-suiters were, according to Octavio Paz, "a symbol of love and joy or of horror and loathing, an embodiment of liberty, of disorder, of the forbidden."[10]

The Zoot-Suit Riots, which were initially confined to Los Angeles, began in the first few days of June 1943. During the first weekend of the month, over 60 zoot-suiters were arrested and charged at Los Angeles County jail, after violent and well publicized fights between servicemen on shore leave and gangs of Mexican-American youths. In order to prevent further outbreaks of fighting, the police patrolled the eastern sections of the city, as rumours spread from the military bases that servicemen were intending to form vigilante groups. The Washington Post's report of the incidents, on the morning of Wednesday 9 June 1943, clearly saw the events from the point of view of the servicemen.

> *Disgusted with being robbed and beaten with tire irons, weighted ropes, belts and fists employed by overwhelming numbers of the youthful hoodlums, the uniformed men passed the word quietly among themselves and opened their campaign in force on Friday night.*

Courtesy of the Library of Congress.

> *At central jail, where spectators jammed the sidewalks and police made no efforts to halt auto loads of servicemen openly cruising in search of zoot-suiters, the youths streamed gladly into the sanctity of the cells after being snatched from bar rooms, pool halls and theaters and stripped of their attire.*[11]

During the ensuing weeks of rioting, the ritualistic stripping of zoot-suiters became the major means by which the servicemen re-established their status over the pachuco's. It became commonplace for gangs of marines to ambush zoot-suiters, strip them down to their underwear and leave them helpless in the streets. In one particularly vicious incident, a gang of drunken sailors rampaged through a cinema after discovering two zoot-suiters. They dragged the pachuco's onto the stage as the film was being screened, stripped them in front of the audience and as a final insult, urinated on the suits.

The press coverage of these incidents ranged from the careful and cautionary liberalism of The Los Angeles Times to the more hysterical hate-mongering of William Randolph Hearst's west coast papers. Although the practice of stripping and publicly humiliating the zoot-suiters was not prompted by the press, several reports did little to discourage the attacks:

> *... zoot-suits smouldered in the ashes of street bonfires where they had been tossed by grimly methodical tank forces of service men. ... The zooters, who earlier in the day had spread boasts that they were organized to 'kill every cop' they could find, showed no inclination to try to make good their boasts. ... Searching parties of soldiers, sailors and Marines hunted them out and drove them out into the open like bird dogs flushing quail. Procedure was standard: grab a zooter. Take off his pants and frock coat and tear them up or burn them. Trim the 'Argentine Ducktail' haircut that goes with the screwy costume.*[12]

The second week of June witnessed the worst incidents of rioting and public disorder. A sailor was slashed and disfigured by a pachuco gang; a policeman was run down when he tried to question a car load of zoot-suiters; a young Mexican was stabbed at a party by drunken Marines; a trainload of sailors were stoned by pachuco's as their train approached Long Beach; streetfights broke out daily in San Bernardino; over 400 vigilantes toured the streets of San Diego looking for zoot-suiters, and many individuals from both factions were arrested.[13] On 9 June, the Los Angeles Times published the first in a series of editorials designed to reduce the level of violence, but which also tried to allay the growing concern about the racial character of the riots.

> *To preserve the peace and good name of the Los Angeles area, the strongest measures must be taken jointly by the police, the Sheriff's office and Army and Navy authorities, to prevent any further outbreaks of 'zoot suit' rioting. While members of the armed forces received considerable provocation at the hands of the unidentified miscreants, such a situation cannot be cured by indiscriminate assault on every youth wearing a particular type of costume. It would not do, for a large number of reasons, to let the impression circulate in*

> *South America that persons of Spanish-American ancestry were being singled out for mistreatment in Southern California. And the incidents here were capable of being exaggerated to give that impression.*[14]

The Chief, The Black Widows and The Tomahawk Kid

The pleas for tolerance from civic authorities and representatives of the church and state had no immediate effect, and the riots became more frequent and more violent. A zoot-suited youth was shot by a special police officer in Azusa, a gang of pachucos were arrested for rioting and carrying weapons in the Lincoln Heights area; 25 black zoot-suiters were arrested for wrecking an electric railway train in Watts, and 1000 additional police were drafted into East Los Angeles. The press coverage increasingly focused on the most "spectacular" incidents and began to identify leaders of zoot-suit style. On the morning of Thursday 10 June 1943, most newspapers carried photographs and reports on three 'notorious' zoot-suit gang leaders. Of the thousands of pachucos that allegedly belonged to the hundreds of zoot-suit gangs in Los Angeles, the press singled out the arrests of Lewis D English, a 23-yearold-black, charged with felony and carrying a "16-inch razor sharp butcher knife;" Frank H. Tellez, a 22-year-old Mexican held on vagrancy charges, and another Mexican, Luis 'The Chief' Verdusco (27 years of age), allegedly the leader of the Los Angeles pachuco's.[15]

The arrests of English, Tellez and Verdusco seemed to confirm popular perceptions of the zoot-suiters widely expressed for weeks prior to the riots. Firstly, that the zoot-suit gangs were predominantly, but not exclusively, comprised of black and Mexican youths. Secondly, that many of the zoot-suiters were old enough to be in the armed forces but were either avoiding conscription or had been exempted on medical grounds. Finally, in the case of Frank Tellez, who was photographed wearing a pancake hat with a rear feather, that zoot-suit style was an expensive fashion often funded by theft and petty extortion. Tellez allegedly wore a colourful long drape coat that was "part of a $75 suit" and a pair of pegged trousers "very full at the knees and narrow at the cuffs" which were allegedly part of another suit. The caption of the Associated Press photograph indignantly added that "Tellez holds a medical discharge from the Army".[16] What newspaper reports tended to suppress was information on the Marines who were arrested for inciting riots, the existence of gangs of white American zoot-suiters, and the opinions of Mexican-American servicemen stationed in California, who were part of the war effort but who refused to take part in vigilante raids on pachuco hangouts.

As the Zoot-Suit Riots spread throughout California to cities in Texas and Arizona, a new dimension began to influence press coverage of the riots in Los Angeles. On a day when 125 zoot-suited youths clashed with Marines in Watts and armed police had to quell riots in Boyle Heights, the Los Angeles press concentrated on a razor attack on a local mother, Betty Morgan. What distinguished this incident from hundreds of comparable attacks was that the assailants were girls. The press related the incident to the arrest of Amelia Venegas, a woman zoot-suiter who was charged with carrying, and threatening to use, a brass knuckleduster. The revelation that girls were active within pachuco subculture led to consistent press coverage of the activities of two female gangs: the Slick Chicks and the Black Widows.[17] The latter gang took its name from the members' distinctive dress, black zoot-suit jackets, short black skirts and black fish-net stockings. In retrospect the Black Widows, and their active part in the subcultural violence of the Zoot-Suit Riots, disturb conventional understandings of the concept of pachuquismo.

As Joan W. Moore implies in *Homeboys,* her definitive study of Los Angeles youth gangs, the concept of pachuquismo is too readily and unproblematically equated with the better known concept of machismo[18]. Undoubtedly, they share certain ideological traits, not least a swaggering and at times aggressive sense of power and bravado, but the two concepts derive from different sets of social definitions. Whereas machismo can be defined in terms of male power and sexuality, pachuquismo predominantly derives from ethnic, generational and classbased aspirations, and is less evidently a question of gender. What the Zoot-Suit Riots brought to the surface was the complexity of pachuco style. The Black Widows and their aggressive image confounded the pachuco stereotype of the lazy male delinquent who avoided conscription for a life of dandyism and petty crime, and reinforced radical readings of pachuco subculture. The Black Widows were a reminder that ethnic and generational alienation was a pressing social problem and an indication of the tensions that existed in minority, low-income communities.

Although detailed information on the role of girls within zoot-suit sub-culture is limited to very brief press reports, the appearance of female pachucos coincided with a dramatic rise in the delinquency rates among girls aged between 12 and 20 years old. The disintegration of traditional family relationships and the entry of young women into the labour force undoubtedly had an effect on the social roles and responsibilities of female adolescents, but it is difficult to be precise about the relationships between changed patterns of social experience and the rise in delinquency. However, war-time society brought about an increase in unprepared and irregular sexual intercourse, which in turn led to significant increases in the rates of abortion, illegitimate births and venereal diseases. Although statistics are difficult to trace, there are many indications that the war years saw a remarkable increase in the numbers of young women who were taken into social care or referred to penal institutions, as a result of the specific social problems they had to encounter.

Later studies provide evidence that young women and girls were also heavily involved in the traffic and transaction of soft drugs. The pachuco sub-culture within the Los Angeles metropolitan area was directly associated with a widespread growth in the use of marijuana. It has been suggested that female zoot-suiters concealed quantities of drugs on their bodies, since they were less likely to be closely searched by male members of the law enforcement agencies. Unfortunately the absence of consistent or reliable information on the female gangs makes it particularly difficult to be certain about their status within the riots, or their place within traditions of feminine resistance. The Black Widows and Slick Chicks were spectacular in a sub-cultural sense, but their black drape jackets, tight skirts, fish net stockings and heavily emphasized make-up, were ridiculed in the press. The Black Widows clearly existed outside the orthodoxies of war-time society playing no part in the industrial war effort, and openly challenging conventional notions of feminine beauty and sexuality.

Towards the end of the second week of June, the riots in Los Angeles were dying out. Sporadic incidents broke out in other cities, particularly Detroit, New York and Philadelphia, where two members of Gene Krupa's dance band were beaten up in a station for wearing the band's zoot-suit costumes; but these, like the residual events in Los Angeles, were not taken seriously. The authorities failed to read the inarticulate warning signs proffered in two separate incidents in California: in one a zoot-suiter was arrested for throwing gasoline flares at a theatre; and in the second another was arrested for carrying a silver tomahawk. The Zoot-Suit Riots had become a public and spectacular enactment of social disaffection. The authorities in Detroit chose to dismiss a Zoot-Suit Riot at the city's Cooley High School as an adolescent imitation of the Los Angeles disturbances.[19] Within three weeks Detroit was in the midst of the worst race riot in its history.[20] The United States was still involved in the war abroad when violent events on the home front signaled the beginnings of a new era in racial politics.

Official Fears of Fifth Column Fashion

Official reactions to the Zoot-Suit Riots varied enormously. The most urgent problem that concerned California's State Senators was the adverse effect that the events might have on the relationship between the United States and Mexico. This concern stemmed partly from the wish to preserve good international relations, but rather more from the significance of relations with Mexico for the economy of Southern California, as an item in the Los Angeles Times made clear. 'In San Francisco Senator Downey declared that the riots may have 'extremely grave consequences' in impairing relations between the United States and Mexico and may endanger the program of importing Mexican labor to aid in harvesting California crops.'[21] These fears were compounded when the Mexican Embassy formally drew the Zoot-Suit Riots to the attention of the State Department. It was the fear of an international incident[22] that could only have an adverse effect on California's economy, rather than any real concern for the social conditions of the Mexican American community, that motivated Governor Warren of California to order a public investigation into the causes of the riots. In an ambiguous press statement, the Governor hinted that the riots may have been instigated by outside or even foreign agitators:

> As we love our country and the boys we are sending overseas to defend
> it, we are all duty bound to suppress every discordant activity which
> is designed to stir up international strife or adversely affect our rela-
> tionships with our allies in the United Nations.[23]

The Zoot-Suit Riots provoked two related investigations; a fact finding investigative committee headed by Attorney General Robert Kenny and an un-American activities investigation presided over by State Senator Jack B Tenney. The un-American activities investigation was ordered "to determine whether the present Zoot-Suit Riots were sponsored by Nazi agencies attempting to spread disunity between the United States and Latin-American countries."[24] Senator Tenney, a member of the un-American Activities committee for Los Angeles County, claimed he had evidence that the Zoot-Suit Riots were "axis-sponsored" but the evidence was never presented.[25] However, the notion that the riots might have been initiated by outside agitators persisted throughout the month of June, and was fueled by Japanese propaganda broadcasts accusing the North American government of ignoring the brutality of US marines. The arguments of the un-American activities investigation were given a certain amount of credibility by a Mexican pastor based in Watts, who according to the press had been "a pretty rough customer himself, serving as a captain in Pancho Villa's revolutionary army."[26] Reverend Francisco Quintanilla, the pastor of the Mexican Methodist church, was convinced the riots were the result of fifth columnists. "When boys start attacking servicemen it means the enemy is right at home. It means they are being fed vicious propaganda by enemy agents who wish to stir up all the racial and class hatreds they can put their evil fingers on."[27]

The attention given to the dubious claims of nazi-instigation tended to obfuscate other more credible opinions. Examination of the social conditions of pachuco youths tended to be marginalized in favour of other more "newsworthy" angles. At no stage in the press coverage were the opinions of community workers or youth leaders sought, and so, ironically, the most progressive opinion to appear in the major newspapers was offered by the Deputy Chief of Police, E.W. Lester. In press releases and on radio he provided a short history of gang subcultures in the Los Angeles area and then tried, albeit briefly, to place the riots in a social context.

> *The Deputy Chief said most of the youths came from overcrowded colorless homes that offered no opportunities for leisure-time activities. He said it is wrong to blame law enforcement agencies for the present situation, but that society as a whole must be charged with mishandling the problems.[28]*

On the morning of Friday 11 June 1943, The Los Angeles Times broke with its regular practices and printed an editorial appeal, "Time For Sanity" on its front page. The main purpose of the editorial was to dispel suggestions that the riots were racially motivated, and to challenge the growing opinion that white servicemen from the Southern States had actively colluded with the police in their vigilante campaign against the zoot-suiters.

> *There seems to be no simple or complete explanation for the growth of the grotesque gangs. Many reasons have been offered, some apparently valid, some farfetched. But it does appear to be definitely established that any attempts at curbing the movement have had nothing whatever to do with race persecution, although some elements have loudly raised the cry of this very thing.[29]*

A month later, the editorial of July's issue of Crisis presented a diametrically opposed point of view:

> *These riots would not occur—no matter what the instant provocation— if the vast majority of the population, including more often than not the law enforcement officers and machinery, did not share in varying degrees the belief that Negroes are and must be kept second-class citizens.[30]*

But this view got short shrift, particularly from the authorities, whose initial response to the riots was largely retributive. Emphasis was placed on arrest and punishment. The Los Angeles City Council considered a proposal from Councillor Norris Nelson, that "it be made a jail offense to wear zoot-suits with reat pleats within the city limits of LA"[31], and a discussion ensued for over an hour before it was resolved that the laws pertaining to rioting and disorderly conduct were sufficient to contain the zoot-suit threat. However, the council did encourage the War Production Board (WPB) to reiterate its regulations on the manufacture of suits. The regional office of the WPB based in San Francisco investigated tailors manufacturing in the area of men's fashion and took steps "to curb illegal production of men's clothing in violation of WPB limitation orders."[32] Only when Governor Warren's fact-finding commission made its public recommendations did the political analysis of the riots go beyond the first principles of punishment and proscription. The recommendations called for a more responsible co-operation from the press; a program of special training for police officers working in multi-racial communities; additional detention centres; a juvenile forestry camp for youth under the age of 16; an increase in military and shore police; an increase in the youth facilities provided by the church; an increase in neighbourhood recreation facilities and an end to discrimination in the use of public facilities. In addition to these measures, the commission urged that arrests should be made without undue emphasis on members of minority groups and encouraged lawyers to protect the rights of youths arrested for participation in gang activity. The findings were a delicate balance of punishment and palliative; it made no significant mention of the social conditions of Mexican labourers and no recommendation about the kind of public spending that would be needed to alter the social experiences of pachuco youth. The outcome of the Zoot-Suit Riots was an inadequate. highly localized and relatively ineffective body of short term public policies that provided no guidelines for the more serious riots in Detroit and Harlem later in the same summer.

The Mystery of The Signifying Monkey

> *The pachuco is the prey of society, but instead of hiding he adorns himself to attract the hunter's attention. Persecution redeems him and breaks his solitude: his salvation depends on him becoming part of the very society he appears to deny.*[33]

The zoot-suit was associated with a multiplicity of different traits and conditions. It was simultaneously the garb of the victim and the attacker, the persecutor and the persecuted, the "sinister clown" and the grotesque dandy. But the central opposition was between the style of the delinquent and that of the disinherited. To wear a zoot-suit was to risk the repressive intolerance of wartime society and to invite the attention of the police, the parent generation and the uniformed members of the armed forces. For many pachucos the Zoot-Suit Riots were simply high times in Los Angeles when momentarily they had control of the streets; for others it was a realization that they were outcasts in a society that was not of their making. For the black radical writer, Chester Himes, the riots in his neighbourhood were unambiguous: Zoot Riots are Race Riots."[34] For other contemporary commentators the wearing of the zoot-suit could be anything from unconscious dandyism to a conscious "political" engagement. The Zoot-Suit Riots were not political riots in the strictest sense, but for many participants they were an entry into the language of politics, an inarticulate rejection of the "straight world" and its organization.

It is remarkable how many post-war activists were inspired by the zoot-suit disturbances. Luis Valdez of the radical theatre company, El Teatro Campesino allegedly learned the "chicano" from his cousin the zoot-suiter Billy Miranda.[35] The novelists Ralph Ellison and Richard Wright both conveyed a literary and political fascination with the power and potential of the zoot-suit. One of Ellison's editorials for the journal Negro Quarterly expressed his own sense of frustration at the enigmatic attraction of zoot-suit style.

> *A third major problem, and one that is indispensable to the centralization and direction of power is that of learning the meaning of myths and symbols which abound among the Negro masses. For without this knowledge, leadership, no matter how correct its program, will fail. Much in Negro life remains a mystery; perhaps the zoot-suit conceals profound political meaning; perhaps the symmetrical frenzy of the Lindy-hop conceals clues to great potential powers, if only leaders could solve this riddle.*[36]

Although Ellison's remarks are undoubtedly compromised by their own mysterious idealism, he touches on the zoot-suit's major source of interest. It is in everyday rituals that resistance can find natural and unconscious expression. In retrospect, the zoot-suit's history can be seen as a point of intersection, between the related potential of ethnicity and politics on the one hand, and the pleasures of identity and difference on the other. It is the zoot-suit's political and ethnic associations that have made it such a rich reference point for subsequent generations. From the music of Thelonious Monk and Kid Creole to the jazz-poetry of Larry Neal, the zoot-suit has inherited new meanings and new mysteries. In his book Hoodoo Hollerin' Bebop Ghosts, Neal uses the image of the zoot-suit as the symbol of Black America's cultural resistance. For Neal, the zoot-suit ceased to be a costume and became a tapestry of meaning, where music. politics and social action merged. The zoot-suit became a symbol for the enigmas of Black culture and the mystery of the signifying monkey:

> *But there is rhythm here*
> *Its own special substance.*
> *I hear Billie sing, no Good Man, and dig Prez, wearing the Zoot suit*
> *of life, the Porkpie hat tilted at the correct angle; through the Harlem*
> *smoke of beer and whisky, I understand the mystery of the Signifying*
> *Monkey.*[37]

The author wishes to acknowledge the support of the British Academy for the research for this article.

Endnotes

1. Ralph Ellison *Invisible Man* New York. 1947 p. 380
2. *Invisible Man* p. 381
3. 'Zoot Suit Originated in Georgia' *New York Times* 11 June, 1943 p. 21

4. For the most extensive sociological study of the zoot-suit riots of 1943 see Ralph H. Turner and Samuel J. Surace 'Zoot Suiters and Mexicans: Symbols in Crowd Behavior' *American Journal of Sociology 62* 1956 pp. 14–20

5. Octavio Paz *The Labyrinth of Solitude* London, 1967 pp. 5–6

6. *Labyrinth of Solitude* p. 8

7. As note 6

8. See KL Nelson (ed) *The Impact of War on American Life* New York 1971

9. OE Schoeffler and W Gale *Esquire's Encyclopedia of Twentieth-Century Men's Fashion* New York, 1973 p. 24

10. As note 6

11. 'Zoot-suiters Again on the Prowl as Navy Holds Back Sailors' *Washington Post* 9 June, 1943 p. 1

12. Quoted in S Menefee *Assignment USA* New York, 1943 p. 189

13. Details of the riots are taken from newspaper reports and press releases for the weeks in question, particularly from the *Los Angeles Times, New York Times, Washington Post, Washington Star* and *Time Magazine.*

14. 'Strong Measures Must be Taken Against Rioting' *Los Angeles Times* 9 June, 1943 p. 4

15. 'Zoot-Suit Fighting Spreads On the Coast' *New York Times* 10 June, 1943 p. 23

16. As note 15

17. 'Zoot-Girls Use Knife in Attack' *Los Angeles Times* 11 June, 1943 p. 1

18. Joan W Moore *Homeboys: Gangs, Drugs and Prison in the Barrios of Los Angeles* Philadelphia, 1978

19. 'Zoot Suit Warfare Spreads to Pupils of Detroit Area' *Washington Star* 11 June, 1943 p. 1

20. Although the Detroit Race Riots of 1943 were not zoot-suit riots, nor evidently about 'youth' or 'delinquency', the social context in which they took place was obviously comparable. For a lengthy study of the Detroit riots see R. Shogun and T. Craig *The Detroit Race Riot: A Study in Violence* Philadelphia and New York, 1964

21. 'Zoot Suit War Inquiry Ordered by Governor' *Los Angeles Times* 9 June, 1943 p. A

22. 'Warren Orders Zoot Suit Quiz; Quiet Reigns After Rioting' *Los Angeles Times* 10 June, 1943 p. 1

23. As note 22

24. 'Tenney Feels Riots Caused by Nazi Move for Disunity' *Los Angeles Times* 9 June, 1943 p. A

25. As note 24

26. 'Watts Pastor Blames Riots on Fifth Column' *Los Angeles Times* 11 June, 1943 p. A

27. As note 26

28. 'California Governor Appeals for Quelling of Zoot Suit Riots' *Washington Star* 1 June, 1943 p. A3

29. 'Time for Sanity' *Los Angeles Times* 11 June, 1943 p. 1

30. 'The Riots' *The Crisis* July, 1943 p. 199
31. 'Ban on Freak Suits Studied by Councilmen' *Los Angeles Times* 9 June, 1943 p. A3
33. *Labyrinth of Solitude* p. 9
34. Chester Himes 'Zoot Riots are Race Riots' *The Crisis* July 1943; reprinted in Himes Black on *Black: Baby Sister and Selected Writings* London, 1975
35. El Teatro Campesino presented the first Chicano play to achieve full commercial Broadway production. The play, written by Luis Valdez and entitled 'Zoot Suit' was a drama documentary on the Sleepy Lagoon murder and the events leading to the Los Angeles riots. (The Sleepy Lagoon murder of August, 1942 resulted in 24 pachucos being indicted for conspiracy to murder.)
36. Quoted in Larry Neal 'Ellison's Zoot Suit' in J Hersey (ed) *Ralph Ellison: A Collection of Critical Essays* New Jersey, 1974 p. 67
37. From Larry Neal's poem 'Malcolm X: an Autobiography' in L. Neal *Hoodoo Hollerin' Bebop Chosts* Washington DC, 1974 p. 9

8

from AIDS Demo Graphics

DOUGLAS CRIMP

In this chapter from a book called AIDS DEMO GRAPHICS *Douglas Crimp with Adam Rolston document the history of the activist graphics produced by ACT UP (AIDS Coalition to Unleash Power), a direct action group that began in 1987 in NYC as a grassroots political effort to end the HIV/AIDS crisis by getting people's attention, demanding better treatment options, and fighting the homophobia surrounding the disease. This chapter demonstrates the in-your-face graphics that artists and activists deployed to resist the public indifference and even hostility toward persons with HIV/AIDS and to change the terms of the public debate. Douglas Crimp is a Professor of Art History/Visual and Cultural Studies at the University of Rochester and a member of ACT UP.*

No More Business as Usual

Wall Street, New York City, March 24, 1987

On March 10, 1987, Larry Kramer agreed to replace Nora Ephron in a monthly speaker's series at New York's Lesbian and Gay Community Services Center. As a founder of the Gay Men's Health Crisis, the author of *The Normal Heart,* and the most vocal critic of both official and community apathy about the AIDS epidemic, Kramer drew a large crowd of mostly gay men—the curious, the frightened, and the furious.

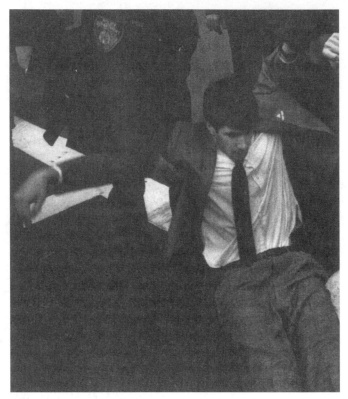

Photo: Tom McKitterick

Kramer began by citing his first call to action, "1,112 and Counting," published four years earlier in the *New York Native*. "Our continued existence," he had written, "depends on just how angry you can get." Now the situation was even more urgent: at the time of the community center speech, officially reported cases of AIDS in the United States had reached 32,000. Kramer produced a number of incitements to the mounting anger: a collapsing New York City health care system, an insurance industry that won't reimburse for home health care or experimental drugs, government officials who can't be bothered. But Kramer's main concern was the unavailability of treatments for AIDS owing to the Food and Drug Administration's snail-paced approval process. He condemned both the National Institutes of Health and the Food and Drug Administration for their inhumane and bureaucratic procedures, and he named a few promising drugs—ampligen, ribavirin, AL-721—on which the FDA refused to act. The exception was AZT (azidothymidine), highly toxic and highly profitable for its maker, Burroughs Wellcome.

Kramer then turned his criticism to New York's leading AIDS service organization, the Gay Men's Health Crisis (GMHC). Six weeks before, he had castigated the organization for a failure of nerve, and now he reiterated his demands: "lobbying, an advocacy division, more public-relations people to get the word out, a change of its tax-exempt status to allow for increased political activities, fighting for drugs. . . ." Discouraged by GMHC's inability to act politically given its corporate structure and service orientation, Kramer posed what turned out to be the crucial question to his audience: "Do we want to start a new organization devoted solely to political action?"

The answer was a resounding yes. Discussion following Kramer's speech ended in the resolve to meet again two days later, a meeting at which nearly 300 people would form the AIDS Coalition to Unleash Power. ACT UP, "a diverse, nonpartisan group united in anger and committed to direct action to end the AIDS crisis," set about immediately to plan its first demonstration, to take place March 24 on Wall Street. The target: BUSINESS, BIG BUSINESS, BUSINESS AS USUAL.

Licensing of the antiviral drug AZT, the only government-sanctioned new therapy for AIDS, was announced by the FDA on March 19. The exceptional rush through the FDA's bureaucratic approval process looked suspicious, since the agency was far from willing to do this for any other drug (AZT took just over two years to approve, as compared to the usual eight to ten). Burroughs Wellcome, the pharmaceutical company granted the monopoly, announced that it would charge each patient upwards of $10,000 annually, making AZT the costliest drug ever.

Over 250 ACT UP novices descended on Wall Street at 7 A.M. on a Thursday to protest the alliance between the FDA and Burroughs Wellcome in the interest of profit rather than saving lives. An effigy of FDA commissioner Frank Young was hung in front of Trinity Church. Traffic was tied up for several hours, and 17 people were arrested for acts of civil disobedience.

Larry Kramer had published an op-ed piece in the *New York Times* the previous day; in it he outlined the same grievances against the FDA that he had presented in his speech at the community center two weeks earlier. Thousands of copies were reproduced and handed out to crowds on their way to work in the financial district. ACT UP also produced its own fact sheet, asserting AIDS IS EVERYBODY'S BUSINESS NOW. The following points explained WHY WE ARE ANGRY:

- For 12 long months AZT was proclaimed as promising but in such short supply that it had to be rationed to a very few mortally ill patients. Once Burroughs Wellcome was licensed to distribute AZT, supply for **30,000** was immediately on hand!

- The National Institutes of Health continue inhumane double-blind placebo-controlled studies on terminal patients, but make no plans to experiment on the hundreds of thousands with AIDS-related complex (ARC) or HIV infection.

- Every major insurance company routinely denies benefits to people with AIDS or at risk for AIDS. That leaves only taxpayer-funded Medicaid, which will not pay for any form of experimental therapy.

- Even the surgeon general says the president must somehow be embarrassed into taking action. **Six years** into the worst pandemic in modern history, there are still no public education programs for everyone—not from the city, not from the state, not from the schools, not from the churches, not from the media.

- **Who is in charge?** The chief executive of this nation has yet to utter the word AIDS.

The demonstration and arrests made national news, and several weeks later, when Commissioner Young announced a speedup of the FDA's drug approval process, CBS anchor Dan Rather credited ACT UP's pressure.

Tax Dollars for AIDS Research

General Post Office, New York City, April 15, 1987

ACT UP's second demonstration was organized for the night of April 15 on the steps of New York City's main post office at Eighth Avenue and 33rd Street. Because the General Post Office stays open around the clock, hundreds of taxpayers go there to file their returns before the midnight deadline—thus becoming a captive audience for a demonstration about how much of their tax money would be spent to fight AIDS. Captive, also, would be the electronic media, who routinely do stories about down-to-the-wire tax-return filers. ACT UP's media savvy thus showed itself from the very beginning, as did our ability to influence coverage by visual means. The Silence = Death Project members, who had printed their posters and wheatpasted them around Manhattan several months earlier, now mounted scores of them on foamcore to make placards for the taxpayer demo. When TV newscasters went to the post office that night, they returned with a new graphic image of ACT UP in action—one that would become increasingly identified with ACT UP as time went on. They also returned with a press release with our demands:

- **Immediate** establishment of a coordinated, comprehensive, and compassionate national policy on AIDS.
- **Immediate** release of drugs that may help save our lives.
- **Immediate** establishment of a $60 million fund to pay for AZT and other drugs as they become available.
- **Immediate** mass national education.
- **Immediate** policy to prohibit discrimination.

ACT UP demonstration at the General Post Office, New York City, April 15, 1987 (photo: Donna Binder).

The taxpayers, too, were given something to take home—a letter addressed to President Reagan, which said, in part:

Dear Mr. President:

As a taxpayer and concerned citizen, I am writing to receive answers to some very pressing questions on your administration's handling of the AIDS epidemic.

Why have the Centers for Disease Control failed to mount a national AIDS-prevention education campaign, even though $70 million was allocated for that purpose this year?

Why is Burroughs Wellcome permitted to charge its asking price of $10,000 annually for AZT when the drug was developed with the help of government funds?

Why haven't you, Mr. President, read your own surgeon general's report on AIDS, which was prepared in October 1986? Since then, over 4,800 Americans have died from this disease.

In all, your administration has witnessed almost 20,000 deaths from AIDS. When will you see fit to have your **first** meeting with the surgeon general to discuss the epidemic?

HOW MUCH LONGER MUST WE WAIT??

Silence = Death, 1986, *Silence = Death Project Poster, offset lithography, 29 × 24″ (also used as placard, T-shirt, button, and sticker).*

115

National AIDS Demo at the White House
Washington, D.C., June 1, 1987

The Third International Conference on AIDS was scheduled to open in Washington, D.C., on June 1, 1987, and activist groups from around the country descended on the capital to protest the Reagan administration's do-nothing record. The White House resident did his part to ensure the demonstration's media success when he addressed the opening ceremonies of the conference the evening of May 31. Speaking the word *AIDS* publicly for the first time since the beginning of the epidemic six years earlier, Reagan's only proposal was to demand widespread routine testing, for which he was loudly booed—not the president's usual reception from doctors, scientists, public health officials, and fundraisers like Liz Taylor, and a sure media story. Reagan's unwelcome call for testing was seconded by then vice president George Bush, speaking at the conference on the following evening; the booing was repeated. Bush, thinking the microphone wouldn't pick up his words, leaned over to an aide and asked, "What is it, some kind of gay group out there?"

But the most visible gaffe was produced by the Washington police. In front of the White House, cops wore bright-yellow rubber gloves as they arrested 64 protesters, thus fueling America's already fever-pitch hysteria about "catching" AIDS through casual contact. The activists, many looking unusually respectable in conservative business clothes, raised the very queer chant

> *Your gloves don't match your shoes!*
>
> *You'll see it on the news!*

The issue, though, was deadly serious. Just one year earlier, Reagan's attorney general, the not-quite-provable criminal Edwin Meese, ruled that a person with AIDS, or anyone suspected of having AIDS, could be fired so long as the employer claimed

Police arrest AIDS activists at the White House, Washington, D.C., June 1, 1987 (photo: Jane Rosett).

ignorance of the medical fact, quoted in the ruling itself, that there is no known health danger from workplace contact. And of course the employer's ignorance could be virtually guaranteed, since the federal government had not yet undertaken a national AIDS education campaign. Nor had it within the ensuing year. ACT UP therefore demanded, on a flier handed out at the White House, both a national education campaign and legislation to prohibit discrimination in employment, housing, insurance, and health care. Also included on the flier were two of the most alarming statistics ACT UP had learned:

- In *one day* the Pentagon spends more than the *total* spent for AIDS research and education since 1982.
- By 1991, more Americans will die from AIDS *each year* than were killed in the *entire* Vietnam war.

The national scandal of the Reagan administration's inaction on AIDS became the subject of the Silence = Death Project's second poster image, produced for the White House demonstration. It was the summer of congressional hearings about secret diversions to the Nicaraguan contras of funds from illegal arms sales to Iran—a series of events variously referred to as Irangate or Contragate, the "-gate" of Watergate having become the colloquial suffix for scandal. For their new graphic, the Silence = Death Project attached the scandal suffix to AIDS and stamped a shocking-pink AIDSGATE over a Warhol-like picture of Reagan's ugly mug—made a little uglier with the repetition of the hot pink in the whites of the president's eyes. A caption at the bottom stated THIS POLITICAL SCANDAL MUST BE INVESTIGATED!

For nearly a year following the White House demonstration, the SILENCE = DEATH and AIDSGATE graphics were the main images at ACT UP's actions. Supplementary posters geared to specific issues were quickly improvised at poster parties prior to particular events, but it was the two Silence = Death Project works that

ACT UP "quarantine camp" in the gay pride march, New York City, June 28, 1987 (photo: Donna Binder).

117

ACT UP demonstration at Federal Plaza, New York City, June 30, 1987 (photo: Donna Binder).

gave ACT UP its well-organized, professional look—all the more so when we wore the two images on T-shirts as well. This look was itself a kind of organizing tool. ACT UP started out fairly small and has always been entirely open, leaderless, grass-roots, anarcho-democratic. But the impressive appearance of the group made people on the sidelines curious: something's happening here; I want to know what it is.

ACT UP was a singular presence in New York's 1987 annual gay pride march during the last weekend in June. A float trimmed with barbed wire and driven by a man in a Ronald Reagan mask represented an AIDS quarantine camp. Surrounding it on the street were internment camp guards wearing gas masks and the now infamous yellow rubber gloves. Scores of activists followed with SILENCE = DEATH and AIDSGATE placards, while others handed out leaflets announcing a rally and demonstration at the Jacob K. Javits Federal Building in lower Manhattan for the following week. Twice as many people were arrested at Federal Plaza for civil disobedience as in ACT UP's first demonstration on Wall Street just a few months before. A handout about THE GOVERNMENT'S **REAL** POLICY ON AIDS gave some of our reasons for risking arrest:

- The Social Security Administration has recently begun denying benefits to persons with AIDS because *"They may be dying, but they might not be disabled."*

- Almost every state is now considering testing or quarantine legislation. Senator Jesse Helms, who sponsored the alien testing bill in Washington, has declared *"The logical outcome of testing is a quarantine of those infected."*

- In 1988, mandatory testing of aliens and Veterans' Administration hospital patients alone will cost over $240 million, *more than Reagan's entire budget for drug research and vaccine development.*

AIDSgate, 1987, Silence = Death Project. Poster, offset lithography, 34 x 22″ (also used as placard and T-shirt).

Perhaps ACT UP's most impressive early appearance was at the massive March on Washington for Lesbian and Gay Rights, Columbus Day weekend, October 1987. AIDS was on nearly everyone's mind that weekend, not only because of the devastation of our communities, but also because of the initial unveiling of the Names Project quilt at dawn before the march. The quilt has grown horrifyingly larger since then—when it occupied the mere space of two football fields on the mall—but because no one had seen it before, it stunned the half million of us at the march.

Leading the 500,000 march participants were people with AIDS, some in wheelchairs pushed by their friends—a reminder that fighting AIDS is now a priority for gay people and that first in the fight are people living with AIDS. ACT UP was positioned toward the back of the march, our legions immediately recognizable from our SILENCE = DEATH T-shirts. SILENCE = DEATH and AIDSGATE posters had been mounted recto-verso on foamcore and hinged together to make a long serpentine of repeated graphic images, like a Chinese new-year dragon adapted for political action. If you were wearing one of our T-shirts, you could be sure to be asked countless times, "Who is that group?" On the following Monday night in New York, the weekly ACT UP meeting swelled to double its usual number—a sure sign that graphics are an aid to organizing.

ATEU Around-the-Clock Vigil

Memorial Sloan-Kettering Hospital, New York City, July 21–24, 1987

For the first six months or more of its existence, ACT UP had one dominant focus: "drugs into bodies." No matter what the occasion or site of a demonstration—Wall Street, the post office, the White House, Federal Plaza—the central issue was getting AIDS treatments out of the NIH and FDA bureaucracies and into the bodies of those who are HIV-infected. Inequalities in access to health care based on class, race, sex, and sexuality; AIDS-related discrimination in housing, jobs, and public accommodations; lack of explicit, culturally sensitive risk-reduction education; the disproportionately high number of people of color with AIDS; the special problems of prisoners, sex workers, drug users, and pregnant women—all these issues were discussed in meetings and mentioned on fact sheets, but the bottom line was treatment.

Treatment issues are extremely complicated and difficult to convey to an uninformed public. But groups within ACT UP began studying the situation intensively at a very early stage. Within the Issues Committee (since split into separate committees for various issues), there were initially two subcommittees working on treatment, one devoted to tracking treatment information generally, another concentrating on the system of AIDS Treatment Evaluation Units (ATEUs) established and funded by the NIH to test new AIDS therapies. In June 1986, Congress appropriated $47 million for the ATEU system of 19 medical centers across the country, where 12,000 people with AIDS were to be enrolled in drug trials. In the summer of 1987, ACT UP learned that after one year only 844 people had been enrolled, and that of these, 92 percent were in ongoing trials for AZT, already approved by the FDA several months before. Meanwhile, our Treatment and Data Subcommittee had researched a whole list of drugs showing promise for the treatment of AIDS that were not being tested. ACT UP decided to target one of the four ATEUs in New York City for a demonstration that would both apply pressure for increased clinical trial enrollment and educate the public about the dysfunctional ATEU system.

Between July 21 and 24, ACT UP staged an around-the-clock vigil at Memorial Sloan-Kettering Hospital, a designated ATEU with $1.2 million of funding from the NIH and a trial enrollment of only 31 patients. A fact sheet cogently outlined the situation, provided statistics detailing under-enrollment, and listed promising drugs not being tested. The response of the Sloan-Kettering medical staff was so positive that ACT UP issued a flier thanking them and providing information about how they could help, including writing to members of congressional committees dealing with health issues. Within the year, Manhattan congressman Theodore Weiss initiated a series of investigations. During one of these, Anthony Fauci, head of the National Institute of Allergy and Infectious Diseases, was forced to admit under oath that the ATEU system was not working, in part owing to staff shortages that he had remained silent about for over a year.

Don't Go to Bed with Cosmo

Hearst Magazine Building, New York City, January 19, 1988

In its January 1988 issue, *Cosmopolitan* magazine published "Reassuring News about AIDS: A Doctor Tells Why *You* May Not Be at Risk." The doctor in question was Robert E. Gould, a psychiatrist whose "concern" about AIDS was how to answer his women patients' growing fears of infection. His comforting answer: straight women have little to worry about, even if their sex partners are infected, and condom use is unnecessary unless there are vaginal lacerations. Gould's lethal advice was based entirely on ignorance and prejudice. It ignored recent statistics showing growing numbers of women infected through heterosexual intercourse; it accused women of lying about their sex lives, claiming, for example, that women won't "admit" to engaging in anal intercourse; and it "explained" the high incidence of heterosexually transmitted HIV infection in Africa with racist presumptions about differing sexual practices (for example, "Many men in Africa take their women in a brutal way, so that some heterosexual activity regarded as normal by them would be closer to rape by our standards."). *Cosmopolitan*'s readership consists of women from ages 18 to 34—15 million of them worldwide; in New York City, AIDS is the leading cause of death in women aged 25 to 34. In January 1988, the Centers for Disease Control reported nearly 2,000 cases of AIDS among women, 26 percent of whom had no risk factor other than unprotected heterosexual intercourse with an infected partner.

By the time of the publication of the *Cosmo* article, a group of ACT UP women had been getting together at informal "dyke dinners" for several months to discuss the role of women, *lesbian* women in particular, in AIDS activism. That role often took the form in Monday night meetings of broadening the debate, keeping inequities determined by class, race, and sex on the agenda. But with the *Cosmo*

ACT UP says no to Cosmo at the Hearst Magazine Building, New York City, January 19, 1988 (photo: Gerri Wells).

121

article, the women had a galvanizing issue specific to the lives of women, and they quickly swung into action to form a Women's Committee and organize a demonstration. On a wintry cold Tuesday nearly 150 activists crowded in front of the Hearst Magazine Building on West 57th Street, where *Cosmopolitan* has its offices. Shouting SAY NO TO COSMO and handing out condoms and fliers to the lunchtime crowds, ACT UP alerted women to the danger *Cosmo* was putting them in and called for a boycott of the magazine and its advertisers (a list of advertisers' addresses was distributed).

The story was taken up—and taken away from the ACT UP women—by the national media. Women activists, who had accumulated extensive knowledge about women and AIDS, were physically ejected from a local talk show, *People Are Talking,* when they protested that the issues were being represented only by men. These same women found themselves blacklisted when they attempted to get into the studio audience of the *Phil Donahue Show* where Gould was appearing as a guest. And only an officially sanctioned expert, Dr. Mathilde Krim, founding chairperson of the American Foundation for AIDS Research, appeared against *Cosmo* editor Helen Gurley Brown and Dr. Gould on ABC's *Nightline.* But the ACT UP women did not simply stand back and watch the representation of their concerns be stolen from them. Members of the ACT UP Women's Committee who had organized the *Cosmo* demo quickly produced the highly praised documentary *Doctors, Liars, and Women: AIDS Activists Say No to Cosmo.* Aired on the Gay Men's Health Crisis weekly cable program *Living with AIDS* and widely circulated at video festivals, universities, museums, and community centers, the video not only presents a counterargument to *Cosmo*'s lies (Gould was naive enough to allow the videotaping of his meeting with ACT UP women), but also provides information on how to organize a demonstration and on the role of women in AIDS activism, including the role of self-representation.

In an open letter to *Cosmo,* Dr. Krim wrote, "The '*You*' to whom Dr. Gould addresses his article are obviously not—in his mind—any of those young minority-group women who give birth to HIV-antibody-positive babies at the rate, now, of **1 out of every 61** births occurring in New York City." That alarming statistic had recently been widely publicized, and, concurrently with the action organized by the ACT UP Women's Committee, Gran Fury produced their first poster, AIDS: 1 IN 61. The poster publicized not only the growing incidence of pediatric AIDS cases, but also the obvious—but apparently not to everyone—concurrent incidence of AIDS in those babies' mothers.

The AIDS Crisis Is Not Over, *1988, Little Elvis. Crack-and-peel sticker, offset lithography, 3⅛ × 11″ (also 1⅝ × 5½″).*

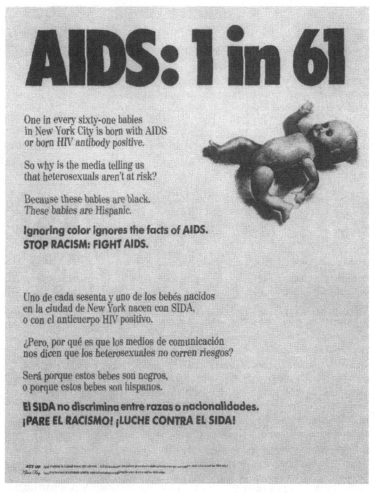

AIDS: 1 in 61, 1988, Gran Fury. Poster, offset lithography, 22 × 17″.

The *Cosmo* article was just one of many media stories that sought to reassure straight people that AIDS wasn't their problem, a homophobic reassurance that also entirely denied the existence of those heterosexuals who *were* getting AIDS, primarily people of color. As Krim implied, the racism of Gould's *Cosmo* article was discernible not only in his portrayal of Africans, but also in his failure to portray what was happening to African—and Hispanic—Americans and to include them among his presumed readership. Gran Fury's poster text, in English and Spanish, therefore linked the fight against AIDS to the fight against racism.

The racist, homophobic tactic of reassuring a presumed white heterosexual audience that AIDS was not and would never become its problem belongs more consistently to the *New York Times* than any other major organ of the U.S. media. In the weeks following the demonstration against *Cosmopolitan,* the *Times* published a series of four front-page feature articles on AIDS that, typically, sought to diminish the scope of the crisis. The ACT UP collective Little Elvis responded with a simple graphic rejoinder: a crack-and-peel sticker insisting THE AIDS CRISIS IS

NOT OVER. Because of the persistence of media presumptions and distortions, the sticker has unfortunately lost none of its relevance as the epidemic has been allowed to continue unabated.

Tracking the Presidential Commission

Metropolitan Life Insurance Building, New York City, February 15, 1988

When Ronald Reagan's Presidential Commission on the HIV Epidemic came to New York to conduct hearings in February 1988, ACT UP showed up to let commission members know angry activists were watching their every move. This was the third time ACT UP had targeted the commission. The first demonstration had been hastily organized two days after the announcement, on July 24, 1987, of those named to the commission, among whom was Cardinal John O'Connor. Because we already knew how dangerous *he* was—with his virulent homophobia and his adamant opposition to safe sex education—we chose St. Patrick's Cathedral as the site for a protest that called for O'Connor's resignation. It soon became clear that Reagan—pressured for several years by Congress and the National Academy of Sciences to establish an advisory group to help form policy on the epidemic—had sought the least informed, most biased commission he could find. Not a single one of the 14-member commission was known to have expertise about AIDS. But for the mainstream media, that wasn't a scandal. What seemed controversial to them, and to many in the administration, was the appointment of the single member who had any qualification at all: Dr. Frank Lilly, a virologist and head of genetics at Albert Einstein Medical Center, former board member of the Gay Men's Health Crisis, and . . . openly gay—hence the "controversy." Others appointed to the commission included:

- Theresa Crenshaw, a sexologist who claimed there was no such thing as safe sex, believed there was danger of contracting HIV from casual contact and supported the notorious Lyndon La Rouche ballot initiative in California requiring quarantine for those testing HIV-positive. Crenshaw's history also includes dismissal from the University of California at San Diego Medical School for misrepresenting her credentials.

- Richard M. De Vos, president of the Amway Corporation, cochairman of the Republican Leadership Council and past finance chairman of the Republican National Committee, and board member of the Robert Schuller Ministries (a televangelist corporation). With no professed knowledge of AIDS, De Vos was chosen, according to an administration spokesperson, because "we wanted to make sure we had folks on the commission with a sense for the average American."

- Cory Servaas, editor and publisher of the *Saturday Evening Post*, in which she made the claim that, working with the NIH, she had discovered a cure for AIDS. The NIH had never heard of her. She also ran a mobile AIDS testing service and was quoted as saying, "It is patriotic to have the AIDS test and be negative."

ACT UP members say "Cut the red tape" to the Presidential Commission on the HIV Epidemic at the Metropolitan Life Insurance Building, New York City, February 15, 1988 (photo: Donna Binder).

- Penny Pullen, associate of right-wing antifeminist ideologue Phyllis Schlafly and Republican leader of the Illinois State House of Representatives, where she sponsored bills requiring HIV testing for marriage license applicants and mandatory contact tracing of the sex partners of HIV-infected individuals.
- Dr. Woodrow A. Myers, Jr., Indiana State health commissioner and advocate of mandatory testing, contact tracing, and quarantine.

This "batch of geeks and unknowns," as they were characterized in the *Village Voice,* met at the National Press Building in Washington, D. C., for the first time on September 9, 1987, and ACT UP went to greet them with calls for their mass resignation. The favored chant of the day found a way to rhyme one commissioner's name with her weird solution for AIDS:

> *Cory Servaas makes us nervous*
>
> *With her mobile testing service*

Within three months, the commission was in total disarray. The staff director was fired, and the chairman and vice chairman resigned. The reorganized commission's new chairman, retired admiral James D. Watkins, former chief of naval operations, was again a man with no special knowledge of AIDS, but he surprised everyone—especially Ronald Reagan—with his willingness to listen to the people with genuine expertise: people working in affected communities, people with AIDS, activists. ACT UP followed the commission around the country, testifying at its hearings when possible and meeting with individual members as they grew more sympathetic. When the commission's final report was issued on June 27, 1988, its recommendations were so reasonable that President Reagan—and later President Bush—decided to ignore them.

He Kills Me, 1987, Donald Moffett. Poster, offset lithography, 23⅜ × 37⅜″ (also used as placard).

Thus when ACT UP member Donald Moffett's HE KILLS ME poster appeared on the picket lines at the February 1988 commission hearings, it was prophetic. Targeting the smirking Reagan for his seven-year neglect of the AIDS crisis, Moffett's poster signaled to the commission and the public that the president kills us in more ways than one: the laughable fool was also a murderer of people with AIDS.

Bush began his term as president by following in Reagan's footsteps, delaying the establishment of *his* AIDS commission by seven months beyond the deadline mandated by Congress. But the commission itself, this time with most members directly appointed by Congress, finally includes people who are knowledgeable about AIDS.

Wall Street II

Wall Street, New York City, March 24, 1988

A year after ACT UP's first demonstration, we went back to Wall Street. Although we had grown enormously, learned much, and managed occasionally to make our demands known to a wide public, and although our new affinity group tactics snarled traffic in the financial district for hours and the number arrested for civil disobedience jumped from 17 to 111, the anniversary demonstration was hardly a time for celebration. New York City police were especially brutal, but we could live with that. What we couldn't live with was the persistent failure of the government to confront the crisis. Our fact sheet detailed the reasons for our frustration

Wall Street Money, *1988, Gran Fury. Flier, photocopy, printed recto-verso (three versions), 3½ × 8½".*

under the heading AFTER EIGHT YEARS OF WAITING, WE ARE STILL WAITING FOR:

Medicine

- **One year ago,** the only drug approved by the FDA for treatment against AIDS was AZT. There were eight other promising drugs, but none were available to people with AIDS.

- **One year later,** the only drug approved by the FDA for AIDS is still AZT. There are now over 40 other promising drugs, but **none** are available to people with AIDS.

Funding

- **One year ago,** this nation had spent less on AIDS education and research over the entire course of this epidemic than the Pentagon spent in one day.

- **One year later,** despite promises to the contrary, the federal AIDS effort is still grossly underfunded.

Education

- **One year ago,** $133 million had been budgeted for AIDS education, promising a comprehensive national education program.

- **One year later,** $296 million has been budgeted, and the government is still promising a national education campaign.

Civil Rights

- **One year ago,** discrimination against people with AIDS and those suspected of having it was widespread.

- **One year later,** even though civil rights protection for people with AIDS has been firmly asserted by the Supreme Court, these rights are under systematic attack by legislators, the Department of Justice, and the Civil Rights Commission.

Leadership

- **One year ago,** after 19,000 deaths, the president of the United States had not publicly acknowledged even the existence of this disease.

- **One year later,** despite the fact that 80 percent of all Americans cite AIDS as the number-one health problem facing the nation today, the president still failed even to mention AIDS in his final state-of-the-union address.

WALL STREET II inspired a number of new graphic interventions. Gran Fury photocopied thousands of $10, $50, and $100 bills to be scattered in the streets, each with caustic words directed at Wall Street brokers on its back. And the simple AID$ NOW placard, generic enough to be used in many demonstrations to come, appeared along with SILENCE = DEATH and AIDSGATE among the ranks blocking downtown business-as-usual traffic.

AID$ Now, 1988, Ken Woodard. Placard, silk screen and stencil, 18 × 24″.

9

Introduction to The Cultural Resistance Reader

Stephen Duncombe

The following portion of the introduction to sociologist Stephen Duncombe's anthology called Cultural Resistance Reader *offers a reflection on the author's own activist involvements, and gestures toward a framework for recognizing and thinking about how various communities deploy diverse forms of culture in ways that might challenge existing social and political conditions. An Associate Professor at New York University's Gallatin School, Duncombe demonstrates how to frame and sustain an inquiry that originates in personal experience and interest.*

> *When I hear the word culture I reach for my revolver.*
>
> attributed to Joseph Goebbels

New York City, October 4, 1998

It's a damp afternoon in early October. The clouds are heavy and low and periodically a light mist rolls down. For the past twenty minutes groups of young people, three here, five there, have been walking up to "The Cube," a large steel sculpture on a traffic island marking the entrance to Manhattan's East Village. Carrying portable radios and dressed in the young hipster uniform of oversized shirt and super-wide pants, they look like they're either coming home from or launching out on an all-night rave. Some look more anxious than others, and the most anxious of the lot scurry around talking too loudly into cell phones or more quietly in little huddles. Radios are tuned to the frequency of a pirate radio station and techno music flows out from fifty boomboxes. Thwump, thwump, thwump. Heads start to nod and feet shuffle. The crowd is visibly excited. Something is going to happen.

Meanwhile, a block south, an old bread truck is parked by the curb, invisibly emanating the pirate signal. Jammed inside its rusting body is a portable radio transmitter, a sound engineer, a couple of DJs, and enough pot smoke to levitate the vehicle. A block west a small crew of people, studiously feigning nonchalance, waits next to a bundle of three, thirty-foot-long steel poles, laid horizontally along the ground and linked at one end. Further down and around the corner stands another small group surrounding what looks like a garden wagon covered in a tarpaulin.

At a little after 3 p.m., as the crowd had grown to more than a hundred, someone gives a signal. Led by a man holding aloft a large orange traffic sign with outlines of a man and woman dancing, the crowd moves tentatively off the curb of the traffic island and on to the street. "Move, move," the anxious ones yell and the crowd breaks into a run down Astor Place. It's one short block and a left turn onto Broadway—the major thoroughfare running the length of Manhattan. In the middle of the street the metal pipes are being pushed into the air to form a tripod. Once the tripod is up and stable a young man scrambles up and seats himself on top. The garden cart is wheeled out, its tarp ripped off, and—after many frustrating tries—a small generator fires up, powering a compact receiver and amplifier. Heavy beats pump from the sound system, echoed by the boomboxes now turned to full volume: THWUMP, THWUMP, THWUMP, Thwumpada Thwumpada Thwumpada. Curious crowds come off the sidewalk, people start to dance, and soon 300 people have turned Broadway on a Sunday afternoon into a street party.

The New York Police Department shows up, at first slowly and then in force. Dressed in riot gear they stand by bewildered, confused by a protest that doesn't look like a protest, mystified by the young man perched precariously twenty-five feet above the pavement, and unsure how to confront a street full of ravers, some with painted faces, a few decked out in Marie Antoinette garb, and one fellow dancing particularly energetically in a bright blue bunny suit.

Propaganda has been handed out to the crowd, proclaiming this as an action of the newly formed New York City chapter of Reclaim the Streets, thrown to protest the Mayor's draconian "Quality of Life" policing campaign and the increased privatization of public space. But such assertions were redundant. The protest itself spoke more eloquently about reclaiming the streets for free and public expression than any photocopied sheet of indictments and demands.

I think it was there, in the middle of that happy, frenetic crowd, holding one of the legs of the tripod steady, that I fully realized the political potential of culture.

I had been a political activist my entire adult life. I began in college, pressuring the State University of New York to pull their money out of businesses in South

Africa. From there I constructed houses in Nicaragua, shut down the City University of New York over tuition increases, protested the Gulf War, got arrested with ACT UP, walked picket lines to support immigrant restaurant and greengrocery workers, formed a community activist organization in the Lower East Side, and would soon assemble direct action affinity groups for world trade demonstrations. For fifteen years I built organizations, planned actions, strategized campaigns, and attended far too many meetings.

I was committed to the struggle for radical change, but also more than a bit disappointed in it: too many defeats, too much defeatism. The "Left" I was part of often seemed stuck in its ways and those ways were not working. But that afternoon with Reclaim the Streets I glimpsed something that filled me with hope. Instead of the exhausted march, chant, and civil disobedience protest model that we (and the police, media, and public) were used to, we had created our own liberatory culture and—at least for a little while—had demonstrated it to the world. In place of the sour Lefty cry of "No! We're against it," we yelled out triumphantly: "Yes! This is what we're for." I went to the first planning meeting of this action as a loyal skeptic, by the end of the afternoon I was a committed believer in the power of cultural resistance.

It wasn't a hard sell. It was culture, punk rock culture, that led me to politics in the first place. I grew up with a supportive family, I went to a good school, I lived in a nice suburb, but I knew something was wrong. Black kids I'd never met stared me down in rage. White kids in work boots were tracked out of my college-bound high-school classes. Boys who were not sufficiently macho were called faggots and girls existed only to fuck. And to top it off, I was bored. For explanation I turned to what culture I had at the time: television. Informed and entertained, I was reassured that these problems are too complex for easy answers, smart men were working on them, it's all being taken care of, it's normal, it might not even exist, you're one of the lucky ones, shut up. I thought I must be crazy.

Then, sometime in my mid-teens, I heard the Sex Pistols.

> Right! NOW! ha ha ha ha ha
> I am an anti-Christ
> I am an anarchist
> don't know what I want,
> but I know how to get it
> I wanna destroy the passer by
> 'cos I, I wanna be . . . anarchy.

Damned if I could figure out what Johnny Rotten was singing about, but I did know that he was angry, and I was angry, and I was not alone. I remember that feeling. That wonderful feeling. A joyous homecoming to a world I hadn't even known existed.

About the same time I was listening to the Sex Pistols I discovered the Ramones. Since they were from the US, I could better understand what they were saying (even through lead singer Joey's affected Cockney accent). But what I got from the Ramones wasn't from their funhouse lyrics—it was their music: high energy, repetitive, rock 'n' roll: G-G-G-G-G-G-G-C—D—. Two bar chords, three positions: "Hey, ho, let's go!" It was simple, it was stupid, anyone could play it . . . and so could I. Within months of listening to the Ramones some friends and I learned to "play" our instruments and we formed a band. I crossed the line from consumer to creator.

And so it was punk rock that taught me my first, and probably most important, political lessons. I learned the importance of community. Alone, I owned my problems: *I* was alienated, *I* was bored, *I* was too sensitive to injustice. But as a punk I found others who also had these problems, and since we all seemed to share them, we reasoned that they must not just be ours, but society's problems. *My* personal problems became *a* social problem. Us punks then supported each other, helping each other face a society we didn't like and working together to create a micro-world that functioned according to different principles. In Lefty parlance, I learned the power of "solidarity." But before I could do anything, I first had to believe I could do it. Initially, I didn't. Like most people growing up in liberal democracies and consumer economies, I was used to politics, products, and entertainment being created and carried out by others *for* me, my own action limited to spending a dollar or casting a vote. Punk taught me to DIY: Do-it-yourself. The idea that I could create my own culture—*do-it-myself*—was for me revolutionary, as it carried within it the promise that I could also create my own politics and my own world.

Punk provided me with political ideas, then ingrained them through experience. The first time I heard the term anarchist used as anything other than an insult was in the Sex Pistols' "Anarchy in the UK." The lyrics of that song, and later ones from more overtly ideological bands like The Clash, Dead Kennedys, and Stiff Little Fingers, lent me new words to interpret and talk about the world. And critically this culture spoke not in the pious slogans of sectarians or the priests' Latin of academics but in a rough, emotional language that was my own. I didn't read about "counterhegemonic cultures," I was surrounded by one: fun, messy, mine. As I spent time immersed within punk culture I internalized a way of looking at and acting in the world that became as "natural" as any set of habits or values I had held before. Smashing the state topped getting a prom date on my things-to-do list for Senior year. And what I learned, I learned by doing. Punk didn't work unless it was performed, and by writing songs, dressing up and playing out I learned to perform my passions. That is, I learned how to transform ideas into action. When I found my way to political activism a few years later, it was an easy step because I was already halfway there.

But only halfway. For just as many aspects of punk pulled me toward political resistance, there were equal forces pushing me away. Punk was a great tool for articulating the problems of my world, and providing a supportive culture where I could develop that critique, but punk in itself did nothing to affect the root causes of the things—racism, sexism, and class inequality—I was so angry about. Punk had no strategic plan; it had no plan at all. In some ways punk rock was merely a release, an escape valve for my political dissatisfaction: "I wanna be anarchy!" OK, I've said that, now I feel better. The culture of resistance that my friends and I had built became a safe place to hide. Fortified by our righteous sense of superiority, stocked with a steady supply of punk rock band, club, and scene trivia to keep us busy, boundaries between "us" and "them" clearly demarcated by dyed hair and leather jackets, we closed off the world. Eventually, however, punk did escape the ghetto walls we had constructed. Following the success of the band Nirvana and the discovery of "grunge" in the early 1990s, the signs and signifiers of punk became a way to market commercial products to a potentially lucrative "Generation X." When I heard Iggy Pop's proto-punk anthem "Search and Destroy" used to sell Nike sneakers I felt sick, but I also learned another important lesson: the politics of culture is not predetermined. Culture is pliable; it's how it is used that matters.

The very word "culture" is elastic. You've probably already noticed that I've been stretching its meaning. Here I'm referring to culture as a thing, there as a set of norms, behaviors and ways to make sense of the world, and, in still other places, I'm describing culture as a process. This is because the word "culture" means all these things.

The term "cultural resistance" is no firmer. In the following pages I use it to describe culture that is used, consciously or unconsciously, effectively or not, to resist and/or change the dominant political, economic and/or social structure. But cultural resistance, too, can mean many things and take on many forms, and before we go much farther it may help to clarify some of its parameters, developing schematically some of the ideas sketched out more casually above and introducing new ones.

Let's begin by considering how cultural resistance works to foster or retard radical political activity. First off, cultural resistance can provide a sort of "free space" for developing ideas and practices. Freed from the limits and constraints of the dominant culture, you can experiment with new ways of seeing and being and develop tools and resources for resistance. And as culture is usually something shared, it becomes a focal point around which to build a community.

Equipped with new ideas, skills, confidence, and comrades, the step into the unknown terrain of political resistance may seem less frightening. And because cultural resistance often speaks in a more familiar and less demanding voice than political dissent it makes this move even easier. In this way cultural resistance works as a sort of stepping stone into political activity.

Cultural resistance can also be thought of *as* political resistance. Some theorists argue that politics is essentially a cultural discourse, a shared set of symbols and meanings, that we all abide by. If this is true then the rewriting of that discourse—which is essentially what cultural resistance does—is a political act in itself.

Taking a more pessimistic view, cultural resistance can be seen as an escape from politics and a way to release discontent that might otherwise be expressed through political activity. From this vantage point, cultural resistance is the creation of a sort of safe sanctuary, a "haven in a heartless world." Within this private utopia an ideal society is conjured up, problems are magically resolved, but outside nothing changes at all.

And finally, continuing the pessimistic slide, you can argue that cultural resistance does not and cannot exist. The dominant system is one of such complete ideological and material hegemony that any cultural expression, even if it appears rebellious, is, or will soon be repackaged and transformed into, a component of the status quo. From this perspective cultural resistance as a political practice is at best a waste of time and at worst a delusional detour from real political resistance.

Next let's look at how culture conveys its politics. A message can travel via the *content* of culture. Returning to the Sex Pistols' "Anarchy in the UK" for example, the band counsels resistance through explicit lyrics. Reading or hearing these words provides you with a political vocabulary, analysis, and even an action plan (although in the case of the Sex Pistols' "I wanna destroy the passer by," a pretty dubious one).

Politics can also be transmitted through the *form* culture takes. It is one thing to read lyrics on a page, quite another to hear them sung with emotion or laid over a danceable beat. Similarly, a different message is conveyed by the same song recorded on a DIY label versus a CD manufactured and distributed by a multi-national corporation. And that song changes yet again depending on whether you are listening to it performed or mixed live at an underground party, or sung in a stadium where you've paid $50 to watch the performer from afar on a wall-sized video screen. To crib from Marshall McLuhan: "the medium is the message."

How culture is received and made sense of—its *interpretation*—determines its politics as well. Even though Malcolm McLaren started the Sex Pistols as an art prank cum rock 'n' roll swindle, it didn't stop a kid like me across the Atlantic from hearing a call to arms. In the same way, Sister Sledge's disco hit "We Are Family" took on new meaning when appropriated as an anthem of gay and lesbian pride and solidarity in the 1980s. Content and medium may carry a message, but the meaning and potential impact of that message lie dormant until interpreted by an audience.

And finally, the very *activity* of producing culture has political meaning. In a society built around the principle that we should consume what others have produced for us, throwing an illegal warehouse rave or creating an underground music label—that is creating your own culture—takes on a rebellious resonance. The first act of politics is simply to act.

Now we can consider the spectrum of political engagement, or what I call scales of resistance. Political self-consciousness is the first one. On one side of the scale is culture that may serve the function of resistance, but was not created with that in mind, nor with the idea that its participants understand it as such. The other pole is occupied by culture consciously created for political resistance and used for that purpose. Somewhere in the middle is culture appropriated for ends for which it was not intended. This can cut both ways: culture that was not meant to be rebellious can be turned and used for those political ends and, conversely, culture that was self-consciously fashioned with rebellion in mind can be made to serve very non-rebellious purposes.

The next scale measures the social unit engaged in cultural resistance. To the left is the individual, creating and perhaps even living out a culture that may—theoretically—challenge the dominant system to its very core. But that person does this in their own head, within their own little world, sharing it with no one. In the middle lies the subculture, a group that has been cut off, or more likely has cut itself off, from the dominant society in order to create a shared, inclusive set of cultural values and practices. To the right is society. If an entire society is engaged in cultural resistance it means one of two things: that the dominant culture and the power it props up are bound to fall away at any moment, or that cultural resistance has been so thoroughly incorporated into a society of spectacle that its practice is one of political futility.

Which brings us to the final scale: the results of cultural resistance. The spectrum here ranges from survival to revolution. Survival is the point at which cultural resistance is merely a way to put up with the daily grind and injustices of life while holding on to a semblance of dignity. Rebellion is where cultural resistance contributes to political activity against the powers-that-be. Results of this resistance may range from suffering repression to forcing meaningful reform, yet all of this occurs within the framework of the dominant power. And revolution, well, revolution is the complete overthrow of the ruling system and a time when the culture of resistance becomes just culture.

The following may help clarify things:

Cultural Resistance and Political Action

- Cultural resistance creates a "free space":

    Ideologically: space to create new language, meanings, and visions of the future

    Materially: place to build community, networks, and organizational models

- Cultural resistance is a stepping stone, providing a language, practice, and community to ease the way into political activity

- Cultural resistance *is* political activity: writing or rewriting political discourse and thus political practice

- Culture resistance is a "haven in a heartless world," an escape from the world of politics and problems

- Cultural resistance does not exist. All culture is, or will immediately become, an expression of the dominant power

Means of Cultural Resistance

- *Content:* the political message resides within the content of the culture
- *Form:* the political message is expressed through the medium of transmission
- *Interpretation:* the political message is determined by how the culture is received and interpreted
- *Activity:* the action of producing culture, regardless of content or form or reception, is the political message

Scales of Cultural Resistance

- unconsciously political   appropriation   self-consciously political
- individual   subculture   society
- survival   rebellion   revolution

10

Negative, 1996

DAVID EYE

In "Negative, 1996" poet David Eye allows readers access to the stream-of-consciousness memories and feelings that come to the narrator as he learns of his HIV/AIDS-negative status. Eye refuses to allow readers to understand AIDS in purely scientific or health policy terms. His poem requires an acknowledgment of the complex subjectivities and communities facilitated through responses to the AIDS epidemic.

The clinic social worker's blond-tipped dreadlocks
are haloed by afternoon light filtering through
the filmy window at 125th and Broadway.
Hard to get an appointment downtown.
With one word comes absolution. But

I am two places at once. I am sitting at this Health
Department desk, sweating in my relief, and I am thinking
of everyone I know who's dead and everyone I know
who knows people who are dead and I can't help wonder
why it is I get to sit at this desk and hear the word
out of her mouth that would have saved them.

She's talking and I hear some of hers, but other words
are floating in the air like a cartoon. Top. Bottom.
Latex. Suck fist carefully needles water-based. And I am thinking

of the letter in 1983 from my college friend, Berkeley postmark,
the weird new disease, the first I'd heard. And oh jesus christ
the Quilt and what happened in DC the moment I set foot

on the canvas margin, like stepping into a glassy ocean
and being pulled under by a riptide of sorrow
you didn't see coming, could not have known was there.
I was let loose, on my knees, like those people in the newsreels
who wail and keen over the remains of their children, their men.
Grief the likes of which we don't know, or aren't allowed.

I am thinking if getting fucked had felt better the first time
in 1977 maybe I would be among the chosen.
I am thinking if I had moved to San Francisco in 1982
(just out of school) instead of San Antonio, I'd be a dead man
and someone would be kneeling by my name.

The social worker's condom admonitions sound like a blessing
but she is drowned out by a march in B-flat minor.
It looks like a parade, but that music. From the backs
of open convertibles, friends, lovers, teachers in prom gowns
and combat gear smile and wave in slow motion.
One after another my comrades fall, seroconverting
with the seasons, T-cells drifting downward
like tickertape in an Armistice Day parade.

11

You Tell Us What to Do

Faiz Ahmed Faiz
Translated by Agha Shahid Ali

Faiz Ahmed Faiz, born in 1911 in what is now Pakistan, was at various times a journalist, government official, political prisoner, and university administrator, but always a poet. "You Tell Us What to Do" is taken from his collection The Rebel's Silhouette *and, like much of his poetry since the 1960s, draws attention to the bloody conflicts that cleaved India, Pakistan, and Bangladesh throughout the 20th century.*

When we launched life
on the river of grief,
how vital were our arms, how ruby our blood.
With a few strokes, it seemed,
we would cross all pain,
we would soon disembark.
That didn't happen.
In the stillness of each wave we found invisible currents.
The boatmen, too, were unskilled,
their oars untested.
Investigate the matter as you will,

blame whomever, as much as you want,
but the river hasn't changed,
the raft is still the same.
Now you suggest what's to be done,
you tell us how to come ashore.

When we saw the wounds of our country
appear on our skins,
we believed each word of the healers.
Besides, we remembered so many cures,
it seemed at any moment
all troubles would end, each wound heal completely.
That didn't happen: our ailments
were so many, so deep within us
that all diagnoses proved false, each remedy useless.
Now do whatever, follow each clue,
accuse whomever, as much as you will,
our bodies are still the same,
our wounds still open.
Now tell us what we should do,
you tell us how to heal these wounds.

12

Building Paranoia

STEVEN FLUSTY

This essay originally appeared in the book Building Paranoia, *where Assistant Professor of Geography at York University Steven Flusty interrogates the connections between the militaristic fortifications of suburban neighborhoods and access to commercial spaces, such as malls, that have come to serve as public commons for some. Flusty models site-based observations and fieldwork—practices which enable an argument to emerge through a sustained engagement with evidence—while also situating those observations in larger trends and conversations.*

Twenty years ago, I was given a premonition of what Los Angeles would be like in the 1990s. My grandparents visited our house, in what was then the far western suburbs of Los Angeles, after returning from a cruise to Rio De Janeiro, Brazil. The stories they told me would have seemed unbelievably dystopian were it not for the fact that I then believed that grandparents do not lie. They spoke of how the houses of the rich Brazilians were surrounded by high walls topped with broken glass. The concierges of apartment buildings carried automatic weapons. The city's outskirts were packed with cardboard and corrugated metal shanties. Children in ragged clothes slept on the sidewalks and ate out of garbage cans in alleys.

My parents still live in that same suburban house, purchased twenty-eight years ago. For eighteen of those years, the house remained much the same. I would pass through a front yard open to the street, unlock and rotate the doorknob, and walk in. Over the past decade, however, the simple act of entering the residence has grown dauntingly complex. Next to the door is a small metal plate with an illuminated red L.E.D., warning of the presence of an activated alarm. Upon disengaging the dead bolt and opening the front door, I have thirty seconds in which to deactivate the alarm by entering a sequence of digits into a small keypad in the entry hall. Should I forget the number, or should the hall be too dark to work the keypad within the prescribed time, a shrieking siren wakes the neighborhood. Next, the dead bolt must be reengaged and a separate switch, located elsewhere in the house, must be tripped to deactivate pressure pads strewn beneath the floor and contacts embedded into the interior doorways. At that point the house's interior becomes safe for passage and the alarm may be safely reactivated as a perimeter defense. At any time, the alarm may be intentionally activated by hitting "panic buttons" sprinkled throughout the house at strategic locations. The exterior of the house, once illuminated only by a porch light, now basks in the glare of multiple 150-watt security lights in the back and side yards, switched on from dusk to dawn by photoelectric sensors.

My parents' house is one of the neighborhood's less obtrusively secured. Many feature lawn signs cautioning passersby of armed response. Some include security lights controlled by motion detectors set to blind anything that moves on the adjacent sidewalk and street. A few have installed spike-topped perimeter fences with remote-controlled, chain-driven gates to allow automobile access without having to exit the vehicle. Patrol cars carrying private security officers pass through the street late at night, watching over only those homes whose owners pay an additional service fee.

This neighborhood transformation did not occur all at once. It was a long, incremental process that only after some ten years has become obvious. A few residences took action in response to specific incidences. Most, however, have reacted to a pervasive sense of insecurity. It is an insecurity at odds with the neighborhood watch maps showing this portion of Police Reporting District 1091 largely free of the *X*'s and *R*'s marking sites of residential and street burglaries.

Meanwhile, three blocks away, people in ragged clothes sleep in the bushes by the side of the freeway and eat from garbage cans behind the supermarket.

"Blockhomes," my term for secured residents like my parents', are one component in the ongoing remaking of L.A.'s landscape as an intrusively nervous place. As we safari through this landscape of elite communities over the next few pages, I will point out a number of these components and try to come to some conclusions about how they add up. Despite the fact that we will be wandering around Los Angeles, the things we will observe could be in Sao Paulo, Manila, indeed any of the long-established colonial cities or newly emerging world cities. Specifically, we will be hunting down interdictory spaces—spaces designed to intercept and repel or filter would-be users. To date, I have found it convenient to distinguish five species:

> Stealthy space—space that cannot be found, is camouflaged or, more commonly, is obscured by such view impediments as intervening objects or grade changes (for example, the Poets' Walk Garden of Citicorp Plaza at Seventh and Figueroa streets, concealed behind an office tower, a department store entrance kiosk, and a flight of escalators).

Slippery space—space that cannot be reached, due to contorted, protracted, or missing paths of approach. Such a strategy is costly, as it may require obfuscating numerous routes of access extending well beyond any single site. Justifying this expense, slippery space provides public-relations benefits in that it may be blamed on preexisting topographical constraints as a means of defraying criticism (for example, California Plaza's Watercourt at 2nd–4th streets and Grand Avenue, looming over Olive Street with no readily apparent means of access from the streets below).

Crusty space—space that cannot be accessed, due to obstructions such as walls, gates, and checkpoints (for example, the Los Angeles County Museum of Art's grounds and sculpture garden at Hancock Park, once open to one another and the surrounding greenswards but now encircled within a series of high wrought-iron and chain-link fences).

Prickly space—space that cannot be comfortably occupied, defended by such details as wall-mounted sprinkler heads activated to clear loiterers or ledges sloped to inhibit sitting (for example, the 380-square-foot park wedged into a southwest-facing pocket between the sidewalk and the Ronald Reagan State Office Building at Third and Spring streets, boasting sparse shade, a highly reflective pavement, and backless benches with seating heights at a leg-numbing twenty-four inches).

Jittery space—space that cannot be utilized unobserved due to active monitoring by roving patrols and/or remote technologies feeding to security stations (for example, the Biddy Mason Pocket Park in the Broadway-Spring Center, a secured through-block connection featuring guarded rest rooms and seventeen video cameras monitoring the park's sitting areas and public sidewalks abutting the park entrances).

In the field, of course, we are unlikely to spot these spaces in isolation. Rather, they tend to be deployed simultaneously, so as to form distinctly unfriendly mutant building typologies. The "blockhome," for instance, is often embedded in an extended jittery perimeter of alarms, video observation cameras, and security lighting. Fast becoming the Angeleno residence of choice, blockhomes are most apparent in gentrifying areas, where new wealthier residents feel threatened by the established poorer community. Venice Beach is dotted with blockhomes forced into compact bunker and tower forms by the expense of beach-adjacent property. The high-style architectural tastes of the area's new residents have resulted in oddly angled concrete walls, Cor-Ten steel gates, and tall, tilted courtyard enclosures collaged of stucco and frosted glass. Witty references to the preexisting community, such as a miniature white picket fence set before a windowless corrugated metal studio/house (as in Dennis Hopper's house) and a home stealthily retrofitted into the unrestored shell of an existing dilapidated house (complete with an address number spray-painted like graffiti across the housefront), abound.

This trend is not confined to locations in flux. In established and affluent foothill neighborhoods like Royal Oak, neighborhood homes sprout such features as crenellated walls and fences comprised of unscalable vertical piping. Some homes include exterior video cameras to communicate the identities of visitors prior to admission through remotely controlled driveway gates. Others employ prickly plantings in "security-oriented gardens" beneath windows and surrounding the property. In areas such as this, the entire neighborhood may be rendered slippery and jittery.

Just five blocks west of my parents' house, Calabasas is an affluent residential community priding itself on its "old west" charm. Most of publicly accessible Calabasas, though, is not somewhere to linger in but to pass through, as the streets are a pointedly inhospitable place to sojourn. Throughout the past decade, these hills have been covered with over 800 homes contained within four walled and gated residential complexes, or "luxury laagers." The public roads of Calabasas Park are confined within a continuous lining of cinder-block walls punctuated only by occasional guardhouses and remotely activated gates. As the luxury laagers face private internal streets, little effort has been made to landscape the public rights-of-way, leaving the spaces between the laagers very prickly—unshaded, hot, and forbiddingly barren. We would see the same thing in all the new hillside developments ringing the L.A. Basin.

These developments sell exclusion. Advertisements tout security features with the Dragnetian brevity of "gated with twenty-four-hour drive-by security" (an entirely novel use of the ominous "drive-by" moniker) or florid prose like, "as you drive through the wrought-iron gates, past the uniformed guard, and over the rushing stream, you will be transfixed by . . ." There is also novelty, like one moated development's "deep twenty-five-acre lake provides total security for the owners of the spacious high-rise condominium homes."

Jittery beneath a crusty shell, sealed luxury laagers with checkpoint entries and private internal security patrols may now be found throughout the L.A. area and beyond. This proliferation has led to an explosion of typological permutations providing high-security residential units in a wide range of prices. High-density multiple-building apartment complexes are refitted with metal fencing stretched between the structures to block access to internal streets. Medium-density stealthy suburban town houses are set atop tall berms landscaped so heavily that you would never know there were houses up

Traditional public spaces are increasingly supplanted by privately produced (although often publicly subsidized), privately owned and administered spaces for public aggregation, most commonly malls.

there. Back in Calabasas, low-density clusters of exurban mansions are accessed by passing through sentried forecourts augmented by video cameras to record visitors' license plates.

One thing we have probably noticed since our walk began is the eerie absence of people, like in one of those "Twilight Zone" episodes where some poor rube wanders around a depopulated theme park. We could try to find ourselves some locals to hang out with. Unfortunately, we are not likely to find any in the very few open spaces we have passed. Public open space has come under assault as privatization has reacted opportunistically to public sector penury. The Proposition 13 property tax "revolt," declines in sales tax due to consumers' loss of purchasing power, the late 1980s collapse of the local real-estate market, and reduced federal assistance have created a state budget deficit of $11 billion, reflected in Los Ange-

Strong point of sale
Eastern Hollywood, California

Luxury laager
Calabasas, California

Crusty space
Labrea Tarpits and L. A. County Museum of Art
at Hancock Park, California

Dennis Hopper House
Venice, California
Brian Murphey, architect

les as a budgetary shortfall of $500 million. As a result, legislators have called for the discontinuation of fiscally burdensome functions of public space and the transfer of potentially profitable functions to the private sector. Such public facilities as parks and libraries have been debilitated by shrinking tax revenues and declining income from user fees, first losing programs, then maintenance, and finally closing entirely.

Traditional public spaces are increasingly supplanted by privately produced (although often publicly subsidized), privately owned and administered spaces for public aggregation,[1] that is, spaces of consumption or, most commonly, malls. In these new, "post-public" spaces, access is predicated upon ability to pay. People without purchasing power, goods that cannot be mass marketed, more-than-passive activities, and ideas narrowly perceived as inimical to the owner's sensibilities (and profit margin) are unaccommodated or ejected by private security as quickly as they are manifested. Exclusivity rules here, ensuring the high levels of control necessary to prevent irregularity, unpredictability, and inefficiency from interfering with the orderly flow of commerce.

The first thing we notice is a new running fence enclosing the mall parking lot, limiting points of access. Spaces of consumption cannot seal themselves off completely, as they are dependent upon customer access for sustenance. Even so, they have imposed tight controls over use, becoming "strong points of sale." The smallest strip mall is a tightly nested series of crusty, jittery, and prickly spaces. The fenced parking lot itself is watched over by armed security guards. Pay phones have been removed to discourage vagrants, and some convenience stores have installed exterior speakers blaring Muzak to drive away adolescent head-bangers. Fast food outlets, equipped with video cameras at pay stations and drive-through windows, feature outdoor eating/playground areas surrounded by outward curving steel bars. Loading docks large enough to enclose delivery vehicles whole are accessed through steel doors set into concrete parapets and watched over by guard towers.

The interior promenades of some larger malls are unremittingly jittery, remotely monitored by both private security and police in on-site substations. One mall substation in Baldwin Hills serves as a base for 200 police officers; another bay immediately across the promenade houses a municipal courthouse. These substations have become central institutions in affluent suburban malls, where the role of shopping as community social focus has provided a site for police contact with the general public. Here, the substations serve as the public hub for community policing and neighborhood watch operations.

Since the 1992 L.A. uprising, this "make-my-day" shopping has undergone accelerated research and development paying special attention to thwarting looting and arson. Wood-frame structures, flammable and easily breached, have been replaced by single or double walls of concrete masonry. Roof lines have been raised to deflect fire bombs thrown from street level. Display windows have been filled in, or set into concrete bulwarks three feet above sidewalk level to prevent automobiles ramming through to the interior. Glass entries have been replaced with armor-plated roll-down doors, pre-graffitied to discourage taggers.

A few blocks east of the still-smoldering wreckage of L.A.'s multicultural mythos, we arrive at Bunker Hill. Bunker Hill was twenty blocks of disintegrating, Victorian, low-income housing until the early 1960s, when it was disconnected from the surrounding street grid, plugged into the freeway, and razed for redevelopment. Now Bunker Hill is the Central Business District, covered in high-rise "citidels" to give L.A. that *sine-qua-non* world city skyline. "Citidels" are the corporate control centers of the global econo-cultural web, the properties administered by management companies competing with one another to attract corporate tenants.

I would take us up Bunker Hill, but the hill's designers are not too keen on pedestrians coming up from down below (except as janitors), so we cannot get there from here. The entire hill is slippery, separated from the adjacent city by an obstacle course of open freeway trenches, a palisade of concrete parking garages, and a tangle of concrete bridges linking citidel to citidel high above the streets. Every path we try confronts us with the blank undersides of vehicular overpasses, towering walls studded with giant garage exhausts, and seating cleverly shaped like narrow sideways tubes so as to be entirely unusable. We could attain the summit from the south, but only by climbing a narrow, heavily patrolled stair "plaza," studded with video cameras and clearly marked as private property. But ignoring the fact that, in the world beyond this text, we would probably find ourselves inadvertently walking onto a freeway offramp (I know I have), we will traverse the plaza on the hill.

The plaza reflects both a shared consciousness between developers and public institutions of the value of user-friendly urban designs and a differing conception of to whom those benefits should accrue. By providing spaces where "office workers will find outdoor areas for noontime relaxation,"[2] attractive site amenities are seen as integral to this competition. Municipal agencies, meanwhile, see plazas as developer-funded additions to the city's open space inventory. Thus attempts are made to extract plazas from private developers in exchange for subsidies provided through below-market-rate land sales or leases, tax abatements, and density bonuses. In negotiations with developers, municipal agencies have been successful in linking public subsidies to the provision of habitable open spaces, in no small part because such spaces enhance the value of the project to the developers. Municipal agencies have not, however, been terribly concerned with assuring right of public access to these spaces. Thus, public subsidies have often been expended to create plazas accessible only at the discretion of private owners; plazas sit stealthy behind hedgerows and grade changes, jittery with blue-blazered private security. Most have small bronze plaques at the property line reading, "Private property. Right to pass by permission, and subject to control, of owners. Sec. 1008 civil code." Inside the plazas we would find malls uniformly equipped with eateries, express mail posts, dry cleaners, and gift shops to relieve office workers of the need to leave the premises. The malls are lushly planted and ornamented with water features. They are graced with high-art plaza-turds signed by some of the best plop-artists. And, once again, they are nearly inaccessible to us.

As we have wandered the streets intent on our destinations, there are some interesting bits that have escaped our notice. I would like to call our attention to a couple of these, starting with the omnipresent whir of helicopter rotors. Across the city, police helicopters maintain a continuous vigil overhead with the aid of gigantic block numeral coordinates painted atop buildings and busses. One helicopter keeps watch over each of the city's three patrol areas at any given time. These helicopters, originally developed for military applications, can cross the L.A. Basin in eleven minutes at a speed of approximately 140 miles per hour. They are equipped with the Spectrolab Nightsun illumination system, producing 30 million peak beam candle power, and the Forward Looking Infra-Red (FLIR) sensing system, capable of detecting body heat at a distance of 1,000 feet, a lit match at 4,000 feet.

We also have not bothered to look closely at the lampposts, freeway signage, and transmission towers, despite the fact that they have been looking at us. Video cameras have become standard equipment at major intersections across the city. Set in bulletproof casings more than forty feet above street level, the cameras are equipped with remotely controlled pan, tilt, and zoom capabilities. They feed to a control center beneath City Hall. These cameras are part of the $300 million Automated Traffic Surveillance And Control (ATSAC) system undergoing installation citywide. ATSAC cameras are presently used to determine the specific cause of traffic delays indicated by in-pavement sensors. Police spokespersons and the mayor's office, however, have been careful not to deny an interest in using the cameras to keep watch over the streets, sidewalks, and adjacent properties. This is not surprising, given that the local police department increasingly shares the rest of the city's love affair with electronic media. Cameras, video recorders, and computer terminals are being installed in LAPD patrol vehicles, enabling mobile street-level surveillance and the instantaneous gathering and transmission of such intelligence as video still images. In essence, the entire region has become jittery space.

So how should we read these symptoms, visible to any peripatetic? Diagnoses require consideration not just of what has happened to us over the course of our excursion, but also of what has not. In all likelihood, we have not been run over or mugged. We have not been verbally abused by beggars, shot by gang members, or had our throats slit in our own driveways by some disgruntled ex-athlete. What we have experienced is ex-aerospace workers pan handling in front of pastel marble clad office buildings, vendors of pirated cassettes and chili'd mangos on the sidewalks in front of overcrowded Spanish revival apartments, billboards and store signs plastered with Spanish, Hangul, or Amaric, and a handful of streets in very poor neighborhoods partially obstructed by unattended police barricades.

The statistics and their ramifications fill in the picture. The population of Los Angeles County increased by nineteen percent to about nine million in the last decade. This mushrooming population cannot sprawl anymore since the infrastructure is too overburdened, so estimated densities in some residential areas have reached those of Manhattan. Population growth has created demand rendering real estate prohibitively expensive for a majority of Angelenos, even in the current depressed market. Resulting land pressures have crowded higher-density development into neighborhoods of traditional, albeit less affordable, suburban homesteads previously isolated along quiet avenues. Development is swallowing up open land: portions of the mountains, beaches, and the few major public parks.

The impact of the increasing demand for limited real estate has been exacerbated by the loss of over half a million jobs since the 1990s began, due to the continued outmigration of industrial investment for more easily exploited locales and the post-cold-war decrease in subsidization of the area's warfare industry. This collapse of the labor market's demand exacerbates the impoverishing effects of more than a decade of upward income redistribution under "trickle down" economic policies, corporate capture of mobile capital, and the resultant expansion of low wage/low skill service work, temporary office or day labor, and the burgeoning informal economy.

The shrinkage of the labor market has increased already substantial differences in quality of life between the city's highly visible elite and expanding poor neighborhoods. It has deformed the geography of resource flows within the city to replicate the distributional inequities of the world economy in general. Thus, portions of L.A., like most world cities, have joined the global economy's exploited and neglected periphery despite being wholly contained within the city itself. Further, in the absence of affordable land and opportunities for significant economic advancement, the parks and streets of neighborhoods in L.A.'s internal periphery have become either the rent-free and accessible sites of informal sector market transactions in "illegally" vended commodities (narcotics and prostitution) or unauthorized temporary sites of homeless encampments.

Reflecting patterns of human displacement throughout the emerging world system, L.A.'s demographic globalization has been a fundamental aspect of its population increase. Los Angeles is the affluent world city most frequently and widely represented (and misrepresented) in electronic media, and the fastest growing on the American continent's West Coast since the 1980s. It has thus become the destination of choice for a disproportionate slice of the planet's estimated one billion immigrants, drawn from regions arrayed around the Pacific Rim and beyond.

There are more Iranians in L.A. than in any city outside of Tehran. Armenian is the first language in pockets of Los Feliz. An Ethiopian three-block stretch of Fairfax now seeks formal recognition as Little Addis. It is the geographical links to Latin America and Asia, however, that have most reconstituted the region's demographics. The "Latin" population is fast reestablishing its long lost majority, comprising 37.8% of the county population as of the 1990 census. It is said that the region boasts more Mexicans than any city outside Mexico City, more Salvadorians than any city but San Salvador. The Asian population has nearly doubled over the past decade to over 10% of the county population. There has emerged a Little Saigon spread across an area half the size of Ho Chi Minh City itself, and a roughly seventy-block swathe of Mid-Wilshire rechristened Koreatown in the map books. Each of these populations brings with it cultural conceptions of urban life differing from the rapidly outmigrating suburban Angeleno ideal.

Previously permitted to settle only in demographically homogeneous, less desirable locations, immigrant communities are more recently atomizing across the L.A. Basin. This dispersion has been facilitated by anti-discriminatory housing policies, by the affordability of clusters of commercial and residential structures depreciated by age, and by the evaporation of local employment bases. Further, many newcomers are of comparatively affluent merchant classes and bring with them assets permitting greater locational choice. An expanding constellation of Little Indias, although concentrated in Artesia, includes outposts from Hollywood to the central San Fernando Valley, with a new Vishnite temple back in Calabasas. New Chinese immigrants have largely bypassed Chinatown; five of the region's incorporated cities are now majority Asian with a preponderance of Cantonese speakers.

Rising population in a limited area, concentrating wealth and poverty (what I like to call the "new world bipolar disorder"), and increasing cultural segmentation at regional and neighborhood levels are producing in Los Angeles, as in other world cities, a densely packed heterogeneous population manifesting dramatic juxtapositions of privation and opulence. This has served to erode the spatial and ideological dominance of an aging, predominantly white "native" elite. The resultant drastic shift in the balance of cultural influence is complicated by the fact that no other group has yet emerged with a sufficient preponderance of members and/or resources to establish itself as the new majority. Lacking such a majority, no one group is empowered to determine new behavioral standards.

Street gangs use spray paint while homeowners associations use neighborhood watch signs; either way we are talking informal militias.

With the decay of previously established cultural standards, and the absence of widely accepted new ones, a wealth of differing ways of life has surfaced, each with its own rules governing spatial use and interpersonal contact. The result is a fluid urban matrix in which likely outcomes of encounters are unpredictable and territorial clues are misread or ignored, causing social friction as individuals and groups continuously encroach upon one another. In response to the uncertainties of a fragmented and dynamic urban milieu, social groups form into "defended neighborhoods" in order to segregate themselves from "danger, insult, and the impairment of status claims."[3] The defended neighborhood is characterized by a homogeneous social group exerting dominance within its boundaries in reaction to perceived threats of territorial violation by outsiders. Street gangs use spray

151

paint while homeowners associations use neighborhood watch signs; either way we are talking informal militias.

In short, the security obsession now pervading our cities is fueled in large part by fears of complex social change and inequitable resource distribution. The concomitant Angeleno "war on crime" may be interpreted as a means of forcibly maintaining, reconstituting, or at least salvaging a challenged and possibly collapsing social consensus while simultaneously protecting the perquisites of that consensus's established beneficiaries. Segmentation of the socio-spatial realm is the critical means to this end.

The luxury laager may thus be seen as the territory of a social group possessing the considerable resources required to assert its spatial claims with walls and mercenaries. Luxury laagers are therefore not intended to exclude merely crime, but a wide range of behavior deviating from the community norms. This overriding concern with conformance to behavioral standards is demonstrated by the fact that residents are subject to covenants, conditions, and restrictions (CC&R's) forbidding such "low class" deviations as painting one's home a color objectionable to the architectural committee, working on one's vehicle outside of one's garage, using overstuffed or other indoor furniture on patios or front lawns, or putting one's garbage cans out early.

Similarly, the blockhome may be interpreted as an attempt by those unwilling to submit to the conformity of the laagers, but unable to afford large lots of their own, to substitute blank walls for wide lawns as a means of establishing a comfortable distance from outsiders. Walls need not even be high for the symbolic exertion of spatial dominance to the owner's satisfaction; many blockhomes' perimeter fences are five feet tall or less with blunt spikes, and interrupted by easily scaled support columns.

It is the unenviable task of the strong point of sale, if it is to survive, to draw prospective tenant merchants and customers into a setting that, by virtue of accessibility to a variety of social groups, precludes the ability of tenants or customers to enforce their own social norms. To resolve this contradiction, the strong point of sale acts to reassure visitors against the likelihood of unpredictable encounters by itself becoming the arbiter of behavioral standards even more conservative than those of the luxury laager.

Like luxury laagers, the plazas of citidels are configured more for the symbolic defense of status then for the physical protection of occupants. This status, however, is not held by individuals within, but must be attained through exhibition to such external constituencies as other businesses and the consuming and investing public at large. The plaza is regarded as a front yard reflecting upon the tenant corporation's aesthetic sensibility and management competence. Thus, management and tenants view a plaza's white-collar user mix adulterated by vagrants or a janitor's family on a picnic as a loss of prestige before the "business community," and a resulting loss of clientele.

Taking a broad perspective on these proliferating spaces of control, it becomes apparent that the sites in which daily life and face-to-face interaction take place—the streets, parks, bazaars, and plazas—are being sacrificed to redundant zones of oversight and proprietary control. This threatens the free exchange of ideas engendering a progressive society. It creates an impediment to the cross-cultural communication necessary to knit together diverse publics. It is a rejection of the individual's right to space in which to be.

In my opinion, what is most ominous about the places we have visited is this: one's permitted passage inside or willingness to step outside is determined by one's actual or apparent affluence. Thus, by employing space as the medium for securing status, we are building material barriers between individuals on the basis of wealth. As the world economic system constitutes a commercial society, access to wealth in the world city is largely a function of professional occupation. Thus, the physical segregation of the world city by criteria of affluence functions to divide society into rigid groups reflecting and reinforcing the local division of labor, while simultaneously impeding mobility and contact between these groups. Therefore, we are not merely witnessing the installation, component by component, of infrastructure restructuring the city into electronically linked islands of privilege embedded in an erratic police state matrix. We may also be observing a warning sign that, in the emerging world cities, class is solidifying into caste.

This essay is adapted from Building Paranoia: The Proliferation of Interdictory Space and the Erosion of Spatial Justice. *Los Angeles: Los Angeles Forum for Architecture and Urban Design, 1994.*

Endnotes

1. Herbert I. Schiller, *Culture, Inc.: The Corporate Takeover of Public Expression* (New York Oxford University Press, 1989)

2. Promotional brochure for Metropolitan Structures West's California Plaza.

3. Gerald D. Suttles. *The Social Construction of Communities* (Chicago: University of Chicago Press, 1972

13

The Politics of Staring: Visual Rhetorics of Disability in Popular Photography

ROSEMARIE GARLAND-THOMSON

In this essay from Disability Studies: Enabling the Humanities, *Garland-Thomson, Professor of Women's Studies at Emory University, offers a framework for analyzing the visual rhetoric enacted in photographs of subjects with disabilities. This essay demonstrates how analytical projects account for the work performed by cultural artifacts—work that might not be immediately obvious.*

The history of disabled people in the Western world is in part the history of being on display, of being visually conspicuous while politically and socially erased. The earliest record of disabled people is of their exhibition as prodigies, monsters, omens from the gods, and indexes of the natural or divine world. From the New Testament to the miracles at Lourdes, the lame, the halt, and the blind provide the spectacle for the story of bodily rehabilitation as spiritual redemption that is so essential to Christianity. From antiquity through modernity, the bodies of disabled people considered to be freaks and monsters have been displayed by the likes of medieval kings and P. T. Barnum for entertainment and profit in courts, street fairs, dime museums, and sideshows.[1] Moreover, medicine has from its beginnings exhibited the disabled body as what Michel Foucault calls the "case," in medical theaters and other clinical settings, in order to pathologize the exceptional and to normalize the ordinary (*Birth of the Clinic* 29). Disabled people have variously been objects of awe, scorn, terror, delight, inspiration, pity, laughter, or fascination—but they have always been stared at.

Staring at disability choreographs a visual relation between a spectator and a spectacle. A more intense form of looking than glancing, glimpsing, scanning, surveying, gazing, and other forms of casual or uninterested looking, staring registers the perception of difference and gives meaning to impairment by marking it as aberrant. By intensely telescoping looking toward the physical signifier for disability, staring creates an awkward partnership that estranges and discomforts both viewer and viewed. Starers gawk with abandon at the prosthetic hook, the empty sleeve, the scarred flesh, the unfocused eye, the twitching limb, but seldom does looking broaden to envelop the whole body of the person with a disability. Even supposedly invisible disabilities always threaten to disclose some stigma, however subtle, that disrupts the social order by its presence and attenuates the bond between equal members of the human community. Because staring at disability is considered illicit looking, the disabled body is at once the to-be-looked-at and not-to-be-looked-at, further dramatizing the staring encounter by making viewers furtive and the viewed defensive. Staring thus creates disability as a state of absolute difference rather than simply one more variation in human form. At the same time, staring constitutes disability identity by manifesting the power relations between the subject positions of disabled and able-bodied.

The rapid flourishing of photography after 1839 provided a new way to stare at disability. In our ocularcentric era, images mediate our desires and the ways we imagine ourselves.[2] Among the myriad, often conflicting, and never indifferent images modernity offers us, the picture of ourselves as disabled is an image fraught with a tangle of anxiety, distance, and identification. As a culture, we are at once obsessed with and intensely conflicted about the disabled body. We fear, deify, disavow, avoid, abstract, revere, conceal, and reconstruct disability—perhaps because it is one of the most universal, fundamental of human experiences. After all, we will all become disabled if we live long enough. Nonetheless, in representing disability in modernity, we have made the familiar seem strange, the human seem inhuman, the pervasive seem exceptional. By the beginning of the twentieth century, for example, public displays of disabled people became inappropriate in the same way that public executions and torture came to be considered offensive. Disabled people were sequestered from public view in institutions and the private sphere as middle-class decorum pronounced it impolite to stare. Photography, however, has enabled the social ritual of staring at disability to persist in an alternate form.

Photographs seem to be transparent windows onto reality that ensnare truth. But like all representations, photographs organize our perceptions, shaping the objects as they depict them by using conventions of presentation that invoke cultural ideas and expectations. Photographs evoke the familiar only to make it seem strange, eliciting a response Alan Trachtenberg describes as "astonishment mingling with recognition" (*Reading* 4). Because disability has such potent cultural resonances, our capitalist democracy has enlisted its imagery to manipulate viewers for a wide range of purposes. Popular photography catapults disability into the public sphere as a highly mediated image shorn from interactions with actual people with disabilities. Photography's immediacy, claim to truth, and wide circulation calcifies the interpretations of disability embedded in the images, at once shaping and registering the public perception of disability.

Photography authorizes staring. Photos are made to be looked at. With the actual disabled body absent, photography stylizes staring, exaggerating and fixing the conventions of display and eliminating the possibility for interaction or spontaneity between viewer and viewed. Photos absolve viewers of responsibility to the objects of their stares at the same time that they permit a more intense form of staring than an actual social interchange might support. Disability photography thus offers the spectator the pleasure of unaccountable, uninhibited, insistent looking. This license to stare becomes a powerful rhetorical device that can be mobilized to manipulate viewers. By exploring some of the purposes to which popular photography's "dialectic of strange and familiar" has been put, I aim here to suggest how modern America imagines disability and disabled people (Trachtenberg, *Reading* 4).[3]

To look at the way we look at disability, I elaborate a taxonomy of four primary visual rhetorics of disability. They are the wondrous, the sentimental, the exotic, and the realistic. This template of visual rhetorics complicates the often restrictive notion of images as being either positive or negative, as communicating either the truth of disability or perpetuating some oppressive stereotype. Thus, I analyze more than evaluate. These visualizations of disabled people act as powerful rhetorical figures that elicit responses or persuade viewers to think or act in certain ways. The wondrous, the sentimental, the exotic, and the realistic converge and inflect one another in individual pictures as well as across all genres of disability photography. These visual rhetorics seldom occur discretely; rather, the photographs blend together in individual photographs. They wax and wane, shift and combine over time as they respond to the purposes for which the photographs are produced. Moreover, these rhetorics constitute part of the context into which all representations of disabled people enter. Not only do these representational modes configure public perception of disability, but all images of disabled people either inadvertently or deliberately summon these visual rhetorics and their accompanying cultural narratives. None of these rhetorical modes operates in the service of actual disabled people, however. Indeed, almost all of them appropriate the disabled body for the purposes of constructing, instructing, or assuring some aspect of a putatively nondisabled viewer.

The first visual rhetoric is the wondrous. The oldest mode of representing disability, the wondrous continues to find a place in modernity's framing of disability. This genre capitalizes on physical differences in order to elicit amazement and admiration. The antecedents of the wondrous disabled figures are the monsters of antiquity, who inspired awe, foretold the future, or bore divine signs, and freaks, who were the celebrities in nineteenth-century dime museums and sideshows (Garland-Thomson, "From Wonder"). The rhetoric of the wondrous springs from a premodern interpretation of disability as either augury or marks of distinction, whether representing good or evil. Oedipus, Teiresias, monsters, giants—even Shakespeare's Richard III—were imposing if ominous disabled figures.

A nineteenth-century example is Charles Tripp, the famous Armless Wonder (Figure 1), pictured eating with his toes in a carte de visite, one of the exceedingly

Figure 1. Surrounded here by the products of his agile feet, the famous nineteenth-century freak show entertainer, Charles Tripp, one of the many "armless wonders," is presented as amazing and yet ordinary. Courtesy of the Robert Bogdan Collection, Syracuse, NY

popular photographic portraits commonly sold to augment and promote live appearances. This carefully choreographed portrait includes samples of his calligraphic skills, paper figures he's cut out, as well as the pen and scissors he used to accomplish such remarkable tasks. The silver tea set in the picture refers to other photos of him drinking from a cup with his toes. The composition is a visual résumé documenting Tripp's supposedly amazing accomplishments. The spectacle tries to elicit awe from the viewers, whose sense of their own clumsy toes makes Tripp's feet feat seem wondrous.

Photography introduced into the rhetoric of wonder the illusion of fusing the ordinary with the extraordinary. This picture invites a relation of identification and differentiation between Tripp and his viewer, making him seem simultaneously strange and familiar. Viewers see a typical man engaged in the quotidian acts of writing, eating, or drinking tea, but—to those with arms—he does this in a most extraordinary manner. Only the single detail of eating with feet rather than hands marks this scene as distinctive. Disability operates visually by juxtaposing the singular (therefore strange) mark of impairment in a surrounding context of the expected (therefore familiar). By telescoping the viewer's eye to the mark of impairment, the picture instructs viewers to stare and coaches them to understand impairment as the exception rather than the rule. Orchestrated and provoked by the photo, staring creates a particular relation between the viewer and the viewed that gives meaning to impairment.

Modernity secularized wonder into the stereotype of the supercrip, who amazes and inspires the viewer by performing feats that the nondisabled viewer cannot imagine doing. Contemporary wonder rhetoric emphasizes admiration rather than amazement, in part because bourgeois respectability now deems it inappropriate to delight in staring at disabled people. One example is a recent ad for adventure tours that features a rock climber using a wheelchair (Figure 2). Here the photographic composition literally positions the viewer as looking up in awe at the climber dangling in her wheelchair. By making the disabled figure exceptional rather than ordinary, the wondrous can estrange viewer from viewed and attenuate the correspondence that equality requires.

Sentimentality has inflected the wonder model, producing the convention of the courageous overcomer, contemporary America's favorite figure of disability. Even though armless calligraphers are no longer an acceptable form of middle-class entertainment, photos of disabled people who have adapted tasks to fit their bodies still ask their viewers to feel a sense of wonder. An advertisement for Habitat for Humanity, for example, pictures a disabled volunteer worker building a house (Figure 3). Like Tripp, this man is portrayed as entirely ordinary except for the detail of the fingerless hands holding the hammer, which occupies the center of interest, at once inviting and authorizing the stare. As is typical in disability photography, the text instructs the viewer how to respond to the picture, with a headline that says, "Extraordinary Volunteer, Unstoppable Spirit." The picture thus combines the narrative of admiration for overcoming disability with the narrative of empowerment characteristic of a post-disability rights movement consciousness. By making disabled subjects masters of ordinary activities such as climbing

Figure 2. This photograph for adventure vacations invokes wonder by inviting the viewer to look up in admiration and awe at the person who can scale rocks while using a wheelchair. Courtesy of Wilderness Inquiry

Figure 3. This photograph of a volunteer worker for Habitat for Humanity, an organization that builds homes for the needy, utilizes the narrative of overcoming to elicit admiration for working despite having a disability. Courtesy of Habitat World

rocks, drinking tea, or using hammers, these photos create a visual context that elicits adulation for their accomplishing what the normalized viewer takes to be a superhuman feat.

The second visual rhetoric is the sentimental. Whereas the wondrous elevates and enlarges, the sentimental diminishes. The sentimental produces the sympathetic victim or helpless sufferer needing protection or succor and invoking pity, inspiration, and frequent contributions. The sentimental disabled figure developed as a part of the larger nineteenth-century bourgeois culture of fine feelings.[4] The pathetic, the impotent, and the suffering confirmed the Victorian bourgeoisie by arousing their finest sentiments. As the increasingly empowered middle class imagined itself capable of capitalizing the world, it began to see itself as responsible for the world as well, a stewardship that launched humanitarian and reform movements to which today's telethons are heir. This discourse of middle-class noblesse oblige operates on a model of paternalism, often trafficking in children and alluding to the cute, the plucky, the long-suffering, and the courageous.

Figure 4. The March of Dimes 1946 poster boy appeals to the rhetoric of sentiment, which often employs pathetic, courageous, or cute children to elicit the viewers' sympathy and money. Courtesy of March of Dimes

The rhetoric of sentiment found an effective home in the photographic conventions of the poster child of mid-twentieth-century charity campaigns. The 1946 March of Dimes poster child (Figure 4) echoes the spunky cuteness of freak figures such as General Tom Thumb. But where Tom Thumb delighted with his miniature adulthood, this poster child breaks hearts as he is propped vulnerably up in a corner of his crib in the before-and-after format. In order to catalyze the adult, to whom the photo addresses itself, this March of Dimes poster presents disability to the middle-class spectator as a problem to solve, an obstacle to eliminate, a challenge to meet. In such appeals, impairment becomes the stigma of suffering, transforming disability into a project that morally enables a nondisabled rescuer. The viewer's dimes, the poster suggests, will literally catapult the unhappy little fellow trapped in braces in his crib into a smiling and spirited tyke, striding with determination and gratitude toward the viewer. Sentimentality makes of disabled people occasions for the viewers' own narratives of progress, improvement, or heroic deliverance and contains disability's threat in the sympathetic, helpless child for whom the viewer is empowered to act. Whereas earlier sentimental literature accentuates suffering to mobilize readers for humanitarian, reform, or religious

161

ends, the poster boy's suffering is only the background to his restoration to normalcy that results from "your dimes." The optimism of cure thus replaces the intensity of sympathy, testifying to an increasing faith in clinical treatment and scientific progress as modernity increasingly medicalizes and rationalizes the body.

The rhetoric of sentiment has migrated from charity to retail in late capitalism's scramble to capture markets. For example, the cover of a 1998 Benetton public relations brochure (Figure 5) distributed in stores employs a chic sentimentality in documenting a school for developmentally disabled children Benetton supports and outfits. This cover girl with both Down syndrome[5] and a stylish Benetton hat fuses sentimental cuteness with high fashion to produce the conviction in the viewer-shopper that Benetton is humanitarian rather than solely commercial. In anticipation of its patron's skepticism, the brochure instructs its viewers that Benetton launched this campaign as social commentary, although people are apt to see it as "cynical advertising." Benetton devotes a whole introductory page to assuring its customers that this brochure is about "the gift of love" (United Colors 3). So while

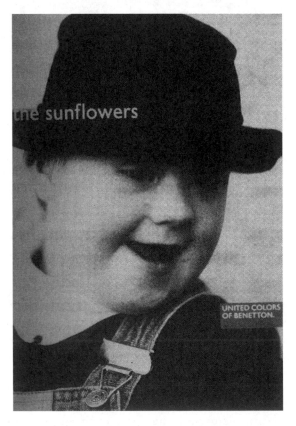

Figure 5. Sentimental cuteness and high fashion come together in this public relations brochure's presentation of a developmentally disabled child in a school supported and outfitted by Benetton clothing stores. Concept: O. Toscani. Courtesy of United Colors of Benetton

commercial fashion marketing demands a certain sophistication and sleekness that precludes the gushy sentiment of the 1940s poster child, Benetton still assures its viewers of their tolerance and allows them to fantasize rescuing this child from the stigma of being disabled by dressing her smartly and supporting her school.

The third visual rhetoric is the exotic. The rhetoric of sentiment domesticates the disability figure, making it familiar and comforting. In contrast, the visual rhetoric of the exotic presents disabled figures as alien, distant, often sensationalized, eroticized, or entertaining in their difference. The exotic reproduces an ethnographic model of viewing characterized by curiosity or uninvolved objectification and informed by the proliferation of popular ethnographic photography that accompanied the era of Western imperialism. For example, nineteenth-century freak photography often transformed disabled people into "wild men" or other exotic "savages," whose impairments were translated into marks of alien ethnicity (Garland-Thomson, "From Wonder" 5). The exotic demedicalizes, fascinates, and seduces with exaggeration, creating a sensationalized, embellished alien.

The introduction of disabled models has exploded the contemporary fashion world in the last several years, returning the rhetoric of the exotic into disability photography. Where the sentimental makes the disabled figure small and vulnerable in order to be rescued by a benevolent agent, the exotic makes the disabled figure large, strange, and unlike the viewer. Ever straining for novelty and capitalizing on titillation, the fashion arm of the advertising world was sure to discover the power of disabled figures to provoke responses from viewers. Advertising has learned that disability sells in two ways. One is by making consumers feel good about buying from a company that is charitable toward the supposedly disadvantaged, which is the Benetton brochure's pitch. The other is to capture the disability market, which is 54 million people and growing fast as the baby boomers age and as their spending power is estimated to reach the trillion-dollar mark in 2000 (J. Williams 29).

The exotic serves this commercial aim by upsetting the earnest, asexual, vulnerable, courageous image of disability that charity rhetoric has so firmly implanted. One image advertising wheelchairs presents a tattooed biker figure brandishing a hockey stick (Figure 6). The image alludes at once to the strong men and tattoo kings of the sideshows and then inflects it with a hyperphallic sexuality, completely rewriting the cultural script of the emasculated invalid and the male who becomes feminized by disability. As is typical with much popular disability photography, the text instructs the viewer on how to read this photo. The exaggeration characteristic of exoticization here marshals ironic hyperbole to mount a brazen, sensational parody, provocatively challenging the viewer by lewdly commanding, "Lick this!" Such representations preclude even a trace of the sentimental or the wondrous, insisting instead on the empowerment of the transgressive, even at the expense of distancing the spectator from the spectacle.

Another venue for disability as the exotic is emerging in the high-fashion market, which is always desperate to keep its edge. These advertisements and magazine features present disabled models in a dual attempt to capture a market and to novelize high fashion by introducing bodies that at once depart from and conform to the exhausted image of the high-fashion body. Alexander McQueen, known in England as the bad boy of fashion design, recently collaborated with other designers and the fashion photographer Nick Knight for a shoot called "Accessible," featuring

Figure 6. The rhetoric of the exotic in this ad for wheelchairs "with an attitude" employs the tattooed biker-jock figure to create a transgressive, hypermasculine image for the wheelchair user. Courtesy of Colours Wheelchairs

eight disabled models. Knight's shots fold the models' impairments into a context of exoticism that extends to the entire frame, as in the shot of Aimee Mullins, the double-amputee celebrity cover girl, rendered as a kind of high-tech bionic mannequin (Figure 7). No attempt is made to disguise her cosmetic prosthetic legs—so she can pass for nondisabled; rather, the entire photo thematically echoes her prostheses and renders the whole image chic. As a gorgeous amputee, Mullins becomes an embodied contradiction. Her prosthetic legs parody, indeed proudly mock, the very idea of the perfect body that has been the mark of fashion until now, even while the rest of her body conforms precisely to fashion's impossible standards. Rather than conceal, normalize, or erase disability, these photos use the hyperbole and stigma traditionally associated with disability to quench postmodernity's perpetual search for the new and arresting image. These transgressive juxtapositions of disability and high fashion, such as the macho chair user and the athletic but legless Mullins, produce a fresh, attention-grabbing brand of exotic radical chic that redefines disabled identity for the disabled consumer.

The fourth visual rhetoric is the realistic. Where the exotic mode cultivates estrangement, realism minimizes distance and difference by establishing a relation of contiguity between viewer and viewed. The wondrous, sentimental, and exotic

Figure 7. The high-fashion layout of the model, sports star, and double amputee Aimee Mullins emphasizes rather than conceals her prosthetic legs, exploiting the exotic mode to make disability seem chic. Courtesy of We Magazine. *Photograph by Nick Knight.*

modes of representation tend to exaggerate the difference of disability to confer exceptionality on the object in the picture. The rhetoric of the realistic, however, trades in verisimilitude, regularizing the disabled figure in order to avoid differentiation and arouse identification, often normalizing and sometimes minimizing the visual mark of disability. Realism domesticates disability. Realist disability photography is the rhetoric of equality, most often turned utilitarian. The use of realism can be commercial or journalistic, and it can also urge the viewer to political or social action.[6]

Realism emerged as a property of portraiture, documentary, and medical photography of the nineteenth century. Documentary photography such as that made famous by Lewis Hine and Jacob Riis aimed photographic realism at the progressive obsession with social reform.[7] Documentary and journalistic photographies differ from charity and commercial photographies in that they do not solicit the exchange of money so directly but rather aim to democratically disseminate information intended to shape the viewers' actions and opinions. Hine and Riis recorded the fabric of the American underclass, exposing the supposed truth of the conditions in which it struggled. Hine photographed wounded workers whose disabil-

Figure 8. Lewis Hine documented wounded workers in 1907–08 by using the rhetoric of realism as a form of social protest against excluding disabled men from the privileges of labor.

ities robbed them of the male privilege and duty of work (Figure 8), and he featured children whose disabilities he felt stole their childhood. The caption below an amputee worker reads, "When a man's hand is mutilated, he keeps it out of sight" (Stange 60). The implied message is that the social mandate to hide disability precludes entry into the workplace. Hine enlists disability in documentary photos ultimately to tell a cautionary tale: disability is a scourge that can and should be avoided in a world that works right. In spite of the political support and social acceptance the picture confers, the photograph nevertheless marks this worker as a person the viewer does not want to be.

A more sensationalized use of realism recently provoked controversy and roused political protests over what constitutes unacceptable looking at women's breasts. The Breast Cancer Fund, a San Francisco-based nonprofit organization dedicated to education about and funding of breast cancer research, mounted a public awareness campaign in January 2000 called Obsessed with Breasts, featuring three posters showing women boldly displaying mastectomy scars. The posters parodied a Victoria's Secret catalog (Figure 9), a *Cosmopolitan* cover, and a Calvin Klein perfume ad, all of which typically parade women's breasts in soft-porn modes that have become an unremarkable staple of commercial magazine advertising. The posters disrupt the visual convention of the female breast as sexualized object for male appropriation and pleasure by replacing the now normative, eroticized breast with the proscribed image of the amputated breast. The powerful visual violation pro-

Figure 9. This controversial 2000 Breast Cancer Fund poster employs the sensationalism often characteristic of realism to protest inadequate breast cancer research and to expose the cultural effacement of mastectomies. Courtesy of the Breast Cancer Fund

duced by exchanging the spectacle of the eroticized breast, which has been desensationalized by its endless circulation, with the medicalized image of the scarred breast, which has been concealed from public view, was so shocking to viewers that many demanded that the images be removed. Of course, the censuring and censoring of images that demand a recognition of the reality of breast cancer ignited a vibrant controversy. The images intensify this forbidden version of the disabled breast by ironically juxtaposing it with the commonplace but virulently sexist eroticization of the breast. The posters thus advance a potent feminist challenge not only to sexism in medical research and the treatment for breast cancer but also to the oppressive representational practices that make erotic spectacles of women's breasts an everyday thing while erasing the fact of the amputation that one woman in eight will have. By mocking the tired sensationalism of pornography, these pictures protest against the refusal of contemporary America to literally and figuratively look at breast cancer.

The visual rhetoric of the ordinary has emerged in a climate of integration and diversity created by the disability rights movement and resulting legislation such as the Americans with Disabilities Act of 1990 (ADA). While the post-ADA era is not without resistance and backlash to the integration of people with disabilities, the social environment is filling with disability in the popular press. Disability not only appears in the sensationalist underbelly of the press, where it always has, but also is tucked with various degrees of conspicuousness into the fabric of common visual culture. Department store and catalog advertising, for instance, has adopted the rhetoric of the ordinary both to appeal to disabled people as a market and to suggest an ethic of inclusion. L. L. Bean promotes a wheelchair backpack in its catalog; Walmart and many other stores feature disabled models and mannequins in everything from frumpy jog suits to evening gowns. Toy lines like Barbie and the upscale American Girl have wheelchair-using dolls. Such routinization of disability imagery not only brings disability as a human experience out of the closet, it also enables people with disabilities—especially those who acquire impairments as adults—to imagine themselves as a part of the ordinary world rather than belonging to a special class of untouchables and unviewables. Images of disability as a familiar, even mundane, experience in the lives of seemingly successful, happy, well-adjusted people can reduce the identifying against oneself that is the overwhelming effect of oppressive and discriminatory attitudes toward people with disabilities.

The most radical reimagining of disability offered by the realist mode is, ironically, the least visually vivid of the images discussed here, perhaps because it is the only mode with no commercial purpose. The genre of disability photography I conclude with is the official portrait, exemplified by the Department of Education's simple photographic portrait of Judith E. Heumann, assistant secretary of education during the Clinton administration (Figure 10). The conventions that govern such pictures strive for the effect of the everyday, inflected with enough dignity and authority to communicate the importance of the position but not enough to separate the official from the constituency. In a democracy, official portraits depict public servants, after all, in no-nonsense black and white, with standard costuming and poses, and flanked unpretentiously by flags. Unlike commercial photographs, these portrayals are neither generalized nor stylized; rather, they are particularized. The photo suggests that here is a real, recognizable person responsible for certain official duties. The radical aspect of this common visual rhetoric is that part of this woman's particularization is the wheelchair that is clearly an aspect of her identity, an integral element of who and what the photograph says she is. The glimpse of her chair is descriptive, as fundamental to her image as the shape of her chin, the cut of her hair, or the tint of her skin. In its ordinariness, the photograph discourages staring without prohibiting it. Indeed, it encourages forms of looking such as glancing, if the viewer is not very interested in the secretary, or perhaps beholding, if the viewer is interested in her. By depicting Secretary Heumann as an ordinary person who has a position of official status in the society, the portrait encourages both viewers who consider themselves disabled and those who consider themselves nondisabled to identify with her. The photograph suggests neither that her accomplishments are superhuman nor that she has triumphantly overcome anything. She thus becomes more familiar than strange. Most important is the picture's message that a woman with a disability can occupy such a position.

Secretary Heumann's picture sits in bold historical opposition to the many now-controversial official photos of President Franklin D. Roosevelt that hide the wheel-

*Figure 10. The contrast between this official portrait of
Assistant Secretary Judith E. Heumann sitting in her
wheelchair and the many photos of FDR that hid the
wheelchair he used daily during his presidency marks the
difference between a pre- and post-civil rights era.
Courtesy of United States Department of Education.*

chair he used daily.[8] Authorized by the cultural changes the civil rights movements
wrought, Heumann's official portrait exemplifies one of several genres in contemporary photography that familiarize disability rather than defamiliarize it. Indeed,
such representations banish the strange and cultivate the ordinary, radically reimagining disability by installing people with disabilities in the realm of human commonality and dismantling the assumption that disability precludes accomplishment.

This taxonomy of four primary visual rhetorics of disability provides a way
to see the way we see disability. These pictures choreograph a social dynamic of
looking, suggesting that disability is not simply a natural state of bodily inferiority and inadequacy. Rather, it is a culturally fabricated narrative of the body, similar to what we understand as the fictions of race and gender. Disability, then, is
a system that produces subjects by differentiating and marking bodies. Furthermore, this comparison of bodies legitimates the distribution of resources, status,
and power in a biased social and architectural environment. As such, disability has
four aspects: first, it is a system for interpreting bodily variations; second, it is a

relation between bodies and their environments; third, it is a set of practices that produce both the able-bodied and the disabled; fourth, it is a way of describing the inherent instability of the embodied self. The category of disability exists as a way to exclude the kinds of bodily forms, functions, impairments, changes, or ambiguities that call into question our cultural fantasy of the body as a neutral, compliant instrument of some transcendent will. Moreover, *disability* is a broad term in which cluster ideological categories as varied as sick, deformed, ugly, old, crazy, maimed, afflicted, abnormal, or debilitated—all of which disadvantage people by devaluing bodies that do not conform to cultural standards. Thus *disability* functions to preserve and validate such privileged designations as beautiful, healthy, normal, fit, competent, intelligent—all of which provide cultural capital to those who can claim such status, who can reside within these subject positions. Thus, the various interactions between bodies and world make disability from the raw material of human variation and precariousness.

All visualizations of disability are mediations that shape the world in which people who have or do not have disabilities inhabit and negotiate together. The point is that all representations have social and political consequences. Understanding how images create or dispel disability as a system of exclusions and prejudices is a move toward the process of dismantling the institutional, attitudinal, legislative, economic, and architectural barriers that keep people with disabilities from full participation in society.

Endnotes

1. For a historical account of the display of disabled people as monsters and freaks, see Altick; Bogdan; Dennett; Garland-Thomson, "From Wonder"; and D. Wilson.

2. For an account of the ocularcentric in Western culture, see Barthes; Crary; Debord; and Jay.

3. I am not including medical or artistic photography here, although both genres inform the visual construction of disability. I am limiting this analysis to popular photography, which I take to be the primary register and shaper of public consciousness. For an analysis of images of insanity, see Gilman.

4. For a discussion of the development of middle-class feeling as a form of distinguishing respectability, see Halttunen; for a discussion of how sentimentality uses disabled figures, see Garland-Thomson, "Crippled Little Girls."

5. The term "Down syndrome" is now preferred over "Down's syndrome" by more politicized parents and guardians looking to mark some distance from the English physician John Langdon Down, who first described the syndrome's characteristic features (i.e., they are challenging his "ownership" of Down syndrome). See, for example, Richards.

6. To use the term *realistic* does not suggest that this visual rhetoric is more truthful, accurate, or real than the other modes discussed here. Real-

ism's function is to create the illusion of reality, not to reproduce or capture reality's elusive and complex substance. Although more subtle perhaps, the rhetoric of realism is just as constructed and convention-bound as the rhetorics of the wondrous, sentimental, or exotic.

7. For further discussion of Hine, see Rosenblum, Rosenblum, and Trachtenberg.

8. For a discussion of Franklin Roosevelt's disability, see H. Gallagher.

Works Cited

Foucault, Michel. *The Birth of the Clinic: An Archaeology of Medical Perception.* Trans. A.M. Sheridan Smith. New York: Vintage, 1975.

Gallagher, Hugh Gregory. *FDR's Splendid Deception.* New York: Dodd, 1985.

Garland-Thomson, Rosemarie. "From Wonder to Error: A Genealogy of Freak Discourse in Modernity." Garland-Thomson, *Freakery* 1–22.

———"Crippled Little Girls and Lame Old Women: Sentimental Spectacles of Sympathy with Rhetorics of Reform in Nineteenth-Century American Women's Writing." *Nineteenth-Century American Women Writers: A Critical Collection,* ed. Karen Kilcup. New York: Blackwell, 1988. 128–45.

Halttunen, Karen. "Humanitarianism and the Pornography of Pain in Anglo-American Culture." *American Historical Review* 100 (1995): 303–34.

Stange, Maren. *Symbols of Ideal Life: Social Documentary Photography in America, 1890–1950.* New York: Cambridge UP, 1989.

Trachtenberg, Alan. *The Incorporation of America: Culture and Society in the Gilded Age.* New York: Hill, 1982.

———*Reading American Photographs: Images as History, Matthew Brady to Walker Evans.* New York: Hill, 1989.

Williams, John M. "And Here's the Pitch: Madison Avenue Discovers the Invisible Consumer." *We Magazine* 3.4 (1999): 28–31.

14

Changing the Face of Poverty

Nonprofits and the Problem of Representation

DIANA GEORGE

Diana George examines the difficulties of adequately documenting poverty, especially for activist purposes. Through a case study of Habitat for Humanity publicity videos, George illustrates the inadequacy of such representations that depict poverty as a radically different from "average" American lives. This scholarly article from the anthology Popular Literacy: Studies in Cultural Practices and Poetics *also suggests possible ways to more accurately capture the complexity of poverty. Diana George works as the Director of Composition Studies at Virginia Tech.*

> *Constructively changing the ways the poor are represented in every aspect of life is one progressive intervention that can challenge everyone to look at the face of poverty and not turn away.*
>
> —*BELL HOOKS, Outlaw Culture.*

ENCLOSED: No Address Labels to Use Up.
No Calendars to Look At.
No Petitions to Sign.

And No Pictures of Starving Children.

Figure 1. Text from the outer envelope of a 1998 Oxfam appeal

s I write this, Thanksgiving is near. I am about to go out and fill a box with nonperishables for the annual St. Vincent De Paul food drive. Christmas lights already outline some porches. Each day my mailbox is stuffed with catalogs and bills and with appeals from the Native American Scholarship Fund, the Salvation Army, WOJB—Voice of the Anishinaabe, the Navaho Health Foundation, the Barbara Kettle Gundlach Shelter Home for Abused Women, Little Brothers Friends of the Elderly, Habitat for Humanity, and more. One *New Yorker* ad for *Children, Inc.* reads, "You don't have to leave your own country to find third-world poverty." Alongside the ad copy, from a black-and-white full-page photo, a young girl in torn and ill-fitting clothes looks directly at the viewer. The copy continues. "Just travel along the hillsides and down through the valleys where the Appalachian coal mines have been shut down. Sad, hungry faces of little children, like Amy's, will haunt you."

The Oxfam promise that I quote above—to use no pictures of starving children—is surely an attempt to avoid the emotional overload of such images as the one *Children, Inc.* offers (Figure 2). Still, those pictures—those representations of poverty—have typically been one way nonprofits have kept the poor before us. In a culture saturated by the image, how else do we convince Americans that—despite the prosperity they see all around them—there is real need out there? The solution for most nonprofits has been to show the despair. To do that they must represent poverty as something that can be seen and easily recognized: fallen down shacks and trashed out public housing, broken windows, dilapidated porches, barefoot kids with stringy hair, emaciated old women and men staring out at the camera with empty eyes. In such images, poverty is dirt and rags and helplessness. In mail, in magazines, and in newspapers, ads echoing these appeals must vie for our time, attention, and dollars with Eddie Bauer, Nordstrom's, the Gap, and others like them whose polished and attractive images fill our days.

In the pages that follow, I offer one way of understanding how the images nonprofits must rely on may, as Stanley Aronowitz has noted about so many public appeals, result in charity but not activism—not in real structural change or an understanding of the systems that remain in place to keep many in poverty even while the culture at large is a prosperous one.[1] I begin with a discussion of what it means to rely on an image to represent an argument about something as complex as poverty and social responsibility—and how nonprofits must convince potential benefactors that they are dealing with the *most* needy, with the "deserving" and not the "undeserving" poor. In the second part of this essay. I examine a particular representation of poverty—publicity videos produced by Habitat for Humanity—in order

Figure 2

to suggest that reliance on stereotypes of poverty can, in fact, work against the aims of the organization producing them. Finally, I look at alternate representations of poverty, especially those offered by the poor themselves and by men and women who work among the poor in this country. If it is possible, as bell hooks suggests above, to constructively change the ways the poor are represented, then such a change must begin with those whose lives are defined by need.

"We Must See Them": The Problems of Representation

Consumer's Union Executive Director Rhoda H. Karpatkin explains her motive for commissioning Eugene Richards's 1985 photo documentary *Below the Line: Living Poor in America* with a workplace anecdote: "In the Consumers Union lunchroom one day, I asked several of my suburban coworkers if they see people who are hungry or homeless. Many do not. Yet we must *see* them before we can care about them. And we must care about them before we are moved to end the intolerable conditions that mark their lives."[2] That motive—to *show* the reality of hard lives in order to move others to act or, at least, react—is an old one.

We might reach back to the paintings of eighteenth-century French moralist Jean-Baptist Grueze, who equated much poverty with moral decay, or to similar representations by Greuze's English contemporary William Hogarth, whose paintings and engravings of English street life linked abject poverty to an unholy and unrepentant lifestyle, one that might lead to the horrors of *Gin Lane,* or the dismal life and ultimate execution of the Idle Apprentice. Or, better yet, we could look to Sir William Beechey's 1793 portrait of the Ford children giving alms to a ragged boy they have encountered in the lane on the edge of their estate.[3] Painted in the manner of Gainsborough, these pretty, delicate upper-class children lean forward to place a coin in the hand of a young beggar—his rags barely covering him, his chest curved inward against hunger and cold.

Paintings, however, are easily understood as interpretations, even fictions—in the case of Grueze and Hogarth, they are eighteenth-century morality tales intended to uplift the monied class at the same time that they reconfirm old prejudices and fears. As industrialization concentrated more poverty and crime in the cities, nineteenth-century journalists and reformers turned to other ways of uncovering the truth and despair of urban poverty, once again, in order to move others to action or at least to sympathy.

Whatever his methods—and they are contested—moving readers to sympathy, if not reform, was certainly a motive for Henry Mayhew when in 1850–1851 he published the first of four volumes of interviews, stories, and firsthand descriptions detailing the lives of London's poor and working poor.[4] In his introduction to the final volume *Those That Will Not Work,* Mayhew writes of beginning with the aim of not simply contributing new facts or with only the hope of making "the solution of the social problem more easy to us, but, setting more plainly before us some of its latent causes, [to] make us look with more pity and less anger on those who want the fortitude to resist their influence."[5] Mayhew reveals with this short statement, and even with the title of this volume, the ambivalence with which even reformers or journalists sympathetic to the plight of the poor approached their subject. "Those that will not work": are they victims to be pitied, or are they simply a drain on resources, a site of criminal behavior, or worse? What Mayhew asks is that his readers, in the least, temper their anger.

At the turn of this century, American novelist and journalist Jack London traveled to England to look again at London street life, to do more than Mayhew and actually *become* one of the London homeless. His accounts, as well, provide almost too vivid moments of the actuality of living in destitution. At one point as London walks beside two men who keep picking things up from the side-walk, he is so taken aback when he understands what they are doing that he pauses in shock and, for his reader, puts his revelation into italics: "*They picked up stray crumbs of bread the size of peas, apple cores so black and dirty one would not take them to be apple cores, and these things these two men took into their mouths, and chewed them, and swallowed them; and this, between six and seven o-clock in the evening of August 20, year of our Lord 1902, in the heart of the greatest, wealthiest, and most powerful empire the world has ever seen.*"[6] For London, in contrast to Mayhew, there was little question of who or what was to blame. Writing in a moment of social realism with such contemporaries as Theodore Dreiser and Frank Norris, whose short stories and novels placed the individual at the mercy of an American capitalist machine out of control, London collects the stories of England's street people, thrown out to hunger and cold when industry has no more use for them: "The unfit and the unneeded! Industry does not clamor for them. There are no jobs going begging through lack of men and women. . . . Women and plenty to spare, are found to toil under the sweat-shop masters for tenpence a day of fourteen hours. Alfred Freeman crawls to muddy death because he loses his job. Ellen Hughes Hun prefers Regent's Canal to Islington Workhouse. Frank Cavilla cuts the throats of his wife and children because he cannot find work enough to give them food and shelter."[7] It is a bleak world made all the more bleak by the assuredness with which London offers his readers little hope.

For reformers, the firsthand account has perennially been the most compelling, for it is through such stark representations that writers and, even more so, photographers challenge their audiences to dare deny the truth before them. Photojournalist Jacob A. Riis's 1890 publication *How the Other Half Lives,* the first thoroughgoing attempt at documenting poverty using photography, certainly marked a turning point for social reform. Using his camera as a way to capture New York tenement life, Riis showed the filth, decay, chaos, and dangerous crowding of which most Americans knew nothing. For Riis, the tenements were "the nurseries of pauperism and crime that fill our jails and police courts; that throw off a scum of forty thousand human wrecks to the island asylums and workhouses year by year; that turned out in the last eight years a round half million beggars to prey upon our charities; that maintain a standing army of ten thousand tramps with all that that implies; because, above all, they touch the family life with deadly moral contagion." Quite bluntly, Riis challenged his readers: "What are you going to do about it?"[8] Riis's photographs are such unflinching documents that they are often credited with forcing housing reform in New York's tenement district.

It was that bluntness, the promise of photography to show what we might not otherwise see, that gave the publisher of Helen Campbell's *Darkness and Daylight: or Lights and Shadows of New York Life* the courage to boast that here we have a volume of uncommon faithfulness to the harsh face of street life in 1892 New

York, brought even more vividly into view by "recent developments in photography [which] have rendered it possible to catch instantaneously all the details of a scene with the utmost fidelity." "It is said," writes this publisher, "that figures do not lie. Neither does the camera. In looking on these pages, the reader is brought face to face with real life as it is in New York; *not* AS IT WAS, but AS IT IS TO-DAY. Exactly as the reader sees these pictures, just so were the scenes presented to the camera's merciless and unfailing eye at the moment when the action depicted took place. Nothing is lacking but the actual *movement* of the persons represented."[9] Despite the publisher's assurance that we have before us what was captured by the untainted lens of the camera, the illustrations for *Darkness and Daylight are,* in fact, engravings made from the photos of Bellevue Hospital photographer O. G. Mason, photojournalist Riis, and others. Still, the claim is crucial to the book's argument that we must be able to *see* the poverty (and depravity) that fills the streets of New York in order to truly understand it and, ultimately, to be moved to end it. The motive is a humanistic one—the belief that seeing is not only believing but understanding as well. Furthermore, such a belief constitutes a faith that, once understood, the problem can—indeed will—be solved.

In depicting the poor, whether in literature, journalism, painting, or photography, representations swing between imaging the impoverished as dangerous, intemperate, low-life street thugs, or as helpless victims. Often, the two representations are somehow set together, as in Mayhew's depiction of those who *will not* work but whose lives must still be looked on with pity. Helen Campbell's volume—while it has much in common with *Riis's How the Other Half Lives* and even takes some of its engravings from those and similar photographs—actually is the story of a Christian temperance mission, suggesting that the true horror of New York Street life begins and ends in the bottle. The pages of this dense book are headed with such running titles as "Human Beasts in Filthy Dens."[10] Of the reformers I mention above, it is only London who rarely strays from the insistence that the impoverished he sees are victims of a larger system. His refrain, "Then the thing happens," is London's way of reminding his readers that the homeless wanderers he spends his days with are only an unfortunate incident away from having been self-supporting working-class or middle-class men and women.

For Hogarth and Grueze, the connection was clear: an immoral life led inevitably to a degraded condition. A return to morality was a return to prosperity and the warmth of hearth and home. Such stories of Penitent Magdalenes and Prodigal Sons might well seem appropriate moralistic tales for eighteenth-century class-conscious English society, and not at all related to what we understand of poverty in the United States today. And yet, the Appalachian child posing for *Children, Inc.* and the unwashed, unshaven, homeless man cautiously leaning into his coffee in a Milwaukee Rescue Mission photo[11] are likely to evoke much the same response as those eighteenth-century images: pity and alms-giving mixed with slight disapproval (Figure 3).

The issue at hand and the difficulty for nonprofits, then, is how to make real the dimensions of poverty and evoke the desire to give or to act without turning benefactors away. The question of seeing remains at the heart of problems of representation. What exactly is it that we see? Here I find Henry Mayhew's words once again useful for understanding what it is we might see. As he introduces

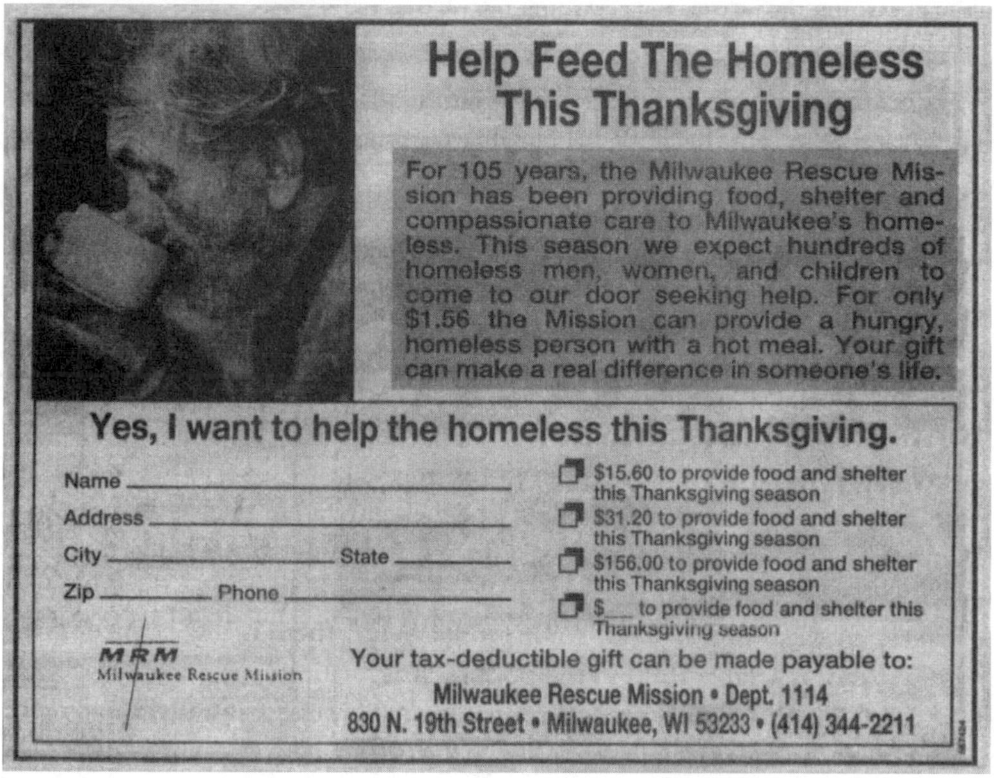

Help Feed The Homeless This Thanksgiving

For 105 years, the Milwaukee Rescue Mission has been providing food, shelter and compassionate care to Milwaukee's homeless. This season we expect hundreds of homeless men, women, and children to come to our door seeking help. For only $1.56 the Mission can provide a hungry, homeless person with a hot meal. Your gift can make a real difference in someone's life.

Yes, I want to help the homeless this Thanksgiving.

Name _____

Address _____

City _____ State _____

Zip _____ Phone _____

□ $15.60 to provide food and shelter this Thanksgiving season
□ $31.20 to provide food and shelter this Thanksgiving season
□ $156.00 to provide food and shelter this Thanksgiving season
□ $___ to provide food and shelter this Thanksgiving season

MRM Milwaukee Rescue Mission

Your tax-deductible gift can be made payable to:

Milwaukee Rescue Mission • Dept. 1114
830 N. 19th Street • Milwaukee, WI 53233 • (414) 344-2211

Figure 3

that final volume devoted to "those that will not work," Mayhew tells his readers,

> *The attainment of the truth, then, will be my primary aim; but by the truth, I wish it to be understood, I mean something more than the bare facts. Facts, according to my ideas, are merely the elements of truths, and not the truths themselves; of all matters there are none so utterly useless by themselves as your mere matters of fact. A fact, so long as it remains an isolated fact, is a dull, dead, uninformed thing; no object nor event by itself can possibly give us any knowledge, we must compare it with some other, even to distinguish it; and it is the distinctive quality thus developed that constitutes the essence of a thing.*[12]

If we think, then, of representation in the way cultural theorist Stuart Hall has explained it—as constitutive of reality or meaning rather than as an attempt to replicate a "fact" already there—easy to see and understand—then Mayhew's remarks must lead us to ask what it is we are representing in the images of poverty most in use by today's nonprofits. What, then, is the essence of this thing poverty as it takes form in the popular imagination?

Certainly this century's most extensive and thoroughgoing attempt to represent poverty in the United States has been the Farm Security Administration's vast photo project documenting the face of rural poverty throughout the Depression and Dust

Bowl years. Following the tradition of earlier documentarists like Riis and Lewis Hine, photographers including Walker Evans, Dorothea Lange, Arthur Rothstein, and others of the FSA created some of the most recognized images we have of America in hardship. These images continue, I would argue, to set the limits for representations of poverty today. Yet, even those images, as historian James Curtis notes in his full-length study of FSA photography, are not mere "facts" recorded with the unflinching eye of the camera lens. The clientele for these images—like the clientele for today's nonprofits—was primarily urban and middle class, and these images, "and entire photographic series," Curtis writes, were manipulated "to conform to the dominant cultural values" of this clientele.[13]

In his analysis of Dorothea Lange's photograph of Florence Thompson, generally known as *Migrant Mother or Migrant Madonna,* Curtis points particularly to the photographic choices Lange made that were "undoubtedly influenced by prevailing cultural biases."[14] The FSA documentary project portrayed the human spirit, the indomitable will of individuals who refused to yield to troubles they could not control, and *Migrant Mother* was certainly that. Florence Thompson, Curtis tells us, was traveling with her husband and seven children in the migrant work camps of California when Lange encountered her, and the choices Lange made in coming to that final shot that is now so recognizable were crucial for the way the image has been read over the years. The series of shots Lange took leading up to the final image indicates, for example, that she made the decision to leave a teenage daughter out, to compose the final group in a classic Madonna and child manner, to eliminate the clutter of the makeshift shelter and more—decisions that, in essence, placed Florence Thompson and her children clearly into the class of *deserving* over undeserving, or shiftless, or any other less acceptable representation that might have been made from the same family. This is an image that America not only accepted but embraced as emblematic of human courage and strength. In fact, this image remains so familiar that in 1998 the United States Postal Service chose it as one of several that would represent the thirties in a run of stamps commemorating each decade of the twentieth century.

In any number of nonprofit appeals, we can see versions of *Migrant Mother,* or of the shacks and bare dirt yards and delicate children in tattered clothing so familiar in Walker Evans's FSA photos. The issue is not that such conditions did not exist then. They did. They do today as well. And yet to rely primarily on these kinds of images while the country, the economy, the conditions, and the dimensions of poverty and need have changed considerably is to limit the ways nonprofits might respond to the need that is there.

Habitat for Humanity: A Case in Point

I have chosen Habitat for Humanity publicity videos for my focus because Habitat is a popular and far-reaching nonprofit with affiliates not only in the United States but throughout the world. Its goal is not a modest one: Habitat for Humanity aims to eliminate poverty housing from the globe. More than that, Habitat puts housing into the hands of the people who will be housed—into the hands of the homeowners and their neighbors. This is not another program aimed at keeping people in what has become known as the poverty or welfare cycle.

To be very clear, then, I am not criticizing the work of Habitat for Humanity. It is an organization that has done an amazing job of addressing what is, as cofounder Millard Fuller tells us again and again, a worldwide problem. What I would draw attention to, however, is how that problem of inadequate housing and its solution are represented, especially in publicity material produced and distributed by the organization, and how those representations can feed into the troubles that Habitat continues to have as it attempts to change the ways Americans think of helping others. What's more, the kinds of visual arguments Habitat and other nonprofits use to advocate for action or change have become increasingly common tools for getting the message to the public, and yet, I would argue, these messages too often fail to overturn cultural commonplaces that represent poverty as an individual problem that can be addressed on an individual basis. Habitat's catch phrase—A Hand Up, Not a Hand-Out—appeals to a nation that believes anyone can achieve economic security with just the right attitude and set of circumstances.

Habitat's basic program has a kind of elegance. Applicants who are chosen as homeowners put in sweat equity hours to build their home and to help build the homes of others chosen by Habitat. The organization then sells the home to the applicant at cost (that cost held down through Habitat's ability to provide volunteer labor and donated materials) and charges a small monthly mortgage that includes no interest. Unlike public assistance, which is raised or lowered depending on the recipient's circumstances, most Habitat affiliates do not raise mortgage payments when homeowners get better jobs or find themselves in better financial shape. And once the house is paid for, it belongs to the home-owner.

Obviously, in order to run a program like this one, Habitat must produce publicity appeals aimed at convincing potential donors to give time, money, and material. Print ads, public service television and radio spots, commercial appeals linked to products like Maxwell House coffee, and publicity videos meant to be played for churches, volunteer organizations, and even in-flight video appeals on certain airlines are common media for Habitat.

Habitat publicity videos are typically configured as problem-solution arguments. The problem is that too many people have inadequate shelter. The solution is community involvement in a program like Habitat for Humanity. The most common setup for these productions is an opening sequence of images—a visual montage—in which we see black-and-white shots of rural shacks, of men and women clearly in despair, and of thin children in ragged clothing. The voice-over narrative of one such montage tells us the story:

> *Poverty condemns millions of people throughout the world to live in deplorable and inhuman conditions. These people are trapped in a cycle of poverty, living in places offering little protection from the rain, wind, and cold. Terrible sanitary conditions make each day a battle with disease and death. And, for this, they often pay over half their income in rent because, for the poor, there are no other choices. Daily, these families are denied a most basic human need: a decent place to live. The reasons for this worldwide tragedy are many. They vary from city to city, country to country, but the result is painfully the same whether the families are in New York or New Delhi.*[15]

181

It is a compelling dilemma.

Organizations like Habitat for Humanity, in order to convey the seriousness of this struggle and, of course, to raise funds and volunteer support for their efforts in addressing it, must produce all sorts of publicity. And in that publicity they must tell us quickly what the problem is and what we can do to help. To do that, Habitat gives us a visual representation of poverty, a representation that mirrors the most common understandings of poverty in America.

Now, there is nothing inherently wrong with that representation unless, of course, what you want to do (as Habitat does) is convince the American people to believe in the radical idea that those who have must care for the needs of others, not just by writing a check, but by enabling an entirely different life-style. For Americans, it is truly radical to think that our poorer neighbors might actually be allowed to buy a home at no interest and with the donated time and materials of others. It is a radical notion that such a program means that these neighbors then own that house and aren't obliged to do more than keep up with payments in order to continue owning it. And it is a radical idea that Habitat does this work not only in our neighborhoods (not isolated in low-income housing developments) but throughout the world. Habitat International truly believes that we are all responsible for partnering with our neighbors throughout the world so that everyone might eventually have, at least, a simple decent place to live. Like the philosophy behind many nonprofits, Habitat's is not a mainstream notion.

Still, that representation of poverty—clinging as it does to commonplaces drawn from FSA photographs in this century, from Jacob Riis's nineteenth-century photos of urban poverty, and from documentaries of Third World hunger—has serious limitations, which must be obvious to those who remember the moment that the Bush administration confidently announced that, after looking everywhere, they had discovered no real hunger in the United States. And that myth that poverty cannot/does not actually exist in the heart of capitalism has once again been reinforced in the 1998 Heritage Foundation report in which Robert Rector echoed the perennial argument that there is little true poverty in this country ("Myth").[16] Heritage Foundation's finding comes despite figures from the National Coalition for the Homeless ("Myths and Facts About Homelessness"), which tell us that in 1997 nearly one in five homeless people in twenty-nine cities across the United States was employed in a full- or part-time job.[17]

In her call for a changed representation of poverty in America, bell hooks argues that in this culture poverty "is seen as synonymous with depravity, lack and worthlessness." She continues, "I talked with young black women receiving state aid, who have not worked in years, about the issue of representation. They all agree that they do not want to be identified as poor. In their apartments they have the material possessions that indicate success (a VCR, a color television), even if it means that they do without necessities and plunge into debt to buy these items."[18] Hers is hardly a noble image of poverty, but it is a true one and one that complicates the job of an organization like Habitat that must identify "worthy" applicants. This phenomenon of poverty in the center of wealth, in a country with its national mythology of hearty individuals facing the hardness of the Depression with dignity and pride, is certainly a part of what Manning Marable challenges when he asks readers not to judge poverty in the United States by the standards of other countries. Writing of poverty among black Americans, Marable reminds us that "the process of impoverishment is profoundly national and regional."[19] It does little good to compare the impoverished of this country with Third World poverty or, for that matter, with Depression Era poverty.

The solution in these Habitat videos is just as visible and compelling a representation as is the problem. The solution, it seems, is a modern-day barn raising. In clip after clip, Habitat volunteers are shown lined up to raise walls, to hammer nails, to cut boards, to offer each other the "hand up not a hand out," as these publicity messages tell us again and again. Like the barn- raising scene from Peter Weir's *Witness,* framed walls come together against blue skies. People who would normally live in very different worlds come together to help a neighbor. It is all finished in record time: a week, even a day. Volunteers can come together quickly. Do something. Get out just as quickly.

The real trouble with Habitat's representation, then, is twofold: it tells us that the signs of poverty are visible and easily recognized. And it suggests that one of the most serious results of poverty (inadequate shelter) can be addressed quickly with volunteer efforts to bring individuals up and out of the poverty cycle.

Of course, if Habitat works, what could be wrong with the representation? It is an organization so popular that it receives support from diametrically opposed camps. Newt Gingrich and Jesse Jackson have both pounded nails and raised funds for Habitat. This is what Millard Fuller calls the "theology of the hammer." People might not agree on political parties and they might not agree on how to worship or even what to worship, Fuller says, but they can all agree on a hammer. All can come together to build houses. Or, can they?

As successful as Habitat has been, it is an organization that continues to struggle with such issues as who to choose for housing, how to support potential homeowners, and how to convince affiliates in the United States to tithe a portion of their funds to the real effort of Habitat: eliminating poverty housing throughout the world, not just in the United States. And, even in the United States, affiliates often have trouble identifying "deserving" applicants or convincing local residents to allow Habitat homes to be built in their neighborhoods. There are certainly many cultural and political reasons for these problems, but I would suggest that the way poverty continues to be represented in this country and on tapes like those videos limits our understanding of what poverty is and how we might address it.

That limitation holds true for those caught in poverty as well as those wanting to help. What if, as a potential Habitat applicant, you don't recognize yourself or you refuse to recognize yourself in those representations? As Stanley Aronowitz points out in *The Politics of Identity,* that can happen very easily as class identities, in particular, have become much more difficult to pin down since World War II, especially with an expansion of consumer credit that allowed class and social status to be linked to consumption rather than to professions or even wages. In his discussion of how electronic media construct the *social imaginary,* Aronowitz talks of the working class with few media representations available to them as having fallen into a kind of "cultural homelessness."[20] How much more true is that of the impoverished in this country who may be neither homeless nor ragged, but are certainly struggling every day to feed their families, pay rent, and find jobs that pay more than what it costs for daycare?

I have been particularly interested in this last question because of a difficulty I mentioned earlier, that of identifying appropriate applicants for Habitat homes or even getting some of the most needy families of a given affiliate to apply for Habitat homes. When I showed the video *Building New Lives* to Kim Puuri, a Copper Country Habitat for Humanity homeowner and now member of the affiliate's Homeowner Selection Committee, and asked her to respond, she was very clear in what she saw as the problem:

> *When I see those pictures I usually think of Africa or a third world country and NOT the U.S. It's not that they can't be found here, it's just that you don't publicly see people that bad off other than street people. If they could gear the publicity more to the geographical areas, it may make more of an impact or get a better response from people. It would mean making several videos. It may not be so much of a stereotype, but an association between Habitat and the people they help. People viewing the videos and pictures see the conditions of the people and feel that their own condition may not be that bad and feel they probably wouldn't qualify.*[21]

What this Habitat homeowner has noticed is very close to what Hall describes. That is, the problem with this image, this representation, is not that it is not real enough. The problem has nothing to do with whether or not these are images of poverty as it exists in the world. There is no doubt that this level of poverty does exist in this country and elsewhere despite the Heritage Foundation's attempts to demonstrate otherwise. The problem is that this representation of poverty is a narrow one and functions to narrow the ways we might respond to the poor who do not fit this representation.

The representation I have been discussing is one that insists on constructing poverty as an individual problem that can be dealt with by volunteers on an individual basis. That is the sort of representation common in this country, the sort of representation Paul Wellstone objects to in a recent call to action when he says "We can offer no single description of American poverty." What it takes to break through such a representation is first, as Stuart Hall suggests, to understand it as a representation, to understand it as a way of imparting meaning. And the only way to contest that representation, to allow for other meanings, other descriptions, is to know more about the many dimensions of poverty in America. "More than 35 million Americans—one out of every seven of our fellow citizens—are officially poor. More than one in five American children are poor. And the poor are getting poorer," Wellstone writes.[22] But we can be certain that much of that poverty is not the sort pictured in those black-and-white images. And if it doesn't *look* like poverty, then how do we address it? How do we identify those "deserving" our help?

Indeed, as Herbert Gans has suggested, the labels we have chosen to place on the poor in this country often reveal more than anything "an ideology of undeservingness," by which we have often elided poverty and immorality or laziness or criminality. "By making scapegoats of the poor for fundamental problems they have not caused nor can change," Gans argues, "Americans can also postpone politically difficult and divisive solutions to the country's economic ills and the need to prepare the economy and polity for the challenges of the twenty-first century."[23] These are tough issues to confront and certainly to argue in a twenty-minute video presentation aimed at raising funds and volunteer support, especially when every piece of publicity must make a complex argument visible.

On the Way to Changing the Face of Poverty

Reflecting on more than thirty years of working among the poor, Dorothy Day once wrote, "Poverty is a strange and elusive thing. . . . We need always to be thinking and writing about it, for if we are not among its victims its reality fades from us."[24] Of course, that impulse—to keep the poor before us—is precisely what has led to the many firsthand accounts and documentary photographs and sociological studies and publicity videos like those I have mentioned above. But Day, who devoted her entire life to working with the poor, continues on in a passage quoted here at length for its directness and clear-headed understanding of what it means now, and has meant in the past, to be truly in need:

> So many good souls who visit us tell us how they were brought up in poverty, but how, through hard work and cooperation, their parents managed to educate all the children—even raise up priests and nuns for the Church. They content that healthful habits and a stable family situation enable people to escape from the poverty class, no matter how mean the slum they may once have been forced to live in. The argument runs, so why can't everybody do it? No, these people don't know about the poor. Their concept of poverty is of something as near and well ordered as a nun's cell.
>
> Poverty has many faces. People can, for example, be poor in space alone. . . . Then there are those who live under outwardly decent economic circumstances but are forever on the fearful brink of financial disaster. . . . No matter how high wages go, a sudden illness and an accumulation of doctor and hospital bills, for example, may mean a sudden plunge into destitution.[25]

What Day tells us here recalls Jack London's warning: "Then the thing happens." It is a reminder that the poor are not only always among us, but at any time might *be* us. At any time so many Americans living on the very edge of financial health might be plunged into destitution.

I suspect some readers wonder why I continue to emphasize the very ordinary nature of those who live in poverty and why I not only consider it so important that nonprofits work to break older stereotypes, but that recipients of those nonprofit appeals learn to read the images of poverty with the knowledge that they are stereotypes and do limit our understanding of need. More than one of the many colleagues and friends I have besieged with my talk of poverty and nonprofit appeals has asked an important question: If nonprofits don't use images that show hunger and need, then how are they to get across the urgency of their message? How do they raise money or awareness? It is a question I have not always answered well or completely. I do believe, however, that an answer might lie in two areas: first, in a knowledge of the actual consequences of relying on those stereotypes to carry a message of need; and second, in an understanding of what we have sometimes called the "visual imperative" of the electronic media.

Once again, as long as people give to nonprofits to support poverty programs, what does the image matter? Does "the vocabulary of poverty," as Michael B. Katz claims, really impoverish the political imagination?[26] I offer one very quick example of how that vocabulary, that stereotype, does indeed impoverish the political imagination. Early in 1999, the Michigan legislature put on fast-track Governor John Engler's most recent plan to cut back the assistance rolls in his state. Engler proposed drug testing for all welfare recipients. Those tested positive would be sent to rehabilitation programs. If they fail to attend those programs or if they are found to continue drug use, they will be dropped from welfare rolls. Despite federal studies that indicate that only about 5 percent of welfare recipients are serious drug and alcohol abusers ("Welfare Drug Test"),[27] this legislation feeds into the notion that if someone is on assistance, there must be something wrong with that person, something that once fixed will make each individual a contributing, self-supporting member of the community.

Democrats' proposed amendments to the Engler bill weren't much better. Amendments asked that only those applicants who have not found a job after participating in Michigan's Work First program be screened "for potential drug and alcohol abuse, learning disabilities, illiteracy, domestic violence, actual or imminent homelessness and mental illness."[28] Clearly, the operative notion here is that only the most deviant, disabled, or disinclined to learn make up the ranks of those who cannot find work.

Although many would argue that such legislation is unconstitutional, it was no idle threat. By July 1999, the legislature has passed Engler's bill and drug testing had begun. Readers might well recall that John Engler's name came to national prominence during his first term in office when he began what has continued to be a deep slashing of public assistance and welfare rolls. His back-to-work or workfare programs have caught on throughout this country, and Engler has been heralded as a governor who takes people off welfare and puts them back into the workplace.

Barbara Ehrenreich's most recent experiment in which she became—Jack London-like—a low-wage employee, not to find out "how the other half lives" but to test out policies like Engler's that claim that "work will lift poor women out of poverty while simultaneously inflating their self-esteem and hence their future value in the labor market," vividly illustrates how impoverished this particular political imaginary actually is. Not only do most jobs held by low-wage employees offer no security and few or no benefits; they are simply not jobs that will provide a living wage. Ehrenreich explains, "According to the National Coalition for the Homeless, for example, in 1998 it took, on average nationwide, an hourly wage of $8.89 to afford a one-bedroom apartment, and the Preamble Center for Public Policy estimates that the odds against a typical welfare recipient's landing a job at such a 'living wage' are about 97 to 1."[29] These are not good odds, and they point again to the reality Dorothy Day wrote of so many years ago: it is important to help individuals, and individuals can certainly raise themselves up out of poverty, but helping the individual without addressing larger structural problems will do little more than help the individual.

The second concern I point to—understanding the role of the media in communicating need—may be even more crucial in changing the face of poverty, for it points directly to how the media work within certain "givens." Speaking on the difficulties of getting United States news media to carry the 1983 story of the

Ethiopian famine, communication scholar Brian Winston addresses one of those givens—what he calls the media myth of being in the "grip of the visual imperative."[30] Winston argues that, if we closely analyze the news media, we will discover that it is only such stories as Third World hunger that are caught in the grip of this visual imperative. Many other kinds of stories get long play with stock—even dull—footage. He names political election stories or stories of economics for which the media will find a number of images that we could not call compelling—the President getting off a plane, for example, or oil wells in a Kansas field. According to Winston, if we were instead to tell the story of hunger as a real story of problems of wealth and distribution and the like, then there would be all kinds of images that would work: wheat fields, graphs, ships moving grain, and more. Instead, however, the story of hunger and poverty exists on the level of crisis reportage so that, according to Winston, this kind of story is *located* in the image.

"Famine," Winston argues, "is a biblical word. We don't have famines in the West. Famines can only come into our collective consciousness . . . if it's in biblical terms." As if to reinforce Winston's point, Michael Buerke, whose BBC report did finally break the Ethiopian famine story in 1984, says much the same: "The curious thing—it came out in the first film we did—is that biblical business. People looked like those depicted in the color illustrations in my old school Bible. Sort of sackcloth color and a certain nobility of features."[31] Winston is much harsher in his assessment. He calls many of these images "masturbatory" images of hunger—a pornography of starvation.

If not those images, then what? Well, I would return to Habitat home-owner Kim Puuri's suggestion that Habitat might have to start making different videos or publicity pieces for different areas/different audiences. In that suggestion, Puuri is actually calling our attention to the most serious problem of such broad representations: they depict poverty as a crisis that we can recognize and address now with just a call, a contribution, a few hours of our time. In addition, these images depict poverty as something that happens to others, people outside the ordinary. As the Michigan legislation suggests, these people are addicts, illiterates and, worse yet, potentially *violent* addicts and illiterates.

Since I have focused many of my comments on Habitat for Humanity publicity, I feel compelled to turn first to Habitat for alternate representations of the people who apply for and get Habitat homes. My own local affiliate published the following fund-raising Christmas card for the 1997 Christmas season (Figure 4). The images of these families are remarkable only for the fact that they are our neighbors. This area, known as the Copper Country, is small enough that families receiving this appeal would recognize some or all of the families pictured on the card. They would have worked with them; many would even be related to them. They are people we know whose financial circumstances are not unlike that of many of their neighbors. What Copper Country Habitat is doing with a card like this one is, in some ways, risky. It is, after all, much easier to imagine need that is far away and desperate in ways that can be seen. Instead this affiliate is counting on the community to know that need looks a lot like the every day. It looks a lot like the people they live with and work with. In fact, it is the people they live and work with.

Other local affiliates do much the same. I have been especially impressed by the work of Chicago's Uptown affiliate. Uptown renovates old apartment houses and

We send thanks—
and thoughts & prayers
for a fine Holiday
and a Good Year—
to your family
from all of ours…

the Kangas family   the Deforge-Harma family

Figure 4

turns them into condos. In forming its homeowner's association, Uptown Habitat homeowners have written their own newsletters, written rules for the condo group, advocated for police attention to the crime outside their doorways, and more. The newsletter *HabiChat* published by Uptown Habitat looks much like many of the newsletters of neighborhood associations throughout suburban America. It includes announcements for Spring Clean-up, marriage and birth announcements, resources for parenting troubles, and more. Such newsletters, sent out as they are to the entire affiliate and not kept isolated within the homeowners association, work to remind Habitat volunteers and donors that Habitat's best work is fundamental to the lives of ordinary people working at one or more low-wage jobs and just trying to get by in safe, inexpensive, decent housing.

Of course, that is Habitat. Despite its goal to eliminate poverty housing on the globe, Habitat can rarely address the needs of the most impoverished. After all, a Habitat homeowner must come up with even a little money for a mortgage, and there are millions of Americans who cannot do that. What of those others? What about that man in the Milwaukee Rescue Mission ad I mentioned earlier? This is clearly a man with little enough to eat much less the resources for a house payment or even the energy for "sweat equity." Perhaps he is a part of those "undeserving" poor, the drunks and addicts Engler would like to push off Michigan's assistance rolls.

Again, I would call attention to how the homeless depict themselves. I offer one last, true story: Outside the San Francisco Hilton just after Christmas a year ago, I bought my third copy of *Streetwise: A Publication of the Coalition on Homelessness San Francisco*. It is not unlike papers sold by homeless men and women in several cities throughout this country. As I tucked the paper into my books, a short, well-dressed woman waiting for a cab turned to ask me if someone was handing out free things. "No. It's a paper. It costs a dollar." In anger, she came closer to me and yelled, "You *paid money* for that trash?"

Stunned both by the suddenness and the volume of her anger, I neglected to ask if she'd read the article on prisons and shelters signed by "Art B, One Homeless Guy, one of the 14,000 in San Francisco living in a shelter or under the freeways." It was pretty good, I wanted to tell her, but she was already off in her cab.

In these street papers, written as this one is by "the homeless and formerly homeless," we are presented with yet another image of desperate poverty. Perhaps because the homeless themselves write articles seeking to uncover the very structures that keep homelessness and poverty alive and well in our cities, some potential readers are driven to the kind of anger I witnessed. More likely, it is that the very sight of a homeless person, so very obviously in need of food, shelter, a recovery program, or more, is enough to frighten away the lady in the cab.

In Tucson during the past year, the City Council threatened to clear the medians of homeless people selling papers. The Council claimed these men and women represented a safety threat. In response Casa Maria, Tucson's Catholic Worker House, distributed a flyer calling for action to block the Council order. In it, Casa Maria accused the Council of acting on the basis of "aesthetics" rather than from any real concern over safety and pointed to the fact that many of the people who sell those papers have actually been able to pay rent and provide themselves with basic necessities just by being allowed to stand on those medians and sell newspapers.

Brian Flagg, a worker from Casa Maria, wrote recently "We won this one! It was cool—We filled their meeting with church people & uppity tramps!"[32]

It might indeed take uppity tramps, local newsletters, and committed activists like Brian to change constructively the ways the poor are represented, as bell hooks asks that we do. As well, however, it will take a clear understanding of need in its many forms, and for this the image of Amy standing in a deserted mining town and looking out from a black-and-white photo does not altogether tell *New Yorker* readers what they need to know.

Endnotes

1. Stanley Aronowitz, interview in the video production *Consumer Hunger: Part III Selling the Feeling* (Maryknoll, N.Y.: Maryknoll World Productions, 1988).

2. Eugene Richards, *Below the Line: Living Poor in America* (Mount Vernon, N.Y.: Consumers Union, 1987), 215.

3. Richard Leppert, *Art and the Committed Eye: The Cultural Functions of Imagery* (Boulder, Co.: Westview Press, 1996), 173–76.

4. Henry Mayhew, *London Labour and the London Poor* (New York: Penguin Books, 1985).

5. Ibid., 447.

6. Jack London, *The People of the Abyss,* facs. edn. (New York: Garrett P, MSS Information Corp., 1970), 78.

7. Ibid., 287–88.

8. Jacob A. Riis, *How the Other Half Lives: Studies among the Tenements of New York* (New York: Dover, 1971), 2.

9. Helen Campbell, *Darkness and Daylight; or Lights and Shadows of New York Life: A Woman's Story of Gospel, Temperance, Mission, and Rescue Work "In His Name"* (Hartford, Conn.: A. D. Worthington, 1892), viii–ix, x–xi (emphasis in the original).

10. Ibid., 99.

11. "Help Feed the Homeless This Thanksgiving," *Milwaukee Rescue Mission* ad appeal, *Milwaukee Journal Sentinel* (Saturday, 14 Nov. 1998), 8A. To be fair to the Milwaukee Rescue Mission, this photograph has been replaced in more recent ads by photos of mothers with children and other single homeless men. In a telephone interview, Pastor Patrick Vanderburgh, Executive Director of Milwaukee Rescue Mission, indicated that the mission has wrestled with the problem of how best to represent the need that is out there. Since this is a fundraising ad, the representation must move the public to charity, but according to Pastor Vanderburgh, even photos of mothers with children have not been nearly as successful in raising funds as this photo of a homeless man who very obviously fits the public's common idea of a street person.

12. Mayhew, *London Labour,* 448.

13. James Curtis, *Mind's Eye: Mind's Truth: FSA Photography Reconsidered* (Philadelphia: Temple University Press, 1989), viii–ix.

14. Ibid., 52.

15. *Building New Lives* (Americus, Ga.: Habitat for Humanity International). This and other Habitat videos are directed primarily at potential volunteers for the organization or might be used to inform local residents about the work of Habitat.

16. Robert Rector, "The Myth of Widespread American Poverty," *The Heritage Foundation Backgrounder* (18 Sept. 1998), no. 1221. This publication is available on-line at <http://www.heritage.org/library/backgrounder/bg1221es.html>.

17. Cited in Barbara Ehrenreich, "Nickel and Dimed: On (Not) Getting by in America," *Harper's* (January 1999), 44. See also Christina Coburn Herman's *Poverty Amid Plenty: The Unfinished Business of Welfare Reform* NETWORK, A National Social Justice Lobby (Washington, D.C., 1999), from NETWORK's National Welfare Reform Watch Project, which reports that most studies of welfare use telephone surveys even though a substantial percentage of those needing aid do not have phone service (41 percent in the NETWORK survey had no operative phone) and, therefore, are not represented in most welfare reform reports. This report is available on-line at <http://www.network-lobby.org>.

18. bell hooks, "Seeing and Making Culture: Representing the Poor," *Outlaw Culture: Resisting Representations* (New York: 1994), 169.

19. Manning Marable, *How Capitalism Underdeveloped Black America* (Boston: South End Press, 1983), 54.

20. Stanley Aronowitz, *The Politics of Identity: Class, Culture, Social Movements* (New York: Routledge, 1992), 201.

21. Kim Puuri, personal correspondence with author.

22. Paul Wellstone, "If Poverty Is the Question," *Nation* (14 April 1997), 15.

23. Herbert J. Gans, *The War Against the Poor* (New York: Basic Books, 1995), 6–7.

24. Dorothy Day, *Loaves and Fishes: The Inspiring Story of the Catholic Worker Movement* (Maryknoll, N.Y.: Orbis Books, 1997), 71.

25. Ibid., 71–72.

26. Michael B. Katz, *The Undeserving Poor: From the War on Poverty to the War on Welfare* (New York: Pantheon Books, 1989), 3.

27. "Welfare Drug Test Bill on Fast Track," *Detroit News* (4 Feb. 1999) <http://www.detnews.com>Metro/State edition.

28. Ibid.

29. Ehrenreich, "On (Not) Getting By," 38.

30. Interviewed in the video production *Consuming Hunger: Part I—Getting the Story* (Maryknoll, N.Y.: Maryknoll World Productions, 1988). These comments and the discussion that follows are drawn from the three-part video *Consuming Hunger* about media representations first of the famine crisis in Ethiopia and then of media representations of hunger in America culminating in the 1986 media event *Hands Across America*. At the time of this taping, Brian Winston was serving as Dean of Penn State's School of Communication.

31. *Consuming Hunger.*

32. Brian Flagg, personal correspondence with author.

15

Attacks on the Homeless Rise, With Youths Mostly to Blame

AMY GREEN

This New York Times *article from 2008 reports on the disturbing increase of assaults against homeless individuals by young people and teenagers, proposed causes for this phenomenon, and attempts by educators, activists, and lawyers to respond to the situation. Despite its brevity, this article demonstrates the complexity that arises when an author draws on multiple sources and perspectives to make sense of a surprising event or trend.*

CROSS CITY, Fla.—Warren Messner was 15 when he and some friends attacked a homeless man and left him for dead. Mr. Messner jumped on a log laid across the man's ribs. He does not know why. He was high, does not remember much and wants to forget the rest.

Today Mr. Messner is a baby-faced 18-year-old serving 22 years for second-degree murder. He used to like skipping school and listening to rap music with friends. He imagined he eventually would help his father install flooring. Now he talks to his parents nearly every night from the maximum-security Cross City Correctional Institution.

"It was just a senseless crime." he said, his eyes down, his shoulders slumped. "I wish it would have never happened. It made no sense. It was stupidity."

Mr. Messner's story is not unusual. Nationwide, violence against the homeless is soaring, and overwhelmingly the attackers are teenagers and young adults. In Florida the problem is so severe that the National Coalition for the Homeless is setting up speakers bureaus to address a culture that sees attacking the homeless as a sport. It is the first time the organization has singled out a particular state.

Of more than 142 unprovoked attacks on homeless people in 2007, the most—at least 32—were in Florida, according to a preliminary count by the coalition and the National Law Center on Homelessness and Poverty. Nationwide, such attacks rose about 65 percent from 2005.

In Fort Lauderdale a group of teenagers captured national attention in 2006 when a surveillance camera caught one laughing as he beat a homeless man with a baseball bat. The teenagers attacked three homeless men that night and face a murder trial in one man's death. A year later in Daytona Beach, a 17-year-old and two 10-year-olds attacked a homeless Army veteran. One 10-year-old dropped a cement block on the man's face, the police said.

"What could possibly be in the mind of a 10- or 12-year-old that would possess them to pick up a rock and pick up a brick and beat another human being in the head?" said Ron Book, chairman of the Miami-Dade County Homeless Trust. "It defies any rational thought process, but it's also why we felt so strongly we had to do something."

The trust has teamed with the local schools to develop a curriculum for elementary, middle and high schools teaching respect for the homeless.

Advocates for the homeless blame a society that they say shuns the homeless through laws that criminalize sleeping in parks, camping and begging.

"I think it reflects a lack of respect for the homeless that has reached such extreme proportions that homeless people aren't viewed as people," said Maria Foscarinis, executive director of the National Law Center on Homelessness and Poverty.

Troubled by news photos showing those two 10-year-olds in Daytona Beach in prison suits and handcuffs, the National Coalition for the Homeless joined with AmeriCorps Vista to open speakers bureaus last fall in Key West, Jacksonville and Tallahassee. Nine more are planned in Florida. The idea is to educate students using speakers who are homeless or once lived on the streets, and the organization wants to open more bureaus nationwide, said Michael Stoops, executive director of the coalition.

"It was just a senseless crime," Mr. Mesaner, right, said of the fatal benting of Michael Roberts. Advocates for the homeless have taken note of a rise in such attacks, particularly in Florida.

The speakers are like George Siletti, who grew up in foster care and lived as a homeless drifter on and off for 25 years, starting at the age of 16. Now 51, Mr. Siletti said he took medication for schizophrenia and depression and lived in subsidized housing in Washington, addressing schools, churches and organizations about homelessness.

"I've had bottles thrown at me. I've had people spit on me, cursed me out for no reason," said Mr. Siletti, who was attacked by teenagers in Fort Lauderdale as he and others slept under a bridge in the 1980s. "People seem to pick on the most vulnerable because they really think that they won't do nothing."

In Miami, students are learning from a weeklong curriculum and a DVD teaching that families are the fastest-growing segment of the homeless population. The curriculum requires younger students to make posters and older students to write essays about what they learned.

Legislation adding the homeless to hate-crime laws has been introduced in Alaska, California, Florida, Maryland, Massachusetts, Nevada, Ohio and Texas. Bills are also pending in Congress.

Mr. Messner, who is an imposing six feet, 240 pounds in his blue prison suit, talks about his crime with quiet resignation.

He and his friends were looking for a place to smoke marijuana near his home in the Daytona Beach area when they stumbled on Michael Roberts. Mr. Messner joined the attack and remembers hearing Mr. Roberts groan when he jumped on the log, but then Mr. Messner tried to pull his friends away, he said.

"He was making noises," Mr. Messner said. "He asked one time why we was doing it to him. Why we was messing with him."

A few days later, Mr. Roberts's body was found. Mr. Messner agreed to a plea bargain and drew the lightest sentence of the four convicted in the attack.

He does not like prison much. He keeps busy doing yard work, exercising and reading. He likes James Patterson novels and murder mysteries. He has dropped at least 40 pounds and developed a penchant for prison tattoos. One arm reads "thug" while the other reads "life." His mother's name, Lori, is on one hand. On one arm is the same cross he wears around his neck, surrounded by the words "hope," "faith" and "love."

"I'm not a killer. I know that," Mr. Messner said. "A lot of people, they see this story and call us killers. I'm not a killer. I regret what I did. I wish I could take it back."

16

Priorities

JOSE MARCIAL GUERRERO

Jose Guerrero's poem, "Priorities," appeared in Xispas, *an online journal of Chicano Culture, Art, and Politics in March 2005. The poem gives voice to the historical and cultural tensions that characterize US-Mexico border culture and border lives.*

On the April side of the year
We returned to the north
Embracing the fifth series
Of dislocated souls

We belong to the corporation
And one more year shall
Bring legal sponsorship
So HE tells us . . .

But my brother and I
Only dream of our little village
And the faces in Oaxaca
Shining with contented sweat
And their hands full of seed

We pray that walmart
And the government won't
Rob anymore land from us
Our people and our ancestors
Cry with cold hunger
And the land begs like a little
Bird still in the nest

17

A Story About the Body

ROBERT HASS

In "A Story About the Body" former U.S. Poet Laureate Robert Hass tells the story of a young man who whose romantic attraction to a much older painter wanes when he learns of her double-mastectomy. This piece comes from Human Wishes, *the third poetry collection by Haas. Hass invites careful reflection on how desires of all kinds—not just romantic—originate, circulate, and change.*

The young composer, working that summer at an artist's colony, had watched her for a week. She was Japanese, a painter, almost sixty, and he thought he was in love with her. He loved her work, and her work was like the way she moved her body, used her hands, looked at him directly when she made amused or considered answers to his questions. One night, walking back from a concert, they came to her door and she turned to him and said, "I think you would like to have me. I would like that too, but I must tell you I have had a double mastectomy," and when he didn't understand, "I've lost both my breasts." The radiance that he had carried around in his belly and chest cavity—like music—withered, very quickly, and he made himself look at her when he said, "I'm sorry. I don't think I could." He walked back to his own cabin through the pines, and in the morning he found a small blue bowl on the porch outside his door. It looked to be full of rose petals, but he found when he picked it up that the rose petals were on top; the rest of the bowl—she must have swept them from the corners of her studio—was full of dead bees.

18

A Dumped Car

GAY HAWKINS

In this essay Gay Hawkins, Professor of Media and Social Theory at University of New South Wales, considers what kinds of ethical relations and imaginative engagements might be established with waste. From the book The Ethics of Waste, *this essay shows how an artistic creation, such as a novel, might generate a framework for inquiry or a set of questions that enables an examination of other specific sites.*

> *I think of how little we can hold in mind, how everything is constantly lapsing into oblivion with every extinguished life, how the world is, as it were, draining itself, in that the history of countless places and objects which themselves have no power of memory is never heard, never described or passed on.*
>
> —W. G. Sebald, *Austerlitz*

In writing about loss W. G. Sebald reminds us of the importance of detritus. For him, abandoned places and things have the power to reveal the reality of vanished lives. But this power is rarely acknowledged; instead, the world seems to be "draining itself." Why is this metaphor of the drain so unsettling? Could it be because drains facilitate such efficient disappearance? It's easy to forget things when elimination is so streamlined, when there is no possibility of careful deliberation. But do all the things we discard lapse into oblivion, drained of power and memory? Or do they outlive us, accumulating across the landscape, dumped but certainly not disappeared?

Don DeLillo finds the answers to these questions in the open landfill. The landfill is a monumental world of soaring garbage, mountains and valleys, trucks and roads with its own distinct smell and soundscape; a place that organizes and frames things *as* waste. A place where "all the appetites and hankerings, the sodden second thoughts came runneling out, the things you ardently wanted and then did not."[1] The open landfill is a landscape in its own right, a "dump" where we confront the forceful presence of things just sinking into themselves, broken and decaying, no longer bound by taxonomy or value.

DeLillo's world isn't drained of things; it's drowning in them, groaning under the weight of excess and obsolescence. In *Underworld* waste generates various new circuits of value: spectacular landscapes, art made out of redundant B52s, and the gangster capitalism of the garbage industry.[2] It also fuels an almost hallucinatory version of Cold War America, in which—despite his fascination with rubbish and waste management—DeLillo seems somehow blind to the materiality of waste. By overstating the case with too much awe and spectacle DeLillo does not so much remember waste as redeem it. His depiction of a Staten Island landfill creates a world in which the monstrous and majestic inhumanness of waste dwarfs the human. The landfill is a landscape visible from outer space, it is a testament to the persistence of waste and to its overwhelming presence in the era of the mass commodity form. DeLillo echoes a familiar trope in much environmentalism about the burdens of materialism. The underworld of capitalist accumulation is waste, the underhistory of American society is waste. By representing waste as things that cannot be removed, that will always return, DeLillo *others* waste, using it as the mirror of the American soul.

Sebald, in contrast, sticks closely to the qualitative character of abandoned things. Consider his reverie on a pile of mattresses:

> *Histories, for instance, like those of the straw mattresses which lay, shadow-like, on the stacked plank beds and which had become thinner and shorter because the chaff in them disintegrated over the years, shrunken—and now, in writing this, I do remember that such an idea occurred to me at the time—as if they were the mortal frames of those who once lay there in that darkness.*[3]

Sebald doesn't situate these abandoned objects in an epic historical narrative. He doesn't fetishize them; rather, he performs a kind of memory work. He apprehends the mattresses in their mundanity, and in the process they become the bodies that lay on them. Sebald gives the mattresses the power of memory.

These are two very different reflections on the nature of wasted objects; Sebald's profoundly melancholic and DeLillo's paranoid and apocalyptic.[4] Their differences are instructive. While DeLillo documents the presence of waste everywhere in overconsuming cultures, Sebald draws attention to the materiality of abandoned objects, reminding us of how little we notice them. For my purposes Sebald is more suggestive. Unlike DeLillo he is not interested in waste as a majestic landscape emblematic of capitalist social relations. Sebald rejects the "landscape function" for waste and all that it entails: the inevitable pull of aesthetics, the constitution of the environment as passively awaiting a human gaze, and human desecration. Instead, he contemplates waste as *things*. He acknowledges the materiality of waste and its ontological unstability.

In exploring the dynamic exchanges between subjects and objects, Sebald captures the translations and displacements that shape human relations with the material world. Ornaments, utensils, dumped car wrecks, mattresses—objects that have outlived their former owners—have what Bill Brown calls "history *in* them."[5] Their dislocation and uncanny presence as remainders makes the traces of their former uses and human attachments visible. Sebald's abandoned things speak of the full magnitude of what happened. He uses cultural debris to confront the past not as moral lesson but as a source of philosophical reflection about loss, destruction, and grief. His "method," if you can call it that, is a powerful evocation of Walter Benjamin's materialist history. For Sebald, like Benjamin, is interested in the phenomenological hermeneutics of cultural debris.[6] Sebald shows what can happen when you notice waste, when you pay close attention to its presence. Suddenly, discarded objects appear animate and able to make claims on us. By refusing to other waste, to reduce it to structure or metaphor, Sebald implicates waste's materiality in questions of affect and ethics.

Could the recognition of waste as *things* change our relations with it? Could it lead to different forms of materialism less concerned with the vagaries of desire or disposability? What would an ethics of waste mean for our material habitus, for how we actually live with things? This chapter explores these questions. While its inspiration is Sebald, its examples are two extraordinary films: Agnes Varda's *The Gleaners and I* and Walpiri Media's *Bush Mechanics*. In both these films people engage with waste. While their motivation is often scarcity and need, the material practices they invent involve an openness to the thingness of waste. It is the possibility of transformation and misuse that makes waste available to other systems of objectification. But you have to be willing to see and feel this. Inventing a new materialism involves a responsiveness to objects that is mutually transformative of both people and things.[7] Waste captures the attention not simply of those in desperate need but also of those able to imagine different uses, able to reanimate it. This is where necessity meets creativity and where ethics meet imagination.

Before we look at these films, the value of thinking about waste as things needs to be considered more carefully. This takes us into the realm of material culture and thing theory. Theories of material culture show how history and biography apply to things. They show how the work of consumption and exchange creates value and how material forms can be coded and recoded to satisfy human needs and desires. This work is invaluable for reminding us how human uses give objects instrumental status. But is there a realm of thingness that exists beyond this material object world? Is there a point where things cannot be reduced to objects, where their presence is asserted in ways that disrupt their object status? And could this nascent thingness be a potential source of different, more ecologically aware practices?

According to Bill Brown, we glimpse thingness in irregularities of exchange, in moments when objects stop working for us, or when we are not quite sure how to identify: all situations that could easily describe waste.[8] These experiences involve an encounter with the anterior physicality of the world, with the sensuous presence that exceeds the materialization and utilization of objects. These are experiences of objects asserting themselves as things, when things provoke and incite, when they capture our attention and demand to be noticed. And in these chance interruptions, these "occasions of contingency," as Brown calls them, different relations surface: "The story of objects asserting themselves as things, then, is the story of a changed relation to the human subject and thus the story of how the thing really names less an object than a particular subject-object relation."[9]

This approach shifts the focus from material culture's anthropological inflections to phenomenology and philosophy. Brown is concerned less with the social life of objects than with how things become "recognizable, representable and exchangeable to begin with," with the mutual constitution of human subject and inanimate object.[10] Elizabeth Grosz's account of the thing takes a similar approach. Like Brown, she is interested in how things assert themselves and how we become enmeshed with them, and she draws on pragmatist philosophers to make her case. Darwin, William James, Bergson, Rorty, and Deleuze all, in different ways, put questions of action and practice at the center of ontology. Here the thing features as a resource for being. We make things with it, leave our trace on it, but this does not mean that the thing is subordinate to human action. For the thing has a "life" of its own that we must accommodate in our activities. "The thing poses questions to us, questions about our needs and desires, questions above all of action: the thing is our provocation to action and is itself a result of our action."[11] Although Grosz doesn't argue this, in her schema things are irrevocably implicated in ethics. For if things pose questions to us then they must also be capable of making us consider what we do.

What, then, of waste? Theories of material culture show us the role of circulation and use in the creation and destruction of value; they illuminate the human and social contexts of objects in motion. But what happens when objects stop moving, when they get stuck on the verge abandoned or when they turn into urban debris? Thing theory explores how the latency of thingness might surface in these moments when objectification breaks down. For if the thing is always a kind of remainder, so too is waste, hence the potential of waste to remind us of the liminality between useful and useless, object and thing. If we noticed waste as things, what sort of new material relations and practices might this trigger? When waste is framed as dead objects and relegated to its proper place in the dump or garbage truck it often fails to provoke. It poses no questions to us because it has been regulated and rendered passive and out of sight. Waste as dead objects throws up few possibilities, but waste as things is full of promise, full of the possibilities of becoming a resource for being.

Getting to Waste

Objects die. And while I'm interested in their afterlife, the causes of death matter. When people classify something as waste they are deciding that they no longer want to be connected to it. Sometimes this is a big decision and sometimes it's not. The plastic cup chucked in the bin walking out of the football stadium is a relief to be rid of. The short life of the disposable object is over—easy come, easy go. The favorite chair handed down from grandparents and now unstable and beyond repair is hard to throw out. It's useless but still connected to the self via circuits of memory and affect. The conversion of objects into waste is complex and complicated. There is a multiplicity of pathways to the limit point at which all function and value are exhausted.

While all cultures need distinctions between valued and valueless, there are multiple and diverse subclassifications within both these categories. Some objects are valueless but we still hang on to them. They are no longer used but their lingering presence in the garage doesn't threaten us. These things aren't unsettling because they are out of sight, occupying a residual status in the microclassifications of rubbish. Then there are the valueless things that we encounter all the time: the dumpster behind the supermarket full of boxes of overripe pears, the perfectly functional but tattered sofa on the pavement; things classified as waste because they are wrecked, in excess of demand, or no longer desired, but still visible in our everyday movements through urban space. Other things are negatively valued; they threaten the stability of self, and we do all we can to eliminate them and render them invisible. As the previous chapter argues, negatively valued waste like shit challenges boundaries and symbolic order, hence its potential to be extremely disturbing. In this chapter it's the valueless rather than the negatively valued, the discarded but still visible waste and rubbish, that is the focus.

Recent writing on material culture has begun to focus on the conversion processes from valued to valueless. While transformations in uses, significations, and values have always been a central concern in this field, the transformations involved in the production of waste and rubbish have been somewhat overlooked. Gavin Lucas, like Nicky Gregson and Louise Crewe, notes the relative lack of interest in waste within studies of material culture.[12] While theorists have been happy to see waste as a historically changing category or as a source of archaeological insight, they have been less interested in comprehending it as a distinct classification or form of value.[13] Now, there is an interesting body of work beginning to investigate how objects become rubbish, how they get to the end of value. My reading of this work identifies several key themes that are worth setting down. The aim is to understand what frames of meaning shape our relations with rubbish and how open these are to transformation. Any possibility of a new materialism and ethics of waste must begin with a different recognition of discarded material. While environmentalism recognizes this in the demand that everybody "reduce, reuse, and recycle," this is only the beginning of the story. The imperative to manage our waste better or avoid the "waste stream" altogether doesn't really get to the heart of how we might come to live differently with things.

The first theme that emerges in recent work in material culture on waste is how reluctant many people are to transfer objects into this category. The rise of a biographical approach to things has documented the myriad of taxonomies, uses, and valuing regimes that objects can move through before they reach the end of their lives, if they ever do. Kopytoff describes the process in this way:

> *In the homogenised world of commodities, an eventful biography of a thing becomes the story of the various singularisations of it, of classification and reclassification in an uncertain world of categories whose importance shifts with every minor change of context. As with persons, the drama here lies in the uncertainties of valuation and identity.*[14]

The creativity of material practices, the constant reincorporation of objects into new classes and systems of exchange and use, makes any essentialist claims about the identity and fixed life cycle of things difficult to sustain. Accounts of the history of things, of their social lives, show that games of value are hard to finish, many things just want to keep on playing. This means that waste, as a point of absolute separation and dematerialization, is often a radical conversion process.

Two studies stand out. Gregson and Crewe's detailed cultural geography of secondhand cultures documents the rich array of classificatory systems and practices that steer things away from the finality of waste. Junk, secondhand, collectables, and retro are a few of the many classifications used to manage and recirculate goods after first-stage consumption.[15] Each classification reflects a specific set of economic, moral, aesthetic, and valuing regimes that work to move objects into various spaces, from the garage to the junk shop to the charity bin; and into different modes of exchange, from philanthropy to barter.

Lucas's study of disposability and dispossession looks at archaeological analyses of waste and comes to similar conclusions: reuse and revaluation are extensive, particularly in relation to things such as clothing, domestic appliances, and furnishings. Dispossession, or the active decision to remove something from one's life and discard it, is as complex a process as possession.[16] What both these studies show is that getting to waste is complicated, and the importance of a material culture perspective is the way it has begun to document this. Gregson and Crewe's research reveals an extraordinary liminal zone in which objects are suspended in time-space awaiting revaluation, their biographies stretched potentially to infinity.[17]

But a biographical perspective cannot evade the question of *de*valuation. Things still get chucked out, constantly, without thought. The ritual of putting out the garbage is one of the markers of the temporality of everyday life. It is also one of the key ways in which we acknowledge the zero degree of value. We need rubbish, as Michael Thompson argues, not just because purification rituals are important to boundaries but also because systems of value depend on a limit point.[18] Thompson's work in *Rubbish Theory* is important because he shows how rubbish makes possible transformations in use and value. Without a category of rubbish it is impossible to generate new and unexpected structures of value. It is impossible for value to move or change. Thompson identifies two major categories of value to which objects are assigned: "transient" for those things that are decreasing in value over time and "durable" for objects whose value increases over time.[19] Most consumer goods would be in the transient category, antiques or art in the durable. The location of different objects in these categories shapes human relationships and uses. The kids can romp around on the worn-out sofa because it's on the downhill slide of value, they can't touch the deco vase on the mantelpiece because it's precious and irreplaceable.

Value is a product of social processes, not the intrinsic properties of things. Just because things decay and wear out does not mean that they automatically lose value. Signs of aging and use can contribute to increased or auratic value. In the same sense the shiny new plastic cup appears to us as imminent rubbish; disposability makes transient value strikingly visible. The fact of malleability and transformation in value is evidence that objects are not locked into categories because of their material qualities. It is *how* their materiality is apprehended and used that is the key to value and its transformation. The question is: What is the role of rubbish in this process of shifting value?

Thompson argues that rubbish is central to accounts of the social control of value because it provides the path for the seemingly impossible transfer of objects from transience to durability. Rubbish is a covert category in between the transient and the durable that functions as a valueless limbo in which, at some point, the object may be rediscovered, given new value, and transferred into the category of durability. The examples Thompson uses to develop this argument are decayed inner-city housing that is gentrified and an obscure kitsch Victorian artifact, the Stevengraph, which suddenly became a collector's item in the mid-1960s. In the case of the Stevengraph two key factors were involved in the transformation of value. First, as economic value increased so too did aesthetic value in the form of research, scholarly publications, exhibitions, and museum acquisitions. And second, men controlled the transfer of value from rubbish to durable. While the Victorian purchase and display of Stevengraphs was a feminine occupation, men dominated the transfer from rubbish to collectable. They wrote the authoritative books, organized the exhibitions, and ran the sales. Changes in value are caught up in wider patterns of distinction and status.[20]

The significance of Thompson's theory is that it offers an explanation of the structural role of rubbish in formations of value. Worthlessness is the condition of possibility for objects to move between different categories. And this movement or process of malleability is grounded *not* in the intrinsic properties of things but in the new and unexpected uses and functions that people bring to them. However, while Thompson acknowledges that innovation and creativity are crucial to the flexibility of value, he doesn't pursue this. John Frow does in a brief but incisive reading of *Rubbish Theory*.[21] Frow develops Thompson's argument by showing how transformations of value are fundamental to person-thing relations: "Objects don't simply occupy a realm of objecthood over and against the human: they translate human interests, carry and transform desire and strategies."[22] For Frow, function is a product of use, and the potential uses of things (appropriate and inappropriate) are infinitely variable; "No single game exhausts their function."[23]

Frow's nuanced account of person-thing relations is concerned with conversion processes, how things pass from one state to another. While this is the central issue in many studies of material culture, Frow's interest is not in tracking the career of objects, their circulation through different uses and patterns of exchange. Rather, he is concerned with understanding the specific *kinds of recognition* that mediate distinctions between person and thing.[24] His analysis of several different examples shows how things and people coproduce each other. Despite the desire for a world of ontological purity and nonhuman authenticity, things are a product of social relations and affect them at the same time. So, if things are caught up in myriad networks and relations and if they can be framed and used in any number of different ways, what does it mean to reframe rubbish?

As Thompson has shown it means a lot in terms of economies of value because of waste's crucial role in generating change. But what does it mean for person-thing relations? What triggers a reframing of rubbish, and what inhibits this? If you looked at examples from environmental education you'd assume that all it took was the voice of abstract moral reason, a television ad instructing you to "think again before you throw that out!" Many of these campaigns take a very simplistic approach to our material habitus and how it might be transformed. They tend to ignore how blind we can be to the everyday materiality of objects, how much we can take their instrumentality for granted, and how this blindness is enhanced when we seek to get rid of things. After all, disposal is a kind of purification ritual that restores us to an ordered state; that is its function and its pleasure. Framing things as rubbish doesn't just help us eliminate things from our lives; it also helps us experience the fantasy of self-sovereignty and ontological separateness. In order to be able to reject we have to convert objects into worthless rubbish simply meeting its fate. As one of our most everyday habits, disposal depends on a particular kind of blindness that helps us *not* see, *not* acknowledge the things we want to be free of. To throw things away is to subordinate objects to human action, it is to construct a world in which we think we have dominion. This doesn't just deny the persistent force of objects as material presence, it also denies the ways in which we stay enmeshed with rubbishy things whether we like it or not.

So, for rubbish to be framed differently it needs first of all to be *noticed,* it has to be become conspicuous. Before other possibilities and potentials emerge, before other games of value and use are activated, the phenomenological reality of rubbish has to be acknowledged. We have to recognize discarded objects not as the passive and redundant context for our lives but as mobile, vital matter open to reconstitution.[25] One pathway toward this, as I've suggested, might be recognizing waste as things. As Brown argues, things become conspicuous when they are in a state of transition between one thing and another, when they are in the process of being reanimated and resignified.[26] Things are different from the material object world and its primary circuits of exchange. They are what's left after objectification breaks down, they are what we suddenly notice when an object seems to drop out of all the systems that give it meaning and value. The tattered sofa on the sidewalk sitting there for days on end awaiting the garbage pickup captures our attention as a thing. Not quite waste yet and definitely out of place, it's just quietly biding its time. Its role in intimate, private lives lingers in the coffee stains on the arms, the permanent slump in the cushions, the secrets it's overhead. Its movement from the living room to the street, from useful to discarded, defamiliarizes it, putting us into a different relationship with it. Its sensuous physicality beckons, you feel like sitting in it as if for the first time.

Following Brown then, it may be the very thingness of rubbish that can save it from abandonment and that can move it into another system of value or allow us to imagine a new objectification for it. Irregularities of exchange and transitional states make thingness visible. Waste is often found in these situations, out of place, on the edges of order, ephemeral and phenomenal. Rethinking waste means rethinking all the practices that blind us to the reality and possibilities of what remains. This is the ethico-political challenge of waste: imagining a new materialism that would transform our relations with the things that we pretend not to see. But we don't have to imagine this from scratch. Agnes Varda's exploration of gleaning shows us how waste is reimagined and reused with great insight and pleasure.

Gleaning

Varda's film *The Gleaners and I* is a waste road movie. At the age of seventy-two this leading figure of French new wave cinema took to the road with a digital camera and collected a series of stories about different ways of living with waste. Part documentary on gleaning and contemporary practices of scavenging in France and part reverie on aging, Varda's film is an extraordinary visual essay on wasted and used things and their ethical force. The film is more than just a story of those living on the margins of excess and affluence, it is also a story of objects and their capacity for constant reclassification. Varda's achievement is to open up the question of person-thing relations in such a way that we are able to see the complexities of a different and radical ethics of waste at work. She does this *not* through moral lesson but through a cinematic technique that celebrates the camera's capacity to glean and the filmmaker's capacity to play with images and stories, to digress, to engage in reverie. Varda calls this *cinécriture*, a kind of "filmic writing."[27] The effect is a series of ethical and aesthetic speculations on waste that is moving and unsettling rather than dogmatic and hectoring. Watching this film we are not being instructed to reform our practices or pity those who live off waste. Rather, we are invited to experience a kind of intimacy and enchantment with the sensuousness of rubbish as things and to witness moments of conversion in which new use values are found for waste.

The value of *The Gleaners and I* for thinking about a new materialism lies in the way this film documents how people become responsive to waste and open to its possibilities. Through interviews and conversations Varda gives us remarkable access to the various ethico-political justifications people have for gleaning. By inviting people to talk about how they glean, where they do it, and why, she enables us to see the different kinds of recognition people have for waste; what makes them notice it, and what makes them imagine new relations with it. This is more than just the discovery of new uses for discarded things. It is also an exploration of how the creation of use values can be infused with ethical impulses. Gleaning becomes a way of translating a moral unease about excess or an ethic of self-sufficiency and survival into a specific set of material practices and habits. It also becomes a way of staying alive. Desperate need is the most compelling motivation for gleaning, and Varda explores it in depth. Consider the potato sequence.

Driving to the potato fields of Beauce in northern France, Varda ponders the reality of contemporary gleaning. While women did it in groups during the nineteenth century, as captured in Millet's famous painting "The Gleaners" (an image Varda cites as an inspiration for her film), now it is often a solitary practice, and men have taken it up. In a landscape of furrowed earth where an enormous commercial potato crop has just been harvested Varda talks to men stooping and searching for potatoes the grubbing machine has missed. They describe the best times and places to glean, foods to go with potatoes, restaurants they sometimes sell to. They also discuss their relationships with farmers, most of whom are happy to have gleaners clean the fields after harvest because of the savings in labor and chemicals.

The film then cuts to interviews with producers who talk straight to camera about the demands of the market, the restrictions supermarkets place on potato size and shape. What we are hearing is a description of the logic of seriality, the ways in which the commodification of food generates a very restricted set of requirements for what counts as a saleable potato. These restrictions lead to twenty-five tons of potatoes being dumped after each harvest in Beauce. We see the reality of this: trucks on the edges of fields emptying out load after load of edible potatoes. Standing around are people with bags ready to glean. A farmer reflects on the importance of the potato as a staple food and says that with the increase in dumping there has been an increase in gleaning. But at other dump sites there are no gleaners. After all, as Varda remarks, you never see a notice about the time and date of dumping in the local newspaper. People find out by word of mouth or observation, and this erratic and informal system means that thousands of potatoes go to waste. The camera pans over a landscape of rotting potatoes green with decay, dangerous to eat—the mortification of matter.

All these potatoes, all these different relationships with them; initially, Varda explores the human framing of the potato as a crop, as something to be sold or gleaned. The emphasis is on how diverse human actions manipulate and subordinate the potato to various systems of exchange. For the farmer the potato is a source of profit, for the gleaner it's a free source of food or something to barter with. Various talking heads tell a story about commodity cultures and the dynamics of different regimes of value. The effect isn't ethnographic; Varda avoids exoticizing gleaning and gleaners with an insistent focus on contexts and economic relations. The film shows how objects mediate social relations and how human interests shape different forms of appropriation: making money, surviving on social security. We could think about this as a kind of cinematic biography of potatoes, an account of their career as material, exchangeable objects—and an account of the different status they confer on people. But then there is a moment when this logic is disrupted, when Varda suddenly notices the thingness of one potato, when she is struck by its material self-evidence.

She's filming a man sorting through a big pile of dumped potatoes. As he discusses their remarkable shapes he encounters a heart-shaped one. Varda is surprised and delighted; she reaches out for it, struck by its phenomenology; its texture and shape captivate her. She attempts an awkward close-up, holding the potato in one hand and the digicam in the other. She then starts scrabbling through the pile looking for more. Cut to a table in Varda's apartment covered in heart-shaped potatoes. The camera explores them in close-up, moving sensuously over their surfaces, tracing the blotches on their skin. It's extraordinarily tactile. The camera brings the materiality of the potato into play—we don't just see the potatoes, we *feel* their dirt and bumps, they seem alive and vital and provocative.[28]

What is going on in this shift from a cultural biography of potatoes as commodities to a startling cinematic rendering of potatoes as material presence? One minute we're hearing people talk about what they *do* with potatoes, the next we're gazing at a pile of potatoes on a table, feeling like we could reach into the screen and pick them up. Is this an effect of the representational techniques of cinema, the camera capturing the world, or has the material force of the thing captured the camera? This if a false opposition, as vigorous debate in film theory has shown; cinema has always been fascinated by objects, and it has always been able to do things with things.[29] It has always been able to move them from the backdrop of human action to central characters in the story. There is a distinct cinematic rendering of things that makes them alluring, mysterious, alive, phantasmatic, *and* strikingly real. But in *The Gleaners* the issue isn't so much cinematic techniques and referentiality, it is witnessing objects becoming things and the ethical implications of this. The power of the heart-shaped potato lies in the way Varda captures the pleasure of surprise. Her chance encounter with a potato produces a response that is suffused with delight in the self-evidence, or the "suchness," of the phenomenon. Suddenly the potato isn't waste, it isn't a discarded object on the edge of decay, it isn't a testament to the excesses of agribusiness—it's a sensuous, wondrous thing. It's what's left over after all those frames of recognition drop away.

This is surely a case of what Brown describes as objects asserting themselves as things. And, following his schema, it is also a case of a changed subject-object relation. In this scene Varda digresses from the role of gleaner of facts, she takes a detour from the journalistic documentation of waste practices. The heart-shaped potato draws her and the audience into another relation. As she searches for more potatoes she pushes the camera closer and closer until we see the close-up pan over the potatoes on the table. It's impossible not to become caught up in the affect of this scene. The links between the visual and the tactile are striking. We are looking at and touching the potatoes, we are perceiving their *texture*. And it's through this imbrication of touch and vision that we experience Varda's sensuous enchantment with the thing. Texture makes trouble for any notion of a disembodied spectator, it foregrounds the ways in which looking and feeling are interconnected. As Eve Sedgwick says, a "particular intimacy seems to subsist between textures and emotions"; touching and feeling go together; "touching" doesn't just mean cutaneous contact, it means being affected, being altered by feelings.[30]

Obviously, it's not just the phenomenological resonances of this scene that reorder our relations with waste, it is also the question of affect. Or, to put it in Sedgwick's terms, it is the ways phenomenology and affect are connected. When we encounter waste as things the affective energy that can accompany this, the sense of wonder or horror, can be the impulse for new relations: a motivation for a different ethics, a sudden inspiration for a new use. In Varda's case the heart-shaped potato triggers a metonymic play from the shape of the heart to charity to those working with the poor and marginalized. The film shifts registers back into documentary mode, and we watch a man discussing how he gleans potatoes to serve in a soup kitchen for the hungry. He talks quietly about being unemployed and wanting to do something useful with his time and about the outrage of good food being dumped while people starve. It's a lovely evocation of a moral framework and motivation that is underlaid with the earlier scene of the beautiful heart-shaped potatoes. To confront the reuse of dumped potatoes as an ethical imperative reverberates with all the associations of them as remarkable physical things. That humble vegetable has got all sorts of holds on us; it can propel us toward acts of generosity and care, entrance us with its beauty and feel. By exploring the multiplicity of ways in which we are mixed up with potatoes— as commodity, as waste, as gift, as things—Varda offers us another way of understanding the ethics of waste. Waste makes claims on us. Reducing waste is not simply a matter of the moral reform of the human, it is also about acknowledging that waste has a kind of agency; that it shares in some of the agency we ascribe only to ourselves.[31]

Varda's Hands

If the surprise of the heart-shaped potato sequence is that it lets us see wasted objects as vital and alive, the surprise of the hand sequence is that it lets us see a living body as dead. In revealing potatoes as things *The Gleaners and I* inaugurates a different kind of vision that is not so much instrumental and objectifying as tactile and intersubjective. The subject-object relation is unsettled by the ways in which the heart-shaped potato scene, in its appeal to texture and contact, evokes the multisensory qualities of perception.[32] It works because we carry sense memories of touching potatoes, because our hands bear the traces of their feel. But in another sequence we see that hands bear the traces of death.

Later in the film Varda is playing around with her digicam, filming objects in her apartment. She talks about their provenance, the pleasure of living with things collected over time. Suddenly, the digicam captures her free hand, the one that has been pointing at different things. She pauses on it, does a close-up, talking with horror about its wrinkles, blotches, and lines. The hand is severed from her body, it becomes a thing separate and alien. In the image of her hand Varda sees her own death—the lines, blotches, and wrinkles are evidence of death at work. The hand appears to us as lifeless and worn out; Varda pauses to mourn her own loss. In that surprise glimpse of her hand we see a body asserting itself as a thing.

The surprise of the hand is that the digicam captures it as already dead. It signals its imminent status as waste. The surprise of the potatoes is that the appear to us as alive. How can this be when the visual techniques in these scenes are so similar? Both involve the contingency of a sudden, unexpected revelation; both involve the intensity of a lingering close-up on skin; both reveal the links between phenomenology and affect. Perhaps the difference between the two scenes has to do with waste. In the potato scene a wasted object asserts itself as a vital thing, in the hand scene a living subject becomes dead matter. What both scenes capture is the instability of waste; wasted objects can be reanimated and brought back to life, living subjects will become waste. Things pass from one state to another; waste, like thingness, is not inherent to things, it's a latency, an effect of certain sorts of recognition. Both these scenes trigger those recognitions, they notice waste in ways that disrupt the boundaries between subject and object, human and non-human, useful and useless, dead and alive.

The effect of this is to open up a very different way of thinking about and living with waste. Moral instruction and mastery of the "waste problem" are not the intentions of this film. These two scenes give waste a recognition and potency that make it much more than the bad object of environmental destruction and capitalist excess. Instead, waste becomes a relation in which we sense the force of conversion and transience, of other possibilities emerging of enchantment *and* disturbance. In waste we see imagination and ethics coinciding: "I wonder what you could do with this?"

Hands and potatoes perform this different recognition of waste well, but so too do the much straighter documentary sequences in the film, in which Varda resists any tendency toward dogmatism. Her interviews with gleaners all over France are suffused with an openness and respect. People talking about their scavenging practices are filmed with unfailing intelligence and tenderness. Men and women found scrounging in bins behind supermarkets or in fields aren't victimized or shamed. Their anonymity and poverty are challenged by a documentary technique suffused with generosity. Varda isn't calculating the moral effect of their stories, the gleaners are not being used to generate sympathy. They're simply telling stories about a different kind of material habitus, a different way of living with things. This way of living is tough; surviving on waste involves a lot of work stooping, searching, and sorting. There's no romance in it, but there is dignity, and Varda's careful documentation of the micro-practices of gleaning, the legalities of it, and the ways of concerting and sharing what's scavenged is a beautiful exploration of the ethic of making do.

Making Do

"Making do" is also the theme of *Bush Mechanics,* but in this documentary the focus is on the pleasure and creativity of this practice more than its ethical import. Made in 1998, the film explores the relationship to cars of a group of young Aboriginal men from the Yuendumu community in remote Australia. Funny, innovative, and full of self-parody, *Bush Mechanics* reveals a completely different set of car practices from those usually seen and celebrated on commercial TV. There are no high-speed chases here, no glossy celebrations of the car as commodity fetish—rather, a set of madcap adventures about driving in the desert in cars chronically on the verge of mechanical collapse. The main content comes from watching these "bush mechanics" solve a variety of technical problems using whatever they can lay their hands on. Punctured inner tubes are replaced with densely matted spinifex grass, brake fluid is made from laundry detergent mixed with water, replacement parts are found on abandoned wrecks that are part of the collective memory in remote desert spaces. All this is evidence of a playful inventiveness prompted not simply by need but also by a robust practical knowledge about various ways of keeping a car moving.[33]

While making do is akin to gleaning because it involves scavenging, the term also implies creative reuse with whatever is at hand. Analyses of this practice, also known as *bricolage,* have been taken up in anthropology (particularly by Lévi-Strauss) and, later, in cultural studies. *Bricolage* describes the human capacity to imagine and create new uses and meanings for things. This process is more than just reclassification, it involves an active reappropriation of things in different contexts that not only produces new meanings but also reveals the social logic of imagination. The capacity to subvert or erase original meanings and make new uses shows that imagination isn't fanciful or an activity restricted to leisure or aesthetics, it's a field of everyday social practice. Michel de Certeau has shown how central the arts of making do are to daily life.[34] Rituals, habits, routines are all a product of adapting ways of doing things with the material resources available.

While no one would question the fact of everyday creativity, cultural studies accounts of bricolage have tended to overvalorize human actions at the expense of a more relational materiality. Human agency is seen as driving the practice of bricolage, often in the interest of creating an oppositional or resistant identity.[35] This has had the effect of making bricolage seem like an act of subversion rather than a quotidian practice driven by pragmatic need. It has also, implicitly, reinforced a sharp opposition between inanimate material and human bodies with consciousness and intention, able to do weird and wonderful things with things.

The question that *Bush Mechanics* raises is: What if we thought of bricolage not as human activity in the service of identity but as evidence of what Latour calls the "networked quality of things?"[36] This is how *Bush Mechanics* represents the arts of making do, and this is what makes it a wonderful exploration of the relations between rubbish, recognition, and reuse. In this film representations of practical ingenuity continually foreground the heterogeneity of things in the world and the fluidity of their classification; things are continually open to new uses and frames of understandings. This is a road movie in which the ontological separation between the humans and the car is flattened, in which distinctions between mechanical, organic, human, and technological get very mixed up. The narrative momentum in the film is triggered by constant car breakdowns and the desperate desire of the five Yuendumu men to make it into town. Keeping the car moving means finding immediate solutions to a series of increasingly tricky technical problems.

While this scenario sounds like the perfect setting for a celebration of indigenous ingenuity, the film avoids this easy, feel-good representation of difference. Instead, it explores the exchanges and relays between a technology that both organizes human action and is subject to human inscription and will. This is a very demanding car. Keeping it on the road involves a radical openness to the technical possibilities of anything and everything. Consider the flat tire sequence—there's no spare or jack, so another solution has to be found. The men collectively lift the car onto a jerry can so they take the wheel nuts off with a pair of pliers. They then head off into the surrounding desert scrub and pull out bunches of spinifex to stuff into the tire. This tough desert grass turns out to be a perfectly reasonable substitute for the punctured inner tube.

In another scene the men wander into the scrub searching for a car wreck they think is nearby. It could provide the spare part that they need to keep moving. What unfolds is an alternative perception of the place of rubbish in natural space. For the bush mechanics, car carcasses are perceived as part of the landscape. Incorporated into the meanings of country, they are understood as traces, and, like rocks and mountains, they remain always available for transformation. Car bodies, like all material and organic things, are regarded as transient. While Western eyes might view these wrecks with moral opprobrium, as evidence of a crude disregard for natural purity, in *Bush Mechanics* they signal the value of traces, of refusing to erase presence. Deborah Bird Rose explains Aboriginal rubbish practices in this way:

> *My Aboriginal teachers in the Northern Territory rarely picked up after themselves, but more to the point they did not seek to erase themselves. When they go fishing they call out to the ancestors and Dreamings saying, "Give us food, the children are hungry, we got kids here!" When they get food, they cook it on the spot. The remains of the dinner camps tell the stories of how they went to that place and called out to country, and how the country fed them. The remains of people's action in country tell an implicit story of knowledgeable action: these people knew where they were, they knew how to get the food that is there in the country. The country responded to their presence by providing for them, and the remains are evidence of the reciprocity between country and people. In contrast, my teachers held self-erasure to be the equivalent of sneaking around the country.*[37]

So rubbish isn't rubbish, it's a literal trace that is available for transformation. It is part of the network of tracks that register movement and tell of events. It is potentiality, it can transform people and people can transform it. In a later television series of *Bush Mechanics* Jack Jakamarra Ross, a Yuendumu leader is filmed wandering in the bush. Suddenly he comes across a defunct engine block. He looks at it closely and says: "This motor grew us up, now it is lying here like a witness looking after us."[38] The moment catches the viewer by surprise—here is someone describing how a car engine brought him up. This is far more radical than the common tendency to anthropomorphize your car with a cute name. Jack Jakamarra's account of his relation to an abandoned engine describes how the technological thing has metamorphosed into an affective agent that continues to watch over him. The thing has exchanged properties with a caring parent.

It's possible to read this scene as evidence of the charming naïveté of indigenous cosmology, but that would involve a denial of its disturbing pleasure and its implications for the meaning of rubbish as nothing but useless matter. The scene is *enchanting*; it disrupts our confident sense of the order of things of the boundaries between human and nonhuman. It frames rubbish not as polluting dead object but as part of the landscape capable of bearing witness and always available for transformation.

I am using Jane Bennett's notion of enchantment here. She argues that the experience of enchantment is often linked to material metamorphoses, and that crossings and admixtures reveal the possibilities of radical shifts in meaning and matter. More important is the capacity of material metamorphoses to reveal the instability of ontology. Enchantment, for Bennett, is much more than a spectatorial delight; it is a moment of potential ethical transformation. "My wager is that if you engage certain crossings under propitious conditions, you might find that their dynamism revivifies your wonder at life, their morphings inform your reflections upon freedom, their charm energizes your social conscience and their flexibility stretches your moral sense of the possible."[39]

Both *The Gleaners* and *Bush Mechanics* satisfy Bennett's stringent checklist for enchantment. These are dynamic, wondrous films full of the pleasures and possibilities of rubbish. They stretch our "moral sense of the possible," as Bennett says, not by a moralizing critique of capitalism's excess and the burdens of waste, but by exploring the implications of framing rubbish differently. They energize our social conscience by giving us a glimpse of what a different materialism looks like.

Endnotes

1. Don DeLillo, *Underworld* (New York: Scribner, 1997), 184–85.

2. John Frow describes DeLillo's account of the waste industry as a form of gangster capitalism in "Invidious Distinction: Waste, Difference and Classy Stuff," in *Culture and Waste: The Creation and Destruction of Value,* ed. Gay Hawkins and Stephen Muecke (Lanham, MD: Rowman and Littlefield, 2002).

3. W. G. Sebald, *Austerlitz* (London: Penguin, 2001), 31.

4. See James Wood, "Black Noise," *New Republic* 217, no. 19 (1997), for an excellent review of *Underworld*.

5. Bill Brown, "How to Do Things with Things (A Toy Story)," *Critical Inquiry* 25 Summer 1998): 935; see also his account of the trace in the same essay.

6. The term *phenomenological hermencutics* comes from Susan Buck-Morss, *The Dialectics of Seeing* (Cambridge, MA: MIT Press, 1991), 3.

7. This is Stephen Meuke's point in "A Landscape of Variability," in *Uncertain Ground: Essays between Art and Nature*, ed. Nicholas Thomas (Sydney: Art Gallery of New South Wales, 1999).

8. Bill Brown, "Thing Theory," *Critical Inquiry* 28 (Autumn 2001): 4–5.

9. Brown, "Thing Theory," 5.

10. Bill Brown, *A Sense of Things* (Chicago: University of Chicago Press, 2003), 4–5.

11. Elizabeth Grosz, *Architecture from the Outside* (Cambridge, MA: MIT Press, 2001), 168–69.

12. Gavin Lucas, "Disposability and Dispossession in the Twentieth Century," *Journal of Material Culture* 7, no. 1 (2002): 5–22; Nicky Gregson and Louise Crewe, *Second Hand Cultures* (Oxford: Berg, 2003).

13. See for example Susan Strasser, *Waste and Want: A Social History of Trash* (New York: Metropolitan Books, 1999); William Rathie and Cullen Murphy, *Rubbish! The Archaeology of Garbage* (New York: Harper Collins, 2001).

14. Igor Kopytoff, "The Cultural Biography of Things: Commoditization as Process," in *The Social Life of Things*, ed. Arjun Appadurai (New York: Cambridge University Press, 1986), 90.

15. Gregson and Crewe, *Second Hand Cultures*, 115.

16. Lucas, "Disposability and Dispossession," 14–19.

17. Gregson and Crewe, *Second Hand Cultures*, 201.

18. Michael Thompson, *Rubbish Theory: The Creation and Destruction of Value* (Oxford: Oxford University Press, 1979).

19. Thompson, *Rubbish Theory*, 7.

20. Thompson, *Rubbish Theory*, 108–9.

21. Frow, *Invidious Distinction*, 34–36.

22. Frow, *Invidious Distinction*, 36.

23. Frow, *Invidious Distinction*, 36.

24. John Frow, "A Pebble, a Camera, a Man Who Turns into a Telegraph Pole," *Critical Inquiry* 28 (Autumn 2001): 275.

25. Jane Bennett, *The Enchantment of Modern Life* (Princeton, NJ: Princeton University Press, 2001), 99.

26. Brown, "How," 954.

27. Chris Darke, "Refuseniks," *Sight and Sound* 11, no. 1 (January 2001): 30–31.

28. For a lovely reading of this scene see Anne Rutherford, "The Poetic of a Potato," *Metro Magazine* 137 (2003): 126–31.

29. For a great exploration of cinematic things see Lesley Stern, "Paths That Wind through the Thicket of Things," *Critical Inquiry* 28 (Autumn 2001).

30. Eve Sedgwick, *Touching Feeling*, vol. 28 (Durham, NC: Duke, 2003).

31. Bennett, *Enchantment*, 99.

32. See Laura Marks, *The Skin of the Film* (Durham, NC: Duke, 2000).

33. See Georgine Clarsen, "Still Moving: Bush Mechanics in the Central Desert," *Australian Humanities Review,* March 2002, at www.lib.latrobe.edu.au/AHR/archive/Issue-March-2002/clarsen.html (accessed March 7 2002), for a great reading of this documentary.

34. Michel de Certeau, *The Practice of Everyday Life* (Berkeley and Los Angeles: University of California Press, 1984).

35. For an example of this see Dick Hebdidge, *Subculture: The Meaning of Style* (London: Methuen, 1979).

36. Bruno Latour, *We Have Never Been Modern* (Cambridge MA: Harvard University Press, 1993).

37. Deborah Bird Rose, "Decolonizing the Discourse of Environmental Knowledge in Settler Societies," in Hawkins and Muecke, *Culture and Waste,* 62 (my emphasis).

38. Quoted in Clarsen, "Still Moving," 4.

39. Bennett, *Enchantment,* 32.

19

From Poster Child to Protester

Laura Hershey

A disability activist and consultant, Laura Hershey writes many articles and authored the book Survival Strategies for Going Abroad: A Guide for People with Disabilities. *Published in a 1997 issue of* Spectacle, *Hershey's essay "From Poster Child to Protester" presents personal stories and observations about, as well as trenchant analysis of, representations of people with disabilities. Taking as her starting point the story of her shift from participation in the annual Jerry Lewis MDA Labor Day Telethon to demonstrating against it, Hershey's unique perspective encourages revaluation of public priorities and policies regarding people with disabilities.*

Orange, pink, and lavender flyers fluttered in the breeze as we handed them to any passer-by willing to take one. "Tune Out Jerry!" the flyers urged. "Boycott the Telethon!" Some two dozen of us lined up in front of the hotel shouting chants, distributing leaflets, and answering questions from the media, while the local segment of the Jerry Lewis Labor Day Telethon broadcast from a ballroom two floors above. Though I would stay outside all afternoon, I remembered all too well the scene that was taking place inside.

The singers croon. The eyelids droop. The money pours in. The firefighters, the Boy Scouts, the business executives, the neighborhood kids, all tiredly smiling proud smiles, carry in their collected funds, in jars, in boots, in oversized checks. The camera rolls. The host smiles. The money pours in. The Poster Child gives awkward answers to inane questions. The host smiles. The Poster Child smiles. The host cries. The money pours in.

You have to keep thinking about the money, because as everyone freely admits, that's what this is all about. The money raised represents hope—year after year, promises of a miracle, the great cure that waits just around the corner. The money manifests faith—faith in the noble research scientists working desperately to identify, and eliminate, flawed genes. The money testifies to human love and compassion, ruthlessly sentimentalized in songs like "They'll Never Walk Alone" which punctuate the twenty or so hours of the telethon.

The money is what justifies, even sanctifies, this annual ritual of tears and guilt. In 1996 the telethon raised over $49 million. That massive amount of money that people—young and old, rich and poor—feel compelled to donate, giving "till it hurts," as Jerry Lewis insists—that money makes it very hard to challenge what is actually going on.

But there we were, back in September 1991, on Denver's busy 16th Street Mall, challenging the Jerry Lewis Labor Day Muscular Dystrophy Telethon. Along with activists in cities around the country, including Chicago, Los Angeles, and Las Vegas, we were protesting the telethon's portrayal of people with disabilities as helpless and pathetic. We were asserting publicly that this colossal begging festival, supposedly carried out on our behalf, is offensive to us and damaging to our efforts to become first-class citizens. Our protests were small, but they would become an annual tradition—much to the annoyance of Jerry Lewis and MDA.

For years we had been protesting against the barriers which keep people with disabilities from using buses, public buildings, and other facilities. Now we were taking on one of the biggest barriers of all: the paternalistic attitudes which prevail in our society, and which are reflected so dramatically in the annual telethon.

It is difficult to raise objections to something like the telethon; people are reluctant to disparage, or even entertain questions about, an effort which they perceive as fundamentally good, or at least well-meaning. That is understandable. It is an uncomfortable truth, in social work, in government activity, and in charitable endeavors, that actions which are intended to help a certain group of people *may actually harm* them. By harm, I mean—among other things—that these actions may reinforce the already devalued status of people with disabilities in this society. Looking closely and critically at the telethon, as some of us have started to do, brings up a number of issues which I feel are essential to understanding the status of people with disabilities as an oppressed minority group in America. These issues include: charity versus civil rights; cure versus accommodation; self-expression and self-determination; and the relationship between pity and bigotry.

The telethon has one goal—to raise as much money as possible for the Muscular Dystrophy Association, or MDA. Conventional wisdom says that the most effective way to do this is to appeal directly to the emotions of viewers—to move people so strongly, with stories of tragic suffering, that they will want to help "save Jerry's kids." Money is tight these days; charitable solicitation is a competitive business. Invoking sympathy sufficient to pry open wallets is not an easy task. But those orchestrating the telethon have a foolproof, not-so-secret weapon: children. Never mind that two-thirds of MDA's 1 million clients are adults—the telethon is not in the business of trying to represent the real lives of people with muscular dystrophy. That's not the point. The point is to paint a picture of a victim so tragic, and at the same time so cute and appealing, that viewers will be compelled to call in a pledge. This victim must also appear helpless, utterly unable to help him/ herself, so that the giver can gain a personal sense of virtue and superiority from the act of giving. Finally, the victim must display something called "courage," which does not resemble the bold, active kind of courage most people aspire to or at least fantasize about, in which one takes one's destiny into one's own hands and, by exercising will and choice, affirms oneself and/or one's place in the universe. No, the "courage" demanded in this instance is the willingness to deprecate oneself; to accept other people's versions of one's own reality; to reject one's own identity in favor of an eagerly anticipated cure (this is also called "hope"); to tolerate and even encourage the assumption that life with a disability is a life scarcely worth carrying on with, except for the generosity of Jerry Lewis and everyone involved in the telethon.

At the age of eleven, I was enlisted into this role of cheerful victim. I was a Poster Child. In 1973–74, I became a mini-celebrity, appearing at fundraisers throughout Colorado. I learned to smile whenever a camera appeared, and to say "thank you"—in other words, I learned to look, sound, and act cute and grateful. And on Labor Day, I became a prop in the TV studio where the local portion of the telethon was broadcast. To whole families, driving by to drop their contributions in a giant fishbowl outside the studio; to the camera's blinking red light; to the anchorman who squatted next to me, holding a huge microphone in my face; to everyone, I gave the same cute-and-grateful act, because that's what they wanted.

So I am no stranger to the telethon. And in the two decades since then, the telethon doesn't seem to have changed much. I watch it every year, just to make sure. It's still chillingly familiar. The sappy music, the camera close-ups of wistful faces, the voice-overs telling us about that person's dream to walk someday, the tearful stories told by parents "devastated" by their children's disability, and the contributors coming forward in droves—it was all just the same as I remember it.

But some things **have** changed; I have changed. I don't know what my politics were as an eleven-year-old, if I had any. But my politics now—which are not merely political but also personal, spiritual, and practical—have led me to question and ultimately reject most of the values which the telethon represents.

Let's start with the money. Does **it** help? Doesn't it make the stereotypes, the appeals to pity, the obnoxious on-air begging worth putting up with?

Yes, the money does help—*some* people, with *some* things. We are talking about a lot of money here. MDA Executive Director Robert Ross asserts that during its 26-year history, the telethon has raised over $600 million. In 1996, the telethon raised $49.1 million.

With all this money coming in, I would expect the direct services provided to people with neuromuscular diseases to be much more extensive, and more relevant, than they actually are. I would expect, for example, that when a person develops a condition which begins to limit his or her mobility, that MDA might come through with some money for access modifications to the home, so that the family wouldn't have to choose between moving to an accessible house (which are hard to find), or hauling the person up and down stairs all day. I would expect some support services for independent living—someone to assist with personal and household needs, training in things like cooking and cleaning from a wheelchair, and help with transportation. I would expect MDA to provide a motorized wheelchair for anyone who wants one. Such a chair can boost a disabled person's quality of life enormously. Instead, MDA has very restrictive criteria for determining who receives a motorized wheelchair.

Far be it from me to advise a multimillion-dollar agency on how to spend its money. But when the telethon tells viewers that by donating money to MDA, they are answering the prayers of people with MD—offering them a friend to turn to in times of need—it exaggerates.

Okay, say the defenders of the telethon, so maybe the money doesn't help people **now** as much as it should. Isn't it still laudable that the telethon raises so much money to help find a cure?

Ah, *the cure*. That's the promise that keeps people sending in those checks. That's what keeps this humiliation going year after year. We're getting closer all the time! Jerry Lewis assures us frenetically. He's been saying it for four decades.

Shortly after my stint as Poster Child was over, I remember meeting a stranger in a store who recognized me from the telethon. He said to me, "I bet you really hope they find a cure soon!" When he said this, I realized that by this time, I almost never even contemplated that possibility anymore, let alone hoped for it. I told him that. I don't think he believed me. I find the same reaction now, when I criticize the telethon for implying that people with disabilities sit around hoping and praying for a cure. I've encountered people who, never having tried it, think that living life with a disability is an endless hardship. For many of us, it's actually quite interesting, though not without its problems. And the majority of those problems result from the barriers, both physical and attitudinal, which surround us, or from the lack of decent support services. These are things that can be changed, but only if we as a society recognize them for what they are. We'll never recognize them if we stay so focused on curing individuals of disability, rather than making changes to accommodate disability into our culture.

Now, I'm not arguing that medical research should halt entirely—I'm just weighing the cost-benefit value, in my life and in the lives of my friends with disabilities, of the millions of dollars spent on the search for a cure, a search that will take decades, versus the things we really need now, on which society spends far less. We will probably never benefit from *the cure*. We will benefit from accessible buildings and transportation systems, job opportunities, and attendant services to provide us personal assistance. So will future generations.

We have begun making progress in those areas. In 1990, for example, the Americans with Disabilities Act became law, putting some legal teeth into our fight for civil rights and access.

But for all our progress in the areas of legal protection and accessibility, there's still this lingering attitude that what people with disabilities **really** need is to be cured. Society wants the problem to go away, so it won't have to accommodate people with long-term disabling conditions. It wants **us** to go away, or at least to "get better." One of my major objections to the telethon is the way it reinforces that attitude.

Sure, some people with muscular dystrophy **do** hope and dream of that day when the cure is finally found. As people with disabilities, we're conditioned just like everyone else to believe that disability is our problem. We've been told over and over that our need for accessibility to buses and buildings, and our need for health services, are too expensive, too unreasonable. Our culture considers it shameful to be physically unable to dress oneself, or to need assistance in going to the bathroom. Rather than demanding that the government provide such helping services, many people with disabilities end up hidden in nursing homes or in our own homes, where personal assistance remains the private "burden" of individuals and families. Rather than insisting on having our personal needs and our access needs met, many prefer to keep quiet about these needs, fearful to show ourselves lacking. The telethon itself encourages such self-defeating thinking. We are primed to regard ourselves as substandard. We therefore hesitate to assert our right to have that which, because of our disabilities, we need. The telethon teaches us to think that others will provide for us because they are kind and generous, not because we are a strong and vocal community. When so many of us feel so negative about our disabilities and our needs, it's difficult to develop a political agenda to get our basic needs met. The **cure** is a simple, magical, non-political solution to all the problems in a disabled person's life. That's why it's so appealing, and so disempowering. The other solutions we have to work for, even fight for; we only have to dream about the cure.

The idea of a cure is at least in part an effort to homogenize, to make everyone the same. To draw a parallel, when I was a child and first learned about racial discrimination, I thought it would be great if people could all be one color so we wouldn't have problems like prejudice. What color did I envision for this one-color world? White, of course, because I'm white. I didn't bear black people any malice. I just thought they'd be happier, would suffer less, if they were more like me.

We all have our own ideas about which human condition is best, based on our own assumptions about other people's lives. These assumptions don't always jibe with reality. People who assume that I live for the day when a cure is found, when I (or future generations) can live disability-free, simply don't understand my reality. It's a question of priorities. On the list of things I want, a cure for my disability is pretty low. Higher up on the list would be achievement of my personal, professional, and social goals, and these are not in any way dependent on a cure.

Besides, there's an issue of pride involved. Disability is a part of my whole identity, one I'm not eager to change. Especially not at the cost of my dignity and personhood, as the telethon implicitly demands.

This gets to another important issue the telethon raises in relation to the oppression of people with disabilities: Whose job is it to tell the story, or stories, of a group of people? The telethon is full of "profiles" of people with various forms of muscular dystrophy and their families. Yet these stories are packaged as products, not told as truth. Favorite subjects are children, for reasons discussed earlier—children can be made to appear more helpless, more pathetic, more dependent on the public's generosity. Children are also cute; therefore they seem more deserving of help.

In comparison with my telethon years, recent telethons do profile more adults with muscular dystrophy. Some are successful, competent adults. Yet somehow, even these individuals were made to look desperate and pitiable.

On any given telethon—both on the national broadcast from Las Vegas, and during the cut-aways to local segments—you will see profiles of children and adults with muscular dystrophy. These spots are all fairly similar in tone and emphasis. As if by a prescribed formula, each one contains several key ingredients. In each, the parents speak about their reactions upon hearing their child's diagnosis—even if, as in most cases, this has occurred years, or even decades, before. Naturally, these reactions include disbelief and grief. Yet there is rarely any discussion of how (or whether) the family has since come to accept the knowledge of their child's condition, to find resources (other than those offered by MDA), to plan for the child's future, or to promote the child's self-esteem. The situation is presented as an unmitigated tragedy.

I'm suspicious of this presentation. I'm not trying to minimize the pain a parent might feel upon learning that a child has a disabling, potentially even fatal, diagnosis. There is a very natural grieving process that goes along with disability at any stage. But when I see those emotions exploited so crassly, I can't help wincing. For most of us, our losses, gains, sorrows and joys are simply part of a rich human life. The telethon works very hard to convince people that our suffering is extraordinary. This produces pity, confusion and misunderstanding.

Another common element in these pieces is the emphasis on "what Johnny can't do." A child, usually a boy, is shown sitting at the edge of a playground. The narrator talks about the games the child can't play, and how he has to watch other children running and jumping. He can only dream, the narrator tells us sadly.

Never mind that the kid might be adept at playing Nintendo, or making rude noises with his mouth. In the real world of children, these skills are valued at least as much as running and jumping. The truth is, all children play at different levels of skill; most can't run as they would like, or jump as high, or play as well. Children in wheelchairs **do** play with other kids on the playground—I did. A child in a motorized wheelchair can be mobile, active—and popular, if willing to give rides now and then. But instead of acknowledging any of this, the telethon encourages viewers to project their own worst fears onto people with muscular dystrophy: "Just imagine what it would be like if **your child** couldn't play baseball."

Finally, each piece puts forward an archaic and gloomy picture of the disabled family member's role, and of the role of the family in a disabled person's life. All the families are described as "courageous"; and they all seem to bear total responsibility for the care and support of the person with MD. Spouses and parents alike are shown carrying the person with MD up and down stairs, pushing their wheelchair, and so on. Rarely if ever is the disabled family member shown making any positive contribution. In these stories, the disabled person's status is clearly (even if the word was never used) that of "burden."

I am all for supportive families. My own parents and brother have stood by me throughout my life, backing me with assistance and encouragement. But I have also built a life apart from them. Many people with disabilities do so, getting educated, working, and having families of our own. I am able to live independently, working toward the goals I choose, as long as I have access to the support services I need—primarily attendant services. I am lucky that the state of Colorado pays someone to come to my home and help me get up in the morning and get to bed at night. Most states do not offer this service, forcing people with disabilities to remain in the care of their families, or to enter nursing homes. Indeed, attendant services is the number one disability rights issue of the 1990's. Activists are demanding that the federal government divert a part of the huge budget which currently subsidizes the nursing home industry, and create a national system of attendant services, available to anyone who needs them.

On the telethon, of course, this is a non-issue. Disability is a private problem, demanding faith and fortitude from families, demanding generosity from viewers, demanding nothing from the government, or from society as a whole. If the need for personal assistance is mentioned at all, it is only to highlight, once again, the purported helplessness of people with MD, as in phrases such as "totally dependent on others for the most basic activities the rest of us take for granted." In fact, the opposite is true: With decent attendant services at my disposal, I become more **independent,** not more dependent. But to present that truth might undermine that vision of the long-suffering, burden-bearing family.

The unvarying tone **and** content of the pieces made it difficult to distinguish one "patient" from another. The profiles put forward a stereotyped view of what it means to have a disability, rather than any genuine stories of real people. We are all individuals, and families are all different. Not on the telethon, though. There we are made to fit the mold. Even the language used on the telethon distorts our reality and thereby dehumanizes us: We are "victims," we "suffer" from our conditions, we are "desperate."

I have firsthand experience of this distortion effect. Six or seven years after my Poster Childhood was over, just before my second year of college, I was asked to be interviewed for a local pre-telethon TV special. At first I said no. I was by now quite leery of the telethon mentality. I had also started becoming politicized, and was now more interested in civil rights than in charity. And I couldn't see any reason to participate once again in the simple-minded propaganda I remembered from my on-camera appearances as Poster Child. Back then, I had been asked questions like, "What would you like to say to all those nice people who are calling in their pledges, Laura?" to which the obvious reply was, "Thank you." Such questions left little room for honest expression.

But the local MDA office promised that the interview would be handled differently in this program: The plan was to take a positive, realistic approach and portray the real lives of three real people. So I agreed.

A TV news reporter conducted the interview in my parents' home. She asked good questions and allowed me to give complete, intelligent answers. It was certainly a different process from my earlier experiences. Afterward, I felt good about the upcoming show. I had been able to discuss issues, describe my life as a college student, and project a strong, positive personality.

Or so I thought. When the program aired, I was horrified. Through careful editing, it had turned into a sob story entitled "Waiting For A Miracle." From that point on, I vowed to have nothing to do with the telethon.

Until 1991, that is. I learned that two Chicago activists, Chris Matthews and Mike Ervin, were interested in coordinating actions against the Jerry Lewis telethon. Like me, they were both former poster children. I urged people from Denver's community to join the campaign. My decision to organize a protest did not come without some thought. In fact, I had for years contemplated doing something like this, but had not. I knew that our message would not be an easy one to convey to the public. Many people are involved with the telethon, either as volunteers or as contributors. I knew that openly criticizing it would cause confusion and anger. The telethon enjoys widespread acceptance, even acclaim.

But that is exactly why it's so important, I feel, to raise our voices against it. Because it **is** accepted *as our reality*. This is my biggest gripe against Jerry Lewis, and against the telethon: the extent to which they claim to tell my story, our stories, without any legitimate authority to do so.

The telethon's hegemony over the image of disability is quite staggering. A 1996 press release issued by MDA states, "According to A.C. Nielsen, last year's Telethon was watched by some 70 million Americans or 27 million households. The MDA

Telethon—considered the granddaddy of all Telethons—ranks in viewership with the World Series and the Academy Awards." Those 70 million people are absorbing a message shaped by greed, deception, and bigotry.

The bigotry of Jerry Lewis is worth discussing. I don't necessarily enjoy attacking another person's motives, but I hear defenders saying, "Jerry Lewis is trying to help so many people. How dare you criticize his methods?" This means-justifies-the-ends argument has a long and despicable history, which I don't need to go into here. Even more dangerous is the attitude that people who are "being helped" have no right to say how they want to be helped, or treated, or thought of. This is paternalism at its worst. By being the object of charitable efforts, do we thereby waive our right to respect, and to free speech? If people are really interested in helping me, wouldn't they want to hear me tell my own story, rather than hearing a distorted version of it from someone who not only doesn't share my experience, but who doesn't even seem to want to listen to me? With the stated goal of "helping" his "kids," Jerry Lewis is helping to keep alive the most pernicious myths about people who have disabilities. He ignores our truth, substituting his own distorted assumptions.

If our protest did nothing else, it allowed some of us the opportunity to say, "No, this is not our reality. If you want to know what our lives are like, listen to us. If you want to know what we need, ask us. If you truly want to help us, let us tell you how. And if you pity and fear us, please own that; then let us work together at changing the world so that disability will not be something to fear, but something to try to understand."

The response to our protest has been interesting. Many people seem to resent our daring to object to these distortions, half-truths, and stereotypes. I have been called "ungrateful," "cruel," and "insensitive"—simply for trying to counter all this with the truth, with my truth. At the very least, I feel that the protest has enabled me and others to begin getting on record our own stories, in contrast to the misleading accounts that come from the telethon.

Media is a powerful thing. It can deceive, or it can enlighten. About a week after that 1991 telethon, a publication arrived in my mailbox called <u>MDA News Magazine</u>, put out by the national Muscular Dystrophy Association office. I started to leaf through it, expecting to find the same kinds of negative stereotypes that permeate the hours of the telethon. Instead, I found articles about job-seeking strategies; profiles of successful individuals who have neuromuscular diseases; honest and thoughtful pieces about families of children with neuromuscular diseases; lists of useful resources; and clinical updates. All of it was written in a positive, realistic tone, using respectful and appropriate language. The phrase "people with disabilities" was used at all times—never "victims," or "sufferers," and certainly not "cripples."

One article, written by Marie Hite, whose son has muscular dystrophy, stood out. Its basic theme was very similar to some of the telethon spots I had viewed: the difficulties a child has in coping with a progressively disabling condition. But Hite's treatment of the subject couldn't have been more different from that presented on the telethon. In her article, her son confided that he could no longer climb a neighbor's tree; he asked his mother for an explanation. She replied that his muscles didn't work the same as other children's.

Whereas the telethon would have used this situation to create pity, this article used it to tell a touching, upbeat story. In it, the focus was not so much on how the boy differs from other children, but on how the author helped her son understand his disability, and on his own resourcefulness in adapting to it. The grief was not denied, but neither was it overdone.

Tears instantly flowed down Petey's cheeks. 'But, Mom, I want to climb trees, too,' his voice pleaded.

Silence. . . .

What to say? . . .

I let him know that it was OK to feel sad, and I stayed with him.

Five minutes later, he was OK again.

'Petey, I'm going to help you climb Mrs. Kurly's tree when I get home from work,' I said. His face lit up. . . .

Her conclusion emphasized the boy's fundamental similarity to other children in struggling to understand and come to terms with himself and his world:

He had accepted his limitation as only a 6-year-old can, with childish grace and fantasy.

There are limits—and tree trunks—that love, with a little ingenuity, can rise above. Like other 6-year-olds, Petey just wanted to play in the tree.

In Hite's piece, Petey got what he wanted, with some assistance and adaptation; in fact, this describes fairly well how most people with severe disabilities live— with assistance and adaptation. Petey was portrayed as a real child, full of humanity. What a different view from that to which telethon viewers are exposed annually!

I was impressed by the sophistication and sensitivity of the writing in this magazine—but also a little baffled. How could the same organization that edits this publication, with its realism and insight, also produce the Jerry Lewis telethon? *They know better!* I thought.

Then I realized the reason for the apparent split personality within MDA. I was seeing two very different presentation, intended for two very different audiences. The magazine is aimed at people with neuromuscular diseases and their families. I commend MDA for offering their clients such a high-quality forum for education, information, and the sharing of experiences.

However, I am dismayed that when it comes to informing the general public, MDA chooses to take the opposite approach. Does the organization fear exposing potential donors to the truths revealed so eloquently in its magazine? Does it foresee a decline in contributions if nondisabled people start to see people with disabilities as we really are? Is respect and awareness bad for the bottom line? Is raising consciousness incompatible with raising money?

Images of people with disabilities sink into the public mind every Labor Day, images of helplessness and eternal childhood. We see children frolicking at summer camp, while an announcer tells us how miserable those children are the rest of the year. We hear tear-jerking stories from parents lamenting their child's condition. Pity is the name of the game in telethonland. Pity brings in big bucks.

So what's wrong with that?

Pity is a complex and deceptive emotion. It pretends to care, to have an interest in another human being. It seems to want to take away pain and suffering. But if you look at pity up close, you notice that it also wants to distance itself from its object. A woman calls in a pledge and boasts, "My two children are perfectly healthy, thank God!" Pity does not share another's reality, only remark upon it.

Pity can be very hostile to the achievement of equality and respect. If you feel sorry for someone, you might pledge a donation, but you are not likely to offer them a good job, or approve of them dating your sister or brother. If emotions were to be grouped into families, pity has some rather unsavory kin. On this emotional family tree, pity is very close to—sometimes indistinguishable from—contempt and fear, which are uncomfortably near to hatred.

That might sound like a strong statement. But I would argue that any reaction which creates separation and inequality between people—which pity certainly does, however benevolent it might appear—is destructive. People cannot live together in community, recognizing and respecting each other as human beings, if one group feels superior to the other for any reason.

Pity paves the way for paternalism, for the attempt to control people on the basis of disability. I have lived with the implications of this reaction, this assumption that I am less able to, have less of a right to, run my own life. I saw it in the eyes of the high school journalism teacher who didn't want me in her class. I see it on the faces of people who pass me on the street, and wonder (perhaps) what I am doing out in public.

Of course, many experiences and many emotions go into the formation of bigotry. I cannot blame all discrimination on pity. Nor can I blame all tendencies toward pity on the Jerry Lewis Telethon. But we need to analyze the way this annual event capitalizes on, and feeds, those tendencies. We need to ask ourselves whether all that money, tracked exuberantly on those giant tally boards, is worth it.

I say it's not.

The effects of our protests on the Jerry Lewis Labor Day Telethon have been mixed. It has become a TV show with a split personality.

Beginning with the 1992 telethon, we began to see some changes from previous years. We saw lawyers, accountants, teachers and journalists with muscular dystrophy, receiving recognition as winners of Personal Achievement Awards. We heard the words "dignity" and "self-respect" used over and over, sometimes in strange contexts—as in "Please call in your pledge to help us save these kids' dignity and self-respect." We heard talk about the Americans with Disabilities Act and the need for a personal assistance program.

But we also saw the old familiar scenes: tuxedo-clad local hosts sweating and beaming, well-groomed two-parent families poised to look brave and desperate, Jerry Lewis mugging and weeping.

The Muscular Dystrophy Association has consistently, obstinately refused to acknowledge the validity of our concerns. Marshalling all its defenses, MDA feverishly protects the decades-old tradition. Those of us identified as the telethon's chief critics continue to be told how ungrateful, unreasonable, vicious, and emotionally disturbed we are.

Yet we'll continue to critique this twenty-plus-hour-long epic. It's a microcosm of so many of our society's attitudes towards disability. It's the details which, for me, sum up the telethon perfectly—both its attempts to change and its intrinsic flaws.

A few examples:

The telethon has often featured a Florida woman named Shelley, an obviously intelligent person with a graduate degree and a professional career. In one typical segment, Shelley and her mother were both interviewed about their hope for a cure for muscular dystrophy. Her mother raised one hand a few inches and, near tears, said something like, "If only she could do this, that would be all I would ask for her." While other mothers wish for their grown children to have personal happiness, professional success, and a family, the telethon encourages the belief that the mother of a disabled adult can only hope for one thing—either total or partial cure.

The mother also stated that she is afraid to leave Shelley at home alone, because she can't use the telephone, or answer the doorbell, by herself. I had to wonder why Shelley did not have access to the relatively simple and inexpensive devices now available, such as hands-free telephones, and doorbell intercoms.

This scene was typical of several telethon segments: In presenting an individual with a neuromuscular disorder, the focus would be on functions the person couldn't do. When I see a story like that, I start this mental process of problem-solving—thinking about adaptive equipment, attendant services, access modifications, etc.—things which could help the person function more independently.

But apparently, the general public takes these things at face value: If Shelley can't answer her own telephone, the only possible solution is to cure her disability.

The telethon certainly doesn't encourage viewers to think of other options. If the person can use equipment and personal assistance to live more independently, then viewers may not feel as sorry for her.

There was another vignette about a family with two sons, one of whom has MD. In focusing on the younger, non-disabled son, the narrator made a statement to the effect that he doesn't have a big brother who can take him places and teach him things—he has a brother he has to take care of.

This statement implies that people with disabilities are incapable of giving to any kind of relationship, that we are undesirable even as siblings. (The telethon also promotes the idea that people with disabilities are miserable parents: Fathers and mothers are shown passively watching as their kids run and play, as if someone in a wheelchair could never provide children with affection, discipline, or moral or financial support. And forget any notion that people with MD can be sexual. The telethon presents even spouses as caretakers, not lovers. The denigration of our potential for relationships is perhaps one of the most dehumanizing and negative aspects of the telethon.

The next day, a different family appeared on the local segment of the telethon. Like the first family, there were two teenage boys, one, named Paul, with MD. The brothers were obviously very close. Again, the host made a major point of talking about how the non-disabled boy "takes care of" and assists his brother Paul. At this statement, the father leaned over to the microphone and said pointedly, "Paul helps him a lot too."

The host ignored this attempt to set the record straight, but I was very moved by it. I feel real compassion for people like that family, who participate in the telethon, yet try (usually in vain) to preserve their own dignity and truth.

MDA representatives have stated again and again that pity works, it makes people give money. They might be willing to change a few things, add some references to the ADA here and there, recognize some "achievers" with MD. But they are not about to tone down, in any significant way, their appeals to pity.

We can take credit, though MDA would never acknowledge it, for the changes that have occurred—they are certainly a direct result of our criticism and protests. But we have to increase the pressure, keep raising awareness, and stop this annual insult once and for all.

20

Seeing and Making Culture

Representing the Poor

BELL HOOKS

In "Seeing and Making Culture: Representing the Poor" from the essay collection Outlaw Culture: Resisting Representations: Resisting Representations, *hooks makes her signature impassioned argument for complicating cultural representations—in this case of the poor—and enacting political and social change. hooks references her own experiences growing up impoverished in Kentucky and attending an elite university on scholarship in order to illuminate the "worlds" of the poor—worlds and experiences that too often are unfairly judged, misrepresented, and uncritically attributed to individual failing.*

Cultural critics rarely talk about the poor. Most of us use words such as "underclass" or "economically disenfranchised" when we speak about being poor. Poverty has not become one of the new hot topics of radical discourse. When contemporary Left intellectuals talk about capitalism, few if any attempts are made to relate that discourse to the reality of being poor in America. In his collection of essays *Prophetic Thought in Postmodern Times,* black philosopher Cornel West includes a piece entitled "The Black Underclass and Black Philosophers" wherein he suggests that black intellectuals within the "professional-managerial class in U.S. advanced capitalist society" must "engage in a kind of critical self-inventory, a historical situating and positioning of ourselves as persons who reflect on the situation of those more disadvantaged than us even though we may have relatives and friends in the black underclass." West does not speak of poverty or being poor in his essay. And I can remember once in conversation with him referring to my having come from a "poor" background; he corrected me and stated that my family was "working class." I told him that technically we *were* working class, because my father worked as a janitor at the post office, however the fact that there were seven children in our family meant that we often faced economic hardship in ways that made us children at least think of ourselves as poor. Indeed, in the segregated world of our small Kentucky town, we were all raised to think in terms of the haves and the have-nots, rather than in terms of class. We acknowledged the existence of four groups: the poor, who were destitute; the working folks, who were poor because they made just enough to make ends meet; those who worked and had extra money; and the rich. Even though our family was among the working folks, the economic struggle to make ends meet for such a large family always gave us a sense that there was not enough money to take care of the basics. In our house, water was a luxury and using too much could be a cause for punishment. We never talked about being poor. As children we knew we were not supposed to see ourselves as poor but we felt poor.

I began to *see* myself as poor when I went away to college. I never had any money. When I told my parents that I had scholarships and loans to attend Stanford University, they wanted to know how I would pay for getting there, for buying books, for emergencies. We were not poor, but there was no money for what was perceived to be an individualistic indulgent desire; there were cheaper colleges closer to family. When I went to college and could not afford to come home during breaks, I frequently spent my holidays with the black women who cleaned in the dormitories. Their world was my world. They, more than other folks at Stanford, knew where I was coming from. They supported and affirmed my efforts to be educated, to move past and beyond the world they lived in, the world I was coming from.

To this day, even though I am a well-paid member of what West calls the academic "professional-managerial class," in everyday life, outside the classroom, I rarely think of myself in relation to class. I mainly think about the world in terms of who has money to spend and who does not. Like many technically middle-class folks who are connected in economic responsibility to kinship structures where they provide varying material support for others, the issue is always one of money. Many middle-class black folks have no money because they regularly distribute their earnings among a larger kinship group where folks are poor and destitute, where elder parents and relatives who once were working class have retired and fallen into poverty.

Poverty was no disgrace in our household. We were socialized early on, by grandparents and parents, to assume that nobody's value could be measured by material standards. Value was connected to integrity, to being honest and hardworking. One could be hardworking and still be poor. My mother's mother Baba, who did not read or write, taught us—against the wishes of our parents—that it was better to be poor than to compromise one's dignity, that it was better to be poor than to allow another person to assert power over you in ways that were dehumanizing or cruel.

I went to college believing there was no connection between poverty and personal integrity. Entering a world of class privilege which compelled me to think critically about my economic background, I was shocked by representations of the poor learned in classrooms, as well as by the comments of professors and peers that painted an entirely different picture. They were almost always portrayed the poor as shiftless, mindless, lazy, dishonest, and unworthy. Students in the dormitory were quick to assume that anything missing had been taken by the black and Filipina women who worked there. Although I went through many periods of shame about my economic background, (even before I educated myself for critical consciousness about class by reading and studying Marx, Gramsci, Memmi, and the like), I contested stereotypical negative representations of poverty. I was especially disturbed by the assumption that the poor were without values. Indeed one crucial value that I had learned from Baba, my grandmother, and other family members was not to believe that "schooling made you smart." One could have degrees and still not be intelligent or honest. I had been taught in a culture of poverty to be intelligent, honest, to work hard, and always to be a person of my word. I had been taught to stand up for what I believed was right, to be brave and courageous. These lessons were the foundation that made it possible for me to succeed, to become the writer I always wanted to be, and to make a living in my job as an academic. They were taught to me by the poor, the disenfranchised, the underclass.

Those lessons were reinforced by liberatory religious traditions that affirmed identification with the poor. Taught to believe that poverty could be the breeding ground of moral integrity, of a recognition of the significance of communion, of sharing resources with others in the black church, I was prepared to embrace the teachings of liberatory theology, which emphasized solidarity with the poor. That solidarity was meant to be expressed not simply through charity, the sharing of privilege, but in the assertion of one's power to change the world so that the poor would have their needs met, would have access to resources, would have justice and beauty in their lives.

Contemporary popular culture in the United States rarely represents the poor in ways that display integrity and dignity. Instead, the poor are portrayed through negative stereotypes. When they are lazy and dishonest, they are consumed with longing to be rich, a longing so intense that it renders them dysfunctional. Willing to commit all manner of dehumanizing and brutal acts in the name of material gain, the poor are portrayed as seeing themselves as always and only worthless. Worth is gained only by means of material success.

Television shows and films bring the message home that no one can truly feel good about themselves if they are poor. In television sitcoms the working poor are shown to have a healthy measure of self-contempt; they dish it out to one another with a wit and humor that we can all enjoy, irrespective of our class. Yet it is clear that humor masks the longing to change their lot, the desire to "move on up" expressed in the theme song of the sitcom *The Jeffersons*. Films which portray the rags-to-riches tale continue to have major box-office appeal. Most contemporary films portraying black folks—*Harlem Nights, Boomerang, Menace II Society,* to name only a few—have as their primary theme the lust of the poor for material plenty and their willingness to do anything to satisfy that lust. *Pretty Woman* is a perfect example of a film that made huge sums of money portraying the poor in this light. Consumed and enjoyed by audiences of all races and classes, it highlights the drama of the benevolent, ruling-class person (in this case a white man, played by Richard Gere) willingly sharing his resources with a poor white prostitute (played by Julia Roberts). Indeed, many films and television shows portray the ruling class as generous, eager to share, as unattached to their wealth in their interactions with folks who are not materially privileged. These images contrast with the opportunistic avaricious longings of the poor.

Socialized by film and television to identify with the attitudes and values of privileged classes in this society, many people who are poor, or a few paychecks away from poverty, internalize fear and contempt for those who are poor. When materially deprived teenagers kill for tennis shoes or jackets they are not doing so just because they like these items so much. They also hope to escape the stigma of their class by appearing to have the trappings of more privileged classes. Poverty, in their minds and in our society as a whole, is seen as synonymous with depravity, lack, and worthlessness. No one wants to be identified as poor. Teaching literature by African American women writers at a major urban state university to predominantly black students from poor and working-class families, I was bombarded by their questioning as to why the poor black women who were abused in families in the novels we read did not "just leave." It was amazing to me that these students, many of whom were from materially disadvantaged backgrounds, had no realistic sense about the economics of housing or jobs in this society. When I asked that we identify our class backgrounds, only one student—a young single parent—was willing to identify herself as poor. We talked later about the reality that although she was not the only poor person in the class, no one else wanted to identify with being poor for fear this stigma would mark them, shame them in ways that would go beyond our class. Fear of shame-based humiliation is a primary factor leading no one to want to identify themselves as poor. I talked with young black women receiving state aid, who have not worked in years, about the issue of representation. They all agree that they do not want to be identified as poor. In their apartments they have the material possessions that indicate success (a VCR, a color television), even if it means that they do without necessities and plunge into debt to buy these items. Their self-esteem is linked to not being seen as poor.

If to be poor in this society is everywhere represented in the language we use to talk about the poor, in the mass media, as synonymous with being nothing, then it is understandable that the poor learn to be nihilistic. Society is telling them that poverty and nihilism are one and the same. If they cannot escape poverty, then they have no choice but to drown in the image of a life that is valueless. When intellectuals, journalists, or politicians speak about nihilism and the despair of the underclass, they do not link those states to representations of poverty in the mass media. And rarely do they suggest by their rhetoric that one can lead a meaningful, contented, and fulfilled life if one is poor. No one talks about our individual and collective accountability to the poor, a responsibility that begins with the politics of representation.

When white female anthropologist Carol Stack looked critically at the lives of black poor people more than twenty years ago and wrote her book *The Culture of Poverty,* she found a value system among them which emphasized the sharing of resources. That value system has long been eroded in most communities by an ethic of liberal individualism, which affirms that it is morally acceptable not to share. The mass media has been the primary teacher bringing into our lives and our homes the logic of liberal individualism, the idea that you make it by the privatized hoarding of resources, not by sharing them. Of course, liberal individualism works best for the privileged classes. But it has worsened the lot of the poor who once depended on an ethic of communalism to provide affirmation, aid, and support.

To change the devastating impact of poverty on the lives of masses of folks in our society we must change the way resources and wealth are distributed. But we must also change the way the poor are represented. Since many folks will be poor for a long time before those changes are put in place that address their economic needs, it is crucial to construct habits of seeing and being that restore an oppositional value system affirming that one can live a life of dignity and integrity in the midst of poverty. It is precisely this dignity Jonathan Freedman seeks to convey in his book *From Cradle to Grave: The Human Face of Poverty in America,* even though he does not critique capitalism or call for major changes in the distribution of wealth and resources. Yet any efforts to change the face of poverty in the United States must link a shift in representation to a demand for the redistribution of wealth and resources.

Progressive intellectuals from privileged classes who are themselves obsessed with gaining material wealth are uncomfortable with the insistence that one can be poor, yet lead a rich and meaningful life. They fear that any suggestion that poverty is acceptable may lead those who have to feel no accountability towards those who have not, even though it is unclear how they reconcile their pursuit with concern for and accountability towards the poor. Their conservative counterparts, who did much to put in place a system of representation that dehumanized the poor, fear that if poverty is seen as having no relation to value, the poor will not passively assume their role as exploited workers. That fear is masked by their insistence that the poor will not seek to work if poverty is deemed acceptable, and that the rest of us will have to support them. (Note the embedded assumption that to be poor means that one is not hardworking.) Of course, there are many more poor women and men refusing menial labor in low-paid jobs than ever before. This refusal is not rooted in laziness but in the assumption that it is not worth it to work a job where one is systematically dehumanized or exploited only to remain poor. Despite these individuals, the vast majority of poor people in our society want to work, even when jobs do not mean that they leave the ranks of the poor.

Witnessing that individuals can be poor and lead meaningful lives, I understand intimately the damage that has been done to the poor by a dehumanizing system of representation. I see the difference in self-esteem between my grandparents' and parents' generations and that of my siblings, relatives, friends and acquaintances who are poor, who suffer from a deep-seated, crippling lack of self-esteem. Ironically, despite the presence of more opportunity than that available to an older generation, low self-esteem makes it impossible for this younger generation to move forward even as it also makes their lives psychically unbearable. That psychic pain is most often relieved by some form of substance abuse. But to change the face of poverty so that it becomes, once again, a site for the formation of values, of dignity and integrity, as any other class positionality in this society, we would need to intervene in existing systems of representation.

Linking this progressive change to radical/revolutionary political movements (such as eco-feminism, for example) that urge all of us to live simply could also establish a point of connection and constructive interaction. The poor have many resources and skills for living. Those folks who are interested in sharing individual plenty as well as working politically for redistribution of wealth can work in conjunction with individuals who are materially disadvantaged to achieve this end. Material plenty is only one resource. Literacy skills are another. It would be exciting to see unemployed folks who lack reading and writing skills have available to them community-based literacy programs. Progressive literacy programs connected to education for critical consciousness could use popular movies as a base to begin learning and discussion. Theaters all across the United States that are not used in the day could be sites for this kind of program where college students and professors could share skills. Since many individuals who are poor, disadvantaged or destitute are already literate, reading groups could be formed to educate for critical consciousness, to help folks rethink how they can organize life both to live well in poverty and to move out of such circumstances. Many of the young women I encounter—black and white—who are poor and receiving state aid (and some of whom are students or would-be students) are intelligent, critical thinkers struggling to transform their circumstances. They are eager to work with folks who can offer guidance, know-how, concrete strategies. Freedman concludes his book with the reminder that

> *it takes money, organization, and laws to maintain a social structure but none of it works if there are not opportunities for people to meet and help each other along the way. Social responsibility comes down to something simple—the ability to respond.*

Constructively changing ways the poor are represented in every aspect of life is one progressive intervention that can challenge everyone to look at the face of poverty and not turn away.

21

Selling Hot Pussy

Representations of Black Female Sexuality in the Cultural Marketplace

BELL HOOKS

In "Selling Hot Pussy," bell hooks examines a wide range of texts, images, and films to illustrate the ways black women's bodies are objectified and sexualized. Author of over thirty books, hooks published this piece as a chapter in her Writing on the Body: Female Embodiment and Feminist Theory. *This essay demonstrates how seemingly progressive moves toward multicultural inclusion or identity-based cultural production might actually result in unintended consequences that reinforce oppressive systems of racism and misogyny.*

Friday night in a small midwestern town—I go with a group of artists and professors to a late night dessert place. As we walk past a group of white men standing in the entry way to the place, we overhear them talking about us, saying that my companions, who are all white, must be liberals from the college, not regular "townies," to be hanging out with a "nigger." Everyone in my group acts as though they did not hear a word of this conversation. Even when I call attention to the comments, no one responds. It's like I am not only not talking, but suddenly, to them, I am not there. I am invisible. For my colleagues, racism expressed in everyday encounters—this is our second such experience together—is only an unpleasantness to be avoided, not something to be confronted or challenged. It is just something negative disrupting the good time, better to not notice and pretend it's not there.

As we enter the dessert place they all burst into laughter and point to a row of gigantic chocolate breasts complete with nipples—huge edible tits. They think this is a delicious idea—seeing no connection between this racialized image and the racism expressed in the entry way. Living in a world where white folks are no longer nursed and nurtured primarily by black female caretakers, they do not look at these symbolic breasts and consciously think about "mammies." They do not see this representation of chocolate breasts as a sign of displaced longing for a racist past when the bodies of black women were commodity, available to anyone white who could pay the price. I look at these dark breasts and think about the representation of black female bodies in popular culture. Seeing them, I think about the connection between contemporary representations and the types of images popularized from slavery on. I remember Harriet Jacobs's powerful exposé of the psychosexual dynamics of slavery in *Incidents in the Life of a Slave Girl*. I remember the way she described that "peculiar" institution of domination and the white people who constructed it as "a cage of obscene birds."

Representations of black female bodies in contemporary popular culture rarely subvert or critique images of black female sexuality which were part of the cultural apparatus of nineteenth-century racism and which still shape perceptions today. Sander Gilman's essay "Black Bodies, White Bodies: Toward an Iconography of Female Sexuality in Late Nineteenth-Century Art, Medicine, and Literature" calls attention to the way black presence in early North American society allowed whites to sexualize their world by projecting onto black bodies a narrative of sexualization disassociated from whiteness. Gilman documents the development of this image, commenting that "by the eighteenth century, the sexuality of the black, male and female, becomes an icon for deviant sexuality." He emphasizes that it is the black female body that is forced to serve as "an icon for black sexuality in general."

Most often attention was not focused on the complete black female on display at a fancy ball in the "civilized" heart of European culture, Paris. She is there to entertain guests with the naked image of Otherness. They are not to look at her as a whole human being. They are to notice only certain parts. Objectified in a manner similar to that of black female slaves who stood on auction blocks while owners and overseers described their important, salable parts, the black women whose naked bodies were displayed for whites at social functions had no presence. They were reduced to mere spectacle. Little is known of their lives, their motivations. Their body parts were offered as evidence to support racist notions that black people were more akin to animals than other humans. When Sarah Bartmann's body was exhibited in 1810, she was ironically and perversely dubbed "the Hottentot Venus." Her naked body was displayed on numerous occasions for five years. When she died, the mutilated parts were still subject to scrutiny. Gilman stressed that: "The audience which had paid to see her buttocks and had fantasized about the uniqueness of her genitalia when she was alive could, after her death and dissection, examine both." Much of the racialized fascination with Bartmann's body concentrated attention on her buttocks.

A similar white European fascination with the bodies of black people, particularly black female bodies, was manifest during the career of Josephine Baker.

Content to "exploit" white eroticization of black bodies, Baker called attention to the "butt" in her dance routines. Phyllis Rose, though often condescending in her recent biography, *Jazz Cleopatra: Josephine Baker In Her Time,* perceptively explores Baker's concentration on her ass:

> *She handled it as though it were an instrument, a rattle, something apart from herself that she could shake. One can hardly overemphasize the importance of the rear end. Baker herself declared that people had been hiding their asses too long. "The rear end exists. I see no reason to be ashamed of it. It's true there are rear ends so stupid, so pretentious, so insignificant that they're good only for sitting on." With Baker's triumph, the erotic gaze of a nation moved downward: she had uncovered a new region for desire.*

Many of Baker's dance moves highlighting the "butt" prefigure movements popular in contemporary black dance.

Although contemporary thinking about black female bodies does not attempt to read the body as a sign of "natural" racial inferiority, the fascination with black "butts" continues. In the sexual iconography of the traditional black pornographic imagination, the protruding butt is seen as an indication of a heightened sexuality. Contemporary popular music is one of the primary cultural locations for discussions of black sexuality. In song lyrics, "the butt" is talked about in ways that attempt to challenge racist assumptions that suggest it is an ugly sign of inferiority, even as it remains a sexualized sign. The popular song "Doin' the Butt" fostered the promotion of a hot new dance favoring those who could most protrude their buttocks with pride and glee. A scene in Spike Lee's film *School Daze* depicts an all black party where everyone is attired in swimsuits dancing—doing the butt. It is one of the most compelling moments in the film. The black "butts" on display are unruly and outrageous. They are not the still bodies of the female slave made to appear as mannequin. They are not a silenced body. Displayed as playful cultural nationalist resistance, they challenge assumptions that the black body, its skin color and shape, is a mark of shame. Undoubtedly the most transgressive and provocative moment in *School Daze,* this celebration of buttocks either initiated or coincided with an emphasis on butts, especially the buttocks of women, in fashion magazines. Its potential to disrupt and challenge notions of black bodies, specifically female bodies, was undercut by the overall sexual humiliation and abuse of black females in the film. Many people did not see the film so it was really the song "Doin' the Butt" that challenged dominant ways of thinking about the body which encourage us to ignore asses because they are associated with undesirable and unclean acts. Unmasked, the "butt" could be once again worshiped as an erotic seat of pleasure and excitement.

When calling attention to the body in a manner inviting the gaze to mutilate black female bodies yet again, to focus solely on the "butt," contemporary celebrations of this part of the anatomy do not successfully subvert sexist/racist representations. Just as nineteenth-century representations of black female bodies were constructed to emphasize that these bodies were expendable, contemporary images (even those created in black cultural production) give a similar message. When Richard Wright's protest novel *Native Son* was made into a film in the 1980s, the film did not show the murder of Bigger's black girlfriend Bessie. This was doubly ironic. She is murdered in the novel and then systematically eliminated in the film. Painters exploring race as artistic subject matter in the nineteenth century often created images contrasting white female bodies with black ones in ways that reinforced the greater value of the white female icon. Gilman's essay colludes in this critical project: he is really most concerned with exploring white female sexuality.

A similar strategy is employed in the Wright novel and in the film version. In the novel, Bessie is expendable because Bigger has already committed the more heinous crime of killing a white woman. The first and more important murder subsumes the second. Everyone cares about the fate of Mary Dalton, the ruling-class white female daughter; no one cares about the fate of Bessie. Ironically, just at the moment when Bigger decides that Bessie's body is expendable, that he will kill her, he continues to demand that she help him, that she "do the right thing." Bigger intends to use her then throw her away, a gesture reinforcing that hers is an expendable body. While he must transgress dangerous boundaries to destroy the body of a white female, he can invade and violate a black female body with no fear of retribution and retaliation.

Black and female, sexual outside the context of marriage, Bessie represents "fallen womanhood." She has no protectors, no legal system will defend her rights. Pleading her cause to Bigger, she asks for recognition and compassion for her specific condition.

> *Bigger, please! Don't do this to me! Please! All I do is work, work like a dog! From morning till night. I ain't got no happiness. I ain't never had none. I ain't got nothing and you do this to me . . .*

Poignantly describing the lot of working-class poor black women in the 1940s, her words echo those of poet Nikki Giovanni describing the status of black women in the late 1960s. The opening line to "Woman Poem" reads: "You see my whole life is tied up to unhappiness." There is a radical difference, however. In the 1960s, the black female is naming her unhappiness to demand a hearing, an acknowledgment of her reality, and change her status. This poem speaks to the desire of black women to construct a sexuality apart from that imposed upon us by a racist/sexist culture, calling attention to the ways we are trapped by conventional notions of sexuality and desirability:

> *It's a sex object if you're pretty and no love or love and no sex if you're fat get back fat black woman be a mother grandmother strong thing but not woman gameswoman romantic woman love needer man seeker dick eater sweat getter fuck needing love seeking woman.*

"Woman Poem" is a cry of resistance urging those who exploit and oppress black women, who objectify and dehumanize, to confront the consequences of their actions. Facing herself, the black female realizes all that she must struggle against to achieve self-actualization. She must counter the representation of herself, her body, her being as expendable.

Bombarded with images representing black female bodies as expendable, black women have either passively absorbed this thinking or vehemently resisted it. Popular culture provides countless examples of black female appropriation and exploitation of "negative stereotypes" to either assert control over the representation or at least reap the benefits of it. Since black female sexuality has been represented in racist/sexist iconography as more free and liberated, many black women singers, irrespective of the quality of their voices, have cultivated an image which suggests they are sexually available and licentious. Undesirable in the conventional sense, which defines beauty and sexuality as desirable only to the extent that it is idealized and unattainable, the black female body gains attention only when it is synonymous with accessibility, availability, when it is sexually deviant.

Tina Turner's construction of a public sexual persona most conforms to this idea of black female sexuality. In her recent autobiography, *I, Tina*, she presents a sexualized portrait of herself—providing a narrative that is centrally "sexual confession." Even though she begins by calling attention to the fact that she was raised with puritanical notions of innocence and virtuous womanhood which made her reticent and fearful of sexual experience, all that follows contradicts this portrait. Since the image that has been cultivated and commodified in popular culture is of her as "hot" and highly sexed—the sexually ready and free black woman—a tension exists in the autobiography between the reality she presents and the image she must uphold. Describing her first sexual experience, Turner recalls:

> *Naturally, I lost my virginity in the backseat of a car. This was the fifties, right? I think he had planned it, the little devil—he knew by then that he could get into my pants, because there's already been a lot of kissing and touching inside the blouse, and then under the skirt and so forth. The next step was obvious. And me, as brazen as I was, when it came down to finally doing the real thing, it was like: "Uh-oh, it's time." I mean, I was scared. And then it happened.*
>
> *Well, it hurt so bad—I think my earlobes were hurting. I was just dying, God. And he wanted to do it two or three times! It was like poking an open wound. I could hardly walk afterwards.*
>
> *But I did it for love. The pain was excruciating; but I loved him and he loved me, and that made the pain less—Everything was right. So it was beautiful.*

Only there is nothing beautiful about the scenario Turner describes. A tension exists between the "cool" way she describes this experience, playing it off to suggest she was in control of the situation, and the reality she recounts where she succumbs to male lust and suffers sex. After describing a painful rite of sexual initiation, Turner undermines the confession by telling the reader that she felt good. Through retrospective memory, Turner is able to retell this experience in a manner that suggests she was comfortable with sexual experience at an early age, yet cavalier language does not completely mask the suffering evoked by the details she gives. However, this cavalier attitude accords best with how her fans "see" her. Throughout the biography she will describe situations of extreme sexual victimization and then undermine the impact of her words by evoking the image of herself and other black women as sexually free, suggesting that we assert sexual agency in ways that are never confirmed by the evidence she provides.

Tina Turner's singing career has been based on the construction of an image of black female sexuality that is made synonymous with wild animalistic lust.

Raped and exploited by Ike Turner, the man who made this image and imposed it on her, Turner describes the way her public persona as singer was shaped by his pornographic misogynist imagination:

> *Ike explained: As a kid back in Clarksdale, he'd become fixated on the white jungle goddess who romped through Saturday matinee movie serials—revealing rag-clad women with long flowing hair and names like Sheena, Queen of the Jungle, and Nyoka—particularly Nyoka. He still remembered* The Perils of Nyoka, *a fifteen-part Republic Picture serial from 1941, starring Kay Alridge in the title role and featuring a villainess named Vultura, an ape named Satan, and Clayton Moore (later to be TV's Lone Ranger) as love interest. Nyoka, Sheena—Tina! Tina Turner—Ike's own personal Wild Woman. He loved it.*

Turner makes no comment about her thoughts about this image. How can she? It is part of the representation which makes and maintains her stardom.

Ike's pornographic fantasy of the black female as wild sexual savage emerged from the impact of a white patriarchal controlled media shaping his perceptions of reality. His decision to create the wild black woman was perfectly compatible with prevailing representations of black female sexuality in a white supremacist society. Of course the Tina Turner story reveals that she was anything but a wild woman; she was fearful of sexuality, abused, humiliated, fucked, and fucked over. Turner's friends and colleagues document the myriad ways she suffered about the experience of being brutally physically beaten prior to appearing on stage to perform, yet there is no account of how she coped with the contradiction (this story is told by witnesses in *I, Tina*). She was on one hand in excruciating pain inflicted by a misogynist man who dominated her life and her sexuality, and on the other hand projecting in every performance the image of a wild tough sexually liberated woman. Not unlike the lead character in the novel *Story of O* by Pauline Reage, Turner must act as though she glories in her submission, that she delights in being a slave of love. Leaving Ike, after many years of forced marital rape and physical abuse, because his violence is utterly uncontrollable, Turner takes with her the "image" he created.

Despite her experience of abuse rooted in sexist and racist objectification, Turner appropriated the "wild woman" image, using it for career advancement. Always fascinated with wigs and long hair, she created the blonde lioness mane to appear all the more savage and animalistic. Blondeness links her to jungle imagery even as it serves as an endorsement of a racist aesthetics which sees blonde hair as the epitome of beauty. Without Ike, Turner's career has soared to new heights, particularly as she works harder to exploit the visual representation of woman (and particularly black woman) as sexual savage. No longer caught in the sado-masochistic sexual iconography of black female in erotic war with her mate that was the subtext of the Ike and Tina Turner show, she is now portrayed as the autonomous black woman whose sexuality is solely a way to exert power. Inverting old imagery, she places herself in the role of dominator.

Playing the role of Aunty Entity in the film *Mad Max: Beyond the Thunderdome,* released in 1985, Turner's character evokes two racist/sexist stereotypes, that of the black "mammy" turned power hungry and the sexual savage who uses her body to seduce and conquer men. Portrayed as lusting after the white male hero who will both conquer and reject her, Aunty Entity is the contemporary reenactment of that mythic black female in slavery who supposedly "vamped" and seduced virtuous white male slave owners. Of course the contemporary white male hero of *Mad Max* is stronger than his colonial forefathers. He does not succumb to the dangerous lure of the deadly black seductress who rules over a mini-nation whose power is based on the use of shit. Turner is the bad black woman in this film, an image she will continue to exploit.

Turner's video "What's Love Got to Do with It" also highlights the convergence of sexuality and power. Here, the black woman's body is represented as potential weapon. In the video, she walks down rough city streets, strutting her stuff, in a way that declares desirability, allure, while denying access. It is not that she is no longer represented as available; she is "open" only to those whom she chooses. Assuming the role of hunter, she is the sexualized woman who makes men and women her prey (in the alluring gaze of the video, the body moves in the direction of both sexes). This tough black woman has no time for woman bonding, she is out to "catch." Turner's fictive model of black female sexual agency remains rooted in misogynist notions. Rather than being a pleasure-based eroticism, it is ruthless, violent; it is about women using sexual power to do violence to the male Other.

Appropriating the wild woman pornographic myth of black female sexuality created by men in a white supremacist patriarchy, Turner exploits it for her own ends to achieve economic self-sufficiency. When she left Ike, she was broke and in serious debt. The new Turner image conveys the message that happiness and power come to women who learn to beat men at their own game, to throw off any investment in romance and get down to the real dog-eat-dog thing. "What's Love Got to Do with It" sung by Turner evokes images of the strong bitchified black woman who is on the make. Subordinating the idea of romantic love and praising the use of sex for pleasure as commodity to exchange, the song had great appeal for contemporary postmodern culture. It equates pleasure with materiality, making it an object to be sought after, taken, acquired by any means necessary. When sung by black women singers, "What's Love Got to Do with It" called to mind old stereotypes which make the assertion of black female sexuality and prostitution synonymous. Just as black female prostitutes in the 1940s and 1950s actively sought clients in the streets to make money to survive, thereby publicly linking prostitution with black female sexuality, contemporary black female sexuality is fictively constructed in popular rap and R&B songs solely as commodity—sexual service for money and power, pleasure is secondary.

Contrasted with the representation of wild animalistic sexuality, black female singers like Aretha Franklin and younger contemporaries like Anita Baker fundamentally link romance and sexual pleasure. Aretha, though seen as a victim of no-good men, the classic "woman who loves too much" and leaves the lyrics to prove it, also sang songs of resistance. "Respect" was heard by many black folks, especially black women, as a song challenging black male sexism and female victimization while evoking notions of mutual care and support. In a recent pbs special highlighting individual musicians, Aretha Franklin was featured. Much space was given in the documentary to white male producers who shaped her public image. In the documentary, she describes the fun of adding the words "sock it to me" to "Respect" as a powerful refrain. One of the white male producers, Jerry Wexler, offers his interpretation of its meaning, claiming that it was a call for "sexual attention of the highest order." His sexualized interpretations of the song seemed far removed from the way it was heard and celebrated in black communities. Looking at this documentary, which was supposedly a tribute to Aretha Franklin's power, it was impossible not to have one's attention deflected away from the music by the subtext of the film, which can be seen as a visual narrative documenting her obsessive concern with the body and achieving a look suggesting desirability. To achieve this end, Franklin constantly struggles with her weight, and the images in the film chronicle her various shifts in body size and shape. As though mocking this concern with her body, throughout most of the documentary Aretha appears in what seems to be a household setting, a living room maybe, wearing a strapless evening dress, much too small for her breast size, so her breasts appear like two balloons filled with water about to burst. With no idea who shaped and controlled this image, I can only reiterate that it undermined the insistence in the film that she has overcome sexual victimization and remained a powerful singer; the latter seemed more likely than the former.

Black female singers who project a sexualized persona are as obsessed with hair as they are with body size and body parts. As with nineteenth-century sexual iconography, specific parts of the anatomy are designated more sexual and worthy of attention than others. Today much of the sexualized imagery for black female stars seems to be fixated on hair; it and not buttocks signifies animalistic sexuality. This is quintessentially so for Tina Turner and Diana Ross. It is ironically appropriate that much of this hair is synthetic and man-made, artificially constructed as is the sexualized image it is meant to evoke. Within a patriarchal culture where women over forty are not represented as sexually desirable, it is understandable that singers exploiting sexualized representations who are near the age of fifty place less emphasis on body parts that may reflect aging while focusing on hair.

In a course I teach on "The Politics of Sexuality," where we often examine connections between race and sex, we once critically analyzed a *Vanity Fair* cover depicting Diana Ross. Posed on a white background, apparently naked with the exception of white cloth draped loosely around her body, the most striking element in the portrait was the long mane of jet black hair cascading down. There was so much hair that it seemed to be consuming her body (which looked frail and anorexic), negating the possibility that this naked flesh could represent active female sexual agency. The white diaper-like cloth reinforced the idea that this was a portrait of an adult female who wanted to be seen as childlike and innocent. Symbolically, the hair that is almost a covering hearkens back to early pictorial images of Eve in the garden. It evokes wildness, a sense of the "natural" world, even as it shrouds the body, repressing it, keeping it from the gaze of a culture that does not invite women to be sexual subjects. Concurrently, this cover contrasts whiteness and blackness. Whiteness dominates the page, obscuring and erasing the possibility of any assertion of black power. The longing that is most visible in this cover is that of the black woman to embody and be encircled by whiteness, personified by the possession of long straight hair. Since the hair is produced as commodity and purchased, it affirms contemporary notions of female beauty and desirability as that which can be acquired.

According to postmodern analyses of fashion, this is a time when commodities produce bodies, as this image of Ross suggests. In her essay "Fashion and the

Cultural Logic of Postmodernity," Gail Faurshou explains that beauty is no longer seen as a sustained "category of precapitalist culture." Instead, "the colonization and the appropriation of the body as its own production/consumption machine in late capitalism is a fundamental theme of contemporary socialization." This cultural shift enables the bodies of black women to be represented in certain domains of the "beautiful" where they were once denied entry, i.e., high fashion magazines. Reinscribed as spectacle, once again on display, the bodies of black women appearing in these magazines are not there to document the beauty of black skin, of black bodies, but rather to call attention to other concerns. They are represented so readers will notice that the magazine is racially inclusive even though their features are often distorted, their bodies contorted into strange and bizarre postures that make the images appear monstrous or grotesque. They seem to represent an anti-aesthetic, one that mocks the very notion of beauty.

Often black female models appear in portraits that make them look less like humans and more like mannequins or robots. Currently, black models whose hair is not straightened are often photographed wearing straight wigs; this seems to be especially the case if the models' features are unconventional, i.e., if she has large lips or particularly dark skin, which is not often featured in the magazine. The October 1989 issue of *Elle* presented a short profile of designer Azzedine Alaia. He stands at a distance from a black female body holding the sleeves of her dress. Wearing a ridiculous straight hair-do, she appears naked holding the dress in front of her body. The caption reads, "they are beautiful aren't they!" His critical gaze is on the model and not the dress. As commentary it suggests that even black women can look beautiful in the right outfit. Of course when you read the piece, this statement is not referring to the model, but is a statement Alaia makes about his clothes. In contemporary post-modern fashion sense, the black female is the best medium for the showing of clothes because her image does not detract from the outfit; it is subordinated.

Years ago, when much fuss was made about the reluctance of fashion magazines to include images of black women, it was assumed that the presence of such representations would in and of themselves challenge racist stereotypes that imply black women are not beautiful. Nowadays, black women are included in magazines in a manner that tends to reinscribe prevailing stereotypes. Darker-skinned models are most likely to appear in photographs where their features are distorted. Biracial women tend to appear in sexualized images. Trendy catalogues like *Tweeds* and *J. Crew* make use of a racialized subtext in their layout and advertisements. Usually they are emphasizing the connection between a white European and American style. When they began to include darker-skinned models, they chose biracial or fair-skinned black women, particularly with blonde or light brown long hair. The nonwhite models appearing in these catalogues must resemble as closely as possible their white counterparts so as not to detract from the racialized subtext. A recent cover of *Tweeds* carried this statement:

> *Color is, perhaps, one of the most important barometers of character and self-assurance. It is as much a part of the international language of clothes as silhouette. The message colors convey, however, should never overwhelm. They should speak as eloquently and intelligently as the wearer. Whenever colors have that intelligence, subtlety, and nuance we tend to call them European.*

Given the racialized terminology evoked in this copy, it follows that when flesh is exposed in attire that is meant to evoke sexual desirability it is worn by a non-white model. As sexist/racist sexual mythology would have it, she is the embodiment of the best of the black female savage tempered by those elements of whiteness that soften this image, giving it an aura of virtue and innocence. In the racialized pornographic imagination, she is the perfect combination of virgin and whore, the ultimate vamp. The impact of this image is so intense that Iman, a highly paid black fashion model who once received worldwide acclaim because she was the perfect black clone of a white ice goddess beauty, has had to change. Postmodern notions that black female beauty is constructed, not innate or inherent, are personified by the career of Iman. Noted in the past for features this culture sees as "Caucasian"[—]thin nose, lips, and limbs—Iman appears in the October 1989 issue of *Vogue* "made over." Her lips and breasts are suddenly full. Having once had her "look" destroyed by a car accident and then remade, Iman now goes a step further. Displayed as the embodiment of a heightened sexuality, she now looks like the racial/sexual stereotype. In one full-page shot, she is naked, wearing only a pair of brocade boots, looking as though she is ready to stand on any street corner and turn a trick, or worse yet, as though she just walked off one of the pages of *Players* (a porn magazine for blacks). Iman's new image appeals to a culture that is eager to reinscribe the image of black woman as sexual primitive. This new representation is a response to contemporary fascination with an ethnic look, with the exotic Other who promises to fulfill racial and sexual stereotypes, to satisfy longings. This image is but an extension of the edible black tit.

Currently, in the fashion world the new black female icon who is also gaining greater notoriety, as she assumes both the persona of sexually hot "savage" and white-identified black girl, is the Caribbean-born model Naomi Campbell. Imported beauty, she, like Iman, is almost constantly visually portrayed nearly nude against a sexualized background. Abandoning her "natural" hair for blonde wigs or ever-lengthening weaves, she has great crossover appeal. Labeled by fashion critics as the black Briget Bardot, she embodies an aesthetic that suggests black women, while appealingly "different," must resemble white women to be considered really beautiful.

Within literature and early film, this sanitized ethnic image was defined as that of the "tragic mulatto." Appearing in film, she was the vamp that white men feared. As Julie Burchill puts it outrageously in *Girls On Film*:

> *In the mature Forties, Hollywood decided to get to grips with the meaty and messy topic of multiracial romance, but it was a morbid business. Even when the girls were gorgeous white girls—multiracial romance brought tears, traumas, and suicide. The message was clear: you intelligent white men suffer enough guilt because of what your grandaddy did—you want to suffer some more! Keep away from those girls.*

Contemporary films portraying biracial stars convey this same message. The warning for women is different from that given men—we are given messages about the danger of asserting sexual desire. Clearly the message from *Imitation of Life* was that attempting to define oneself as sexual subject would lead to rejection and abandonment. In the film *Choose Me*, Rae Dawn Chong plays the role of the highly sexual black woman chasing and seducing the white man who does not desire her (as was first implied in *Imitation of Life*) but instead uses her sexually, beats her, then discards her. The biracial black woman is constantly "gaslighted" in contemporary film. The message her sexualized image conveys does not change even as she continues to chase the white man as if only he had the power to affirm that she is truly desirable.

European films like *Mephisto* and the more recent *Mona Lisa* also portray the almost white, black woman as tragically sexual. The women in the films can only respond to constructions of their reality created by the more powerful. They are trapped. Mona Lisa's struggle to be sexually self-defining leads her to choose lesbianism, even though she is desired by the white male hero. Yet her choice of a female partner does not mean sexual fulfillment as the object of her lust is a drug-addicted young white woman who is always too messed up to be sexual. Mona Lisa nurses and protects her. Rather than asserting sexual agency, she is once again in the role of mammy.

In a more recent film, *The Virgin Machine*, a white German woman obsessed by the longing to understand desire goes to California where she hopes to find a "paradise of black Amazons." However, when she arrives and checks out the lesbian scene, the black women she encounters are portrayed as mean fat grotesques, lewd and licentious. Contemporary films continue to place black women in two categories, mammy or slut, and occasionally a combination of the two. In *Mona Lisa*, one scene serves as powerful commentary on the way black sexuality is perceived in a racist and imperialist social context. The white male who desires the black prostitute Mona Lisa is depicted as a victim of romantic love who wishes to rescue her from a life of ruin. Yet he is also the conqueror, the colonizer, and this is most evident in the scene where he watches a video wherein she engages in fellatio with the black male pimp who torments her. Both the black man and the black woman are presented as available for the white male's sexual consumption. In the context of postmodern sexual practice, the masturbatory voyeuristic technologically based fulfillment of desire is more exciting than actually possessing any real Other.

There are few films or television shows that attempt to challenge assumptions that sexual relationships between black women and white men are not based solely on power relationships which mirror master/slave paradigms. Years ago, when soap operas first tried to portray romantic/sexual involvement between a black woman and a white man, the station received so many letters of protest from outraged viewers that they dropped this plot. Today many viewers are glued to the television screen watching the soap opera *All My Children* primarily to see if the black woman played by Debbie Morgan will win the white man she so desperately loves. These two lovers are never portrayed in bedroom scenes so common now in daytime soaps. Morgan's character is competing not just with an old white woman flame to get her white man, she is competing with a notion of family. And the story poses the question of whether white male desire for black flesh will prevail over commitments to blood and family loyalty.

Despite this plot of interracial sexual romance on the soaps, there is little public discussion of the connections between race and sexuality. In real life, it was the

Miss America pageant where a black woman was chosen to represent beauty and therefore desirability which forced a public discussion of race and sex. When it was revealed that Vanessa Williams, the fair-skinned straightened-hair "beauty," had violated the representation of the Miss America girl as pure and virtuous by having posed nude in a series of photographs showing her engaged in sexual play with a white woman, she lost her crown but gained a different status. After her public "disgrace," she was able to remain in the limelight by appropriating the image of sexualized vamp and playing sexy roles in films. Unmasked by a virtuous white public, she assumed (according to their standards) the rightful erotic place set aside for black women in the popular imagination. The American public that had so brutally critiqued Williams and rejected her had no difficulty accepting and applauding her when she accepted the image of fallen woman. Again, as in the case of Tina Turner, Williams's bid for continued success necessitated her acceptance of conventional racist/sexist representations of black female sexuality.

The contemporary film that has most attempted to address the issue of black female sexual agency is Spike Lee's *She's Gotta Have It*. Sad to say, the black woman does not get "it." By the end of the film, she is still unable to answer the critical question, posed by one of her lovers as he rapes her, "whose pussy is this?" Reworded the question might be: How and when will black females assert sexual agency in ways that liberate us from the confines of colonized desire, of racist/sexist imagery and practice? Had Nola Darling been able to claim her sexuality and name its power, the film would have had a very different impact.

There are few films that explore issues of black female sexuality in ways that intervene and disrupt conventional representations. The short film *Dreaming Rivers,* by the British black film collective Sankofa, juxtaposes the idealized representation of black woman as mother with that of sexual subject, showing adult children facing their narrow notions of black female identity. The film highlights the autonomous sexual identity of a mature black woman which exists apart from her role as mother and caregiver. *Passion of Remembrance,* another film by Sankofa, offers exciting new representations of the black female body and black female sexuality. In one playfully erotic scene, two young black women, a lesbian couple, get dressed to go out. As part of their celebratory preparations they dance together, painting their lips, looking at their images in the mirror, exulting in their black female bodies. They shake to a song that repeats the refrain "let's get loose" without conjuring images of a rotgut colonized sexuality on display for the racist/sexist imagination. Their pleasure, the film suggests, emerges in a decolonized erotic context rooted in commitments to feminist and antiracist politics. When they look in the mirror and focus on specific body parts (their full thick lips and buttocks), the gaze is one of recognition. We see their pleasure and delight in themselves.

Films by African American women filmmakers also offer the most oppositional images of black female sexuality. Seeing for a second time Kathleen Collin's film *Losing Ground,* I was impressed by her daring, the way she portrays black female sexuality in a way that is fresh and exciting. Like *Passion of Remembrance* it is in a domestic setting, where black women face one another (in Collin's film—as mother and daughter), that erotic images of black female sexuality surface outside a context of domination and exploitation. When daughter and mother share a meal, the audience watches as a radical sexual aesthetics emerges as the camera moves from woman to woman, focusing on the shades and textures of their skin, the shapes of their bodies, and the way their delight and pleasure in themselves is evident in their environment. Both black women discreetly flaunt a rich sensual erotic energy that is not directed outward, it is not there to allure or entrap; it is a powerful declaration of black female sexual subjectivity.

When black women relate to our bodies, our sexuality, in ways that place erotic recognition, desire, pleasure, and fulfillment at the center of our efforts to create radical black female subjectivity, we can make new and different representations of ourselves as sexual subjects. To do so we must be willing to transgress traditional boundaries. We must no longer shy away from the critical project of openly interrogating and exploring representations of black female sexuality as they appear everywhere, especially in popular culture. In *The Power of the Image: Essays on Representation and Sexuality,* Annette Kuhn offers a critical manifesto for feminist thinkers who long to explore gender and representation:

> *In order to challenge dominant representations, it is necessary first of all to understand how they work, and thus where to seek points of possible productive transformation. From such understanding flow various politics and practices of oppositional cultural production, among which may be counted feminist interventions . . . there is another justification for a feminist analysis of mainstream images of women: may it not teach us to recognize inconsistencies and contradictions within dominant traditions of representation, to identify points of leverage for our own intervention: cracks and fissures through which may be captured glimpses of what in other circumstance might be possible, visions of "a world outside the order not normally seen or thought about?"*

This is certainly the challenge facing black women, who must confront the old painful representations of our sexuality as a burden we must suffer, representations still haunting the present. We must make the oppositional space where our sexuality can be named and represented, where we are sexual subjects—no longer bound and trapped.

22

I, Too, Sing America

LANGSTON HUGHES

In this much-anthologized poem, Langston Hughes speaks to the cultivation of community and resources in the midst of blatant racism. This short piece presents an instance of racial discrimination and the reflections and plans of the man discriminated against. Hughes suggests in this poem the strategic usefulness of pursuing multiple approaches for social change, including material accumulation and moral indictment. Well-known as a great American poet, Hughes also wrote about the political nature and function of art.

I, too, sing America.

I am the darker brother.
They send me to eat in the kitchen
When company comes.
But I laugh,
And eat well,
And grow strong.

To-morrow
I'll sit at the table
When company comes
Nobody'll dare

Say to me,
"Eat in the kitchen"
Then.

Besides, they'll see how beautiful I am
And be ashamed—

I, too, am America.

23

Nobody Mean More to Me Than You and the Future Life of Willie Jordan

JUNE JORDAN

June Jordan, author of over twenty collections of poetry and essays, presents here the story of how she and a group of her college students came to explicitly study the features and politics of "Black English." The students also deploy their linguistic prowess to protest the police killing of one student's brother and the lack of accountability that followed the shooting. In this essay from On Call: Political Essays, *Jordan promotes the study of how language shapes identity, forms community, and enables activism.*

Black English is not exactly a linguistic buffalo; as children, most of the thirty-five million Afro-Americans living here depend on this language for our discovery of the world. But then we approach our maturity inside a larger social body that will not support our efforts to become anything other than the clones of those who are neither our mothers nor our fathers. We begin to grow up in a house where every true mirror shows us the face of somebody who does not belong there, whose walk and whose talk will never look or sound "right," because that house was meant to shelter a family that is alien and hostile to us. As we learn our way around this environment, either we hide our original word habits, or we completely surrender our own voice, hoping to please those who will never respect anyone different from themselves: Black English is not exactly a linguistic buffalo, but we should understand its status as an endangered species, as a perishing, irreplaceable system of community intelligence, or we should expect its extinction, and, along with that, the extinguishing of much that constitutes our own proud, and singular identity.

What we casually call "English" less and less defers to England and its "gentlemen." "English" is no longer a specific matter of geography or an element of class privilege; more than thirty-three countries use this tool as a means of "intranational communication." Countries as disparate as Zimbabwe and Malaysia, or Israel and Uganda, use it as their non-native currency of convenience. Obviously, this tool, this "English," cannot function inside thirty-three discrete societies on the basis of rules and values absolutely determined somewhere else, in a thirty-fourth other country, for example.

In addition to that staggering congeries of non-native users of English, there are five countries, or 333,746,000 people, for whom this thing called "English" serves as a native tongue. Approximately 10% of these native speakers of "English" are Afro-American citizens of the U.S.A. I cite these numbers and varieties of human beings dependent on "English" in order, quickly, to suggest how strange and how tenuous is any concept of "Standard English." Obviously, numerous forms of English now operate inside a natural, an uncontrollable, continuum of development. I would suppose "the standard" for English in Malaysia is not the same as "the standard" in Zimbabwe. I know that standard forms of English for Black people in this country do not copy those of whites. And, in fact, the structural differences between these two kinds of English have intensified, becoming more Black, or less white, despite the expected homogenizing effects of television and other mass media.

Nonetheless, white standards of English persist, supreme and unquestioned, in these United States. Despite our multi-lingual population, and despite the deepening Black and white cleavage within that conglomerate, white standards control our official and popular judgements of verbal proficiency and correct, or incorrect, language skills, including speech. In contrast to India, where at least fourteen languages co-exist as legitimate Indian languages, in contrast to Nicaragua, where all citizens are legally entitled to formal school instruction in their regional or tribal languages, compulsory education in America compels accommodation to exclusively white forms of "English." White English, in America, is "Standard English."

This story begins two years ago. I was teaching a new course, "In Search of the Invisible Black Woman," and my rather large class seemed evenly divided between young Black women and men. Five or six white students also sat in attendance. With unexpected speed and enthusiasm we had moved through historical narratives of the 19th century to literature by and about Black women, in the 20th. I had assigned the first forty pages of Alice Walker's *The Color Purple,* and I came, eagerly, to class that morning:

"So!" I exclaimed, aloud. "What did you think? How did you like it?"

The students studied their hands, or the floor. There was no response. The tense, resistant feeling in the room fairly astounded me.

At last, one student, a young woman still not meeting my eyes, muttered something in my direction:

"What did you say?" I prompted her.

"Why she have them talk so funny. It don't sound right."

"You mean the language?"

Another student lifted his head: "It don't look right, neither. I couldn't hardly read it."

At this, several students dumped on the book. Just about unanimously, their criticisms targeted the language. I listened to what they wanted to say and silently marvelled at the similarities between their casual speech patterns and Alice Walker's written version of Black English.

But I decided against pointing to these identical traits of syntax; I wanted not to make them self-conscious about their own spoken language—not while they clearly felt it was "wrong." Instead I decided to swallow my astonishment. Here was a negative Black reaction to a prize-winning accomplishment of Black literature that white readers across the country had selected as a best seller. Black rejection was aimed at the one irreducibly Black element of Walker's work: the language—Celie's Black English. I wrote the opening lines of *The Color Purple* on the blackboard and asked the students to help me translate these sentences into Standard English:

> *You better not never tell nobody but God. It'd kill your mammy.*
>
> *Dear God,*
>
> *I am fourteen years old. I have always been a good girl. Maybe you can give me a sign letting me know what is happening to me.*
>
> *Last spring after Little Lucious come I heard them fussing. He was pulling on her arm. She say it too soon, Fonso. I ain't well. Finally he leave her alone. A week go by, he pulling on her arm again. She say, Naw, I ain't gonna. Can't you see I'm already half dead, an all of the children.*

Our process of translation exploded with hilarity and even hysterical, shocked laughter: The Black writer, Alice Walker, knew what she was doing! If rudimentary criteria for good fiction includes the manipulation of language so that the syntax and diction of sentences will tell you the identity of speakers, the probable age and sex and class of speakers, and even the locale—urban/rural/southern/western— then Walker had written, perfectly. This is the translation into Standard English that our class produced:

> *Absolutely, one should never confide in anybody besides God. Your secrets could prove devastating to your mother.*
>
> *Dear God,*
>
> *I am fourteen years old. I have always been good. But now, could you help me to understand what is happening to me?*
>
> *Last spring, after my little brother, Lucious, was born, I heard my parents fighting. My father kept pulling at my mother's arm. But she told him, "It's too soon for sex, Alfonso. I am still not feeling well." Finally, my father left her alone. A week went by, and then he began*

bothering my mother again: pulling her arm. She told him, "No, I won't! Can't you see I'm already exhausted from all of these children?"

(Our favorite line was "It's too soon for sex, Alphonso.")

Once we could stop laughing, once we could stop our exponentially wild improvisations on the theme of Translated Black English, the students pushed me to explain their own negative first reactions to their spoken language on the printed page. I thought it was probably akin to the shock of seeing yourself in a photograph for the first time. Most of the students had never before seen a written facsimile of the way they talk. None of the students had ever learned how to read and write their own verbal system of communication: Black English. Alternatively, this fact began to baffle or else bemuse and then infuriate my students. Why not? Was it too late? Could they learn how to do it, now? And, ultimately, the final test question, the one testing my sincerity: Could I teach them? Because I had never taught anyone Black English and, as far as I knew, no one, anywhere in the United States, had ever offered such a course, the best I could say was "I'll try."

He looked like a wrestler.

He sat dead center in the packed room and, every time our eyes met, he quickly nodded his head as though anxious to reassure and encourage me.

Short, with strikingly broad shoulders and long arms, he spoke with a surprisingly high, soft voice that matched the soft bright movement of his eyes. His name was Willie Jordan. He would have seemed even more unlikely in the context of Contemporary Women's Poetry, except that ten or twelve other Black men were taking the course, as well. Still, Willie was conspicuous. His extreme fitness, the muscular density of his presence underscored the riveted, gentle attention that he gave to anything anyone said. Generally, he did not join the loud and rowdy dialogue flying back and forth, but there could be no doubt about his interest in our discussions. And, when he stood to present an argument he'd prepared, overnight, that nervous smile of his vanished and an irregular stammering replaced it, as he spoke with visceral sincerity, word by word.

That was how I met Willie Jordan. It was in between "In Search of the Invisible Black Woman" and "The Art of Black English." I was waiting for Departmental approval and I supposed that Willie might be, so to speak, killing time until he, too, could study Black English. But Willie really did want to explore Contemporary Women's Poetry and, to that end, volunteered for extra research and never missed a class.

Towards the end of that semester, Willie approached me for an independent study project on South Africa. It would commence the next semester. I thought Willie's writing needed the kind of improvement only intense practice will yield. I knew his intelligence was outstanding. But he'd wholeheartedly opted for "Standard English" at a rather late age, and the results were stilted and frequently polysyllabic, simply for the sake of having more syllables. Willie's unnatural formality of language seemed to me consistent with the formality of his research into South African apartheid. As he projected his studies, he would have little time, indeed, for newspapers. Instead, more than 90% of his research would mean saturation in strictly historical, if not archival, material. I was certainly interested. It would be tricky to guide him into a more confident and spontaneous relationship with both language and apartheid. It was going to be wonderful to see what happened when he could catch up with himself, entirely, and talk back to the world.

September, 1984: Breezy fall weather and much excitement! My class, "The Art of Black English," was full to the limit of the fire laws. And, in Independent Study, Willie Jordan showed up, weekly, fifteen minutes early for each of our sessions. I was pretty happy to be teaching, altogether!

I remember an early class when a young brother, replete with his ever-present pork-pie hat, raised his hand and then told us that most of what he'd heard was "all right" except it was "too clean." "The brothers on the street," he continued, "they mix it up more. Like 'fuck' and 'motherfuck.' Or like 'shit.' " He waited. I waited. Then all of us laughed a good while, and we got into a brawl about "correct" and "realistic" Black English that led to Rule 1.

Rule 1: *Black English is about a whole lot more than mothafuckin.*

As a criterion, we decided, "realistic" could take you anywhere you want to go. Artful places. Angry places. Eloquent and sweetalkin places. Polemical places. Church. And the local Bar & Grill. We were checking out a language, not a mood or a scene or one guy's forgettable mouthing off.

It was hard. For most of the students, learning Black English required a fall-back to patterns and rhythms of speech that many of their parents had beaten out of them. I mean *beaten*. And, in a majority of cases, correct Black English could be achieved only by striving for *incorrect* Standard English, something they were still pushing at, quite uncertainly. This state of affairs led to Rule 2.

Rule 2: *If it's wrong in Standard English it's probably right in Black English, or, at least, you're hot.*

It was hard. Roommates and family members ridiculed their studies, or remained incredulous. "You *studying* that shit? At school?" But we were beginning to feel the companionship of pioneers. And we decided that we needed another rule that would establish each one of us as equally important to our success. This was Rule 3.

Rule 3: *If it don't sound like something that come out somebody mouth then it don't sound right. If it don't sound right then it ain't hardly right. Period.*

This rule produced two weeks of compositions in which the students agonizingly tried to spell the sound of the Black English sentence they wanted to convey. But Black English is preeminently, an oral/spoken means of communication. *And spelling don't talk.* So we needed Rule 4.

Rule 4: *Forget about the spelling. Let the syntax carry you.*

Once we arrived at Rule 4 we started to fly because syntax, the structure of an idea, leads you to the world view of the speaker and reveals her values. The syntax of a sentence equals the structure of your consciousness. If we insisted that the language of Black English adheres to a distinctive Black syntax, then we were postulating a profound difference between white and Black people, *per se*. Was it a difference to prize or to obliterate?

There are three qualities of Black English—the presence of life, voice, and clarity—that testify to a distinctive Black value system that we became excited about and self-consciously tried to maintain.

1. Black English has been produced by a pre-technocratic, if not anti-technological, culture. More, our culture has been constantly threatened by annihilation or, at least, the swallowed blurring of assimilation. Therefore, our language is a system constructed by people constantly needing to insist that we exist, that we are present. Our language devolves from a culture that abhors all abstraction, or anything tending to obscure or delete the fact of the human being who is here and now/the truth of the person who is speaking or listening. Consequently, *there is no passive voice construction possible in Black English*. For example, you cannot say, "Black English is being eliminated." You must say, instead, "White people eliminating Black English." The assumption of the presence of life governs all of Black English. Therefore, overwhelmingly, *all action takes place in the language of the present indicative*. And every sentence assumes the living and active participation of at least two human beings, the speaker and the listener.

2. A primary consequence of the person-centered values of Black English is the delivery of voice. If you speak or write Black English, your ideas will necessarily possess that otherwise elusive attribute, *voice*.

3. One main benefit following from the person-centered values of Black English is that of *clarity*. If your idea, your sentence, assumes the presence of at least two living and active people, you will make it understandable because the motivation behind every sentence is the wish to say something real to somebody real.

As the weeks piled up, translation from Standard English into Black English or vice versa occupied a hefty part of our course work.

> *Standard English (hereafter S.E.): "In considering the idea of studying Black English those questioned suggested—"*
>
> *(What's the subject? Where's the person? Is anybody alive in there, in that idea?)*
>
> *Black English (hereafter B.E.): "I been asking people what you think about somebody studying Black English and they answer me like this:"*

But there were interesting limits. You cannot "translate" instances of Standard English preoccupied with abstraction or with nothing/nobody evidently alive, into Black English. That would warp the language into uses antithetical to the guiding perspective of its community of users. Rather you must first change those Standard English sentences, themselves, into ideas consistent with the person-centered assumptions of Black English.

Guidelines for Black English

1. Minimal number of words for every idea: This is the source for the aphoristic and/or poetic force of the language; eliminate every possible word.

2. Clarity: If the sentence is not clear it's not Black English.

3. Eliminate use of the verb *to be* whenever possible. This leads to the deployment of more descriptive and therefore more precise verbs.

4. Use *be* or *been* only when you want to describe a chronic, ongoing state of things.
   He *be* at the office, by 9. (He is always at the office by 9.)
   He *been* with her since forever.

5. Zero copula: Always eliminate the verb *to be* whenever it would combine with another verb, in Standard English.
   S.E.: She is going out with him.
   B.E.: She going out with him.

6. Eliminate *do* as in:
   S.E.: What do you think? What do you want?
   B.E.: What you think? What you want?

Rules number 3, 4, 5, and 6 provide for the use of the minimal number of verbs per idea and, therefore, greater accuracy in the choice of verb.

7. In general, if you wish to say something really positive, try to formulate the idea using emphatic negative structure.
   S.E.: He's fabulous.
   B.E.: He bad.

8. Use double or triple negatives for dramatic emphasis.
   S.E.: Tina Turner sings out of this world.
   B.E.: Ain nobody sing like Tina.

9. Never use the *-ed* suffix to indicate the past tense of a verb.
   S.E.: She closed the door.
   B.E.: She close the door. Or, she have close the door.

10. Regardless of intentional verb time, only use the third person singular, present indicative, for use of the verb to *have*, as an auxiliary.
    S.E.: He had his wallet then he lost it.
    B.E.: He have him wallet then he lose it.
    S.E.: We had seen that movie.
    B.E.: We seen that movie. Or, we have see that movie.

11. Observe a minimal inflection of verbs. Particularly, never change from the first person singular forms to the third person singular.
    S.E.: Present Tense Forms: He goes to the store.
    B.E.: He go to the store.
    S.E.: Past Tense Forms: He went to the store.
    B.E.: He go to the store. Or, he gone to the store. Or, he been to the store.

12. The possessive case scarcely ever appears in Black English. Never use an apostrophe ('s) construction. If you wander into a possessive case component of an idea, then keep logically consistent: *ours, his, theirs, mines.* But, most likely, if you bump into such a component, you have wandered outside the underlying worldview of Black English.

S.E.: He will take their car tomorrow.
B.E.: He taking they car tomorrow.

13. Plurality: Logical consistency, continued: If the modifier indicates plurality, then the noun remains in the singular case.
S.E.: He ate twelve doughnuts.
B.E.: He eat twelve doughnut.
S.E.: She has many books.
B.E.: She have many book.

14. Listen for, or invent, special Black English forms of the past tense, such as: "He losted it. That what she felted." If they are clear and readily understood, then use them.

Do not hesitate to play with words, sometimes inventing them; e.g., "astropotomous" means huge like a hippo plus astronomical and, therefore, signifies real big.

15. In Black English, unless you keenly want to underscore the past tense nature of an action, stay in the present tense and rely on the overall context of your ideas for the conveyance of time and sequence.

16. Never use the suffix -*ly* form of an adverb in Black English.
S.E.: The rain came down rather quickly.
B.E.: The rain come down pretty quick.

17. Never use the indefinite article *an* in Black English.
S.E.: He wanted to ride an elephant.
B.E.: He want to ride him a elephant.

18. In variant syntax: In correct Black English it is possible to formulate an imperative, an interrogative, and a simple declarative idea with the same syntax:
B.E.: You going to the store?
You going to the store.
You going to the store!

Where was Willie Jordan? We'd reached the mid-term of the semester. Students had formulated Black English guidelines, by consensus, and they were now writing with remarkable beauty, purpose, and enjoyment:

I ain hardly speakin for everybody but myself so understan that.

—KIM PARKS

Samples from Student Writings:

"Janie have a great big ole hole inside her. Tea Cake the only thing that fit that hole. . . .

"That pear tree beautiful to Janie, especial when bees fiddlin with the blossomin pear there growin large and lovely. But personal speakin, the love she get from starin at that tree ain the love what starin back at her in them relationship."
(Monica Morris)

"Love is a big theme in *They Eye Was Watching God*. Love show people new corners inside theyself. It pull out good stuff and stuff back bad stuff. . . . Joe worship the doing uh his own hand and need other people to worship him too. But he ain't think about Janie that she a person and ought to live like anybody common do. Queen life not for Janie." (Monica Morris)

"In both life and writin, Black womens have varietous experience of love that be cold like a iceberg or fiery like a inferno. Passion got for the other partner involve, man or woman, seem as shallow, ankledeep water or the most profoundest abyss." (Constance Evans)

"Family love another bond that ain't never break under no pressure." (Constance Evans)

"You know it really cold/When the friend you/Always get out the fire/Act like they don't know you/When you in the heat." (Constance Evans)

"Big classroom discussion bout love at this time. I never take no class where us have any long arguin for and against for two or three day. New to me and great. I find the class time talkin a million time more interestin than detail bout the book." (Kathy Esseks)

As these examples suggest, Black English no longer limited the students, in any way. In fact, one of them, Philip Garfield, would shortly "translate" a pivotal scene from Ibsen's *Doll House*, as his final term paper:

NORA: I didn't gived no shit. I thinked you a asshole back then, too, you make it so hard for me save mines husband life.

KROGSTAD: Girl, it clear you ain't any idea what you done. You done exact what once done, and I losed my reputation over it.

NORA: You asks me believe you once act brave save you wife life?

KROGSTAD: Law care less why you done it.

NORA: Law must suck.

KROGSTAD: Suck or no, if I wants, judge screw you wid dis paper.

NORA: No way, man. (Philip Garfield)

But where was Willie? Compulsively punctual, and always thoroughly prepared with neatly typed compositions, he had disappeared. He failed to show up for our regularly scheduled conference, and I received neither a note nor a phone call of explanation. A whole week went by. I wondered if Willie had finally been captured by the extremely current happenings in South Africa: passage of a new constitution that did not enfranchise the Black majority, and militant Black South African reaction to that affront. I wondered if he'd been hurt, somewhere. I wondered if the serious workload of weekly readings and writings had overwhelmed him and changed his mind about independent study. Where was Willie Jordan?

One week after the first conference that Willie missed, he called: "Hello, Professor Jordan? This is Willie. I'm sorry I wasn't there last week. But something has come up and I'm pretty upset. I'm sorry but I really can't deal right now."

I asked Willie to drop by my office and just let me see that he was okay: He agreed to do that. When I saw him I knew something hideous had happened. Something had hurt him and scared him to the marrow. He was all agitated and stammering and terse and incoherent. At last, his sadly jumbled account let me surmise as follows: Brooklyn police had murdered his unarmed, twenty-five-year-old brother, Reggie Jordan. Neither Willie nor his elderly parents knew what to do about it. Nobody from the press was interested. His folks had no money. Police ran his family around and around, to no point. And Reggie was really dead. And Willie wanted to fight, but he felt helpless.

With Willie's permission I began to try to secure legal counsel for the Jordan family. Unfortunately Black victims of police violence are truly numerous while the resources available to prosecute their killers are truly scarce. A friend of mine at the Center for Constitutional Rights estimated that just the preparatory costs for bringing the cops into court normally approaches $180,000. Unless the execution of Reggie Jordan became a major community cause for organizing and protest, his murder would simply become a statistical item.

Again with Willie's permission, I contacted every newspaper and media person I could think of. But the William Bastone feature article in *The Village Voice* was the only result from that canvassing.

Again with Willie's permission, I presented the case to my class in Black English. We had talked about the politics of language. We had talked about love and sex and child abuse and men and women. But the murder of Reggie Jordan broke like a hurricane across the room.

There are few "issues" as endemic to Black life as police violence. Most of the students knew and respected and liked Jordan. Many of them came from the very neighborhood where the murder had occurred. All of the students had known somebody close to them who had been killed by police, or had known frightening moments of gratuitous confrontation with the cops. They wanted to do everything at once to avenge death. Number One: They decided to compose personal statements of condolence to Willie Jordan and his family, written in Black English. Number Two: They decided to compose individual messages to the police, in Black English. These should be prefaced by an explanatory paragraph composed by the entire group. Number Three: These individual messages, with their lead paragraph, should be sent to *Newsday*.

The morning after we agreed on these objectives, one of the young women students appeared with an unidentified visitor, who sat through the class, smiling in a peculiar, comfortable way.

Now we had to make more tactical decisions. Because we wanted the messages published, and because we thought it imperative that our outrage be known by the police, the tactical question was this: Should the opening, group paragraph be written in Black English or Standard English?

I have seldom been privy to a discussion with so much heart at the dead heat of it. I will never forget the eloquence, the sudden haltings of speech, the fierce struggle against tears, the furious throwaways and useless explosions that this question elicited.

That one question contained several others, each of them extraordinarily painful to even contemplate. How best to serve the memory of Reggie Jordan? Should we use the language of the killers—Standard English—in order to make our ideas acceptable to those controlling the killers? But wouldn't what we had to say be rejected, summarily, if we said it in our own language, the language of the victim, Reggie Jordan? But if we sought to express ourselves by abandoning our language, wouldn't that mean our suicide on top of Reggie's murder? But if we expressed ourselves in our own language, wouldn't that be suicidal to the wish to communicate with those who, evidently, did not give a damn about us/Reggie/police violence in the Black community?

At the end of one of the longest, most difficult hours of my own life, the students voted, unanimously, to preface their individual messages with a paragraph composed in the language of Reggie Jordan. *"At least we don't give up nothing else. At least we stick to the truth: Be who we been. And stay all the way with Reggie."*

It was heartbreaking to proceed, from that point. Everyone in the room realized that our decision in favor of Black English had doomed our writings, even as the distinctive reality of our Black lives always has doomed our efforts to "be who we been" in this country.

I went to the blackboard and took down this paragraph, dictated by the class:

> . . . *You Cops!*
> *We the brother and sister of Willie Jordan, a fellow stony brook student who the brother of the dead Reggie Jordan. Reggie, like many brother and sister, he a victim of brutal racist police, October 25, 1984. Us ap pall, fed up, because that another senseless death what occur in our community. This what we feel, this, from our heart, for we ain't stayin' silent no more.*

With the completion of this introduction, nobody said anything. I asked for comments. At this invitation, the unidentified visitor, a young Black man, ceaselessly smiling, raised his hand. He was, it so happens, a rookie cop. He had just joined the force in September and, he said, he thought he should clarify a few things. So he came forward and sprawled easily into a posture of barroom, or fireside, nostalgia:

"See," Officer Charles enlightened us, "most times when you out on the street and something come down you do one of two things. Over-react or under-react. Now, if you under-react then you can get yourself kilt. And if you over-react then maybe you kill somebody. Fortunately it's about nine times out of ten and you will over-react. So the brother got kilt. And I'm sorry about that, believe me. But what you have to understand is what kilt him: over-reaction. That's all. Now you talk about Black people and white police but see, now, I'm a cop myself. And [big smile] I'm Black. And just a couple months ago I was on the other side. But see it's the same for me. You a cop, you the ultimate authority: the Ultimate Authority. And you on the street, most of the time you can only do one of two things: over-react or under-react. That's all it is with the brother. Over-reaction. Didn't have nothing to do with race."

That morning Officer Charles had the good fortune to escape without being boiled alive. But barely. And I remember the pride of his smile when I read about the fate of Black policemen and other collaborators in South Africa. I remember him, and I remember the shock and palpable feeling of shame that filled the room. It was as though that foolish, and deadly, young man had just relieved himself of his foolish, and deadly, explanation, face to face with the grief of Reggie Jordan's father and Reggie Jordan's mother. Class ended quietly. I copied the paragraph from the blackboard, collected the individual messages, and left to type them up.

Newsday rejected the piece.

The Village Voice could not find room in their "Letters" section to print the individual messages from the students to the police.

None of the tv news reporters picked up the story.

Nobody raised $180,000 to prosecute the murder of Reggie Jordan.

Reggie Jordan is really dead.

I asked Willie Jordan to write an essay pulling together everything important to him from that semester. He was still deeply beside himself with frustration and amazement and loss. This is what he wrote, un-edited, and in its entirety:

> *Throughout the course of this semester I have been researching the effects of oppression and exploitation along racial lines in South Africa and its neighboring countries. I have become aware of South African police brutalization of native Africans beyond the extent of the law, even though the laws themselves are catalyst affliction upon Black men, women and children. Many Africans die each year as a result of the deliberate use of police force to protect the white power structure.*
>
> *Social control agents in South Africa, such as policemen, are also used to force compliance among citizens through both overt and covert tactics. It is not uncommon to find bold-faced coercion and cold-blooded killings of Blacks by South African police for undetermined and/or inadequate reasons. Perhaps the truth is that the only reason for this heinous treatment of Blacks rests in racial differences. We should also understand that what is conveyed through the media is not always accurate and may sometimes be construed as the tip of the iceberg at best.*
>
> *I recently received a painful reminder that racism, poverty, and the abuse of power are global problems which are by no means unique to South Africa. On October 25, 1984 at approximately 3:00 p.m. my brother, Mr. Reginald Jordan, was shot and killed by two New York City policemen from the 75th precinct in the East New York section of Brooklyn. His life ended at the age of twenty-five. Even up to this current point in time the Police Department has failed to provide my family, which consists of five brothers, eight sisters, and two parents, with a plausible reason for Reggie's death. Out of the many stories that were given to my family by the Police Department, not one of them seems to hold water. In fact, I honestly believe that the Police Department's assessment of my brother's murder is nothing short of absolute bullshit, and thus far no evidence had been produced to alter this perception of the situation.*

Furthermore, I believe that one of three cases may have occurred in this incident. First, Reggie's death may have been the desired outcome of the police officer's action, in which case the killing was premeditated. Or, it was a case of mistaken identity, which clarifies the fact that the two officers who killed my brother and their commanding parties are all grossly incompetent. Or, both of the above cases are correct, i.e., Reggie's murderers intended to kill him and the Police Department behaved insubordinately.

Part of the argument of the officers who shot Reggie was that he had attacked one of them and took his gun. This was their major claim. They also said that only one of them had actually shot Reggie. The facts, however, speak for themselves. According to the Death Certificate and autopsy report, Reggie was shot eight times from point-blank range. The Doctor who performed the autopsy told me himself that two bullets entered the side of my brother's head, four bullets were sprayed into his back, and two bullets struck him in the back of his legs. It is obvious that unnecessary force was used by the police and that it is extremely difficult to shoot someone in his back when he is attacking or approaching you.

After experiencing a situation like this and researching South Africa I believe that to a large degree, justice may only exist as rhetoric. I find it difficult to talk of true justice when the oppression of my people both at home and abroad attests to the fact that inequality and injustice are serious problems whereby Blacks and Third World people are perpetually short-changed by society. Something has to be done about the way in which this world is set up. Although it is a difficult task, we do have the power to make a change.

WILLIE J. JORDAN JR.
EGL 487, SECTION 58, NOVEMBER 14, 1984

It is my privilege to dedicate this book to the future life of Willie J. Jordan Jr.

August 8, 1985

24

Helping Students Use Textual Sources Persuasively

MARGARET KANTZ

*In this essay, Kantz explores the difficulties students often face when try-
ing to compose an academic essay that relies on research as well as possible approaches for enabling student to produce more sophisticated texts.
An Associate Professor of English at University of Central Missouri, Kantz
shows how students might write with sources heuristically and rhetorically so that research is marshaled to address a question or solve a problem. This article originally appeared in a 1990 issue of* College English.

Although the researched essay as a topic has been much written about, it has
been little studied. In the introduction to their bibliography, Ford, Rees,
and Ward point out that most of the over 200 articles about researched
essays published in professional journals in the last half century describe classroom methods. "Few," they say, "are of a theoretical nature or based on research,
and almost none cites even one other work on the subject" (2). Given Ford and
Perry's finding that 84% of freshman composition programs and 40% of advanced
composition programs included instruction in writing research papers, more theoretical work seems needed. We need a theory-based explanation, one grounded
in the findings of the published research on the nature and reasons for our students' problems with writing persuasive researched papers. To understand how to

269

teach students to write such papers, we also need a better understanding of the demands of synthesis tasks.

As an example for discussing this complex topic, I have used a typical college sophomore. This student is a composite derived from published research, from my own memories of being a student, and from students whom I have taught at an open admissions community college and at both public and private universities. I have also used a few examples taken from my own students, all of whom share many of Shirley's traits. Shirley, first of all, is intelligent and well-motivated. She is a native speaker of English. She has no extraordinary knowledge deficits or emotional problems. She comes from a home where education is valued, and her parents do reading and writing tasks at home and at their jobs. Shirley has certain skills. When she entered first grade, she knew how to listen to and tell stories, and she soon became proficient at reading stories and at writing narratives. During her academic life, Shirley has learned such studying skills as finding the main idea and remembering facts. In terms of the relevant research, Shirley can read and summarize source texts accurately (cf. Spivey; Winograd). She can select material that is relevant for her purpose in writing (Hayes, Waterman, and Robinson; Langer). She can make connections between the available information and her purpose for writing, including the needs of her readers when the audience is specified (Atlas). She can make original connections among ideas (Brown and Day; Langer). She can create an appropriate, audience-based structure for her paper (Spivey), take notes and use them effectively while composing her paper (Kennedy), and she can present information clearly and smoothly (Spivey), without relying on the phrasing of the original sources (Atlas; Winograd). Shirley is, in my experience, a typical college student with an average academic preparation.

Although Shirley seems to have everything going for her, she experiences difficulty with assignments that require her to write original papers based on textual sources. In particular, Shirley is having difficulty in her sophomore-level writing class. Shirley, who likes English history, decided to write about the Battle of Agincourt (this part of Shirley's story is biographical). She found half a dozen histories that described the circumstances of the battle in a few pages each. Although the topic was unfamiliar, the sources agreed on many of the facts. Shirley collated these facts into her own version, noting but not discussing discrepant details, borrowing what she assumed to be her sources' purpose of retelling the story, and modelling the narrative structure of her paper on that of her sources. Since the only comments Shirley could think of would be to agree or disagree with her sources, who had told her everything she knew about the Battle of Agincourt, she did not comment on the material; instead, she concentrated on telling the story clearly and more completely than her sources had done. She was surprised when her paper received a grade of C–. (Page 1 of Shirley's paper is given as Appendix A.)

Although Shirley is a hypothetical student whose case is based on a real event, her difficulties are typical of undergraduates at both private and public colleges and universities. In a recent class of Intermediate Composition in which the students were instructed to create an argument using at least four textual sources that took differing points of view, one student, who analyzed the coverage of a recent championship football game, ranked her source articles in order from those whose approach she most approved to those she least approved. Another student analyzed various approaches taken by the media to the Kent State shootings in 1970, and was surprised and disappointed to find that all of the sources seemed slanted, either by the perspective of the reporter or by that of the people interviewed. Both students did not understand why their instructor said that their papers lacked a genuine argument.

The task of writing researched papers that express original arguments presents many difficulties. Besides the obvious problems of citation format and coordination of source materials with the emerging written product, writing a synthesis can vary in difficulty according to the number and length of the sources, the abstractness or familiarity of the topic, the uses that the writer must make of the material, the degree and quality of original thought required, and the extent to which the sources will supply the structure and purpose of the new paper. It is usually easier to write a paper that uses all of only one short source on a familiar topic than to write a paper that selects material from many long sources on a topic that one must learn as one reads and writes. It is easier to quote than to paraphrase, and it is easier to build the paraphrases, without comment or with random comments, into a description of what one found than it is to use them as evidence in an original argument. It is easier to use whatever one likes, or everything one finds, than to formally select, evaluate, and interpret material. It is easier to use the structure and purpose of a source as the basis for one's paper than it is to create a structure or an original purpose. A writing-from-sources task can be as simple as collating a body of facts from a few short texts on a familiar topic into a new text that reproduces the structure, tone, and purpose of the originals, but it can also involve applying abstract concepts from one area to an original problem in a different area, a task that involves learning the relationships among materials as a paper is created that may refer to its sources without resembling them.

Moreover, a given task can be interpreted as requiring an easy method, a difficult method, or any of a hundred intermediate methods. In this context, Flower has observed, "The different ways in which students [represent] a 'standard' reading-to-write task to themselves lead to markedly different goals and strategies as well as different organizing plans" ("Role" iii). To write a synthesis, Shirley may or may not need to quote, summarize, or select material from her sources; to evaluate the sources for bias, accuracy, or completeness; to develop original ideas; or to persuade a reader. How well she performs any of these tasks—and whether she thinks to perform these tasks—depends on how she reads the texts and on how she interprets the assignment. Shirley's representation of the task, which in this case was easier than her teacher had in mind, depends on the goals that she sets for herself. The goals that she sets depend on her awareness of the possibilities and her confidence in her writing skills.

Feeling unhappy about her grade, Shirley consulted her friend Alice. Alice, who is an expert, looked at the task in a completely different way and used strategies for thinking about it that were quite different from Shirley's.

"Who were your sources?" asked Alice. "Winston Churchill, right? A French couple and a few others. And they didn't agree about the details, such as the sizes of the armies. Didn't you wonder why?"

"No," said Shirley. "I thought the history books would know the truth. When they disagreed, I figured that they were wrong on those points. I didn't want to have anything in my paper that was wrong."

"But Shirley," said Alice, "you could have thought about why a book entitled *A History of France* might present a different view of the battle than a book subtitled *A History of British Progress*. You could have asked if the English and French writers wanted to make a point about the history of their countries and looked to see if the factual differences suggested anything. You could even have talked about Shakespeare's *Henry V*, which I know you've read—about how he presents the battle, or about how the King Henry in the play differs from the Henrys in your other books. You would have had an angle, a problem. Dr. Boyer would have loved it."

Alice's representation of the task would have required Shirley to formally select and evaluate her material and to use it as proof in an original argument. Alice was suggesting that Shirley invent an original problem and purpose for her paper and create an original structure for her argument. Alice's task is much more sophisticated than Shirley's. Shirley replied, "That would take me a year to do! Besides, Henry was a real person. I don't want to make up things about him."

"Well," said Alice, "You're dealing with facts, so there aren't too many choices. If you want to say something original you either have to talk about the sources or talk about the material. What could you say about the material? Your paper told about all the reasons King Henry wasn't expected to win the battle. Could you have argued that he should have lost because he took too many chances?"

"Gee," said Shirley, "That's awesome. I wish I'd thought of it."

This version of the task would allow Shirley to keep the narrative structure of her paper but would give her an original argument and purpose. To write the argument, Shirley would have only to rephrase the events of the story to take an opposite approach from that of her English sources, emphasizing what she perceived as Henry's mistakes and inserting comments to explain why his decisions were mistakes—an easy argument to write. She could also, if she wished, write a conclusion that criticized the cheerleading tone of her British sources.

As this anecdote makes clear, a given topic can be treated in more or less sophisticated ways—and sophisticated goals, such as inventing an original purpose and evaluating sources, can be achieved in relatively simple versions of a task. Students have many options as to how they can fulfill even a specific task (cf. Jeffery). Even children can decide whether to process a text deeply or not, and purpose in reading affects processing and monitoring of comprehension (Brown). Pichert has shown that reading purpose affects judgments about what is important or unimportant in a narrative text, and other research tells us that attitudes toward the author and content of a text affect comprehension (Asch; Hinze; Shedd; Goldman).

One implication of this story is that the instructor gave a weak assignment and an ineffective critique of the draft (her only comment referred to Shirley's footnoting technique; cf. Appendix A). The available research suggests that if Dr. Boyer had set Shirley a specific rhetorical problem such as having her report on her material to the class and then testing them on it, and if she had commented on the content of Shirley's paper during the drafts, Shirley might well have come up with a paper that did more than repeat its source material (Nelson and Hayes). My teaching experience supports this research finding. If Dr. Boyer had told Shirley from the outset that she was expected to say something original and that she should examine her sources as she read them for discrepant facts, conflicts, or other interesting material, Shirley might have tried to write an original argument (Kantz, "Origi-nality"). And if Dr. Boyer had suggested that Shirley use her notes to comment on her sources and make plans for using the notes, Shirley might have written a bet-ter paper than she did (Kantz, "Relationship").

Even if given specific directions to create an original argument, Shirley might have had difficulty with the task. Her difficulty could come from any of three causes: 1) Many students like Shirley misunderstand sources because they read them as stories. 2) Many students expect their sources to tell the truth; hence, they equate persuasive writing in this context with making things up. 3) Many students do not understand that facts are a kind of claim and are often used persuasively in so-called objective writing to create an impression. Students need to read source texts as arguments and to think about the rhetorical contexts in which they were written rather than to read them merely as a set of facts to be learned. Writing an original persuasive argument based on sources requires students to apply mater-ial to a problem or to use it to answer a question, rather than simply to repeat it or evaluate it. These three problems deserve a separate discussion.

Because historical texts often have a chronological structure, students believe that historians tell stories and that renarrating the battle cast them as a historian. Because her sources emphasized the completeness of the victory/defeat and its deci-sive importance in the history of warfare, Shirley thought that making these same points in her paper completed her job. Her job as a reader was thus to learn the story, i.e., so that she could pass a test on it (cf. Vipond and Hunt's argument that generic expectations affect reading behavior. Vipond and Hunt would describe Shirley's reading as story-driven rather than point-driven). Students commonly misread texts as narratives. When students refer to a textbook as "the story," they are telling us that they read for plot and character, regardless of whether their texts are organized as narratives. One reason Shirley loves history is that when she reads it she can combine her story-reading strategies with her studying strategies. Students like Shirley may need to learn to apply basic organizing patterns, such as cause-effect and general-to-specific, to their texts. If, however, Dr. Boyer asks Shirley to respond to her sources in a way that is not compatible with Shirley's understanding of what such sources do, Shirley will have trouble doing the assignment. Professors may have to do some preparatory teaching about why certain kinds of texts have cer-tain characteristics and what kinds of problems writers must solve as they design text for a particular audience. They may even have to teach a model for the kind of writing they expect.

The writing version of Shirley's problem, which Flower calls "writer-based prose," occurs when Shirley organizes what should be an expository analysis as a narrative, especially when she writes a narrative about how she did her research. Students frequently use time-based organizing patterns, regardless of the task, even when such patterns conflict with what they are trying to say and even when they know how to use more sophisticated strategies. Apparently such common narra-tive transitional devices such as "the first point" and "the next point" offer a reas-suringly familiar pattern for organizing unfamiliar material. The common strategy of beginning paragraphs with such phrases as "my first source," meaning that it was the first source that the writer found in the library or the first one read, appears to combine a story-of-my-research structure with a knowledge-telling strategy

(Bereiter and Scardamalia, *Psychology*). Even when students understand that the assignment asks for more than the fill-in-the-blanks, show-me-you've-read-the-material approach described by Schwegler and Shamoon, they cling to narrative structuring devices. A rank ordering of sources, as with Mary's analysis of the football game coverage with the sources listed in an order of ascending disapproval, represents a step away from storytelling and toward synthesizing because it embodies a persuasive evaluation.

In addition to reading texts as stories, students expect factual texts to tell them "the truth" because they have learned to see texts statically, as descriptions of truths, instead of as arguments. Shirley did not understand that nonfiction texts exist as arguments in rhetorical contexts. "After all," she reasoned, "how can one argue about the date of a battle or the sizes of armies?" Churchill, however, described the battle in much more detail than Shirley's other sources, apparently because he wished to persuade his readers to take pride in England's tradition of military achievement. Guizot and Guizot de Witt, on the other hand, said very little about the battle (beyond describing it as "a monotonous and lamentable repetition of the disasters of Crecy and Poitiers" [397]) because they saw the British invasion as a sneaky way to take advantage of a feud among the various branches of the French royal family. Shirley's story/study skills might not have allowed her to recognize such arguments, especially because Dr. Boyer did not teach her to look for them.

When I have asked students to choose a topic and find three or more sources on it that disagree, I am repeatedly asked, "How can sources disagree in different ways? After all, there's only pro and con." Students expect textbooks and other authoritative sources either to tell them the truth (i.e., facts) or to express an opinion with which they may agree or disagree. Mary's treatment of the football coverage reflects this belief, as does Charlie's surprise when he found that even his most comprehensive sources on the Kent State killings omitted certain facts, such as interviews with National Guardsmen. Students' desire for truth leads them to use a collating approach whenever possible, as Shirley did (cf. Appendix A), because students believe that the truth will include all of the facts and will reconcile all conflicts. (This belief may be another manifestation of the knowledge-telling strategy [Bereiter and Scardamalia, *Psychology*] in which students write down everything they can think of about a topic.) When conflicts cannot be reconciled and the topic does not admit a pro or con stance, students may not know what to say. They may omit the material altogether, include it without comment, as Shirley did, or jumble it together without any plan for building an argument.

The skills that Shirley has practiced for most of her academic career—finding the main idea and learning content—allow her to agree or disagree. She needs a technique for reading texts in ways that give her something more to say, a technique for constructing more complex representations of texts that allow room for more sophisticated writing goals. She also needs strategies for analyzing her reading that allow her to build original arguments.

One way to help students like Shirley is to teach the concept of rhetorical situation. A convenient tool for thinking about this concept is Kinneavy's triangular diagram of the rhetorical situation. Kinneavy, analyzing Aristotle's description of rhetoric, posits that every communicative situation has three parts: a speaker/writer (the Encoder), an audience (the Decoder), and a topic (Reality) (19). Although all discourse involves all three aspects of communication, a given type of discourse may pertain more to a particular point of the triangle than to the others, e.g., a diary entry may exist primarily to express the thoughts of the writer (the Encoder); an advertisement may exist primarily to persuade a reader (the Decoder). Following Kinneavy, I posit particular goals for each corner of the triangle. Thus, the primary goal of a writer doing writer-based discourse such as a diary might be originality and self-expression; primary goals for reader-based discourse such as advertising might be persuasion; primary goals for topic-based discourse such as a researched essay might be accuracy, completeness, and mastery of subject matter. Since all three aspects of the rhetorical situation are present and active in any communicative situation, a primarily referential text such as Churchill's *The Birth of Britain* may have a persuasive purpose and may depend for some of its credibility on readers' familiarity with the author. The term "rhetorical reading," then (cf. Haas and Flower), means teaching students to read a text as a message sent by someone to somebody for a reason. Shirley, Mary, and Charlie are probably practiced users of rhetorical persuasion in non-academic contexts. They may never have learned to apply this thinking in a conscious and deliberate way to academic tasks (cf. Kroll).

The concept of rhetorical situation offers insight into the nature of students' representations of a writing task. The operative goals in Shirley's and Alice's approaches to the term paper look quite different when mapped onto the points on the triangle. If we think of Shirley and Alice as Encoders, the topic as Reality, and Dr. Boyer as the Decoder, we can see that for Shirley, being an Encoder means trying to be credible; her relationship to the topic (Reality) involves a goal of using all of the subject matter; and her relationship to the Decoder involves an implied goal of telling a complete story to a reader whom Shirley thinks of as an examiner—to use the classic phrase from the famous book by Britton et al.—i.e., a reader who wants to know if Shirley can pass an exam on the subject of the Battle of Agincourt. For Alice, however, being an Encoder means having a goal of saying something new; the topic (Reality) is a resource to be used; and the Decoder is someone who must be persuaded that Alice's ideas have merit. Varying task representations do not change the dimensions of the rhetorical situation: the Encoder, Decoder, and Reality are always present. But the way a writer represents the task to herself does affect the ways that she thinks about those dimensions—and whether she thinks about them at all.

In the context of a research assignment, rhetorical skills can be used to read the sources as well as to design the paper. Although teachers have probably always known that expert readers use such strategies, the concept of rhetorical reading is new to the literature. Haas and Flower have shown that expert readers use rhetorical strategies "to account for author's purpose, context, and effect on the audience . . . to recreate or infer the rhetorical situation of the text" (176; cf also Bazerman). These strategies, used in addition to formulating main points and paraphrasing content, helped the readers to understand a text more completely and more quickly than did readers who concentrated exclusively on content. As Haas and Flower point out, teaching students to read rhetorically is difficult. They suggest that appropriate pedagogy might include "direct instruction . . . modeling, and . . . encouraging students to become contributing and committed members of rhetorical communities" (182). One early step might be to teach students a set of heuristics based on the three aspects of the communicative triangle. Using such questions could help students set goals for their reading.

In this version of Kinneavy's triangle, the Encoder is the writer of the source text, the Decoder is the student reader, and Reality is the subject matter. Readers may consider only one point of the triangle at a time, asking such questions as "Who are you (i.e., the author/Encoder)?" or "What are the important features of this text?" They may consider two aspects of the rhetorical situation in a single question, e.g., "Am I in your intended (primary) audience?"; "What do I think about this topic?"; "What context affected your ideas and presentation?" Other questions would involve all three points of the triangle, e.g., "What are you saying to help me with the problem you assume I have?" or "What textual devices have you used to manipulate my response?" Asking such questions gives students a way of formulating goals relating to purpose as well as content.

If Shirley, for example, had asked a Decoder-to-Encoder question—such as "Am I in your intended audience?"—she might have realized that Churchill and the Guizots were writing for specific audiences. If she had asked a Decoder-to-Reality question—such as "What context affected your ideas and presentation?"—she might not have ignored Churchill's remark, "All these names [Amiens, Boves, Bethencourt] are well known to our generation" (403). As it was, she missed Churchill's signal that he was writing to survivors of the First World War, who had vainly hoped that it would be war to end all wars. If Shirley had used an Encoder-Decoder-Reality question—such as "What are you saying to help me with the problem you assume I have?"—she might have understood that the authors of her sources were writing to different readers for different reasons. This understanding might have given her something to say. When I gave Shirley's source texts to freshmen students, asked them to use the material in an original argument, and taught them this heuristic for rhetorical reading, I received, for example, papers that warned undergraduates about national pride as a source of authorial bias in history texts.

A factual topic such as the Battle of Agincourt presents special problems because of the seemingly intransigent nature of facts. Like many people, Shirley believes that you can either agree or disagree with issues and opinions, but you can only accept the so-called facts. She believes that facts are what you learn from textbooks, opinions are what you have about clothes, and arguments are what you have with your mother when you want to stay out late at night. Shirley is not in a position to disagree with the facts about the battle (e.g., "No, I think the French won"), and a rhetorical analysis may seem at first to offer minimal rewards (e.g., "According to the Arab, Jewish, and Chinese calendars the date was really . . .").

Alice, who thinks rhetorically, understands that both facts and opinions are essentially the same kind of statement: they are claims. Alice understands that the only essential difference between a fact and an opinion is how they are received by an audience. (This discussion is derived from Toulmin's model of an argument as consisting of claims proved with data and backed by ethical claims called warrants. According to Toulmin, any aspect of an argument may be questioned by the audience and must then be supported with further argument.) In a rhetorical argument, a fact is a claim that an audience will accept as being true without requiring proof, although they may ask for an explanation. An opinion is a claim that an audience will not accept as true without proof, and which, after the proof is given, the audience may well decide has only a limited truth, i.e., it's true in this case but not in other cases. An audience may also decide that even though a fact is unassailable, the interpretation or use of the fact is open to debate.

For example, Shirley's sources gave different numbers for the size of the British army at Agincourt; these numbers, which must have been estimates, were claims masquerading as facts. Shirley did not understand this. She thought that disagreement signified error, whereas it probably signified rhetorical purpose. The probable reason that the Guizots give a relatively large estimate for the English army and do not mention the size of the French army is so that their French readers would find the British victory easier to accept. Likewise, Churchill's relatively small estimate for the size of the English army and his high estimate for the French army magnify the brilliance of the English victory. Before Shirley could create an argument about the Battle of Agincourt, she needed to understand that, even in her history textbooks, the so-called facts are claims that may or may not be supported, claims made by writers who work in a certain political climate for a particular audience. She may, of course, never learn this truth unless Dr. Boyer teaches her rhetorical theory and uses the research paper as a chance for Shirley to practice rhetorical problem-solving.

For most of her academic life, Shirley has done school tasks that require her to find main ideas and important facts; success in these tasks usually hinges on agreeing with the teacher about what the text says. Such study skills form an essential basis for doing reading-to-write tasks. Obviously a student can only use sources to build an argument if she can first read the sources accurately (cf. Brown and Palincsar; Luftig; Short and Ryan). However, synthesizing tasks often require that readers not accept the authors' ideas. Baker and Brown have pointed out that people misread texts when they blindly accept an author's ideas instead of considering a divergent interpretation. Yet if we want students to learn to build original arguments from texts, we must teach them the skills needed to create divergent interpretations. We must teach them to think about facts and opinions as claims that are made by writers to particular readers for particular reasons in particular historical contexts.

Reading sources rhetorically gives students a powerful tool for creating a persuasive analysis. Although no research exists as yet to suggest that teaching students to read rhetorically will improve their writing, I have seen its effect in successive drafts of students' papers. As mentioned earlier, rhetorical reading allowed a student to move from simply summarizing and evaluating her sources on local coverage of the championship football game to constructing a rationale for articles that covered the fans rather than the game. Rhetorical analysis enabled another student to move from summarizing his sources to understanding why each report about the Kent State shootings necessarily expressed a bias of some kind.

As these examples suggest, however, rhetorical reading is not a magical technique for producing sophisticated arguments. Even when students read their sources rhetorically, they tend merely to report the results of this analysis in their essays. Such writing appears to be a college-level version of the knowledge-telling strategy described by Bereiter and Scardamalia *(Psychology)* and may be, as they suggest, the product of years of exposure to pedagogical practices that enshrine the acquisition and expression information without a context or purpose.

To move students beyond merely reporting the content and rhetorical orientation of their source texts, I have taught them the concept of the rhetorical gap and some simple heuristic questions for thinking about gaps. Gaps were first described by Iser as unsaid material that a reader must supply to/infer from a text. McCormick expanded the concept to include gaps between the text and the reader; such gaps could involve discrepancies of values, social conventions, language, or any other matter that readers must consider. If we apply the concept of gaps to Kinneavy's triangle, we see that in reading, for example, a gap may occur between the Encoder-Decoder corners when the reader is not a member of the author's intended audience. Shirley fell into such a gap. Another gap can occur between the Decoder-Reality corners when a reader disagrees with or does not understand the text. A third gap can occur between the Encoder-Reality points of the triangle if the writer has misrepresented or misunderstood the material. The benefit of teaching this concept is that when a student thinks about a writer's rhetorical stance, she may ask "Why does he think that way?" When a student encounters a gap, she may ask, "What effect does it have on the success of this communication?" The answers to both questions give students original material for their papers.

Shirley, for example, did not know that Churchill began writing *The Birth of Britain* during the 1930s, when Hitler was rearming Germany and when the British government and most of Churchill's readers ardently favored disarmament. Had she understood the rhetorical orientation of the book, which was published eleven years after the end of World War II, she might have argued that Churchill's evocation of past military glories would have been inflammatory in the 1930s but was highly acceptable twenty years later. A gap between the reader and the text (Decoder-Reality) might stimulate a reader to investigate whether or not she is the only person having this problem; a gap between other readers and the sources may motivate an adaptation or explanation of the material to a particular audience. Shirley might have adapted the Guizots' perspective on the French civil war for American readers. A gap between the author and the material (Encoder-Reality) might motivate a refutation.

To discover gaps, students may need to learn heuristics for setting rhetorical writing goals. That is they may need to learn to think of the paper, not as a rehash of the available material, but as an opportunity to teach someone, to solve someone's problem, or to answer someone's question. The most salient questions for reading source texts may be "Who are you (the original audience of Decoders)?"; "What is your question or problem with this topic?"; and "How have I (the Encoder) used these materials to answer your question or solve your problem?" More simply, these questions may be learned as "Why," "How," and "So what?" When Shirley learns to read sources as telling not the eternal truth but a truth to a particular audience and when she learns to think of texts as existing to solve problems, she will find it easier to think of things to say.

For example, a sophomore at a private university was struggling with an assignment that required her to analyze an issue and express an opinion on it, using two conflicting source texts, an interview, and personal material as sources. Using rhetorical reading strategies, this girl discovered a gap between Alfred Marbaise, a high school principal who advocates mandatory drug testing of all high school students, and students like those he would be testing:

> *Marbaise, who was a lieutenant in the U.S. Marines over thirty years ago . . . makes it very obvious that he cannot and will not tolerate any form of drug abuse in his school. For example, in paragraph seven he claims, "When students become involved in illegal activity, whether they realize it or not, they are violating other students . . . then I become very, very concerned . . . and I will not tolerate that."*
>
> *Because Marbaise has not been in school for nearly forty years himself, he does not take into consideration the reasons why kids actually use drugs. Today the social environment is so drastically different that Marbaise cannot understand a kid's morality, and that is why he writes from such a fatherly but distant point of view.*

The second paragraph answers the So what? question, i.e., "Why does it matter that Marbaise seems by his age and background to be fatherly and distant?" Unless the writer/reader thinks to ask this question, she will have difficulty writing a coherent evaluation of Marbaise's argument.

The relative success of some students in finding original things to say about their topics can help us to understand the perennial problem of plagiarism. Some plagiarism derives, I think, from a weak, non-rhetorical task representation. If students believe they are supposed to reproduce source material in their papers, or if they know they are supposed to say something original but have no rhetorical problem to solve and no knowledge of how to find problems that they can discuss in their sources, it becomes difficult for them to avoid plagiarizing. The common student decision to buy a paper when writing the assignment seems a meaningless fill-in-the-blanks activity (cf. Schwegler and Shamoon) becomes easily understandable. Because rhetorical reading leads to discoveries about the text, students who use it may take more interest in their research papers.

Let us now assume that Shirley understands the importance of creating an original argument, knows how to read analytically, and has found things to say about the Battle of Agincourt. Are her troubles over? Will she now create that A paper that she yearns to write? Probably not. Despite her best intentions, Shirley will probably write another narrative/paraphrase of her sources. Why? Because by now, the assignment asks her to do far more than she can handle in a single draft. Shirley's task representation is now so rich, her set of goals so many, that she may be unable to juggle them all simultaneously. Moreover, the rhetorical reading technique requires students to discover content worth writing about and a rhetorical purpose for writing; the uncertainty of managing such a discovery task when a grade is at stake may be too much for Shirley.

Difficult tasks may be difficult in either (or both of) two ways. First, they may require students to do a familiar subtask, such as reading sources, at a higher level of difficulty, e.g., longer sources, more sources, a more difficult topic. Second, they may require students to do new subtasks, such as building notes into an original argument. Such tasks may require task management skills, especially planning, that students have never developed and do not know how to attempt.

The insecurity that results from trying a complex new task in a high-stakes situation is increased when students are asked to discover a problem worth writing about because such tasks send students out on a treasure hunt with no guarantee that the treasure exists, that they will recognize it when they find it, or that when they find it they will be able to build it into a coherent argument. The paper on Marbaise quoted above earned a grade of D because the writer could not use her rhetorical insights to build an argument presented in a logical order. Although she asked the logical question about the implications of Marbaise's persona, she did not follow through by evaluating the gaps in his perspective that might affect the probable success of his program.

A skillful student using the summarize-the-main-ideas approach can set her writing goals and even plan (i.e., outline) a paper before she reads the sources. The rhetorical reading strategy, by contrast, requires writers to discover what is worth writing about and to decide how to say it as or after they read their sources. The strategy requires writers to change their content goals and to adjust their writing plans as their understanding of the topic develops. It requires writers, in Flower's term, to "construct" their purposes for writing as well as the content for their paper (for a description of constructive planning, see Flower, Schriver, Carey, Haas, and Hayes). In Flower's words, writers who construct a purpose, as opposed to writers who bring a predetermined purpose to a task, "create a web of purposes . . . set goals, toss up possibilities . . . create a multidimensional network of information . . . a web of purpose . . . a bubbling stew of various mental representations" (531–32). The complex indeterminacy of such a task may pose an intimidating challenge to students who have spent their lives summarizing main ideas and reporting facts.

Shirley may respond to the challenge by concentrating her energies on a familiar subtask, e.g., repeating material about the Battle of Agincourt, at the expense of struggling with an unfamiliar subtask such as creating an original argument. She may even deliberately simplify the task by representing it to herself as calling only for something that she knows how to do, expecting that Dr. Boyer will accept the paper as close enough to the original instructions. My students do this frequently. When students decide to write a report of their reading, they can at least be certain that they will find material to write about.

Because of the limits of attentional memory, not to mention those caused by inexperience, writers can handle only so many task demands at a time. Thus, papers produced by seemingly inadequate task representations may well be essentially rough drafts. What looks like a bad paper may well be a preliminary step, a way of meeting certain task demands in order to create a basis for thinking about new ones. My students consistently report that they need to marshal all of their ideas and text knowledge and get that material down on the page (i.e., tell their knowledge) before they can think about developing an argument (i.e., transform their knowledge). If Shirley's problem is that she has shelved certain task demands in favor of others, Dr. Boyer needs only to point out what Shirley should do to bring the paper into conformity with the assignment and offer Shirley a chance to revise.

The problems of cognitive overload and inexperience in handling complex writing tasks can create a tremendous hurdle for students because so many of them believe that they should be able to write their paper in a single draft. Some students think that if they can't do the paper in one draft that means that something is wrong with them as writers, or with the assignment, or with us for giving the assignment. Often, such students will react to their drafts with anger and despair, throwing away perfectly usable rough drafts and then coming to us and saying that they can't do the assignment.

The student's first draft about drug testing told her knowledge about her sources' opinions on mandatory drug testing. Her second draft contained the rhetorical analysis quoted above, but presented the material in a scrambled order and did not build the analysis into an argument. Only in a third draft was this student able to make her point:

> *Not once does Marbaise consider any of the psychological reasons why kids turn away from reality. He fails to realize that drug testing will not answer their questions, ease their frustrations, or respond to their cries for attention, but will merely further alienate himself and other authorities from helping kids deal with their real problems.*

This comment represents Terri's answer to the heuristic "So what? Why does the source's position matter?" If we pace our assignments to allow for our students' thoughts to develop, we can do a great deal to build their confidence in their writing (Terri raised her D + to an A). If we treat the researched essay as a sequence of assignments instead of as a one-shot paper with a single due date, we can teach our students to build on their drafts, to use what they can do easily as a bridge to what we want them to learn to do. In this way, we can improve our students' writing habits. More importantly, however, we can help our students to see themselves as capable writers and as active, able, problemsolvers. Most importantly, we can use the sequence of drafts to demand that our students demonstrate increasingly sophisticated kinds of analytic and rhetorical proficiency.

Rhetorical reading and writing heuristics can help students to represent tasks in rich and interesting ways. They can help students to set up complex goal structures (Bereiter and Scardamalia, "Conversation"). They offer students many ways to think about their reading and writing texts. These tools, in other words, encourage students to work creatively.

And after all, creativity is what research should be about. If Shirley writes a creative paper, she has found a constructive solution that is new to her and which other people can use, a solution to a problem that she and other people share. Creativity is an inherently rhetorical quality. If we think of it as thought leading to solutions to problems and of problems as embodied in questions that people ask about situations, the researched essay offers infinite possibilities. Viewed in this way, a creative idea answers a question that the audience or any single reader wants answered. The question could be, "Why did Henry V win the Battle of Agincourt?" or, "How can student readers protect themselves against nationalistic bias when they study history?" or any of a thousand other questions. If we teach our Shirleys to see themselves as scholars who work to find answers to problem questions, and if we teach them to set reading and writing goals for themselves that will allow them to think constructively, we will be doing the most exciting work that teachers can do, nurturing creativity.

Appendix A: Page 1 of Shirley's Paper

The battle of Agincourt ranks as one of England's greatest military triumphs. It was the most brilliant victory of the Middle Ages, bar none. It was fought on October 25, 1414, against the French near the French village of Agincourt.

Henry V had claimed the crown of France and had invaded France with an army estimated at anywhere from 10,000[1] to 45,000 men.[2] During the siege of Marfleur dysentery had taken 1/3 of them[3], his food supplies had been depleted[4], and the fall rains had begun. In addition the French had assembled a huge army and were marching toward him. Henry decided to march to Calais, where his ships were to await him[5]. He intended to cross the River Somme at the ford of Blanchetaque[6], but, falsely informed that the ford was guarded, he was forced to follow the flooded Somme up toward its source. The French army was shadowing him on his right. Remembering the slaughters of Crecy and <u>Poictiers</u>, the French constable, Charles d'Albret, hesitated to fight[8], but when Henry forded the Somme just above Amiens[9] and was just

Endnotes

1. Carl Stephinson, *Medieval History,* p. 529.
2. Guizot, Monsieur and Guizot, Madame. *World's Best Histories-France, Vol II,* p. 211.
3. Cyrid E. Robinson. *England-A History of British Progress,* p. 145.
4. Ibid.
5. Winston Churchill. *A History of the English-Speaking Peoples. Volume 1: Birth of Britain,* p. 403.
6. *Ibid.*
7. *Ibid.*
8. Robinson, p. 145.
9. Churchill. p. 403.

Works Cited

Asch, Solomon. *Social Psychology.* New York: Prentice, 1952.

Atlas, Marshall. *Expert-Novice Differences in the Writing Process.* Paper presented at the American Educational Search Association, 1979. ERIC ED 107 769.

Baker, Louise, and Ann L. Brown. "Metacognitive Skills and Reading." *Handbook of Reading Research.* Eds. P. D Person, Rebecca Barr, Michael L. Kamil, and Peter Mosenthal. New York: Longman, 1984.

Bazerman, Charles. "Physicists Reading Physics: Schema-Laden Purposes and Purpose-Laden Schema." *Written Communication* 2.1 (1985): 3–24.

Bereiter, Carl, and Marlene Scardamalia. "From Conversation to Composition: The Role of Instruction in a Developmetal Process." *Advances in Instructional Psychology.* Ed. R. Glaser. Vol. 2. Hillsdale, NJ: Lawrence Erlbaum Associates, 1982. 1–64.

———. *The Psychology of Written Composition*. Hillsdale, NJ: Lawrence Erlbaum Associates, 1987.

Briscoe, Terri. "To test or not to test." Unpublished essay. Texas Christian University, 1989.

Britton, James, Tony Burgess, Nancy Martin, Alex McLeod, and Harold Rosen. *The Development of Writing Abilities (11–18)*. Houndmills Basingstoke Hampshire: Macmillan Education Ltd., 1975.

Brown, Ann L. "Theories of Memory and the Problem of Development: Activity, Growth, and Knowledge." *Levels of Processing in Memory*. Eds. Laird S. Cermak and Fergus I. M. Craik. Hillsdale, NJ: Laurence Erlbaum Associates, 1979, 225–258.

———, Joseph C. Campione, and L. R. Barclay. *Training Self-Checking Routines for Estimating Test Readiness: Generalizations from List Learning to Prose Recall*. Unpublished manuscript. University of Illinois, 1978.

——— and Jeanne Day. "Macrorules for Summarizing Texts: The Development of Expertise." *Journal of Verbal Learning and Verbal Behavior* 22.1 (1983): 1–14.

——— and Annmarie S. Palincsar. *Reciprocal Teaching of Comprehension Strategies: A Natural History of One Program for Enhancing Learning*. Technical Report #334. Urbana, IL: Center for the Study of Reading, 1985.

Churchill, Winston S. *The Birth of Britain*. New York: Dodd, 1956. Vol. 1 of *A History of the English-Speaking Peoples*. 4 vols. 1956–58.

Flower, Linda. "The Construction of Purpose in Writing and Reading." *College English* 50.5 (1988): 528–550.

———. *The Role of Task Representation in Reading to Write*. Berkeley, CA: Center for the Study of Writing, U of California at Berkeley and Carnegie Mellon. Technical Report, 1987.

———. "Writer-Based Prose: A Cognitive Basis for Problems in Writing." *College English* 41 (1979): 19–37.

Flower, Linda, Karen Schriver, Linda Carey, Christina Haas, and John R. Hayes. *Planning in Writing: A Theory of the Cognitive Process*. Berkeley, CA: Center for the Study of Writing, U of California at Berkeley and Carnegie Mellon. Technical Report, 1988.

Ford, James E., and Dennis R. Perry. "Research Paper Instruction in the Undergraduate Writing Program." *College English* 44 (1982): 825–31.

Ford, James E., Sharla Rees, and David L. Ward. *Teaching the Research Paper: Comprehensive Bibliography of Periodical Sources*, 1980. ERIC ED 197 363.

Goldman, Susan R. "Knowledge Systems for Realistic Goals." *Discourse Processes* 5 (1982): 279–303.

Guizot and Guizot de Witt. *The History of France from Earliest Times to 1848*. Trans. R. Black. Vol. 2. Philadelphia: John Wanamaker (n.d.).

Haas, Christina, and Linda Flower. "Rhetorical Reading Strategies and the Construction of Meaning." *College Composition and Communication* 39 (1988): 167–84.

Hayes, John R., D. A. Waterman, and C. S. Robinson. "Identifying the Relevant Aspects of a Problem Text." *Cognitive Science* 1 (1977): 297–313.

Hinze, Helen K. "The Individual's Word Associations and His Interpretation of Prose Paragraphs." *Journal of General Psychology* 64 (1961): 193–203.

Iser, Wolfgang. *The act of reading: A theory of aesthetic response*. Baltimore: The Johns Hopkins UP, 1978.

Jeffery, Christopher. "Teachers' and Students' Perceptions of the Writing Process." *Research in the Teaching of English* 15 (1981): 215–28.

Kantz, Margaret. *Originality and Completeness: What Do We Value in Papers Written from Sources?* Conference on College Composition and Communication. St. Louis, MO, 1988.

———. *The Relationship Between Reading and Planning Strategies and Success in Synthesizing: It's What You Do with Them that Counts*. Technical report in preparation. Pittsburgh: Center for the Study of Writing, 1988.

Kennedy, Mary Louise. "The Composing Process of College Students Writing from Sources." *Written Communication* 2.4 (1985): 434–56.

Kinneavy, James L. *A Theory of Discourse*. New York: Norton, 1971.

Kroll, Barry M. "Audience Adaptation in Children's Persuasive Letters." *Written Communication* 1.4 (1984): 407–28.

Langer, Judith. "Where Problems Start: The Effects of Available Information on Responses to School Writing Tasks." *Contexts for Learning to Write: Studies of Secondary School Instruction*. Ed. Arthur Applebee. Norwood, NJ: ABLEX Publishing Corporation, 1984. 135–48.

Luftig, Richard L. "Abstractive Memory, the Central-Incidental Hypothesis, and the Use of Structural Importance in Text: Control Processes or Structural Features?" *Reading Research Quarterly* 14.1 (1983): 28–37.

Marbaise, Alfred. "Treating a Disease." *Current Issues and Enduring Questions*. Eds. Sylvan Barnet and Hugo Bedau. New York: St. Martin's, 1987. 126–27.

McCormick, Kathleen. "Theory in the Reader: Bleich, Holland, and Beyond." *College English* 47.8 (1985): 836–50.

McGarry, Daniel D. *Medieval History and Civilization*. New York: Macmillan, 1976.

Nelson, Jennie, and John R. Hayes. *The Effects of Classroom Contexts on Students' Responses to Writing from Sources: Regurgitating Information or Triggering Insights*. Berkeley, CA: Center for the Study of Writing, U of California at Berkeley and Carnegie Mellon. Technical Report, 1988.

Pichert, James W. "Sensitivity to Importance as a Predictor of Reading Comprehension." *Perspectives on Reading Research and Instruction*. Eds. Michael A. Kamil and Alden J. Moe. Washington, D.C.: National Reading Conference, 1980. 42–46.

Robinson, Cyril E. *England: A History of British Progress from the Early Ages to the Present Day*. New York: Thom Y. Crowell Company, 1928.

Schwegler, Robert A., and Linda K. Shamoon. "The Aims and Process of the Research Paper." *College English* (1982): 817–24.

Shedd, Patricia T. "The Relationship between Attitude of the Reader Towards Women's Changing Role and Response to Literature Which Illuminates Women's Role." *Diss.* Syracuse U, 1975. ERIC ED 142 956.

Short, Elizabeth Jane, and Ellen Bouchard Ryan. "Metacognitive Differences between Skilled and Less Skilled Readers: Remediating Deficits through Story Grammar and Attribution Training." *Journal of Education Psychology* 76 (1984): 225–35.

Spivey, Nancy Nelson. *Discourse Synthesis: Constructing Texts in Reading and Writing.* Diss. U Texas, 1983. Newar DE: International Reading Association, 1984.

Toulmin, Steven E. *The Uses of Argument.* Cambridge: Cambridge UP, 1969.

Vipond, Douglas, and Russell Hunt. "Point-Driven Understanding: Pragmatic and Congnitive Dimensions of Literary Reading." *Poetics* 13, (1984): 261–77.

Winograd, Peter. "Strategic Difficulties in Summarizing Texts." *Reading Research Quarterly* 19 (1984): 404–25.

25

Girl

JAMAICA KINCAID

Novelist and short story writer Jamaica Kincaid often takes up issues of gender relations and colonialism in her much celebrated work. One example includes her short fiction piece "Girl" from her collection At the Bottom of the River. *This story presents a string of dialogue in which a mother forcefully instructs her daughter about her place in the world and behaviors appropriate to her gender without honestly listening to the concerns and questions her daughter raises. This exchange raises questions about how familial and social conventions and expectations influence actions and desires.*

Wash the white clothes on Monday and put them on the stone heap; wash the color clothes on Tuesday and put them on the clothesline to dry; don't walk barehead in the hot sun; cook pumpkin fritters in very hot sweet oil; soak your little cloths right after you take them off; when buying cotton to make yourself a nice blouse, be sure that it doesn't have gum on it, because that way it won't hold up well after a wash; soak salt fish overnight before you cook it; is it true that you sing benna in Sunday school?; always eat your food in such a way that it won't turn someone else's stomach; on Sundays try to walk like a lady and not like the slut you are so bent on becoming; don't sing benna in Sunday school; you mustn't speak to wharf-rat boys, not even to give directions; don't eat fruits on the street—flies will follow you; *but I don't sing benna on Sundays at all and never in Sunday school;* this is how to sew on a button; this is how to make a buttonhole for the button you have just sewed on; this is how to hem a dress when you see the hem coming down and so to prevent yourself from looking like the slut I know you are so bent on becoming; this is how you iron your father's khaki shirt so that it doesn't have a crease; this is how you iron your father's khaki pants so that they don't have a crease; this is how you grow okra—far from the house, because okra tree harbors red ants; when you are growing dasheen, make sure it gets plenty of water or else it makes your throat itch when you are eating it; this is how you sweep a corner; this is how you sweep a whole house; this is how you sweep a yard; this is how you smile to someone you don't like too much; this is how you smile to someone you don't like at all; this is how you smile to someone you like completely; this is how you set a table for tea; this is how you set a table for dinner; this is how you set a table for dinner with an important guest; this is how you set a table for lunch; this is how you set a table for breakfast; this is how to behave in the presence of men who don't know you very well, and this way they won't recognize immediately the slut I have warned you against becoming; be sure to wash every day, even if it is with your own spit; don't squat down to play marbles—you are not a boy, you know; don't pick people's flowers—you might catch something; don't throw stones at blackbirds, because it might not be a blackbird at all; this is how to make a bread pudding; this is how to make doukona; this is how to make pepper pot; this is how to make a good medicine for a cold; this is how to make a good medicine to throw away a child before it even becomes a child; this is how to catch a fish; this is how to throw back a fish you don't like, and that way something bad won't fall on you; this is how to bully a man; this is how a man bullies you; this is how to love a man, and if this doesn't work there are other ways, and if they don't work don't feel too bad about giving up; this is how to spit up in the air if you feel like it, and this is how to move quick so that it doesn't fall on you; this is how to make ends meet; always squeeze bread to make sure it's fresh; *but what if the baker won't let me feel the bread?;* you mean to say that after all you are really going to be the kind of woman who the baker won't let near the bread?

—1983

26

Language

AMITAVA KUMAR

The essay "Language" comes from Amitava Kumar's Passport Photos. *Kumar, Professor of English at Vassar College, opens up some of the complexities of language and its ties with identity and legacies of imperialism and contemporary racialized violence. This essay draws on wide-ranging source material, including fictional works, films, and personal experience to explore language as a transnational territory fraught with violence.*

Everytime I think I have forgotten,
I think I have lost the mother tongue,
it blossoms out of my mouth.
Days I try to think in English:
I look up,
paylo kallo kagdo
oodto oodto jai, huhvay jzaday pohchay
ainee chanchma kaeek chay
the crow has something in his beak.
Sujata Bhatt

Name

Place of Birth

Date of Birth

Profession

Nationality

Sex

Identifying Marks

My passport provides no information about my language. It simply presumes I have one.

If the immigration officer asks me a question—his voice, if he's speaking English, deliberately slow, and louder than usual—I do not, of course, expect him to be terribly concerned about the nature of language and its entanglement with the very roots of my being. And yet it is in language that all immigrants are defined and in which we all struggle for an identity. That is how I understand the postcolonial writer's declaration about the use of a language like English that came to us from the colonizer:

> *Those of us who do use English do so in spite of our ambiguity*
> *towards it, or perhaps because of that, perhaps because we can find*
> *in that linguistic struggle a reflection of other struggles taking place*
> *in the real world, struggles between the cultures within ourselves and*
> *the influences at work upon our societies. To conquer English may*
> *be to complete the process of making ourselves free.*

I also do not expect the immigration officer to be very aware of the fact that it is in that country called language that immigrants are reviled. I'd like to know what his thoughts were when he first heard the Guns N' Roses song:

> *Immigrants*
> *and faggots*
> *They make no sense to me*
> *They come to our country—*
> *And think they'll do as they please*
> *Like start some mini-Iran*
> *Or spread some fuckin' disease.*

It is between different words that immigrants must choose to suggest who they are. And if these words, and their meanings, belong to others, then it is in a broken language that we must find refuge. Consider this example.

I took this photograph while standing outside an Arab grocery store in Brooklyn. While pressing the shutter I was aware of another grocery store, in the film *Falling Down*, where the following exchange took place between a white American male, played by Michael Douglas, and a Korean grocer:

MR. LEE: Drink eighty-five cent. You pay or go.

FOSTER: This "fie," I don't understand a "fie." There's a "v" in the word. It's "fie-vah." You don't got "v's" in China?

MR. LEE: Not Chinese. I'm Korean.

FOSTER: Whatever. You come to my country, you take my money, you don't even have the grace to learn my language?

What Foster doesn't realize is that not only is it not his country alone, it is also not his language anymore. (That should be obvious to the ordinary American viewer, except that it *wasn't* obvious to every one. And it isn't.) But what I'm interested in asking is this: what is it that Mr. Lee is saying?

In saying "Not Chinese. I'm Korean," Mr. Lee is talking about difference. He is trying to tell another story. His story. Except that Foster won't listen. He is more interested in taking apart Mr. Lee's store with a baseball bat—the same way that, as Rita Chaudhry Sethi reminds us, others destroyed Japanese cars before Vincent Chin died. Vincent Chin was a young Chinese American who was murdered, also with a baseball bat, by two white autoworkers in Detroit. Chin was called a "Jap" and told "It's because of you motherfuckers that we're out of work." When I say Mr. Lee is talking about differences, I don't simply mean the difference between someone who is Chinese and someone else who is Korean. Instead, by difference I mean a sense of where it is a person is coming from. Both in terms of a location in place and in history.

Vincent Chin was an American of Chinese origin. The year he was killed marked the hundred-year anniversary of the Chinese Exclusion Act; in the year 1882, lynch mobs had murdered Chinese workers who were working on the West Coast.

Chin's murderers, Ronald Ebens and Michael Nitz, were autoworkers in Detroit, the city that entered the annals of early U.S. industrialism through its success in manufacturing cars. Ebens and Nitz did not know the difference between a worker and a capitalist. They were kept ignorant of the world of transnational capitalism, their very own world in which "General Motors owns 34 percent of Isuzu (which builds the Buick Opel), Ford 25 percent of Mazda (which makes transmissions for the Escort), and Chrysler 15 percent of Mitsubishi (which produces the Colt and the Charger)." Chin's killers did not spend a single night in prison and were fined $3,780 each. A Chinese American protesting the scant sentence is reported to have said, "Three thousand dollars can't even buy a good used car these days."

What does the word "Jap" mean? What is the difference between a Japanese and a Chinese American? What is the difference between a Chinese American and a used car? How does language mean and why does it matter?

As the Swiss linguist Ferdinand de Saussure argued very early in this century, language is a system of signs. And any sign consists of a signifier (the sound or written form) and a signified (the concept). As the two parts of the sign are linked or inseparable (the word "camera," for instance, accompanies the concept "camera" and remains quite distinct in our minds from the concept "car"), what is prompted is the illusion that language is transparent. The relationship between the signifier and the signified, and hence language itself, is assumed to be natural.

When we use the word "alien" it seems to stick rather unproblematically and unquestioningly to something or someone, and it is only by a conscious, critical act that we think of something different. Several years ago, in a public speech, Reverend Jesse Jackson seemed to be questioning the fixed and arbitrary assumptions in the dominant ideology when he reminded his audience that undocumented Mexicans were not aliens, they were *migrant workers*.

E.T., Jackson said emphatically, was an *alien*.

That is also the point made, albeit with more special effects than political ones, by the opening sequence of the film *Men in Black*.

The empty legs of the trousers hung up to dry in my birthplace, Ara, can be seen as just that, empty, lacking the fullness of meaning. But the image of the trousers—or the *signifier*—can also, however, be imaginatively joined to the concept of the bourgeoisie—or the *signified*—in whose service the half-clad washermen, not to mention the washerwoman with her back turned to us, labor in the river. These men who are poor do not wear the trousers they wash. The critical reader can fill the empty legs of these trousers with another meaning, the meaning born of a class and caste analysis of contemporary Indian society.

If you have been patient with my exposition so far, we might ask the same question of the object called the passport. How do we understand it as a term of language?

Let me, somewhat polemically, establish its meaning precisely by foregrounding a difference. For those who live in affluent countries, the passport is of use for international travel in connection with business or vacations. In poorer nations of the world, its necessity is tied to the need for finding employment, mainly in the West.

Once the process of acquiring a passport is over, you are reminded by friends and relatives that the real hurdle is getting the visa to enter that country that has now become this real place in your dreams. The passport is without any value if it does not have the visa. In other words, it is meaningless as a passport.

Abraham Verghese, writing in the *New Yorker*, had this report from the U.S. consulate in his home city of Madras, India:

> *One morning, the visa officer turned down six consecutive doctors and told the seventh, who happened to be a friend of mine, and whom I'll call Vadivel, "Spare me the crap about coming back with specialized knowledge to serve your country. Why do you really want to go?" Vadivel, who had held on to his American dream for so long that he could speak with the passion of a visionary, said, "Sir, craving your indulgence, I want to train in a decent, ten-story hospital where the lifts are actually working. I want to pass board-certification exams by my own merit and not through pull or bribes. I want to become a wonderful doctor, practice real medicine, pay taxes, make a good living, drive a big car on decent roads, and eventually live in the Ansel Adams section of New Mexico and never come back to this wretched town, where the doctors are as numerous as fleas and practice is cutthroat, and where the air outside is not even fit to breathe." The consul gave him a visa. The eighth applicant, forewarned, tried the same tactic but was turned down.*

If, on the one hand, the meanings of words like passport and visa are tied to dreams and fantasies, they are also, on the other, inextricably woven into the fabric of power and social prejudice. Americans learned recently of what one commentator called the "State Department visa 'profiles' of foreign applicants based on skin color, ethnicity, looks, speech—and remarkably enough—fashion sense." A Federal District Court judge had questioned the legality of State Department manuals that, apart from encouraging "special handling" of blacks, Arabs, and others, provide a list of abbreviations to help sort applicants: "RK=rich kid, LP=looks poor, TP=talks poor, LR=looks rough, TC=take care." In the case in which the judge had provided his ruling, among the evidence submitted were rejected applications with notations like "slimy looking," "Wears jacket on shoulders w/earring" and "No way . . . poor, poor, poor."

A fictional tale that takes place against the background of the humiliating drama of getting a visa is Salman Rushdie's marvelous short story "Good Advice Is Rarer than Rubies." It is also a tale about an old man's falling in love with a young woman who is a stranger. The beautiful Miss Rehana, whose "eyes were large and black and bright enough not to need the help of antimony," arrives at the gates of the British Consulate to apply for a visa. As we learn later in the story, she is about to go to what she calls "Bradford, London" to join a man who she had been engaged to as a child. She is approached outside the gates by Muhammad Ali who specialized in wheedling money from unsuspecting, illiterate women who had no skills in the language of the state.

The old man is struck by Miss Rehana's singular charm. "Her innocence made him shiver with fear for her." He is bewitched by her beauty, and he finds himself moving beyond the set speech in which he would warn applicants of the kinds of questions the British authorities would ask. "Muhammad Ali spoke brutally, on purpose, to lessen the shock she would feel when it, or something like it, actually happened."

"The oldest fools are bewitched by the youngest girls," writes Rushdie. And Muhammad Ali offers Miss Rehana, almost helplessly, a forged British passport, gratis.

But Miss Rehana does not accept Muhammad Ali's gift; it is only his advice she wants, for, as she says, "good advice is rarer than rubies." As she turns away from him, Muhammad Ali says to Miss Rehana, "Bibi, I am a poor fellow, and I have offered this prize because you are so beautiful. Do not spit on my generosity. Take the thing. Or else, don't take, go home, forget England, only do not go into that building and lose your dignity."

I do not think that what would cause Miss Rehana to lose her dignity is only the violence of a particular inquiry by immigration agents, say about her virginity, a subject of inquiry vehemently protested in the 1980s; instead, it is also the violence of the immense erasure of differences, historical particularities, and the individual humanity that is at the heart of Muhammad Ali's fears for her.

You start with an inquiry into the meaning of a word and you enter a world of difference. What are the answers to the question of an Indian woman's identity? Similar to the point about difference raised in the context of the Korean grocer, Mr. Lee, this question, too, finds an answer only in the form of more questions—at least in this brief fragment from an epic poem "Aay Wha' Kinda Indian Arr U?" written by a Sri Lankan-Canadian poet, Krisantha Sri Bhaggiyadatta:

> *am i the Indian wearing salwar or a sari, a turban or a pottu*
> *   on the subway platform at 10 p.m.*
> *am i the mother awaiting the scalpel-wielding*
> *   C-section surgeon at Scarborough hospital?*
> *am i the baby who puts off being born*
> *   from June to October to February to June*
> *   awaiting a Jullundur Spring*
> *am i the self-sacrificing monogamous Sita*

> or *am i the strong-willed and passionate*
> *revengeful polyandrous Draupadi*
> *(& her five Pandavas),*
> *or am i the "we shoulda met earlier" Usha of Urvashi*
> am i the *Indian who must submit to virginity tests*
> *from immigration's con/insultants?*
> am i the *sponsored Indian whose husband owns her*
> *for ten years or else . . .*
> *thanks again, to the immigration department's*
> *department of familiar values*
> am i the *Indian who is kept 5 oceans apart from her lover?*
> am i the *Indian hiding in a women's shelter*
> *from her "til death do us apart" husband. . . .*

The question asked by the poet are important not only because they are so heterogeneous. They also hold a special appeal for their ability to returns us to language as the terrain on which difference is constructed or resisted. That is what I see, for example, in the poet's novel splitting of the word "con/insultants." Or in this anthropological account from 1924 about an early Sikh migrant in the U.S., which is cited by the Asian American scholar Ronald Takaki: "In one of the camps [for migrant workers in California], an Asian Indian told a visiting lady: 'We eat no meat, that is, no beef—the cow is sacred.' 'But you drink milk?' she snapped skeptically. 'And your cow gives you the milk!' 'Yes,' he countered, 'we drink our mother's milk also, but we do not eat her!'"

When you turn to me in the bus or the plane and talk to me—*if* you talk to me— you might comment, trying to be kind, "Your English is very good."

If I am feeling relaxed, and the burden of the permanent chip on my shoulder seems light, I will smile and say, "Thank you" (I never add, "So is yours"). Perhaps I will say, "Unfortunately, the credit goes to imperialism. The British, you know . . . " (Once, a fellow traveler widened her eyes and asked, "The British still rule over *India*?").

It was the British who, in the first half of the nineteenth century, under the imperative of Lord Macaulay, introduced the systematic teaching of English in India in order to produce a class of clerks. In Rushdie's novel *The Moor's Last Sigh,* a painter by the name of Vasco Miranda drunkenly upbraids the upper-class Indians as "Bleddy Macaulay's Minutemen. . . . Bunch of English-Medium misfits, the lot of you. . . . Even your bleddy dreams grow from foreign roots." Much later in the novel, the protagonist, Moor Zogoiby, reflects on Macaulay's legacy as he is leaving for the last time the city of his birth, Bombay:

> To form a class, *Macaulay wrote in the 1835 Minute on Education,* . . . of persons, Indian in blood and colour, but English in opinions, in morals, and in intellect. *And why, pray? O, to be* interpreters between us and millions whom we govern. *How grateful such a class of persons should, and must, be! For in India the dialects were* poor and rude, and a single shelf of a good European library was worth the whole native literature. *History, science, medicine, astronomy,*

geography, religion were likewise derided. Would disgrace an English farrier . . . would move laughter in girls at an English boarding-school.

This historical reverie is an occasion for Zogoiby to declare retrospective judgment on the drunken Miranda, to assure the reader and posterity that "We were not, had never been, that class. The best, and worst, were in us, and fought in us, as they fought in the land at large. In some of us, the worst triumphed; but still we could say—and truthfully—that we had loved the best."

But what is it that was judged the best—in English?

The answer to that question can be sought in the pages of another Third-World writer, Michelle Cliff, who in writing about a Jamaican childhood describes how the schoolteacher's manual, shipped year after year from the London offices, directed the teacher

> *to see that all in the school memorized the "Daffodils" poem by William Wordsworth. . . . The manual also contained a pullout drawing of a daffodil, which the pupils were "encouraged to examine" as they recited the verse. [Cliff rightly adds,] No doubt the same manuals were shipped to villages in Nigeria, schools in Hong Kong, even settlements in Northwest Territory—anywhere that "the sun never set". . . . Probably there were a million children who could recite "Daffodils," and a million more who had actually never seen the flower, only the drawing, and so did not know why the poet had been stunned.*

I was one of those children, though I cannot remember being shown even a drawing of the flower! And this in an independent nation, still unable to shrug off, when it comes to education in English, its colonial heritage. I can, therefore, understand the critique of that education lying at the heart of the Jamaican cultural theorist Stuart Hall's observation: "When I first got to England in 1951, I looked out and there were Wordsworth's daffodils. Of course, what else would you expect to find? That's what I knew about. That is what trees and flowers meant. *I didn't know the names of the flowers I had left behind in Jamaica.*" In some ways, admittedly, we cannot speak of the postcolonial experience as only limited to the idea of the absent daffodil. A more adequate representation of that experience would encompass, at the same time, that moment when the Indian child thinks of the daffodil as a bright marigold—or when, as in Cliff's novel, a student in the Caribbean colors it "a deep red like a hibiscus. The red of a flame." In that instant, which I can only call one of creative appropriation, language does not remain an instrument of cultural domination. It is transformed, knowingly or unknowingly, into a weapon of protest.

But let me return to that particular moment when, as his plane banks over the smoky landscape of Bombay, Moor Zogoiby finds himself thinking of the doings of the Indian elite in the past ("In some of us, the worst triumphed; but still we could say—and truthfully—that we had loved the best"). His thought can also be seen as a protest. His Bombay was a Bombay that is no longer. For his Bombay was, as he says, "a city of mixed-up, mongrel joy." That vision of the city is in direct conflict with the Bombay, or Mumbai as it has now been renamed, of the right-wing, Hindu rule of the Shiv Sena in Maharashtra. The Shiv Sena's vision of Mumbai is essentially a purist one. It is intolerant of those that fall outside its own, arbitrary, even atavistic, frame of reference. What Zogoiby seems to be savoring in his past, as he leaves his city behind him with no companion other than a stuffed mutt by the name of Jawaharlal, is the kind of modern liberal-democratic vision we associate with an earlier India led by Nehru. "Unlike many other nationalists who had come to a sense of their Indianness through the detour of the West," Sunil Khilnani points out, "there is no trace in Nehru of that inwardly turned rage of an Aurobindo or Vivekananda, political intellectuals who strove to purge themselves of what they came to regard as a defiling encounter with the modern West—an encounter that had first planted in them the urge to be Indian." Against the memory of Jawaharlal Nehru, the mongrel visionary, we have the reality of the Shiv Sena supremo, Bal Thackeray, who lists Hitler among his models.

And yet there is one detail that deserves commentary. The Shiv Sena leader's own name owes its origins to his Hindu father's admiration for the English novelist William Makepeace Thackeray. I recall that detail not in order to point out that the Shiv Sena leader is hypocritical—though he might be that, and he can certainly be accused of much else—but to point out that, in the postcolonial condition, contradictions are inescapable.

To begin to *see* the contradictions is to become aware of history and, therefore, of another relation that this history has with the present. And to think of these contradictions *as inescapable* is to abandon a naive and dangerous view of history that inevitably harbors in its heart murderous longing.

Let's take the fairly banal example of the name of the street on which I passed most of my youth in India. My parents' house in Patna was on a street that is still called "Hardinge Road" by the city's mail carriers, the ricksha pullers, and a wide variety of the city's citizenry. The road was named by the British after Charles Hardinge, the viceroy in India around 1914. In the 1980s, forty years after independence, the provincial government renamed the street "1942 Kranti Marg" (literally, 1942 Revolution Street). This was in honor of the high school students who, while participating in the 1942 Quit India movement, had fallen to British guns. For as long as I can remember, their historic statues have stood at the mouth of the street.

For me, this renaming wasn't without significance: it attached me to a history of nationalist struggle and its local roots. It made more real and meaningfully concrete what otherwise remain grand and empty proclamations of patriotism. However, at the same time, while indeed calling that street "1942 Kranti Marg," I cannot ever forget that there are in use in that town, and in the country as a whole, other names that are, if not English, at least *in English*. To deny that would be once again to deny our history. It would be to succumb, perhaps as hypocritically as the Shiv Sena chief does, to a purism that, at least in his case, has no role other than sanctifying the persecution of those that are relegated to the role of Others in his history. They are the Muslims, the untouchables, Communists, progressive women . . .

Which is not to say that any defense of the use of English should be uncritical. In a fine, witty novel, *English, August,* written by Upamanyu Chatterjee, the narrator's amusement at the use of English in small-town India is designed to mock the pretensions and the complacencies of the petty bourgeoisie. The narrator, while certainly very much an elitist, does not remove himself from the circle of critique. Take his own name, for example. He was named Agastya after a famous sage in the Hindu vedas. While in school, he told his friends he had wished he was a part of Westernized "Anglo-India, that he had Keith or Alan for a name, that he spoke English with their accent." From that day, he had been given among other names—which included "last Englishman" or just "English"—the name that stuck, "August." In the novel, even while baring his own repressed Anglo-envy or expressing his enjoyment at the spicy masala mix of his tongue, August does not fail to lampoon the affectations of his friend, a member of the metropolitan Americanized bourgeoisie in India:

> *"Amazing mix, the English we speak. Hazaar fucked. Urdu and American," Agastya laughed, "a thousand fucked, really fucked. I'm sure nowhere else could languages be mixed and spoken with such ease." The slurred sounds of the comfortable tiredness of intoxication, "'You look hazaar fucked, Marmaduke dear.' 'Yes Dorothea, I'm afraid I do feel hazaar fucked'—see, doesn't work. And our accents are Indian, but we prefer August to Agastya. When I say our accents, I, of course, exclude yours, which is unique in its fucked mongrelness—you even say 'Have a nice day' to those horny women at your telephones when you pass by with your briefcase, and when you agree with your horrendous boss, which is all the time, you say 'yeah, great' and 'uh-uh.'"*

The one named August is "hazaar fucked," the other, if I may hazard a guess, "plainly fucked." It is for the latter, from the position, perhaps of the former, that I had coined an (im)proper name, a name for a dog that is, and yet isn't, a cousin to the mongrel we encountered beside Zogoiby's legs:

LORD MACAULAY'S TAIL

TheEnglishlanguage was the second name
of Lord Macaulay's pet dog.
So we became its tail.

The mistake was
that we believed this tail
actually wagged the dog.

Now the condition is such
that on that side the teeth of the dog might well be
devouring someone

but on this side
we keep wagging the tail vigorously.

Those of Lord Macaulay's breed occupy the missionary position in relation to Indian education in the English medium. They are the ones who receive their training in convents from Christian priests described by the writer Shashi Tharoor as those "who serve their foreign Lord by teaching the children of the Indian lordly." Those priests might not be the ones, however, who teach in schools with names like Bright Future English School—a name noticed by Pankaj Mishra during his travels through small towns in India, narrated in his book *Butter Chicken in* **Ludhiana**. Or even in institutions with names more like St. Joseph's Cross School—a name that, with the word "cross," has connotations not only of Christ but also of an unstable hybridity or mixing. The name draws Mishra on this speculative path:

> *St. Joseph's Cross School? Even the name sounded dubious. I couldn't recall a school with that name in Meerut. It was probably very recent, cleverly exploitative of the Indian regard, not entirely misplaced, for Christian schools and English-medium education. Scores of such schools, more than half of them fraudulent, had come up all over small-town India, some with incomplete buildings that frequently collapsed and left in their stead a turbid dust of recriminations and denials hanging over buried bodies.*

In this contemporary rewriting of the colonial project of missionary education, new fraudulent acts forge the consciousness of small-town India in the name of older, more legitimized, acts of moral uplift and business as usual. Mishra imagines only the pile of collapsing rubble on children's bodies, but in the decades that followed Indian independence there were many deaths as a part of what was called "language riots." In the demand of various groups for separate states under the federal Indian government, one bone of contention quite often was the existence of "English-medium" schools. If India was now free, did we need to have schools that prided themselves on teaching only English?

Among my earliest memories of going to school is of a rainy day when I was perhaps five. The car taking us to school suddenly stopped. Men, shouting slogans and waving their arms, smeared the license plate with tar. The driver turned the car around and brought my sisters and me back home. We were off from school; and, though not entirely unshaken by the event, I remember being very happy at the prospect of playing with paper boats.

Those men, although I did not know at that time, were part of the "Hindi Only" movement that considered the use of English in India a throwback to the imperialist era of the British. In *Midnight's Children* Rushdie's hero, the boy Saleem Sinai, finds himself crashing on his bicycle into one of the protest marches. The narrative is unable to hide the fact that grave issues of class identity gave intensity to what would be described as a merely cultural demand for a "linguistic state":

> *Hands grabbing handlebars as I slow down in the impassioned throng. Smiles filled with good teeth surround me. They are not friendly smiles. "Look look, a little laad-sahib comes down to join us from the big rich hill!" In Marathi which I hardly understand, it's my worst subject at school, and the smiles asking, "You want to join S.M.S. [Samyukta Maharashtra Samiti, or United Maharashtra Party], little princeling?" And I, just knowing what's being said, but dazed into telling the truth, shake my head No. And the smiles, "Oho! The young nawab does not like our tongue! What does he like?"*

Sinai, in Rushdie's novel, makes his escape from his predicament by giving to the crowd a nonsense rhyme in Gujarati, the language of the crowd's opponents.

> *Soo ché? Saru ché!*
> *Danda lé ké maru ché!*

A nonsense rhyme—"How are you? I am well! / I'll take a stick and thrash you to hell!"—and cleverly designed to mock the rhythms of Gujarati, it gets adopted as a slogan, a war cry, an insult. Soon the first language riot is underway, leaving fifteen killed and over three hundred wounded.

When I was a schoolboy and confronted by the faces outside the windows of the car taking us to school, I was unable, lacking the prescience of Saleem Sinai, to read in those faces, in their words and gestures, the signs of social disenfranchisement and anger. Nor was I involved with those people in exchanges that would impress me with premonitory messages about the power of words. But a somewhat jagged line joins that event with the more immediate reality in which I find myself: an immigrant speaking a language that, even when it is the one that my listeners speak, still *sounds* different from theirs. As I stand in front of a classroom filled with English-speaking, mostly white-skinned, students—we could be engaged in a discussion about a writer, the sounds of whose name are utterly alien and distant not only to to my illiterate grandparents but also, it sometimes seems, to my own lips—I might be composing my own nonsense rhyme to give those I see ringed around me.

> *I leave the door open*
> *when I teach. And turn back*
> *to spell on the board the word*
> *they said they "didn't get."*
> *"Oh that!" they say, moving*
> *quickly to the next point. Sometimes*
> *I apologize. They understand*
> *I don't have to. "No big deal."*
> *"Doesn't bother me." We agree*
> *to hide our embarrassment.*
> *And put everything within*
> *quotes (like "they" and "I")*
> *to keep things manageable.*
> *I turn from the board: black*
> *wall with weak ribs of chalk.*
> *My voice rises, fills the room*
> *and moves out of the door.*
> *It dances in the corridor, tripping*
> *with its foreign accent*
> *those calmly walking past.*

I took this photograph very close to the U.S.-Mexico border, somewhere between San Diego and Tijuana. There was a tear in the fence; I climbed under it and came up close to the highway to get a better shot. When I went back to the place in the fence, I was startled out of my skin by a Border Patrol van that was very slowly driving past. The officer did not see me, however, and I was soon back in the bar next to my motel.

    While sipping my beer, I imagined a conversation with the border patrol officer who had only narrowly missed catching me.

OFFICER: I saw you photographing that sign. That was good, an excellent idea. What do you think about the sign though?

ME: Mmm. I don't know. It's just that—this is the first time I saw that sign. In my country, we have family-planning signs with figures like that. Father, mother, kid. The Health Ministry has a slogan painted it, One or Two kids. Then Stop.

OFFICER: That's very interesting. This is what I like about multiculturalism. You get to learn about cultural difference.

ME: You really think so? Yes, that's great. What can I learn from *this* sign?

OFFICER: Well, you've gotta get into the semiotics of it, you know what I'm saying?

ME: Uh-huh.

OFFICER: I'll be damned if language is transparent. That's the bottom line here. Just look at that sign—in English it's Caution, but in Spanish, it's *Prohibido*. You don't think those two words mean the same thing, do you?

ME: I don't know. I don't know Spanish.

OFFICER: Okay, well, I'll be patient with you. The sign in English is for folks who drive. They're being cautioned. Now, the sign in Spanish—

ME: Yes, yes, I see what you're driving at! The *Prohibido* sign is for the Spanish speaker—

OFFICER: There you go! Bingo! Bull's eye! They don't have the word *Caución* there. It's plain Prohibited: pure and simple. The picture, the image—it splits, right before your eyes!

ME: The scales have fallen . . .

OFFICER: Well, but you gotta stay alert. 'Cause culture is a moving thing, meaning change. Or sometimes, just get plain run over. All the time.

ME: Yes, yes.

OFFICER: What work do you do?

ME: I teach English.

OFFICER: No kidding! See, this is America! You teaching *English* to our kids, I love it. Say, did you ever watch *Saturday Night Live* when it first came on?

ME: No, I don't think so.

OFFICER: Michael O'Donoghue played a language instructor. He was teaching this confused immigrant played by John Belushi. You know the sentence that O'Donoghue used to introduce the language?

ME: What was it?

OFFICER: I will feed your fingers to the wolverines.

We could have gone on, the officer and I. If we were swapping stories today, I'd have mentioned the news report that the telephone company Sprint, in its billing letter in Spanish, threatens customers with phone cutoff unless their check is received by the end of the month. According to the news report, the Anti-Defamation League and the National Council of La Raza have filed complaints. Why? Because the billing letter in English is somewhat differently worded: "As a customer you are Sprint's number one priority. We . . . look forward to serving your communication needs for many years to come."

And, if the officer had had more time, we might have arrived at an understanding that language, especially English, has been used as a racial weapon in immigration.

To cite a historical example: in 1896 a colonial official argued against the restrictions imposed on the entry of Indians in South Africa, adding that this would be "most painful" for Queen Victoria to approve. At the same time, he sanctioned a European literacy test that would automatically exclude Indians while preserving the facade of racial equality.

Almost a hundred years later a Texas judge ordered the mother of a five-year-old to stop speaking in Spanish to her child. Judge Samuel Kiser reminded the mother that her daughter was a "full-blooded American." "Now, get this straight. You start speaking English to this child because if she doesn't do good in school, then I can remove her because it's not in her best interest to be ignorant. The child will only hear English."

Who is permitted to proceed beyond the gates into the mansion of full citizenship? And on what terms? These are the questions that the episode in the Texas courthouse raises. Apart from the issue of gross paternalism and an entirely injudicious jingoism, what comes into play here is the class bias in North American society that promotes bilingualism in the upper class but frowns on it when it becomes an aspect of lower-class life.

More revealing of the ties between language and U.S. Immigration is the following newspaper report: "School and city officials expressed outrage this week over the Border Patrol's arrest of three Hispanic students outside an English as Second Language class."

For the Chicano poet Alfred Arteaga, the above story about arrest and deportation has a double irony: "irony, not only that 'officials expressed outrage' at so typical an INS action, but irony also, that the story made it into print in the first place." Arteaga knows too well that what Chicanos say and do in their own language is rarely found worthy of printing.

I think it is equally significant to remark on the fact that the officers who conducted the arrest were patrolling the borders of the dominant language to pick up the illegals. They are ably assisted by the likes of the California state assembly-man William J. Knight, who distributed among his fellow legislators a poem, "I Love America." That poem begins with the words "I come for visit, get treated regal, / So I stay, who care illegal." This little ditty makes its way through the slime of a racist fantasy. Its landscape is filled with greedy swindlers and dishonest migrant workers. The breeding subhumans speak in a broken syntax and mispronounce the name Chevy, the heartbeat of America, as (call the National Guard, please!) Chebby. The poem ends with a call that emanates like a howl from the guts of the Ku Klux Klan:

> *We think America damn good place,*
> *Too damn good for white man's race.*
> *If they no like us, they can go,*
> *Got lots of room in Mexico.*

If the immigration officer were to ask me about my language, what would I say? That any precious life-giving sense of language loses all form in this arid landscape of Buchanan-speak? Perhaps. That any answer I could possibly give is nothing more defined than a blur moving on the infrared scopes of those guarding the borders of fixed identity.

Homi Bhabha writes: "The enchantment of art lies in looking in a glass darkly—a wall, stone, a screen, paper, canvas, steel—that turns suddenly into the almost unbearable lightness of being." But where is this buoyancy, the refulgence, the mix of new life and new art? As the case of Fauziya Kasinga reminds us—the young woman who fled Togo to avoid genital mutilation and was held for long in detention by the U.S. Immigration authorities—grim reality so often persists in its unenchanting rudeness.

In such conditions to speak is only to declare any speech a station of loss.

> *I brought two bags from home, but there was a third that I left behind.*
> *In this new country, apart from the struggles that made me a stranger,*
> *were your needs, of the ones who bid me goodbye, those I left behind.*
> *Among the papers I collected, you had put a small bag of sweets, I left*
> *behind.*
>
> *There were divisions at home, there were other possibilities; there*
> *were communities in my town, there were communities where I came;*

> *I found a job, called it a struggle for survival, everything else I left*
> *behind. I didn't want to forget my traditions, the tradition of forget-*
> *ting I left behind.*
>
> *Bags, passport, my shoes crossed the yellow lines, something was left*
> *behind.*
>
> *Here I am, a sum of different parts; travel agents everywhere are sell-*
> *ing ads for the parts that were left behind.*

And yet, while speaking of the patrolling of the borders of dominant identity, I must note the presence of one who is still eluding arrest: a border-artist/
poet-performer/hoarder-of-hyphens/warrior-for-Gringostroika. Officer, meet Guillermo
Gómez-Peña. You have been looking for him not only because Gómez-Peña declares
"I speak in English therefore you listen/I speak in English therefore I hate you." But
also because, like a "Pablo Neruda gone punk," this "border brujo" threatens
mainstream America with the swaggering banditry of language, demanding as ransom a pure reality-reversal:

> *What if the U.S. was Mexico?*
> *What if 200,000 Anglo-Saxicans*
> *Were to cross the border each month*
> *to work as gardeners, waiters*
> *3rd chair musicians, movie extras*
> *bouncers, babysitters, chauffeurs*
> *syndicated cartoons, feather-weight boxers, fruit-pickers*
> *and anonymous poets?*
> *What if they were called Waspanos*
> *Waspitos, Wasperos or Waspbacks?*
> *What if literature was life, eh?*

27

Epiphany of the Other

DAVID LEVI STRAUSS

Chair of Art Criticism and Writing at the School of Visual Arts, David Levi Strauss presents here a short yet sophisticated treatment of the photography of Sebastiao Salgado. Levi Strauss draws on a variety of sources to help him contextualize and explain the complexity of representation and political effort present in Salgado's documentary efforts. From Between the Eyes: Essays on Photography and Politics, *this essay explores the difficulty and complexity of moving from compassion for the suffering to recognition of their dignity and power.*

> *The light was there, illuminating the roses and the portrait, and flags around them, perhaps, bundled up,* in the humblest popular solemnity. . . .
>
> —Pier Paolo Pasolini, *The Divine Mimesis*[1]

The photographs of Sebastião Salgado leave remarkably durable afterimages that reappear long after one walks away from them. One that recurs to me often is from a Mexican cemetery. Centered in the foreground is a mongrel dog, seated like a sphinx on the raised concrete slab of a gravestone. Lighted tapers and funereal flowers surround him as several cloaked mourners move off into the mist above. The closest mourner glances over her shoulder at the devoted dog, whose humble offering has stopped time. It is an image of great solemnity, but it is not at all ponderous or stale. The dog will soon rise and trot away, sniffing the bases of the stones, and the other mourners will begin their long work days, as usual.

Sebastião Salgado, Cemetery of the town of Hualtla de Jiménez. Mexico, 1980

In one of Salgado's magnificent images from the Serra Pelada gold mine in his native Brazil, one worker pauses briefly amid the hiving bodies in the pit. The resting worker's stance—feet together and arms folded, backed against an upright timber—evokes a crucifixion, and the Boschian spectacle of the mine confirms this solemn evocation. But at the same time, and equally, the foregrounded man is never more nor less than a worker at rest. This extraordinary balance of alterity and likeness, of metaphoric and documentary functions, is part of the Salgado signature. It allows his subjects to be themselves and more than themselves at once.

Like the mud-covered miners of Serra Pelada, Salgado's images come up out of the earth, bringing the earth with them. From the sands of the Sahel to the mountains of Ecuador and Bolivia, his frames are filled with earth and the people who live close to the earth, who know how hard it is to make a living from it.

One of the most telling differences between these photographs and those of one of Salgado's principle progenitors, W. Eugene Smith, is the comparative *cleanliness* of the latter's images. Even when photographing the smudged faces of coal miners in Wales, Smith made the lines clean and the contrasts sharp. Despite all the "Family of Man" rhetoric applied to Smith's oeuvre, he was an illuminator of contrasts more than of commonalities. Most of his essays tend to focus on individual heroes rising above the mediocrity that surrounds them. Smith's subjects are pulled up out of relation into his photographs, while Salgado's subjects are seen only and always *in relation*.

If there is a family of man today, most of its members live in the Third World, and Salgado is its family photographer. He has said that the world's goods are produced by "one family" that is spread out all over the world, and for his epic documentation of the end of large-scale manual labor in mining and other industries due to mechanization, he has photographed laborers in the Soviet Ukraine, Brazil,

Cuba, India, Bangladesh, Poland, and Venezuela. This massive undertaking, which Salgado calls "the archaeology of the industrial age," is intended to be "a kind of homage to the working class and the old ways of producing that are disappearing."[2] He works at a grueling pace, obsessively driven to document the workers of the world before they disappear, as the second industrial revolution sweeps them before it like sand. Like all great documentarians, Salgado has a passion to *save* an image of these people and these particular ways of living before they vanish forever. The impulse is essentially conservative. But unlike lesser practitioners who are drawn only to the drama and the tragedy of loss, Salgado's understanding of the geopolitical and economic backgrounds of the situations he documents gives his images an urgency of address. Single images may appear nostalgic, but relations among the images in Salgado's ongoing essays reveal a conflicted and often concealed history.

Behind the epic grandeur of the Serra Pelada images lies the history of European exploitation of Latin America. Greed for gold and silver motivated the Conquest. On October 13, 1492, one day after stumbling upon the New World and discovering he was lost, Columbus wrote in his diary: "I was attentive and worked hard to know if there was any gold." Later on he refers to the purpose of his trip as "our activity, which is to gather gold."[3] Gold and slave labor have always gone together. It was Brazilian gold that allowed England to confront Napoleon. As Eduardo Galeano concludes: "The Indians have suffered, and continue to suffer, the curse of their own wealth; that is the drama of all Latin America."[4]

> *Everyone knows that when the exploiters (by means of the exploited)*
> *produce goods, in reality they produce human beings (social relations).*
> —Pasolini, *Lutheran Letters*[5]

The exploitation that Pasolini decried in Italy is now happening on a global scale. Pasolini identified a guiding principle common to both the old Fascism in Italy and what he called the "new Fascism" of consumerist conformism, namely, "the idea that the greatest ill in the world is poverty and that therefore the culture of the poorer classes must be replaced by the culture of the ruling class."[6]

Most photojournalism and "social documentary" photography originating in the United States begins from this assumption. The photographer operates as a distanced, superior, "objective" witness to war, poverty, labor, and exotic cultural practices in other parts of the world. There is a big market for this kind of photography. As Galeano notes: "Poverty is a commodity that fetches a high price on the luxury market."[7] Photographs taken from this position may elicit pity, sorrow, or guilt in their viewers, but they will never provide information for change. They only work to reinforce the construction of the center and the periphery; north and south, rich and poor, superior and inferior. It cannot be otherwise. As Salgado says: "You photograph with all your ideology."[8]

What sets Salgado's images apart from most social documentary work is his relation to the other. Because of his background in Brazil and his understanding, as an economist, of the social and political background of the people and situations he photographs, his relation to his subjects is substantially different, and he has found a way to register this difference photographically.

The exploitation of the other that occurs in most (North American and European) documentary photography is partly a result of the political relation of photographer to subject. The difficult questions arising from such representations do not disappear with Salgado's images; they are in fact intensified, clarified, and made more insistent. The static that allows us to turn away from other photographs of starving people, for instance—their exploitation, crudity, and sentimentality—will not protect us from Salgado's images. We are, in turn, put in a different position in relation to the faces in these photographs, and we are forced to acknowledge that relation.

At the same time, Salgado's devotion to the people he photographs often transforms them into images of the sacred. A coal miner in India, with his lighted hat and pilgrim's staff, could be Saint James in a fifteenth-century illumination, and the skeletal corpses of the Sahel in their winding clothes resemble the ones fought over by guardian angels and demons in a medieval Book of Hours. The three angels of Juazeiro do Norte, the Condor-men of Ecuador, and Lot's wife in Mali in 1985 are all depicted in transformation, as aspects of the divine.

The spiritual issues involved in the struggle between cultures are dealt with in Salgado's many depictions of spiritual practices, from Coptic burial rites in Ethiopia to Tarahumara trance and animal sacrifice; from first communion in Brazil to a thanksgiving prayer to the Mixe god Kioga in Oaxaca.

These images of spiritual transcendence are perhaps the most troublesome for contemporary North American viewers, who are accustomed to that materialist dualism that finds a contradiction between radical politics and metaphysics, between history and mythology, between justice and transcendence. This materialist fix does not hold away from the center. The Argentinian philosopher and historian Enrique Dussel might have had Salgado's photographs before him when he wrote:

> *Beyond phenomenology the road of epiphany opens: revelation (or apocalyptic) of the other through the other's face, which is not merely a phenomenon or manifestation, a presence, but an epiphenomenon, vicarious, trace or vestige of the absent, of the mysterious, of one beyond the present. Ontology (phenomenology) gives way to metaphysics (apocalyptic epiphany of the other). . . . epiphany fulfills itself as a revelation of the one who makes decisions beyond the horizon of the world or the frontier of the state.*[9]

The sacred lies behind nearly every image in Salgado's most difficult series: his photographs from the famine-ravaged Sahel region of Africa in 1984 and 1985. Salgado did not set out to make sacred images, any more than the military photographers who documented the liberation of the death camps in Poland did. He set out, as a dedicated documentarian, to show the world what was going on so that they would pressure their governments to put a stop to it. Unlike the hundreds of "shooters" from all over the world who dropped in to "cover" the famine, Salgado became involved at a different level. The political repression following the military coup in Brazil in 1964 forced Salgado to flee to Paris with his wife in 1969. A radical student activist, Salgado's passport was revoked and he was not allowed to return to Brazil for ten years. Having already begun his education as an economist in Brazil, he continued this course of study in France, earning his doctorate at the University of Paris in 1971. He went to work for the International Coffee Organization, attempting to aid in the diversification of coffee production in Africa, in collaboration with the European Development Fund, the United Nation's Food and Agriculture Organization, and the World Bank. At some point, he took a camera he had borrowed from his wife to Africa and at age twenty-nine he made the decision that he could do more good for the people he was trying to help as a photographer than as a development economist. His first photographic assignment was a report on starvation in Africa for the World Council of Churches in 1973. He began to work extensively in Latin America and other parts of the world for the Sygma and Gamma photo agencies, finally joining Magnum in 1979.

While working on a series documenting the effects of famine in northern Brazil, Salgado realized that this was a world problem and needed to be approached as a world problem. In 1984, the French medical relief group Médecins sans Frontières (Doctors Without Borders) asked Salgado to return to Africa to record the famine relief work they were doing. He photographed in the huge refugee camps in the Sudan and elsewhere in Ethiopia, Chad, and Mali for fifteen months, traveling with medical teams and living with the dying. In an interview dealing with his experiences in Ethiopia, Salgado said:

> *What I found was beyond my imagination. In the first camp I visited, there were 80,000 people. They were starving. You would see the debris of the dying—bodies of men and women and many, many children. More than 100 people were dying every day.*
>
> *In the first few days at a camp like this, making photographs was impossible, because of the emotional situation. You are too stunned to shoot. But after a few days you stop crying. And after a few more days you know you have a job to do. It is a job just like the job of the doctors who have come to treat the sick or the engineers who have come to build housing.*[10]

It is not easy to look at these documents from the Sahel, but looking, one realizes how very different they are from other photographs of starving people in Africa. Whereas those other images end at pity or compassion, Salgado's images begin at compassion and lead from there to further recognitions. One of the first of these further recognitions is that starvation does *not* obliterate human dignity. A young boy, naked and gaunt, stands nevertheless tall, supported by a walking stick, rhyming shadows with a tree. A mother in an Ethiopian refugee camp, her bald skull mapped with pain, cradles her clear-eyed child and waits, defiantly. Salgado did not photograph passive victims, and pity does not suffice.

Salgado desperately wanted these images to be published and widely distributed at the time they were made, to raise a cry of alarm. Even though by that time, 1985, Salgado was winning prize after prize and his work was being published in all the top news magazines (his inconsequential photograph of John Hinkley's inept assassination attempt on Ronald Reagan was published thousands of times all over the world), the photographs from the Sahel were judged to be "unsaleable" in most markets. Though they were published as a book in France under the title *L'Homme en détresse* (Man in distress) in 1986, and in Spain as *El Fin del Camino* (The end of the road) in 1988, very few of them were published in the United States at the time (aside from two pages in the *New York Times* and four pages in *Newsweek*). Salgado's editor, curator, and collaborator, Fred Ritchin, has commented on the irony that these documents, which were judged by publishers and most magazine picture editors to be "too disturbing" when they were made, can only now, five years later, be seen, in a museum retrospective exhibition of a "famous" photographer.[11] Ritchin calls this evidence of "an unfortunate tendency to elevate the messenger while denying the message."[12]

At a time when the "message" and even the evidential veracity of documentary photography itself is disappearing into the pixels of digital imaging, and the efficacy of social documentary photography is being fundamentally questioned, the photographs of Sebastião Salgado appear almost as a new kind of document, with a very different address and relation to the other, and yielding quite different information about difference. Eschewing entirely the vaunted "objectivity" of photojournalism, Salgado works in the realm of collective subjectivities, aspiring to that "transcendence of self which calls for epiphany of the Other."[13] It is an aspiration that could breathe new life into the documentary tradition.

Endnotes

1. Pier Paolo Pasolini, *The Divine Mimesis*, trans. by Thomas Erling Peterson (Berkeley: Double Dance Press, 1980), p. 5.
2. Sebastião Salgado, in an interview with John Bloom, *Photo Metro 9*, November 1990, p. 4.
3. Tzvetan Todorov, *The Conquest of America: The Question of the Other*, trans. by Richard Howard (New York: Harper & Row, 1984), p. 8.
4. Eduardo Galeano, *Open Veins of Latin America: Five Centuries of the Pillage of a Continent*, trans. by Cedric Belfrage (New York: Monthly Review Press, 1973), p. 59.
5. Pier Paolo Pasolini, "Intervention at the Radical Party Congress," *Lutheran Letters*, trans. by Stuart Hood (London: Carcanet, 1983), p. 123.
6. Ibid., p. 16.
7. Eduardo Galeano, "Salgado, 17 Times," trans. by Asa Zatz, in *Sebastião Salgado: An Uncertain Grace* (New York: Aperture, in association with the San Francisco Museum of Modern Art, 1990), p. 11.
8. Salgado, quoted in Fred Ritchin, "The Lyric Documentarian," in *Sebastião Salgado*, p. 147.
9. Enrique Dussel, *Philosophy of Liberation*, trans. by Aquiliana Martinez and Christine Markovsky (Maryknoll, NY: Orbis Books, 1985), p. 58.
10. Salgado, in "The Sight of Despair," *American Photo*, January/February 1990, p. 40.
11. If then NEA chairman John Frohnmayer had had his way, they may not have been seen there either. I refer to a statement Frohnmayer made in August of 1990 that a display of images that "leads to confrontation . . . would not be appropriate for public funding." Asked to clarify, he gave the example of a photograph of Holocaust victims displayed "in the entrance of a museum where all would have to confront it, whether they chose to or not." ("Don't Confront the Holocaust?" *Time*, August 13, 1990).
12. Ritchin, "Lyric Documentarian," p. 149.
13. Emmanuel Levinas, *L'Humanisme de l'autre homme* (Montpelier: Fata Morgana, 1972).

28

Marking the Spot

LUCY LIPPARD

Lucy Lippard is a life-long artist, activist, and public intellectual with twenty books published since 1966, including The Lure of Local: Sense of Place in a Multicentered Society *from which the following chapter is excerpted. With a collage-like arrangement of text and images, this chapter considers some of the ways societies choose what events and sites to memorialize. By challenging the taken-for-granted nature of memorials, Lippard invites an understanding of history not as past, but as something actively participated in through contemporary choices about what and who to remember.*

> *Past and present are linked by a contract, a covenant between the people and their leaders, and this covenant is given visible form in monuments and a temporal form in a series of scheduled holidays and days of commemoration.*
>
> *—J. B. Jackson*

The celebration of the past can easily be made to play politics, and monuments are linchpins of this process. Most monuments favor mythology and are even further from "reality" than historical preservation. Nationalist and conservative forces are particularly fond of manipulating meaningful regional forms and histories to bolster their chauvinistic agendas, often denigrating modern life and blaming its faults on recent immigrants and ethnic minorities. Loyalty to "homeland" and "the unity-in-diversity discourse" still serve to ease immigrants

> *There are no conventional monuments outside the cemeteries in Georgetown, but there is a modest predilection for (recent) bronze plaques, publicly commemorating those (often summer) residents who have contributed to the town, or privately commemorating those who lived or died on site. On an island off Hunnewell Beach a Bates College student who drowned there is remembered. In the depths of the woods on Long Island are three plaques to the memories of former residents.*

into assimilation. Sometimes buildings themselves are monuments, but for the most part a monument is a structure built on top of memory relating to it only super-structurally, or even beyond memory—creating compulsory recall. Usually a sorry substitute for any actual remains, it can serve several contradictory purposes—resurrecting history, laying it to rest, and attracting tourists.

While monuments are often sterile pronouncements of the obligation to honor a truly dead past that occupies only a static place in the ongoing present, they can also recall the dead in order to make the survivors responsible to the living. Commemorating a place can have the same effect, as it did with a 1967 event staged by the New York State Council on the Art's visual art director, Allon Schoener, to commemorate the sesquicentennial of the Erie Canal—931 miles of heroic engineering and endangered waterway. The cultural and economic role of the canal in the state's history was dramatized by the voyage of the Erie Maid, a twin-decked "exhibition boat' carrying a lively audiovisual show that stopped at thirty communities between Albany and Buffalo with much fanfare, costume pageantry, and a pseudo-historical newspaper handout called *The Canal Courier.*

Is it more important to preserve the sites of pleasure or of pain? Monuments to social tragedies should intervene in daily public space, lest responsibility be dis-

Houston Conwill, Estella Conwill Majozo, and Joseph De Pace, Stations of the Underground Railway, 1992–93, New *York State, Niagara Region: Lewiston, Niagara Falls, Niagara-on-the-Lake, Ontario, Pekin, Parker, and Niagara University (Photo: Biff Henrich, courtesy Castellani Art Museum, Niagara University). Each site has a historical connection to the Underground Railroad—the escape route taken by enslaved African Americans to reach free territory in the North or in Canada. The installation of each shrine-like sculpture was accompanied by a "response poem" by Estella Majozo and a symbolic libation—the pouring of water.*

> *Our real monuments are of another order, still on the move. Boats are a big part of Maine's attraction. "Tall Ships" and "windjammers" (perceived as "clipper ships" though they are often old cargo coasters) ply the coast as mobile inns, or dock here and there for paying tours. The Maine Maritime Museum in Bath is homeport to the fishing schooner Harvey Gamage and there is talk of creating a "naval historic park" based on the first destroyer designed to carry missiles, built at the Bath Iron Works in 1959. For as long as I can remember, the Wiscasset*

placed, whereas celebratory monuments may blend more harmoniously. Monuments to victories are often less moving than those to losses, and monuments are not always in place; sometimes the event memorialized, like the Holocaust, happened far away. The gleaming black angle and fifty-eight thousand chronologically listed names rising from or descending into the earth of Maya Lin's Vietnam Memorial in Washington, D.C., is a rare monument that has become a place in itself rather than a reference to another place and time. It overwhelms the conventional bronzes nearby—Frederick Hart's heroic soldiers and Glenna Goodacre's noble nurses—demanded by conservatives who were outraged by the great black wall and its youthful Asian designer. Most literal representations are melodramatic and banal to an extreme, but abstracted monuments can seem to deny experience. Monumental architecture and sculpture rarely hold their own against space or time. The feeling of reverence sought by monument makers is not easy to come by in our irreverent society.

Where Lin's Vietnam Memorial and her smaller but equally impressive Civil Rights monument in Atlanta create places of memory and mourning, the squat

Maya Ying Lin, Civil Rights Memorial, *1988–89, black granite and water, Southern Poverty Law Center, Montgomery, Alabama (Photo: Hubert Murray). Maya Lin's name has become synonymous with the "new monument," since her Vietnam Memorial was built in Washington D.C. in 1982. In this more intimate Civil Rights Monument, water is the theme and the content, as it runs down a wall behind the oval black table and bubbles up from the table itself—a form inviting dialogue and touch, on which the movement's open-ended history is documented. Incised on the wall are the words that inspired the work, Dr. Martin Luther King quoting the Bible: "We are not satisfied and we will not be satisfied 'until justice rolls down like water and righteousness like a mighty stream.'" Water becomes a healing, purifying agent as it flows gently over the names of forty men, women and children slain during the struggle for civil rights, showing, as Lin says, "how individual people helped to change history." This picture shows visitors from Project Hip-Hop in Boston: Nancy Murray, Wyatt Jackson, Nick Andrade, Sandra Marcelino, and Ravi Dixit.*

> *waterfront on the Sheepscot River has been centered on the ghostly hulks of two 80'-long, four-masted sailing ships. The Hesper and the Luther Little were built in 1917–18 and brought to Wiscasset in 1932 as part of a lumber-hauling scheme that fell victim to a post-Depression economy. They were towed close to shore and abandoned, gradually becoming much-loved landmarks. Even listing in the mud, they provided one of the most romantic images in the area. Year by year, however, saw increasing depradations. The masts and rigging went first, but even*

volcanic rock obelisk marking ground zero at the Trinity site in southern New Mexico, where the atomic age began, cannot compete with the place itself. Dwarfed by the vast landscape of White Sands Missile Range, which is dotted with military bunkers and ominously unidentifiable structures, the Trinity monument makes no references to Hiroshima and Nagasaki—and no plaque has been added for Chernobyl. Evocation of the planetary consequences of the event of 1945 are left to the place, the space itself, the blue mountains in the distance, thunderclouds on the horizon, the dust devils rolling across the desert.

> *Older jish [ceremonial bundles, or kits] belong in the community where they were originally acquired . . . Some of these have a history that goes back 200 years. A jish contains rare elements from all over Navajoland and beyond. In a way it is a miniature version of Navajoland that concentrates the power of its rare elements and species.*
>
> —*Klara Kelley and Harris Francis*

American Indian history, so integrally entangled with place, has been ill served by the ubiquitous brave-on-a-horse monuments (especially James Earle Fraser's dispirited *End of the Trail,* which began as a life-size bronze but has since become ubiquitous, reproduced in many scales and mediums). Gutzon Borglum's Mount Rushmore defiles rather than commemorates the sacred Paha Sapa, or Black Hills, by transforming them into a monument to American colonialism. It is rather ineffectively parried by the in-progress monument to Crazy Horse near Rapid City, South Dakota—a generic image since the great Lakota warrior refused ever to have his picture taken. For many Native American nations, the land itself provides the monuments, marked by innumerable sacred sites where mythical and historical events took place, known only to those who care.

Making the connections between the genocide of Native Americans, Jews, and the living death of African American slavery, James Young has suggested that we might all share "common spaces of memory, if not common memory itself. As a result, every group in America may eventually come to recall its past in light of another group's historical memory, each coming to know more about their compatriots' experience in the light of their own past." The Washington Mall will eventually provide a panoply of cultural contributions, with the addition of Smithsonian museums dedicated to American Indian and African American culture. Those who see multiculturalism as divisive rather than inclusive oppose this panhumanism as "Balkanization of the Mall."

the rotting hulls had an imposing profile. Then they too began to disintegrate. Finally, in 1996, the town admitted that the old ships were more of a liability than an attraction. Their fate is still undecided. Some propose to salvage them, bring them on land, and start a waterfront museum. Local opinion ranges from get-rid-of-that-eyesore to nostalgic reluctance to see them go.

A recent arrival in Bath is a 17' section of the 35' bow of the Snow Squall— the last known clipper ship. Built in Cape Elizabeth in 1851, she sank near the

Charles Smith, African-American Heritage Cultural Center, Aurora, Illinois, 1986 to the present (Photos: Dave Kargl). Smith, who holds a BA in social sciences and is an ordained minister, is a Vietnam veteran. He began to make sculpture while struggling with post-traumatic stress disorder and now his ever-growing yard environment includes some 75 works commenting on history and current events. Despite a focus on activism and tragedy (slavery, Vietnam, Somalia, Rodney King), the museum is also a healing place, including among its many figures an arched gateway spelling "We Shall Overcome," and historical figures representing various virtues: "Grandma Hands" (Heritage and Remembrance), "Ms. Sassy" (Dignity), Gwendolyn Brooks (Character) and Louis Armstrong (Achievement). The Center is dedicated to "those of African ancestry that paid the price with their lives and their commitment to the struggle for liberation of African-Americans here and in Africa," says Smith. "I see this facility being the first African-American art institute in the United States that is free from all outsiders explaining, telling, and controlling it, because it is designed to tell the raw truth. Nor will we have anyone telling us these pieces are too graphic, that there is too much blood, or there's too much hatred. There is none of that. All of it is history." Smith welcomes groups, gives tours of his museum, and uses his sculptures as teaching aids for neighborhood youth. The environment continues indoors, where living space merges with work space and Smith shares his life with sculptural companions.

Only an avid military buff would be moved by the ubiquitous war memorials that dot the nation's small town squares and parks. In the late sixties, I suggested that all the equestrian statues in Central Park be brought together in a single field, like toy soldiers, strength in unity being the last hope for obsolete statuary. It was a time when a number of Minimalist, Conceptual, and Pop artists (Dan Graham, Robert Smithson, Carl Andre, and Claes Oldenberg, among others) had become interested in monuments, precisely because of their often absurd vacancy and loss of meaning. For a municipal art project in New York City in 1967, Oldenburg had a hole dug by union gravediggers behind the Metropolitan Museum—negative spatial comment on the mausoleum role of the museum and monuments in general. Since then, some of the most impressive ideas for monuments have dealt directly with the fact that absence can be more powerfully evoked than presence. The jury for the Free Speech Movement monument at Berkeley (I was on it) recommended Mark Brest van Kampen's project: a small circle of dirt marked by an inscription on marble: "This soil circle and the air space extending above it are not part of any nation and are not subject to any entity's jurisdiction." A decade later, a jury recommending public art for the Atlanta Olympics (I was there again) gave a prize to a similarly "artless" delineation of a space that nullified all zoning laws. These awards were not just nods to clever gestures of resistance but critiques of the lack of inventiveness in proposals presented for built monuments. Writing about several artists' spatially negative Holocaust monuments in Germany, Young has called this kind of work the "counter-monument," since it mocks "the traditional monument's certainty of history . . . Memory is thus sustained, not denied, by a sense of human temporality."

While monuments tend to be the results of complex social processes (including design competitions, political maneuvering, community approval, massive fundraising, and endless compromises), the marker offers a small-scale, subtler, and potentially subversive way of recalling the history of a place. The brown wooden roadside historical markers, illegible from a speeding car (despite the addition of "warning' signs so that people will be able to slow down and stop) are sometimes inaccurate and do little to provoke those who already think "there is nothing to see." Here again, however, the place itself, changed or apparently unchanging, is the monument.

Bronze plaques on urban buildings can be seen as subtexts to the houses themselves, "a part of the system of inscriptions that institutions of power write about themselves." When we read them without entering the house, they take precedence over the primary artifact. Signage pushes interpretation in one direction or another and often quells associative ponderings. But a more imaginative use of signs could ask questions, connect the site to the place itself. Firsthand accounts are always the *hotel"), inherited via several Dalrymple "boys" from its original owner, Anne Lauriat. The boat was built in the 1870s, and when time finally took its toll, Jud couldn't bear to have her end up as a rotting monument or beach toy (or worse still, a planter). So we gave her a Viking burial at the annual July 4th picnic on the Cross's beach in 1952. She burned for a long time. Everyone else went home. Four of us sat by her side until just at midnight, with the Popham bell ringing, the waves broke over her embers. We drank a toast to her long life heading*

most riveting. For example, the signs at a restored adobe ruin of a seventeenth-century mission church at Quarai, New Mexico, range from the predictable to the informative. But only one captures the last decade of the mission's and the pueblo's existence—a first-hand account by Fray Bernal, who wrote back to Spain that for two years both Spaniards and Indians had eaten toasted hides and leather while they lived in constant fear of Apache attacks. What now is a beautiful, peaceful spot was the scene of slavery, battle, and starvation. In fact, every place is the site of both contentment and despair, and it is this complexity that historical preservation and signage should convey.

Contemporary morality tends to interfere with realistic impressions. Josie Bassett's little homestead ranch in Utah has been swallowed by Dinosaur National Park. Her boarded-up cabin still stands in its idyllic site with a Parks Department sign showing a photo of the grandmotherly type who settled and ran the place alone in the early years of the century. It takes a book in the visitor's center to fill out the picture: Josie had four husbands, may have murdered one of them, and might have engaged in cattle rustling with her mother and sister. In an area known for its outlaws (heroes of novels and movies who are well documented in local museums or

Repohistory (James Malone and Tom Klem), Sarah Lena Echols Malone, from the "Entering Buttermilk Bottom Project," 1995, Atlanta (Photo: copyright Frank Niemier). Signs marking well-known and anonymous lives, created in collaboration with local residents, were accompanied by an installation in Piedmont Park and a parking lot painted with the life-size outlines of houses and streets that had occupied that site before demolition, including house numbers and family names, based on a 1959 city directory. Klem was inspired at an early project meeting by James Malone pulling out a tattered snapshot of his mother sitting on a porch in Buttermilk Bottom, where he was raised. The text reads simply: "Mrs. Sarah Lena Echols Malone raised her family on 267 Pine Place, Apt. #3, in the early thirties."

> *jauntily into the wind. I still have some of her ashes, my cousin Anne has her transom as a coffee table, and my 12-foot broad-beamed, gaff-rigged Beetle Cat named Rosita looks and sails just like the Anne L.*
>
> *John Bunker, an amateur historian from Palermo, Maine, collects living monuments—"antique apple trees" he plants on his property. "The apples are a link with the past," he says. "Each has a history. They are a living incarnation of amazing things that happened 100 or more years ago . . . Looking at an apple*

roadside attractions), a woman's crimes apparently are not so marketable. Far more informative and evocative of place than most signage are the "history trails" through cities that have appeared in the last decade. Designed to unearth the lost histories of women, minorities, or workers, they bring historical landscapes up into view from under the concrete, but without substantial architectural and landscape components, they tend to float. Markers may be inadequate on their own, but like unmarked walking tours of historical areas, they have one foot in the past and one in present reality. What one tours is the remains, sometimes almost invisible, but at least visualizable with a little help. Physical movement through streets and past buildings, even when they offer a mixed bag in terms of chronology and remodeling, brings the tourist closer to the past than history books can. Gail Lee Dubrow has proposed to introduce innovative, "nondidactic" interpretive panels in historic places for a Women's Heritage Trail in Boston, a city that already boasts a Black Heritage Trail (including little about black women) and other historical itineraries. Her proposals, supported by grassroots activities in the public school system, have been influenced by the Power of Place project and other public artists.

Appropriation of the signage styles of the bureaucracy is a popular strategy for artists to enter the picture. Edgar Heap of Birds's confrontational texts force passersby to acknowledge genocidal tragedies and the histories of stolen lands. **Repo** history (replaces the neutral markers of the bureaucracy with lively and opinated visual-verbal commentaries on historical events up to the present. Scott Parsons and David Greenlund confounded expectations by offering a sign in the Lakota language, among others in their skeletal tipi project, which was pivotal in the cancellation of Denver's Columbus Day parade in 1992. Gloria Bornstein and Donald Fels provided critical "viewpoints" on the historic development of the Seattle waterfront. Ilona Granet, who makes her living as a sign painter, also makes signs as art that comment with wickedly straightforward humor on male behavior toward women in public places. Since these are not functions art is expected to fill, the artist's sign becomes an effective mediator between general expectations of public information and of art.

For all the talent and sophistication that goes into such artworks, none have achieved the public appeal of the Burma Shave signs, which began in Minnesota in 1926. Just as anonymous advertising artists have more cultural influence than the biggest names among fine artists, popular culture is way ahead of "public art" in representing the past to millions of North Americans. In her scholarly and entertaining book *The Colossus of Roads: Myth and Symbol Along the American Highway,* Karal Ann Marling celebrates the sculptural counterparts of the tall tales that

318

is almost like looking into a crystal ball and seeing who's there." Like the sumacs that grow thick in disturbed ground, gnarled apple trees are often our first clues to old cellar holes and wells buried in the woods.

Tourists now go to see the monuments of tourist history. Tourist cabins emerged with the advent of the Model A—the "tin can tourist" that ended Maine's exclusivity as a summer playground for the wealthy. By 1930 there were about 150 motor courts in the state. Traffic-clogged Route One (known

fuel American folklore. Her talisman is a fifteen-foot tall statue of Paul Bunyan and Babe the Blue Ox on the shore of Lake Bemidji, Minnesota: built in 1937, it is the model for many others of its kind that define Midwestern space and assert local identity. Such behemoths are particularly well-suited to the Great Plains, where

Scott Parsons And David Greenlund, in cooperation with members of the Oglala Lakota nation and Augustana College, The Reconciliation Project, *1992, Sioux Falls, South Dakota. 29 charred skeletal tipi frames, 25' tall, were placed near the Nobel Institute Peace Prize Forum, recalling the fact that Native Americans had not been invited to attend. The lodgepoles (already burned) came from the sacred Black Hills, recalling the massacres that took place all over the west. They were accompanied by nine simulated National Park Service Historical Markers with text and image that included quotations from Native writers, including Leslie Marmon Silko, Russell Means and Leonard Peltier. Greenlund and Parsons recreated the tipis (90 of them this time, plus 29 markers) in Civic Center Park in Denver at the time of the 1992 Columbus Day Parade, providing a spiritual center for Native American protests against the parade, which was called off at the last minute and has not taken place since. The ghostly monuments reached into the sky and cast long shadows on the earth, combining visual poetry and harsh fact, directly affecting the cultural memories of those who experienced them, and overshadowing a bronze cowboy in the background. The artists intended the piece as a counter-memorial, "not stuck in the past, [but] a springboard to reconciliation for the next 500 years. . . . We wanted to imagine what apologies and historical accountability looked like."*

as America's Main Street), which runs up the coast and then inland, from Kittery to Fort Kent, is rich in roadside rustic cabins, stylized motels, diners, movie theaters, and 1950s-era gas stations. They are being surveyed for a State Historic Preservation Commission listing of vernacular roadside architecture and possible inclusion in the National Register of Historic Places. "Every generation rebels against the taste of its parents and prefers the taste of its grandparents," says commission director Earle Shettleworth.

they are visible for miles, breaking highway monotony and luring tourists to towns that may have little else to offer outsiders. They are counterparts of postcards advertising local produce: the giant potato on a railway flatcar, the pair of huge, breastlike navel oranges flanking a happy small boy, the ear of corn looming over a tractor, the barn-sized loaf of bread in a Kansas wheatfield, the huge fish or grasshoppers that may be caught nearby, and mythical animals like the "Jackalope" (the gigantic antlered jackrabbit invented in Douglas, Wyoming, in 1934 and since immortalized in postcards, a band, and a Southwestern gift store). These artistic creations may have taken a cue from their found-object siblings, symbols of the past too large or too ordinary to fit in museums—the locomotives, cannons, cable cars, airplanes, and missiles that dot local public parks.

Roadside sights are created independently by local artists as well as by entrepreneurs and chambers of commerce. Some evoke distant sites (in Washington state, in the seventies, I saw a roadside miniature Egyptian desert, complete with camels and pyramids); some evoke the local past (in a New Mexican village a little painting of a church stands on a mound of rubble where an earlier church stood (pl. 2). Elaborate yard displays of bottles and crockery embedded in cement or fantastic found-object sculptures and gardens featuring stone or shell castles, religious shrines set in upended bathtubs, whole hills painted and transformed into paeans to Jesus—these loving and obsessive works may lack the scale of the commercial offerings but make up for it with a marvelous degree of detail and subtlety, and far more connection to local place than imposed commercial monuments.

> *All of Polynesia is represented on forty-two acres of the Hawaiian island Oahu, at the Polynesian Cultural Center, which claims that "more people come to know and appreciate Polynesia while touring these beautifully landscaped grounds than will ever visit those fabled islands.*
>
> *—Barbara Kirshenblatt-Gimblett*

The president of Colonial Williamsburg once boasted that the flourishing souvenir market was "proof that history could be sold." There has been little doubt since then: from the reenactment of the gunfight at OK Corral in Tombstone, Arizona, to antebellum belles guiding visitors through plantation gardens on Louisiana's River Road, to the Graceland phenomenon, history is decidedly for sale in this country. Grady Clay points out that no city is complete (or economically viable) without an "epitome district" characterized by a name ("Old Town"), a center, local history explained in maps, pamphlets, signage, mythology, and costumed celebrations.

"The Big Indian," *40' high, Freeport (Photo: Peter Woodruff). Commissioned by the Casco Bay Trading Post and sculpted in Pennsylvania, it arrived on Route 1 in 1969 and has survived two owners since. The Indian is Plains generic, unrelated to Maine tribes.*

The most spectacular challenge to this trend involved the Walt Disney Corporation's projected American history theme park near the Bull Run/Manassas Battlefield in Prince William County, Virginia. "Disney's America" (not a misplaced possessive) raised questions of land use in the rural (and bedroom community) borderlands around a densely populated urban center. The corporation secretly bought up three thousand acres before announcing its plans to capitalize on the nineteen million tourists who visit nearby Washington, D.C. annually, some of whom might prefer an ersatz rural version to the real thing located in an inner city. Ironically, the history park would have endangered a dozen battlefields and sixty-four National Register sites from America's most popular war, not to mention destroying a beautiful rural landscape (which includes many wealthy fox-hunting

Yeibichai, *painted aluminum with lights, 1990, 36' high, made by Hinkley Signs for the Gallup Visitors and Convention Center, New Mexico (Photo: Richard Hooker). Popularly known as "the yellow Yei," and inscribed "Gallup, New Mexico, Heart of Indian Country," this monumental figure of a Navajo deity is a near replica of an earlier figure on the outskirts of Gallup. Both were made with no Indian consent or input and there was opposition to yet another unauthorized representation of sacred imagery.*

estates), and threatening some six thousand local farms on its peripheries. The prospect of three thousand new jobs was weighed against water, sewage, air pollution, and traffic congestion. District residents polled early on were 52 percent undecided, with 32 percent for and only 16 percent against. Governor George F. Allen was all for Disney, though, and in the spring of 1994 the state legislature agreed to financial incentives for the corporation.

But the real battle was over views of history. Despite claims to the contrary, Disney's track record suggested that the park would have constituted a counterrevolution against the gains made in broader and more critical views of history by trivializing and rescripting the events that have formed North America. The "Industrial Revolution" attraction was to be (literally) a roller coaster ride through a turn-of-the-century steel mill "culminating in a narrow escape from a fiery vat of molten steel," not plant closure; an Ellis Island recreation was to celebrate the "immigrant heritage." The "Native America" exhibit was to end in 1810, thereby omitting much of the bad news, and implying that indigenous people's histories came to an end almost two hundred years ago. All of which tends to confirm Jean Baudrillard's whimsical assertion that "Disneyland is there to conceal the fact that the 'real' country, all of 'real' America, is Disneyland. Disneyland is presented as imaginary to make us believe that the rest is real, when in fact all of Los Angeles and the America surrounding it are not any longer real but of the order of the hyper-real and of imagination."

In summer 1994, Disney Chairman Michael Eisner wrote a nationally published op-ed piece quoting Thomas Jefferson, appealing for Disney's right to "freedom of expression" and citing the popularity of their Lincoln talking doll exhibit at Disneyland: "At the Disney's America we will open in 1998," he boasted, "we will use all of our new technology, our creativity, our film and theater techniques and, yes, our entertainment skills to create a place that we hope will inspire renewed interest in American history and a renewed pride in American institutions." When the battle heated up, fueled by reports of Disney's avoidance of taxes and broken promises in Florida, the corporation surrendered and withdrew the project.

Endnotes

Conwill, De Pace, Majozo: See *Stations of the Underground Railroad,* a booklet for the public produced by the Castellani Art Museum and the Niagara communities in which the works were situated. See also **Susan Krane,** *Art at the Edge: Houston Conwill,* Atlanta: High Museum, 1989.

Maya Lin: See **Tom Finkelpearl,** "The Anti-Monumental Work of Maya Lin," *Public Art Review,* Fall/Winter, 1996; *Maya Lin Public/Private,* Columbus: Wexner Center for the Arts, Ohio State University, 1994.

Crazy Horse monument: The project was begun in 1947 by sculptor Korczak Ziolkowski who was asked by Lakota authorities, including Chief Henry Standing Bear, to create a work of art that would show "the white man the red man has great heroes too." The Boston-born Ziolkowski died in 1982, but work has been continued by his family. So far 8.4 million tons of rock have been removed (in comparison to Mount Rushmore's mere 450,000 tons). (**Daniel Gibson,** "Crazy Horse Memorial: Tribute or Tourist Trap?", *Indian Artist,* Winter 1997.)

James Young, "Holocaust Memorials in America . . . " in *Survey of Jewish Affairs* 1991, **William Frankel,** ed. Thanks to judy Chicago for introducing me to James Young's scholarly and deeply moving work

"war memorials": see **Lippard,** "Within Memory," in *Athena Tacha: Massacre Memorials and Other Public Projects,* New York: Max Hutchinson Gallery, 1984.

On Conceptual monuments: See **Lippard,** *Six Years. . . .*

Charles Smith: see **David Kargl, Debra N. Mankoff, Thomas Skwerski,** *Straight at the Heart: Charles Smith's African/American Heritage Museum,* Beloit, Wisconsin: Wright Museum of Art, Beloit College, 1995

James Young, "The Counter-Monument: Memory Against Itself in Germany Today," *Critical Inquiry,* Winter 1992. See also Young's "When a Day Remembers: A Performative History of *Yom ha-Shoah, History and Memory*", Winter 1990.

Josie Bassett: see **Diana Allen Kouris,** *The Romantic and Notorious History of Brown's Park,* Greybull, Wyoming: Wolverine Gallery, 1988.

John Bunker, quoted in MST, Oct. 6, 1996.

Parsons and **Greenlund:** Quotations from letters to the author from **Scott Parsons.**

Earle Shettleworth, quoted in PPH, July 5, 1995.

"the real battle": As **David Harvey** has bluntly stated, "All history is, after all, the history of class struggle." ("Monument and Myth," *Annals of the Association of American Geographers,* September 1979.)

Jean Baudrillard, quoted by **Kyong Park** in brochure for his lecture on "Nuclear Heritage Park: Weapon-Based Entertainment," at the Cooper Hewitt Museum, New York, 1994.

Michael Eisner, op-ed piece in *Portland Press Herald,* August 5, 1994.

29

The Cinema of
Suburban Paranoia

STEVE MACEK

Steve Macek works as an Associate Professor of Speech Communication at North Central College. In this chapter from Urban Nightmares: The Media, the Right, and the Moral Panic Over the City, *Macek argues that major films participate in and help amplify mainstream culture's class-based and racialized fears about urban cities. This chapter also illustrates how an argument about popular culture might identify trends and locate those trends in specific social and historical tensions.*

> *The imagined landscape of the city has become, inescapably, a cinematic landscape.*
>
> —*James Donald,* Imagining the Modern City

> *In Hollywood film the city has long functioned to focus psychic processes of paranoia, hysteria and repression.*
>
> —*Liam Kennedy,* Race and Urban Space in Contemporary American Culture

Consider the following scene from director David Fincher's hugely successful and critically acclaimed 1995 thriller *Seven*.[1] It is nighttime and it's pouring rain. It is almost impenetrably dark. We see a seedy boulevard that looks vaguely like it belongs on the Lower East Side of Manhattan (see Figure 1). Detective William Sommerset (played by Morgan Freeman)—a dour, weary-looking old man wearing a trench coat and fedora—is shown dashing from the door of his apartment building, past a couple of grubby homeless men sharing a bottle, to hail a cab. He sighs upon entering the vehicle and gazes out onto the street with a look of utter exhaustion as the cab moves slowly into traffic. Through the backseat window we catch a passing glimpse—from Sommerset's point of view—of uniformed cops dressed in clear plastic rain gear bending over what appears to be a corpse sprawled out on a glistening, crowded sidewalk. We hear a siren. On the opposite side of the cab, a police cruiser pulls into view, its lights flashing. "Where you going?" asks the driver, glancing into the rearview mirror. "Far away from here," responds Sommerset still staring out the window. The camera then lingers for two or three seconds more on his furrowed, bone-tired face before cutting away.

This particular sequence isn't especially central to the action of the film that follows Sommerset and his inexperienced new partner from "upstate," Detective David Mills (Brad Pitt), as they track the perpetrator of a series of demented, biblically inspired murders through a murky, rain-soaked metropolis. In terms of the plot, the scene serves merely to convey the character of Sommerset from his apartment, where he restlessly ponders the exotic details of the slayings, to the library where he does the research that eventually leads him to the murderer, Jonathan Doe (Kevin Spacey). Nor is the scene—drawing as it does on the well-worn conventions of film noir (tired, trench coat-clad detective, slick streets, looming darkness, bleak tone etc.)—especially innovative aesthetically. However, it *is* emblematic of

Figure 1. Detective William Sommerset's view from the cab in Seven.

the way *Seven* constructs its "big city" setting as an oppressive space of gloom and ambient violence, a locus of quotidian horror, the kind of place any sane person would want to stay "far away from."

Since the early '80s, Hollywood has produced a spate of enormously popular movies that share *Seven's* nightmarish vision of the American urban scene. Dark, comic book-inspired films such as *Batman* (1989), *Darkman* (1990), and *The Crow* (1994), along with their respective sequels, cast their imagined cities as breeding grounds for criminality, bloodshed, and moral chaos that can only be tamed by merciless superhero vigilantes. A cycle of ghetto crime dramas such as *Colors* (1988), *New Jack City* (1991), *Menace II Society* (1993), *Trespass* (1992), and *Sugar Hill* (1993) depict the inner city as little more than a battleground for warring youth gangs; action thrillers like the *Dirty Harry* and *Death Wish* series, Steven Segal's many movies and their low-budget imitators like *Street Justice* (1989) all present a similar and similarly chilling picture of our metropolitan centers wracked by murder and mayhem. Meanwhile, America's suburban schools are pictured as veritable combat zones in movies like *The Substitute* (1996), *187* (1997), and *Dangerous Minds* (1996). And current cinematic science fiction can envision only two possible futures for the American metropolis: either its current trajectory of decline and dilapidation is extrapolated into the near future, as in *Escape from L.A.* (1996) and *Johnny Mnemonic* (1995), or, more usually, it is subjected to the kind of spectacular annihilation witnessed in *Independence Day* (1996), *Volcano* (1997), *Deep Impact* (1998), *Armageddon* (1998), and *Godzilla* (1998).[2] As Douglas Muzzio notes, the dominant cinematic images of U.S. cities in the 1980s and 1990s "have been grim, almost irrespective of genre, location and director" (Muzzio 1996, 196). This is not to say there weren't other, more sanguine representations of urban life in Hollywood film during this period. Movies like *Sleepless in Seattle* (1993), *You've Got Mail* (1998), *It Could Happen to You* (1994) and *Desperately Seeking Susan* (1985) imagined New York City as a magical place of adventure, self-discovery, and romance. Yet, these upbeat urban stories were exceptions to the gloomy, blood-drenched vision of the city that was the norm on the big screen.

Of course, edgy, apprehensive portrayals of city life are hardly unique in the history of Hollywood film. The mean streets and cutthroat mob underworld of '30s' gangster films like *Little Caesar* (1930) or *Public Enemy* (1931) were hardly a good advertisement for the pleasures of urbanity. Nor, for that matter, was the horrified, expressionist vision of urban existence that pervades classic film noir. The noir pictures of the 1940s and '50s—films like *Scarlet Street* (1946), *The Woman in the Window* (1945), *The Big Sleep* (1946), and *Kiss Me Deadly* (1955)—notoriously depicted the city as "a shadow realm of crime and dislocation in which benighted individuals do battle with implacable threats and temptations" (Krutnik 1997, 83). But the menacing cities on display in mainstream movies during the '80s and '90s articulated a shrill anti-urbanism unprecedented in the most pessimistic of the classic noirs and unusual even in the long annals of Hollywood's distrust of the city. So, for instance, *The Crow* (1994) presents us with a hyperbolically degenerate Detroit ruled by a sinister mastermind who sleeps with his half-sister, grills the gouged-out eyeballs of his victims, and every Halloween has his lecherous, drug-addicted henchmen set fire to the city for the sheer joy of it. Similarly, *Batman*'s Gotham City is a sunless, brooding playground for muggers and super-criminals that one character frankly admits is unfit for habitation by "decent people." The barbarous urban wasteland of *Escape from L.A.* is presided over by (pseudo-revolutionary) gangs, con men, and psychotics. And in *The Devil's Advocate* (1997), Satan is a Park Avenue lawyer and New York is crawling with his demonic minions. According to Hollywood, it seems, cities haven't merely fallen on hard times, they've been condemned to the fires of eternal damnation.

It is worth asking why such hysterically terrified representations apparently resonated so well with the movie-going public of the past two decades. What meanings do they convey? What exactly is at stake ideologically in these images? How do they, to use a phrase of Douglas Kellner's, "transcode political discourses and in turn mobilize sentiment, affection, perception and assent toward specific political positions" (Kellner 1995, 60)? What anxieties, what fears are being allegorized in these dark visions?

These questions take on added weight if we bear in mind the enormous cultural and ideological power of Hollywood's considerable output. Though not the "total environment" that television is for most Americans, film nevertheless plays an important cultural role as an interpreter of social experience and a promoter of values. As Graeme Turner has argued:

> [i]t is now more or less accepted that film's function in our culture goes beyond that of being, simply, an exhibited aesthetic object. . . . Popular films have a life beyond their theater runs or reruns on television; stars, genres, key movies become part of our personal culture, our identity. Film is a social practice for its makers and its audience; in its narratives and meanings we can locate evidence of the ways in which our culture makes sense of itself. (Turner 1988, xiv–xv)

That Hollywood film exerts a profound ideological, moral, and psychological influence on its audiences is in fact recognized by the leaders of the industry. Thus, former head of Columbia Studios David Puttnam once candidly admitted that "Whether we like it or not filmmakers are in the propaganda business . . . film sets the social agenda—more so, in my view, than television. Attitudes are altered by film, particularly kids' attitudes" (Puttnam 1986, 45). And while it would be a mistake to treat mainstream films as automatically "reflecting" or "mirroring" the prevailing values and hegemonic ideology of a given historical moment, it can't be denied that they frequently do assume, reproduce, and lend credibility to concepts and myths drawn from dominant ideological discourses.[3] This "propaganda" function is clearly in evidence in the movies employing "the city as nightmare" trope dissected below.

In this chapter I argue that the dominant images of American cities and urban space circulating through Hollywood film in the 1980s and '90s derived their shared fantasy about contemporary urban reality largely from the conservative interpretation of street crime, gangs, and the "underclass" that became so prominent in news reporting and public discourse during this period. Along with welfare-bashing politicians and "if it bleeds it leads" journalism, these representations catered to and amplified the panic of a mostly suburbanized, mostly white middle class over the mayhem supposedly raging in America's largely black and Latino central cities. Like the moralistic interpretation of ghetto poverty offered by Myron Magnet and William Bennett or the coverage of the "crack epidemic" on network news shows, they mystified the source and nature of the real social and economic problems faced by our major cities even as they selectively exaggerated their severity. And, like the shrill rhetoric spouted by the conservative demagogues of the era, Hollywood's framing of the social and economic troubles of our metropolitan areas during the Reagan, Bush, and Clinton years offered a series of ideological justifications for the punitive attitude toward the ghetto poor and the urban working class that prevailed under those administrations.

This chapter demonstrates the extent to which Hollywood has perpetuated reactionary mystifications of urban woes by surveying a broad range of films produced during the 1980s and '90s. To begin with, I examine the tendency of mainstream movies to imagine the city—and particularly the distressed urban core—as a racialized zone of unfettered criminality and social pathology. I also briefly consider the appropriation and exploitation of this vision of urban space in African American-directed "ghetto-centric" gangster films like *New Jack City* and *Menace II Society*. I go on to argue that the conservative politics of Hollywood's conception of inner-city ills is thrown into high relief by a group of films—*Judgment Night* (1993), *Falling Down* (1993), *Grand Canyon* (1991)—each of which center around the story of middle-class white men who find themselves lost in the wilderness/jungle of the postindustrial metropolis and are forced to fight their way out. Next I show how a number of popular films of the '90s postulate urban violence and criminality as a threat to an embattled and besieged middle-class family. Finally, the chapter concludes by examining the now-common cinematic trope of the city as the embodiment of an absolute, often supernatural evil—as Babylon, Sodom and Gomorrah, or even Hell itself—deployed in David Fincher's hit thriller *Seven*.

The City as Police Problem

Since at least the early '70s, Hollywood films have tended to define the ever-more socially heterogeneous American city as a police problem, an unruly place overrun by dangerous, amoral, usually minority undesirables from whom the rest of society must be vigilantly protected. In many of these films, the old racist, imperialist image of the anonymous mass of natives against whom "is always counterpoised the isolated white figure" (Hall 1995, 21) gets resurrected and set in a modern metropolitan context. Such movies depict the (usually black and brown) residents of the city as self-destructive and "out of control," as not merely people in trouble but "people who make trouble." The result, in film after film, is "a pervasive sense that life in the urban center is a self-made hell" (McCarthy et al. 1997, 285). Rarely is this characterization of the "urban crisis" put on screen without an accompanying plea for brutally repressive state action as a response.

A perfect example of this tendency is John Carpenter's dystopian thriller *Escape from New York* (1981), in which the island of Manhattan has become a giant prison governed by its own depraved inmates. Its residents live in squalor, dress in outrageous, tattered punk attire, and hoot and scream wildly at the gladiatorial contests staged for them by the settlement's overlord, the Duke. The film's city is, as Douglas Kellner and Michael Ryan correctly observe, "a conservative nightmare of minorities and criminals run rampant" (Kellner and Ryan 1990, 258). Indeed, all the urban specters that haunt the middle-class imagination are there: the homeless psychotics, the punk rock hooligans, the gangbangers, the angry mobs. The narrative leaves little doubt about how best to restore order to this mutinous assemblage. Forced against his will to descend into the city in order to rescue the president of the United States, who has fallen into the clutches of Manhattan's gangs, a Rambo-esque martial arts expert named Snake (Kurt Russell) shoots first and asks questions later. Snake is conservative ideology's archetypical strong individual; a former military hero and renegade who has nothing but disdain for both the government he is helping and the dehumanized low-lifes he has to kill to complete his mission. Throughout, the film asks us to identify with Snake's point of view, and from his perspective New York appears mainly as a collection of assaults to be repelled and pitfalls to be avoided.[4] One could hardly ask for a better metaphoric rendering of the conservative interpretation of America's central cities.

A more recent example of Hollywood's definition of the city as a space of violent criminality is the 1990 sci-fi action picture *Predator 2*, which also takes as its narrative premise the conservative fantasy of a "fallen city" run by hoodlums. As Christopher Sharrett explains, the film dramatizes:

> *the true conscience of the commercial industry in conflating the blood-thirsty, unstoppable alien invader (whose head armor resembles dreadlocks) with Jamaican, Colombian and other Third World "drug posses" whose chaotic gun battle with police opens the film and sets its tone. The Predator is an Other as comprehensive as Coppola's Dracula, with a different focus. Los Angeles, the postmodern hellscape besieged by crime (not grounded in the social), the Babel whose conscientious and multi-ethnic law enforcement apparatus must do battle with bureaucracy and entertainment media, incarnates a scapegoat in the predator, who not incidentally is viewed by the bemused Third Worlders as a deity and whose predatory tactics mimic their own. (Sharrett 1993b, 108–9)*

The chaos and savagery that neo-imperialist fictions like *Rambo II* (1985) or *Clear and Present Danger* (1994) impute to Vietnam or Colombia has here invaded the imperial homeland. Indeed, there's virtually no difference between the film's black and Latino villains and, say, the swarthy enemies that populate the *Rambo* cycle; the threat to American civilization posed by the foreign armies and the domestic underclass, it is intimated, is identical. The fact that the original *Predator* (1987) was set in the battle-torn jungles of Central America only strengthens the parallel *Predator 2* tries to draw between the ghettos of L.A. and the hostile Third World imagined by apologists for the New World Order. The idea that the ghetto constitutes a "combat zone" as perilous and volatile as any in Southeast Asia is a point that is made often and bluntly in the course of the story. For instance, the television reporter (Morton Downey Jr.) whose alarmed voice-over accompanies *Predator 2*'s frenetic opening gun battle, concludes his report by observing, "It's a fucking war down here." The detective leading the campaign against the Jamaican and Colombian drug dealers (played by Danny Glover) echoes the reporter's view, telling a new member of his team that "metro command is a war zone."

Characterizing the city as an unruly Third World "battlefield" naturally invites no-holds-barred military intervention (at least according to the twisted "logic" of the new American imperialism of the 1980s and '90s). After all, if the city, or—more specifically—the ghetto, is as treacherous and uncivilized as Vietnam, Iraq, or Central America, if it is a place of "guerrilla combat" and "unconventional warfare" populated with devious, bloodthirsty natives, then almost any atrocity committed against its inhabitants can be justified. The trope of the inner city as war-torn jungle forms a significant common thread running through Hollywood's treatment of the subject over the past two decades or so. As Scott Forsyth has argued, in the openly Reagan-esque action thrillers of the 1980s and early '90s "the black and increasingly Hispanic masses . . . are the exact equivalent to the exotic masses of the third world; repeatedly, the ghetto is labeled a jungle" (Forsyth 1992, 280–81).

Take, for instance, Dennis Hopper's *Colors* (1988), which depicts the black and Latino neighborhoods of South Central Los Angeles as a staging ground for perpetual combat between feuding youth gangs. Although the film's claim to fame is the "realism" of its representations of L.A.'s notorious youth gangs, the real heroes (and narrative focus) of the story are the police, particularly a likeable old veteran of the LAPD's special anti-gang task force named Bob Hodges (Robert Duvall). Endlessly patrolling the ethnically balkanized communities of South Central, Hodges and his tough, trigger-happy partner Danny McGavine (Sean Penn) unsuccessfully try to head off an escalating war between the Crips and the Bloods. The African American and Latino neighborhoods that Hodges and McGavine patrol are depicted exclusively as graffiti-covered alleys overflowing with junk, settings for drive-by shootings, abandoned buildings or crumbling houses that have been transformed into gang hangouts, and street corner drug markets. Every youth the pair encounters is either a member of a gang (as signified by their "colors," sartorial badges of gang membership) or wants to be one. In more than one scene, several of these teens drink beer and smoke pot to the point of near collapse. Meanwhile, most of the adults Hodges and McGavine encounter in such communities are either the broken, disheartened parents of the victims of street violence or anti-gang activists whose efforts to steer community youth away from gang activity are depicted as utterly ineffectual. The viciousness and pathology of the inner city is further reinforced by its contrast with the warm, safe, comfortable domesticity enjoyed by "normal people" like Hodges and his wife (which we are invited to witness when they entertain McGavine and his girlfriend in their suburban home).

In the final analysis, the central message of the movie is one of hopelessness. The residents of the inner city, the film suggests, are powerless to change the endless cycle of violence and victimization in which they find themselves caught. This is made clear by the scene in which a gang from a small Latino neighborhood attacks the headquarters of a ruthless group of Crips. After the Latino gang has blown up and machine-gunned several Crips, one of their leaders—Loony Tunes—faces down the remaining Crip: both are armed with machine guns and both have an opportunity to turn away and save themselves; instead they simultaneously shoot each other to pieces (in slow motion, of course). This senseless mutual slaughter stands as a fitting symbol of the incorrigible "self-destructiveness" that the film—in an obvious echo of the right's discourse on the problem of the underclass—repeatedly attributes to inner-city youth. The police, we learn, are also relatively powerless to change the tragic dynamics of the ghetto: they might be able to save a few kids from getting involved in crime and drug abuse but they can do little to stop the majority of inhabitants of the ghetto from inevitably annihilating each other.

Yet even as it acknowledges the limits of the LAPD's power to address the problems of the postindustrial ghetto, the film seems to endorse police measures like the anti-gang task force as better than nothing. Indeed, it heroizes the character of Detective Hodges. He is gentle, sensitive, and tolerant; he relates to and is respected by most of South Central Los Angeles's gangs; he does them favors and they do him favors in return; he is intent on preventing the children of the communities he patrols from imitating the "creeps" who belong to gangs. By having Hodges senselessly murdered by a PCP-crazed gangbanger, *Colors,* unwittingly or not, turns him into a martyr for the cause of the (nearly all-white) police force who appear to be the only institution working for peace in the midst of the South Central's bloody killing fields. And this, Ed Guerrero has pointed out, ultimately amounts to "a cop's view of the 'hood'" (Guerrero 1993, 185).

The View from the 'Hood?
The City in Ghetto-centric Action Films

In contrast to the alarmist law-and-order message of films like *Predator 2* and *Colors,* one might expect African American–directed films dealing with the same central city terrain to articulate something like a critical, anti-racist alternative to the mainstream perspective. But, in fact, such are the constraints of the for-profit film industry that the "new wave" of commercially viable black filmmakers like John Singleton, Mario Van Peebles, and the Hughes brothers have found it difficult to break entirely with the hegemonic Hollywood definition of the inner city as a lawless killing zone. To be sure, the work of these filmmakers often tries to contextualize ghetto poverty and street crime in a way that appropriately lays blame for the growing urban crisis on official government policy, institutional racism, and the deindustrialization of the cities. Yet just as often these efforts at critical recontextualization of the standard stereotyped image of the inner city fail, allowing spectators to read the new wave of ghetto-centric movies as so many vindications of conservative discourse on the urban crisis. As Liam Kennedy observes, in such films "efforts to critique racism are blurred by spectacular displays of black-on-black violence and other forms of autodestruction" (Kennedy 2000, 117).

Van Peebles's *New Jack City* illustrates this tendency nicely. The film begins with a long aerial shot of downtown Manhattan accompanied by rap music by Queen Latifah and snatches of radio news items on various hot social issues of the day. The information conveyed by the news blurbs is of the sort that's absolutely necessary for any critical understanding of the urban crisis: we hear statistics about the high rate of black unemployment, discussions of the growing gap between the rich and poor in Reagan's America, and a factoid about the rising black murder rate. The film then goes on to tell the fairly predictable saga of the rise and fall of drug lord Nino Brown (Wesley Snipes) and his ruthless Cash Money Brothers crime syndicate. A mise-en-scène foregrounding the trappings of hip-hop culture—from a rap music club that doubles as the syndicate's headquarters to the omnipresent gold chains on Nino's henchmen—and an "inside look" at the manufacture and distribution of crack are the only things that distinguish *New Jack City* from any number of other formulaic gangster films. Throughout, the social context for the rise of black gangsterism that was briefly invoked at the film's outset all but disappears. It resurfaces briefly in the concluding trial scene, when Nino points to the oppression and denied opportunities of his ghetto childhood as a rationale for his criminality, but his flippant attitude cues the audience not to take this explanation seriously. Further compromising the film's critical force is the fact that Van Peebles seems to support a retributive, "take no prisoners" approach to the Ninos of the world. Ed Guerrero comments that "[t]he biracial cops (Ice-T and Judd Nelson) of *New Jack City* are depicted as the violent, institutionally sanctioned, extralegal solution to the black community's drug and crime ills" (Guerrero 1993, 187). And, one might add, their rough, vigilante justice is the only viable solution even entertained in the movie.

The films of other widely acclaimed black directors go beyond the token dissent from the conservative stigmatization of the city we see in Mario Van Peebles's neo-Blaxsploitation vehicle. John Singleton's *Boyz in the Hood* (1991), a coming-of-age story set in a black neighborhood in South Central Los Angeles, offers an unapologetically oppositional, black-identified interpretation of the inner-city's problems. Its adolescent protagonist, Tre Styles (Cuba Gooding, Jr.), struggles through one "rite of passage" after another in a quest to avoid getting caught up in gang violence or assassinated by vicious cops and survive long enough to attend college in Atlanta. Tre fortunately has the guidance of a loving but somewhat authoritarian father, Furious Styles (Laurence Fishburne) to help him negotiate this treacherous journey. His two good friends, half-brothers Ricky (Morris Chestnut) and Doughboy (rap star Ice Cube), are not as fortunate: their fathers are absent from their lives and by the conclusion of the story both have met violent ends.

In its sympathetic attention to the myriad forms of oppression endured by those forced to live in the ghetto, *Boyz* couldn't be more different from a movie like *New Jack City*. It is, as Paula Massood has argued, a film focused intently on "the power relations inherent in space and geography" (Massood 1996, 90). As she notes, the film's mise-en-scène is filled with signs—from "Stop" and "One Way" signs to yellow police tape around a murder scene—which signify the various obstacles that work to isolate the residents of the 'hood from the rest of society. In addition, the LAPD is everywhere, a ubiquity signaled by "a proliferation of aural and visual signs . . . most notably through the repeated searchlights and off-screen sounds of police surveillance helicopters" (90). The police themselves are repeatedly shown to be predatory and sadistic in their relations with community members. In one pivotal scene, for instance, Tre is arbitrarily stopped by a pair of cops, one of whom roughs him up and thrusts a gun in his face just to scare him. By drawing attention to the constraints imposed by the ghetto on his characters' movements and life opportunities, Singleton attempts to expose the social conditions and economic realities driving the urban crisis that are effaced in the standard Hollywood treatments of the subject. That this is part of Singleton's agenda is underscored by a didactic speech about crack, liquor stores, and the Asian American–led gentrification of black neighborhoods that Furious delivers to his son in one scene. Speaking from a position recognizable as "black nationalist," he condemns the incursion of Asian stores into South Central on the grounds that their presence diverts capital and consumer dollars that should be going to struggling black-owned businesses. It is the sort of radical, "community control" position on the ghetto economy once espoused by the Black Panthers.

Be that as it may, some critics have, rightly in my view, taken even the critical politics of a film like *Boyz in the Hood* to task for accepting too readily an essentially conservative definition of contemporary black urban experience. In their article "Danger in the Safety Zone: Notes on Race, Resentment, and the Discourse of Crime, Violence, and Suburban Security," Cameron McCarthy, Alice Rodriguez, and their colleagues contend that "the images of the inner city produced by the current new wave black cinema corroborate rather than critique mainstream mass media" (McCarthy et al. 1997, 282). They note that Singleton's *Boyz* and the Hughes brothers' *Menace II Society* echo the themes of television news and play to the prejudices of the suburban middle-class spectators by constructing the inner city as "a harbinger of violence, danger and chaos" (279). The "realism" of *Boyz* and other ghetto-centric action films, they argue, is in fact predicated on a mainstream "reality code" defined by a conservative preoccupation with inner-city violence, sexual license, and drug use. As a consequence, "[t]he gangster film has become paradigmatic for black filmic production coming out of Hollywood" (283), so much so that even a talented auteur like Spike Lee has felt compelled to try his hand at the genre (in *Clockers*).[5] Furthermore, McCarthy and his co-authors point out that in the work of black directors like Singleton and the Hughes brothers, the problems of the black community are all too often laid at the feet of single mothers who, it is implied, "cannot properly raise their sons" (286). This too seems to corroborate the conservative discourse on the inner city and the underclass. Though a generation of commercially successful African American filmmakers in the '90s critically interrogated certain elements of Hollywood's mythology about contemporary urban existence, that mythology was powerful enough that their portrayals of the inner city all too often "transformed it into a space marked by a stylized nihilism" (Massood 2003, 152), an embodiment of white fears about reckless, antisocial ghetto youth.

Not Safe for Normal (White, Middle-Class) People

The demonization of urban life in mainstream '80s and '90s film is even more evident in a set of films—among them *After Hours* (1985), *Something Wild* (1986), *Bonfire of the Vanities* (1990), *Bad Influence* (1991), and *Judgment Night* (1993)—that critic Barry Keith Grant has dubbed the "yuppie horror film" (Grant 1996).[6] According to Grant, the yuppie horror film "addresses the anxieties of an affluent culture in an era of prolonged recession" (4). The typical yuppie horror film pits a young, usually male, professional against a monstrous doppelgänger (or a monstrous situation) that disrupts their anal-retentive predilection for self-mastery as well as their comfortable lifestyles. In keeping with the generic conventions of the horror film, it often thrusts its protagonists into a "terrible place," which in the case of the yuppie horror film is almost always some desperately impoverished slum or ghetto. Thus, to cite just three examples, *Trespass* traps its white middle-class main characters in an abandoned East St. Louis factory where they are forced to do battle with an Uzi-wielding black gang, *Bonfire of the Vanities*'s rich anti-hero, Sherman McCoy, gets into trouble when he takes a wrong turn in the Bronx, and *After Hours* chronicles the misadventures of a white-collar professional named Paul who gets stranded in the strange, bohemian world of Soho. As Grant argues, "These scenes of crossing over into the nether world of urban decay 'exude the Manichean, middle-class paranoia that once you leave bourgeois life, you're immediately prey to crime, madness, squalor and poverty'" (5). In constructing their "nether worlds," most yuppie horror films—regardless of their ostensive political commitments—deploy the conservative myths and ideologically overdetermined images that are so central to the hegemonic discourse on urban life. Consider the following examples of the (sub)genre that diverge dramatically in their overt politics while sharing a profoundly conservative conception of the postindustrial city and its problems: *Judgment Night*, a formulaic "road movie" about a group of middle-class suburbanites being chased through the mean streets of Chicago; *Grand Canyon*, a liberal social message film about the fractiousness and social divisions that shape life in contemporary Los Angeles; and *Falling Down*, a film about an "angry white male" who lashes out at his multicultural urban environment.

Judgment Night's themes, settings, and choice of cast make it an almost perfect (and perfectly formulaic) example of Grant's "yuppie horror" genre. Premised on a crudely drawn binary opposition between the safe comforts of suburbia and the mortal dangers of the inner city, it tells the story of a group of suburban men driving to a boxing match who take a wrong turn into a "bad neighborhood" on Chicago's South Side, witness a murder, and spend the rest of the film running from the drug dealers who are responsible for the killing. The persecuted suburbanites represent a cross-section of middle-class manhood: Frank (Emilio Estevez), the responsible, level-headed leader of the group, has a baby and a wife who doesn't approve of his wild friends; John (Stephen Dorff), Frank's troubled, slightly rebellious brother; Ray (Jeremy Piven), a fast-talking salesman; and Mike (Cuba Gooding, Jr.), a macho African American womanizer. Soon after the group takes to the road in a state-of-the-art RV—which is obviously meant as a metaphor for and constant reminder of the luxurious suburban neighborhood that Frank and the others call home—a traffic jam forces them to take a detour. Once they turn off the highway (in an area of Chicago that the knowledgeable viewer immediately recognizes as somewhere near the notorious "vertical slums" of the Robert Taylor Homes), they enter into a truly nightmarish urban landscape of dimly lit streets, vacant lots littered with blowing paper, and loitering bums. As they are driving along, someone dashes into the path of the RV; after stopping the vehicle, the group finds an injured man on the road and, when they take him on board, discovers that he has been shot. Shortly after, the drug dealers who shot him, led by a sneering hood named Fallon (Denis Leary), crash their car into the RV, kill the injured man, and then decide to eliminate the witnesses as well, setting off the chase that takes up the remainder of the film.

It is typical of the "yuppie horror" genre that the battle of wits that ensues between Fallon's gang and the frightened suburbanites is presented as a test of the group's collective manhood. In an early scene, Mike asks Frank if "married life" is making him "soft"; in the rest of the film the anxiety expressed in that question—anxiety about the potentially "emasculating" effects of suburban domesticity, affluence, and a life of comfort—is dramatized and, in the end, assuaged. The urban landscape Frank and his friends stumble into is a lawless environment, a "Wild West," in which only the "strongest" and most "masculine" will survive. Fallon alludes to this fact when, while hunting through a rail yard for Frank and company, he tauntingly refers to them as "ladies" and asks, "what do ya think of the neighborhood?" The conceit of making the inner city into a breeding ground for a

Figure 2. In Judgment Night *Frank and his friends race through the inner city.*

particularly aggressive, pathological form of hyper-masculinity echoes the fables that conservatives like Charles Murray and William Bennett spent decades spinning about underclass neighborhoods and urban "superpredators." Indeed, the standard, demonized image of the inner city and its inhabitants forms the template for the film's vision of Chicago's near South Side. For instance, in the rail yard, Frank and his friends meet a band of homeless men (one of whom babbles incoherently through most of the sequence) who greedily take their money in return for not revealing their whereabouts to Fallon. Next, to the sound of rap music, they wander into a foreboding housing project composed of brick tenement buildings illuminated by low-key, infernal sulfurous lighting (see Figure 2). They go into one of the buildings and roam through the halls desperately banging on doors, begging for help, but no one responds to their pleas. Eventually they find a couple of women who grudgingly agree to let them use their phone. Meanwhile, the housing project's resident gang tells Fallon and his crew how to find Frank's group in return for a roll of bloodstained hundred dollar bills. With the exception of the two women who let Frank and his pals use their phone, then, the denizens of the inner city are presented as morally on par with the ruthless Fallon and his gang. As Ray exclaims at one point, "This is hell."

Naturally, Frank and his friends don't survive their trip through the urban netherworld unscathed. The first to go, predictably, is Ray, the slick dealmaker. He gets caught by Fallon on the roof of one of the tenements and tries unsuccessfully to sweet talk his way out of the inevitable. "You're the kind of milk-fed fucker I hate," Fallon tells him before tossing him off the roof. While the death of the effete Ray seems almost preordained according to the gendered logic of the narrative, tough guys Mike and John also find themselves injured and incapacitated in the lead-up to the final showdown in an empty downtown marketplace. The sole remaining healthy member of the group, Frank, is thus left to fight it out with Fallon alone. The climactic hand-to-hand battle turns out to be pretty standard action-movie fare: Frank nearly succumbs but at the last minute, after Fallon threatens to hurt his family, he summons up the strength to shove Fallon to his death. In the end, the police and the paramedics arrive, Mike and John are wheeled off to a waiting ambulance, and a cop tells Frank, "Your wife's outside." At the most obvious level of interpretation, Frank's triumph signals a victory of "normal" middle-class suburban manhood over the deviant, violent manhood associated with the inner city. But beyond that, it implies that the middle-class nuclear family, far from rendering Frank "soft," is what gives him the strength to defeat Fallon. It is hard not to see such an ending as vindicating the conservative "family values" preached by the likes of Dan Quayle and Charles Murray. If *Judgment Night* has a coherent politics, it surely centers on its valorization of the suburban domesticity over and against the deviance and wildness of urban life.

As one would expect from the man who created *The Big Chill,* the definitive Hollywood post-mortem on the cultural and political upheavals of the sixties, the main ideological thrust of director Lawrence Kasdan's *Grand Canyon* is considerably more "liberal" than *Judgment Night's* celebration of vigilantism in the service of the middle-class family. The film chronicles a few months in the lives of a cross-section of Los Angeles residents coping with a variety of existential crises (most of which are precipitated by the pressures of urban life). As in *After Hours* and *Judgment Night,* the story's main animating crisis occurs when a middle-class white man, in this case an immigration lawyer named Mack (Kevin Kline), takes a wrong turn and ends up in the heart of the ghetto. Soon after he is passed by a car blasting rap music and loaded with hostile-looking young black men, Mack's car breaks down. A short while later, the same group spots him stranded and circles back around to harass him. The gun-wielding leader of the gang is about to force him out of the car when Simon (Danny Glover), a black tow-truck driver, arrives on the scene to defuse the situation. The whole episode is, as Lisa Benton has observed, "the quintessential white, middle-class urban nightmare" and "reveals Los Angeles as a landscape of tension and conflict, of emerging language and custom barriers, of contests over space and 'turf rights'" (Benton 1995, 156). But unlike most yuppie horror flicks, in which the sanctioned response of the white middle-class protagonist to the threat posed by the city is always some Rambo-esque flurry of violence, *Grand Canyon* holds out hope that the city's divisions can be bridged and conflicts healed. Thus, Mack eventually seeks out Simon to thank him for saving his life and the two strike up a (somewhat awkward) friendship. Mack manages to find an apartment for Simon's sister, allowing her to move out of her dicey, crime-ridden neighborhood, and even arranges a date between Simon and a secretary who works in his building that sparks the beginning of a relationship. By the end of film the two men and their families take a joint vacation to the Grand Canyon. The final shot pictures the two families on the edge of the Grand Canyon, black and white, affluent and working class, united in their awe of nature's wonders, a fitting symbol of *Grand Canyon's* personalized, therapeutic approach to social conflict and polarization. All the divided metropolis needs to escape its problems, this ending suggests, is more goodwill, personal warmth, and "camaraderie" among its residents.

Interestingly, though, *Grand Canyon's* patina of liberalism does not prevent the film from taking at face value what is an essentially conservative understanding of the urban crisis. The South Central neighborhood where Simon's sister and her children live, in particular, is envisioned as a veritable "landscape of violence." As Simon's sister and her daughter walk home one day, they pass a woman scrubbing bloodstains off the sidewalk. On another occasion, a salesman who sells life insurance policies that cover funeral expenses for children shows up at her door. And, in an especially terrifying scene, the family's house is riddled with bullets during a late night drive-by shooting. Nor are the dangers of urbanity confined exclusively to South Central. A demented, disheveled assailant shoots Mack's movie-producer friend Davis (Steve Martin) in the thigh outside a swank restaurant in order to steal his watch. Mack's wife Claire repeatedly encounters a sullen, muttering homeless man camped out in the alleyway behind an upscale shopping street (see Figure 3).

Inevitably, as in the television news stories discussed in chapter 4, the film interprets the city's dangers as emanating from the underclass. It is an underclass that *Grand Canyon* candidly admits is the product of the widening gap between the affluent and the rest of society, between the white suburbs and the racially heterogeneous city. As the character of Davis explains: "There is an ever-widening gulf between people who have stuff and people who don't have shit. It's like a big hole in the ground—like the Grand Canyon—what comes out of this hole is an eruption of rage, and rage creates violence, and violence is real." Despite this shocking admission, the film makes no moral or political judgment about, and assigns no social agent responsibility for, the widening gulf itself. The city's social tensions and the explosive conflicts such tensions create are presented simply as evidence that things are, as Mack puts it, mysteriously "going to shit." In this way, the film can allow its white upper-middle-class characters to lament the urban crisis without registering their own complicity in its creation. At most, they feel terror and confusion mingled with a vague, inchoate sense of guilt, as when Claire declares, "The world doesn't make sense to me. Babies lying in the streets, people who sleep in boxes. People are ready to shoot you if you look at them and we are getting used

Figure 3. Claire crosses paths with a deranged homeless man in Grand Canyon.

to it. The world is so nuts. It makes me wonder about the choices we made." Despite its liberal leanings, in the end *Grand Canyon* elaborates no critique of the structural forces driving the urban decline it laments.

The frequency with which the yuppie horror film's nightmare world adopts the guise of "bad neighborhoods" in the inner city suggests a return of the repressed: it is a coded acknowledgment that the lavish upper-middle-class lifestyle depends (to some degree, at any rate) on the very economy responsible for immiserating those neighborhoods and exploiting the black and Latino working people who reside there. The accidental voyages into those areas that the white middle-class protagonists in *Judgment Night* and *Grand Canyon* undertake allow them to face down the specter of the monstrous underclass nemesis. The conservative politics of *Judgment Night* requires that this meeting end in a fight to the death from which the middle-class subject necessarily emerges victorious; in the case of *Grand Canyon,* the encounter gives rise to therapeutic soul searching and individual good deeds that nonetheless pose no challenge to the prevailing arrangement of political and social power. Yet despite the surface political differences between the two films, their rhetorical construction of the inner-city menace is similarly alarmist and similarly indebted to the right's interpretation of the urban crisis.

Though differing from the standard "yuppie horror film" in some key respects, the controversial hit movie *Falling Down* (1993) shares with *After Hours* and *Judgment Night* the organizing story-arc of a white man's embattled odyssey through a multicultural urban wilderness. Dubbed by one reviewer "a *Taxi Driver* for the '90s," it tells the story of a day in the life of Bill Foster (known in the film as D-Fens for his personalized license plate), a divorced, laid-off defense worker played by Michael Douglas, whose rage and frustration with everyday life in Los Angeles finally boils over in the form of a cross-town rampage that puts him into conflict with a Korean shop owner, a Latino gang, a neo-Nazi, and a pushy panhandler, among others. As Carol Clover describes the plot, "like Odysseus, [D-Fens] is heading home, except that instead of Scylla and Charybdis there are Chicano gangs and homeless people, and instead of Penelope waiting patiently in Ithaca there is a former wife with a restraining order in Venice Beach" (Clover 1993, 6).

At its most obvious, *Falling Down* dramatizes the much-publicized crisis of white male authority that pundits in the '90s alleged had been precipitated both by the forces of "political correctness" (i.e., feminism and identity politics) and by changing demographics that were gradually rendering white men a minority in many areas of the country. D-Fens is, as critic Jude Davies asserts, "a specific type, the Average White Male facing a crisis of power at a particular moment in U.S. history" (Davies 1995, 216). Indeed, *Falling Down*'s notoriety in the spring of 1993 helped launch a thousand polemics about the plight of "angry white men." *Newsweek*'s March 29 cover story titled "White Male Paranoia" used the film as a touchstone for a discussion of the question of whether these discontented white men are "victims of multiculturalism or . . . just bad sports" (Gates 1993, 48). As the article explained, "'Falling Down', whether it's really a message movie or just a cop film with trendy trimmings, pushes white men's buttons. The annoyances and menaces that drive D-Fens bonkers . . . are a cross-section of white-guy grievances" (48).

What the film leaves maddeningly unclear is whether such grievances are actually being endorsed or, as Davies would have it, "ironized" (215). The fact that D-Fens ends the film, as he himself puts it, in the position of "the bad guy," and is gunned down in the closing scene ostensibly gestures toward a condemnation of his actions. Yet, as Liam Kennedy has argued, "in its depiction of ethnic and racial stereotypes the film sends out very mixed, confused messages about the hysterical white male subject it constructs at its center" (Kennedy 1996, 92). Moreover, the film participates in Hollywood's ongoing backlash against feminism by presenting D-Fens's problems as caused at least in part by his neurotic ex-wife's assertion of control over the family home and their daughter, Adele (Mahoney 1997; Clover 1993).

Falling Down's vision of Los Angeles territorializes the objects of D-Fens's animus, an animus that by its very intensity manages to outshine and perhaps even negate the film's political ambivalence. Throughout, Los Angeles is presented, in the words of critic Peter Rainer, as a smog-choked "melting pot nightmare" (Rainer 1993, F7). The film opens with the scene of the nerdish D-Fens—decked out in a buzz cut, blindingly white shirt and tie, and black-rimmed plastic glasses—trapped in a gridlocked L.A. traffic jam, one that a quick pan indicates is as multiracial and cacophonous as the city itself. As repeated intercutting between the tense, sweating face of D-Fens and the stalled traffic around him underscores, he is a time bomb with a perilously short fuse. Soon enough he leaps out of his car and clambers up the highway embankment, telling an irate driver behind him that he is "going home." Thus begins his journey by foot across most of downtown L.A. to Venice Beach, where he hopes to be reunited with his daughter and estranged wife in time to celebrate his daughter's birthday.

One thing that becomes apparent in the course of his journey is that D-Fens "has no sense of ownership or rootedness; the space of the city has been taken over by racial and/or sexual 'others' " (Mahoney 1997, 174). Everywhere he turns, he encounters (spatial as well as social) barriers and exclusive enclaves standing in his way. At one point, he stumbles onto the graffiti-marked turf of a Latino gang who demand a toll (see Figure 4). Later, he is forced to walk through a public park crowded with homeless people (see Figure 5). It is worth quoting Liam Kennedy's description of this scene in full:

> *The camera surveys these people and foregrounds excessive images of poverty: there is an emaciated white man holding a sign which reads "We are dying of AIDS please help us!"; there is a black man in a wheelchair holding a sign reading "Homeless Vet Needs Food Money"; there are two young black men with a trolley full of empty cans, being arrested by the police—and the background is filled with predominantly African-American and Latino people. (Kennedy 1996, 95)*

As he traverses the park, D-Fens is accosted by an annoying panhandler (munching happily on a sandwich) who badgers him until he turns over his briefcase and then complains when it contains nothing but a bag lunch. As Kennedy points out, this entire scene constitutes "an obscene depiction of collective 'underclass' existence, with these people represented as degenerative signifiers of social immiseration and victimization" (Kennedy 1996, 95). In what one guesses is a half-hearted effort at "even-handedness," *Falling Down* implies that the rich are as much to blame for D-Fens's alienation from the urban landscape as the abject poor: "D-Fens breaches two high walls in the course of his long walk home," Clover notes, one surrounding a country club and the other surrounding a plastic surgeon's mansion (Clover 1993, 9).

Figure 4. D-Fens on gang turf in Falling Down.

Figure 5. Homeless people in the park in Falling Down.

D-Fens's "homelessness" and complete alienation is further underscored by the fact that his ex-wife replies to his telephone call announcing his impending return by telling him "this is not your home anymore" and by asking the police for protection.

D-Fens responds to the annoyances and obstacles the city places in his way with escalating violence. He smashes up the store of a Korean shopkeeper who refuses to give him change and charges exorbitant prices for sodas. He uses a baseball bat to repel the Latino gang members who accost him and later shoots one of them in the leg after they try unsuccessfully to gun him down. He murders a neo-Nazi storekeeper who mistakes him for some sort of kindred spirit. Finally, he chases his ex-wife and daughter out onto a pier and traps them there (with the intention, the viewer supposes, of killing them both). There he is cornered by the aging white male cop, Prendergast, who has been tracking him for much of the movie and who kills D-Fens when the latter challenges him to "draw."

Yet, as I have already implied, it would be a mistake to read *Falling Down* as a critique of the white male anger simply because D-Fens dies in the end. First of all, by pointedly contrasting D-Fens to the character of the viciously racist, homophobic Nazi storekeeper, the film shows him in at least a partially sympathetic light. Moreover, as Kennedy has argued, "even as the film parodies the tale of regeneration through violence in the narrative of D-Fens, it reproduces it more soberly in the narrative of his double within the film, the white policeman Prendergast" (Kennedy 1996, 98). Prendergast begins the story as an ineffectual detective, a henpecked husband, and a general object of ridicule on the police force who regains his authority (both on the job and in the home) precisely by hunting down and killing D-Fens. While the film ostensibly repudiates D-Fens's vigilantism, it clearly approves Prendergast's legally sanctioned (liberal-minded) violence and, as such, "ensures the reproduction of white masculine authority in a new register" (99). And even the repudiation of D-Fens's violence is lukewarm at best. The harassment he endures at the hands of the Latino gang and in the person of the homeless man at least appear to excuse his rough reactions. Indeed, his actions all respond in one way or another to irritations of urban living that, as in the opening traffic jam, he can no longer shut out. As in *Batman* or *Predator 2,* the city in *Falling Down,* to quote Peter Rainer, is "made to stand in for all that [is] rotting and malevolent in society" (Rainer 1993, F7); it is an equation that, circulating widely throughout contemporary popular culture, goes a long way toward legitimating the white male rage that D-Fens embodies. As McCarthy and his coauthors put it, in the film "the discourse of crime, violence and suburban security has come . . . to justify suburban revenge and resentment. We now have a white man [D-Fens] who enters the 'hood to settle moral scores with anything and anyone that moves" (McCarthy et al. 1997, 284).

Demonizing the Urban Public Realm

As with the park scene in *Falling Down,* Hollywood over the past two decades has typically projected urban public amenities like parks and playgrounds as dangerous, dirty, and in ruins, as symptomatic of the blight of the contemporary American city as a whole. In particular, the spaces defined by public schools and public transit—arguably two of the signature achievements of American urban civilization—have been singled out for unflattering treatment. In mainstream film of the Reagan era and after, big city schools are uniformly lousy and the subways are all stalked by muggers.

Exemplary of this trend is the grim portrayal of urban schools in the 1996 movie *Dangerous Minds,* the story of a white ex-Marine turned teacher-in-training named LouAnne Johnson (Michelle Pfeiffer), who is doing her student teaching in an inner-city high school. Hired as an English teacher in a program for students who are considered "unteachable," Johnson is immediately confronted with an out-of-control classroom full of black and Latino youth who blast loud music, rap, dance, shout, and generally disregard her authority. As presented by the film, these are kids who, to quote Henry Giroux, "have brought the 'worst' aspects of their culture into the classroom" (Giroux 1997, 47). As Giroux explains, the initial scenes of Johnson and her class "work powerfully in associating black and Hispanic kids with the culture of criminality and danger. They also make clear that whiteness as a racial identity is both vulnerable and under siege, as well as the only hope these kids have for moving beyond the context and character of their racial identities" (47). Taking a page from the standard ghetto action-picture, *Dangerous Minds* underscores the (minority) violence that haunts Johnson's school both by means of the graffiti that appears to cover its every available surface (which functions here, as in other media texts, as a generic signifier of gang activity) and by means of the ubiquitous rap soundtrack featuring hard-core gangster rapper Coolio among others.

Johnson eventually wins the respect of her class and manages to inculcate them with a love of (white) poetry, but only after she impresses the students with her old Marine uniform and demonstrates her knowledge of karate moves. As Giroux explains, "[t]hrough her assumption that fear and danger are the only emotions the kids recognize as important, LouAnne crosses a racial divide by rooting her sense of authority in a reactionary notion of discipline" (48). Significantly, Johnson's struggle to uplift her underclass charges is opposed every step of the way by the school's black principal, Mr. Grandey (Courtney Vance), a rigid and unfeeling bureaucrat. In the end, *Dangerous Minds* "reinforces the highly racialized . . . mainstream assumption that chaos reigns in inner-city public schools and that white teachers alone are capable of bringing order, decency, and hope to those on the margins of society" (49).

Dangerous Minds's basic formula of a tough white teacher acting as savior to otherwise hopeless underclass kids is taken to absurd extremes in another 1996 release, *The Substitute*. In *The Substitute* it is not an ex-Marine turned student teacher but, even more implausibly, an unemployed mercenary named Shale (Tom Berenger) masquerading as a substitute teacher who brings order to a stereotypical inner-city high school. As in *Dangerous Minds*, the film's high school is dominated by (in this case, largely Latino) gangs who intimidate and terrorize the teachers, among them Shale's girlfriend Jane (Diane Verona), all to the accompaniment of a hard-core rap soundtrack. Shale gets drawn into this toxic environment when Jane is attacked "by a six-foot-six Seminole" in what he suspects is a hit orchestrated by her student Juan Lacas (Marc Anthony), leader of the bluntly named Kings of Destruction gang. No sooner has Shale infiltrated the school posing as Jane's substitute than he is breaking his students' fingers and twisting their arms in an effort to subdue his unruly classroom. "I'm in charge of this class," he announces after he has sent a couple of disobedient teens to the nurse's office, "I'm the warrior chief. I'm the merciless god of anything that stirs in my universe. Fuck with me and you will suffer my wrath." Again echoing *Dangerous Minds*, Shale's strong-arm classroom reforms—depicted in the film as being unequivocally successful—are thwarted by an African American principal, Claude Rolle

(Ernie Hudson), who Shale eventually discovers is running a massive cocaine ring out of the school's basement with the Kings of Destruction's cooperation. This premise is so outrageous that one almost hesitates to draw attention to its obvious racism. Yet, Rolle's depiction as a slick personification of evil is only slightly more hyperbolic than the generally negative portrayal of most of the nonwhite students and teachers in the film. In the end, Shale and his band of mercenary buddies "clean up" the school in a pitched battle with Rolle's hired guns. Again, as so often in Hollywood films of the '80s and '90s, the answer to the inner city's problems proposed by *The Substitute* is an orgy of violence directed at people of color.

The treatment of the crisis in urban public education in both *The Substitute* and *Dangerous Minds* harkens back to an earlier film, *Lean on Me* (1988), based on the life story of black New Jersey high school principal Joe Clark. In early 1988, Clark—whose habit of carrying around a baseball bat as he patrolled the halls and screaming at students through a bullhorn earned him the nickname "Crazy Joe"—burst into the limelight when he summarily expelled sixty-six of his students without due process. The action provoked a confrontation with the school board; the board's disapproval of his methods was further exacerbated by Clark's characterization of the dismissed students as "hoodlums, thugs, and pathological deviants." His severe brand of discipline did, however, endear him to prominent conservatives. As *Time* magazine reported shortly after Clark's run-in with the school board, "President Reagan has commended Clark as an exemplar of the tough leadership needed in urban schools. In the wake of the school board battle, U.S. Secretary of Education William Bennett telephoned to urge Clarke to 'hang in there'" (Bowen 1988, 53). Clarke was even offered a post as a White House policy adviser (which he turned down).

Lean on Me celebrates Clark (played by Morgan Freeman) and his strong-arm methods in a morality tale as didactic and reactionary as a parable from Bennett's own *Book of Virtues.* From the opening sequence on, we are given an impression of Clark as a stern, stubborn, but energetic teacher who is willing to buck convention to help his students reach their potential. East Side High circa 1982, the school Clark takes over, is constructed as a place as wild and disorderly as he is strong-willed. We're introduced to it by means of a chilling montage encapsulating what is supposed to be the beginning of a typical class day. It begins with a shot of a brawl in the main hallway, cuts to two large black students hurling a sink through a bathroom window, then to kids playing with a terrified white teacher's tie, and is followed by a shot of a white woman accosted by four black women in a bathroom who rip off her shirt and bra. This is followed by shots of a student making a drug deal on the school steps with what looks like a teacher, a student selling pills in the cafeteria, a teenage boy checking his revolver, and a skirmish between some students that results in the beating of a teacher. The montage ends with a young kid being locked into his locker.

Shortly after taking charge, Clark, using his trademark tactics, transforms this mayhem and squalor into the picture of cleanliness and order. The delinquents and drug dealers are banished, the graffiti cleaned up, the kids develop an eagerness to learn, and a collection of former troublemakers learns to proudly sing an *a cappella,* "soulified" version of the school song on demand. The last third of the film centers, therefore, not on Clark's struggles with his students—they have by that point willingly submitted to and even learned to love his tough authority—but on his clashes with a sleazy white mayor, an opportunistic black school board member, and a racist fire chief. This, of course, bestows on Clark's authoritarianism the status of "rebellion" against a corrupt status quo; indeed, from the moment we first see Clark as a young teacher in the 1960s wearing an Afro and dashiki, the film makes an effort to associate Clark, however tenuously, with the tradition of radical black nationalism. The film's Reagan-esque message of "discipline" and "no excuses for failure" is thus all the more nefarious because it is packaged (especially in the final scene of students cheering Clark and singing the new *a cappella,* Eastside anthem) as an organic and triumphant expression of black pride.

If *Dangerous Minds, The Substitute,* and *Lean on Me* all endorse force and strict discipline as answers to the problems of urban public education, the bleak 1997 release *187* suggests that those problems are at bottom intractable and that city schools are beyond rescuing. The film tells the story of a dedicated high school science teacher, Trevor Garfield (Samuel Jackson), who struggles to cope with his anxieties and manage an unruly urban classroom after being viciously stabbed by a student. The film opens, appropriately enough, with a nightmare sequence—shot in a gloomy, diffuse blue light—in which Trevor relives the circumstances that lead up to his stabbing: teaching physics in a Brooklyn high school to a group of boisterous, mostly minority students, he discovers that one of his students has scrawled the numbers "187"—the police code for homicide—on one of the textbooks. Shortly after, we see Trevor being stalked down the school hallway by a tough-looking black kid wearing a stocking cap who sneaks up behind him and sticks a homemade "shiv" in his back. Trevor awakens, sweating, from his nightmare not in New York but in sun-baked Los Angeles where he has taken a job as a substitute teacher (and where, we soon learn, the school system is even more vile).

The inner-city school to which he is assigned overflows with all the stock horrors: thuggish looking minority teens (some of whom he spots spray painting graffiti on the school basketball court); a nasty Latino gang that appears to run the place; a teacher who—for self-protection—keeps a handgun in his desk; and a by-the-book principal who cares more about students filing lawsuits against the school district than about the safety of his teachers (see Figure 6). Trevor, committed pedagogue that he is, tries to make the best of it, succeeds in "reaching" a promising young Latina student named Rita, and engages a fair number of his other students. Nevertheless, from his confrontation with the resident troublemakers on his first day of class onward, Trevor seethes with frustration and barely contained rage. When the one friend he makes on the faculty, a pretty white computer teacher named Ellen (Kelly Rowan), tells him that gang leader Benny Chicon (Lobo Sebastian) has been terrorizing her because she testified against him in a school disciplinary hearing, the audience is prepared for Trevor to take matters into his own hands. Benny soon goes missing and we naturally suspect that Trevor had something to do with it. Benny's gang, it turns out, has similar suspicions, and under the new leadership of Cesar Sanchez (Clifton Gonzalez Gonzalez), a truly loathsome character who in one scene beats his own mother, they trash Trevor's lab, destroying the desks, spray painting obscenities on the walls, tearing apart books, even impaling the class's pet rat with scalpels. Later, when Cesar kills Ellen's dog, Jack, Trevor retaliates by drugging him and cutting off his "trigger" finger. Cesar and his

Figure 6. Trevor's new school in 187.

gang naturally come gunning for him shortly thereafter (having painted the fatal number "187" all over his garage as a portent of things to come).

Given the basic narrative pattern of the teacher-as-savior genre, one would expect a happy, uplifting resolution to this conflict, one in which Trevor's actions are shown to be necessary and heroic, the gang is vanquished, and the school is restored to a state of prelapsarian tranquillity. But it is here that *187* diverges sharply from the generic mold established by films like *Dangerous Minds* and *Lean on Me*. First of all, Ellen begins to suspect Trevor of killing Benny and distances herself from him as a result. Meanwhile his "special project," Rita, decides she doesn't want to graduate. Then the principal, fearing a potential sexual harassment lawsuit, fires Trevor after finding out about his private meetings with Rita. Moreover, if killing Benny and slicing off Cesar's finger are not proof enough, Trevor's actions at the end of the film confirm that he is dangerously unbalanced, perhaps even insane.

After Cesar and his henchmen break into Trevor's house, Cesar, reenacting a scene from *The Deerhunter*, forces Trevor to play Russian roulette, which he does willingly. Trevor proclaims that he is "crazy" and acts it; when Cesar hesitates to take his turn, Trevor grabs the gun and shoots himself in the head (after which, Cesar, not wanting to be beaten at the game, also shoots himself in the head). Thus, *187* can be read as something of an immanent critique of the conventions of the teacher-as-savior genre. The intolerable situation—and the sense of frustration and hopelessness—that in *Lean on Me* or *The Substitute* finds its antidote in order imposed by a judicious use of force here triumphs in the end. The teacher does not conquer but instead is conquered by the horrible conditions in inner-city schools. Even vigilante violence makes no difference. This despairing message is made explicit by the closing scene in which shots of Ellen clearing out her desk and throwing away her teaching credentials are intercut with Rita reading a heartfelt eulogy for Trevor at the graduation ceremony. "You can push a good teacher too far," Rita says tearfully. "Teachers don't get no respect." The film closes with a text informing the audience that "[o]ne in nine teachers have been attacked at school. Ninety-five percent of those attacks were committed by students. A teacher wrote this movie."

Where *Dangerous Minds* and *Lean on Me* at least held out the possibility that city school systems (and by implication the cities that operate them) could be renewed by getting tough on troublemakers, *187* can be read as arguing that the only sensible course of action is a wholesale evacuation of and retreat from public schools and from the degenerate metropolitan culture they represent. Such a view would no doubt resonate with the growing sector of both the urban and the suburban middle class who are placing their children into private schools at record rates and are clamoring for government-funded vouchers to help pay for it. As Henry Giroux comments, the film "capitalizes on the popular conception . . . that public education is not safe for white, middle-class children, that racial violence is rampant in the public schools, that minority students have turned classroom discipline into a joke, that administrators are paralyzed by insensitive bureaucracies, and the only thing that teachers and students share is the desire to survive the day" (Giroux 1999, 49).

Like its portrayal of urban schools, the film industry's view of public mass transit—that other iconic fixture of the modern metropolis—has been uniformly bleak. For those who ride public transit in the movies, bloodshed, gun fights, hijackings, and catastrophic accidents are apparently par for the course. Thus, *The Warriors* (1979) features a series of gang battles on the trains between the Bronx and Coney Island. *Blue Steel* (1990) climaxes with a chilling gunfight on a New York subway platform. The 1994 blockbuster *Speed* features a Los Angeles city bus wired with a bomb rigged to explode if it slows down and culminates in scenes of hand-to-hand combat aboard a runaway train. *Die Hard: With a Vengeance* has a group of demonic criminals blow up a New York subway to create a diversion for a robbery. The awful *Money Train* (1995) follows two disgruntled New York Transit cops as they round up the veritable army of criminals who appear to populate the subways and dream up ways to rob the "money train" (the train that collects all the cash from the transit system's daily operations). This latter film, it should be noted, was blamed for a group of "copycat" arsons in which one New York Transit police officer was killed. But *Money Train* is hardly the most disturbing story about public transportation created by the celluloid dream factory; that distinction is properly reserved for the chilling 1997 horror flick *Mimic*.

In some ways, *Mimic* is little more than an updated version of the Frankenstein story (or, better, of the '50s horror classic *Them*): in order to stop a deadly outbreak of a cockroach-borne illness that's killing off the children of New York, entomologist Dr. Susan Tyler (Mira Sorvino) releases a species of insect genetically engineered to kill roaches, the "Judas" bug, into the city's subway system; the Judas bugs wipe out the roaches but, true to their name, turn on their creators. We soon learn that the Judas bugs have metamorphosed from the tiny, innocuous creatures Tyler created into six-foot tall man-eating predators who can disguise themselves as humans. It turns out they have set up an enormous colony in the dark, dank bowels of the New York subway system and the colony's "warrior" bugs are busy picking off priests, street kids, and sweet little retarded boys. Unlike the creature in the original Frankenstein story, the monsters here are irreducibly "Other" and thoroughly demonized; from their unintelligible language of clicks to their grotesque cockroach-like appearance and their frenzied, mechanical method of dismembering their victims, the Judas bugs are presented as abnormal in a way that bolsters rather than challenges hegemonic conceptions of normalcy. In this, *Mimic* participates in what Christopher Sharrett has identified as the neoconservative "cooption of the horror film's radicalism" (Sharrett 1993b, 100).

What is especially interesting here is how the film maps the repellent Otherness of the Judas bugs onto the subway system itself.[7] One way that it does this is by representing the subways quite literally as the murderous insects' hunting ground. Thus, in one terrifying scene, we see two kids scavenging through the system's service tunnels savagely butchered, and, in another, Dr. Tyler is snatched off a subway platform by a flying Judas bug. Another way *Mimic* projects the monstrousness of the bugs onto the subway system is by establishing the tunnels themselves as a realm of near total darkness. Most of the underground action takes place in murky abandoned tunnels and closed stations; even the active platforms are equipped with dim, flickering lights. The tunnels are marked off as alien territory in other ways as well: the passages leading to the heart of the colony are pictured not only as choked with garbage but as covered with the bugs' excrement and offal (the scatological symbolism serving to underscore just how abhorrent and deserving of annihilation the bugs really are). There's even a room stacked from floor to ceiling with sticky Geiger-esque "egg pods." By the end of the film Dr. Tyler finds herself, her husband, and a few other hearty souls being hunted by the Judas bugs through this dark maze as it dawns on her that the insects are planning to colonize the rest of the country. Luckily, the world is saved when her husband chances upon the colony's central nest in some sort of giant furnace room and blows it up. The underworld threat is vanquished but an unrelieved sense of foreboding—fostered by the moaning music of the sound track and the dour expressions on the actors' faces—lingers on even after Tyler and her husband are reunited at the end.

Together, images like those in *Mimic* or *Money Train* reinforce the undeserved bad reputation public transit has gotten in the suburbanriented news media. And beyond that, they help fuel a general suspicion of public places that is snuffing out what remains of urban civic culture. In light of such depictions, it is understandable that at least a few managers of urban public transportation systems have begun to fight back: New York Transit Authority chief Alan Kiepper has frequently denied filmmakers' requests to use the city's subways as showcases for violent chase scenes and has refused to let them paint graffiti on his meticulously clean fleet of cars (Pierce 1994, 5). Unfortunately, such small gestures can do very little indeed to dispel the myths that *Mimic* and films like it help to perpetuate.

Under Siege: The Threat to the (Suburban) Middle-Class Family

If Hollywood over the past few decades of conservative ascendancy has increasingly framed the big city as hostile territory, it has also tended to present the sparkling clean, well-lit world of the suburban middle-class family as "under siege" from a range of sexual, criminal, and moral threats that are typically urban in origin. Alan Nadel has noted that the "house-at-risk motif" was "common to many films of Reagan's America" (Nadel 1997, 195) and, I might add, remained popular in the Bush and Clinton eras as well. For instance, *Home Alone* (1990) centers on a little boy defending his well-appointed home from a pair of inept burglars; *Unlawful Entry* (1992) tells the story of a middle-class couple terrorized by a working-class police officer after he investigates a break-in at their suburban residence; *Pacific Heights* (1990) is about a demented tenant who ruins a yuppie pair's turn-of-the-century house and nearly ruins their lives; and *The Hand That Rocks the Cradle* (1992) shows us an affluent family menaced by their live-in nanny.

Perhaps no film exemplifies the siege narratives of the 1980s and 1990s as well as Adrian Lyne's 1987 thriller *Fatal Attraction*. This story of a single professional woman, Alex (Glenn Close), who seduces and then persecutes a married man, Dan Gallagher (Michael Douglas), has been correctly diagnosed by most critics as an assault on feminism and a naked celebration of "family values" (Faludi 1991, 112–23; Nadel 1997, 184–90). Spurned by Dan after their one-night stand, Alex kidnaps his daughter and eventually invades his home with a butcher knife. In a frenzied final confrontation, Dan and his wife are forced to kill the interloper in order to save their own lives. The obvious, anti-feminist message of all this is that independent career women and casual sex are potentially lethal, especially to families. Significantly, the threat personified by Alex issues from outside the stereotyped setting of middle-class existence: she lives in a trendy downtown loft apartment surrounded by art and the haunting sounds of Puccini's *Madame Butterfly*, a milieu that is almost the diametric opposite of the cozy, suburban one Dan and his family are in the process of settling into. The film thus implies a moral equivalence between the "feminist" woman and the downtown vice that the news media of the 1980s and '90s warned was "spreading" to nice middle-class neighborhoods.

Interestingly, the excessive brutality that *Fatal Attraction* authorizes Dan and his wife to use in defense of their home—which results in Alex being beaten, drowned in their bathtub, and then shot—parallels the sort of spectacular violence movies like *Judgment Night* or *New Jack City* recommend as a solution to the problem of ghetto crime. As Nadel has pointed out, although most "siege" films—like *Fatal Attraction*, *Pacific Heights*, and *Unlawful Entry*—"reject the specifics of the black menace to the neighborhood, they evoke the narrative of the black menace as the context in which white psychopaths are supposed to be striking and shocking anomalies" (Nadel 1997, 197). Indeed, given a social context in which the news media and the political establishment consistently fixate on inner-city crime, the siege narrative's focus on what Nadel terms the "pathology of the perverse stranger" can't help but activate the specter of an out-of-control underclass for most audiences. That this is so can be seen even more clearly in two popular siege narratives, *Eye for an Eye* and *Ransom*, both released in 1996.

Eye for an Eye dramatizes the imagined danger to middle-class security posed by the pathologically depraved Other in terms even more heavy-handed than *Fatal Attraction* and associates this threat even more closely with the city. It tells the story of Karen McCann (Sally Field), a busy professional with a loving husband (Ed Harris), two beautiful daughters, and a palatial home in the suburbs (an early establishing shot of which, as in many a conservative siege narrative, singles it out as a privileged, almost sacred site of warmth and familial harmony).[8] This domestic idyll is soon shattered when a psychotic delivery man brutally rapes and then kills the older daughter on the living room floor as Karen, stuck downtown in a traffic jam, listens helplessly to her screams on a cellular phone. As Detective Sgt. Denillio (Joe Montegna) tries to track down the murderer, the McCanns attempt to cope with this horrible violation by installing a security system and joining a support group for people who've lost loved ones to violence. Denillio eventually discovers and arrests the killer, Robert Doob (Kiefer Sutherland), a smirking, sleazy career-felon who, Karen tells her husband, "has been in and out of jail his entire life." He is so evil that at one point in the film he gratuitously pours hot coffee on a stray dog (see Figure 7). Yet, because—in an obvious reference to the O. J. Simpson trial—the L.A. County prosecutors failed to share DNA evidence with the defense, Doob goes free.

Beside herself, Karen becomes obsessed with Doob and begins spying on him, eventually following him to the seedy, downtown flophouse where he lives. Doob's neighborhood—L.A.'s notorious Skid Row area—is pictured as the grotesque antithesis of Karen's tranquil, bucolic suburb. While Karen's neighborhood is preternaturally quiet, Doob's is rocked by the sounds of rap music, yelling, traffic noise, and Mexican pop tunes. The McCann house stands alone amidst a picturesque lush green landscape; in contrast, the rundown hotel Doob calls home is surrounded by streets full of bumper-to-bumper traffic and sidewalks teeming with raucous multiethnic, multiracial crowds. The people milling around in these crowds—many of whom are drinking beer or stronger liquor from bottles in brown paper bags—look uniformly disheveled and sullen; at least one, a large African American woman in a ragged housedress, is a raving lunatic who berates passers-by

Figure 7. Doob pours coffee on a stray dog in Eye for an Eye.

in every scene in which she appears. Doob's association with this milieu naturalizes his violence and psychosis as a normal feature of the inner city, as the "law" of the "urban jungle." In *Eye for an Eye,* as in countless other movies like it, threats to middle- and upper-middle-class safety and comfort arise almost exclusively from the urban poor and environments like Doob's grungy neighborhood.

Eye for an Eye leaves little doubt about the best method of counteracting the urban Other's brutal disruption of suburban domestic bliss. When Doob discovers Karen has been trailing him he begins harassing her surviving daughter and this spurs Karen to seek out members of a support group who may be taking justice into their own hands. At their urging, she practices shooting at a firing range. Eventually they obtain a gun for her and draw up plans for a "hit" on Doob. Karen appears to agonize over the deed and calls the vigilante group to back out after being tipped off about an undercover FBI investigation into their activities. But this is just a ruse to trick the authorities and she subsequently lures Doob into her home, where—according to Hollywood's version of the law—killing intruders is always justified. "This is personal!" she screams before pumping four slugs into the attacking Doob. Detective Denillio, who arrives on the scene later to investigate, correctly suspects that the shooting was a set-up, but ultimately signals his approval by telling another police officer that "it looks like a clear-cut case of self-defense" (as does Karen's husband, who reluctantly takes her hand when he arrives back at the house). As with conservative crime dramas since *Dirty Harry* and *Death Wish,* *Eye for an Eye* endorses violence and vigilantism as the only solution to crime and blames the "liberal" judicial system for failing to lock up the "scumbags."

In Ron Howard's blockbuster *Ransom,* which pulled in box office revenues in excess of $125 million in 1996, it is not an upper-middle-class family but an extremely wealthy one that finds itself "under siege" by hostile Others; however, the framing of and final solution to the problem is nearly identical to that proposed by *Eye for an Eye.* At the beginning of the film, we're introduced to self-made millionaire Tom Mullen (Mel Gibson) who is enjoying what appears to be an ideal life: he owns a successful airline and has a penthouse apartment overlooking Central Park, a gorgeous wife, and an intelligent son. He even stars in his own television advertisements. All that changes when kidnappers seize his son, Sean, one day when he and Tom are out playing in the park (another not-so-subtle attempt to brand urban public space as unsafe). The FBI is called in and head agent Lonnie Hawkins counsels a terrified Tom to comply with the kidnappers' demands. There's immediate tension between Tom and Lonnie, in part because the FBI had spent the previous three years investigating Tom for possibly giving a bribe to the head of one of the unions at his airline. Meanwhile, the kidnappers—a gnarly looking collection of petty criminals who are working for a crooked cop named Jimmy Shaker (Gary Sinise)—keep Sean locked up in a squalid basement apartment somewhere in the "bad part" of Brooklyn. The first time Tom attempts to pay the $2 million ransom he follows the kidnappers' orders meticulously, but just as he is about to hand over the money he realizes the kidnappers have no intention of handing over the boy.

At this point, Tom decides to get tough with his son's abductors. He goes on television to offer a $2 million reward for the kidnappers' capture. Just as Tom had hoped, this stratagem subverts Shaker's plans and sows discord in his gang. As a result, Shaker ultimately kills off his partners and poses as Sean's liberator in order to claim the bounty himself. There are at least three things worthy of note about the way *Ransom* stages the standard family-under-siege narrative. First, there is the characterization of the kidnappers themselves, a group which is a veritable typology of urban criminality (but which is cast as all white). Shaker is not only shrewd and backstabbing but is driven by a palpable and all-consuming class hatred. Maris (Lili Taylor), Shaker's second-in-command, is utterly callous, insists on keeping Sean tied up, refuses to feed him, and comes close to killing him a couple of times. Clark (Liev Schreiber) and Chubby (Donnie Wahlberg) are archetypal stocking-cap-wearing small-time hoods but at least Chubby has a soft spot in his heart for the boy. The group's computer whiz, who's responsible for throwing the FBI off the kidnappers' trail, is perpetually drunk. And as Krin Gabbard points out, "the kidnappers regularly adopt speech patterns and a metalanguage associated with African Americans" (Gabbard 2001, 19), suggesting a connection to the ghetto underclass and its "tangle of pathology." There's not a sympathetic character in the bunch and Shaker and Maris in particular are framed as richly deserving of their respective violent ends.

Second, the film is obsessed with the contrast between Shaker's run-down lower-class world and Tom's luxurious one, repeatedly juxtaposing the Mullens' affluent apartment with the kidnapper's basement lair. The contrast is remarked on by Shaker when he compares Tom's house in the sky to that of the elite Eloi in H. G. Wells's *Time Machine* and again as he admires the Mullen place when he shows up there to pick up the reward check.

In the end, though, the spatial contrast between Tom's penthouse and Shaker's basement becomes a metaphor not just for the class differences between the millionaire and the crooked cop but for the moral differences between them as well. Though Tom as a representative of his class is not without flaws (it turns out Tom did pay off the unions, just as the FBI suspected), the moral and psychological shortcomings of the rich are excused in light of the atrocities perpetrated by creatures of the street like Shaker and his gang. Tom, after all, loves his wife and child; Shaker, on the other hand, shoots his own lover in order to get his hands on the reward money. Finally, in siding with and ultimately rewarding Tom's "no compromise" approach to Shaker's domestic terrorism over the FBI's ineffectual strategy of appeasement, *Ransom* like *Eye for an Eye* can be read as an argument for the fascistic approach to crime control advocated by William Bennett and Rudy Giuliani, for retribution and repression rather than prevention, rehabilitation, and social justice.

Despite the absence of minority villains, *Eye for an Eye* and *Ransom* are fairly open about their politics and about the (racist, anti-urban) fears they aim to conjure up. Both in their idealized, sentimental conception of the normal, white nuclear family and in the way that they locate the source of the threat to this family in a stereotypically slum-like space, these films openly echo the conservative discourse on the underclass with its construction of the inner city as an uncivilized space responsible for dissolving the bonds of family and community. That there is, to use Stuart Hall's term, a certain *inferential racism* to such constructions, no matter what color skin the menacing urban Other in these films happens to have, almost goes without saying (Hall 1995).

"A deadly sin on every street corner": *Evil and Urbanity in* Seven

The association between cities and metaphysical evil has grown so strong in popular consciousness since the early 1980s that a number of successful Hollywood films have taken up the trope of the damned or hellish city as their central theme and narrative pretext. I'm thinking here of what could be called "urban gothic" films like *Batman* (1989), *The Crow* (1994), or the Hughes brothers' *From Hell* (2001) that picture the city as a brooding, Stygian world haunted by "creatures of the night." Rendering the imagined menace of the urban center visually as a *shimmering darkness,* these films break with the codes of cinematic "realism" in order to give full expression to the most hysterical fantasies about the horror of contemporary city life. Indeed, the fact that these representations of the city are openly fantastic, cartoonish, even surreal makes them uniquely suited as vehicles for the rising middle-class moral panic over urban conditions. Following critic Robin Wood's remarks on the social meaning of horror films, I'd like to argue that it is precisely the "fantastic" nature of films like *The Crow* or *Batman*—indeed, of any film that purports to be simple entertainment, pure spectacle, or mere illusion—that allows them to give voice to fears and anxieties habitually repressed or disavowed by viewers in their more rational moments. As Wood puts it, in the unreal world of the horror film, "the censor (in both the common and the Freudian sense) is lulled to sleep and relaxes vigilance" (Wood 1985, 203). The "urban gothic" movies of the '80s and '90s, I want to suggest, articulated in a coded way the creeping, semi-conscious, media-generated paranoia about urban disorder that increasingly troubled the affluent comfort of the suburban middle-class. There's arguably no better example of this than David Fincher's *Seven*.[9]

As the sequence cited at the beginning of the chapter indicates, the makers of *Seven* represent its unidentified, New York–style urban setting as a thoroughly noxious, menacing place, an allegorical Hell as full of suffering and anguish as the *Inferno* of Dante on which it appears to have been modeled. This contributes to the film an oppressively despairing, apocalyptic mood. But the function of the urban environment in *Seven* goes beyond providing a suitably expressive backdrop for the film's bleak story. In the course of the film, the city's nastiness and immorality—and the sense of defeated resignation it imposes on its residents—emerges as an explicit and recurring theme. In *Seven,* as Amy Taubin has argued, "cities are cesspools of contagion, spreading sin faster than TB" (Taubin 1996, 23). And no one, whether innocent or not, escapes the city's contaminating influence. In fact, the "moral breakdown" that characterizes *Seven*'s metropolis provides the motivation for the actions of more than one of the main characters.

The first hint the viewer is given of the malevolence of the film's city occurs immediately before the opening credits. After meeting Mills at the scene of a routine domestic shooting, Sommerset lounges in his apartment reading. As he lies there on his bed, the sounds of distant shouting, of tires squealing, of a dog barking, and finally of a car alarm blaring invade his bedroom. Even before the first of Jonathan Doe's grotesque murders is discovered, these noises—which Sommerset habitually drowns out using a metronome—signal the relentless brutality of the surrounding milieu. Equally important, the fact that similar sounds of distress penetrate the space of Sommerset's bedroom again in later scenes underscores just how inescapable and quotidian such ambient violence actually is (which is precisely the point of the casually displayed corpse in the scene with the cab driver described at the start of this chapter). Such sounds—together with the jarring, post-punk theme song by Nine-Inch Nails—define our initial image of the cinematic city and continue to inflect our experience of it throughout the film.

That experience is even more heavily colored by the graphic and incomprehensibly sadistic violence that drives the plot. Thus, following the opening credits, Sommerset and Mills are called in to inspect the bloated, discolored remains of Doe's first victim, an incredibly obese man who has been forced to literally eat himself to death (that is, until his stomach bursts). This begins their futile race to track down the killer before he claims yet another victim. Each clue they uncover, each step they take, only leads them belatedly to the scene of another of Doe's series of meticulously planned, artistically carried-out slayings. There appears to be a definite ethico-religious logic to Doe's killings, each of which dispatches an individual who epitomizes one of the deadly sins using a symbolically "appropriate," Dante-esque method of punishment: a greedy uptown lawyer bleeds to death after being made to slice out a pound of his own flesh; a prostitute is killed with a razor-tipped dildo that Doe makes one of her hapless clients use on her; a vain fashion model has her nose sliced off ("to spite her face," as Sommerset notes), and so on. Doe's murders are, as Sommerset correctly discerns, a form of "preaching" and the film's big mystery is whether he'll get a chance to finish his sermon.

Interestingly, Doe's savagery is rarely represented directly on the screen; the sort of dramatically choreographed action that is so omnipresent in slasher films and standard *policiers* is—with the exception of a single chase scene—virtually absent here. Rather than give us gun play and acrobatic fight scenes, from the opening shot to the last, the film confronts us with the gruesome "physical evidence" of mind-boggling acts of violence slowly and gradually revealed. Not only does this create tension and uneasiness, it compels the viewer to linger over the gore. Much of the terrifying visual impact of *Seven* relies on the vividly depicted and often hideously mutilated bodies, and pieces of bodies, Doe leaves behind. These grisly tableaus owe much of their distinctive look to visceral "body horror" of genre films like *Hellraiser* as well as, perhaps, to the necrophilic aesthetic of avant-garde photographer David Watkins. The camera records each hideous wound and disfiguration with unflinching, pornographic, almost clinical accuracy. Among other things, we see the dissected and reassembled body of the fat man, an amputated hand, and the skeletal, barely alive body of a man covered with oozing bedsores. One could argue that the real suspense in the film has more to do with the anticipation of the inevitable spectacle of horror that awaits the investigators at each new crime scene than it does with actually locating the killer. And this, in turn, endows the city—which is presented above all else as a collection or network of crime scenes—with a pronounced sense of foreboding.

Meanwhile, the built environment projected by the film as the showcase for all this butchery radiates a definite aura of decay and despair. *Seven*'s metropolis appears to be in an advanced state of decrepitude. Its buildings are filthy, weathered, crumbling, and moldy, their walls full of cracks and holes, their paint peeling and stained, their floors creaking. The fat man's house, to cite a memorable example, has windows so heavily streaked with dirt they barely admit light. The apartment building where the detectives find the man murdered for personifying "sloth" has hallways and stairwells covered with litter and slick from rain that has seeped in through fissures in the roof. Piles of overflowing black plastic garbage bags, disintegrating cardboard boxes, and abandoned pieces of furniture crowd the streets. Graffiti is present in nearly every outdoor shot; even the lampposts appear to have been "tagged." Even those buildings that don't appear to be decomposing—like the police station or the lawyer's office or the library where Sommerset hunts for clues—look old and exhausted, their paint fading and their decor and fixtures dated.

Nicholas Christopher argues that the city in classic film noir and in more recent noir revivals is frequently constructed as a nightmarish labyrinth, one which perpetually threatens to enmesh, engulf, and overwhelm the hero (Christopher 1997, 16–17). This is certainly true of *Seven,* in which Mills and Sommerset confront a metropolis that is not only in the process of collapsing in on itself but is punctuated by spaces that are maze-like, disordered, and disorienting in the extreme (see Figure 8). Thus, after the pair discover Doe's apartment, he leads them on a confusing chase through several floors and rooms of the building, over a roof top, through what looks like an abandoned ballroom, across a busy thoroughfare, and into an alleyway where Doe knocks Mills unconscious. It is, as Amy Taubin has observed, "a chase scene so dark that we can't tell one good guy from another, let alone good from bad" (Taubin, 1996, 24). The layout of Doe's apartment, which the partners search shortly after the failed chase, likewise proves difficult to negotiate. The place is a maze of clothes racks, bookshelves, cabinets, rooms, and hallways connected in one instance by what seems to be a secret (or at least carefully

Figure 8. A dark, rainy alley in Seven.

obscured) doorway. Even more disturbing, every single window in the apartment is covered and the walls appear to be painted pitch black. Small wonder, then, that it takes Mills what seems like an eternity to track down the phone when it starts ringing in the middle of the detectives' search of the premises. The omnipresent clutter—the piles of garbage, the paper strewn everywhere—render the film's disordered spaces even more chaotic. And the multiplicity of labyrinthine spaces adds to the perceived hostility of the setting by holding out the possibility of unforeseen pitfalls and dangers hidden in their shadowy recesses.

Other elements of the mise-en-scène, most notably the lighting, also strengthen the impression of *Seven*'s city as unwelcoming and perilous terrain. Noir-inspired lighting plays a key role in defining the film's tone.[10] Night shots are bathed in blackness and even in daytime shots the lighting is murky and muted.[11] Direct sunlight is virtually absent. Hard back- and side-lighting is used frequently to create ominous silhouettes and shadows. Crime scenes in particular are typically darker than the rest of the film and depend on low-key lighting and available sources of illumination like floor lamps, neon signage, and flashlights. Moreover, what light is allowed to enter a scene often enters at odd angles and in the form of jagged slices, odd patches, and narrow beams. Even the darkest of the classic noirs—films like *T-Men* (1947) or *Touch of Evil* (1958)—were never quite this dark. So, for instance, when Mills and Sommerset examine the body of Doe's first victim, it is in a room so dimly lit that the only details of the scene we can really make out are those illuminated by the thin beams of their flashlights. The movie's color palette—which runs from black to an infinite variety of browns and grays to putrid greens with blood and wounds rendered in a deep, inky crimson—highlights the sinister associations of the lighting scheme. In the brothel where the prostitute is found murdered, a red neon light provides her room with suitably infernal illumination. Similarly, in Doe's apartment a bright red neon cross and an assortment of dim lamps provide most of the light. The apprehensive atmosphere created by this use of light and color is rendered gloomier by the fact that the unidentified metropolis is deluged by what seems like perpetual rainfall. As in film noir, the darkness and the inclement weather echo and indeed become an "objective correlative" of the metropolis's climate of moral decline.

Seven's grim urban wasteland exerts a profound, tangible pressure on the psyches of the main characters. And no one exhibits the strain of life in the metropolis as clearly as Detective William Sommerset. Kevin McNamara writes that the detective in film noir, from Philip Marlowe to *Blade Runner*'s Rick Deckard, is "a man who has seen everything but is powerless to change much of anything" (McNamara 1996, 177). Sommerset certainly fits this description. As the archetypal cynical, world-weary yet all-knowing career cop, he possesses a vast store of accumulated knowledge about the moral depravity of the streets, which he is perpetually trying to share with his naive young partner (and, through him, with the audience). It is significant, then, that one of first things we learn about him is that he has decided to quit the police force and retire to the country. Throughout the film, Sommerset wants nothing more than to escape the city: when Mills's wife, Tracy (Gwyneth Paltrow), asks him over dinner, "how long have you lived here?" his only rejoinder is "too long." His running commentary makes it clear that he regards the film's shadowy metropolis as incomprehensibly vicious. Thus, when his captain attempts to dissuade him from retiring, Sommerset tells him a story about a man who just the night before was randomly attacked while walking his dog and stabbed in both eyes, concluding that "I don't understand this place anymore." As he sees it, the apathy and callousness of "this place" gives the Jonathan Does of the world freedom to operate. "In any major city," he explains to Mills as they discuss the case, "minding your own business is a science. The first thing they teach women in rape prevention is to yell fire. Nobody answers to 'help.'"

Sommerset is not the only character in the film who finds the city unbearable. Tracy too views her surroundings as loathsome. Early in the film she complains to David about the excessive traffic noise outside their apartment, commenting that "I thought we moved here to get away from tractor pulls." Later this annoyance with city life turns to open repugnance. At one point she arranges to get together with Sommerset behind David's back because he is the only person in town she knows and she needs desperately to talk. When they meet, Tracy, who was a fifth-grade teacher when she lived "upstate," describes how she has looked for work in the local school system but discovered that "the conditions are just horrible." Then, revealing that she is pregnant and having second thoughts about carrying the pregnancy to term, she tearfully confesses that "I hate this city." The tortured, helpless expression on her face speaks volumes about her feelings toward her new home.

Jonathan Doe, we discover, basically shares Tracy and Sommerset's perspective on urban existence. We are hardly surprised to learn, therefore, that the two thousand handwritten notebooks the detectives find in his apartment include page after page of misanthropic diatribe in which the city figures prominently (an allusion, perhaps, to Dostoyevski's *Notes from Underground*). "On the subway today a man came up to me to start a conversation," Sommerset reads out loud from one of Doe's journals. "He made small talk, this lonely man, talking about the weather and other things. I tried to be pleasant and accommodating but my head began to hurt from his banality. I almost didn't notice it had happened but I suddenly threw up all over him. He was not pleased. And I couldn't stop laughing." Doe's solution to the horror around him is an apocalyptic one. In keeping with millenarian Christian fantasy, he believes that only total violence can redeem a fallen, godless social world.[12] Fittingly, he sees himself as a sort of avenging angel, insisting that "I did not choose. I was chosen." He had to resort to such extreme measures, Doe tells Sommerset and Mills, because "wanting people to listen you can't just tap them on the shoulder anymore, you have to hit them with a sledge hammer." After he has turned himself in to the police and is guiding Sommerset and Mills to the alleged location of his latest victims, Doe justifies his deeds by pointing to the pathologies and moral failings of the city. "Don't ask me to pity them. We see a deadly sin on every street corner, in every home and we tolerate it," explains Doe. "We tolerate it because it's common, it's trivial. We tolerate it morning, noon and night." His victims, he argues, are as deserving of punishment (and as undeserving of sympathy) as "the thousands who died at Sodom and Gomorrah."

The film itself stakes out a profoundly ambiguous stance toward Doe's murders and toward his justification for them. What Doe does is clearly monstrous, but the depiction of the metropolis as a vast den of iniquity implies that at least some of his violence is an appropriate reaction to the monstrousness of his social environment. His first few victims are, after all, hateful, immoral people with whom the audience feels absolutely no connection. Indeed, with the exception of the pathetic Tracy, none of the denizens of *Seven*'s city—Sommerset and Mills included—come off as even remotely sympathetic. However revolted we are by Doe's brutality, the film more or less demands that the audience adopt a position from which the regeneration of the world through some sort of cleansing conflagration or orgy of bloodshed perversely makes sense.

Of the major characters, only Mills with his boundless enthusiasm and bravado seems totally oblivious to the malevolence of his surroundings. Impulsive, not very bright, emotional to a fault, and basically optimistic, he is the diametric opposite of Sommerset's stoic reserve and cynical realism; next to Sommerset, he appears as a regular country yokel. His ignorance of the pitfalls and depravity of the big city and his lack of self-control appear fated to get him into trouble from the start. Thus, it seems perfectly fitting that he and Tracy have been tricked into renting an apartment next to a noisy subway line. Nor is it accidental that Mills's explosive temper threatens to compromise the Doe investigation on more than one occasion: first, when he almost refuses to give Sommerset the money to obtain an FBI computer list of people reading about deadly sins and then again when he kicks in the door to Doe's apartment without a warrant, potentially tainting the evidence inside. Moreover, without the aid of his knowing, street-smart partner, Mills's investigation of Doe's murders would go nowhere. It is Sommerset, after all, who spots all the important clues, who figures out Doe's *modus operandi,* and who leads the pair to the suspect's lair. Given his persistent disregard for Sommerset's warnings about the treacherous nature of *Seven*'s metropolis, it is entirely predictable that Mills becomes the film's most abject victim.

Seven's ending essentially vindicates the despairing outlook already manifest in Doe and Sommerset's view of urban life (while at the same time repudiating Mills's strutting confidence and macho posturing). Throughout the film, Doe remains in charge and in control, dictating the action and easily eluding his pursuers even after they have tracked him to his apartment. When Doe allows himself to be taken into custody, it is only so he can complete his "masterpiece" (by revealing that he has killed Tracy out of envy, thereby provoking Mills to "become wrath" and execute him). That Doe successfully carries his plan to its bloody conclusion confirms what we already know: that the guardians of public order are helpless to contain the elemental forces of violence and barbarity being bred at the heart of the metropolis. The fact that he manages to destroy Mills's life in the process symbolizes the fate in store for those who underestimate the power of those forces. Despite a tacked-on voice-over by Sommerset avowing that the world is "worth fighting for,"[13] and despite an indication that he might not leave the police force after all, the film's conclusion leaves us emotionally exactly where we began: with a gloomy, unrelieved sense of foreboding about the threat posed by the city. No other outcome is even imaginable. In a sense, the fatalistic ending was already implied by the visual and thematic emphasis given to the urban setting. As Christopher has pointed out, in classic film noir, "the labyrinth . . . the city-as-world is made to appear implacable and unassailable, and the hero puny and vulnerable" (Christopher 1997, 32). Naturally, this way of framing the confrontation between the individual and the environment bodes ill for the individual. In this respect *Seven* once again pushes the basic noir formula to its logical limit: the looming omnipresence of the film's latter-day Sodom and Gomorrah from the very first frame suggests that all the protagonists' efforts will be losing ones and that the protagonists themselves will come to bad ends.

Seven's portrayal of the city as a blighted, decaying zone of unfettered criminality and vice, as a place where one finds "a deadly sin on every street corner," more or less directly transcodes the reactionary view of urban problems promoted by the mainstream news media and the conservative punditocracy. Like countless other Hollywood films that have come out since the early 1980s, it validates middle-class suburbia's revulsion for a (mostly poor, mostly of color) urban core understood as *essentially* unruly and beyond hope. As Homi Bhabha points out, "the conservative suburban attitude is founded on the fear of difference; and a narrow-minded appeal to cultural homogeneity. It is a kind of national paranoia that draws the boundary between what is acceptable and what is unacceptable ever more tightly around the norm of the 'known' . . . " (Bhabha 1997, 299). A number of different currents of ideologically motivated anxiety feed the "national paranoia" Bhabha refers to here. Concern about the economic decline of America's metropolitan regions (along with concomitant concerns about national decline), racialized fear of street crime, anxiety about the "breakdown" of the family and civilized morality in the ghetto, apprehension about the threat to social order posed by "inner-city" drugs like crack, skepticism about government's capacity to address urban problems—all figure prominently in the conservative discourse that *Seven* and other contemporary cinematic representations of urban life confirm and circulate.

To begin with, the dilapidated structures and litter-filled alleys we see in *Seven*—and, even more hyperbolically, in the post-apocalyptic L.A. of films like *Escape from L.A.* and *Blade Runner*—give visual form to the suspicion that our central cities are now economically obsolete. In the conservative suburban imagination, the nation's downtowns and the neighborhoods that surround the downtowns are not merely struggling but already in ruins, reduced to vast dumping grounds for marginal populations of various sorts. As explained in chapter 3, this image of postindustrial urban failure performs some important ideological functions for the middle class, most notably by providing them with a justification for distancing themselves from urban minorities and inner-city neighborhoods. Moreover, by "siting" economic and social decline in central cities, the dominant, right-wing interpretation of urban reality obscures both the deeper causes of such decline and its real scope (since the forces of economic decline and deindustrialization are now doing to our suburbs, especially our older, inner-ring suburbs, exactly what they did to the central cities). *Seven*'s city functions as a symbol of decline not merely because it is falling apart and overflowing with garbage, but also because it appears quite literally to be stuck at an earlier moment in the history of urban development. Most of the film's interiors appear to date from the 1940s or before (as, for that matter, do most of Sommerset's and Mills's suits). This anachronism is obviously meant to evoke the dark universe of classic film noir. But it is also, I think, a reflection of the discourse that treats central cities and the lifestyles associated with them as hopelessly out of date and on the verge of extinction. In this age of mega-malls, Wal-Mart, and "telecommuters," the official voices of mainstream America—writers like journalist Joel Garreau or conservative pundit George Gilder—often charge that cities are doomed because they have failed to evolve to keep up with the sweeping changes wrought by information-age capitalism; as Garreau claims in *Edge City,* classic central cities like Manhattan and San Francisco "are relics of a time past. They are aberrations" (Garreau 1991, 25). By envisioning its metropolis as a relic from the 1940s, *Seven* makes a similar accusation.

Of the popular fears surrounding the contemporary American city that are tapped into by *Seven,* the fear of urban crime articulated by the film perhaps resonates most powerfully with middle-class suburbanites. I have already detailed how paranoia about street crime has spurred the growth of the private security industry, the rapid spread of gated communities from Los Angeles to New York, and rising public support for punitive crime-fighting legislation. Crime hysteria has also played and continues to play a major role in the ongoing out-migration of middle-class families fleeing urban neighborhoods for the greener pastures of suburbia. For instance, a 1993 *Chicago Tribune* series on the motives of people leaving Chicago for the suburbs found that fear of urban crime was more of a motivating factor for most migrants than any positive feature of their new homes. As one person interviewed for the report put it, "We became worn out by the traffic, parking hassles, noise, crime, lack of being able to feel safe, etc. We did not feel the City of Chicago was a good place to start a family" (Reardon 1993, 10). Sentiments like these are clearly and approvingly echoed in *Seven* and in films like it. When Sommerset talks longingly about retiring to the country or when Tracy worries out loud about raising a child in the city, they are speaking from the ideological position of all those families who have fled or dream about fleeing the city for the perceived safety and comfort of the suburbs.

Moreover, a movie like *Seven* takes the gory, blood-drenched image of urban life painted by law-and-order politicians and local television news shows at face value—and then renders it even bloodier. The film indulges right-wing fantasies about the violence of the city to the point where violence becomes the city's sole distinctive feature. In this, *Seven* follows a well-established Hollywood trend. The identification of the American metropolis with violence in films like *Trespass, Predator 2, Menace II Society,* or *New Jack City* is so complete that, as Jerry Herron has argued, "a city without violence would be irrelevant because it would appear unreal to the majority of contemporary Americans" (Herron 1993, 186).

But *Seven* doesn't just exaggerate the extent of urban violence. It also decontextualizes (and thereby mystifies) it. In the film, as in reactionary discourse on crime in general, violent criminality is seen as the result of individual psychological aberrations or personal moral failing rather than as the product of systemic social and economic forces. Though Doe's misguided vigilantism is provoked by the wickedness around him, the fact that he is independently wealthy, white, and totally psychotic renders any sociological understanding of his bizarre killings moot. And the other murders we learn about—the man who is shot by his wife, the corpse Sommerset sees from the cab, the man who is attacked while walking his dog—appear inexplicable and unmotivated if not outright random. But we know, as a matter of fact, that criminal behavior is rarely truly random and that poverty and joblessness are at the very least contributing factors to most sorts of street crime. As noted in chapter 1, rates of crime, and particularly rates of violent crime, are generally higher in poor neighborhoods than in middle-class and wealthy ones,[14] and residents of economically distressed inner-city black and Latino neighborhoods are much more likely to become victims of crime than other city-dwellers.[15] In other words, the assaults and muggings that so terrify suburbia—the quotidian street crime that *Seven* makes such a point of showing us—are properly seen as stemming directly from the deepening poverty and contracting opportunity structure that has accompanied the deindustrialization of our nation's inner-city communities of color. Yet *Seven,* like most films that deal with the subject, conspicuously avoids confronting the underlying dynamics of the urban violence and criminality it is so preoccupied with depicting. As framed by the film's narrative, the imputed barbarism of the city is utterly unrelated to entrenched racial oppression or a dysfunctional economy; rather, it is a manifestation of pure evil. This moralistic view of crime jives perfectly with the perspective championed by conservatives like Charles Murray and William Bennett, which in a not-so-subtly racist way insists that the social problems of America's minority communities are caused by their own moral failings and not by institutional racism of the larger society or the inherent contradictions of capitalist development.

It is noteworthy that in *Seven* the perpetrators of violence are all, as far as we know, white, and that the main representative of law and order, Sommerset, is black. This appears to break with the standard right-wing narrative in which heroic white cops defend the white, suburban public against the implicitly black violence of the city. However, I would argue that the film's pointed and excessive association of bloodshed with the big city—which in the current universe of political discourse has become synonymous with the deviant racial "Other"—subtly *codes* its violence as black (or, better, reinforces stereotypes about criminality and violence that are often applied exclusively to inner-city people of color). The rundown tenements and the garbage-choked streets one sees throughout the film likewise can be read as connoting "the ghetto" or ghetto-like conditions even in the absence of African American "bad guys." And the sheer pervasiveness of cops and crime scenes in the film is bound to conjure up images of rampant black lawlessness to the suburban viewer weaned on *Cops* and television coverage of the "crack crisis." In this way, hysterical white fear of black street crime perhaps receives in the film a kind of displaced, deracialized expression that avoids opening up questions about the systemic causes of the very real violence tearing apart poor, urban, minority neighborhoods.[16]

But more than anything else, it is the fatalism one finds in *Seven* and other recent Hollywood attempts to deal with American urban reality that dovetails with the most reactionary sentiments of the suburban middle class and articulates the worst aspects of the hegemonic discourse on the urban crisis. As I argued in chapter 1, the epochal migration of the American population away from the central cities to the suburban fringe has been above all a flight from communal, public life to the comforts of a privatized existence centered around the single family home, the automobile, and the TV set. As William Schneider notes, "Suburbanization means the privatization of American life and culture. To move to the suburbs is to express a preference for the private over the public" (Schneider 1992, 37). In the political realm, this fondness for the private becomes skepticism about how much municipal government can do to address nagging social ills like crime, poverty, and illicit drug use. "A major reason people move out to the suburbs is simply to buy their own government," explains Schneider. "These people resent it when politicians take their money and use it to solve other people's problems, especially when they don't believe that government can actually solve those problems" (37). The image of the city as beyond redemption, as hopelessly dysfunctional, justifies the generally individualistic, antisocial bent of suburban politics. Thus, when *Seven* portrays the city as locked in a downward spiral of decay and shows the police as hopelessly ineffectual, it vindicates the suburbanite's hostility to "government spending" and "money for cities." Likewise, Sommerset's longing for retirement (which, remember, he intends to spend in the country) echoes the increasingly respectable middle-class desire to simply abandon (politically, materially, and culturally) those left behind by suburbanization. Along the same lines, the celebration of apocalyptic vigilantism in *Batman* and *The Crow,* and the fantasy image of a feral metropolis safely cordoned off from the rest of America that one sees on display in *Escape from New York* and its sequel, each express in their own way a deep sense of hopelessness about the future of the city.

Conclusion

The alarmist images of and rhetoric about cities on display in so many Hollywood films of the 1980s and '90s replicated and amplified the fear and loathing of all things urban so adroitly exploited (and encouraged) by the forces of the political right. Sometimes, as in *Predator 2* or *Falling Down* or *The Substitute,* such films are nakedly racist in their terrified depictions of vice-ridden black and brown inner cities. More often than not, though, as in *Eye for an Eye* and *Ransom,* they give white, middle-class fears of the urban underclass a coded, disguised form of expression. As we have seen, even ostensibly liberal films like *Grand Canyon* and movies made by the "new wave" of black filmmakers find it difficult to free themselves from the terms of the conservative discourse on the urban crisis.

Nowhere in the Hollywood cinema of the past two decades are reactionary nightmares about the postindustrial city more in evidence than in the proliferation of "urban gothic" thrillers such as *Seven*. Like the malevolent urban environment in *Batman, The Crow,* and other movies of its ilk, the dark, decaying, crime-ridden metropolis constructed by Fincher's film reflects the terrified perspective of people who over the past few decades have done their utmost to "get far away from" the city and the collective responsibilities and human solidarities upon which the city is based. *Seven*'s vision of its metropolis confirms the middle-class suspicion that our cities are overrun by violence, morally degenerate, economically moribund, and essentially beyond repair. When Sommerset gives his junior partner a photocopied version of a diagram of Dante's *Inferno* to aid him in the investigation of the Doe killings, the gesture makes explicit what is clear throughout the film and is axiomatic for many of its suburban middle-class viewers: the city is Hell. This bleak vision—which dovetails so perfectly with right-wing discourse on social problems and which so thoroughly mystifies the problems facing America's metropolitan areas—wasn't just confined to films and television news reports. As the next chapter demonstrates, it even seeped into the eye-catching imagery and thirty-second narratives of advertising.

Endnotes

1. *Seven* grossed over $100 million in 1995 in the U.S. market alone, making it one of the top ten domestic money-makers that year. (http://www. boxofficereport.com/ybon/1995.shtml [accessed November 27, 2005]).

2. In his brilliant *Ecology of Fear,* Mike Davis notes that the destruction of Los Angeles has been such a popular theme in recent cinema that "[t]he entire world seems to be rooting for Los Angeles to slide into the Pacific or be swallowed by the San Andreas fault" (Davis 1998, 276–77).

3. Whether or not the process by which films assume elements of the dominant ideology should be described as a process of "reflection" is open to debate. To talk about a film "reflecting" the dominant ideology assumes that a) that ideology is a closed, preconstituted system of ideas, meanings, etc. and b) that this preconstituted system of meanings is imported into the film untransformed. Neither proposition stands up to scrutiny: first because the dominant ideology is always evolving and in flux; and second, because a film's "operationalization" of ideological concepts always changes, deepens, and expands their meanings. It would therefore perhaps be better to speak of film as helping to define the dominant ideology rather than as merely reflecting it.

4. This becomes even clearer in the *Escape from New York* video game based on the film. In the video game, literally every street, every alleyway, and every subway car harbors potential attackers that the player/Snake must destroy; indeed, in the game's rendition of the film's carceral New York, there are no safe spaces at all.

5. As I point out in the conclusion to this book, Lee's film uses the conventions of the ghetto-centric gangster film in a way that breaks politically with the genre's acceptance of key aspects of the right's pathologizing discourse on the underclass. In this respect, *Clockers* is the exception that proves the rule.

6. Technically speaking, Grant's designation is something of a misnomer because the protagonists of many of these films, while they ostensibly share the lifestyle, mentality, and values typically associated with yuppies, live in the suburbs— making them *young suburban professionals* as opposed to *young urban professionals*.

7. As Andrew Ross remarks, the subways and sewers of New York and other metropolitan centers have often been linked to "the alien presence of immigrant populations busily breeding mutant Americans" and, as he points out, "the rich zoological life of the underworld has continued to be a source of representation for threats to the urban racial order" (Ross 1994, 135–36).

8. Alan Nadel has argued that "the establishing shot is the representation of the Establishment, in that it presents the unchallenged assumptions necessary to allow the scene to unfold. It frames the framing of the subsequent shots by delimiting the imaginary space in which they are situated" (Nadel 1997, 143). In the case of *Eye for an Eye,* the reverential establishing shot of the McCanns' giant upper-middle-class house doesn't merely specify the imagined space of the

house as the site of much of the film's action but also posits the house and the lifestyle that centers around it as essentially good and decent.

9. This section of the chapter draws on my article on *Seven* and fear of the city in contemporary Hollywood film (Macek 1999).

10. For more on the expressionistic use of light and shadow to develop distinctively bleak urban settings in classic film noir see Ford 1994, Christopher 1997, and Krutnik 1997. It is important to point out that the sort of lighting and black and white color palette one sees in *Seven* is not exclusively associated with film noir. This particular style owes as much to directors who've come to film from working in advertising (and, in Fincher's case, music videos) as it does to noir.

11. Fincher's desire to foreground darkness in the film led him to employ the rarely-used silver retention method of processing that, as Amy Taubin explains, "produces more luminosity in the light and more density in the darks" but is also extremely expensive (Taubin 1996, 24). The process is so costly and time-consuming, in fact, that only a few hundred of the prints of *Seven* in circulation are silver retention.

12. In this respect, at least, Doe's solution to urban problems resembles Travis Bickel's famously violent, apocalyptic response to the mean streets of New York in Scorsese's *Taxi Driver*. For more on the apocalyptic "redemption" of the city in *Taxi Driver* (1976) see Sharrett 1993a.

13. According to Richard Dyer, whose excellent monograph on *Seven* appeared at roughly the same time as my *College Literature* article on the film, this tacked-on and utterly unpersuasive voice-over was "a cap desired by the studio, intended to give some crumb of Hollywoodian comfort in a film so extraordinarily un-American in its pessimism" (Dyer 1999, 77). I have been unable to confirm this claim but the voice-over at the end is so incongruous with the bleak spirit of the movie that it would be surprising if it were not the result of some sort of studio tampering.

14. Lauren Krivo and Ruth Peterson have recently conducted research confirming that "extremely disadvantaged communities have higher levels of crime than less disadvantaged areas, and that this pattern holds for both black and white communities" (Krivo and Peterson 1996, 640).

15. For further discussion of the social factors driving high levels of black street crime, see Hacker 1992, 179–98.

16. In this respect, the film bears some resemblance to *Batman,* which, as Andrew Ross has argued, depends heavily on a veiled racial subtext to construct its vision of a crime-threatened Gotham City (Ross 1990).

30

What We Talk About When We Talk About Race

MANNING MARABLE

Manning Marable works as a Professor of History at Columbia University. The essay "What We Talk About When We Talk About Race" from The Great Wells of Democracy: The Meaning of Race in American Life *names the social and legal processes that created white privilege and that continue to prevent the full participation of black Americans and other minority groups in civil society. Arguments calling for color-blindness or simple celebrations of diversity ignore these processes. Marable's essay illustrates how to take commonsense arguments, read them rhetorically, and locate them within a history of social power.*

> *It is an historical fact that privileged groups seldom give up their privileges voluntarily. Individuals may see the moral light and voluntarily give up their unjust posture; but, as Reinhold Niebuhr has reminded us, groups tend to be more immoral than individuals.*
>
> —Martin Luther King, Jr.
> "Letter from Birmingham Jail," April 16, 1963

W**hen I was twelve years old,** growing up in an African-American community in Dayton, Ohio, something happened at our church one Sunday afternoon that I've never forgotten. My family and I attended

St. Margaret's Episcopal Church, which had a congregation that was almost completely black. Occasionally after mass, we'd go downstairs to the church basement and have Sunday dinner for the members of the congregation. On this particular afternoon, the church had organized a raffle. Each ticket cost fifty cents, and the first prize was a $100 U.S. savings bond.

My allowance at the time was about one dollar and fifty cents per week. I calculated that I could afford to buy one raffle ticket. Before dinner was served, everybody gathered for the drawing. Much to my amazement, I had purchased the winning ticket.

As I walked forward to receive my savings bond, church members and family friends stood up to applaud. One elderly, somewhat heavyset church lady with a beautiful broad smile hugged me and proudly pinched my cheeks. She exclaimed, "Son, this must be your lucky day!"

There are moments like that in everyone's life. Like when you're standing at a city crosswalk and, looking down, see a crumpled twenty-dollar bill on the pavement. The event is unexpected, something that is unusual. I don't know what happened to that savings bond; it's probably somewhere in my mom's basement back in Dayton. But that doesn't diminish how I felt that special day when I was twelve.

Four decades have passed since then. I usually speak about once or twice each week, and I travel more than 120 days every year. Because of deregulation and the new post-9/11 security regulations, air travel for most Americans is nothing less than a kind of torture: long lines, surly ticket agents, uncomfortable seats, terrible meals, and constant delays. Sometimes I can observe the corporate executives sitting up in first class. They're usually chilled out. They seem pampered, well fed, and on especially long flights, generally intoxicated. Then I realize the obvious. For them, almost every day is their lucky day. These are the material benefits of whiteness and upper-class privilege in twenty-first-century America.

Sociologists often use a concept called "life chances." These are things that are likely to happen to you simply because you are identified with a particular group. If you're black or Latino in a racist society, where whiteness is defined as the social norm, you are statistically far more likely to experience certain unfortunate and sometimes even life-threatening events—not based on your behavior, but merely because of your identification with an oppressed social category. The Marxist philosopher Louis Althusser once described this process as "overdetermination." You become a social actor in the real world not on the basis of any objective criteria, but by the stereotypes imposed on you externally by others. The boundaries of one's skin become the crude starting point for negotiating access to power and resources within a society constructed around racial hierarchies. And after a period of several centuries, a mountain of accumulated disadvantage has been erected, a vast monument to the pursuit of inequality and injustice that to most black Americans is the hallmark of our "democracy."

Sitting back into my uncomfortable coach middle seat, I looked again at the first-class section. I then recalled the plot of comedian Bill Murray's movie *Groundhog Day* (1993). In the film, Murray plays an obnoxious weatherman who becomes trapped in a small Pennsylvania town on February 2, Groundhog Day. Despite every effort, he finds that he can't escape. The day repeats itself over and over again. The real world is similar, I thought: People wake up to the same racial discrimination or white upper-class privilege day after day. Affluent whites usually experience a lucky day and, with some minor variations, enjoy that same day repeatedly. The structure of white privilege sets certain parameters of existence that guarantee a succession of lucky days.

Then I began to have second thoughts. Are the overweight white guys in the first-class section *personally* responsible for an entire race being placed permanently back in coach, figuratively speaking? I recalled that Connecticut senator and former Democratic vice presidential candidate Joe Lieberman had traveled south in 1964 to participate in the "Mississippi Freedom Summer," organizing and registering African-American voters. And after all, more than 3 million white people did vote for Jesse Jackson in 1988. Some whites even endorsed Louis Farrakhan's 1995 "Million Man March."

But sympathy for the oppressed is not the same as having a shared or linked fate. We can only truly understand someone else's pain when we step outside the protected confines of our lives to take risks. The political culture of whiteness is conformity. Let's accept the way things are—because things aren't too bad. Power translates itself into "merit." Privileged access and opportunity create spaces for comfortable lives.

Conversely, the structural limitations and restrictions on black life have been continuous in this country. The effects can be seen in many realms, especially in the arts. Racism has produced aesthetically some of this country's most powerful music: for example, the blues. The politics behind this art form, simply put, are based on the harsh reality of having a "bad day" over and over again.

To take this example further, why were the blues produced by oppressed black sharecroppers in the Mississippi Delta, but not by the privileged families of George W. Bush and Dick Cheney? According to 2002 estimates, President Bush's personal assets are between $11.1 million and $21.6 million; Vice President Cheney's total assets are between $19.3 million and $81.8 million. Perhaps we might understand why Bush and Cheney don't sing the blues by reconsidering the real life chances of most African Americans who live under a system most of us call "democracy."

African Americans and Latinos constitute 25 percent of the U.S. population but represent nearly 60 percent of the 2 million Americans currently in prison. Statistically, blacks account for only 14 percent of all illegal drug users. Yet we make up over one-third of all drug arrests and 55 percent of all drug convictions. Are blacks just unlucky in the courts, or is something else at work here?

If it's bad luck, it must start before birth. White Americans in 1995 had an infant mortality rate of 6.3 deaths per 1,000 live births. The African-American infant mortality rate that same year was 15.1 deaths per 1,000 live births—a higher rate than in such places as Taiwan, Portugal, Cuba, Chile, or Bulgaria. Are black babies just unlucky, or are their deaths an inevitable consequence of inadequate health care, poor housing, and the destructive impacts of poverty, unemployment, and the extreme stresses of everyday life for pregnant black women?

The stresses are financial as well as emotional and physical. In several recent studies, major insurance companies were found to charge black homeowners significantly higher rates than whites to insure homes of identical value. Supermarket chains routinely charge higher prices for most groceries in minority urban neighborhoods than in predominantly white, upper-class suburbs. Are African-American consumers in the marketplace just unlucky, or is it the logical result of "equity inequity," the racial profiling of credit and capital investment in our communities? "Bad luck" clearly has nothing to do with the unequal outcomes that construct the normal conditions of our existence. If President George W. Bush and his buddies in the first-class seats who voted for him experienced what we see and feel in our daily lives—omnipresent racial inequality in the courts, in health care, education, employment, and many other areas—they might have invented the blues, too.

The two distinct sections of the airplane also symbolized for me the two strikingly different narratives that have evolved about the character of U.S. democracy and the nature of our social contract, the written and unwritten rules governing relations between the American people and their leaders that theoretically protects their collective interests. For most white Americans, especially those in the first-class seats, U.S. democracy is best represented by enduring values such as personal liberty, individualism, and the ownership of private property. For most of us African Americans and other marginalized minorities, the central goals of the Black Freedom Movement have always been equality—the eradication of all structural barriers to full citizenship and full participation in all aspects of public life and economic relations—and self-determination—the ability to decide, on our own terms, what our future as a community with a unique history and culture might be.

"Freedom" to white Americans principally has meant the absence of legal restrictions on individual activity and enterprise. By contrast, black Americans have always perceived "freedom" in collective terms, as something achievable by group action and capacity-building. "Equality" to African Americans has meant the elimination of all social deficits between blacks and whites—that is, the eradication of cultural and social stereotypes and patterns of social isolation and group exclusion generated by white structural racism over several centuries.

The airplane metaphor is somewhat useful in understanding the problems of race, gender, and class, but in other ways it is limited. The vast majority of the passengers in the coach section are also white, middle-class males. Perhaps one-quarter of the passengers are women. There are several Asian Americans, one or two Latinos, and maybe three other African Americans sitting side by side in two separate rows. As part of the middle class, we have the means and the resources to fly to our destination in relative comfort. But the vast majority of the African-American population, and a significant number of women and other racialized minorities, never board the plane at all. Their physical and social mobility is severely and deliberately restricted. During the era of Jim Crow segregation, the "white" and "colored" signs were the demarcation of society's racial fault line, and black "travelers" were restricted by the boundaries of color. Today, the segregationist signs have been taken down, but the ugly patterns of racialized inequality and white privilege persist in most respects. Through extraordinary efforts, those who never had access to the airplane fought and sacrificed to get some of us on board. Our tickets were purchased at an exorbitant price. Yet those of us fortunate enough to gain that access should recognize that the monopoly of power that severely restricts the mobility of our own community is still in place.

Think for a moment about the individuals in the first-class section. Relative to nearly everybody else, they have a privileged lifestyle. They have set up trust funds for their children, and they take advantage of elitist policies such as "legacies" to guarantee that their descendants will have access to the best university education. They lobby vigorously for the elimination of the inheritance tax to preserve the accumulation of their wealth over several generations. For the most part, they control the national discourse about politics and public policy, and they largely determine the outcomes of national elections. But despite their privileges and power, they nevertheless do not own the plane. They are favored customers, privileged "frequent flyers," but not the owners. They don't control the airplane's schedule or the direction the flight is taking. In fact, those who own the airliner are rarely on it, because they have their own private jets. In the 1990s, 90 percent of the total income gain of the upper one-fifth of U.S. households went to the top 1 percent. As Kevin Phillips observed, "Attention should focus on the top one-tenth of 1 percent, because these are the raw capitalists and money-handlers, not the high-salaried doctors, lawyers and Cadillac dealers." About 250,000 Americans have annual incomes above $1 million. As Phillips noted, "The 30 largest U.S. family and individual fortunes in 1999 were roughly *ten times* as big as the 30 largest had been in 1982, an increase greater than any comparable period during the 19th century."

We are living in a period when the concentration of wealth and economic power is unprecedented in human history. Wal-Mart, which in 1979 had $1 billion in sales for an entire year, now sometimes generates that amount in a single day worldwide. In 2001, Wal-Mart netted $219.81 billion in revenue, outdistancing the second-largest corporation, Exxon-Mobil, which had 2001 revenues of $191.58 billion. General Motors, which held the top spot for fifteen years until 2000, had $177.26 billion in revenues. Enron, the nation's largest energy corporation, which filed for bankruptcy in December 2001, nevertheless reported 2001 earnings of $130.9 billion. For many of the hundreds of thousands of Americans, regardless of race, who lost all or part of their pensions and life savings from the Enron fiasco, it may be difficult to reconcile such vast inequalities generated by this concentration of wealth within a political system that still claims to be a democracy. The racialized inequality that African Americans have brutally experienced and deeply feel is only one important dimension to the larger problem of inequality that is structured across the entire American social order.

The profound differences between the two narratives about the meaning of the American project are often reflected in our conflicts over historical symbols. For example, several years ago, the New Orleans School Board announced the renaming of one of its oldest elementary schools. What was previously George Washington Elementary had become the Dr. Charles Drew Elementary School. The name change was initiated and enthusiastically supported by the school's students, teachers, and parents. The school's African-American History Club had proposed the name to commemorate a famous black surgeon who had established research procedures for processing and storing blood plasma. Drew had been the leading organizer of blood-bank programs during World War II and was responsible for saving millions of lives.

When it became public knowledge that the first U.S. president had been symbolically "dumped" in favor of a black man, many local whites were outraged. But the white "Founding Fathers" aren't the only ones at the center of the school-naming controversies in New Orleans. Over the past 100 years, New Orleans public schools have been named for a series of white racists, slaveholders, and former Confederate army officers. A short list includes: John McDonogh, a wealthy

Louisiana slaveholder who freed many of his slaves only on the condition that they would return to Africa; Henry W. Allen, a sugarcane planter and Confederate general; Confederate army commander Robert E. Lee; and Confederate president Jefferson Davis. Some people who have supported racial name changes have argued that the overwhelmingly black student population of the New Orleans public school system should be presented with positive role models from their own history and culture. Certainly this is a valid point. By cultivating greater awareness and appreciation among African-American young people about their heritage, they may acquire valuable lessons about black achievement against the odds.

But perhaps the greatest beneficiaries in the changing of public honorific names are white Americans. "Whiteness" imposes blinders that shut off the full spectrum of social reality, the shared experiences of people from different racialized backgrounds in the making of a common history. The symbolic act of naming makes a public statement about our relationship to the past and about the principles and values that should be preserved.

The larger political issue that lies just behind the debate over names is far more disturbing. The United States, from its origins to the present, has consistently lied to itself about what it actually is. We claimed to be a "democracy" in the early nineteenth century, even while denying voting rights to the majority of citizens. We claim "equal protection under the law" while millions of black, brown, and poor people have been and continue to be unjustly treated in our courts and prisons. Our economic system favors the privileged few, while allocating greater poverty and unemployment along the unequal boundaries of race.

There have always been Americans who have challenged the political hypocrisy of this nation. They have been black, brown, and white. In the 1960s, they were activists in civil rights, in the antiwar movement against U.S. involvement in Vietnam, in women's rights, and in the welfare-rights movement. In the nineteenth century, they were the abolitionists who fought to outlaw human bondage. They are the "Other America," those who dreamed of a truly democratic, pluralistic society. Their names— such as W.E.B. Du Bois, Cesar Chavez, Fannie Lou Hamer, Ida B. Wells-Barnett, Eugene V. Debs, William Lloyd Garrison, Joe Hill, and Paul Robeson—represent an alternative perspective on what America has been and what it could become. Our debate over history therefore is a debate about the future of the country itself.

I

"E Pluribus Unum": Out of many, one. Americans have been taught to believe that they have always been champions of religious, ethnic, and cultural pluralism. "Diversity" has become our multicultural mantra about America's past as well as its future. Offices of student life and student activities groups throughout the United States now fund thousands of celebrations promoting diversity, from the annual birthday events honoring Dr. Martin Luther King, Jr., to Cinco de Mayo, from programs for lesbian, gay, bisexual, and transgender awareness to those honoring the heritage of American Indians. Administrators in the private sector now routinely talk about "managing diversity," of creating workplace environments in which "difference" is not coded into institutional hierarchies. Yet there's a crucial difference between the recognition of "difference" and the acknowledgment that the reality of difference has produced unequal outcomes and divergent life chances for citizens within the same society. As Ron Wakabayashi, the executive director of the Los Angeles County Commission on Human Relations, has observed: "Politicians like to say that diversity is our greatest strength. That is b.s. Diversity simply *is*. The core question is how do we extract its assets while minimizing its liabilities."

Instead of "celebrating diversity," we must theorize it, interrogate it, and actively seek the parallels and discontinuities in the histories of the people who over many centuries have come to call themselves "Americans." Instead of talking abstractly about race, we should be theorizing about the social processes of racialization, of how certain groups in U.S. society have been relegated to an oppressed status, by the weight of law, social policy, and economic exploitation. This process of subordination has never been exclusively or solely grounded in a simplistic black-white paradigm. Although slavery and Jim Crow segregation were decisive in framing the U.S. social hierarchy, with whiteness defined at the top and blackness at the bottom, people of African descent have never experienced racialization by themselves.

As ethnic studies scholars such as Gary Okihiro and Ronald Takaki have observed, the 1790 Naturalization Act defined citizenship only for immigrants who were "free white persons." Asian immigrants who were born outside the United States were largely excluded from citizenship until 1952. U.S. courts constantly redefined the rules determining who was "white" and who was not. For example, Armenians were originally classed as "Asians" and thus were nonwhite, but they legally became "whites" by a 1909 court decision. Syrians were "white" in court decisions in 1909 and 1910; they became "nonwhite" in 1913, and became "white" again in 1915. Asian Indians were legally white in 1910, but they were classified as nonwhite after 1923. Historians such as David Roediger and Noel Ignatiev have illustrated how a series of ethnic minorities, such as the Irish and Ashkenazi Jews, experienced fierce racialization and discrimination but over several generations managed to scale the hierarchy of whiteness.

What many white Americans still refuse to consider is that their numerical majority in the United States is rapidly eroding. By approximately 2016, the population category defined by the U.S. Census Bureau as "non-Hispanic whites" will peak in size, and then it will gradually decline. As Asian Americans, Caribbean people, Latin Americans, Arab Americans, and other nationalities enter the national dialogue about democracy, we will inextricably move away from history's old honorific icons toward new names and symbols of political accomplishment. American democracy is still an unfinished project. Navigating within that new diversity will not be easy. One central reason is that oppression in the United States—or anywhere else, for that matter—has been constructed around interlocking systems of prejudice, power, and white heterosexual male privilege in which the vast majority of the population has been defined outside the acceptable boundaries of the mainstream.

There was, of course, the hierarchy of race: the social construction of whiteness as a category of privilege, the racial stereotyping of the vast majority of non-Europeans, the genocidal elimination of most American Indians, and the enslavement of people of African descent. But there was also a hierarchy of gender oppression or patriarchy: the beliefs of heterosexist male authority and domination, and female inferiority and subordination; the absence for centuries of voting rights and property rights for women; the deliberate uses of violence, such as rape, sexual harassment, and physical intimidation, to preserve patriarchal power.

The hierarchy of heterosexism and homophobia relied on beliefs and practices that reinforced heterosexual superiority and power and promoted institutional discrimination and subordination against lesbian, gay, bisexual, and transgendered people. It permitted the systematic use of violence of different types and degrees to intimidate and control people based on their sexual orientation. And there was the hierarchy of class: the unequal distribution of the bulk of all private property, productive resources, factories, banks, and financial institutions into the hands of a small minority of the population, with the great majority forced to live and exist only by its labor power; the development of an ideology of class privilege that masquerades by calling itself "merit"; and, increasingly, the monopolization and exploitation of global resources and transnational corporations to manufacture and preserve the privileges of class.

The key to properly understanding and theorizing what "racialization" has meant in our historical past and still means today was first conceptualized by legal scholar Cheryl Harris: "Whiteness as Property." To be white is not essentially a biological or genetically based, fixed social category; it is the social expression of power and privilege, the consequences of discriminatory policies in the past, and the practices of inequality that exist today. Thus we will never dismantle structural racism as a system unless we are also willing to address the transformation of the American social structure and the full democratization of our political and economic institutions.

The dynamics of socioeconomic and political marginalization and of social isolation and exclusion inevitably impact the behavior of any oppressed group. Oppressed people are constantly forced to define themselves, largely unthinkingly, by the crude boundaries of the formal, legal categories that have been imposed on them. Any people dwelling at the bottom of a social hierarchy will see themselves as the "Other," as individuals outside of society's social contract, as subordinated, marginalized, fixed minorities. Frequently, oppressed people have used these categories, and even terms of insult and stigmatization, such as "nigger" or "queer," as a site for resistance and counter-hegemonic struggle.

The difficulty inherent in this kind of oppositional politics is twofold. First, it tends to anchor individuals to narrowly defined, one-dimensional identities that are often the "inventions" of others. For example, how did African people become known as "black" or, in Spanish, "Negro"? Europeans launching the slave trade across the Atlantic 400 years ago created the terminology as a way of categorizing the people of an entire continent with tremendous variations in language, religion, ethnicity, kinship patterns, and cultural traditions. Blackness, or the state of being black, was completely artificial; no people in Africa prior to the transatlantic slave trade and European colonialism called themselves "black." Blackness only exists as a social construct in relation to something else. That "something else" became known as whiteness. Blackness as a category relegates other identities—ethnicity, sexual orientation, gender, class affiliation, religious traditions, kinship affiliations—to a secondary or even nonexistent status.

In other words, those who control or dominate hierarchies, whether by ownership of the means of production or by domination of the state, have a vested interest in manufacturing and reproducing categories of difference. An excellent recent example of this occurred in the United States in 1971, when the U.S. Census Bureau "invented" the category "Hispanic." The term was imposed on a population of 16 million people reflecting divergent and even contradictory nationalities, racialized ethnicities, cultural traditions, and political loyalties: black Panamanians of Jamaican or Trinidadian descent, who speak Spanish; Argentines of Italian or German descent; anti-Castro, white, upper-class Cubans in Miami's Dade County; impoverished Mexican-American farm workers in California's Central Valley; and black Dominican service and blue-collar workers in New York City's Washington Heights. Yet when states or hierarchies name the "Other," the act of naming creates its own materiality for the oppressed. Government resources, economic empowerment zones, and affirmative-action scholarships are in part determined by who is classified as Hispanic, and who is not. Identities may be situational, but when the power and resources of the state are used to categorize groups under a "one-size-fits-all" designation, the life chances of individuals who are defined within these categories are largely set and determined by others.

II

In post–civil rights era America, most white commentators on issues of race emphasize the necessity for all of us to become "color blind." That is, we should be "blind" to any imputed differences that tend to divide people by skin color or phenotype, by physical appearance, or by genetic background. The political version of this argument is that any special measures that created privileged classes based on racial categories are inherently unfair and discriminatory.

The color-blind thesis almost always is accompanied by an appeal to "forgive and forget." The logic of this argument goes as follows: Black Americans were certainly terribly oppressed during slavery and Jim Crow segregation. But no white Americans alive today owned slaves. There's been much social progress in recent years, thanks to the constructive cooperation between the races. It's time for us to move beyond ancient grievances and racial bitterness, toward taking greater personal responsibility for our own lives. All of us bear part of the blame for the burden of prejudice—that is, the minorities themselves are partly responsible for getting themselves into their current predicament.

With certain variations, this basic argument is repeated over and over again in the white media by white political leaders and institutions about the dynamics of race. Their thesis is that African Americans must stop being so "sensitive" and "defensive" about the problems of their people and communities. Whites have nothing to apologize for, and African Americans have little really to complain about.

In popular films and culture, the message is largely the same. At the beginning of *Die Hard with a Vengeance* (1995), a white actor, Bruce Willis, stands in Harlem, just off Amsterdam Avenue, wearing a huge sign that reads: "I Hate Niggers." A cluster of justifiably outraged young black men surrounds the undercover white cop. Yet the film, remarkably, portrays not the white cop, but the African-American males, as emotional, dangerous, unstable, and threatening. In the award-winning film *Pulp Fiction* (1994), a white criminal played by John Travolta "accidentally" blows off the head of a young black man when his gun discharges. Covered with blood and gore, the white killer and his black partner (Samuel L. Jackson) take refuge in the suburban home of a white criminal associate (Quentin Tarantino). The suburban mobster is outraged that this "dead nigger" has been dragged into his home. Yet to display that he could not really be a racist, the film then cuts away to show that this bigot is married to an African-American woman. The fact that he has a sexual relationship with a black woman is supposed to clear up any mis-understandings about his repeated stream of utterances about "dead niggers"!

The white corporate-oriented media loves to publicize stories about "black bigotry." Several years ago, for instance, when the Oakland, California, board of education suggested that African-American young people may learn best in an environment that validates the language they actually speak ("ebonics") in their neighborhoods and in daily interactions with friends, blacks everywhere were attacked for "rejecting" standard English, as if none of us speak it. When African-American students now demand black studies courses, or advocate campus hous-ing emphasizing Caribbean, African, and black American cultural traditions and identity, they are subjected to ridicule as proponents of "self-segregation."

We will never uproot racism by pretending that everyone shares an equal and common responsibility for society's patterns of discrimination and inequality. Black people were never "equal partners" in the construction of slavery, Jim Crow seg-regation, and ghettoization. We weren't individually or collectively consulted when our criminal-justice system imprisoned one-third of our young men, or when we continue to be burdened with twice the unemployment rate of whites. To be "color blind" in a virulently racist society is to be blind to the history and reality of oppres-sion. To forget the past and to refuse to acknowledge the color-coded hierarchies that constitute our parallel racial universes is to evade any responsibility for racial peace in the future.

Perhaps the greatest lie in the arsenal of the "color-blind" proponents of racism is the assertion that black people can be understood only as part of the larger nar-rative of standard American history. That is to say that "black history" is some-how inferior to or at odds with "American history." To be part of the national project, culturally and ideologically, means that we must surrender and abandon those lessons we've learned in our struggles along the way.

While it is certainly true that black Americans are survivors of a very destruc-tive historical process from slavery, Jim Crow segregation, and ghettoization, we know within ourselves that we have never stood silently by, succumbing to the forces of white oppression. Any understanding of black history illustrates that we have consistently fought to maintain a unique set of cultural values that have shaped and continue to define our core identities as a people. We have, in effect, always been not only the makers of "our" history but also central to the con-struction and evolution of the larger American experience.

What are the cultural reservoirs that create the psychological, emotional, and cultural foundation of the strength and vision that the adventure of blackness in American life has produced? Even in the shadows of slavery, we found our human-ity in the gift of song. Our music tells us much about who we are, how we have worked, how we have loved, where we've been, and where we're going. From the blues of the Mississippi Delta, to the soaring sounds of bebop in Harlem in the

1940s, to the provocative rhythms of today's hip hop, black music reflects the pulse and sensibility of blackness.

Black history and culture reveal the gift of grace, the fluidity of motion and beauty that an oppressed people have claimed as their own. It is constantly recreated in many ways: from the artistry of dance to the spectacular athleticism of Michael Jordan. Grace is the ability to redefine the boundaries of possibility. We as a people were not supposed to survive the ordeal of oppression and Jim Crow segregation, yet our very existence speaks to the creative power of our collective imagination. That power is reflected in our language, the rhythm of gospel, and the power of black preachers on Sunday morning in our churches. That power is found in the creative energy of our poets and playwrights. The gift of grace can be heard in the writings of Toni Morrison, James Baldwin, Amiri Baraka, and Alice Walker.

The experience of work has always been the foundation of black strength and capacity-building throughout history. Slavery was the only moment in American history when people of African descent experienced full employment: Everybody worked. If financial gain was commensurate with hard work, African Americans would undoubtedly be among the wealthiest people on earth. Yet despite our economic marginalization, despite the historic pattern of receiving barely 60 cents for every dollar of wages that comparable white work commands, we nevertheless have found real meaning in the world of work. Black labor, more than any other, is responsible for establishing much of the foundations of the economic productivity of this country. Black working-class women and men have for generations been at the forefront of the trade-union movement and collective efforts to improve the quality of life and the conditions of work for all Americans.

And then there is the historical strength of family and community, kinship and neighbors within the black experience. An oppressed people cannot survive unless there is close cooperation and mutual support by and for each other. The reservoir of strength within the black family has been anchored in our recognition that kinship is collective, not nuclear, in structure.

Throughout black history, along with the strength of family there has been the strength of our faith. During slavery, a prayer was in many ways an act of resistance. When we sang "Steal Away to Jesus," our eyes looked to the North Star, to the faraway promised land of freedom. Today that faith still resounds as the cultural heart of black community life in thousands of towns and cities across the country. From the courage of Dr. Martin Luther King, Jr., to the contemporary activism of a Jesse Jackson or an Al Sharpton, black faith has been most powerful as a historical force when spirituality reinforces fundamental social change.

It is only through the telling of our stories about the destructive dynamics of racialization that many white Americans will be able finally to come to terms with the social costs of "whiteness," for themselves, their children, and for the larger society. No genuine dialogue about race is possible when millions of whites are taught to believe that blacks have been marginal to the construction of American society, or that the "race problem" has now been solved.

No meaningful dialogue can take place when some whites still think about race as a "zero-sum game," where any economic or political advances by racial minorities must come at their expense. I believe that the only way for us to move toward a nonracist society is for white Americans to acknowledge that the struggles and sacrifices that blacks have made to destroy structural racism in all of its forms throughout history have directly contributed to enriching and expanding the meaning of democracy not just for ourselves, but for everyone within our society. As Martin Luther King, Jr., observed in the "Letter from Birmingham Jail," the "real heroes" of American democracy are those who actively challenged the immorality and injustices of racial inequality:

> *One day the South will recognize its real heroes. They will be the James Merediths, with the noble sense of purpose that enables them to face jeering, and hostile mobs, and with the agonizing loneliness that characterizes the life of the pioneer. They will be old, oppressed, battered Negro women, symbolized in a seventy-two-year-old woman in Montgomery, Alabama, who rose up with a sense of dignity and with her people decided not to ride segregated buses, and who responded with ungrammatical profundity to one who inquired about her weariness: "My feets is tired, but my soul is at rest." They will be the young high school and college students, the young ministers of the gospel and a host of their elders, courageously and nonviolently sitting in at lunch counters and willingly going to jail for conscience' sake. One day the South will know that when these disinherited children of God sat down at lunch counters, they were in reality standing up for what is best in the American dream and for the most sacred values in our Judeo-Christian heritage, thereby bringing our nation back to those great wells of democracy which were dug deep by the founding fathers in their formulation of the Constitution and the Declaration of Independence.*

Endnotes

1 *"Groups tend to be more immoral than individuals"*: Martin Luther King, Jr., "Letter from Birmingham Jail," in *Why We Can't Wait* (New York: Harper & Row, 1964).

4 *Under a system most of us call "democracy"*: See "The State of the Estate Tax," *Washington Post*, June 6, 2002.

7 *"Doctors, lawyers and Cadillac dealers"*: Kevin Phillips, "Dynasties! How Their Wealth and Power Threaten Democracy," *The Nation*, July 8, 2002, pp. 11–14.

7 *"Greater than any comparable period during the 19th century"*: Kevin Phillips, "The New Face of Another Gilded Age," *Washington Post*, May 26, 2002.

7 *Inequality that is structured across the entire American social order*: See Matt Moore, "Wal-Mart Passes Exxon to Top Fortune 500 List," *Washington Post*, April 1, 2002.

10 *Classified as nonwhite after 1923*: See Gary Okihiro, "Cheap Talk, er, Dialogue," *Souls*, vol. 1, no. 3 (Summer 1999), pp. 52–58; and Ronald Takaki, *A Different Mirror: A History of Multicultural America* (Boston: Little, Brown, 1993).

31

Country Roads Lined with Running Fences

A Dozen Story Problems about the Place of Place

MICHAEL MARTONE

Director of Creative Writing at University of Alabama, Michael Martone presents a set of reflections on "place" in this piece. From his book Racing in Place, *this annotated list offers a series of connected reflections on the nature and function of place. This piece speaks to the complex interplay of physical locations and how people imagine their relationships to them as well as what competing or conflicting desires these constructs of place evince.*

1. ***Where to have lunch?*** One summer, in Centerville, Iowa, I had supper in a restaurant on the largest town square in the world. At one time, chances were good that on most town squares of the Midwest there would be a steak place, or a pizza parlor, soda fountain, or newsstand, run by a Greek family. Perhaps the only indication would be a special salad on the menu, a gyros machine by the grill, or a fading picture of a white island and blue water tacked to the wall. Ten years before, George, the restaurant owner, came to Centerville from the Peloponnese by way of the Quad Cities, where he had family in the restaurant business. He worked most of the year but shut down to return to Greece with his family. He told me he sent his wife and child back for good since he

wanted the boy to grow up there. One day, he thought, he'll return for good, too. It was the winter he had never grown used to. Though Centerville had been very good for business, it could never be home. When I told him how much I'd liked traveling in Greece, how I'd look to make it over there again, he did something remarkable. He scribbled down his name and the addresses of cousins in Athens, folks in his village, and told me where to find them when I am in Kalamata. "Ask for Yiorgos," he said. "Say that you are from Iowa."

2. *Iowa is where exactly?* Actually, I am from Indiana—that's where I was born and grew up. I know the feel of the Midwest. In Ireland, in Poland, in Italy one can sense a loss and a resignation to the fact that much of the country's population lives somewhere else. America as a nation has never suffered a diaspora, but natives of Iowa, of Indiana, and of the Midwest know of this fate. Our migrations are internal, our shifts of population covered by an easy freedom to move about and an illusion that most places are the same or can be made to feel the same. Talking with George in Centerville, Iowa, reminded me of Greece, where most everyone has a friend or relative who has gone away. And being reminded of that brought me home, back to Iowa, to Indiana, to my midwestern home, where people have not gone to a new country but have certainly gone away.

3. *Where exactly is this Midwest?* Where are its borders? What are its colors on the map? It depends on whom you ask. Iowans generally sketch roughly the Big Eight states—Iowa, Nebraska, Kansas, Missouri, and the Dakotas—as the prime midwestern states. Sometimes they will reach for Oklahoma. When asked about Indiana or Ohio the usual consensus is that those places lie in the East. They are surprised to learn that Hoosiers think of the Midwest as the Big Ten—Michigan, Ohio, Indiana, Illinois, Wisconsin, and part of Iowa. Iowans want to know what "Easterners" from Indiana would call what they call the Midwest. I say the Plains, of course. It becomes more interesting when I ask what defines a midwestern state. It must be rooted in agriculture, they say. I answer that it should be a balance between farming and manufacturing. They narrow their definition. The agriculture must be a special kind. It must be corn. Their definition of the Midwest derives from their home state, of course. It hasn't defined anything at all, but has been shaped to fit the place.

4. *Where exactly is the Midwest?* We should perhaps be more interested in what the confusion reveals than in pinning down the actual boundaries of the place, though it is probably wise to spend a few moments in definition. Again, where is the Midwest? And beyond that, what does characterize the region? How does it differ from other regions? Does it differ at all? These are important questions in developing a sense of place. Perhaps we assign an identity too easily, use the names without thinking what we want them to represent. Despite the confusion about its location, people agree that the Midwest is a good place to be *from*. It is as if we keep the region purposely vague in order to include as many people as possible as natives. "I am *from* the Midwest": that coin is worth collecting.

5. *What is the real question?* So the real question is: Why do so many of us want to be from a place that is nowhere and everywhere? The preposition is

important, the *from.* Even those of us who still live in the Midwest, no matter how you define it, still would say we are from the Midwest, as if its special properties rub off on us only at birth and that since birth we have been getting farther and farther away.

6. *What is what it is not?* Dorothy realizes when she bumps down in Oz that she is not in Kansas anymore. If there is anything that characterizes a literature of the Midwest, it is this sense of discovery through absence. Nick Carraway, the narrator of F. Scott Fitzgerald's *The Great Gatsby,* realizes as the story ends that it is a tale of the Midwest and of a midwesterner in New York totally unequipped to live in the East. As the novel ends, he is preparing to return home. Leaving home, the Midwest, in order to see home clearly is a driving force in the themes of midwestern literature and life. Stories of the Midwest often begin at the moment of turning back from afar and the hero gaining sight for the first time of a distant beauty. Living in the Midwest, we know a truth about this coming and going. Many, many people have left, but few actually return. Though Dorothy keeps demanding to be sent home, though she tells us once she is home that there is nothing like it, we are uneasy. It is a black and white world in Kansas. Why would she, why would we leave the technicolor of Oz?

7. *What does New Jersey have to do with anything?* A friend who grew up in New Jersey noticed right away that the Midwest had no walls. There are picket fences, strung wire, cyclone mesh, the red staves of snow fence, chicken wire, barbed wire, even electric line. But no walls. My friend defines the Midwest that way—a country woven in wire fence—and he always argues that beyond the lack of boulders in the ground to build walls, the fences reflect something else inherent in the people who live here. You can see through fences, he says. They do not block out the subtle and endless beauty of the prairie and field. But at the same time the fence breaks up that vast and overwhelming horizon into bits of manageable places. The fence builders want it both ways. It is an aesthetic compromise between private property and being part of a neighborhood. A fence allows its builder to say, "I am alone. Separate, not different. I've got nothing to hide, but don't come too close." It is a delicate balance. There are many such balances here between the individual and the community. The fences of the Midwest give us tangible evidence of the web of these relationships.

8. *What does the current disappearance of fences and fence rows tell us about the state of affairs now?* The disappearance of fence rows could be written off to the use of larger machines with broader turning radii, the lack of animals on farms, the trouble of maintaining the wire. But does it reveal something deeper? The simplest definition of place carries within it the notion of limits, of boundary. Part of what we believe as Americans, indeed what brought many people here in the first place, includes the contradictory idea of a country unbounded, a place of limitless opportunity. In the realm of advertising's easy diction, *you can have it all.* The disappearance of physical fences in the midwestern landscape might represent a transformation, a shift in interior space as well. A rickety, rusty wire fence was the product of the

meeting between the irresistible force of individual enterprise and the immovable object of community. Fences snare and enmesh but are flexible, movable, many-gated. Their disappearance could signal to us the release of an unbridled force that is dangerous to community. An article in the *Des Moines Register* on the obsolescence of the township included a picture showing the entire government and voting body of a township in Iowa: a farmer, his wife, and their daughter. The question that arises is this: When does a town stop being a town? What is the critical mass of a community? The presence of fences tells us finally that there are people here, that the land is divided up among them. As people have left the Midwest the fences have come down. Their absence does not bring people closer together but only indicates that there is no one here. Someone will always own the land but someone will not always live here.

9. *Where did they go?* The roads that have taken people away can also be thought of in the same way as fences—as physical manifestations of our interior feelings about place and the land. As we've seen, they are the quickest way out of town for our writers, our children, our friends, ourselves but also the way back. Roads too form our boundaries. The section roads lie like a net over the land, divide it, define it, parcel it out, and impose the order of place. But the road is also a common way owned by no one and everyone. When we usually think of the literature of the road, say of Kerouac, we think of the road as a conveyor, as something that moves through, something that is part of somewhere else. Yet, it is also part of the things that stay put. We treat the road as Euclideans would have us treat a line—the distance between two points having no width. But the road, the sidewalk, the corners, the squares are rich with metaphoric meanings where once again the individual meets the group of which he or she is a part. The road may bound us, but it also binds us together. The road is a place itself, as a fence row is, and both must be thought of more as transmitting membranes, like skin, at once tough and intimate.

10. *Can you be more specific?* Good writing is always specific. Henry James wrote that good writing is "selected perception and amplification." There is literally a world of difference between using one word over another, "a" instead of "the." As a writer selects words, he or she is making a series of choices that include or exclude parts of the world. William Faulkner called the county in Mississippi he wrote about his "postage stamp of land." Though writers narrow and select, they often cordon off a precinct sacred to them. Readers discover that within those boundaries there are areas of human experience that seem unlimited. Perhaps it is a quirk in the way we are made, but it appears the more specific a writer is, the easier it is for a reader to generalize. In geometry, we know that a finite plane bounded on all sides still contains infinite points. Stories, poems, essays work that way, too. The more tightly bounded, the more restricted a work is, the richer we find it. Author and authority are related words. To be author of a specific place is, in a way, to be its god, its creator. But the place a god creates can never be as detailed as the larger world it is part of, for the writer faces the fact that he or she is

limited, mortal. Writing then, by its limitation, by acknowledging its human scale, still participates in something grand. The writer shares in the creation of the universe by creating a postage stamp. In Thornton Wilder's *Our Town,* a character receives a letter addressed to her, her street, her town, her state, her country, her planet, her solar system, and on until it ends with the mind of God. Her thrilled response is that it got *here* anyway. It got here.

11. *Can you tell us a story?* If books are like places, then places are like books. Let me tell you a story. I was helping a farmer during planting. I was driving a tractor vibra-shanking a field of soybean stubble as the farmer followed behind me planting corn. The operation I was asked to do was an easy one, but I don't have much aptitude for machines. I wound up during one pass almost sliding into a ditch of water when I tried to make the turn. Braking, I stalled the engine, and shaken, I couldn't get the thing in gear to start up again. The farmer all this time was steadily catching up. The harder I tried to free myself and prove my competence, the worse things got. The farmer's son was working in the next field. He yelled to me that he was on his way to help. In a few minutes I saw him poling down the ditch on a raft made of old fence posts, and he saved the day. There isn't much to the story. That's not why I told it. What is interesting is that when I visit that farm now sooner or later that little story is told again—how Michael got stuck and Eric came to the rescue. Sometimes it is told to people who haven't heard the story. But more often than not, we tell it to ourselves. It is as if the story is another building constructed a few springs ago. It is a part of the layout of the place, part of the map. This little story takes its place with hundreds of others. The field where I had my adventure is called Cottonwood for the tree that used to be there sixty years ago. When Farmer Brown tells Eric to cultivate Cottonwood, it is a one-word story. The tree no longer exists. The story does. Places exist in two dimensions. They exist in the physical realm, but also in time. I will exist as part of a place on that farm as long as people tell the story. Though the dirt, the ditch, the crops exist; a place needs a person to name it. Cottonwood. It is interesting what we call the documents that transfer land: deeds and titles. The land itself carries its own deeds and titles. To gain a sense of place is to be sensitive to stories about places.

12. *Here's your hat; what's your hurry?* A sense of place is a complex idea further confounded by our relationship to it. We all labor to resolve two opposing forces in our lives. On one hand we have a desire to be rooted, to belong—literally to be long—in a place. On the other hand, we wish to be free of those connections, to keep moving through. As with all compelling conflicts, this one is not easily resolved, probably not to be resolved. People now move far more than they stay put. By moving we find it easier to ignore those limits imposed on our lives. The fences on either side of the road seem more like a chute channeling us on to some wonderful future. To have a sense of place is to sense limits, to sense our own deaths, a specific plot of ground where we will be buried and where our bodies will become part of the plot of ground. By accepting the limits a place imposes, we gain the ability to leave a mark. By being part of a place, we become it.

32

Rodents

ANNA MCCARTHY

Anna McCarthy's brief reflection "Rodents" appeared in a 2007 issue of the Journal of Visual Culture. *McCarthy, an Associate Professor of Cinema Studies at New York University, makes several comparisons between the computer mouse and common rats. Such an unexpected juxtaposition enables an insightful analysis of and argument about a problem—the environmental impact of the computer mouse—and the human attitudes that produced it.*

Abstract

The computer mouse is the latest rodent on municipal vermin lists. The poisonous electronic waste that piles up on our city streets makes digital humanity seem as much an urban infestation as the common rat.

Keywords
digital culture • electronic waste • environmentalism • new media • rats • urban space

Roadkill. A rodent, squashed and eviscerated, splayed flat in the gutter. It's a common enough sight in New York and other big cities. Perhaps the most recent addition to the urban vermin list is the computer mouse. Mice, according to University of Florida scientists, leak enough lead to be classified as hazardous waste under current EPA guidelines (Hoover, 2004). They are a plastic pestilence.

Like the rat problem, the electronic waste infestation is a problem of human making. In industrialized places, rats and electronics follow people wherever they go. Rats, in fact, exhibit a powerful affinity for the wired worlds we make. As Robert Sullivan (2004) explains in his transfixingly detailed account of the history and habitat of *Rattus norvegicus* (the common brown rat), 'rats, like mice, seem to be attracted to wires' (p. 7). It seems that rodent mice, as well as electronic ones, are part of the urban digital infrastructure.

There are differences, of course. The urban rat eats garbage, but e-waste *is* garbage. And while rats succumb to poison, the mouse *is* poison. Still, both are creatures that creep and dart along the everyday surfaces of our lives, accompanying our late-night wanderings through the pages of the internet or along empty city streets. They are long-tailed, clicking, red-eyed companions to our most solitary selves.

For both rats and computer mice, touch is a powerful sense. Rats, Sullivan tells us, are 'trigmophilic'—touch loving (p. 12). As they travel through tunnels and down alleys, they are in almost constant contact with the walls along which they move. Rats use this ongoing communication with their environment as a vehicle for memory, retaining in their muscles tactile maps of the routes they travel. The mouse we use to interact with the screen is similarly motivated by touch, requiring constant contact if it is to navigate space successfully. The mouse also extends the human hand into the virtual world of the screen—a situation which, when you think about it, makes digital life a trigmophilic kind of experience.

Something has been gnawing at me ever since I saw my first computer mouse on the street, and the digital trigmophilia of the mouse user has helped clarify what it is. All this e-waste drives home the terrifying ways that humans themselves resemble rodents, infesting the earth and corrupting it with our filthy leavings. I'm not particularly prone to eco-paranoia, but the tangled nests of dead electronics that litter the streets of Manhattan seem to encourage apocalyptic thinking.

References

Hoover, A. (2004) 'Discarded Cell Phones, Printers, Keyboards, Etc. May Be Hazardous Waste', *UF News*, 1 March. URL (consulted Oct. 2006): http://www.napa.ufl.edu/2004news/ewaste.htm

Sullivan, R. (2004) *Rats: Observations of the History and Habitat of the City's Most Unwanted Inhabitants*. New York: Bloomsbury Publishing.

33

In Public: The Street and Spaces of Pleasure

LINDA McDOWELL

Linda McDowell is Professor of Human Geography at University of Oxford. In this chapter from Gender, Identity and Place: Understanding Feminist Geographies *McDowell presents an account of the social forces, gendered assumptions of women in particular, that shape public spaces and how various populations experience those spaces differently. This chapter demonstrates how inquiries into social life and power can originate in the physical arrangement of both public and domestic or private space.*

Introduction

In this chapter we move from the internal spaces of the home and the workplace back outside, to the public or open spaces of the street and the park, and the public or quasi-public spaces of leisure: bar, cafés, swimming pools and pool or snooker clubs, the department store and the public house. Here many of the themes that we have already examined in previous chapters reoccur: about the ideal and beautiful female body, for example, from chapter 2, and about the social constitution and gendered nature of different spaces and activities. However, I suggest that it is important to distinguish public and quasi-public spaces of leisure because they are a different *kind* of space than either the home or the workplace, and in them the constitution and maintenance of gender relations take particular forms. Thus, according to Neil Smith's (1993) definition which I introduced earlier, these spaces are spaces at a different scale from the ones we have considered already. This is not to deny that spaces or scales are social constructions, with complex and messy overlaps between them. The public spaces of leisure that we shall consider here, for example, are also workplaces for the many waged employees who maintain the services provided within them, but in this chapter the focus will be solidly on the gendered social relations of consumption.

When we turn to public spaces we clearly see the effect of the associations of the public/private divide with gender divisions. Because of the strong associations between women and the home, those interior spaces of domesticity, feminist investigations of public spaces have often focused on the problems and dangers that women experience 'outside' compared with an assumption that men may take for granted their freedom in and dominance of these spaces. Thus there is a significant literature about the ways in which women experience fear and anxiety, as well as physical danger, harassment and attack in streets and open spaces. I want to discuss this work but I also want to show that, paradoxically, the public spaces of the city have been significant locations in women's escape from male dominance and from the bourgeois norms of modern society. Indeed, I want to start with this latter area and return to the connections between gender divisions and the establishment and growing dominance of the norms of bourgeois respectability during the modern era. First, however, it is important to remember, as I have emphasized elsewhere, that here too the division between the public and private, just like the distinction between geographical scales, is a socially constructed and gendered division that feminist scholarship has challenged and attempted to overturn.

As you may remember, I suggested earlier that industrial societies, in the mid to late nineteenth century, witnessed the establishment of an ideology that constructed women (or rather so-called decent women) as angels of the hearth. This ideology has dominated Western thought, housing provision and urban planning since that period. Its significance for definitions of 'the home' was outlined in chapter 3, and some of the implications for urban land-use divisions in chapter 4. Here I want to look at the converse as it were: at how women who did not conform or keep to their place were constructed as wicked or fallen, subjected to abuse or vulnerable to physical danger, forcing them to reconsider their decision to participate in the public sphere. But I also want to show how semi-public spaces, such as the large department stores that began to be built in nineteenth century cities, created a place where women might escape from the confines of domesticity and male presence/control, even if only for short and temporary periods. Thus the public and semi-public arenas of industrial towns and cities were paradoxical spaces for women, where danger but also relative freedom awaited them.

I then want to move on to twentieth-century spaces and contemporary issues about gender and the public arena, through a discussion of women's relationship to open spaces, as seen variously through the eyes of women artists and writers. I also want to look at men's relationship to open spaces, to streets and to parks, especially the relationship of those men who cannot or choose not to conform to hegemonic notions of masculinity. Finally I want to assess the effects of the images of familialism and heterosexuality that pervade a wide range of spaces of pleasure. Here I shall focus in particular on beach holidays and other holiday places, and on urban spectacles presented in spaces of pleasure and desire.

Citizenship and Public Space

In this chapter the predominant emphasis is on the case-study material, as the theoretical basis of the divisions between public and private space and their implications for gender have been thoroughly discussed already. But here I want to blur that sharp association between gender and space and suggest that there is a messier and more complicated set of relationships to be uncovered since so many activities transgress the clear associations between feminity and privacy on the one hand, and masculinity and public spaces on the other. Men and women are variously divided and united by social characteristics—their race, age and sexuality, for example—and so do not always line up clearly on one side or other of a gender divide.

Here, in this chapter, I also want to introduce debates about the definition of citizenship and human rights, because conflicts over the use of public spaces often revolve round differential claims about the right of occupation. Liberal theorists argue that each and every individual as a member of the polity has an equal right to be in the public arena, but as feminists and others have pointed out, this right is often denied in practice. There is, in the operation of state-defined rules and in common practices, an assumption of moral worth in which *de facto* as opposed to *de jure* rights of citizenship are defined as open to those who are deserving or who are capable of acting responsibly. The less deserving and less responsible are defined as unworthy of or unfitted for the privileges of full citizenship. Thus in practice, as critics from both the left and the right have recognized (Sandel 1996; Sklar 1991; Young 1990b), citizenship is not an inclusive but an exclusive concept.

A range of individuals and particular social groups are excluded from the widest spectrum of access to public spaces and arenas, on the grounds either of their transgressive behaviour and their refusal to recognize the common rights of all or, alternatively, on the grounds of their need for protection from the hurly-burly of the public arena. It is on this latter set of grounds that women have been, and continue to be, excluded from equal access to the public arena. Thus women's construction as dependent on men, both economically and morally, or as lesser beings—as fragile or in need of protection—reduces their rights to freedom (Pateman 1988, 1989). A clear illustration here lies in the judgments made in cases of rape and harassment, when judges often argue that women should remain indoors for their own protection. Calls for curfews for women and girls when men who are suspected to be dangerous are 'loose' are common. Feminist campaigns to 'reclaim the streets' or 'reclaim the night', along with counterclaims for curfews for men, challenge the assumed greater freedom for men to occupy open and public space.

Interestingly, in these cases of rape or murder, women also appear as transgressors who through their actions should also be excluded from the public sphere. Thus the British judiciary often indicates in such cases that a woman who has been out too late or in the wrong place deserves what happened; the element of fault, it is implied, is on her part rather than on the part of the man who attacked her (see J. Smith 1989). A number of feminist geographers have looked at questions of women's safety on the streets (Valentine 1990; Pain 1991), although it is also salutary to remember that abuse and physical harm are more likely to be perpetrated by someone known to the victim, often within the 'haven' of the home, than by a stranger in a public arena.

A range of other groups are also discriminated against in terms of access to particular spaces. Young people, people of colour and 'countercultural' groups often find that they are harassed and moved along (McKay 1995; Valentine 1996) as urban public spaces become increasingly less accessible and privatized through, for example, the use of private security firms to patrol the spaces between corporate buildings (see M. Davis's vivid description of this in Los Angeles (1989) and Zukin's work on New York (1995)). For the growing number of homeless people living on the streets, in doorways, subways and other tunnels (Morton 1995), increasing surveillance of urban spaces causes great problems.

Feminist political theorist Nancy Fraser has argued that if we are to take these exclusions seriously, then we have to rethink our notion of public space as sets of multiple and differentiated public arenas to which some groups have access but from which others are excluded. Like the postcolonial theorists who argue that there are subaltern subjects who are able to challenge the power and discourses of colonialism, Fraser suggests the notion of 'subaltern counterpublics', which are public spaces where marginalized groups might articulate their needs, so constructing them in opposition to the dominant or legitimate uses of these spaces (Fraser 1990).

Some subaltern counterpublics perhaps exist already. We might include spaces of protest, such as New Age encampments perhaps, or the tunnels and trees of road protesters, although the work of the geographer Don Mitchell (1995) on the history of the People's Park in Berkeley, which was claimed by countercultural groups in the late 1960s, shows how hard it is to preserve spaces like these in the face of the state and private property interests. Protest movements trying to maintain subaltern spaces in Britain have had the same experience, as participants are torn out of trees and tunnels or evicted from squatted houses by police and specialist security firms.

But public spaces are important in that they are where the diversity that constitutes 'the public' is most apparent and where idealized notions of 'the public interest' are challenged. As David Harvey (1992) showed in his analysis of the use of Tompkins Square, a park in Manhattan, the multiple users of this space—young women and children, Hell's Angels and bikers, the deinstitutionalized, people who abuse a variety of substances, the homeless and business people—found mutual and tolerant coexistence impossible. Harvey drew on a range of sources for his paper and made vivid use of press coverage. He starts, for example, with extracts from an article in the *International Herald Tribune* (1 August 1989) by John Kifner. At the time Kifner wrote his report, as well as three hundred homeless people living in the park there were also:

> *Skateboarders, basketball players, mothers with small children, radicals looking like 1960s retreads, spikey-haired punk rockers in black, skinheads in heavy working boots looking to beat up the radicals and punks, dreadlocked Rastafarians, heavy metal bands, chess players, dog walkers all occupy their spaces in the park, along with profes-*

*sionals carrying their dry-cleaned suits to the renovated 'gentrified'
buildings that are changing the character of the neighbourhood.
(Quoted in Harvey 1992: 588)*

Two years later an article in the *New York Times* pointed out the dilemma that
faced the city's planners in attempting to resolve the conflicts arising from these multiple users:

> *There are neighborhood associations clamouring for the city to close the
> park and others just as insistent that it remain a refuge for the city's
> down-trodden. The local Assemblyman yesterday called for a curfew
> that would effectively evict more than a hundred homeless people camped
> out in the park. Councilwoman Miriam Friedlander instead recom-
> mended that Social Services, like healthcare and drug treatment, be
> brought directly to the people living in the tent city. 'We do not find the
> park is being used appropriately,' said Deputy Mayor Barbara J. Fife, 'but
> we do recognize that there are various interests.' There is, they go on to
> say, only one thing that is a consensus, first that there isn't a consensus
> over what should be done, except that any new plan is likely to provoke
> more disturbances, more violence. (Quoted in Harvey 1992: 590)*

Clearly issues about the multiple occupancy of urban spaces raise difficult questions
about how to adjudicate between conflicting notions of appropriate access and
use. As I shall show below, twentieth-century concerns about differential access to
particular spaces and places in the city have historical precedents.

Modernity and Urban Public Spaces: The City Flâneur and the Flâneuse

At the end of the millennium when issues about difference and diversity are central
in geographic research agendas, there is a noticeable retrospective flavour to many
analyses in their return to how these issues developed a century previously. Although
the turmoil of a postmodern world seems challenging to many, the huge social and
economic upheavals that wrenched people from the land and from their homelands
in the vast expansion of industrial urbanization in Western Europe and the US in
the nineteenth and early twentieth centuries not only reshaped the relations between
space, gender and identity but also transformed cultural representations. One of
the reactions to the huge and unprecedented growth of cities in the nineteenth century was a set of new movements in the arts, in painting, poetry and literature, and
the development of new cultural forms such as photography and the cinema in
which reactions to the vast social changes were explored. Thus Raymond Williams
has argued that

> *the facts of the development of the city into the metropolis are basic. We
> can see how certain themes in art and thought developed as specific
> responses to the new and expanding kinds of nineteenth-century city and
> then, as the central point of analysis, see how these went through a vari-
> ety of actual artistic transformations . . . in certain metropolitan con-
> ditions of the early twentieth century. (Williams 1989: 39)*

During this period, between about 1850 and 1920, modernism as an artistic move-ment became established, challenging previous ideals of artistic representation and culminating in movements such as Dadaism, surrealism, cubism and so on. It was also a key period of political unrest and social ferment in Western Europe and the US, of which the suffrage movement was an important part. So changes in women's status and their everyday lives were also a key part of urbanization and modernity.

The artistic and cultural movements of modernity, as well as the social upheavals, have attracted a great deal of research attention recently from a range of disciplinary perspectives, including geography. In the so-called 'cultural turn' in our discipline, for example, there has been a new interest in literature and art as source materials (see, for example, the work by Cosgrove and Daniels (1988) on painting and architecture) and in the built environment of the period (see, for example, Mona Domosh's book about New York and Boston (1996a) that I men-tioned in chapter 4) in understanding modernity. It has been argued, however, that in this work in general, the experiences of women have received insufficient atten-tion. The key reason for this, Janet Wolff (1985) has suggested, is an overwhelm-ing focus on the public arena of life, that is the sphere dominated by men, since industrial urbanization was accompanied by a growing spatial separation of men's and women's lives. In the great new cities of the nineteenth century, a new male fig-ure appeared, that of the flâneur or voyeur who took pleasure in his role as an urban onlooker. I want to examine some of the arguments about the place of these male urban observers and, in particular, assess the possibility that they might have had a female counterpart.

The writings of French poet and commentator, Charles Baudelaire, were crucial in the recognition of the significance of urban change. Indeed, modernism as an urban artistic movement drew some of its earliest inspiration from his work. In an essay 'The painter of modern life', written between 1859 and 1860, Baudelaire (1963) outlined a set of arguments about the fleeting and transitory nature of urban experience. He suggested that the artificiality of urban life was based on a confu-sion between images and reality in cities where dreams and spectacles were the basis of consumption. The quintessential figure of the modern metropolis, according to Baudelaire, was that of the flâneur: the strolling observer, who gazed at but did not participate in the spectacular developments in the city. The flâneur was an anony-mous figure in the urban crowd, invisible but all-seeing, a spectator who was, accord-ing to Frisby, 'a prince who everywhere rejoices in his incognito' (1985:19).

These ideas about the fleeting and anonymous nature of social interactions in the metropolis became an important element in the sociology of urbanism developed later in the century, predominantly in Germany, by Simmel, Tönnies and others, whose work so influenced the Chicago School of urban sociology in the US in the first two decades of the new century, and later the development of urban geography. (Interestingly Simmel was one of the first academics to permit women to attend his seminars at the University of Berlin before they were formally admitted as students.)

For Baudelaire, and succeeding theorists, the flâneur inevitably was a man, as it was only men at that time who had the freedom to 'hang out' and spectate. Women in the mid-nineteenth century, or rather respectable middle-class women, were not accepted participants in the urban spectacle, but instead were those angels of the hearth confined to the sylvan peace of suburbia. Their less respectable sisters, however, joined the flâneur, or the urban dandy, as urban outsiders. As well as the flâneur, these outsiders or observers included, according to Baudelaire, poets, rag-pickers, lesbians, old women and widows (this group presumably assumed to be free from the unwanted heterosexual gaze) and prostitutes or whores, all of whom lived on their wits in the developing metropolises. The latter group of women, commonly and accurately termed 'streetwalkers', were regarded as fallen women in the hypocritical sexual double standard of the Victorian era. The very act of their appearance on the streets left the status of women open to interpretation and, often, to unwanted sexual attentions. In late Victorian Cambridge, for example, the early women students were required to wear gloves and hats when they ventured out into public in an attempt to distinguish them from the many women of 'easy virtue' in the city.

In her interesting paper, Janet Wolff pursued her claim that the sociology (and we might add the geography) of modernity neglects the specificities of most women's experiences of urban living. In her view 'the flâneur can only be male' (1985: 37). She suggests that the heroes of modernity, and modern urbanization—the flâneurs, the migrant and the stranger, who 'share the prospect and possibility of lone travel, of voluntary uprooting and of anonymous arrival at a new place' (p. 40)—are all men. It is perhaps her emphasis on the voluntary nature of travel that is significant here, as during the nineteenth and twentieth centuries as I describe in the next chapter, millions of women also became migrants, but more often through necessity than choice. But in Wolff's view the insistence in a wide range of writing on the transitory and fugitive nature of encounters as typical of life in the modern metropolis did not match the experience of most women.

In her book *The Sphinx in the City* and in a specific response to Wolff, Elizabeth Wilson (1991, 1992) disagreed with Wolff's contention that a female flâneur—a flâneuse—was an impossibility. She suggested that women actually had a great deal more freedom in nineteenth- and twentieth-century cities than Wolff allows, as the city was an arena where the strict and hierarchical ties of small towns and villages were relaxed and dissolved. Consequently, women too were able to experience something of the rootlessness and displacement at the heart of the urban experience.

In her edited collection of women's twentieth-century fiction about the city, Liz Heron (1993) also argues that the city is an important locus in the challenge to gender divisions. The city is, Heron suggests, a crucible for destabilizing the dichotomies that traditionally divide women's and men's lives. Thus, she suggests,

> the classic narrative of the city as a new beginning, a stage embarked upon in early adult life, has specific features for women in that the very notion of female self-invention defies the nature-culture divide; women being traditionally the stable, fixed point in a universe whose spaces wait to be explored by men, so that woman endures while man transcends. (Heron 1993: 3)

Instead, in the city the active independent woman came into her own. In the fiction that Heron included in her collection, associations between migration to the city and urban living and women's sexual and economic freedom are a central theme.

As Wilson noted, as the nineteenth century ended, women became increasingly visible in cities, passing through the streets on their way to the new employment opportunities afforded by the rise of clerical occupations and to go shopping in the growing number of department stores, where solitary women were able to linger, gazing at the goods in a manner reminiscent of the flâneur. This is not to deny, however, that women were still subjected to and constrained by the intrusive male gaze and, on occasion, actual verbal or physical harassment. However, as Heron notes, 'this can be less of a feature of city life than of a narrower social environment like that of the provincial town' (1993: 7). The very anonymity of the urban crowd may protect women, while at the same time that edge of danger is a lure to explore the city landscape.

Interestingly, Wilson has extended the argument about the significance of gender by suggesting that, far from being a representative of solid hegemonic masculinity, the figure of the flâneur was actually a transgressive one, a sexually insecure figure, and a passive spectator rather than, as is more commonly associated with masculinity, a participant. Indeed with his interest in clothes and shopping, the flâneur represented an unstable and unsettling version of a feminized masculinity. Heron also argued that the socially marginal female figures that dominate a large number of women's writings about the city are androgenous figures: independent and hard-pressed working-class women, artists' models or writers, if not deviants and misfits, outside the conventional bounds that define femininity. These female protagonists are women without family, often without men, and certainly escapees from the stultifying bonds of domesticity.

The work of scholars such as Elizabeth Wilson and writers such as Liz Heron, and now many others who are exploring the neglected aspects of women's experiences in the transformations associated with modernity, is crucial in countering previous dominantly male-centered accounts of these changes. Indeed the central burden of Wolff's original argument about the impossibility of a female flâneur was the theoretical impact this denial had on the development of the social sciences. Wolff documented the long disciplinary neglect of the private sphere and analysis of the reasons for women's exclusion from and/or limited participation in the public worlds of work and politics in the social sciences in general. This neglect, as I have noted already, was also a central feature of the history of geographical thought.

Transgressive Spaces for Men

The association of city spaces with the possibility of transgressing hegemonic versions of sexuality has not only been documented by feminist scholars as important for women. For men too the city is an arena permitting greater sexual freedoms, and the associations have been explored by several urban and gender theorists in different ways. Mapping the spatial significance of particular parts of a city for both hetero- and homosexual behaviour is a feature of some of this work. In, for example, her fascinating examination of paradoxical responses to nineteenth-century cities entitled *City of Dreadful Delight* (1992) Judith Walkowitz has looked at the ways in which bourgeois and ruling-class young men in Victorian England were drawn to particular urban spaces in their attempts to escape from what they saw as the stifling codes of conventional Victorian morality. For example, young men who lived in upper-class residential districts in the West End of London used the East End as their playground. Here they engaged in gambling and forbidden sports such as cockfighting and bearbaiting, as well as in varieties of heterosexual and homosexual experience outside the bounds of their 'normal' social and sexual relations with women of their own class background.

Other researchers have concentrated on uncovering the histories of public displays of homosexual behaviour and their urban associations. Thus in the expanding scholarship about gay men by queer theorists and others, an important emphasis is placed on the significance of particular places and spaces in the city which are identified with non-heterosexual identity. Indeed in some of the earliest work about gay gentrification, it was even claimed that gay men were not gay unless they had a visible territorial identity that marked them out as different.

Gay New York by the historian George Chauncey (1995) is a recent and interesting book that charts the significance of different spaces in the city for gay men between 1890 and 1940. Chauncey argues that gay men in the period before the Second World War were involved in a public world of gay social relationships that took place in certain parts of the city, especially in working-class areas. He shows how, in the Bowery for example, middle-class men were able to act out a gendered performance that both threatened and reinvented hegemonic notions of straight and gay masculinity. Chauncey used a wide array of sources, from newspapers to diaries, to reveal a network of clubs, bars, rooming houses, restaurants, YMCAs, areas in Central Park and public baths in New York City that were part of the landscape of gay sexuality. Over the period he studied, however, the visibility of gay cultures disappeared as gay men were forced back into the closet, especially through the strict enforcement of a public discourse about 'vice'.

His book is a welcome attempt to connect the social construction of alternative sexual identities to the symbolism and meaning of the urban landscape and also an important corrective to the idea that a visible gay male identity in New York City had to await the Stonewall riot of 1967 when the police raided a gay bar. Chauncey is currently working on a second volume to bring his analysis up to the present. Indeed it may be published before this book: if you are interested in contemporary New York, keep an eye out for it.

In a somewhat similar project in London, Frank Mort (1995) has constructed a series of what he termed 'archaeologies of city life'. Focusing on the Soho district in central London in the 1980s, he has shown how a regime of gendered commerce drew on a range of cultural constructions of urban space as an arena of consumption to create Soho as an area associated with a series of particular versions of masculine identity. Mort argues that a distinctive breed of media professionals and cultural entrepreneurs was responsible for the promotion of London as a renewed site of conspicuous wealth during the 1980s, creating a plurality of identities for men. Homosexual men were particularly important actors as their social and sexual identities were shaped by the new consumer regime. These new consumer-based forms of masculine identity were mapped on to the urban landscape, creating particular zones in the city which became closely associated with the new configurations of gendered culture and business. Mort identified Soho as an area that had long been associated with gendered regimes, although, at least visually, it was dominantly a seedy form of heterosexuality in previous decades. In the post-war period, however, and especially in the 1980s, Soho became a crucial quarter for the development of a particular type of homosexual identity.

Using a similar set of sources to Chauncey, Mort uncovered the uneven archaeology of Soho as a space with a history of sexual dissidence and cultural hybridity. In the early twentieth century, it was an area of bohemian habits and behaviour where an early mixture of immigrants, artists, theatre people, prostitutes, and jazz musicians rubbed shoulders. This bohemian and avant-garde culture, according to Mort, 'privileged a range of masculine types, [and] revolved around the personalities of the bohemian, the flaneur, and the man about town' (1995: 577). From the late 1960s onwards an organized sex trade dominated the area, but in its 1980s renaissance its older bohemian character was resurrected. The new consumer culture that developed in that decade drew on 'the gendered representations of city life which had been laid down at different historical moments'. Distinctive heterosocial and homosocial spaces were constructed, with differential access for particular versions of masculine identity.

But it was a particular version of homosexual masculinity that came to dominate the area. According to Mort there was a

> *growing commercialization of homosexuality. Bars and clubs, cafes and shops held out the promise of a homosexual life, shaped by the world of goods. In these commercial spaces the carnival promised a 'mixed' utopia—a co-mingling of lesbians, gay men, and their friends. But it was one constituency—young homosexual men—who laid particular claim to the streets of Soho. Despite the visibility of lesbians on the February Parade (an annual Queer Valentine Carnival), it was a masculine perspective on public space which predominated, even though this masculinity was defined as irregular and transgressive. (1995: 581)*

Entrepreneurs welcomed this spatial concentration of gay consumption although, as Mort noted, 'the absence of an accompanying residential population in Soho made it unlikely the district would foster the type of ethnically centred gay communities which had emerged in San Francisco's Castro district, or in New York's Greenwich Village' (p. 581). But its development was important, nevertheless, in making a gay identity visible and in involving gay men in planning issues in London.

Conspicuous Consumption and Spectacular Cities

The significance of the city as an arena of consumption has been a continuing theme through urban history and not only in the development of what Mort termed a 'regime of gendered commerce'. I want to trace some of the history of conspicuous consumption by returning to Baudelaire, or rather to his influence on Walter Benjamin, a German critic writing between the 1920s and 1940s, to sketch a brief outline of some of the relationships between consumption, urbanization and gender relations over the twentieth century. Benjamin drew, in his work on shopping and display in what is now known as the arcades project (see Buck-Morss's book *The Dialectics of Seeing* (1991)), on Baudelaire's ideas of the city as a magical and mythical spectacular display. In his work on what we now term conspicuous consumption, Benjamin analysed the rise of the department store at the end of the nineteenth century, looking in particular at the significance of glass arcades where goods were displayed for the voyeuristic pleasure of the passing spectator. Benjamin also studied fairs and exhibitions such as the one held at Crystal Palace for Queen Victoria's silver jubilee in 1851. Here, too, fabulous arrays of exotic goods, and even 'exotic' people, were displayed before the curious gaze of the passers-by. In such exhibitions, Benjamin saw the origins of a pleasure industry in which advertising based on spectacle and fantasy manipulated the desires of the masses.

As the twentieth century progressed, the significance of consumption and advertising became a central aspect of economic and urban development, and in the 1960s the French social theorist Guy Debord wrote about the rise of 'a society of the spectacle' (Debord 1994). Later, postmodern theorists such as Baudrillard have pointed to the rise of hyperreality, where images have become even more important than reality as places are marketed through the construction of image and fantasy. Perhaps the extreme example here is Las Vegas where visitors may sit in a pastiche of a Roman forum and watch the sun rise and set every twenty minutes. In waterfront developments across the globe, consumers may eat in Italian tavernas or buy clothes in mock Parisian shops and streets. But as David Harvey argued in his classic text *The Condition of Postmodernity* (1989), image and spectacle are the basis of more mundane urban economies near the end of the millennium. The mechanics of capitalist accumulation grind on as usual below the glittering surface of these displays and spectacles.

Almost all these theorists, however, have tended to underplay the significance of gender relations in the development of new urban spectacles. For women the rise of consumerism paradoxically not only rooted them in their place as consumers rather than producers, as frivolous not serious—as well as women actually being the consumers of the growing range of items, their images were used both to sell and display goods and as a metaphor for exotic otherness—but also led to the development of spaces of pleasure which women might visit without male escorts. I have already suggested that the department store is a location of great significance here. It is explored in more detail in the next section.

Shopping for Pleasure: Consumption as (Partial) Liberation

One of the most indispensable documents in the recent renewal of interest in the nineteenth-century shift to economies based on consumption is the novel *Au bonheur des dames* by Émile Zola, first published in 1882. A century later the University of California Press published a new edition *The Ladies Paradise,* with an introduction by the cultural critic Kristin Ross (Zola 1982). As Ross details, a number of technological and urban changes paved the way for Paris to lead the way in the development of department stores. The great public works of Baron Haussmann transformed the city's streets, and wide boulevards were carved through the heart of Paris. New pavements or sidewalks were laid down, allowing pedestrians to stroll and pause to gaze in the windows of the new stores. Developments in glass and iron technology permitted large windows to be inserted in shop frontages, and electrification enhanced the spectacular nature and theatricality of the displays that were constructed behind them. Changes in the internal layout of the new stores, too, combined with the great variety of goods assembled under one roof, increased the impression of shopping as a pleasurable leisure activity (see plate 6.1).

Plate 6.1 Contemporary shopping spaces: Brent Cross, North London

Ross argues that Aristide Boucicault, the French entrepreneur who took over the Bon Marché retail store in 1852 (it was later to become a major chain)

> *could be called the inventor of "browsing": passers-by could, for the first time, feel free to enter a store without sensing an obligation to buy something. Goods were rotated frequently, with a low mark-up in price; high volume and frequent rotation created the illusion of a scarcity in supply among what were in fact mass-produced and plentiful goods. (Ross in Zola 1982: vii–viii)*

The consumers who were the clientele of these new shops were predominantly women. The net result, as Rachel Bowlby (1985) argued in her analysis of consumer culture in the novels of Dreiser, Gissing and Zola, was that for middle-class women the fantasy world created in department stores, those 'colossal phantasmagoric dream factories' (Ross in Zola 1982: ix), became a 'second' home and a place of escape from their everyday lives and domestic routines. Tea rooms, lounges and powder rooms were provided for the comfort and respite of the consumers. But as Zola observed in his own notes to the novel, the desires of these female consumers were manipulated by male entrepreneurs, owners and floorwalkers: this paralleled women's construction as consumers rather than producers in the developing social relations of capitalism. Douglas, quoted in Domosh (1996b: 259), notes that 'the lady's function in a capitalist society was to appropriate and preserve both the values and commodities which her competitive husband, father, and son had little time to honor or enjoy; she was to provide an antidote and a purpose for their labour'.

Thus women's participation in the semi-public arena of the store and the street reinforced rather than challenged the developing separate spheres of Victorian industrial societies. And yet Zola also noticed, in this and his other novels, the potentially transgressive aspects of women's presence on the streets of expanding cities. He emphasized the feminine and volatile nature of the urban crowd, its delirious and contagious energy, and threatening female sexuality, which might spill over into violence. Elizabeth Wilson (1991), recognizing this threatening aspect of the urban crowd, has even suggested that this fear lay behind the development of town planning, resulting in women's reconfinement in the suburbs. It was believed in the nineteenth century that ' "public" woman, unlike public man, who is a serene and rational figure, is a woman prey to savage and violent impulses' (Ross in Zola 1982: xviii). Susanna Barrows (1981) has also suggested that behind this particular portrayal of a threatening feminine urban crowd lay the shadow of an even more intimidating group of women: French feminists and their association with moments of revolutionary fervour. In Britain too, especially in the suffrage movement at the beginning of the twentieth century, the women who took public action, marching and protesting in the streets, were portrayed as a huge threat to civil order, as well as unfeminine traitors to their sex.

In contemporary feminist analyses, the centrality of advertising and consumption in the social construction of feminine identities continues to be an important research focus, and as Robin Dowling (1993) has argued, a more nuanced understanding of the significance of place than is common in cultural studies work distinguishes the recent geographical scholarship. As she suggests, 'the construction of femininity occurs as part of the creation of place, and the characteristics of a place have an impact on the meaning of commodities and their associated femininity. [Thus] retailing is uniquely suited to an analysis of the links between femininity, place and commodities' (p. 296). In her own empirical study of Woodwards, a department store in downtown Toronto, Dowling shows how contradictory discourses of familialism (women as wives and mothers) and modernity (the superiority of scientific rationality) led to a particular notion of the feminine consumer in changes in the design and management of the store's food section in the period between 1945 and 1960.

In Britain, there is a growing collection of studies in what has been termed the 'new retail geography' and by other social scientists looking at the construction of gendered identities, of both consumers and retail assistants (see, for example, Michelle Lowe and Louise Crewe's (1996) work on The Gap and Paul Du Gay's (1996) case studies of the construction of hybrid subjects in clothing stores), in which the distinctions between leisure and work are blurred. In the new work, however, the fluidity of gendered identities, rather than the differences between women and men, are explored in particular circumstances. Indeed, at the end of the twentieth century, consumption, advertising and shopping have become identified as the essence of postmodernity, in which spectacle and desire combine to produce fluid subjects who are ambiguously gendered. As Simpson (1994) and Mort (1996), among others, have shown, the idealized male body is now as much an object of the male (both homoerotic and straight) gaze as the female body, and shopping has become an ambiguously gendered activity. However, as Wilson pointed out and I noted earlier, the flâneur himself more than a century earlier was a decentred and irresponsible subject, perhaps the forerunner of the new postmodern subject that is coming into being at the turn of the millennium.

Out (of Place) in the Open

I want now to illustrate a different aspect of the relationship between place, femininity and leisure, by looking at women's relationship to the 'great outdoors'. As the social construction of gender has been so bound up with a public/private distinction, it raises questions about a woman's place in the countryside and in the semi-rural parks and other green spaces in cities and on the urban fringe. I have shown, in chapter 2, how women's participation in particular sporting activities tends to be based on assumptions about decorum and the lack of physicality in the construction of ideal feminine bodies. Here I want to change the emphasis and focus on active and physical pleasures, looking specifically at questions about the place of women in the British countryside and in recreational woodlands on the urban-rural fringe. First we turn to the work of the British geographer Jacquelin Burgess and her colleagues (Burgess 1996; Burgess et al. 1988; Harrison and Burgess, 1994) and then to the specific responses of women of colour to the British countryside illustrated by photographer Ingrid Pollard.

For a number of years Burgess and her colleagues have explored the social and cultural dimensions of attitudes to and the use of a range of open spaces in southern England, including urban parks and semi-wild areas such as marshlands and recreational woodlands on the urban fringe. Gender, age and ethnic differences were explored in their work. Both the men and the women whom they interviewed for their research expressed fears of sexual attack: the women were fearful for their own safety, the men for their women friends and family—although official Home Office statistics show that teenage boys are actually the group most vulnerable to personal assault in public spaces. At the same time, however, young men, especially when gathered in large numbers, are also seen as threatening by other people. Burgess found that for Asian and Caribbean women the fear of racial attack from gangs of white men and/or youths inhibited their use and enjoyment of woodland areas even when they visited in family groups. So as we found in urban parks, like Tompkins Square in New York City, 'community' spaces are dominated by certain groups who exclude others, either by their actual behaviour or by the implicit threats that their presence poses.

While participation in rural activities such as woodland walks raises questions about safety for all women, for women of colour there is a further and more complex issue to explore, related to the representation and meaning of the British countryside, and to their exclusion from these representations. Although the meaning of landscapes is mobile and changing (think, for example, of the representation of the Lake District as barren and forbidding in the eighteenth century compared with its contemporary idyllic majesty), representations of the countryside are bound up with images of the nation. The protection of Britain's countryside is seen as part of the preservation of a national heritage. Indeed, the association is often specifically with an idealized version of England, rather than nation as a whole. One of the significant institutions in this field, for example, is the Council for the Protection of Rural England (CPRE). But as Paul Gilroy has pointed out, images of Englishness, of being British, exclude black British citizens: 'there ain't no black in the Union Jack' (Gilroy 1987). The celebration of, for example, 'Constable country'—rolling acres in rural Suffolk—or the greensward of 'Shakespeare's England' is based on a cultural heritage that denies slavery and racism (Malik 1992). (A more general discussion of the representation of nationality and its exclusions in literature may be found in Edward Said's *Culture and Imperialism* (1994), and I shall discuss the connections between gender and national identity in the next chapter.)

In Britain the black population is specifically urban-based, living predominantly in the larger cities of the UK: in 1991, according to the census, no less than half of all non-white people lived in Greater London. In an exhibition called *Pastoral Interludes,* first shown in 1984, the black artist Ingrid Pollard (1989) explored her relationship to the British countryside in a series of captioned photographs. Pollard was born in Guyana in the 1950s but came to England as a small girl. Phil Kinsman, a geographer at the University of Nottingham who is interested in the social construction of the countryside, interviewed Pollard in 1992 and has published both a working paper and an article, which I have drawn on here (Kinsman 1993, 1995).

This is how Kinsman describes the exhibition:

> [It] consists of five tinted pictures of black figures, both male and female, in rural landscapes, accompanied by a text which speaks of a sense of dread in visiting the countryside, of not belonging, of a threat of violence, even death, and of the history of slavery which brought black people to Britain. The title is of course ironic, and refers to the whole area of the pastoral ideal in English culture . . . Pollard attributes Pastoral Interludes to her personal holiday experiences, a particular conversation with a black friend about black people confining themselves to some parts of England and the complex readings of some viewers of early showings of the pictures. They saw in them metaphors of exclusion—barbed wire and stone walls—which she had not at first intended to be their content. (1995: 301–2)

Pollard suggests that black people's experience of the British countryside is as 'a landscape of fear': a concept used by feminist geographers describing the general experience of women (Pain 1991) and lesbians in particular (Valentine 1990). Interestingly, however, both Pain and Valentine focused on urban rather than rural environments. Pollard's critique of the countryside depends on an examination of the social construction of black British identities. According to Kinsman,

> She testifies that it is not considered to be part of the black experience to visit the countryside, and if it is to be visited, there are barriers of confidence to be overcome. She stresses that going to the countryside is a cross-cultural activity, that there is a country code that has to be learned, which proves to be a barrier to black people. Although there are also very material barriers preventing black people going to the countryside, much of what prevents them is indeed ideological, and a part of this is how black senses of identity are perceived in relation to the countryside. (1995: 307).

Stuart Hall, a renowned British sociologist, born in Jamaica, has argued that experiences of alienation from the land and a sense of not belonging, either to Britain or to the Caribbean, are a common experience for migrants. I shall discuss this experience in more detail in chapter 8 where questions of displacement and the formation of diasporic identities will be considered. Although Pollard concentrated explicitly on race in her work, in the reactions to the exhibition she recorded she noted that working-class people and white middle-class women found echoes of their own experiences in her photographs. This illustrates the complexity of the ways in which class, race and gender divisions both divide and unite groups in their experiences of different places.

Gendered Beaches

The main alternative to the countryside as a public site of leisure is the seaside, and specifically the beach. With the rise in living standards and average wages, and improvements in mass transport during the twentieth century large numbers of people in the 'West' travel annually to the edge of continents to take a break from their regular routine. As I have argued in this and previous chapters, assumptions about sexuality—the appropriate relations between the sexes and their permitted visibility— are writ large in the built environment. Explicit and implicit rules and regulations about whose bodies are permitted in which spaces and the interactions between them are set into the nature and form of buildings, the spaces between them and their internal divisions. In all but exceptional cases and places, these regulations are based on heterosexual social relations and women's assured inferiority. Perhaps the most visible display of hegemonic sexuality in the public arena is on the beach and in its associated holiday developments. Here, in that liminal place between the land and the sea—literally a place on the edge—the sets of binary associations that structure Western social relations are made visible, and in some cases trangressed.

The beach is a place of freedom, where the usual (for holiday makers, at least) division of life between work and home is totally or partially disrupted. Here, in a space between land and sea, the boundary between nature and culture is also fluid. At low tide, the beach may be 'civilized' with chairs, rugs, food and games equipment, but this colonization is fragile and temporary and all signs of it are washed away twice daily. On this anomalous strip, other signs of the civilized side of the nature—culture divide are also challenged, as the temporary occupants strip away many of the signs of their class position with their clothes; they are reduced merely to bodies of various shapes and signs, and pleasure becomes primarily a physical, rather than cerebral, experience. Fiske, in a paper entitled 'Reading the beach' (in Fiske 1992), suggests that the following list of binaries is challenged by the anomalous categories of the beach (p. 57; 'bathers' in the list refers to swimming costumes):

A	Anomalous category	Not A
SEA	Beach	LAND
NATURE		CULTURE
NAKED	Topless/Bathers	CLOTHED
FUR	Tan	SKIN
SWIMMING	Surfboard	BOATING
FISH	Scuba	MAN
ANIMALS	Pets (dogs)	MAN

The use of 'man' is perhaps a little irksome in these divisions.

There is one binary category, however, which is not challenged on the beach. Gender differentiations, of course, loom even more significant on stripping, as the beach becomes a display of sexuality and a locus dominated by the gaze. Above all, beaches are arenas for looking (indeed doing more is often explicitly forbidden by notices of public by-laws): men look at women, women at women, men at men, women at men, and adults at children. In all but the exceptional locations, however, it is the heterosexual male gaze that dominates the displays, although beaches are often distinguished by the dominance of a certain group—the surfers' beach by young men, for example, or a family beach by adults and children. In his paper, Fiske, a sociologist working in Australia, perhaps not unsurprisingly chose to focus on the sexist nature of the surfers' culture.

> *The surfboard is perhaps the perfect example of a category anomalous between nature and culture. It is carefully designed, with a scientific approach to the placement of fins and shape of the hull, yet it is also the most minimal object that enables man to float on the sea [that man again, but as we shall see in a moment, this time Fiske means exactly that]. . . . As befits its anomalous status, the surfboard is both sacred and taboo. To the surfie it is an object of near worship, and there are strong taboos that prevent girls, or the too young or the too old, from riding it.*

Fiske continues:

> *we are not interested here in a Freudian reading of the surfboard with male sexuality, but it is worth remarking on the sexist nature of most youth subcultures, where male and female behaviour is clearly distinguished, and where males are active and dominant and females passive and subordinate. Vans, motorbikes and surfboards are conventionally driven/ridden by males and the size, skill, decoration involved in them is part of the male status order. Females are passengers, spectators, there to be won, possessed, flaunted by the male. Surfers' writing mingles accounts of mastering waves with ones of easy mastery of girls. They have an exclusive language for each . . . but the key term is hunting, which applies equally to waves and females. Hunting is where man first denotes his mastery over nature: it is the prerequisite of cooking, which, in turn, becomes the resonant metaphor for the process of culturizing nature. And consequently it is seen as a natural activity—man hunting for food, hunting for females, hunting for waves is man behaving 'naturally' because he is acting according to his bodily needs. (1992: 60)*

Thank goodness for the inverted commas round naturally. Fiske seems so taken with the masculinity of surfers in his discussion of their attitudes and language that I felt he almost believed their arguments about the 'naturalness' of women's passive and inferior position.

If you are interested in a further exploration of some of the reasons for the sexist rituals among youth subcultures, you might turn to my social geography reader *Undoing Place?* (McDowell 1997b), where I have reprinted studies of, among others, bikers and mods, and to the edited collection by Skelton and Valentine, *Cool Geographies* (1997).

Conclusions

In this chapter it has become clear that there is a series of complex relationships between gender, sexuality and space. The divisions and associations are more complicated than a simple binary division between the public and the private, where each sphere is associated respectively with men and with women. Instead there are complex and paradoxical associations between gender and locale, between identity and particular places, for men as well as women. For both sexes, the city and its public spaces are associated both with fear and with delight, with danger and heady freedoms, whereas the beach is an anomalous space. Definitions of gender, identity and place, as well as the relationships between them, have always been more fragmented, complex and fluid than suggested in some of the earlier feminist analyses and in conventional liberal theory. The particular division between the workplace and the home, the city and the suburbs, private family life and the public arena that was established in the industrial revolution in 'the West', made concrete in nineteenth-century cities—and which perhaps reached its apotheosis in the urban areas of the US and UK in the 1950s—was always cross-cut by a more fractured set of lines and divisions than has sometimes been recognized in theoretical analyses.

Further, urban space itself is not just the straightforward, legible or scientific space of the urban planners and cartographers. It is also constructed through sets of myths and representations which are given meaning by everyday spatial practices, as De Certeau (1988) and Lefebvre (1991) have suggested. Spaces have different meanings for different groups, and each space may, over the course of a day, a week or longer, be occupied by a series of different social groups whose practices imbue the same spaces with different meanings at different times. The street and the park, for example, in the day and in the evening, or the holiday resort in and out of season, are different spaces in practice, in the everyday experiences of those who live in and use them.

At the end of the twentieth century, the profound reorganization of space and time that is taking place, albeit unevenly, through the development of global communications and information technologies has, for some at least, prised social relations and gender divisions free from the hold of specific locales, recombining them across huge space-time distances in hitherto unforeseen ways. These changes, migrations and movements—of capital, people and ideas—have placed new questions about the spatialization of everyday life at the centre of contemporary social theory in a wide range of disciplines. Thus geographic concerns have become central questions for the millennium. In the penultimate chapter I shall turn to some theoretical and empirical questions about the effects of movement, travel and displacements, but first, in chapter 7, I want to leave the scale of the city and address some of the relationships between gender and the nation-state.

Further Reading

Mapping Desire by David Bell and Gill Valentine (1995) was perhaps the first collection of papers by geographers that seriously considered the multiple geographies associated with different sexualities. It includes papers about lesbian and gay relationships in a range of locations, as well as discussions of strategies of resistance. Frank Mort's *Cultures of Consumption* (1996), drawn on in this chapter, is an excellent excavation of the history of Soho. The fictional portraits of the Castro district in 1980s San Francisco by Armistead Maupin (1980, 1984, 1986) that I mentioned in chapter 4 provide an insight into 'alternative' life in that city, whereas Frances Fitzgerald's discussion of the same area in her book *Cities on the Hill* (1986) is a more serious look at the same area. They are relevant to the material discussed here as well as that in the earlier chapter.

Lifestyle Shopping, a collection of papers edited by Rob Shields (1992), includes a range of chapters on different types of spaces of consumption and draws on ideas from Henri Lefebvre, Michel Maffesoli, Walter Benjamin and Mikhail Bakhtin; it might be useful for readers interested in the current relevance of the work of these 'great men'. On the lure and power of advertising, however, it is hard to beat Judith Williamson's journalism. *Consuming Passions* (1985) is a collection of her pieces from newspapers and journals such as *New Society* in the 1980s. David Bell and Gill Valentine's recent book *Consuming Geographies* (1997) is an interesting assessment of the relationship between location and eating. The collection edited by Rosa Ainley (1998) includes papers on a wide range of public spaces including open space in London, shopping centres in New Zealand, dance halls in Kingston, Jamaica, and real and virtual streets in California. Finally Neil Wrigley and Michelle Lowe's book *Retailing, Consumption and Capital: Towards the New Retail Geography* (1996) is, as the title indicates, a collection of papers by the 'new' retail geographers.

Works Cited

Barrows, S. 1981: *Distorting Mirrors: Visions of the Crowd in Late Nineteenth Century France.* New Haven: Yale University Press.

Baudelaire, C. 1963: The painter of modern life (1864). In *The Painter of Modern Life and Other Essays,* ed. J. Mayne. Oxford: Phaidon Press.

Bowlby, R. 1985: *Just Looking: Consumer Culture in Dreiser, Gissing, and Zola.* London: Methuen.

Burgess, J. 1996: Focusing on fear. *Area,* 28, 130–135.

Burgess, J. et al 1988: People, parks and the urban green: a study of the popular meanings and values for open spaces in the city. *Urban Studies,* 25, 455–73.

Chauncey, G. 1995: *Gay New York: The Making of the Gay Male World 1890–1940.* London: Flamingo.

Cosgrove, D. and Daniels, S. 1988: *The Iconography of Landscape.* Cambridge: Cambridge University Press.

Davis, M. 1989: *City of Quartz.* London: Verso.

Debord, G. 1994: *The Society of the Spectacle.* New York: Zone Books.

De Certeau, M. 1988: *The Practice of Everyday Life,* trans. S. Rendall. Berkeley: University of California Press.

Domash, M. 1996a: *Invented Cities: The Creation of Landscape in Nineteenth Century New York and Boston*. New Haven and London: Yale University Press.

Domash, M 1996b: The feminized retail landscape: gender, ideology, and consumer culture in nineteenth century New York City. In N. Wrigley and M. Lowe (eds), *Retailing Consumption and Capital: Towards the New Retail Geography*. Harlow: Longman.

Dowling, R. 1993: Femininity, place and commodities: a retail case study. *Antipode*, 25, 295–319.

Du Gay, P. 1996: *Consumption and Identity at Work*. London: Sage.

Fiske, J. 1992: *Reading the Popular* (1989). London: Routledge.

Fraser. N 1990: Rethinking the public sphere: a contribution to the critique of actually existing democracy. *Social Text*, 25–6, 56–80.

Frisby, D. 1985: *Fragments of Modernity*. Cambridge: Polity Press.

Gilroy, P. 1987: *There Ain't No Black in the Union Jack*. London: Hutchinson.

Harrison, C. and Burgess, J. 1994: Social constructions of nature: a case study of the conflict over Rainham Marshes SSSI. *Transactions of the Institute of British Geographers*, 19, 291–310.

Harvey, D. 1989: *The Condition of Postmodernity*. Oxford: Blackwell.

Harvey, D. 1992: Social justice, postmodernism, and the city. *International Journal of Urban and Regional Research*, 16, 588–601.

Heron, L. (ed) 1983: *Streets of Desire: Women's Fiction in the Twentieth Century City*. London: Virago.

Kinsman, P. 1993: Landscapes of national non-identity: the landscape photography of Ingrid Pollard. Working Paper 17, Department of Geography: University of Nottingham.

Kinsman, P. 1995: Landscape, race, and national identity: the photography of Ingrid Pollard. *Area*, 27, 300–10.

Lefebvre, H. 1991: *The Production of Space,* trans. D. Nicholson-Smith. Oxford: Blackwell.

Lowe, M. and Crewe, L. 1996: Shop work: image, customer care, and the restructuring of retail employment. In N. Wrigley and M. Lowe (eds), *Retailing Consumption and Capital: Towards the New Retail Geography*. Harlow: Longman.

Malik, S. 1992: Colors of the countryside—a whiter shade of pale. *Ecos*, 13, 33–9.

Mitchell, D. 1995: The end of public space? People's Park, definitions of the public, and democracy. *Annals of the Association of American Geographers*, 85, 109–33.

McKay, G. 1995: *Senseless Acts of Beauty*. London: Verso.

Mort, F. 1995: Archaeologies of city life: commercial culture, masculinity, and spatial relations in 1980s London. *Environment and Planning D: Society and Space*, 13, 573–90.

Mort, F. 1996: *Cultures of Consumption: Masculinities and Social space in Late Twentieth-Century Britain*. London: Routledge.

Morton, M. 1995: *The Tunnel: The Underground Homeless of New York*. New Haven: Yale University Press.

Pain, R. 1991: Space, sexual violence, and social control. *Progress in Human Geography,* 15, 415–31.

Pateman, C. 1988: *The Sexual Contract*. Cambridge: Polity Press.

Pateman, C. 1989: *The Disorder of Women*. Cambridge: Polity Press.

Pollard, I. 1989: Pastoral interludes. *Third Text: Third world Perspectives on Contemporary Art and Culture,* 7, 41–6.

Said, E. 1994: *Culture and Imperialism*. London: Vintage.

Simpson, M. 1994: *Male Impersonators*. London: Cassell.

Smith, J. 1989: *Misogynies*. London: Faber.

Smith, N. 1993: Homeless/global: scaling places. In J. Bird, B. Curtis, T. Putnam, G. Robertson and L. Tickner (eds) *Mapping the Futures: Local Cultures, Global Change*. London: Routledge.

Sandel, M. 1996: *Democracy's Discontent: America in Search of a Public Philosophy*. Cambridge, MA.: Belknap Press.

Sklar, J. 1991: *American Citizenship: The Quest for Inclusion*. Cambridge: Harvard University Press.

Valentine, G. 1990: Women's fear and the design of public space. *Built Environment,* 16, 288–303.

Walkowitz, J. 1992: *City of Dreadful Delight*. London: Virago.

Williams, R. 1989: *The Politics of Modernism*. London: Verso.

Wilson, E. 1991: *The Sphinx in the City*. London: Virago.

Wilson, E. 1992: The invisible flaneuse. *New Left Review,* no. 191, 90–110.

Wolff, J. 1985: The invisible flaneuse: women and the literature of modernity. *Theory, Culture and Society,* 2, 37–46.

Young, I.M. 1990b: *Justice and the Politics of Difference*. Princeton: Princeton University Press.

Zola, E. 1982: *The Ladies Paradise,* trans. from *Au bonheur des dames* (1882), introd. Kristin Ross. Berkeley: University of California Press.

Zukin, S. 1995: *The Cultures of the City*. London: Blackwell.

34

I Knew I'd Sing

HEATHER MCHUGH

A poet, translator, and visiting creative writer at Warren Wilson College, Heather McHugh presents a humorous, yet intense, scenario in her poem "I Knew I'd Sing" from Hinge and Sign. *In this poem, the narrator details her mother's harsh reaction to her use of the word "cunt" and how that reaction further convinced her of the power of particular words. McHugh suggests in this piece that socially transgressive and often derogatory words might actually perform a wide range of work, depending on the speaker and audience.*

A few sashay, a few finagle.
some make whoopee, some
make good. But most make
diddly-squat. I tell you this

is what I love about
America—the words it puts
in my mouth, the mouth where once
my mother rubbed

a word away with soap. The word
was *cunt*. She stuck that bar
of family-size in there
until there was no hole to speak of,

so she hoped. But still
I'm full of it—the cunt,
the prick, short u, short i,
the words that stood

for her and him. I loved the thing
they must have done, the love they must
have made, to make
an example of me. After my lunch of Ivory I said

vagina for a day or two, but knew
from that day forth which word
struck home like sex itself. I knew
when I was big I'd sing

a song in praise of cunt—I'd want
to keep my word, the one with teeth in it.
Forevermore (and even after I was raised) I swore

nothing—but nothing—would be beneath me.

35

History with a Small "h"

A Conversation with Glenn Ligon

RACHEL MIDDLEMAN

In "History with a Small 'h'" Rachel Middleman, a PhD candidate in Art History at the University of Southern California, interviews Glenn Ligon, a multimedia artist who interrogates intersections of race and sexuality. Ligon discusses how his artistic project Lest We Forget *works against the common practice of memorializing one version of a historically significant event. He memorializes ordinary, ambiguous moments of gay male cruising, demonstrating how to conduct history (with a small "h") and to use such histories to potentially disrupt public memory. This exchange originally appeared in a 2006 issue of* GLQ: A Journal of Lesbian and Gay Studies.

The publication of this interview with the artist Glenn Ligon coincides with his current midcareer exhibition, "Glenn Ligon: Some Changes," which opened in 2005 at the Power Plant in Toronto.[1] Ligon remains best known for his conceptual text paintings, which explore the construction of identities through language and representation. The work documented here, *Lest We Forget* (1998), is a rarely exhibited, somewhat ephemeral addition to his oeuvre. Ligon conceived the series during a two-month residency at Artpace San Antonio in Texas. There he created metal plaques inscribed with personal anecdotes about cruising and desire. He installed the plaques in the public space of the city where they visually resembled the historical markers found in abundance in the downtown tourist area. He then photographed them and left them behind to be discovered, stolen, or removed by whoever encountered them subsequently. The plaques have since disappeared, but the photographs he took of them in situ and a second set of the plaques remain and were exhibited at Artpace in 1998. I had the opportunity to talk with Ligon in February 2005 about how *Lest We Forget* relates to his larger body of work, his process in making the series, and how it challenges received ideas of history, identity, and communication.

RACHEL MIDDLEMAN: How did this project, *Lest We Forget,* begin for you?

GLENN LIGON: At Artpace there wasn't a mandate to do projects that were specifically geared toward San Antonio, but there was definitely a sense that they wanted some kind of interaction with the city. And I guess I just took that literally. I thought I should use what was available, and I found out that the bronze plaque makers were in Texas, right in San Antonio. I don't know if you've ever been to San Antonio, but basically it's a tourist town. Artpace is on the edge of downtown near the River Walk, and I was very aware of that being a tourist neighborhood and having all these historic markers—they're everywhere. Also, I don't drive, so that was another factor in the project. I walked around a lot. All those things came together to start me thinking about doing a project using bronze plaques. And as for the texts themselves . . . I mean the truth is sort of funny there. Like the one where I'm talking about meeting a guy and I said something like, "shuffling a little bit, a little something-something between us," but I don't know exactly what happened. Maybe nothing happened. The plaques read like you're in somebody's head, but the actual interaction between me and whoever it was is ambiguous.

RM: What did you imagine someone passing by would think when they read the plaques?

Figure 1. Glenn Ligon, "Hunky Guy," Lest We Forget (1998). All photographs courtesy of the artist

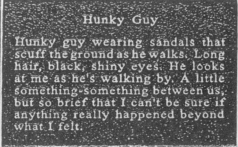

Figure 2. Glenn Ligon, "Hunky Guy" (detail)

Figure 3. Glenn Ligon, "A Guy in Uniform," Lest We Forget

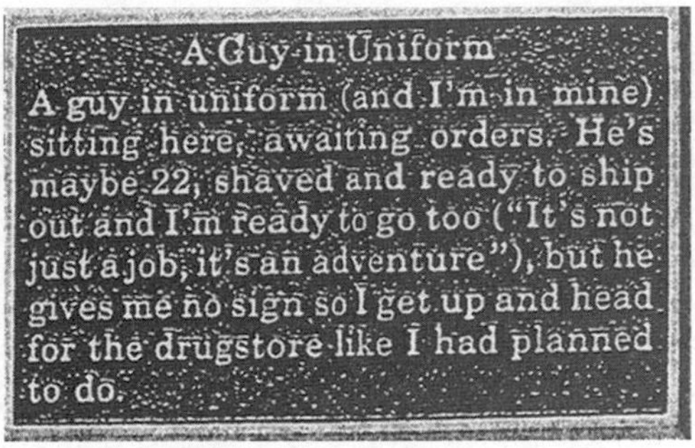

Figure 4. Glenn Ligon, "A Guy in Uniform" (detail)

GL: First of all, I wasn't sure that people would read them at all. Imagine a public park that has this plaque on a concrete pedestal and there are five other things like that in the park. The form of the plaque was just mimicking what was already there. They are so ubiquitous I don't think anyone really reads them anymore. It was funny to imagine how they could just be there forever without being noticed, or, if they were read, it would be because they were at odd sites like the side of the bus station. I wanted people to think about uses of public spaces, particularly queer uses of public spaces, because there was some cruising going on in the downtown area. Not that I ever really saw it in any sustained way, but it was supposedly there. I was thinking that rock plaques are about the official record and asking what it would mean to do things that were in the same language but were about the temporary, the transient, and the illicit. And even beyond that, about things that were so ephemeral maybe they didn't even really happen, things that don't really leave a trace.

RM: I see a humor in that, too, because it's not what you expect to read on a metal plaque. It's not commemorating some historical event, and we don't know if the event even took place. Monuments are intended to remember the past, but that is something that we can never fully grasp. Where was *A Guy in Uniform* placed?

GL: That was Travis Park, which is about five blocks from Artpace. All the other plaques in the park look like that. I think they were soldier monuments, but I'm not really sure. The "D" from one of the plaques is my friend Dario Robleto. He's an artist who lived in San Antonio, and he helped me make this project. I thought we should install it at night, but he suggested going out during the day because I wanted to photograph it. We just walked out there in the middle of the day and put it down. It's amazing what you can do if you act like you know what you're doing.

RM: You took the photographs yourself?

GL: Yes.

411

Figure 5. Glenn Ligon, "A Boy," Lest We Forget   Figure 6. Glenn Ligon, "A Boy" (detail)

RM: And did you see what happened to the plaques?

GL: No. I think some lasted about a week. *A Guy in Uniform* weighed one hundred pounds. So it's not like someone was going to pick it up. It was probably someone from the parks department who eventually figured it out. But I don't know what happened to them.

RM: Did you have an audience? Did you draw any attention?

GL: Nope.

RM: How do you think humor plays into this work?

GL: I don't think I thought about it when I was writing them up. The experience was real, but the writing up was influenced by other things. Honestly with *A Boy*, I was thinking about the Narcissus myth. I was reading myths at the time, and I was particularly interested in doing a project around Narcissus. That whole question about whether he's looking at himself in the glass or looking at another person or not is filtered through the Narcissus myth. I was just reading this book *Vertigo* by the German writer W. G. Sebald, and he talks about this guy who's trying to remember a battle scene and the landscape. He draws this memory map for himself—it's diagrammed in the book—and at a certain point he realizes that the map corresponds directly to an etching he had seen. Basically, it's about how visual images take over one's memories. I was thinking about that because you were talking about the unreliability of memory, and I think it's interesting that images sometimes replace one's memory. Also, my memories are sort of tied up with reading the Narcissus myth, and so what I'm writing about in the plaque is being partially structured by the structure of that myth.

RM: *Lest We Forget* was exhibited with some of the *Stranger in the Village* series. Did you also do those while you were in San Antonio?[2]

GL: Yes, they were done at the same time.

RM: Did you see a relationship between the two projects?

GL: There is a tangential relationship between the two because the *Stranger* paintings are so much about defeat or frustration. I shouldn't say defeat

. . . the end of communicating in a way. And the plaques are about starting to communicate and making something visible that may not be visible to people. That's one way to connect them. I notice I've done a lot of projects that are very clear for lack of a better word. I did a series of rubbings [*Schwartzmannstrasse Drawing*] of a street sign when I was in Munich. The street was called Schwartzmannstrasse, "black man's street," and that was the street that I actually lived on when I was in Munich doing a residency. I did some research and found out a Jewish family from the turn of the century had the alley named after them when they gave some money to the government. I liked that there was this weird misapprehension of what that sign meant. Suddenly it was about me because I was living there, but it wasn't about me at all. But people didn't know the history or anything about that family. Some of my projects are much more about trying to communicate, and the paintings are more about the difficulty of language.

RM: I did get a sense of difficulty in communication with *Lest We Forget* because of the events you choose to describe. They're not about actually meeting a person or having some kind of relationship with them. They're only what you [Ligon] think happened.

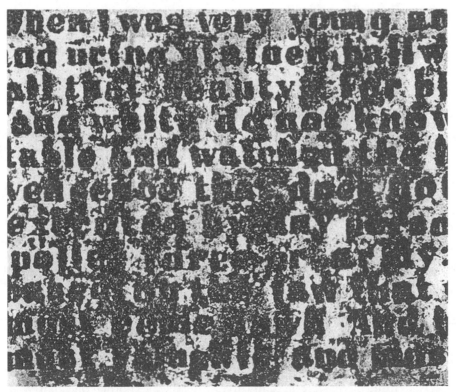

Figure 7. Glenn Ligon, Untitled (The Fire Next Time/Hands #1) *(2000), ink, glue, and coal dust over screen print. St. Louis Art Museum, Museum Minority Artists Purchase Fund*

GL: Yeah, there's no connection. I guess I'm not very good at cruising! I think the piece is about facts. Plaques are about facts, though those facts are always contested. If you read the plaques at the Alamo, you know there is a whole other story there that is not represented. I wanted to be true to my encounters, which were about, "well, I didn't really connect with this guy," and also put the facts in all those plaques into question.

RM: The plaques don't necessarily say that nothing came of the encounter, but the assumption is there. Of course, I don't know what really happened; maybe you went and introduced yourself.

GL: That's an interesting way to think about it because it's about memorializing a moment, but it doesn't memorialize the before and after. I think historical plaques are trying to memorialize the whole event. "This happened on this spot. Here are the players involved. This changed history, and we're marking this spot." But my plaques are more about, "Something happened here. I'm not sure if it was what it was exactly. And did it have an effect on those people after? I'm not sure." They are much more about the ephemeral.

RM: I was thinking that you could read the work two ways: as being about the more general search for recognition from another person and the missed connections that happen between people all the time, or more specifically it could be about the idea of remapping the city through an experience of cruising. How did you find the cruising spots?

GL: People who lived there told me. San Antonio has a big gay population, so I knew something had to be going on somewhere. I was told that sometimes the park and the River Walk at night are downtown cruising spots. But another part of it was that I had to walk in order not to be dependent on the staff at Artpace. There was an art supply place and a bookstore I could walk to.

RM: How did you come up with the title *Lest We Forget*?

GL: It was on a monument in the town. I don't remember what it was a monument to, though; it might have been a Civil War monument. It was carved on the granite base. It's funny because it sounds kind of romantic and nineteenth century.

RM: There is something poetic about the word *lest*. It lends a feeling of importance. Why is it that we shouldn't forget what you describe in the plaques?

GL: I guess there has to be room for history with a small "h." All the other bronze plaques are about the big "H," the official history.

RM: How many plaques were made?

GL: I think there were actually five. There was another one that was on a bench right outside Artpace.[3]

RM: How did you imagine the relationship between the gallery exhibit and the plaques out in public space?

GL: As documentation I wanted to create the sense of an important thing that had been out in the world but was already gone. Because the sites were around Artpace, you could figure out the locations. People would imagine that if they went there they would see the plaque, but actually it had already disappeared. I wanted a way to indicate what had been there. It's kind of ridiculous to put up a bronze plaque and let it be stolen. I kind of liked that, so much of the work was about the disappearance of that thing. Again, part of that may have been the people who are in charge of places like the bus station. It lasted there I think about three days, and then someone read it and realized it wasn't supposed to be there. Or maybe they didn't, and it just fell off because they're not attached permanently at all.

RM: How did you adhere the plaques?

GL: Double-sided tape. And they're bronze. So that's a lot of tape.

RM: I was thinking about how you were saying that you didn't know if people would even notice them. This brought to my mind the difference between sanctioned public art and a more interventionist type of public art. This seems to me like it's not entirely either. It wasn't sanctioned because you just put it out there, and, at the same time, it doesn't demand attention or disrupt public space the way some interventionist art can. But I liked the subtlety of that. It's not that every single person who passes by is going to receive a particular message from Glenn Ligon.

GL: Yeah, I think that is what the activities that are being documented in my plaques are about. That's why you're looking at someone looking into the window of a deli and you have no idea whether he's really looking at you (well, sometimes you do!). You don't really know if he's interested in you. You don't know what his sexuality is. It seemed to me that cruising is about the risk of misreading something. Or it could be one-sided if the person is not who you think he is, or he's not interested. Or he is who you think he is, but he's not interested! Also it happens surreptitiously initially,

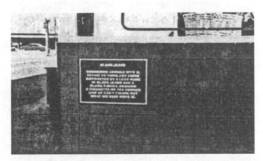

Figure 8. Glenn Ligon, "Black Jeans," Lest We Forget

even if people are going out to cruise each other. It's happening in public spaces but has to remain undercover at the same time. So I think the plaques have to be about this "notice me, don't notice me." They have to remain a bit obscure. They have to mimic, to look like other things, like cruising in public space has to look like you're just going to the bathroom or like you're just reading your book on the bench. As for the questions of the race and gender of the person speaking in the plaques, I didn't think it through that way, that's the way the text came out. But it's interesting to have to think about these things more, afterward.

RM: I think it's interesting to look at it both ways. I don't want to ignore where the work is coming from, but the first time I read this [the plaques] I couldn't assign it immediately to a particular identity. I was trying to look at it both knowing who the artist is and as an anonymous text as if I were a passerby.

GL: The problem of art historians! How to decide what's relevant. Is the biography relevant? Or how do you deal with biography without determining the work? The work is "x" because he's "x."

RM: I really like the idea of putting something so personal into a public form of address, especially if you never really know if it's truth or fiction.

GL: It's interesting because people imagine that art can't be acted. The part one plays in a movie is not the actor; it's the part. Art can do that, too, sometimes. The plaques point to it more than other works. I think there has always been this strain in my work. It's seemingly autobiographical but always about quotation, someone else's text, or someone else's description of me. It's always mediated by something so that it's autobiographical and resists autobiography at the same time. But I have to tell you that it's interesting to me to talk about those things as not being sexed and gendered, on my part, because I don't think I wrote thinking that I would not reveal myself in them. It just sort of happened that way. I mean it's sort of funny to me to think of them in retrospect. I don't think I really had any sense of doing that as a strategy when I was writing those texts.

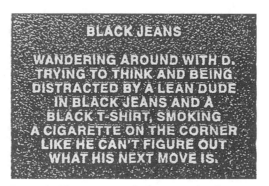

Figure 9. Glenn Ligon, "Black Jeans" (detail)

RM: I want to go back to something you said before about this work being about making something visible as opposed to the difficulty or frustration of communication in the text paintings. And I wonder if you could say a little more about that.

GL: This is the first time that I actually wrote something that I used directly for the text. I had always resisted that. Maybe that's why in the text it's hard to locate the person in terms of race and gender. It's the first time I'm actually using my own words, and so I have to sort of hold back from it. Whereas the text paintings hold back because it's already a quotation, it's already someone else's text even though it says "I." It pretends to be the artist's, but it's really a quote. Then there is another level of removal because the text disappears, creating another barrier to the meaning of the text. The plaques were much more direct. The text is quite legible and out in a public place. So in that sense they're about a certain visibility, but in another way they're sort of, as you said, they're so in my head that they're kind of like removed in that sense. Someone daydreaming. It's funny because I hadn't really thought about the work in that way and why it doesn't locate me more specifically. I think partially because so much of my work has been quotation that I felt like I needed to remove the biographical details, even though they seem very autobiographical. It's funny because I think sometimes artists don't know what their work is about. I mean that whole thing about writing the text. . . . it's funny to me . . . but I think that's what keeps you going. I guess I sort of figure things out as I make work, so often those things don't get figured out until after the work is made, and I can say, "That's what that was about."

RM: I don't think much has been written about this work. Do you know why that is?

GL: They haven't been exhibited a lot. They were shown at Artpace and at Riverside in a show that Charles Gaines just curated [Remembering, Group Exhibition, Sweeney Art Gallery at the University of California, Riverside, October 1–December 11, 2004].

RM: Where is *Lest We Forget* now?

GL: Under my bed. In the studio.

Endnotes

This interview was occasioned by a paper on Glenn Ligon's *Lest We Forget* written for a graduate seminar, "Twentieth-Century Art in Public and Private," taught by Richard Meyer at the University of Southern California in the fall of 2004.

1. "Glenn Ligon: Some Changes" is traveling to the Contemporary Arts Museum, Houston (January 14–April 19, 2006); the Warhol Museum, Pittsburgh (September 30–December 31, 2006); the Wexner Center for the Arts, Columbus, Ohio (January 27–April 22, 2007); and Mudam—Musée d'Art Moderne Grand-Duc Jean, Luxembourg (October 6–December 17, 2007). Co-curators

of the exhibition are Wayne Baerwaldt (formerly of the Power Plant) and Thelma Golden (Studio Museum in Harlem, New York).

2. This series includes text taken from James Baldwin's essay "Stranger in the Village" (1953). Ligon's layering of text and materials, including coal dust, creates a luminescent field of gray and black in which Baldwin's words become almost illegible. Ligon creates a similar effect in *Untitled (The Fire Next Time/Hands #1)* (fig. 7), which also borrows text from Baldwin.

3. An image of the fifth plaque was not available for reproduction.

36

Ancestors

Cesare Pavese

Cesare Pavese was a beloved writer in Italy, publishing novels and poems in the first half of the 20th century. "Ancestors" appears in Disaffections: Complete Poems 1930–1950, *and it showcases Pavese's signature interests and style—the intimacies and tensions that develop among family members and neighbors in rural Italy, rendered in an accessible, almost conversational poetic voice.*

Stunned by the world, I reached an age
when I threw punches at air and cried to myself.
Listening to the speech of women and men,
not knowing how to respond, it's not fun.
But this too has passed: I'm not alone anymore,
and if I still don't know how to respond,
I don't need to. Finding myself, I found company.

I learned that before I was born I had lived
in men who were steady and firm, lords of themselves,
and none could respond and all remained calm.
Two brothers-in-law opened a store—our family's
first break. The outsider was serious,
scheming, ruthless, and mean—a woman.
The other one, ours, read novels at work,

which made people talk. When customers came,
they'd hear him say, in one or two words,
that no, there's no sugar, Epsom salts no,
we're all out of that. Later it happened
that this one lent a hand to the other, who'd gone broke.

Thinking of these folks makes me feel stronger
than looking in mirrors and sticking my chest out
or shaping my mouth into a humorless smile.
One of my grandfathers, ages ago,
was being cheated by one of his farmhands,
so he worked the vineyards himself, in the summer,
to make sure it was done right. That's how
I've always lived too, always maintaining
a steady demeanor, and paying in cash.

And women don't count in this family.
I mean that our women stay home
and bring us into the world and say nothing
and count for nothing and we don't remember them.
Each of them adds something new to our blood,
but they kill themselves off in the process, while we,
renewed by them, are the ones to endure.
We're full of vices and horrors and whims—

37

Abandoned Women and Spaces of the Exception

GERALDINE PRATT

This essay, published originally in Antipode, *a radical Geography journal, takes up the philosophical claim of Agamben that some bodies/some citizens are more valued even in liberal democracies than others—that some bodies/some citizens are rendered what he calls "bare life." Geraldine Pratt, a Professor of Geography at the University of British Columbia, applies this claim to two cases of bare life that she has studied—the murder of 69 sex workers in Vancouver over a 20 year period of time and the contemporary treatment of Filipina domestic workers also in Vancouver. This essay not only illustrates how to explore a philosophical claim through empirical research, but also analyzes the effects of symbolic and material geographies on lived lives.*

> *I consider two cases of legal abandonment in Vancouver—of murdered sex workers and live-in caregivers on temporary work visas—in light of Agamben's claim that the generalized suspension of the law has become a dominant paradigm of government. I bring to Agamben's theory a concern to specify both the gendering and racialisation of these processes, and the many geographies that are integral to legal abandonment and the reduction of categories of people to 'bare life'. The case studies also allow me to explore two limit-concepts that*

> *Agamben offers as a means to re-envision political community: the refugee who refuses assimilation in the nation-state, and the human so degraded as to exist beyond conventional humanist ethics of respect, dignity and responsibility.*

Women began to go missing from the Downtown Eastside in Vancouver in 1978. The media and the police were oddly inattentive. It was not until 1998—roughly 69 murders later—that they began to pay attention. Subsequently, the DNA of 31 women has been identified on a suburban Vancouver property, and the owner has been charged with their murders and currently awaits trial. Vancouver's Missing Women, as they are now called, have finally and fully captured the public imagination. In January of 2004, for instance, artist Kati Campbell exhibited an installation called 67 Shawls. The artist had laboriously embroidered text onto 67 shawls; each shawl memorializes one missing woman, and each was to be delivered to a missing woman's mother when the exhibit closed. Yet, at the moment that Campbell's shawls were being displayed, a new case involving women in the Downtown Eastside came to light. Another Vancouver man was found to have brutally assaulted an astonishing number of women in the same neighbourhood (*Vancouver Sun* 2004)[1]. He had video recorded 12 of these assaults, which was a convenience of sorts for the Vancouver police.

My research with domestic workers in Vancouver calls attention to this same uncanny incapacity on the part of the state to regulate and police certain types of violence and illegal behaviour. In 1995 I began working with women who have come from the Philippines on temporary work visas to care for middle class Canadian children in their homes. This was an exciting time to start this research because, after years of lobbying, activists were finally beginning to exact some significant legislative reforms. In 1995 in British Columbia, for instance, the Employment Standards Act was amended so that live-in domestic workers were covered by minimum hourly wage and overtime regulations from which they previously had been excluded. However, almost a decade after these legislative reforms, local activists think that the situation of live-in domestic workers in Vancouver has worsened. The state has neglected to enforce the new regulations, and many live-in caregivers are working longer hours under even more exploitative conditions. The Director of the Philippine Women Centre argues that it is now harder to organize domestic workers than it was in 1995, precisely because domestic workers work longer hours than they did before the new labour regulations were put in place. A decade ago, domestic workers used to gather together at the Philippine Women Centre on weekends; now, desperate phone calls come into the Centre on an individual, emergency basis. In the Director's words, every phone call is "as if they're calling 911."[2]

The reference to '911' is ironic because this is the telephone number that is used in Canada to connect a caller to emergency state services. Yet it is precisely the inadequacy of state regulation that leads live-in domestic workers to place emergency calls to the Philippine Women Centre. I want to pursue this issue of absences and lapses in state policing and regulation in particular spaces of the city. Rather than viewing such lapses as aberrations from normal practice, I want to ask how such irregularities become the norm for certain people in certain places. This raises, in the context of everyday life in Vancouver, a paradox that Foucault identified for the modern biopolitical state. The paradox is that there is a positive relation between the state's assurances of life (eg, protecting the rights and freedoms of citizens, as well as the health of the nation), and the state's right to kill: "the more you kill [and] . . . let die, the more you will live" (quoted in Stoler 1995:84). The relation between the production of citizenship and the state's sovereignty over life is therefore not incidental but productive and fundamental.

I pursue this paradox by means of Giorgio Agamben's theorizing of the state of exception. I bring to Agamben's theory a concern to specify the gendering and racialisation of these processes. As a feminist frustrated by both the everyday violence exacted on certain categories of women and the seeming inability to reform the Live-in Caregiver Program, I turn to Agamben's theory for fresh ideas about political strategy.

Suspending the Law

According to Agamben, what most characterizes modern biopolitics is the generalized suspension of the law—the state of exception—as a basis of liberal sovereignty. In his book *Homo Sacer,* Agamben theorises this sovereign ban through the example of ancient Roman law and the figure of *homo sacer,* a legal designation for one who was excluded by and from juridical law.[3] The possibility of suspending the law allows the elimination "of entire categories of citizens who for some reason cannot be integrated into the political system" (2005:2). Such people are rendered as bare life and legally abandoned. Abandonment is not equivalent to exclusion. It has a more complex topological relation of being neither inside nor outside the juridical order. The difference between exclusion and abandonment turns on the fact that abandonment is an active, relational process. The one who is abandoned remains in a relationship with sovereign power: included through exclusion. It is thus "impossible to say clearly whether that which has been banned is inside or outside the juridical order" (Mills 2004:44).

The interest and force of Agamben's theorizing comes from his insistence that the technologies of abandonment have contemporary relevance. One source of this continuing relevance lies within what Agamben sees as a structural contradiction at the heart of modern democratic societies. This is the promise and simultaneous failure to reconcile biological life and political life: "it [modern democracy] wants to put the freedom and happiness of men into play in the very place—'bare life'— that marked their subjection" (Agamben 1998:10). But this reconciliation is never entirely effected and distinctions are persistently made between active and passive citizenship, between lives with and without political and economic value. The "highest political task" within modern democratic societies, he argues, becomes that of defining a threshold of who is inside active citizenship and who is excluded, whose life is politically relevant and whose life ceases to be relevant. Because entry into political life in modern democratic societies is in the first instance through the body's birth, much of this struggle about the worth of different types of human lives takes place through medicalised, gendered and racialized discourses about the health, vigour, and civility of the body. The health of the body politic is maintained through the regulation and maintenance of individual bodies. Impure, poor and aging bodies can be seen as costly to the social body; hence the logic of Foucault's observation about the intimate relation between death and life within the modern biopolitical state.

Agamben argues that certain events of the 20th century are both evidence of and cause for nation states to police the nation's biological body ever more vigorously. In particular, he notes the growing numbers of refugees, who have been cast out by certain nations and can be seen as a threat to the integrity of other nation-states. He notes as well the increasing tendency, starting in 1915, for states to legalise the denaturalization of certain groups of citizens.[4] We might add current tendencies within neo-liberalism to judge moral worth in terms of self-care, such that a 'mis-managed' life is itself evidence of and grounds for abandonment (Brown 2003).[5]

Not only is there a proliferation of cases of legal abandonment in the contemporary world, Agamben argues that we live in more intimate spatial terms with those who have been abandoned.[6] He cites the concentration camp as the paradigmatic space of exception where the suspension of the law becomes localized. He claims that the camp is now widespread and, in fact, is "the hidden matrix of the politics in which we are . . . living" (175). He urges us to "learn to recognize [the camp] in all its metamorphoses" (175) within the spaces of the city. He cites as examples zones of detention in airports and "certain outskirts of our cities" (1998:175). And he alerts us to the fact that "we must expect not only new camps but also always new and more lunatic regulative definitions of the inscription of [bare] life in the city. The camp, which is now securely lodged within the city's interior, is the new biopolitical *nomos* of the planet" (original emphasis, 1998:176).

Embodying Homo Sacer

Agamben is offering a philosophical analysis, and is preoccupied with a general topological process that produces exclusion within inclusion in liberal democratic societies. This is a process "in which what was presupposed as external (the state of nature) now reappears, as in a Mobius strip or a Leyden jar, in the inside (as state of exception)" (1998:37). I would like to contribute to a fuller empirical specification of his argument by considering how power works to target and manage certain groups in concrete spaces. As one aspect of this, I argue that geographies do more than contain or localize bare life. Geographies are part of the process by which certain individuals and groups are reduced to bare life. They are therefore integral to the process that Agamben describes.

Empirical specification also suggests that legal abandonment takes different forms, which need to be both noted and theorized. I pursue in particular the gendering of legal abandonment. As Catherine Mills has noted, Agamben is "not at all sensitive to the gendered dimension" (2004:58). This is perplexing because Agamben develops his analysis of legal abandonment through a distinction between public and private, which he maps onto the categories of political and biological life. In the classical Roman world, he argues, politics were anchored by and operated through these distinctions. Political life emerged in the public sphere of the city, while other systems of (pre-political, patriarchal) authority operated in the home.[7] The figure of *homo sacer* was produced as bare life through the sovereign ban. Bare life is not equivalent to biological life: it is life reduced to matter, "an exposure of natural life to the force of the law in abandonment . . . . the irreparable exposure of life to death in the sovereign ban" (Mills, 2004:46). In Agamben's account of modern democracy, it is the unstable blurring of biological and political life (which takes form as the sovereign citizen) that creates the conditions of modern biopower, in which the state administers the health of the national body through and in the name of the health of individual bodies.

Given the gendered nature of the public/private divide, so amply explored within feminist scholarship (Landes 1998; Marston 1990; Pateman 1988), it is inconceivable that these processes work in a uniform way for men and women.[8] As Rooney notes, "it is only in living memory" that the domestic and family has been "genuinely subject to the rule of law" (2002, 141). Recasting private domestic issues such as childcare and domestic assault as public ones remains an area of intense political contest. Feminists have long explored the paradox that women's issues are often depoliticized by being enclaved within the private sphere, while women are simultaneously less able than men to maintain the stability of the distinction between private and public (eg, they are more vulnerable to having their 'private' selves made into a spectacle through publicity (Fraser 1992)). Brown (2004) underlines the fact that it is not simply the case that women have had troubled access to the public sphere. Rather, women's formal equality within the public sphere has been entirely dependent on their subordination within the home. Comparing the political incorporation of women and Jews in 18th and 19th century Europe, she concludes that, while

> *racialization [may first appear as] a more powerfully determining discourse than sexualization in establishing limits to nation-state incorporation, . . . sexualization functions as a more relentlessly subordinating discourse and is therefore precisely what permits women's enfranchisement as political equals without the risk of substantive equality—and more importantly, without a risk of a challenge to the masculinist, heterosexual, and Christian norms at the heart of the putative universality of the state (23).*

Bare life and legal abandonment are not equivalent to the private sphere, but the wealth of feminist theorizing on the way that the private-public divide works *within* modern democracy has to be brought to bear on processes of legal abandonment. Both the production of the home as a gendered private space, and women's especial difficulty in maintaining the border between private and public, are key resources for the legal abandonment of women. The point here is not only that many of those who are placed in the position of bare life are women. It is also that both admission to citizenship and rendering individuals as bare life are accomplished through—and often in the name of—gendered and heterosexual norms. Legal abandonment occurs through a complex and gendered layering and enfolding of geographies of public and private, one into the other. I am not claiming that women's gender subordination creates the most egregious instances of legal abandonment. I am suggesting that there are real limitations to generalizing across the experiences of men and women, and across racialized and gendered forms of abandonment, and—most importantly—that gender hierarchies support and relay the split between biological and political life, which is both cause and effect of abandonment. As Lisa Sanchez comments, "the law of exclusion, far from being an equal-opportunity subordinator, targets gendered and racialized bodies most persistently, but it does so partially and differentially" (2004:879).

I would like to develop this argument in relation to the two examples with which I began, the missing women in Vancouver's Downtown Eastside, and the circumstances of Filipina domestic workers. My desire to work with the two cases emerges first from the uncanny ways that the stories haunt each other. One of the stories that the media has circulated about the fate of the missing women is that their remains were consumed by pigs on the farm of the accused, and that the pigs were then slaughtered and distributed for human consumption. Although it is estimated that the pig meat was distributed to 40 acquaintances of the accused murderer (Pynn 2004:A1), the media has identified one Filipino man—Crisanto Diopita—as a key recipient, and suggest that the accused murderer was "well known in the Filipino community" (Skelton and Fong 2004:A4). The fact that Diopita is both the only acquaintance named and is identified as Filipino is, I think, significant, given a long colonial history of marking Filipino 'primitivism' through habits of food consumption.[9] Cannibalism—even second order and accidental cannibalism—is yet another iteration of this marking. So too, the experience of being stigmatized as a prostitute haunts Filipino domestic workers, who speak of ongoing battles against being cast as prostitutes or otherwise immoral women (Pratt 2004; Pratt in collaboration with the Philippine Women Centre 2005). The cases are provocative to read against each other for additional reasons. In both cases the women's claims to rights are compromised by the fact that they embody particular racialised historical geographies. These racialized geographies nonetheless locate them at the limits of the Canadian nation in different respects: many of the missing women were aboriginal and domestic workers are prospective immigrants. One haunts the nation-state from 'within' as a reminder of the inability of the state to conclude the act of colonization, the other marks a troubled passage from 'outside'. They thus collaborate to call into question the completeness of the territorialization of the nation-state.[10]

The differences between the cases are particularly productive in another respect. Both examples draw our attention to the fact that it is often women who are cast into bare life, but sex workers and domestic helpers lie at and play upon provocative extremes within gendered norms: that of public whore and domesticated mother. The locations of the case studies call up these same extremes. The Downtown Eastside includes the poorest census tract in Canada, and is the site of high concentrations of drug addiction, prostitution, HIV-AIDS and Hepatitis B. It is where one expects to find the state of exception.[11] I want to unsettle this expectation by looking as well at a more banal, less predictable and less sensationalized place of exception: the middle-class home. Each case also offers opportunities to explore how conventional attempts to bring abandoned subjects back from bare life can be limited by the ways that they re-enact gender and class norms. They bring to each other doubts about conventional political strategy: the ineffectiveness of the legislative victories of domestic workers suggest the violence of exclusion through non-citizenship; the case of the murdered women tells domestic workers that citizenship is no protection. Finally, each case brings us close to one of two figures that Agamben offers as a means to re-envision political community, such that we might tentatively explore them. These are the refugee and the human being so degraded as to demand an ethics beyond liberal humanism. Different zones of exception offer different opportunities for thought.

Producing Vancouver's Missing Women as Bare Life

For many years the police insisted that the missing women had not been killed: they were merely transient (de Vries 2003; Pitman 2002). That police could lose track of so many of these women is in some ways astonishing, especially given that the women were for the most part sex workers, whose bodies were undoubtedly closely surveilled. Activists argue that gentrification pressures in this area have only increased the policing of prostitution in this part of the city (this has had the effect of forcing sex workers into more isolated and more dangerous areas) (Pitman 2002). Women living in the Downtown Eastside interviewed by Jennifer England (2004) speak of daily police harassment that follows from the fact that they are invariably read as prostitutes. Lana, a 52 year old aboriginal woman, describes standing on the street with her daughter:

> *And then when I'm standing there, this cop goes to me like this, 'come here'. He says 'you standing out here again?' And I said, 'What the hell are you talking about?' 'Can you give me your names, both of you give me your names. Cause if you're going to act smart you're going to come with us'. I say 'no I rather not come with you, but I'd rather report you to your supervisor'. And yet they still intimidated me because they didn't think I would. My daughter went over there and says, 'what's the problem here' . . . and then pretty soon, because they had made a mistake, they tried to cover up to her (quoted in England, 2004:308).*

England traces what she calls a "trope of visibility/invisibility", of the women's feelings that they are both hyper-visible and invisible, both inside and outside the gaze of the state. Their inclusion within the law as sex workers is simultaneously an act of exclusion.

In the case of the missing women, police and civic officials were slow to accept that they were not simply transient. In response to public requests for a concerted police investigation, the mayor, Philip Owen, reportedly stated, "We are not running a location service" (de Vries 2003:217), and first suggested that any reward that might be offered be framed as a $5,000 incentive for women to "call home" (de Vries 2003:221). These comments can be understood to reflect some unfounded geographical assumptions about the inherent mobility of drug addicts[12] and sex workers, based on speculation that they may have entered a treatment program, or may be seeking to distance themselves from their stigmatized lives as prostitutes, in another location under another identity.[13] Lisa Sanchez (2004) contends that the sex worker is "a subject who is always already out of place . . . an eternal outsider who cannot be displaced [because she has no place], a figure of eternal motion, elusive and ghost-like, both illegal and impossible." One part of this illusive mobility is a suspicion that prostitutes lead double lives. Wright (2004) traces how police in Ciudad Juarez, Mexico have justified their failure to stop the flow of murders of hundreds of women by casting doubt on their morality. Family and friends are often asked, "Are you sure that she didn't lead a double life?" (377). Similarly (but in reverse), in Vancouver the suspicion of their return to respectable life justified police inaction.

Another geographical way of making sense of the police argument about transience is to note that at least 39 of the missing women were aboriginal, and to trace the colonial geography that their aboriginality implies. There has been a long history in Canada of assuming that aboriginals and cities are mutually exclusive. It is often assumed that aboriginals in cities are merely transient, en route to their legislated 'camp', which is the Indian reserve (Peters 1996:1998)[14]. In other words, the presumption of transience made sense because of other geographical assumptions. All of these spatialities undergird legal abandonment.

By 1998, however, more and more women had disappeared, and family, friends and community activists continued to call for state action. The media uncovered the story of police operating very differently in different spaces of the city and in relation to different categories of citizens[15]. Under increasing pressure, the attorney general and Vancouver police produced and distributed a poster about the missing women, and announced a reward of up to $100,000 for information leading to the arrest and conviction of a person or persons responsible for the women's disappearance. These representations of the missing women nonetheless undermined their claims to be citizens with rights to police protection. On the missing persons page of the Police Department website, for instance, there appeared two lists on opposite sides of the screen: missing persons on the right, missing sex workers on the left. A sister of one of the missing women has interpreted this as evidence that: "Sex workers were excluded from the 'persons' category" (de Vries 2003:104).

The missing women poster continues to shape media images of the women even to this day. Its enframing of the missing women has important effects because it is arguable that the photos, text, and layout contribute to produce the missing women in less than a human subject position. Jennifer England (2004) has argued that the poster criminalized the missing women because the photographs that appeared on this poster were in a mug shot format that either were or resemble those taken when a person is processed during arrest. They thus trace (or suggest) a history and microgeography of bodies that already have been processed and administered by the police for their social deviancy.[16] The mug shot format continues to be used even after the women's fate has been well established; in January 2004, for instance, the local newspaper, *The Vancouver Sun*, reused it when reporting that the remains of nine more women had been verified (Figure 1; Culbert 2004). Cropped closely around the head, de-contextualised, and arrayed in a grid, these photographs report on the state's administration of already deviant bodies, and not on individual lives lost.[17] The compulsion to quantify is so great that the women whose DNA has been found but not identified, for whom there is no photograph, are also represented on the grid.

At the heading of the original poster ran the title: "Missing Downtown Eastside Women." The poster thus explicitly located the women within a particular space: the Downtown Eastside. This has also persisted in media reportage. For instance, when it was reported in the national newspaper, *The Globe and Mail*, that Dawn Crey's remains had been identified in January 2004, the first fact that we learnt was that Crey was "a drug addict who lived in a residential hotel in Van-

Figure 1. Locating missing women

couver's seamy Downtown Eastside (Armstrong 2004:A7). Identification with the Downtown Eastside is problematic because media representations of the neighbourhood tend to be uniformly negative and sensational. Rather than presenting its complexities, including a rich and diverse tradition of artistic production and political organizing, media regularly present the Downtown Eastside as the epicenter of a national crisis in illegal drug use (England, 2004), and "probably Canada's worst neighbourhood." It has been described as outside "civilization," literally beyond "the boundary into hell" (quotes are taken from the *Vancouver Sun* in summer 1998; Sommers and Blomley 2003:19). Simply being in this space is taken as evidence of the women's degeneracy. This is an argument that Sherene Razack has made in relation to the 1995 murder of Pamela George, an aboriginal women working as a sex worker in another western Canadian city. Trying to understand why the two white middle-class 19-year-old men who killed Pamela George received relatively light sentences, Razack states succinctly: "[s]he was of the space where murders happen; they were not" (2000:126).

A complex layering of imaginative geographies has led to the reduction of missing women to bare life, such that the police failed to investigate their disappearances, in some cases for over twenty years. First, there was the assumed mobility of sex workers. Second, there are the colonial geographies that make First Nations women almost naturally disappear in an urban context. Third, there is the unremitting stigmatization of the Downtown Eastside, and the persistent association of the women with it. Finally, women were and continue to be represented almost exclusively as diseased, criminalized, impoverished and degenerate bodies, now—literally—as disembodied DNA or as dead contaminating meat. It is not only that geographies contain bare life—that camps localize states of the exception. Imaginative and material geographies are part of the process of constructing certain categories of people as bare life.

In the case of the missing women, the location of the accused murderer's home, which is also the site where the women's remains have been found, has only cemented the reduction of the women to bare life. The accused murderer owned and lived on a pig farm, which was also the site of notorious parties to which the murdered women were allegedly transported directly from the Downtown Eastside. Aerial photographs of the farm have appeared in local newspapers (and are reprinted in Oleksijczuk (2003)). These distanced aerial photographs show the farm framed by neat rows of suburban housing developments, and thus excite the viewer to speculate on their own proximity to danger and to explore their vulnerability to the barbarism living right next door.[18] There is an odd symmetry between this photograph and popular understandings of the spatial order of the Downtown Eastside, as a bounded area of disorder at the heart of the city or civilized life. In February 2002, the *Vancouver Sun* began to explore a story that played on fears of an inability to contain this disorder: there was speculation that fragments of some of the women's bodies had entered the food chain through a local rendering plant to which the accused delivered pig entrails. The director of the Canadian Food Inspection Agency was quoted as speculating: "I can't imagine any testing that would distinguish, um, you know—animal matter one from another" (Bolen and Kines 2002:A6; quoted in Oleksijczuk 2003:112). Bare life indeed.

Reclaiming the Missing Women from Bare Life, and Erasing them Once Again

Not all of the media coverage has reduced the Missing Women to bare life. These women are often returned to their full humanity through the caring and grieving voices of their family members. Because these family members are typically located outside the Downtown Eastside, they also reconnect the women—typically as sisters and daughters—with non-stigmatized places.[19] Bev Pitman (2002:176) has argued that the sympathy evoked by these stories created in 1999 "an uncommon kind of [cross-class, inter-racial] community" in Vancouver. We can see this community at work still in Kati Campbell's art piece with which I began. In a newspaper review of her show (Laurence 2004:35), Campbell is quoted as saying: "I was thinking really hard about how to deal with these losses in a way that does not add to the media spectacle." "What could I give,' she asks, "that would be a real aid to mourning?" She settled on crafting 67 shawls, one for each murdered or missing woman's mother. Each shawl is embroidered with lines of text that are words and phrases that refer to the names of the missing women. "The most prevalent middle name of all the women," Campbell tells us, "is Louise—it turns up at least a dozen times . . . . Louise means 'brave warrior', so it's a wonderful refrain that works its way through the piece." The reviewer of Campbell's work recognises her politicized intent, namely to address "our culture's refusal to empathize with drug addicts and prostitutes, as if they have somehow forfeited their humanity and their emotional ties" (35). Still, she presses Campbell to link the specifics of her personal life to the grief of the mothers of the murdered women. In particular, she invites her to compare their grief to her own grief over the accidental death of her 15-month old daughter. We are told that Campbell is "reluctant" to do this. She tells the reviewer that, "the first time my partner made the connection, I couldn't even see it.' Pressed by the journalist, "she does agree that her understanding of grief and mourning made empathy possible" (Laurence 2004:35).

Campbell's hesitation to equate her grief with that of the murdered women's mothers is one that I want to pursue. It is not that empathy is misguided, but that the generalized grieving solicited by the journalist potentially abstracts the murdered women's lives in troubling ways. Empathy through normalised family loss humanizes the murdered women by locating them within narratives of the middle-class family. Not only is this a gendered and heteronormative narrative, it privatizes, individualizes, and potentially depoliticizes aboriginal women's and sex workers' specific marginality in the Downtown Eastside. In short, it is too easy to empathize in a generalized way as mothers (or sisters or fathers or brothers) if it allows us to evade the specificity of sex workers' lives and their particular (state regulated) vulnerability to violence.[20]

The propensity to neutralize specific race and class experiences was demonstrated in a striking way when *America's Most Wanted,* a US reality television program, focused its sights on the Vancouver Missing Women case in 1999. Halfway through the segment, there was a dramatic re-enactment of the disappearance of Sarah de Vries, one of the missing women. A young white woman was shown stepping into a brown van. Given her mixed African-Canadian and aboriginal heritage, this is a curious portrayal of Sarah de Vries. Bev Pitman (2002) understands this whitening of Sarah de Vries to reflect an attempt to increase audience identification among white middle-class viewers. But, as Pitman notes, this enacts "for a second time" (179) the violence of removing an aboriginal woman from the streets of Vancouver. This is also a tactic of re-incorporating the missing women into the social body by assimilating them within the space of the white middle-class family. It establishes the family as the criterion by which their life is grieveable, and it resituates the missing women—not as citizens within the city—but within the private sphere of pre-political life.

I want to turn now to the case of Filipina domestic workers because it thoroughly disrupts the middle class home as an unambiguous space from which to build inclusion. It possibly also provides another model for thinking about returning those who have been cast into bare life to full humanity.

Producing Filipina Domestic Workers as Bare Life

This is little doubt that those who come through the Canadian federal government's Live-in Caregiver Program are in an ambiguous legal state. They are on temporary work visas, living in Canada as citizens of another country. As such, their residency in Canada is carefully monitored, and periodically there is a high profile deportation that makes visible through example the discretion and force of state power. Most live-in caregivers come to Canada from the Philippines. As is the case for most sending countries, the Philippines has been largely ineffectual in protecting the rights of its citizens working abroad as domestic workers (Pratt 2004). Domestic workers' rights within Canada are on equally shaky ground. For example, employers are told by the Canadian federal government that "Citizenship and Immigration Canada is not party to, nor does it bear responsibility for, the enforcement of" their employment contract with the domestic worker (cited in Stasiulis and Bakan 2004:250). In other words, protection of employee rights is a provincial, and not a federal, responsibility. Critics argue that this position signals to employers "implicit permission to violate contract provisions" (Stasiulis and Bakan 2002:250). In any case, the employment contract is itself paradoxical because it is a contract to assume the status of live-in servant, "at which point," in the words of a Canadian legal scholar, "the contractual model (with its assumption of juridical equality) ceases to inform the internal operation of the relationship" (Macklin 1992:749). It is not, as one activist put it, "that all employers are mean, nasty, dirty, evil people in comparison with lovely domestic workers. The point is, the way the system is set up, it's very easy to abuse domestic workers because they are in powerless position" (quoted in Macklin 1992:729). "That many (perhaps most) employers choose not to mistreat their domestic workers does not negate the availability of the option" (Macklin 1992:729). This is precisely the state of exception of which Agamben writes, where law is decided and administered in a discretionary way and those who are abandoned are both inside and outside the jurisdiction of the law.

One of the issues that I have explored over the last decade is how and why this program of indentured servitude persists in a liberal democratic society such as Canada. Not only does it persist without much censure or popular protest, but it is usually perceived in positive terms. This is a space of exception that liberal middle-class Canadians seem to administer with a clear conscience. This clear conscience is in part due to the fact that domestic workers can apply for citizenship after 24 months in the program. The policy is thus a time-limited period of legal abandonment for which citizenship is judged as compensation (Pratt in collaboration with the Philippine Women Centre 2005). But it is also intimately bound up with the material and symbolic spaces in which domestic work occurs and the geographies that are read into Filipinas (Pratt 2004).

The point about the literal spaces in which domestic work is carried out is simply this: in many ways the home is still perceived to be a private, non-political space that ought to be free from state interference. Domestic labour is typically not seen as work. Employers have a very difficult time distinguishing whether the labour of live-in caregivers is waged labour, the work of social reproduction or gifts of labour time. This is especially so when domestic workers are compelled to live in the employer's home. It seems reasonable to ask domestic workers to watch children for an extra half hour or so, when they are, in any case, present in the home. It may seem reasonable to ask a domestic worker to clean the family's dishes after meals because she presumably needs to do at least some of this labour as a means of reproducing herself. Domestic workers labour in a zone of indistinction between work and leisure, private and public space, between biological and political life.

But it is not only that domestic work is done within the home; there are other geographies at work that systematically reduce Filipinas to bare life, so as to make their ambiguous legal status unremarkable. One plays on a discourse of primitivism, another on their utter desperation as 'third world women'. There are many ways into the primitivism argument because it is so pervasive. I have been told about it by many nanny agents operating in Vancouver (Pratt 2004). For example: Filipina nannies [as compared to European nannies] will "let your children pee in the park. They just take their pants down in the park." (Interview with Nanny Agent E, June 1994). Or:

> By our standards . . . the adults who are coming over, were not raised how we would raise our children at all . . . There's none of this, you know, 'Would you please sit and eat?' No, they can run all over the house eating something. . . . so it's a hell of a life . . . They're kind and caring and loving and that sort of thing. But there is no discipline and structure . . . You know, you don't line up for a bus. You push aside some little old lady getting on the bus. When you sit at the table, you don't see that there's so much food, so you take proportionately. No. You make sure you get yours first. So there's none of that, you see, which fits in more with a Canadian society. And there's a lot of learning that a lot of Filipino people have to do. (Interview with Nanny Agent H, June 1994).

This primitivism also operates in media representations that are meant to be critical of it. Take, for example, an in-depth article that appeared in 2001 in the major national newspaper, *The Globe and Mail* (Figure 2; Saunders 2001). The article

A week in the life

The nanny
Salary: **$200**
Rent: **$50**
Food: **$50**
Medical: **No insurance or coverage**
Transportation: **City bus**
Amount sent home to El Salvador:
$50 or more

The dog
Boarding: **$490**
Walking: **$200**
Food: **$50 (incl. treats)**
Medical: **$25 vet fees (when healthy)**
Grooming: **$100 per session**
Other services available:
**psychiatrist, masseuse, spa,
antidepressants, human sleeping companions**
Transportation: **Car or limo**

You wouldn't wish it on a dog

Figure 2. A curious comparison between nanny and dog
Note: This is a rendering of the photograph which appeared in the newspaper. It was not possible to obtain permission to use the orginal photograph.

advocates for domestic workers in Los Angeles by comparing the deplorable wages and conditions of domestic workers with the expenses that affluent households willingly pay for the care of their dogs. The comparison should be made between children and dogs on the one hand, and domestic workers and the various groomers, dog walkers, etc. who are hired to care for dogs on the other. But both the text and visuals work differently. Because the dog caregivers are absent from the visuals, we pair the domestic worker with the dog, a reading that is prompted by the title, "You wouldn't wish it on a dog". This reading is particularly problematic in Canada, where the majority of foreign domestic workers are Filipino, and one means of primitivising Filipinos is precisely through their reputation as 'dogeaters'.

There is a second characteristic of their geography that sticks to Filipinas so as to turn their indentured servitude in Canada into a kind of rescue mission: this is the assumption of utter destitution of life in the Philippines. Again, various nanny agents whom I have interviewed in Vancouver voiced this assumption. Explaining why established labour standards of minimum wage and overtime provisions cannot be applied to domestic work, one nanny agent reasoned: "[this] would not work at all. There's not the money there [within the household budgets of prospective Canadian employers]. It will just cut down on the amount of immigration from the Philippines tremendously, because that [the Live-in Caregiver Program] is the foot in the door for many immigrants . . . You know, things are not good back in the Philippines. . . . They would be doomed to a life there" (Interview with Nanny Agent H, June 1994).

Domestic workers are certainly coming to Canada for the opportunity to immigrate and for economic opportunities, but destitution is not an accurate representation of many of their circumstances given the program requirements that they have linguistic competence in one of the two national languages and two years of post-secondary education. Rhacel Parrenas (2005) has argued that it is in fact the middle classes in the Philippines who are most prone to do overseas contract work. They do this in order to maintain their middle class standing in the face of massive privatization of state services in the Philippines, especially health and education services, occurring under the discipline of the IMF and World Bank. The educational credentials of the 15 domestic workers with whom I have worked closely over the last decade (Pratt and the Philippine Women Centre 2005) certainly bear this out: considering their educational qualifications from the Philippines, one was trained as a social worker, one as a registered nurse, five as midwives, seven as school teachers and one as a nurses' aid. Yet media fascination with poverty in the Philippines, for example with the sale of body organs, does nothing to convey this message of middle-class labour migration—of the basic similarity between middle class Canadians and the Filipinas whom they employ as servants.

I have argued, then, that practices of legal abandonment do not simply happen anywhere; they are always accomplished through particular material and symbolic geographies. Assumptions about the inherent transience of the missing women led to police neglect. Live-in caregivers have precarious claims to workers' rights because they work and live in their employers' homes. In both cases, the space of the home disrupts claims to full active citizenship. For domestic workers, labour in the home is indistinct from social reproduction and leisure activities, and they tend to be conceived with familial relations. The home is a private space to some extent presumed to be beyond state regulation. For missing women, it was their inability to claim home in the Downtown Eastside that rendered them invisible. But subsequent efforts to bring these women into visibility tend to relocate them in their familial homes, in private depoliticized spaces that equally strip them of their status as public citizens. Such forms of legal abandonment are gendered and racialized. Although Agamben claims that the very distinction between public and private is deactivated in the state of exception, the continuing gendering of the distinction is itself a resource for legal abandonment. The instability of women's passage from private into political life haunts these women and returns to produce them as bare life. Layers of taken-for-granted gendered and racialised geographies make unremarkable the abandonment of certain groups of women.

An End to Civil War?

While Agamben's insensitivity to gender is perplexing and limiting, I do not want to under estimate the significant opportunities that he brings to feminist theorizing and strategizing. Legal abandonment is not another way of telling the story of the private sphere, and bare life is not equivalent to a feminized social existence of toil within the domestic realm. Bare life describes a human life reduced to matter, a life in many ways beyond gendered existence. I am particularly interested by the ways in which his theorizing challenges feminists to rethink political strategy for bringing abandoned women back to social life, as fully human beings. How, in particular, might Agamben's theorizing provoke us to think beyond conventional means of bringing *homo sacer* back to life through the production of similarity within liberalism? My own efforts in the last section to retrieve Filipino domestic workers as professionals operates within this circuit of producing inclusion through similarity. The danger of rehabilitating the goodness of middle-class professional immigrants is that it potentially reinstates a division between good and bad immigrants (Honig 1998; Ong 1996), and thus continues the process of nation-building through the production of bare life. Might Agamben's theorizing enable us to rethink more profoundly our relationship to biopolitical sovereignty, a form of sovereignty that is driven to abandon more and more citizens as a way of purifying and enhancing the health of the nation, a form of sovereignty that wages a kind of continual civil war through the production of bare life?

The two cases that I have considered are intriguing because they bring us close to two limit-concepts that Agamben uses to re-imagine political community. One is the human so degraded as to exist beyond conventional humanist ethics of respect, dignity and responsibility (Agamben 2000b). Another is the refugee who refuses assimilation within the nation state. With respect to the latter, Agamben goes so far as to recommend that we "build our political philosophy anew starting from the one and only figure of the refugee" (2000a:15). The importance of this figure is that it severs the connection between personhood and the nation-state, a link that is forged in liberal societies through the concept of the citizen and territorialisation of individual rights within the nation-state. The figure of the refugee who refuses assimilation is of one who refuses to submit their personhood to the territorializing biopolitical state.

I want to think with the figure of the refugee in relation to foreign domestic workers because it provokes a different line of political strategy than the one pursed in recent years by the Philippine Women Centre. Their main strategy has been to lobby for the eradication of the Live-in Caregiver Program. A second strategy is to force the Canadian government to allow Filipinos to migrate to Canada on the basis of their professional credentials, typically within the health professions. In other words, they are attempting to force the Canadian government to admit Filipinos as citizens rather than as labour migrants. Agamben asks us to think about political strategy in other terms because seeking inclusion as citizens does nothing to disrupt a political community based on a process of abandonment. Agamben urges the need to imagine fully political subjects outside of and beyond specifically liberal notions of citizenship.

What might this mean for domestic workers? Without really knowing the answer to this question, I have become increasingly interested in the refusals voiced by Filipina domestic workers once they have received Canadian citizenship. Over the decade I have worked with a number of the women who came through the Live-in Caregiver Program and are now permanently settled in Canada, but who received their Canadian citizenship very unwillingly. They feel that their migration was forced on them by economic circumstances brought on by the corruption of the Philippine government and the stranglehold of the World Bank and IMF, and they remain bitter about their experiences in Canada as live-in domestic workers (Pratt and the Philippine Women Centre 2005). In short, they are ambivalent Canadian citizens.

In recent years, I have also worked with Filipino-Canadian immigrant youth, some who are children of these domestic workers. Feeling alienated from what they perceive to be a racist Canadian society, they have sought different, extra-territorial attachments in their identification as Filipino (Pratt in collaboration with the Filipino-Canadian Youth Alliance 2004). This identification takes them on regular visits to the Philippines and they gather political strength from a history of student activism in the Philippines. The tenth annual cultural evening of the Filipino-Canadian Youth Alliance in May 2005, for instance, was organized under the theme of 'Ipagpatuloy: Living the Storm', to reference that this year also marks the 35th anniversary of the First Quarter Storm, a three month period in 1970 of mass mobilization in the Philippines to protest the Marcos regime, and to draw a line of continuity between this struggle and their own in Canada. They have also crafted a strong network of linkages in Europe and the United States. Linkages to Amsterdam, where Professor Jose Maria Sison lives in the state of exception[21], are strong. But I am particularly interested in the ways that these youth articulate their transnational Filipino identity with other youth groups in Vancouver. At the moment, one of their strongest alliances is with First Nations youth organizations. They articulate their alliance around a common theme of displacement and forced migration, as well as a shared critique of liberal norms and the uneven application of them. I want to argue that this process of alliance building offers a moment for imaging political community within Canada, not based in identification through an abstract notion of national belonging or citizenship rights, but as a series of incomplete translations across partially overlapping issues and concerns. That process of translation requires a laboured process of reading across particular embedded histories, for example, the displacement of First Nations in Canada and the land question in the Philippines. Political solidarities are constructed, but social and political identification is always excessive to these alliances. Perhaps this is one model for realizing what Agamben urges for all of us: that is, "to recognize the refugee that he or she is" (2000a:25), namely a person whose identifications and claims to social and political life exceed citizenship.

The missing women may offer another way to think through the aporia of the irreconcilability of political and biological life within liberalism. Consider a poem written by Sarah de Vries, one of the murdered women:

> *Woman's body found beaten beyond recognition*
> *You sip your coffee*
> *Taking a drag of your smoke*
> *Turning the page*
> *Taking a bite of your toast*
> *Just another day*
> *Just another death*
> *Just one more thing you so easily forget*
> *You and your soft, sheltered life*
> *Just go on and on*
> *For nobody special from your world is gone*
> *Just another day*
> *Just another death*
> *Just another Hastings Street whore*
> *Sentenced to death*
> *The judge's gavel already fallen*
> *Sentence already passed*
> *But you*
> *You just sip your coffee*
> *Washing down your toast.*
> *She was a broken-down angel*
> *A child lost with no place*
> *A human being in disguise*
> *She touched my life*
> *She was somebody*
> *She was no whore*
> *She was somebody special*
> *Who just lost her way*
> *She was somebody fighting for life*
> *Trying to survive*
> *A lonely lost child who died*
> *In the night, all alone, scared*
> *Gasping for air.*

Sarah de Vries (de Vries 2003:233–4)

Sarah anticipated our neglect. She imagined us reading about a murdered sex worker's death as we eat our breakfast toast. The woman has been legally abandoned: the judge's gavel has already fallen. She is beaten beyond recognition, and dies scared and all alone. In a book memorializing her sister's life and death, Maggie de Vries agonizes over this aloneness, and expresses a desire to have borne witness to Sarah's murder.

This resonates, in an uncanny way, with Agamben's (2000b) discussion of the ethical force of the testimony of survivors from Auschwitz. He argues that such survivors speak by proxy for those who did not survive. Further, the dehumanizing process of Auschwitz reduced many prisoners to a state in which they had lost their capacity to observe and testify. Witnessing, on the part of survivors, entails bringing into language that which does not have a language because the victims were rendered mute, beyond speech. Its ethical force lies in resisting biopolitical efforts to separate those abandoned in bare life from speaking, fully human beings. The terrible burden of Sarah de Vries' poem comes from the fact that she is testifying (before the fact) about an event (murder) that she cannot witness. She speaks in proxy for herself, and her authority undoubtedly comes from her very own death (Felman 2001).

How might we respond to the poem's call for recognition, of a body beaten beyond recognition? And how might such recognition open up, in Judith Butler's words, "another kind of normative aspiration in the field of politics," one that lies beyond a claim for individual rights tied to the autonomy of our bodies (2004:26)? Sarah de Vries' poem is shocking and provokes shame because it bears witness to our neglect. Had we heeded her poem, would so many women have died? Would we have read her poem if she had not? Witnessing is an intersubjective process, and key to the possibility for political transformation through witnessing is the understanding that the act of public testimony transforms those who witness such testimony (Butler 2004). Butler develops this analysis through the concept of mourning. Mourning involves an acceptance to undergo a transformation, to be beside oneself through grief. Rather than returning the murdered women to us—through the conventions of family, or abstract ideals of human dignity and respect, or paranoid fears about a generalized vulnerability to sexual predators—mourning the missing women would involve allowing our relationship to them to change us, to become dispossessed from ourselves. A key moment of dispossession might be to recognize what these women experienced long before their murders. This is the chilling process of abandonment within the everyday spaces of our cities, and a normalized passing across the threshold into bare life.

Acknowledgements

I thank Nick Blomley, Derek Gregory, and Joel Wainwright for their close readings of earlier drafts of this manuscript, and Heidi Nast for her comments as referee. I have benefited hugely from thoughtful and probing responses to presentations given at U.B.C., Tokyo Keizai University, the University of Minnesota and University of Toronto. Thanks very much to Noel Castree and Melissa Wright for their editorial assistance, and for the opportunity to bring this paper to completion as the *Antipode* Lecture at the 2005 annual meetings of the Association of American Geographers. I thank Maggie de Vries for permission to reprint her sister's poem.

Endnotes

1. Twelve of these assaults took place in the Downtown Eastside in Vancouver, and the rest in Southeast Asia. The accused, Donald Bakker, is the first Canadian to be charged under Canada's new "sex tourism law", which

makes it possible to prosecute Canadians for sexual abuse of children outside of Canada.

2. This comment was made in casual conversation with Cecilia Diocson in July 2003.

3. To modern ears the name is deceptive. *Homo sacer* was a position conferred by ancient Roman law upon those who could not be ritually sacrificed (because they were outside divine law and their deaths thus had no value to the gods), but could be killed (or let die) with impunity (because they had been excluded from juridical law).

4. Bhabha (2004) chronicles more recent attacks on birthright citizenship in the United States, Canada and Ireland.

5. Brown (2003) is cautioning for more rigour in conceptualizations of neo-liberalism, arguing that neo-liberalism draws on a very specific and especially brutal variant of economic liberalism. Unlike earlier variants of political liberalism, neo-liberalism collapses moral and political rationalities into the economic. She argues that citizenship has been reduced to an entrepreneurial responsibility for well-being, and the consequences of such freedom and responsibility are both individualized and moralized.

6. This simplifies Agamben's argument because he is claiming that every individual now contains an unstable mix of bare life and political subjecthood, given that entry into citizenship is via bare life. "Bare life is no longer confined to a particular place or a definite category. It now dwells in the biological body of every living being" (Agamben 1998:140). However, it is also clear that he believes that some lives are barer than others, and it is this distinction that I am pursuing here. As Peter Fitzpatrick (2001) notes, Agamben offers two modes of conceiving bare life: one totalizing, and another that comes in varied instantiations.

7. Another boundary defined a threshold between civilized life and a state of (uncivilized) nature. I bracket this at the moment but this clearly becomes important to an analysis of the racialisation of legal abandonment and in particular the ways that discourses of primitivism naturalise legal abandonment. In the case of racialised women, the state of nature returns and is enfolded into the geographies of private and public in especially problematic ways.

8. Lisa Sanchez (2004) takes a stronger stance and argues that *homo sacer* is gendered as masculine. She writes that "the expulsion of *homo sacer* is the displacement of one who was already imagined to be inside—he is a useful enigma—an included exclusion". In her view, certain excluded women—she writes in particular about sex workers—dwell in an entirely different conceptual and legal space than *homo sacer*. They are, she argues, utterly excluded, with no possibility of return. I want to take a somewhat different tact, and argue that contemporary *homo sacer* is a much more complicated figure in practice than imagined by Agamben, and to pursue what a gendered analysis of *homo sacer* might look like.

9. Consider US Senator Henry Cabot Lodge's remark in 1900: "a native [Filipino] family feeds; it does not breakfast or dine, it feeds" (quoted in Doty 1996:39).

10. I thank Joel Wainwright for this phrasing, and for sharpening my thinking on this point.
11. Consider an email that one of my undergraduate students sent me as I began writing this paper. He was participating in a theatre workshop—ironically, one entitled: Practicing Democracy—that was being held in the Downtown Eastside. He writes:

> Today was even more intense, one of the defining moments being the extreme use of force in the arrest of a young woman right outside the rehearsal hall. The group was on a smoke break while a couple of policeman were making what appeared to be a routine arrest across the road, until suddenly the young woman was taken down to the pavement and put into a choke hold. As she started screaming and yelling, a bunch of us ran over just in time to see one of the officers smack the girl in the back of the head. There must have been about fifteen of us who went over, to see what could be done. The scene was pretty crazy . . . but it was amazing how fast the young woman calmed down once she realized that there was a huge crowd of witnesses. The police seemed a little taken aback as well and suddenly everything was strictly by the book. One in our group is a first aid attendant and was able to convince the police to let him make sure the young woman (who couldn't have been more than sixteen) was physically okay, as she was spitting up blood and vomiting. We were also able to get the badge numbers of the policemen and called the young woman's lawyer, telling him that several of us had witnessed the affair. Anyway, just another day in the downtown eastside, I guess . . . (email communication, February 2, 2004).

The role of middle class observers as witnesses who rehabilitate the rights of those who have been cast into bare life is an important one. But this understanding also reinforces the idea that the Downtown Eastside is truly exceptional.
12. de Vries (2003:189) argues that this displays a misunderstanding of the geographies of survival sex work and drug addiction insofar as "as women get older and become addicted to drugs, they become less transient, to the point where they are more or less rooted in one spot."
13. These speculations found some slight support in 1999 when four of the missing women were located: two dead and two alive (de Vries 2003:189).
14. Indeed, this assumption has been formalized in Canadian laws that have made access to aboriginal rights contingent on residence on a First Nation's reserve. Yet more than 50% of First Nation's people in Canada now live in urban areas, and Peters (1998) has argued that the city is especially important to First Nation's women and to their efforts to create a space for themselves beyond patriarchal relations on reserves. There is however a persistent inability on the part of non-aboriginal Canadians to imagine First Nations' peoples permanently settled within the space of the city, and a tendency to assume a continuing link between aboriginality and the space of the reserve. As an index of this, in the province of Manitoba the 1996 census found that

35% of the province's natives live in cities, but about 90 percent of government funding is aimed at reserves (Smith 2004). A recent federal decision not to appeal a court decision about government discrimination against off-reserve natives in relation to a specific training program has been taken by some Native advocates as a decision that will "completely change the way that Ottawa deals with urban communities," whilst "[e]xperts are divided about whether the court's decision will oblige the federal government to directly fund urban aboriginal groups" (Smith 2004:A7).

15. It should be acknowledged that some media coverage was both effective and highly praised—in fact, one journalist (Wood 1999a:1999b) received a national award for his investigative reporting on this issue. However, the media have abandoned the missing women in numerous ways, including some that I do not explore. Young and Pritchard (2005), for instance, puzzle over the small number of US media violations of the media ban in relation to the trial of the man accused of murdering the missing women (relative to an earlier sensationalized Canadian serial murder case). They reason that US media have evinced less interest in the current case because the victims were sex workers and many were aboriginal, whereas the victims of the earlier serial murderer were white and middle class.

16. It would be unfair to overextend this point, because some of the photos were provided by family members.

17. This stands in striking contrast to the treatment in New York newspapers of those missing after the September 11, 2001 attacks on the World Trade Center. "The newspaper portraits were of a necessity uniform. As in a high school yearbook, everyone memorialized was given equal space and equal treatment" (Miller 2003:114). There are, however, two telling differences. First, these (typically smiling) portraits were accompanied by written anecdotes that were meant to individuate, and provide what Miller calls "a narrative DNA". Second, the newspaper editors of the *New York Times* publicly "pondered the best strategy for identifying the singularity of each life within the constraints of the form" (Miller 2003:114) and lamented the fact that such profiles were but "a single frame lifted from the uncountable complexity of a lived life" (quoted in Miller).

18. The media has deployed the same tactic with respect to Donald Bakker, the Vancouver man accused of sex torture in January 2004. He is invariably described as a "short and balding" "father of a young child" who lives in a middle-class neighbourhood (*Vancouver Sun* 2004). In other words, he could be living next door.

19. This is also a common strategy among oppositional groups in the Downtown Eastside. In her assessment of photographic representations of women in the Downtown Eastside, for instance, Jennifer England (2004) contrasts two photography shows exhibited in Vancouver in 1998. She argues that one by a well-known Vancouver photographer, Lincoln Clarkes, eroticizes women's poverty within the confined spaces of the back alleys of the Downtown Eastside. She contrasts this to a collaboration between an artist and nine Downtown Eastside women, and notes in particular the productive way that the latter exhibit "challenges an outsider's view of the community as

a homogeneous, tightly bounded space" (91) by showing images of Downtown Eastside women with their families moving in and out of this neighbourhood (on public transit for instance). This disrupts the stereotype that these women are entrapped by and in fact synonymous with the space of the Downtown Eastside. A similar comparison could be made between two important and widely aired films that have been made about the Downtown Eastside: *Through a Blue Lens,* and *Fix: Story of an Addicted City.* The former video—made in collaboration with Vancouver police—plays directly with the theme of frontier (England 2004) and the latter begins, significantly, with the trip by advocates for drug addicts outside of the Downtown Eastside into the centre of official local political life: City Hall.

20. For instance, the changing regulation of prostitution in Vancouver over the last 30 years has forced sex workers into increasingly marginal and deserted locations in the city (de Vries 2003).

21. An exiled Filipino revolutionary, Professor Sison exists within the state of the exception. He was stranded while visiting Holland in 1987 when the Aquino government cancelled his passport and thus legally abandoned him as a citizen of the Philippines. Sison was recognized by the Dutch government as a political refugee and is thus protected from expulsion. The Dutch government continues, however, to refuse admission and rights of residence. Professor Sison is currently included on the US list of "Specially Designated Nationals and Blocked Persons" and on the list of terrorists of the Council of the European Union and Commission of the European Communities. He has made a complaint to the European Court of Justice demanding that his name be removed and that he be paid damages.

References

Agamben G (1998) *Homo Sacer: Sovereign Power and Bare Life.* Translated by D Heller-Roazen. Standford: Standford University Press

Agamben G (2000a) *Means without End: Notes on Politics.* Translated by V Binetti and C Casarino. Minneapolis: University of Minnesota Press

Agamben G (2000b) *Remnants of Auschwitz: The Witness and the Archive.* Translated by D Heller-Roazen. New York: Zone Books

Agamben G (2005) *State of Exception.* Translated by K Attell. Chicago: University of Chicago Press

Armstrong J (2004) Woman's remains identified on B C farm. *Globe and Mail,* January 17:A7

Bhabha J (2004) A "mere fortuity" of birth? Are children citizens? *differences: A Journal of Feminist Cultural Studies* 15:91–117

Brown W (2003) Neo-liberalism and the End of Liberal Democracy *theory&event* 7:1, n.p.

Brown W (2004) Tolerance and/or Equality" The "Jewish Question" and the "Woman Question." *differences: A Journal of Feminist Cultural Studies* 15:1–31

Butler J (2004) *Precarious Life: The Powers of Mourning and Violence.* London: Verso

Culbert L (2004) Nine more women linked to Pickton case, total 31. *The Vancouver Sun,* January 28:A1

de Vries M (2003) *Missing Sarah: A Vancouver Woman Remembers Her Vanished Sister.* Canada: Penguin

Doty R L (1996) *Imperial Encounters.* Minneapolis: University of Minneapolis Press

England J (2002) "Representation and the Production of Space: Aboriginal Women in Downtown Eastside, Vancouver." MA Thesis, Department of Geography, University of British Columbia

England J (2004) Disciplining subjectivity and space: Representation, film, and its material effects. *Antipode* 36:295–321

Felman S (2001) Theatres of justice: Arendt in Jerusalem, the Eichmann Trial, and the redefinition of legal meaning in the wake of the holocaust. *Critical Inquiry* 27:201–238

Fitzpatrick P (2001) Bare sovereignty: *Homo Sacer* and the insistence of law. *Theory and Event* 5:5.2

Fraser N (1992) Sex, lies, and the public sphere: Reflections on the confirmation of Clarence Thomas. *Critical Inquiry* 18:595–612

Honig B (1998) Immigrant America? How foreignness 'solves' democracy's problems. *Social Text* 16:1–27

Landes J (ed) (1998) *Feminism, the Public and the Private.* Oxford and New York: Oxford University Press.

Laurence R (2004) The fabric of memory. *The Georgia Straight,* January 1–8:35

Macklin A (1992) Foreign domestic workers: Surrogate housewife or mail order servant? *McGill Law Journal* 37:681–800

Marston S (1990) Who are 'the people'?: Gender, citizenship, and the making of the American nation. *Environment and Planning D: Society and Space* 8:449–458

Miller N (2003) 'Portraits of grief": Telling details and the testimony of trauma. *differences: A Journal of Feminist Cultural Studies* 14:112–135

Mills C (2004) Agamben's messianic politics: Biopolitics, abandonment and happy life. *Contretemps* 5:42–62

Oleksijczuk D (2003) Haunted spaces. In R Shier (ed) *Stan Douglas Every Building on 100 West Hastings* (pp 96–117). Vancouver: Vancouver Art Gallery/Arsenal Press

Ong A (1996) Cultural citizenship as subject-making: Immigrants negotiate racial and cultural boundaries in the United States. *Current Anthropology* 37:737–751

Parrenas R (2005) *Children of Global Migration: Transnational Families and Gendered Woes.* Stanford: Stanford University Press

Pateman C (1988) *The Sexual Contract*. Cambridge: Polity Press

Peters E J (1996) 'Urban' and 'aboriginal': An impossible contradiction? In J Caulfield and L Peake (eds) *City Lives and City Forms: Critical Research and Canadian Urbanism* (pp 47–62). Toronto: University of Toronto Press

Peters E J (1998) Subversive spaces: First nations women and the city. *Environment and Planning D: Society and Space* 16:665–685

Pitman B (2002) Re-mediating the spaces of reality television: *America's Most Wanted* and the case of Vancouver's missing women. *Environment and Planning A* 34:167–184

Pratt G (2004) *Working Feminism*. Edinburgh: Edinburgh University Press and Philadelphia: Temple University Press

Pratt G in collaboration with Ugnayan ng Kabataang Pilipino sa Canada/Filipino-Canadian Youth Alliance (2003) Between homes: Displacement and belonging for second generation Filipino-Canadian youths. *B C Studies* 139:41–68

Pratt G in collaboration with the Philippine Women Centre (2005) From migrant to immigrant: Domestic workers settle in Vancouver, Canada. In L Nelson and J Seager (eds) *Companion to Feminist Geography* (pp 123–137). Oxford: Blackwell

Pynn L (2004) Ottawa rates health risk from human remains in farm meat. *The Vancouver Sun*, October 29:A1–2

Razack S (2000) Gendered racial violence and spatialized justice: The murder of Pamela George. *Journal of Law and Society/Revue canadienne droit et societe* 15:91–130

Rooney E (2002) A semiprivate room. *differences: A Journal of Feminist Cultural Studies* 13:128–156

Sanchez L E (2004) The global e-rotic subject, the ban, and the prostitute-free zone: Sex work and the theory of differential exclusion. *Environment and Planning D: Society and Space* 22:861–883

Saunders D (2001) You wouldn't wish it on a dog. *Globe and Mail*, June 23:F1, F8

Skelton C and Fong P (2004) Meat contamination a new blow to families. *The Vancouver Sun*, March 12:A1, A4

Sison J M and Rosca N (2004) *Jose Maria Sison: At Home in the World. Portrait of a Revolutionary. Conversations with Ninotchka Rosca*. Greensboro, North Carolina: Open Hand Publishing

Smith G (2004) Urban aboriginals celebrate decision. *Globe and Mail*, February 18:A7

Sommers J and Blomley N (2003) "The worst block in Vancouver" in *Stan Douglas Every Building on 100 West Hastings*. Edited by R. Shier. Vancouver: Vancouver Art Gallery/Arsenal Press, pp, 18–58.

Stasiulis D and Bakan A (2002) Negotiating the citizenship divide: Foreign domestic worker policy and legal jurisprudence. In R Jhappan (ed) *Women's Legal Strategies in Canada: A Friendly Assessment* (pp 237–294). Toronto: University of Toronto Press

Stoler A L (1995) *Race and the Education of Desire: Foucault's History of Sexuality and the Colonial Order of Things*. Durham and London: Duke University Press

Vancouver Sun (2004) Sex-torture suspect first to be charged under Canada's new sex-tourism law. July 24:A2

Wood D (1999a) Missing *Elm Street* November:97–107

Wood D (1999b) The case of the vanishing women. *Georgia Straight* November 25–December 2:15–17

Wright M (2004) From protests to politics: Sex work, women's worth and Ciudad Juarez modernity. *Annals of the Association of American Geographers* 94:369–386

Young M L and Pritchard D (2005) "A Cross-border Crime Story: New Technologies, National Sovereignty and Murder." Unpublished manuscript. Available from author

38

Artificial Assimilation

Representational Politics of the Gayby Boom

MARGARET PRICE

Margaret Price, Assistant Professor of Composition and Rhetoric at Spelman College, published "Artificial Assimilation" in a 2003 issue of the magazine Bitch. *Price illustrates how most mainstream representations of queer parents position this group as white and affluent couples who fit normative ideals of family life. This article also points to more complicated portrayals of genderqueer parents who work at refashioning what it means to parent and who, Price suggests, invite others to do the same.*

Five years ago, I wrote an indignant letter to the *New York Times Magazine* expressing my hope for some lesbian-parent visibility (they had just published a special issue on motherhood, and had failed to include any representations of queer moms). Well, be careful what you wish for.

Now queer parents[1] are all over the media: Custody disputes in Florida. Adoption documentaries on PBS and Cinemax. Smiling, sweaty dykes giving birth on *Friends* and *Queer As Folk*. And with the recent progress toward the legalization

---

[1] By "queer parents" I mean parents who are queer, as opposed to parents of queer kids. Queer parents, as this article loosely defines them, are those whose sexuality or gender is bent in some way. This includes gays and lesbians, transpeople, bi- and pansexuals, queer parents who had kids while straight, and Marilyn Manson, who is not a parent, but we can always hope.

of gay marriage, we can expect even more queering of the crib in the months and years to come. This surge of attention to queer parents mirrors a rise in actual numbers. According to the nonprofit Adoption Family Center, in 1976 there were only about 500,000 biological children of gay and lesbian parents. As noted by Suzanne Johnson and Elizabeth O'Connor in *The Gay Baby Boom: The Psychology of Gay Parenthood,* as of 2002, as many as 14 million kids (biological, foster, and adoptive) have at least one gay or lesbian parent.[2] As David Elliott of the National Gay and Lesbian Task Force said proudly in a 2001 *Washington Post* article headlined "Lesbians Find Haven in Suburbs," "We are indeed everywhere."

But who is this "we," and how are they represented? If you refer to the available media images of queer parents, what do you see? I've spent the last couple of months reading magazines, searching the web, talking to queer parents, and watching innumerable episodes of *Queer As Folk* on DVD. And from where I sit, it seems that queer parents—in both fictional and nonfictional representations—are an awfully *Brady*-like bunch.

They're predominantly white, middle- or upper-class, and partnered; moreover, they usually don't push boundaries of gender or sexuality. For example, "Lesbians Find Haven in Suburbs" eagerly documents all the ways in which lesbians are discovering their inner soccer moms: "They're active in the PTA of their daughter's school," reads the piece. "They drive a minivan and help at block parties. Neighborhood children flock to the huge trampoline in their backyard." Now, there's nothing diabolical about helping at block parties or having a trampoline, but the real point of the article seems to be to underscore what these moms are not doing: namely, shaking things up.

Queer parents tend to be portrayed in ways that play up their normativity. "We're just like you" is the rallying cry—or, depending upon who is producing the images, "They're just like us." Author and columnist Dan Savage, who adopted a son with his partner, Terry, has commented on the pressure that's placed on queer parents to seem as uncontroversial as possible. "Some [gays and lesbians] felt that Terry and I—young, urban types—weren't the 'right' kind of gay couple to be adopting," he explained in an online interview with ABC News. "They felt that, due to the political controversy surrounding gay men and lesbians adopting, that older, 'safer,' cozier gay couples should adopt." Although in that interview Savage didn't elaborate on what "safer" and "cozier" might mean, he does say more in his 1999 book, *The Kid,* which details his and Terry's experience. One objection came from a queer activist who argued, in Savage's words, that gay adoptive parents should be "men in their forties, together at least eight years, monogamous, professional, irreproachable, and unassailable." Dan and Terry failed to meet the specs of this hypervirtuous profile on a number of counts, particularly given Savage's career as a sex columnist. Writing about bondage and anal fisting, apparently, does not mix with parenting. Or isn't supposed to.

---

[2] A couple disclaimers about these numbers: First of all, statistics overwhelmingly refer to parents who are "gay or lesbian," with virtually no numbers available on parents with other queer identities (e.g., bisexual or trans). Also, although the gayby boom is to some degree a real boom, it's worth noting that the rising numbers are also due to increasingly accurate data collection. But, however flawed its outlines, a new demographic is undeniably emerging.

This is a conflict familiar to many groups battling for civil rights: Is the best strategy to assimilate with mainstream culture, or to try to radicalize it? Often, the urge is to downplay difference and therefore avoid conflict. But the fact is, queer parenting is itself a paradox. It's both conventional and radical, a gesture toward joining mainstream culture and a way to transform it. Johnny, who narrates the 2002 documentary *Daddy & Papa*, and who adopts two sons with his partner, William, in the course of the film, sums up this perspective: "My most revolutionary act would be the most traditional thing in the world."

How does this paradox emerge in mainstream portrayals of queer parents? In a word, rarely. Most representations either explicitly or implicitly focus on the seemliness of their subjects. It's almost as if, having decided to focus on one freak factor (the queerness), those shaping the stories feel compelled to keep everything else (race, class, gender, family structure) as bland and unremarkable as possible.

The Unbearable Whiteness of Being a Queer Parent

QUEER PARENTS NOW HAVE THEIR VERY OWN GLOSSY magazine, *And Baby,* and the images on the pages of its May/June 2003 issue look like a family reunion in Iowa. On the contributors page, for instance, seven people are pictured, all of whom are white; in the table of contents, photos of no fewer than 17 people appear, only one of whom even *might* be a person of color. Television isn't much better: The parents in the Lifetime movie *What Makes a Family,* HBO's dyke drama *If These Walls Could Talk 2,* Showtime's *Queer As Folk,* the ubiquitous *Friends,* and the Cinemax documentary *He's Having a Baby* are, to a person, overwhelmingly Caucasian.

And the problem goes beyond quantity and into quality. Most portrayals of queer parents not only underrepresent parents of color, they downplay the ways that race can complicate the lives and choices of queer parents and their kids. This deficiency is unnervingly apparent throughout *He's Having a Baby,* which follows a white father, Jeff Danis, as he adopts a Vietnamese son. Danis decides early in the film that he wants to adopt a child from abroad, but fails to make even a peep about the issues inherent in cross-cultural and cross-racial adoption. Instead, his concerns are shown to be shallow to the point of absurdity. To wit: "The pictures of kids from China and Guatemala were very cute," Danis reports, "but the one from Cambodia, the kid wasn't that cute. So I'm like, Oh, god, what if I don't get a cute kid? He has to be a cute kid. Or at least kind of cute. He can't be ugly. I can't have an ugly kid." As far as I can tell, this is meant to be a flattering portrayal of Danis, but with biographers like that, who needs enemies?

The racial/cultural questions that come up over the course of *He's Having a Baby* are all but brushed off, and Danis's apparent ignorance of them is never questioned by the filmmakers. In a scene where he is deciding on a future son, Danis holds up two photos provided by the adoption agency and explains, "One is called Duong Dinh Tan, but I'm going to change his name to Bruce, or Harvey. And this one's name is Lam Xuan Chinh, who might be named Bob." (Ultimately, he and his partner go with the name Joe.) Of course, it's fine to rename your adoptive baby, but here it's done in a boorish, let's-get-that-scary-foreign-name-out-of-here kind of way. (In another scene, Danis takes a poll at his office to help him choose his kid, and when he asks office mates for a "celebrity look-alike" for one of the pictures, someone shouts out, "The Little Emperor!")

Fortunately, the documentary *Daddy & Papa,* which was shown both at the 2002 Sundance Film Festival and more recently on PBS, is an exception. It follows four families, each of which has one or two gay men as parents. Three of the families have adopted black children; of these three families, only one includes a nonwhite parent. (The fourth family is two white men who had a daughter through a white surrogate mother.) Instead of glossing over the issue as a common consequence of the foster care and adoption system (as, for instance, Rosie O'Donnell does when publicly discussing her adoptive children), *Daddy & Papa* takes a serious look at this phenomenon. One of the white parents, Kelly, notes that he deliberately adopted brothers so that his sons, who are black and Latino, would each have a family member of the same race. Another parent, William, who is biracial, comments on the politics of white parents adopting children of color: "I have mixed feelings about it. I think a lot of these [white] men believe that they can just raise African-American kids in a color-blind way, so that they don't really have to deal with race, and as long as there's love, it shouldn't matter. Well, that's bullshit. I mean, the reality is that their child is going to be treated differently." *Daddy & Papa* presents all four families in a highly positive light, but doesn't offer pat solutions or bromides.

An unnerving side effect of parents choosing children, whether they are flipping through catalogs of foster children or of potential sperm donors, is that the racist attitudes underlying so much mainstream discourse suddenly pop out. For example, there's the third segment of HBO's *If These Walls Could Talk* 2,[3] which stars Ellen DeGeneres and Sharon Stone as Kal and Fran, two Southern California dykes with a pronounced case of baby fever. The most bizarre moment in this short film comes when Fran proposes to Kal, "Maybe we should think about having an ethnic baby. Ethnic babies are so beautiful." Given the daffiness of this comment (all babies are "ethnic," folks), not to mention its conventional racist attitude that babies of color are somehow ornamental, it's hard to discern its purpose. Is it meant unproblematically? Or perhaps to show that queer adoptive parents are susceptible to the same foibles as straight ones? Hard to say; the issue is not discussed any further.

. . . And the Unbearable Wealth

ACCORDING TO MOST POP CULTURE REPRESENTATIONS, not only are queer parents overwhelmingly white, they're also extraordinarily well-off. One of the more egregious examples I've seen, among fictional representations, is *Walls* 2. Neither Fran nor Kal appears to be employed. However, they live in a large, well-appointed house, drive an SUV, and apparently have no concerns about undertaking a project whose dollar-suckage per month will run them somewhere between a car payment and a mortgage. Sitting in their kitchen next to a brushed-aluminum refrigerator,

---

[3]The three segments that compose this film are separate stories. When I refer to *Walls* 2 from here on, I mean the third segment, which takes place in 2000.

among yards of glowing blond-wood cabinetry, they get on the phone with a sperm bank. Kal's end of the conversation goes like this: "We want it. Yes. We want it. All of it! All of it! How much is it? Wow. Okay, whatever."

Just to put this dialogue in perspective, sperm banks charge between $150 and $300 for a single vial. Apparently, these dykes are in a position to order thousands of dollars' worth of jizz without thinking twice about it. *Walls* 2 concludes when Kal and Fran discover that they are pregnant after their fourth attempt. They do a dance of victory together in their bathroom (which, in case you're interested, has hardwood floors, a sink shaped like a large calla lily, and walls of blue tile and textured concrete).

The narrative struggle focuses solely upon whether Fran and Kal are able—biologically—to get pregnant. Although they're shown making multiple attempts, expressing frustration at their lack of success, and finally stepping up their efforts by visiting a fertility specialist, all of this is untrammeled by financial constraints. Their upper-middle-class standing allows them—and, by extension, viewers—to ignore the problems that might arise in a more complex (i.e., less moneyed) scenario. Thus, the audience can cheer wholeheartedly for them without having to consider difficult questions such as: Do Fran and Kal have health insurance? Can one of them cover the other through domestic partnership? Does their policy have implicit penalties for using donor sperm (for instance, a required 12-month waiting period in which they must try to get pregnant before any coverage kicks in)? What options are open to the gals if they can't afford that nice fertility specialist—or the sperm bank in the first place? How much does second-party adoption cost, and is it even legal in the state where they live? What safeguards can they put in place if Kal can't adopt Fran's baby, and how much would the legal fees for those safeguards run?

Admittedly, *Walls* 2 would be as dull as dirt if it addressed every one of those questions. But the film avoids the topic of money to such an extreme that Fran and Kal seem to exist in a sunny, airbrushed paradise where tanks of frozen sperm, helpful medical professionals, and surgical procedures simply appear for the taking. And this omission, in turn, allows the heterosexist policies and laws that are built into our medical and legal systems to go unnoticed.

On the nonfiction side, *He's Having a Baby* once again disappoints. Potential dad Danis, who is "gay, nearing 50," is a Hollywood (do I sense a pattern?) talent agent who has discovered a sudden longing to have a child. The opening scenes of the film are taken up with luscious shots of his home, which includes an in-ground swimming pool, abstract sculptures, and enough square footage of hardwood floor to play roller hockey. Much of the film's action takes place in his BMW, from which he conducts impatient, agency conversations on the phone while driving from adoption interview to adoption interview. A later sequence shows his partner, Don, mulling over the idea of having a child. It's hard to tell whether the directors meant this montage cynically or not, but it's framed as a series of pensive shots of Don and Jeff on vacation, each with a subtitle to identify the posh locale: Saint Barts. Palm Springs. The Hamptons. Big Sur. When Danis eventually gets on the telephone to inform the adoption agency which of two Vietnamese orphans he wants, the conversation sounds disturbingly as if he is purchasing a piece of real estate: "I'm going to go for Lam Xuan Chinh. . . . Karen, thanks so much, I'll be back in touch with you real soon. Let's put a hold on Lam Xuan Chinh."

These representations of free-spending queer parents are problematic in that they simply don't mention the issue that is uppermost in so many parents' minds: How the fuck am I going to afford this? When parents get pregnant for free (i.e., sperm meets egg without any further complications), money tends to become an issue after conception. But for queers, money is often a barrier to getting sperm near egg in the first place. Inseminating with sperm from a sperm bank runs—depending on where you live and what kind of specimens you want—between $300 and $1,000 a month. This might be manageable if one could count on getting pregnant immediately, but the average number of tries before conception, using frozen sperm, is between 6 and 12.[4] Adoption is still pricier, usually costing between $10,000 and $20,000. And surrogacy costs the most of all, generally coming in at more than $30,000. Even if you're lucky enough to go the cheap route—that is, you possess a healthy reproductive system and a male friend who is willing to deliver his sperm into that system by some means or other—you're still looking at legal fees for a donor agreement and, if you're partnered, second-party adoption.

I can't find one example of queer parenting in the media in which the issue of money is addressed in any depth. There are occasional glancing references; for example, in *Daddy & Papa* it's mentioned that adopting hard-to-place foster children is less expensive than private adoption or trying to adopt a more "desirable" (i.e., young, white, healthy) baby. And in the Lifetime movie *What Makes a Family,* although there is no discussion between the two dykes of the cost of sperm-bank sperm, some attention is given to the financial strain that ensues after one parent becomes ill with systemic lupus. But the most common approach is simply to ignore money as a factor. Asked by an *Advocate* interviewer why more gay men don't have children, actor and parent B.D. Wong responds, "I guess a lot of gay people have issues with their parents, and that must color their ideas about whether they want to be parents or not." Well, sure—but could it also be, perhaps, that they don't have $10,000 lying around?

Queer Queers

DID YOU KNOW THAT TRANSPEOPLE HAVE BABIES? YOU wouldn't, if you got your information from television, films, and most print media. Generally, representations of queer parents show them to be extremely gender-determinate gay men or lesbian women, without a hint of genderfuck anywhere in the picture. Sometimes this phenomenon is jacked up to the level of unintentional self-parody, as with the superfemmey lesbian moms in *Friends* and *Queer As Folk.* More often, it's simply taken for granted.

Every once in a while, though, a queer queer shows up with a kid. One instance is the 2002 Norwegian documentary *Alt Om Min Far (All About My Father),* which traces a series of conversations between Esben/Esther, a doctor who identifies as both a man and a women, and his/her son Even, the filmmaker, who struggles to reconcile his own view of his father with the out transperson who now

---

[4]Since there are few studies of queer parents, and those that exist often contradict one another, many of the numbers I've collected for this article are approximate. Medical facts have been checked with at least one OB/GYN.

confronts him. Another example comes from the *New York Times Magazine,* which in 2001 ran an article titled "When Debbie Met Christina, Who Then Became Chris," about a transman, Chris, and his partner, Debbie. When the article was published, the couple had a 4-year-old daughter and were expecting another child in a few months.

Both *All About My Father* and "When Debbie Met Christina" pay substantial attention to the ways that genderqueer life is materially different from conventionally gendered life. While they don't paint being genderqueer as either tragic or bizarre, they do acknowledge that it's a different row to hoe, both as a person and as a parent. Esben/Esther and Even, for instance, are shown engaged in passionate debate about the ways that Esben/Esther's shifting gender identification has affected both their lives: Esben/Esther insists that his/her son accept him/her as he/she is now, and Even insists, just as firmly, that he cannot accept Esben/Esther as anything but a man and a father. Admirably, the film refuses to conclude their struggle with a pat resolution. Instead, it ends in a kind of stalemate, which is then further tempered by an outtake, shown with the credits, in which Even and Esben/Esther hug each other, and Even asks half-jokingly, "Are you all right?"

In "When Debbie Met Christina," the couple is described with care; the story doesn't simply check off a diversity box for the magazine (the article was part of a special issue called "Love in the 21st Century"), but constructs a full and complicated portrait of Debbie's and Chris's lives. For instance, author Sara Corbett notes that when Chris transitioned from female to male, Debbie's sexuality and identification were affected as well. "I really questioned who I was, suddenly, this lifelong lesbian living with a man," Debbie explains. And Corbett observes, astutely, that the "daily contradictions" of genderqueer life are faced by Debbie as well as Chris. As parents, Debbie and Chris build the genderqueer aspects of their lives into their raising of their daughter, Hannah. Corbett explains, for instance, that Debbie and Chris tend to "switch the genders of the characters in Hannah's children's books to keep things more fluid, more equitable—and as they like to see it, more true to life."

Both *All About My Father* and "When Debbie Met Christina" are sensitive portrayals of genderqueer parents, but both are third-person accounts, narrated in the first case by the genderqueer person's son and in the second case by a journalist. A first-person account comes courtesy of a 2000 *Village Voice* article, in which writer Patrick Califia describes his own queer family: "We are both transgendered men (female-to-male or FTM), and my boyfriend [Matt] is the mother of my child." Not only does he identify his family's queerness, but Califia spends considerable time exploring the implications of being the queer dads of a baby, one of whom gave birth to the child. One stereotype he refutes is the notion that queer dads will meet their fiercest opposition from straight people; in fact, Califia reports, his and Matt's straight acquaintances "have been pretty sweet." Their most hostile responses have been from FTMS they know. (Members of an online FTM group, for instance, "started calling Matt by his girl name, because real men don't get pregnant.") Other transpeople have been more supportive, however, Califia notes; in fact, many FIMS have contacted them to ask about the experience of getting pregnant and coparenting. Califia's article goes beyond "We're here, we're queer, we gave birth" and explores much deeper implications of identity that are shared not only by transgendered parents but by queer parents as a whole.

In a different article, originally published in the magazine *Skin Two,* Califia discusses BDSM,[5] another queer-parenting issue that doesn't get much play (so to speak). Outraged at the common assumption that people who are part of the leather community cannot also be responsible parents, Califia points out that this assumption relies upon a simplistic view of leatherpeople as "two-dimensional caricatures of vanilla people's erotic paranoia, emerging from our warrens only after dark, always clad in body-hugging fetish gear, having no real lives outside of public dungeon clubs and 'violent' pornography." As much as any parent, Califia argues he is perfectly capable of drawing appropriate boundaries between his sex life and his life as a parent. In fact, he maintains, his experience as a responsible member of the leather community is an asset, because it has required him to develop qualities such as empathy, patience, flexibility, and, above all, the ability to negotiate relationships in an open and ethical way. Califia's assertion that pervs can be parents—and good parents—is welcome and rare. However, because his article appeared in a fetish magazine, this point remains confined to a sort of journalistic ghetto, and does not emerge in mainstream representations of queer parents.

Most portrayals of queer parents keep sex out of the picture; when it does appear, it tends to be handled with extreme, well, normativity. The Fran-and-Kal segment of *Walls 2,* for example, shows them naked in bed, but the sexual activity resembles an animated Hallmark card, with golden light suffusing the scene as they kiss each other's smooth bodies and Dido croons "Thank You" in the background. Similarly prissy action occurs between Lindsay and Melanie, the dyke-mom couple on *Queer As Folk.* Occasionally they're naked in bed together, but, as with Fran and Kal, pretty much all that happens is in the realm of (not to put too fine a point on it) tongue-plus-nipple. This is partly to do with gender (girl-on-girl sex on television or in movies is often presented as cleaner, simpler, somehow *nicer* than boy-on-boy), but more to do with the fact that most portrayals of queer parents seem to fear allowing them any complexity as people, and that precludes showing them as individuals with active and varied sex lives. Most straight parents represented in the media don't appear to have active and varied sex lives, either, so I would guess this to be a final frontier of queer-parent representation.

Making the Baby

PERHAPS BECAUSE THE PRODUCTION OF OFFSPRING by queers so rarely involves sexual intercourse, media representations of queer parents seem positively obsessed by the issue of where the baby comes from. The swell of media attention accompanying the gayby boom focuses not on queer parents who already have children, or queer stepparents joining existing families, but queer people who are making or obtaining children (usually babies). In other words, what you will see on television, in film, and in print is the *procurement* of babies by queer parents. If you're a 37-year-old mother of two, you've just left your husband, and you're trying to coordinate babysitting schedules with dating your first girlfriend, not to mention

---

[5]BDSM is an acronym that refers to three pairings: bondage/discipline, dominance/submission, and sadism/masochism. People who practice some variation of BDSM are often said to be part of "the leather community," the phrase I'll use here.

the issue of coming out to your kids—well, there are plenty of you out there, but your story's not going to show up next week on *Queer As Folk*.

So, for instance, on *QAF*, we have Lindsay, fresh from labor, being visited in the hospital by the donor dad. In *Walls 2*, we have Fran leaping around her house with a turkey baster while Kal visits the sperm bank to pick up the specimen. In *Daddy & Papa* and *He's Having a Baby*, we see gay men deciding to adopt, choosing names, meeting their kids for the first time, and learning their way around a Snugli. In his *Advocate* interview, B.D. Wong delivers the apotheosis of this attitude: "There are no accidental kids of gay parents. Every single gay parent passionately wanted to be a parent." Oh, really? Did you ask the single dyke on food stamps who has three kids from a former marriage? Or the gay man who just came out to his two teenage kids? Wong's comment assumes that gay parenting involves a predetermined order of events: First, be gay; second, decide to parent; third, become a parent. Scenarios in which the order of these steps may be shuffled are erased.

Not that people who come out after having children didn't want their kids, but let's remember, not all children of queer parents sprout magically in the petri dish. Some of them are already hanging around the house, asking, "What's rimming?" or squirming during the coming-out talk and then saying dismissively, "What*ever*, Mom, everyone at my school is bisexual." However, most stories about queer parenting center upon a single glimpse: the moment of becoming. It's as though the plot arc of TLC's *A Baby Story*—pregnancy, baby shower, birth, next episode—has taken over the queer-parenting narrative. Sometimes there are variations—in adoption stories, the peak moment is not birth but the first contact between parent and child—but the central focus remains the same.

A similar proclivity is demonstrated by the pictures of queer parents (sometimes author photos, sometimes cover art) on books such as Rachel Pepper's *The Ultimate Guide to Pregnancy for Lesbians*, Judy Dahl's *River of Promise: Two Women's Story of Love and Adoption*, and the aforementioned *The Gay Baby Boom*. In these pictures, parents are shown with their newly procured babies, which are cuddled lovingly against a cheek or held up like a prize. It's a money shot, with baby as climax.

So what's going on here? Why this obsession with getting the goods, and the simultaneous downplaying of living with the result? Again, it seems to stem from an impulse to make things as normal and as unqueer as possible. The parents in these portrayals mouth platitudes that align them with depressing heteronormative myths, such as the belief that a potential parent should feel empty and lonely without a child. "Without [parenthood]," mourns Jeff in *He's Having a Baby*, "I feel very empty. Without it, I feel very incomplete." The next shot shows him walking sadly on his treadmill, while in the background we hear the opening bars of "You're Nobody 'til Somebody Loves You." As the film goes on, Jeff's partner, Don, is shown to be reluctant to have children. However, he agrees to the adoption of little Joe (né Lam Xuan Chinh), and much of the latter half of the film is taken up with heartwarming scenes that show Don's conversion to delighted dad. Parenthood, according to this scenario, is not only something that all normal adults should desire; it's something that the appearance of a small, soft baby will magically make desired. This myth insults those (queer or straight) who choose not to have children; it also insults those who choose to have children for reasons other than to fill a yawning void in their lives.

But there's more going on. Joe becomes just another consumer acquisition to go with Jeff's treadmill, artworks, and potted palms; children in general become yet another means by which queers can be folded into a larger, homogeneous American culture—one in which there are differences, sure, but nothing that a little "tolerance" and a few "Celebrate Diversity!" bumper stickers can't overcome. If queers have Subarus, house payments, and daycare schedules to attend to, how threatening can they be?

Daddy & Papa offers an entertainingly self-aware account of William and Johnny's absorption into baby-related consumer culture when they attend a picnic for gay dads and their kids. "It's raaanch-style," William singsongs as they pull up to the suburban home where the picnic will take place. They park behind and take notice of a neat lineup of three Volvo station wagons. Johnny muses in voiceover: "Were we mimicking straight people, trying to prove that we could be good parents, too? Or was this just the life of a parent, gay or straight, doing our best for our kids?" Shortly thereafter, Johnny ruefully reports, he and William bought a Volvo station wagon. This segment is insightful in the way it both documents and comments upon the connections between babies and consumer goods. However, like most representations of queer parenting, it avoids the topic of babies *as* consumer goods, thus failing once again to answer the question of why it's more appealing to watch queers get their kids than to watch them living with their kids.

And is there one answer? It's hard to say for sure. But maintaining a focus on the acquisition of a baby allows the creators of and audience for TV shows, magazine articles, and books to maintain a tacit connection between consumer items and legitimate membership in society. If queers can pile up the possessions that signal capitalist citizenship—babies, houses, Volvos, even our very own "Rainbow" Visa card—then we can assure ourselves that we have indeed been given the proverbial place at the table.

Finally, there's one more issue tangled up with the repetitive theme of baby-making. Focusing on the moment of acquisition allows creators of queer-parenting stories to—you guessed it—keep things simple, and this simplicity allows normativity to prevail yet again. If the image of queer parents is kept to the relatively brief moments surrounding their acquisition of babies, then there are no messy consequences to consider. How does the first coming-out talk go (or is a coming-out talk even necessary)? What happens when the kids get harassed at school? In what ways do the kids rebel against their parents, or not, and how do parents' sexualities and genders play into these events? What might older kids of queer parents have to say about their lives? We rarely get to hear answers to such questions—though Even's side of the discussion in *All About My Father* is a welcome exception—because when queer parents appear in the media, their offspring are usually preverbal.

Straightness Becomes You

THIS PUSH TOWARD NORMATIVITY ISN'T SIMPLY something that is thrust upon queer parents by a homophobic media empire. In some cases, it's an impression that queer parents themselves seem eager to embrace. For instance, a 1996 *People* magazine article arguing that queer (excuse me, "gay or lesbian") families are "so different, so much the same" presents a gay father, Ron Frazier, who enthusiastically endorses

People's safety-in-sameness angle. "We weren't stereotypical gays," he explains. "So when people saw that we were just two ordinary men, they realized there was no cause for alarm."[6] Well, I can think of a few reasons to be alarmed by his remark. But no one on the Fraziers' block is, and I guess that makes the barbecues a lot more comfortable for everyone. *People* certainly isn't going to call our attention to the problems with this viewpoint; it's too busy assuring us that it "helped" (helped what?) that Heidi Frazier's dads "live their day-to-day lives in relative anonymity."

But the issue is more complex than simple avoidance. This *People* article points—albeit not very thoughtfully—to an ongoing problem faced by queer parents. Like oil and water, queerness and parenting seem to resist blending. "Becoming a parent was the straightest thing I ever did," a friend wrote me when she found out I was working on this article. As writer Mary Martone, a new queer mom, argues, "Babies make lesbians disappear." She describes herself as a "big, short-haired gal," but notes that the social stigma she usually encounters tends to evaporate when she's with her small daughter. She's often placed into some acceptable social narrative—for example, that she has a husband who happens to be somewhere else. The usual view of parents tends to adhere to the logical syllogism "If parent, then straight," as well as its corollary, "If queer, then not a parent."

Queer as well as mainstream cultures perpetuate the assumption that queerness and parenthood don't mix. In *Daddy & Papa*, when Johnny and William try to take their toddler, Zach, to Gay Day at the Great America theme park, they discover (after paying $20 for Zach's ticket) that all the rides for children have been closed for the day. Another of *Daddy & Papa*'s dads walks through his neighborhood in San Francisco's famously gay Castro district, saying ruefully, "We go to the park three or four nights a week, and I would say there's been twice in a year and a half that there's been other kids there." And the saddest part of the *People* article about Heidi Frazier's gay dads, for me, is the passage that recounts Ron and Tom's loss of their gay community:

> *Though Frazier and McCulley have lost some of their gay friends because of their mutual commitment to parenthood, that doesn't seem to have bothered them much. Between dashing off for school functions, helping shuttle Heidi and her friends to choir practice and church affairs, they discovered that they had more in common with the straight families in their neighborhood. Parenthood trumped sexual preference as the governing social factor in their lives. "Now our friends are mostly heterosexual couples," says Frazier.*

Regardless of how common this phenomenon is (many areas have relatively few other queer families to befriend), it's outrageous that this loss is marked not as an isolation that Ron and Tom must live with, but merely as something that "doesn't seem to have bothered them much."

---

[6] The term "stereotypical" isn't elaborated on, but I assume it means "throwing large house parties with 'it's Raining Men' turned up to ear-shattering levels" or "wearing a feather boa to the Stop & Shop."

Now, I'll be the first to say that hanging out with straight folks is not a horrible fate. But the point is that queer parents are being forced to make an either/or choice. "Being a parent has put me in between gay and straight communities," writes Patrick Califia. In queer spaces, he reports, people are often "hostile to children"; in straight spaces, people who see him and his partner parenting often "[invent] some reason to think we are not queer." Areas of overlap are difficult—often impossible—to find.

Media representations of queer parents create an inaccurate and damaging impression of normativity—white, middle- or upper-class, and so forth. Without a doubt, we need more varied representations in the future. But we should also pay attention to the grain of truth in such portrayals: that queer parents are simultaneously thrust inside and kept out of mainstream culture. The queer parents in TV shows, films, articles, and books that I admire are those who can acknowledge the paradoxes they live with, those who give me some insight into what life is like when such paradoxes must be negotiated every day. I laugh when Johnny and William shamefacedly include a shot of their new Volvo station wagon. I'm unable to side wholly with either Esben/Esther or Even, each of whom passionately defends a compelling position. And I feel relief when Dan Savage and Patrick Califia remind me that pervs are parents, too. These are the kinds of queer-parenting lives I want to see: messy, complicated, flawed. They don't simply announce that queers can be parents; they queer the institution of parenthood itself.

39

When Girls Will Be Boys

ALISSA QUART

Alissa Quart writes for publications such as Atlantic Monthly *and* Mother Jones *and wrote the book* Hothouse Kids: The Dilemma of the Gifted Child. *Her feature story "When Girls will Be Boys" appeared in a 2008 issue of the* New York Times Magazine. *Quart introduces readers to a few of the issues, concepts, and terminologies that touch the lives of traditional college-age transgender students by highlighting the complicated story of Rey, a transman, who initially enrolled in a women's college. This piece speaks to the multiplicity of gender variations and calls on readers to thoughtfully consider what constitutes gender.*

It was late on a rainy fall day, and a college freshman named Rey was showing me the new tattoo on his arm. It commemorated his 500-mile hike through Europe the previous summer, which happened also to be, he said, the last time he was happy. We sat together for a while in his room talking, his tattoo of a piece with his spiky brown hair, oversize tribal earrings and very baggy jeans. He showed me a photo of himself and his girlfriend kissing, pointed out his small drum kit, a bass guitar that lay next to his rumpled clothes and towels and empty bottles of green tea, one full of dried flowers, and the ink self-portraits and drawings of nudes that he had tacked to the walls. Thick jasmine incense competed with his cigarette smoke. He changed the music on his laptop with the melancholy, slightly startled air of a college boy on his own for the first time.

Rey's story, though, had some unusual dimensions. The elite college he began attending last year in New York City, with its academically competitive, fresh-faced students, happened to be a women's school, Barnard. That's because when Rey first entered the freshman class, he was a woman.

Rey, who asked that neither his last name nor his given name be used to protect his and his family's privacy, grew up in Chappaqua, the affluent Westchester suburb that is home to the Clintons, and had a relatively ordinary, middle-class Jewish childhood. Rey, as he now calls himself, loved his younger brother, his parents were together and he was a good student, excelling in English and history. But he always had the distinct feeling that he wasn't the sex he was supposed to be. As a kid, he was often mistaken for a boy, which was "mostly cool," Rey said. "When I was 5, I told my parents not to correct people when strangers thought I was a boy. I was never a girl, really—I questioned my own gender, and other people also questioned my gender for me." When Rey entered puberty, he felt the loss of the "tomboy" sobriquet acutely.

"My body changed in freshman year of high school, and it made me depressed," Rey said. That year, he started to wonder whether he was really meant to become a woman. His friends in high school were almost all skater boys and musicians, and he related to them as if he were one of them. He began to define himself as "omnisexual," although he was mostly attracted to women.

The idea that he might actually want to transition from female to male began to take shape for Rey when he was 14 or 15; he can't quite remember when exactly. "A transmale speaker guy" gave a talk at a meeting of his high school's Gay Straight Alliance, and Rey was inspired. Then he took a typical step for someone going to high school in the first years of this century. He went home and typed "transgender" into Google.

At the end of his freshman year in high school, he met Melissa, a student at Smith College who was back in Westchester for summer break and later became his girlfriend. During one of their days together, Melissa, who was immersed in campus gender activism, mentioned the concept of being a "transman" and spoke of her transmale friends. Rey confided his questions about his gender identity to her, and she encouraged him to explore them further. For most of high school, Rey spent hours online reading about transgendered people and their lives. "The Internet is the best thing for trans people," he said. "Living in the suburbs, online groups were an access point." He also started reading memoirs of transgendered people. He asked Melissa to explain the gender theory she was learning in college.

In his senior year, he took on the name Rey. At 17, he finally felt ready to come out as trans to his family, who according to Rey struggled to understand his new identity. Around that time, he also visited a clinic in Manhattan, hoping to start hormone therapy. He was told that unless he wanted his parents involved in the process, he'd have to wait until he was 18. In the meantime, Rey began to apply to colleges. He wanted to go to "a hippie school," as he put it, yet he felt pressure to choose a school like Barnard that hewed to an Ivy League profile. Though he decided on Barnard, he still planned to start on testosterone as soon as he turned 18. When I asked him why he wanted to start hormone therapy so soon, he replied simply, "You live your life and you feel like a boy." Of course, living life like a boy is not what an elite women's college has historically been about.

At 18, Rey is part of a growing population of transgender students at the nation's colleges and universities. While still a rarity, young women who become men in college, also known as transmen or transmales, have grown in number over the last 10 years. According to Brett-Genny Janiczek Beemyn, director of the Stonewall Center at the University of Massachusetts, Amherst, who has studied trans students on college campuses, adults who wished to transition historically did so in middle age. Today a larger percentage of transitions occur in adolescence or young adulthood. The National Center for Transgender Equality estimates that between a quarter of a percent and 1 percent of the U.S. population is transgender—up to three million Americans—though other estimates are lower and precise figures are difficult to come by. Still, the growing number of young people who transition when they are teenagers or very young adults has placed a new pressure on colleges, especially women's colleges, to accommodate them.

The number of young people who openly identify as transgendered has grown for a few reasons. Some parents of young children who are "gender nonconforming"—usually children who identify psychologically with the opposite sex but also children who have hermaphroditic traits, like indeterminate sex organs—now allow their kids to choose whether they are referred to as "he" or "she" and whether to wear boys' or girls' clothing. And some of these parents, under a doctor's supervision, have even begun to administer hormone blockers to prevent the arrival of secondary sex characteristics until a "gender variant" child is old enough to make permanent choices. The Internet also offers greater access to information about transmale and gender-variant identities.

In addition, 147 colleges and universities nationwide now include "gender identity and expression" in their nondiscrimination policies, and students will often use gender-neutral pronouns like "ze" and "hir"—especially if they post on campus message boards. At Wesleyan last year, students initiated a survey of bathrooms, checking to see if they were transgender-friendly—open to all sexes. Many colleges now have Transgender Days of Remembrance in memory of victims of gender-identity-related hate crimes. Students at the University of Vermont hold a yearly "Translating Identity Conference" for trans college students that draws hundreds of people from around the country. The increasing number of trans college students has even given rise to a surprisingly deft reality television show, "Transgeneration," on the Sundance Channel, which featured a transmale student at Smith College.

The conventional thinking is that trans people feel they are "born in the wrong body." But today many students who identify as trans are seeking not simply to change their sex but to create an identity outside or between established genders—they may refuse to use any gender pronouns whatsoever or take a gender-neutral name but never modify their bodies chemically or surgically. These students are also considered part of the trans community, though they are known as either gender nonconforming or genderqueer rather than transmen or transmale.

At many of America's first-tier women's colleges, the growth of the trans community has led to campus workshops on transgender identity. According to students at Smith, a good number of restrooms have been made over as "gender neutral." And some professors make sure to ask students to fill out slips indicating their preferred names and pronouns. Students at several women's colleges have also created trans groups to reflect their experiences and political views.

According to one transmale student I talked to at Wellesley, there are at least 15 gender-nonconforming students at the college, ranging from full-on trans to genderqueer, who have formed their own group. Other women's colleges, like Smith, have in the last few years had on-campus gender-nonconforming groups with up to 30 members, more than 1 percent of that school's population.

Which doesn't mean it isn't sometimes a struggle to be trans or gender-nonconforming on campus. Many trans students feel themselves to be excluded or isolated at women's schools and at coed colleges. Some talk of being razzed or insulted by fellow students. And even within a college's gender-nonconforming population, students are often divided among those who define themselves as men but don't transition medically, those who do and those who prefer not to define themselves as either male or female.

These difficulties are a natural part of being a minority that is still fighting for acceptance. But trans students' problems can also be institutional. The presence of trans students at women's colleges can't help raising the question of whether—or to what degree—these colleges can serve students who no longer see themselves as women.

From his first week at Barnard, Rey told me, he felt he was struggling. The women on campus seemed to Rey to be socially conservative and archly feminine, and he felt he had to seek solace elsewhere. At the Callen-Lorde Community Health Center in downtown Manhattan—the medical facility for gay, lesbian, bisexual and transgender people that he visited while he was still in high school—he began to get biweekly testosterone "T" shots (he turned 18 in September). Rey had psychological counseling elsewhere first; typically a letter of referral from a mental-health professional is required before anyone between 18 and 24 can receive hormone therapy. Rey also began to bind his breasts. But binding hurt, he said; it made it hard for him to breathe. He especially hated "having to alter your body every morning so you can go through the world and people will accept you."

But as a transmale student in a sea of women at Barnard, he felt alone. He longed to be with his girlfriend, Melissa, and with transmale friends, some of whom, like Rey, were attending women's colleges. Even as he sought to adopt a more conventionally male appearance, he wanted to maintain his ties with his former self. "I am all for not rubbing out my past as female," he told me.

But it was not to be that simple. As a transmale college student, he was something of a pioneer. And he began to hit some walls.

In the first week of September, he found out that his roommates had complained to the college's freshman housing director about being asked to share their rooms with a man. They wanted Rey to find somewhere else to live. According to Dorothy Denburg, the dean who spoke to Rey about the situation, these young women were disturbed when Rey told them on the first day "that he was a transboy and wanted to be referred to by male pronouns." Rey's roommates had, after all, chosen to attend a women's college in order to live and be educated in the company of other women. Barnard doesn't have singles for freshmen. As Rey saw it, he was simply shut out by his two roommates—and by the rest of the school. A week after learning of his roommates' disapproval, Rey, together with the dean and his parents, decided that Rey should transfer to Columbia's School of General Studies.

Rey felt lost. He slept on people's couches and stayed with one friend, a Columbia student and fellow trans activist, for a week. The story of his rooming travails ultimately wound up on the gossip pages of The New York Post. The Post squib cast Rey as an infiltrator in one of the last girls-with-pearls bastions.

"They were very typical feminine girls," explained Rey. "I didn't fit in. It's why I didn't hang out with straight girls for most of high school—I hung out with queer women. Around the Barnard women, I felt extremely other."

Rey described the days that followed as "the worst semester ever." As his new hormone regime began to take effect, he started to go through male puberty, which meant increased bone mass and a deepening voice and facial hair. He struggled to lead the normal life of an arty college student: eating vegan, going to clubs, keeping his grades up. Only recently, Rey says, has his life brightened. Indeed the transformation from the person he was to who he has become is startling. The second time we met, on a street corner near Columbia in Upper Manhattan, was a cold but sunny day in January, and Rey was aglow, smiling and laughing. Accompanied by his girlfriend, Melissa, now a graceful college senior, he greeted me with a hug.

The reason for this cheer, he said, was that he finally felt on the way to becoming who he really is. The testosterone shots he had received every other week since October had lowered his voice a few octaves. He was in the process of legally changing his name to a male name, although he couldn't decide whether to go casual (Rey) or Old Testament (Asher). And in December Rey underwent what he called "chest reconstruction surgery," also known as "top surgery," which he paid for out of pocket.

Melissa helped Rey through it, feeding him antibiotics and massaging his postsurgery chest with arnica cream. He joined a campus trans organization, GendeRevolution. In a few short months, he had become a full-blown activist. He quit smoking. To cap it off, he was bar-mitzvahed in Israel in January. He'd had his bat mitzvah at 13, but as Rey put it, he didn't feel "connected to the experience." He was bar-mitzvahed without his parents in attendance, but he took the rite of passage to heart. After all, at 13 he'd become a woman. Now, at 18, he was a man.

Despite the seriousness of the issues Rey has dealt with, all in such a short time, he often seemed like a giddy teenager, probably because he still was one. Clad in his usual uniform of baggy pants and a B-Boy cap covered with images of euros, he gossiped about his friends, music, sex and food, from time to time throwing his arm around Melissa, who is pixielike, slim and Rey's height—a little over five feet. She was wearing skinny jeans and ballet flats. She was so supportive of Rey's transformation that she was taken aback when I asked if his period of postoperative recovery had been hard for her.

"He's so much happier now," she said. Even though Melissa always defined herself as a lesbian, she said her partner's transition made sense to her. Part of the couple's sangfroid is generational—she and Rey see themselves as genderqueer rather than gay. For them, sexual orientation is fluid. Like some of their peers, Melissa and Rey want to be—and sometimes imagine they already are—part of the first generation to transcend gender.

On the face of it, it's not surprising that students like Rey would choose to attend a women's college. Same-sex colleges have always been test beds for transformations among American women. Set up as places where women could flourish without men, colleges like Barnard, Wellesley, Smith and Mount Holyoke have always had dual personalities, serving both as finishing schools and as incubators of American feminism. Smith College's alumnae include not only Barbara Bush and Nancy Reagan but also Betty Friedan, Gloria Steinem and Catharine MacKinnon.

The schools that decided to remain single-sex in the 1970s, when many colleges around the country went coed, represented a significant and even controversial challenge to liberal ideas about gender equality. And in refashioning their identities for the time, many became loci for the interrogation of gender roles. It was, after all, at all-female schools that many young women first began to question the very notion of femininity. And this questioning found echoes in the curriculum. Scholars like Esther Newton, Gayle Rubin, Anne Fausto-Sterling and Judith Butler ushered in an era that reconceived gender as a social construct, distinct from both a person's sex and sexuality. For Butler and others, femaleness did not automatically produce femininity and maleness did not produce masculinity: gender was fluid and variable, something to be fashioned, and could shift in character depending on the culture or the time period. As some see it, the presence of trans students at single-sex colleges is simply a logical extension of this intellectual tradition.

Indeed, as one transmale student I spoke to at Wellesley pointed out, women's colleges are uniquely suited to transgender students. "There's no safer place for transmen to be than a women's college because there's no actual physical threat to us," he told me, adding, "I have more in common with women because of that shared experience than I do with men." And even though Rey chose to leave Barnard for a coed school, he also says that women's schools can—and should— act as havens for transmale students, that they are, in fact, natural beacons for trans people, because "feminists and trans activists are both interested in gender."

In a sense, transgender and genderqueer students could be said merely to be holding women's colleges to their word: to fully support women's exploration of gender, even if that exploration ends with students no longer being female-identified. As Judith Halberstam, a professor of English and gender studies at the University of Southern California and the author of "Female Masculinity," put it, feminist theory offers students a way to think about gender as performance, to create a trans self or a genderqueer one—and give that self contours, definition— in a way that was simply unavailable 30 years ago. Indeed, Rey discovered his own trans identity reading queer theory, and even transitioning to be a man hasn't changed his core sense of himself. "I'm still queer even though I am a man now— it's the beauty of the term," Rey said.

"I think gender is a spectrum—gender is more complicated than sex," Rey continued. He sees everyone, and not just transmen, as having "their own gender," just as they might have their own personality or temperament. Rey's point isn't merely academic. A good number of gender nonconforming students I spoke to at women's colleges agreed with him. Most did not have operations but rather defined gender simply by how they experienced it, seeing themselves as existing on a "gender continuum" with their more conventionally feminine college friends. I met with one such student, Jordan Akerley, a 22-year-old senior at Wellesley. As we sat in the student-run on-campus cafe where Akerley works, Akerely explained what it is like to live out a theory of identity that doesn't exactly conform to one gender or the other.

"I find pronouns cumbersome and self-limiting," Akerley told me, which is why friends use the name Jordan, a name that Akerley says she intends to make official this year. Akerley, a co-captain of the school's soccer team, takes no hormones and has no plans to have an operation. Akerley's look and entire manner is quite unremarkable, even conservative: hair combed in a modified Tin Tin do, sporty, plain cotton shirt, jeans and sneakers. The only sign of an "alternative" or outsider identity—other than appearing masculine enough to be frequently mistaken on campus for a female student's boyfriend—is Akerley's eyebrow ring. Akerley's affect could be that of an aspiring politician: amiable, physically attractive, clean cut, inoffensive and articulate.

"My identity is fluid; it may evolve and fluctuate," Akerley explained. "My preference is not to use gender pronouns. My work is not always grammatically correct because of the lack of pronouns."

Though women's colleges may seem a haven for trans or gender-nonconforming students, accommodating such students requires balancing a complex set of needs and expectations—inside and outside the college. Barnard, like many women's colleges, has an admissions policy of accepting only "legal" women. The college's president, Judith Shapiro, who wrote an article on transsexualism in the 1980s, is clearly sympathetic to the trans population in general, but when I spoke to her she wondered aloud why a transmale or male-identified student "would want to be in a woman's college." She went on to explain her position this way: "Having been very involved in second-wave feminism, I am interested in gender revolutionaries, but I still think gender is a major category in our society." In many ways, Shapiro could be said to represent the position women's colleges now find themselves in: caught between wanting to embrace a campus minority that their own interrogation of gender roles has helped to shape and defending the value of institutions centered on the distinct experience of being female.

Colleges must also navigate the attitudes and expectations of their alumnae. While some alumnae have readily accepted the presence of trans students on their campuses, others, like Suzanne Corriell and Regis Ahern, graduates of Mount Holyoke, see it as a betrayal of the foundational principles of their alma mater. Corriell and Ahern recently wrote an angry letter to The Mount Holyoke Alumnae Quarterly, charging that admitting transmale students was, in effect, a way of "passively going coed" and that the "lifestyle choices" of these students was a bald negation of a women's college charter. Trans students, they wrote, were simply "men seeking to take advantage of Mount Holyoke's liberal and accepting atmosphere."

When I called Corriell, who is 28, at the law library at the University of Richmond, where she works, she explained her feelings to me this way: "I am a strong believer in women's education, and I think the colleges are a dying breed that need protection. I respect their agenda, which is educating women." She paused, then said: "Educating trans students in a same-sex residential community produces difficulty—when a student no longer identifies as a woman, the privilege to attend these schools is lost. Men have lots of schools they can go to—why must transmen go to women's schools?"

Of course, many trans students identify first as women—as lesbians or feminist activists. They are attracted to women's schools precisely because of their reputation as safe harbors for exploring these identities. As a result, many transmale students apply to women's schools and attend them before they have fully come out as "gender nonconforming"—and this is likely to be the case for years to come.

Denburg, the Barnard dean, acknowledges that women's colleges have always been places "where women can explore definitions and dimensions of gender." But it is only in the last five years of her tenure as dean, she says, that she has encountered transmale students. She had, she said, no objection to Rey's attending Barnard. The school has helped other gender-nonconforming students, among them a resident adviser in his senior year, who had to inform his female dorm mates about his gender transition over the summer. Denburg described her work with these students "as an educational journey for me as well, that has helped me to better understand the drive of someone who feels they are in the wrong body."

That said, Barnard does not have the kind of groups for trans students or awareness campaigns and gender-neutral bathrooms that some of the other women's colleges do. And it has not been as affiliated with women's and gender activism as some of its sister schools. Rey's case, as Denburg put it, "caught us off guard," mostly because administrators had never encountered a student who wanted to transition physically at such a young age. To Denburg, 18 still seems very young for such a decision.

Many people would agree that going on hormones carries risks: there are few studies on the long-term effects of hormone therapies on transmen. Some transmen in their 20s and 30s have told me they worry about the hormones' potential side effects—an increase in "bad" cholesterol and the risk of heart disease and stroke. For transmen, finding appropriate health care is complicated by the fact that student health services typically need to refer such students to outside clinics or hospitals for their care—and transmen may need additional insurance or be required to bear at least some of the medical costs themselves.

Rey always expected to go off-campus for his transition. He wound up being operated on by a private surgeon in New York City. (He received no "bottom surgery," as it is known—few transmen do, in part because the operation is thought to be too rudimentary and in part because many transmen view it as unnecessary.) While many gender-nonconforming students don't have "top surgery" in their freshman years, they may still struggle with their colleges' medical services, not because they want specialized treatments but because they want health care that is sensitive to their new identities. As one gender-noncomforming student complained to me, he hated that health services insisted on treating him "like a girl."

Colleges, trans activists and advocates say, are even less prepared for advising students on how their gender-variant identities may affect their futures, including their professional lives. After all, many states don't have protection for gender-nonconforming people in the workplace, and "gender identity" was recently dropped from the 2007 Employment Non-Discrimination Act, or ENDA. "There's no professional development for trans kids at colleges," said Shannon Sennott, a founder of Translate, a Brooklyn-based nonprofit group that holds workshops on trans awareness at women's colleges. "The majority disappear into big cities, working as bartenders with advanced degrees because there's real prejudice against trans workers." Hadley Smith, a recent Wellesley graduate and a Translate founder who describes himself as gender-nonconforming, said that unemployment or limited employment is par for the course for many transgendered people, but those limits may seem starker when high-achieving graduates from educationally competitive schools like Smith College feel, out of fear of discriminating employers, that they have to abandon, at least temporarily, their professional aspirations.

Some transmale students ultimately go "stealth" after graduation, not mentioning their earlier lives as women. When I asked Rey how he hoped to handle it, he said he had no intention of hiding and was planning to be out as a transman for the rest of his life. With all the bravado of youth, he said: "I won't get a career that I can't be out and trans in. I'm not planning to go into business.

"I've learned not to try to see my future—to do the best I can in the space I am in," he continued, and then added shyly, "I would like to, you know, make public art."

On a winter afternoon, I visited Rey at his new workplace at Columbia University's Office of Multicultural Affairs, where he was organizing a series of trans awareness events on campus. Rey was being paid by the college to create the series, and at the moment he had two chores on his list: booking a transmale photographer as a speaker and creating signage for gender-neutral bathrooms. To achieve the latter, Rey was busy sketching possible new symbols. Melissa, his girlfriend, was helping him. First they turned the familiar female stick figure into a rocket ship, making her legs into a flame. Rey created a few variations of the sign with a ballpoint pen. Then he drew a confused-looking person standing in front of both a male and a female bathroom, not knowing which one to pick. Next, he tried a single circle with the male and female symbols attached to it. Melissa laughed mockingly at the drawing of the confused man, but she nodded her head in approval at the two other symbols.

The dynamic between the two is often like this—teasingly supportive. Earlier at lunch, Melissa joked about whether they were even in a relationship, "I'm not sure: Rey doesn't do labels." Then she told Rey, "I've saved 20 voice mails of your voice changing over the last four months." He looked at her adoringly as they ate French fries in sync: Melissa was not only his girlfriend but also the historian of his identity.

"Before I was on hormones, people would get confused when I spoke over the phone—they thought I was male, and then they'd start asking questions about how old I was," Rey said. "I didn't want to stay a prepubescent boy."

When talk turned to the couple's plans for the future, Melissa was more concerned about Rey leaving "wet towels on the floor," she said, and "tracking mud in the house" than about his medical transition. His lack of housekeeping skills was particularly on her mind, since the two are planning to move in together over the summer. "We'll stay together," Melissa said. "That's unless you go gay . . . again." She laughed. She was talking about the possibility of Rey's coming out a second time—going from being a woman who loves women to a man who loves women to a man who loves men. The remark was meant lightly, but nonetheless it got to the heart of the radical gender leaps both she and Rey were making in their everyday lives.

Then Rey grew more serious.

"Some transmen want to be seen as men—they want to be accepted as born men," he said. "I want to be accepted as a transman—my brain is not gendered. There's this crazy gender binary that's built into all of life, that there are just two genders that are acceptable. I don't want to have to fit into that."

40

Maps of the Everyday: Habitual Pathways and Contested Places

NEDRA REYNOLDS

How are place and identity linked? What kinds of imagined geographies have we constructed in our heads that tell us what places are desirable, or danger-ous, or contested? Where do we feel included or excluded—and why? How do students straddle the borders of many communities at once? Composition and Rhetoric scholar Nedra Reynolds reports here on an ethnographic study she conducted with eight undergraduate students at the University of Leeds in the UK to understand the mix of memory and experience that led students to define places as no-go, ethnic, conflict, and normal. This is a chapter from Geographies of Writing: Inhabiting Places and Encountering Difference.

> *Mapping is too important to be left to cartographers . . .*
>
> —*J. B. Harley,* "Deconstructing the Map"

> *What the map cuts up, the story cuts across . . .*
>
> —*Michel de Certeau,* The Practice of Everyday Life

Who is felt to belong and not to belong contributes in an important way to the shaping of social space . . .

—*David Sibley,* Geographies of Exclusion:
Society and Difference in the West

In one episode of the popular television drama *The West Wing,* White House officials meet with groups that wouldn't normally have the ear of the White House.[1] The character C. J. is assigned the group "Cartographers for Social Equality" and meets with them reluctantly. The Cartographers for Social Equality had come to the White House asking for a mere million dollars or so to replace the thousands of Mercator projection maps still hanging in classrooms across the country with Peters projection maps that depict continents with more accuracy. In a scene where three (geeky) geographers demonstrate the different views of the world as evidenced by the Mercator projection map and the Peters projection map (Peters), C. J. is mesmerized, her "world view" decidedly shaken up, especially by an image where the map is flip-flopped so that the northern hemisphere occupies the "bottom" of the map, and the southern takes over the map (see Figure 1).

While some may be skeptical that different maps, created through different projection systems, could alter world politics or influence social justice (Lemann), critical geographers insist on the connection. J. B. Harley, in Deconstructing the Map," asserts the rhetoricality of maps:

> *rhetoric is part of the way all texts work and . . . all maps are rhetorical texts. . . . All maps strive to frame their message in the context of an audience. All maps state an argument about the world, and they are propositional in nature. All maps employ the common devices of rhetoric such as invocations of authority. This is especially so in topographical maps. . . . Rhetoric may be concealed but it is always present. . . . (242, his emphasis)*

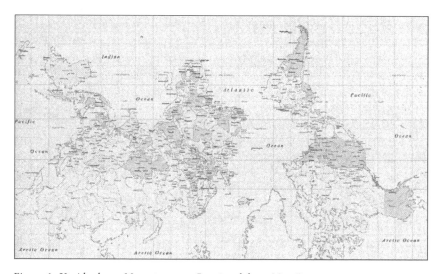

Figure 1. Upside-down Mercator map. Reprinted from Map Resources,
<www.mapresources.com>

Many areas of geographic study have changed dramatically in response to both poststructuralist claims about knowledge-making and new technologies, but perhaps none more than the science of maps and attitudes toward mapping. Our ideas about maps need to change in order to reflect how technology is revolutionizing map-making as well as map-reading, document design, and technological reproduction.

For decades if not centuries, the dignified authority of library atlas cabinets, flat drawers with neat stacks of two-dimensional maps, as well as the generally reliable accuracy of glove-compartment maps, led to dominant notions about maps not as "texts" to be interpreted but as documents to be trusted. Following Harley's lead, critical geographers address the politics of mapping and admit that map-making is a political and interpretive act, and scholars in human geography and cartography have acknowledged in recent years the rhetoricality of map-making. The collection *Writing Worlds: Discourse, Text, and Metaphor in the Representation of Landscape* (Barnes and Duncan), for example, engages with the cross-disciplinary emphasis on intertextuality, signification, and deconstruction to argue that *discourse* creates maps and dominant images of regions, not measurements, surveys, or instruments. In *The Power of Maps*, Denis Wood asserts that maps work by serving interests, and this "interested selectivity," embodied in the map as both presences and absences, allows the map to work, to have meaning, and in turn, to reproduce the culture that creates them in the first place (1). In nearly every field or discipline, scholars use the language of mapping to show how the field is configured, where the borders lie, and who works where. (In rhetoric and composition studies, for example, see Phelps; Lauer; Sullivan and Porter; Glenn.)

As academics and the writers of *The West Wing* recognize, mapping is an important spatial practice that illustrates the link between geography and culture, between images of the world and world power, between the concept of space and actual places. Maps and their significance loom large in both traditional assumptions about the discipline of geography and in people's habitual ways of navigating the world. This chapter concentrates on mapping as another spatial practice that informs geographies of rhetoric and writing and that illustrates the complexity of thirdspace, where maps can be informative and useless, accurate and empty, image and text, exemplary of logic and measurement but also unreadable to a first-time user.[2] The maps we spread out onto a dashboard or view on a screen have very little to do with our mental maps, the images and associations of places that we carry around in our heads.

This disparity means that we must change our notions of mapping, just as we must re-imagine acts of writing, to account for paradoxical and contested places and for places that are laden with risk or the perception of risk for trespassers, the unwelcome, or "intruders" marked by difference. People move through space, in large part, very cautiously, particularly if their (visible) identity puts them at risk in certain areas or neighborhoods. Movement through the spatial world is determined largely by contested places and geographies of exclusion, by (invisible) markers of boundaries. In addition, even the finest maps—created via satellite and updated every twenty-four hours—cannot capture the contested places that are difficult even for insiders to characterize or predict.

Computer technologies and Geographic Information Systems have made maps more public and democratic, easy to reproduce, available in more than one dimension, and, via satellite technology, precisely "accurate." Like most advances, this presents a double-edged sword, and the dual nature of these advances encapsulates the changing nature of geography and the complications of place and space. Maps achieved much of their cultural capital in colonialist and imperialist enterprises; obviously much rarer in ink on parchment, maps and mapping services are consumed today by many professional groups as well as by farmers or fishermen and all those whose income and livelihood depends on the weather. The group of consumers gets larger, too, when you add in the avid gardeners, boaters, golfers, and other middle-class outdoor enthusiasts who now want maps that move, as on weather sites, where radar images of rain march from west to east, illustrating a "speeding up" of weather patterns and the projected paths of fronts or storms. Maps are colorful, often portable, collectible, or valuable, but their value comes, of course, from the culture's demand for positivist, precise, measurable, and reproducible forms of "reality" and representations of regions that are meaningful to people.

Familiar to some readers, a poststructuralist critique of mapping is offered here alongside a practical fondness for maps, an admiration for their logic, and a confidence in their usefulness. Despite the wealth of persuasive arguments that maps are everything from inaccurate to instruments of oppression, I don't want to dismiss something that we depend on so much in the everyday. The image of travelers and tourists poring over maps is a common one, but walkers and residents also depend on different types of maps, memories, or landmarks to find their way around, even for such mundane activities as errands or appointments: street names, subway maps, big trees, crosswalks, billboards, hills or rivers, bus stops or benches, shops or stores, signs of all types. Habitual pathways, of course, are characterized by signs that have faded with familiarity; the routine byways of a pedestrian, for example, may have originally been marked by signs of the built environment, but they are no longer needed when the routine becomes naturalized.

The dignified authority of maps dies hard, but it has by now been challenged rigorously by a number of geographers and cartographers—and also by revolutionary technologies of map-making. Affordable software, increasing access to GIS databases, and a growing reliance on satellite imagery might be making possible the "democratization" of cartography, but technological advances, while they may be useful in settling disputes over boundaries and borders, do not alone make new maps "more" accurate or true. Harley worries, in addition, that the

> *effect of accelerated technological change—as manifest in digital cartography and geographical information systems—has been to strengthen its positivist assumptions and it has bred a new arrogance in geography about its supposed value as a mode of access to reality. (231)*

In other words, there is a danger of investing in technologically sophisticated maps as the new source of truth without also acknowledging the shifting, fragmentary nature of all forms of knowledge and information.

If we assume that people who never leave their neighborhoods don't really need maps, that assumption ignores the power of a globe or atlas for armchair travel, for dreaming about traveling or imagining other places. Those who do explore unfamiliar places, by choice or by circumstance, often depend on a map and often have the experience of "Hey, here it is! Just like on the map, just like the map says." Something about maps is hugely satisfying, and there's nothing quite like "a good map" to a hiker, tourist, new resident, or real estate agent. However, as this chapter will argue, mapping takes many different forms, and we need to look beyond published and copyrighted two-dimensional maps to understand mapping as a spatial practice. Rhetorical mapping addresses questions of "How do you get there from here?" that have more to do with practices of the everyday than with expeditions of the Royal Geographical Society or van trips on blue highways. "Which bus will take me to Stop and Shop?" "Don't go that way during rush hour." "How far to a good flea market?" "Turn right where the old post office used to be." Since maps have been the subject of intense debate within human geography for several years now, it's important to contextualize that debate and to come to terms with the kinds of information that maps can and cannot give us.

Mental Mapping, Maps That Move

While print and electronic maps are the most familiar forms, "mapping" is increasingly used as a metaphor for charting, understanding, exploring, or organizing. Mental mapping and cognitive mapping are both terms used by educators and researchers to refer to a person's cognitive capacity to understand where things are in relationship to one another, sense of direction, or sense of distance. It's the ability to carry around in our heads organized information or images of cities, especially images that are "soaked in memories and meanings" (Lynch 1).[3] A form of imagined geography, mental maps hold the cognitive images in our minds about a place, a route, or an area. We have mental maps of our hometowns or the most familiar places of our childhoods; we have mental maps of our current neighborhoods or campuses. Based on these mental maps, many of us could give directions to a stranger or could sketch the way from A to B. In *The Image of the City*, Kevin Lynch introduced the concept of cognitive mapping to city planning by testing the idea of "imageability" through interviews with inhabitants. Principles for urban design, Lynch believed, would develop from a comparison between group images of their city and visual reality. Residents were asked to describe places, sketch locations, or take an imaginary trip through the area.

The techniques of mental mapping are not only useful to city planners. Educators, like the fictional cartographers portrayed on *The West Wing*, know the importance of teaching children spatial sense: children should be able to make a short trip alone to the school library or tell a driver how to get to their house; or know how far it is to other neighborhoods reported to have better playgrounds. The point of teaching "spatial sense" is not to turn schoolchildren into cartographers, but to make them safe in their lifeworlds and to expand those lifeworlds gradually without endangering or intimidating them. In geographic education, mental mapping usually begins with freehand drawings of a place, proceeds to fieldwork or other types of investigation, and then returns to revising or redrawing the original map, based on new knowledge and understanding (see Mental Mapping and Mental Mapping Project).

Geography educators argue, rightly, that it is an important form of visual and global literacy to be able to read maps. Children should understand something about the relative size of countries, the differences among continents, the way that the sun, for example, affects cultures in dramatically different ways. It matters, for purposes of employment or to increase one's opportunities, to have good map literacy or a strong spatial sense. For example, the navigational skills required for reading a map are similar to those found on a computer interface, but also in very practical terms, how can someone get to a job interview without finding their way there? Here's the case that geography educator Patrick Wiegand makes for children's spatial literacy:

> *Children's need to understand the spatial relationships of the Earth's land masses will become more important. For example, increasing school use of the Internet and the opportunities offered by videoconferencing will enable children to undertake interactive investigations around the world. They will need a sharper awareness of where places are in relation to each other and how time zones operate. Having a reasonably accurate image of the way the continents are arranged around the globe and the limitations of world maps not only allows us to make better sense of travel and world events, it is [also] one of the building block of international understanding. (6)*

Using mental maps, researchers have learned about people's ability to navigate space and to remember places based on mental maps. Wiegand and Bernadette Stiell, in "Mapping the Place Knowledge of Teachers in Training," asked geography student-teachers to draw a freehand sketch map of the British isles—a "mental map" or "free recall" map as an admittedly partial test of place knowledge. The results, while varied in theme and significance, showed that "all students in the sample drew England 38 percent larger than its actual relative size. The Republic of Ireland and Scotland were shown 45 percent and 20 percent smaller respectively" (195). Similarly, in a large-scale study of mental mapping, researchers collected 3,568 maps of the continents drawn by students in seventy-five universities in fifty-two countries (Monastersky 222). A predictable "home-turf exaggeration" emerged, but even more striking was the consistent pattern by which Europe was enlarged in scale while Africa's dimensions shrank. No matter where students lived, they exaggerated the size of Europe, and a full 80 percent of the maps featured Europe in the middle (Monastersky 222). The point is not, then, that students need to be taught the right scale, but that mental mapping can tell us a great deal about how people perceive the world, and how ideology (i.e., Eurocentrism) is reproduced in images and school exercises.

The legitimate criticisms of mental maps are that most exercises or experiments using them require people to draw, and then drawing ability comes into the picture. Some research subjects may have very accurate and even unique mental maps but not feel comfortable with the activity of drawing or putting those images on paper. This has always been a disadvantage in using mental maps for research, and, of course, as composition readers know very well, cognitive research is often problematic when divorced from the social production of knowledge.

Mental maps, however cognitively housed, are socially constructed. They are a particular form of "imagined geography" that illustrate the complex relationships between the social and the spatial. Most importantly, maps and spatial memory have been shown to relate to gender and class. This means they are not "cognitive" topics but social ones. The research of Peter Orleans from 1967 in Los Angeles provides the most striking example of this: asking residents of L.A. to share their mental maps of urban space, Orleans questioned a wide range of groups and then created composite maps from their responses (Gould and White). Unsurprisingly, the higher the income and the whiter the neighborhood, the richer and more wide-ranging were residents' knowledge of LA. White respondents from Westwood represented tourist areas and the coast, for example, while black residents in Avalon identified main streets leading to downtown, but other districts were vague entities. Finally, Spanish-speaking residents in Boyle Heights constructed the smallest mental maps of all, representing only the immediate area, the City Hall, and the bus depot (Gould and White 17). In other words, leisure time, access to affordable transportation, and above all, feelings of empowerment and safety allow people to explore little-known regions and to broaden and deepen their own "mental maps" of a place or region.

Soja pins a fondness for mental mapping on secondspace epistemologies,

> *immediately distinguishable by their explanatory concentration on conceived rather than perceived space and their implicit assumption that spatial knowledge is primarily produced through discursively devised representations of space, through the spatial workings of the mind. (*Thirdspace *78–79)*

Artists and architects, urbanists and designers can be found in secondspace, according to Soja, where "the imagined geography tends to become the 'real' geography, with the image or representation coming to define and order the reality" (79). Despite his criticisms, others believe that mental maps and a variety of forms of mapping can become vital tools in exploring people's understanding of space, or the cultural and social spaces that mark inclusions or exclusions: "Just as individuals need cognitive maps of their cities to negotiate their spatial environment, so we need maps of society to intelligently analyse, discuss and intervene in social processes" (Gregory, Martin, and Smith 10).

One form of mapping can be found in William Least Heat-Moon's *PrairyErth*. Subtitled "A Deep Map," his book captures the character, history, and richness of Chase County, Kansas, in the Flint Hills, "the last remaining grand expanse of tallgrass prairie in America" (12). Using the image of a grid to organize Chase County into twelve quadrangles, and hoping that coordinates would lead to connections (15), Least Heat-Moon's chapters—his in-depth visits to each quadrangle—all begin with sections "From the Commonplace Book" and "In the Quadrangle." His deep map is mostly textual rather than visual; the rare visual maps he includes are two-dimensional and not even in color. But to make this map, for thirty months Least Heat-Moon walks across approximately 780 square miles of landscape and explores a dozen small towns; he searches country records, talks to residents, and collects Native American legends. Partly geographic and partly anthropologic, the deep map merges botany, geology, history, and anthropology; Least Heat-Moon is explorer and recorder and narrator. Least Heat-Moon's deep map is a story written geographically, and illustrates vividly how much we need stories for our maps as well as maps for our stories.

Within rhetoric and composition studies, Ralph Cintron uses mapping to situate his ethnographic study of *Angels' Town:* Chero *Ways, Gang Life, and Rhetorics of the Everyday*. His second chapter, titled "Mapping/Texting," uses a map of Angelstown (the size of a double bed) as an example of the discourses of measurement, particularly reduction (17); distinctions between grids and circuity; and the rhetoric of place names (20). A map is "one kind of optical knowledge that comes into being after real space overwhelms the eye" (29); it is a material representation of space, one that furthers "the desire to conquer and colonize," desires made possible by the process of mapping and texting (35).

Influenced by Lynch, Least Heat-Moon, Cintron, and others, I rely in this chapter on overlapping versions of mapping to argue that mapping as a concept helps us understand the social production of space and people's experiences in space, but our concept of mapping must include the realandimagined and needs to be drawn from the actual experiences of sociospatial beings. Mental maps are drawn by people's experience in space and with specific places or locations—experiences that have everything to do with class, race, gender, age, mobility, and sexuality. Identity is constructed in place, via place, and I hope to build on that assertion both by qualitative research methodologies and through the rich literatures of cultural geography.

A Study: Mental Maps and Living in Leeds

I often rode the bus in Leeds from St. Michael's to the Headrow, observing the politics of space even on a double-decker bus: young adults in groups, probably students, always go upstairs. Young men riding alone go up, too. Young women alone, though, stay down. Do the students and younger riders consciously leave the lower level seats for pensioners or mothers with children—those who cannot navigate the stairwell—or do they want to "claim" the upper deck, where the view is better and the driver's gaze removed?

In order to explore the relationship between the spatial and the social in a concrete and practical way, I interviewed eight students in a cultural geographies class at Leeds University about their experiences in Leeds, with getting around the city, with living and working there as students.[4] My purpose was to explore the everyday material existence of university students in the "mundane landscape" of the campus, the surrounding area, their housing, and the other places of their social and spatial lifeworlds. What places did these students see as contested, desirable, or dangerous? Which places did they avoid or feel excluded from? How are their experiences in space shaped by their identities as students, who are typically transient members of learning communities? In what ways do students—straddling the borders of a number of communities—describe geographically-constructed difference? My analysis of the interview transcripts suggests that an awareness of the workings of geographic exclusion helps us

476

come to terms with the "invisible" types of difference that are the hardest to identify and understand. Geographies of exclusion (Sibley) are worth far more of our attention as we attempt to understand the various ways in which difference is encoded.

I asked for volunteers and conducted managed conversations with eight students from the third-year cultural geographies module in which I was a participant observer in the spring term of 2000. While participants were certainly not randomly selected, they were all third-years, all seeking BA degrees in geography, and all white. With the social advantages of race and excellent educational backgrounds (only about the top 10 percent of all eligible college-age students are accepted into university), the students with whom I worked were very representative of "the student body" at Leeds.

Here's how the interview project began: during a workshop early in the term, the lecturer asked students to do a version of a mental mapping exercise as a sort of pre-writing activity to their research project on a place new to their experience. "Tom" (all names are pseudonyms) gave students, in pairs, a photocopy of an Ordnance Survey map of Leeds (see Figure 2) and asked them to identify four types of areas: no-go, ethnic, conflict, and normal. Using colored markers, students were to shade in or outline these types of areas and then get together to compare and discuss their shadings.

I was immediately struck—and troubled—by Tom's terms for these categories. "Normal to whom?" I wanted to ask. "No-go for whom?" "Doesn't it depend on gender, race, class, modes of transport, and abilities?" I didn't raise these questions that day, but the classroom activity—observing students and listening in on their decisions about what to mark—sparked my interest in one-on-one interviews with students about their mental maps of Leeds. I combined, then, a form of mental mapping with one-to-one semistructured interviews.[5] The interviews, like the activity in class, asked students to sit with a map of Leeds and colored markers and to talk about their *personal* definitions of and experiences with the following categories (changed slightly from those in class): "no-go," "ethnic," and "desirable."

The interview transcripts (a total of approximately seventy-eight pages) touch on a range of issues well beyond the three categories. The eight students (four males and four females) talked about their main modes of transport and their habitual routes in getting around the city; they described types of housing that worked as signifiers for them; they shared anecdotes of feeling fearful or excluded; they discussed how they had "come to know" about certain places; and they made comparisons between Leeds and their own hometowns. One of the striking findings of this data is that these students, despite their training as human geographers, stuck to a very limited area within Leeds and were either reluctant or totally uninterested in exploring other parts of the city. They also held strong opinions—some of those uninformed—about particular neighborhoods. The interview data I share below supports the argument of feminist geographers Geraldine Pratt and Susan Hanson, "that most people are fixed in and by space. Understanding these processes provides one way of seeing differences as socially constructed" (12).

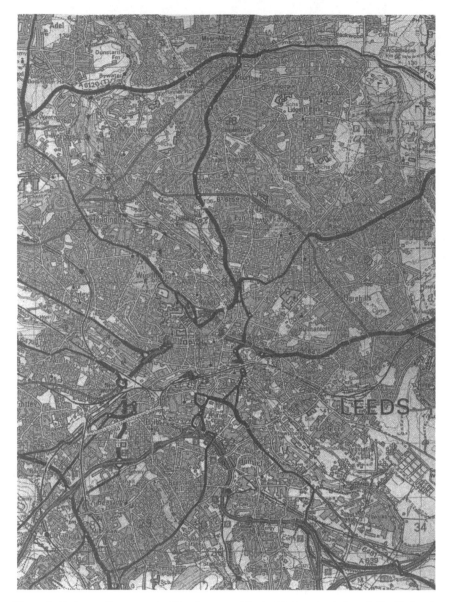

Figure 2. Ordnance Survey map of Leeds proper. Used with the permission of Her Majesty's Stationery Office, © Crown Copyright, NC/01/577.

The (Confined) Spatiality of Social Lives

In "Geography and the Construction of Difference," Geraldine Pratt and Susan Hanson point out the tension between postmodern views of experiencing space and more everyday and down-to-earth realities:

> *Much has been made of the shrinking world, of the increasing ease of travel and communication, and of the resulting homogenisation of space around the globe. Although the world is indeed increasingly*

> *well connected, we must hold this in balance with the observation*
> *that most people live intensely local lives; their homes, work places,*
> *recreation, shopping, friends, and often family are all located within*
> *a relatively small orbit. The simple and obvious fact that overcoming*
> *distance requires time and money means that the everyday events of*
> *daily life are well grounded within a circumscribed arena. (10–11, my*
> *emphasis)*

A passage from my interview with "Elaine," which highlights students' reluctance to stray from well-defined student areas, offers considerable support for Pratt and Hanson's assertion. Here's the passage in full.[6]

I: Anything else you want to say about your map of Leeds?

E: Not many details is there? [laughs]

I: Well, why do you say that or why do you suppose that is?

E: It's just a general knowledge that I don't really have of the area; I think I know Leeds well, but all I know is like Headingley to the city center— I know the city center quite well, but there's a general lack of details thing.

I: Well, do you think that's because . . . you're a student?

E: Uh-huh.

I: And your particular place and time in life?

E: I think so but not necessarily 'cause when I was working in Comet [a retail store] back in the summer, there were people there that didn't have a clue about north of Leeds or where I live.

I: Any part?

E: Yeah, and most of them had lived their all their lives.

I: So it's not necessarily about being a student; it's about . . .

E: It's like your neighborhood is your whole life, isn't it? . . . People identify with their neighborhood, and if you've got everything there, then you didn't need to go out of it, and you're safe in this area where you live 'cause that's where the home is.

I: So you haven't really felt compelled to explore . . . the areas of Leeds that you don't know.

E: No, not really, no. I suppose it bring questions of home into it, doesn't it? 'cause Headingley is my home at the minute, so therefore that's where I'm going to spend the majority of my time.

All eight of the participants commented on their own neighborhoods and their limited knowledge of the city of Leeds. Mitchell says, "I don't really know too many areas of Leeds because when you're a student you're only really going between the university, your house, and into the city center," and he repeats the point about his ignorance of Leeds twice more. Anna puts the issue rather succinctly: "because I have no need to go very far out, I mean my knowledge of Leeds is pretty much concentrated into that student area or where students live."

Zoe compared her limited sense of place in Leeds with her similar experience in London:

> *I don't really feel like I know Leeds at all really 'cause I only know a narrow corridor; . . . a bit strange really [. . .] but I suppose like if you're living in London, I mean I only knew my borough, I only knew that really well; I didn't know that much of the rest of London at all.*

Julian believes that most people's familiar territory occurs within a limited radius:

> *I only know sort of a limited, I think you'll find this with everybody else, they've got a sort of chunk of Leeds that they know quite well [. . .] You've got a sort of radius—if you live in that, like I live in that so I've got a radius of about five miles either side of that which I know quite well, which is everywhere within walking distance basically.*

Some were quite matter-of-fact about their ignorance of the city while others seemed a bit regretful that they had not done more to explore a wider range of places. Sheila, in particular, seemed to feel that she had failed somehow as a geographer in her tendency to stick to student areas, but she explains her behavior in terms of security and convenience.

S: I'm totally ashamed of myself for the fact that I've just basically been on this road here which is just basically where students live—the town center and—

I: Between the city center and—

S: And I'd say even as far as Headingley—

I: Just up the A660, right?

S: That's it. That's the area where students all live; that's where all the pubs are, the clubs are in town and basically I mean, I've been, the area that I've functioned in is so restricted I'm almost ashamed of myself, but—

I: It's not because you're afraid, it's because—

S: No, it's because I can't, it's because . . . everything I want is here [taps finger on map] which is really bad. I've got friends who've gone out into the countryside and explored all around, but I'm bored with that because that's what it's like when I'm at home [in Wales]. Everything I want is, has been along this road, and students do feel like quite secure there I suppose as well.

I: Well it's their, their culture.

S: Yeah, put it this way: [. . .] I wouldn't *not* go to Bramley for the day 'cause I'm a student, but I wouldn't want to live there amongst . . . I'd want to live—

I: With students?

S: Yeah! Definitely and that's probably some sort of security issue there and also because you know it's just that there's four cinemas, . . . there's all my friends, there's loads of pubs, and it's just—

I: Convenient?

S: It's convenient, yeah, which I'm quite, I am ashamed of it, I should've been around a bit more but—

I: Well, it's about who you are right now, I guess.

Students were able to name the reasons for their restricted knowledge of Leeds, namely the convenience and a desire to share in "student life," defined in part by being surrounded by other students. If "everything they need is there" in the student neighborhoods, why should (white, middle-class) college students venture into unknown territory? They relied very much on what friends and acquaintances had told them about certain places, and "things they'd heard" as well as their own impressions of places formed through their regular routes through Leeds. Except for Sheila, they accepted their confined spatiality as a fact of life, a reality connected either to their position as students or to the geographic given that "for many people in the world, everyday life continues to take place within a restricted locale" and that "the 'localization' of most of everyday life is indisputable" (McDowell, *Gender* 2–3).

Students' identities as students—their embodied practices—kept them from venturing into certain areas where they had strong feelings that they weren't welcome or would feel "out of place." At my suggestion, students used the term "no-go" to name and discuss places where they personally would not feel safe.[7] Anna talks about one no-go area, determined for her by one (accidental) drive through the area and information from others:

> *I wouldn't feel comfortable walking down Chapletown at any time just because I'm obviously not [a resident]; I don't think I would fit in there, I mean the kids that hang about on the streets there [. . .] the people who are sort of my age tend to be hanging around in, we call 'em pikeys which is like Adidas pants and all the girls have their hair scraped up onto their heads and spiral perms with blonde hair and I'd be, just by standing there it'd be obvious that I wasn't one of them, so I just wouldn't stop.*

Students were well aware of the features that marked them as students and used these differences to explain their isolation from many areas of the city. Elaine can't really name the areas but says "some of the ones down here [in south Leeds] because, just because of my position in Leeds at the moment as a student they wouldn't appreciate us going there." When I asked her to elaborate, she admits that she is stereotyping the areas or basing her notions on hearsay but also is clear that her reluctance to enter these areas comes from her identity: "just because I'm, mind, a student with student feelings putting myself into one of these like council estates it wouldn't be a wise thing to do; you just don't go there, just for your own safety."

These students have good reasons to worry about their own safety, as most of the participants mention incidents where they had abuse directed at them or felt vulnerable because of crimes against students. Elaine clarifies that things can happen even in daylight, even in residential areas: "I've had little groups of kids throw stones at you and stuff." Liam talks about being spat upon as he walked by "kids who sit on walls," but he emphasized that he didn't take it personally. In naming no-go areas, Liam describes an area near his house: "There's footpaths down at the bottom of that—I wouldn't actually go up there for fear of being, well, I get abuse shouted at me, every now and again, all students do I suppose, but then there's bricks in there and I wouldn't walk down that way at night." While he seems quite casual about the verbal abuse, Liam avoids an area where greater physical harm could be done. In addition, both Sheila and Anna narrate the details of a crime scheme in this area of Leeds where (male) students are grabbed off the streets at night and taken to cash points, where they are forced to withdraw money to give to their attackers. This pattern had been repeated three or four times over a few months, and most students were well aware of it.

In less threatening ways, however, students were also made aware that they were unwelcome in certain areas, that they were trespassers in areas that "belonged" to other social groups. Half of the students interviewed talked about their tentative status, even in neighborhoods—in this case, Hyde Park—full of student dwellers. Hyde Park, a neighborhood near the university occupied by both students and Asians,[8] is the epitome of a contested place, where the local businesses' economic dependence on students bred an attendant feeling of resentment of them. In this space, students realize their economic clout but are equally aware of their temporary status as residents. In the next section, I try to illustrate further the complexities of Hyde Park as both realandimagined space, where the construction of difference can be illustrated by conflicts related to liminal spaces and residential segregation.

Contested Spaces

On a gray afternoon in February, taking my usual route from campus to Headingley, I overheard one side of a mobile phone conversation, where a male student said to his caller, "I'm walking through Hyde Park. . . . No, the dodgy one. In *Leeds*."

Hyde Park is most often associated with London, but that confusion is only one of many layers of complicated meaning affixed to this place. I begin with Hyde Park, the dodgy one in Leeds, because it emerged in these interviews as a place marked by contestation and controversy, while it was also obviously a gathering place and a playground. It served the functions that city parks fulfill—it was a pleasantly green respite from the otherwise brick and stone environment—and it was also perceived to be a dangerous place. As one geographer has noted, "Parks are typical of those spaces that make the edge of the street ambiguous, that extend the space the street signifies" (Crouch 165). It was often filled with people using the space in various ways; on a nice day, you could see dogs being walked, children on the playground, older teens on the skateboard ramp or basketball court, pick-up football matches, and many people just passing through on their way to and from the university or towards the Hyde Park bus stop on one edge of the park. However, at dusk or after dark, it took on a different identity, and for women, at least, even the streets surrounding the park take on a sinister quality.

For residents of Leeds, "Hyde Park" refers to both a park, with clear borders, and a neighborhood, with boundaries less obvious. Hyde Park is both a clearly bound green space, with playground areas and trees lining the sidewalks, and also a residential area characterized by red-brick terraced housing, a shopping area, and at least one major traffic artery (the Otley road). I often had to ask students to clarify whether they meant Hyde Park as *park* or as neighborhood, and this distinction is just one layer of the contestations surrounding this space. On the city of Leeds ward map, Hyde Park is part of the Headingley ward. One would have to "know the area," in experiential ways, to distinguish the boundaries between Hyde Park and other parts of the Headingley ward (including Headingley the residential and commercial district within the voting ward of Headingley) (Leeds City Council). Rates for rentals, higher in Headingley, and the number of "ethnic" shops, higher in Hyde Park, can serve to distinguish between the two areas.[9] On the northwestern edge of the university, the park serves as *a space in between* the campus and some of the most student-populated neighborhoods in Leeds—streets that are also more permanently occupied by a very diverse group of residents.

Hundreds of pedestrians and cyclists, making their way to or from the university, walk through Hyde Park, both as a shortcut to certain parts of campus and to avoid or take a break from the busy and noisy main road. My first reaction to it was a very pleasant one—after a mile of walking on an exhaust-fumed main road, I welcomed a calmer green space. However, I was to learn later that Hyde Park is considered by most students to be unsafe at certain times or in certain situations. In addition, students consider Hyde Park the neighborhood to be, simultaneously, terrible, rundown, and full of character. Even though those I interviewed called it "student land," it is also presented in social geography lectures as one of the most ethnic areas in Leeds, occupied mostly by South Asians, many of whom run businesses: shops, taxi stands, takeaway restaurants. I want to write about Hyde Park here to illustrate how contested places can be. Hyde Park operates as a complicated signifier for the students I interviewed and supports the argument that even the most precise, sophisticated map cannot represent much about a place except where it exists in (geometric) relationship to other places.

My own understanding of Hyde Park, and all its contestations, comes from walking through the area a few days a week and from living in Headingley, adjacent to Hyde Park the neighborhood. But none of my experiences as a transient resident prepared me for the strong reactions most of the students I interviewed had towards Hyde Park or the strong associations or a particularly resonant sense of place.

When asked how she knew that Hyde Park was an ethnic area, Elaine replied, "I know about Hyde Park because we live round there, so we have to walk through that." She doesn't pause to clarify what "*that*" is, but given her wording and tone, it is clearly distasteful (why didn't she say "we have to walk through *there*"?). Elaine also says: "I've been in Hyde Park in the middle of the night, and it's like oh my gosh I'm so scared." When I asked her whether she meant the park itself or the neighborhood, she said "both really," but she emphasized that "when it goes dark, you don't walk through the park, you walk around it."

Elaine lives nearby, in Headingley, but she doesn't hesitate to draw firm boundaries between the two (despite the fact that firm boundaries are not drawn by the city). Headingley is, in fact, considered by Elaine to be a desirable area: "I suppose at the minute, I'd say Headingley is desirable to me because it is a student area and it's very accessible to the center of town. Hopefully when I finish next year I want to stay in Headingley; I don't want to move out; everything is just there for you." She clarifies that it's not so much physical attractiveness that makes the area desirable but "it's just everything's there in a community; there's young people and lots of services, like good bus routes into town and takeaways, the cinema, everything." Elaine ignores the fact that Hyde Park is also accessible to the city center; also has a cinema (see Figure 3) as well as a number of shops. What Hyde Park does not have, unlike Headingley, is a number of pubs; what it *does* have are a number of nonwhite and nonstudent residents.

Anna's boyfriend lives in Hyde Park, but she attributes her avoidance of the area to her upbringing in a small village, a small-town experience that cultivated in her a sharp awareness of her surroundings for city life: "Because I'm from a little country village I'm more aware of that than a lot of other people; I never walk through Hyde Park even though a lot of my friends don't believe it's violent."

Figure 3. Hyde Park cinema. Photo by Randy Blackburn.

Her geographic upbringing and gender make Anna notice many of the details that then contribute to her judgment about Hyde Park:

> *Even walking through Hyde Park, you can see that it's not a desirable place to live. It's the sort of place that people go and live when they're students, and they're fine 'cause they can treat it as student land, but then when they leave, you know, as soon as they stop being students they want to go somewhere nice. The reason it's not nice is because there's bars over all the windows, there's robberies and people driving around in cars with darkened windows a lot with the music coming out— . . . so I'm going to ring that in ethnic as well. I don't know if that's because it's ethnic or not, or if it's just because it's so run down . . . there's rubbish in the streets; there's stray cats everywhere; there's gangs and gangs of Asian kids playing behind the terraced houses on the back streets.*

According to Anna and others, Brudenell Road (see Figure 4) is the clearest signifier of an "Asian street," but Anna says, "To be honest, the students and the Asians live side-by-side."[10] Brudenell Road is characterized by, says Liam, "a lot of ethnic shops and food places—there's a big concentration of them. When I walk round there I've got a couple of friends who live down there—there's always more ethnic minorities walking around than you see white people." Mitchell, who calls Hyde Park "definitely one of the ethnic areas," also specifically mentions "a lot of Asian shops like grocery shops and meat shops' Halal signs."

Sheila was the only student of the eight interviewed who lived in Hyde Park by choice: "I live in this area here—it's Hyde Park and it's definitely ethnic 'cause there's a lot of like Asian families that live in and around here; I've been there so I know." Since all of her friends live there too, Sheila is careful to distinguish between Hyde Park the neighborhood and Hyde Park the park.

Figure 4. A small section of Brudenell Road, Hyde Park. Photo by Randy Blackburn.

I: Would you walk in Hyde Park, at night?

S: Hyde, the actual park? No, you never walk through Hyde Park, that's definitely a no-go area; I'll mark that one actually. . . . The actual park is not lit; it's really dark; actually the council should probably spend a bit of money on lighting. Of course I'd walk through at night but in a massive gang. I'm talking four plus. Walk through coming back home from the university union Old Bar and go home; I'd walk through there if there's more than four of us usually—usually if there's a lad as well but *never* just me and my friends walking in from the union, always round the side of the park, never through the park.

I.   Even in the daytime you go around?

S: The worst time apparently for like student muggings or other incidents is around five or six o'clock at night when it's dark, so going home from uni, that's the time I usually go, between half five and seven at night I'm usually on my way home so then I would always go around the side.

I: And that's better lit?

S: It's better lit and there's just traffic and houses.

I: More people?

S: Yeah, there's loads of students walk down there; I mean 'cause it's terrifying when you're walking through the park and it's dark and someone comes from the opposite direction and you're oh no, and you realize that there's students so it's okay, and you think oh it's just students so they're legitimate, which is a bad thing to think anyway. [laughter]

Sheila's relief at seeing other students, which she admits is problematic, may illustrate the high ethnic population of Hyde Park. Even Sheila, who enjoys living in Hyde Park for its diversity, expresses her sense of relief at encountering other students at night—rather than, one assumes, other locals who may not be white.

Mitchell and Anna both talk about the contested claims to residency status or about the contestation over who belongs in this neighborhood and who doesn't. Mitchell says,

> *I know people who live in the Hyde Park area, and their next door neighbors who're Asian come round and knock on their door and say, "Why are you living here, this is an Asian area." So I think as well as white people saying it's is an ethnic or Asian area, Asians see it as an ethnic area themselves.*

Anna relates her own experience as a visitor and nonresident:

A: Basically I went to a friend's house there [in the Hyde Park area], and we're all sitting in the lounge having a cup of tea or something, and these kids were climbing on the bars in front of the windows climbing across the bars [imitates them]. "Oy mister, mister, give us this, give us that," and they [my friends] can't put any, any of their washing out, and there are literally—there are sort of bars over the windows to stop the kids coming in, and they're inside the house and that's their territory—soon as you step outside the house then it's almost like it's Asian people's territory, really, . . . so

I: They'll ask you things like—

A: What are you doing here, what are you doing here. If you're in the way, or if you're wanting to get past them, it's fine if . . . you, you know, keep yourself to yourself and you've been quite separate about it, but if you—if there's any attempt to mix in any sense then, that, you know, I'd be nervous about it, definitely, so you tend to sort of keep yourself to yourself and walk with your head high and hopefully no one will bother you.

Anna identifies in this passage what David Sibley, in *Geographies of Exclusion*, calls a liminal zone, spaces of ambiguity where the categories of inside/outside, public/private, or home/street become blurred or uncertain. Sibley asserts "for the individual or group socialized into believing that the separation of categories is necessary or desirable, the liminal zone is a source of anxiety" (33). If students are in their homes, they are "safe," but Anna's anxiety begins when she has to cross the threshold, enter the streets, and move through the neighborhood.

In these mixed residential areas, where races and classes share limited space, inevitable conflicts arise, not just from racial or economic differences but from a whole set of issues that are deeply embedded in English culture and the experience of immigrants. Elaine tells a story that illustrates these layers of tensions:

> On our street, there's an Asian lady that lives opposite us, and we've always said "Oh look, she's got a lot of plants." Everything in her garden looks really nice. We had a friend come and stay with us and she gave us a window box, so we put it out on the back of our kitchen window which doesn't face her house—we put it inside. Well, one day in the summer came a knock on our back door, and we never use our back door, so it's like, oh, who's that? So we open the door, and there's this lady, and she accused us of stealing her window box, and we were just like [laughs], "Come on now this is ridiculous." And then she started going on about how we were students and we come from middle-class families, which isn't necessarily true, and how just that we think we're better than everybody else and tra la la.

Several things about Elaine's brief narrative give us some insight into the sociospatial construction of difference and everyday conflicts related to coexisting in shared neighborhoods. The permanent resident takes great pride in her garden and works hard at maintaining the flowers and plants, which the students do notice and appreciate; however, one assumes that the student residents have never shared their appreciation with their neighbor in a conversation that may have preceded this encounter. When a single window box appears on the students' otherwise unadorned flat, the gardener notices, even though it doesn't face her house. The gardening neighbor comes to the back door, a door that the students never use, giving an immediate sign that this visitor does not belong—and doesn't want to. (Does she walk around to the back because she wants this conversation to take place "off the street"? Because she feels unworthy to come in the front? Or because she wants to make her case next to the window box in question?) For whatever reason, the neighbor woman resists the students' habitual spatial practice of always using the front door. Her decision to knock at the back door forces students to encounter her in different territory, somewhat unfamiliar to them. As this woman's confrontation of her student neighbors suggests, Asians' own exclusions from so many neighborhoods and from "middle England" in general leads them to want to claim Hyde Park as their own. They see students as trespassers in the streets where they, in fact, feel somewhat protected, by virtue of residential segregation, from confrontations with non-Asians. They want to keep students out to increase their own sense of belonging.

The students I interviewed did not openly challenge others' claims that they didn't belong; they recognized that other residents were far more permanent, with more of a stake in the area. Some students were willing to admit that they didn't always make "good neighbors"; Mitchell talks about how students don't care for their houses (because they'll lose their security deposit anyway). Elaine, however, describes an "antistudent sentiment" that she claims is held by most locals: "The locals think that we come in and make loads of noise and create rubbish and get drunk and we're hooligans; and they've just got quite a lot of negative feelings against us."

Sheila thinks the antistudent attitudes result from a very limited form of contact between the two groups: the Asian businesses provide services to students, and students are interested in or dependent on the Asians only as "service providers." The students are consumers, and the businesses need them to survive.

> *Yeah, the only thing I do dislike about [Hyde Park] a lot is the fact the community's so divided, students and you know, the Asian families and businesses. The only thing you ever come into contact with people for unfortunately is buying burgers from the takeaway or taxis; that's the only contact. [. . .] I think that students, well I know that students are really resented by the locals—cause we can really misbehave.*

For the residents, students' economic clout often overrides residents' resentment of their noise and "hooligan" behaviors. Sheila remarks about how "welcomed" the students feel when they return to Leeds in September: "We come back and the taxi drivers always say 'Oh I'm so glad to have you back.' You know, students do bring most of the money into the area and businesses, especially all the takeaways."

As Sibley says, "In the interaction of people and the built environment, it is a truism that space is contested but relatively trivial conflicts can provide clues about power relations and the role of space in social control" (xiii). It's impossible to tell how serious or how trivial some of these encounters were between students and the Hyde Park residents; however, it's clear that the mix of social differences, beyond "race" or "class," causes boundaries or borders to shift and slide; those unsure of their place use tactics, like Anna's, of "keeping herself to herself" in order to get through territory that belongs to others.

These students' accounts of their experiences in and reactions to contested places like Hyde Park can tell us a great deal about the construction and reproduction of cultural difference. Places can only be contested, however, if there is some conflict, a mix and diversity that some students will find unnerving while others will find it refreshing. With one exception, these students were willing, theoretically, to live in Hyde Park, or they knew plenty of students who did; it was convenient and relatively inexpensive. Other places in Leeds, however, were no-go, a category that Tom introduced in the initial mapping activity in the class workshop and that I also used to question students about areas of Leeds into which they would not venture.

No-Go Areas

As I walked to and from campus that spring, geography lectures in my head, I tried to pay attention to my habitual pathways and variations from it. In one spot along the Otley Road, in front of several billboards, pedestrians had worn a path between the billboards and the backs of several buildings. Shadowed and often damp, it was a mathematical shortcut but too intimidating for me, too narrow and deserted looking. I couldn't make myself walk through it alone.

In the mid-1980s, following violent clashes between the police and the black community in London, the press and political discourse used repeatedly the term "no-go area," as Michael Keith explains, a phrase with roots in Northern Ireland, "a phrase that implied that there were parts of British cities which the police were unwilling or unable to patrol" (39). Calling it a term surrounded with mystification, Keith acknowledges the pejorative use of the term but presents two fallacies of its use: "one that this phenomenon is new to mainland Britain, the other that it is causally related to the number of crimes committed by black people" (40). These students did report one such area in Leeds, an area that the police entered only reluctantly and therefore a distinct no-go area, in keeping with the evolution of the term. For this mental mapping exercise, however, I encouraged students to define no-go areas (and the others as well) with whatever terms they chose; Liam, for example, defines no-go areas as those where "I wouldn't feel safe at night, but I suppose in the daytime as well." Elaine says for her, no-go areas are all about fear, "whether or not I've got myself in a position of vulnerability."

Liam identifies Chapletown as "notorious," something he knows by reputation rather than experience. Chapletown was, in fact, the most often named no-go area for these students. Elaine says that there's a special police force unit there, and Mitchell refers to information they received in the halls of residence during first year:

> *There was quite a big thing about not going to Chapletown during the day, and don't even think about going at night, because it's unsafe and you'll get mugged. Also in lectures on social geography, we were told that it's an area where if you do get mugged the police won't do anything because they'll say, "Well, what are you doing here in the first place?"*

Sheila confirms this, that first-years are advised to stay out of there, and that social geography lectures identified Chapletown as a site of deviance and crime, that it is a no-go area for the police.

Liam and Sheila and most of the group agree about what constitutes a no-go area in terms of the physical characteristics. Sheila lists "some of the characteristics of urban deprivation like more graffiti, more litter, vandalism; . . . and the shops tend to have physical barriers like grilling on the windows." Liam mentions twice the feature of terraced housing as well as vandalism: "housing is terraced, . . . litter everywhere, kids running around screaming." Note the similarity to Julian's description of a no-go area: "Everything's boarded up, and there's nobody about. . . . You see burned out cars and broken windows; you see high security fences everywhere and rubbish strewn everywhere and a few kids perhaps running around the place looking wild." Zoe mentions litter repeatedly to describe no-go areas, as well as "back-to-back houses, really run down."

Although there was considerable agreement about one no-go place (Chapletown) and about the physical signs of urban deprivation, no-go, like all neat and tidy categories for capturing a sense of place, didn't quite apply to some more nuanced or complex places. Mitchell: "So I suppose although Hyde Park's quite a green area, it's seen as an undesirable park with undesirable houses around it." Liam makes it very clear that he considers Burley "quite a scrubby area," but he's not exactly frightened to be there: "I mean if I walked through Burley, I wouldn't think someone's gonna come at me. I just don't like the feel of the place; I just don't like it."

Anna explains that for her, Hyde Park is not exactly no-go but that she approaches it with some trepidation or what she calls "provisos"—her own improvised rules for navigating the area:

> So yeah, I walk a lot, I walk from university home to Headingley, but I always walk along the Otley Road; I don't walk through Hyde Park, unless someone's walking through Hyde Park with me and they prefer to go that way. Once I'm out of Hyde Park, I walk up Cardigan Road without a problem; Cardigan Road's fine, it's just . . . it's just Hyde Park that I don't like, and walking down Victoria Road's fine as well 'cause it's on the edge, isn't it?

"On the edge" is safer, then, than being in the thick of it. Liam is one of the few students who acknowledges that people actually *live* in no-go areas:

> Having said that [about Burley], I live in Woodhouse, and a lot of people think of Woodhouse as being a not very nice area because it's inner city and it's not aesthetically pleasing to look at, but in fact, living there I know it's really only kids that cause trouble. I feel quite safe walking around Woodhouse, but I suppose that's only because it's my home. . . . I think of Burley as being quite a scrubby area, for want of a better word, but people who live there might not think so.

Mitchell also mentions Burley, but as a no-go area based on "what people told me about it, because of the riots that happened there." According to newspaper accounts, however, the riots were in Hyde Park.

Riots in Leeds erupted in both July 1995 and May 1997. According to newspaper accounts, the 1995 conflicts, in Hyde Park, left a pub in smoking ruins and on successive nights, attracted between fifty and a hundred youths to the area, where they attacked police with stones (Wilkinson). Those who set the pub alight were reacting to police raids on The Jolly Brewer and claimed that it was "the center of a police surveillance operation" for drug dealing and robbery, which the reporter confirmed. Although there were no arrests and only one person slightly injured, these are the "riots" that Zoe, for example, referred to in trying to name her aversion to Hyde Park.

The 1997 riot was more complicated. Centered in Harehills, where the minarets of a new mosque are visible on the skyline, an Indian shop owner made a "'tactless' decision to stock a video about the Indo-Pakistan conflict which features a Koran being flung to the ground" (Wainwright). A crowd of three hundred Muslim youths gathered, throwing stones and threatening arson. The police response, a "high-profile response" (i.e., with riot police) was blamed for making the situation worse, and officials called it the worst violence among British Muslims since *The Satanic Verses* was publicly burned in Bradford. None of the students I interviewed lived in Harehills, but one group did explore part of it for their streetwork projects.

Liam also assumes that there have been riots in Chapletown, though he's quick to point out that he hasn't actually been there himself. From his knowledge of Manchester, Liam draws parallels between the worst by reputation areas of Manchester (Northside and Hume) with Leeds's Chapletown and assumes that the area is defined by drugs and prostitution. But the main marker for no-go areas for Liam, is that of housing: "See, I'd actually go around Burley rather than walking through the center, you know there's quite a lot of terraced housing near the bottom of the hill from the university; . . . there's a lot of housing around there that I wouldn't walk through at all."

In describing where she lives and how she gets around Leeds, Zoe mentions an area that, while surrounded by places she considers safe, is nevertheless an island of no-go. Near her home in Meanwood, this area represents a complicated set of boundaries.

> Z: This is Meanwood Road, and I live just off the ridge just up here, but as you walk into the center of town like here, it's not nice—actually I shouldn't have put that bit as desirable 'cause that's Little London there, in here [see Figure 5].
>
> I: Is Little London good or not?
>
> Z: No, it's horrible. [laughs]
>
> I: Why?
>
> Z: Little London is . . . , well it's in Woodhouse I suppose . . . Little London is like here.
>
> I: Okay.
>
> Z: I live just before Little London; it's not nice at all.
>
> I: So what characterizes Little London, I mean how do you *know* that that's Little London?
>
> Z: Because all the houses are the same—it's all council houses; there's a lot of tower blocks as well; I mean there's about five tower blocks;

Figure 5. A part of Little London. Photo by Randy Blackburn.

they're all—all the roads are called after London stations, and there's a Little London community center, but basically all the houses look the same, and then it suddenly changes when you get out of that. But it's not nice at all because I suppose a very poor area and what people have said about it as well; I think there's quite a lot of crime that goes on round there.

I: Okay, so, in getting from your house to the city center, do you avoid Little London?

Z: Oh, yeah, definitely. Where I live it would be quicker for me to just walk down the main road to get on to the interchange here, and then there's this sort of pedestrian park that goes through the tower blocks of Little London towards the city center, but there's no way I'd walk there because, I just wouldn't want to.

Desire and Place

Despite students' claims not to know much about Leeds, they could be quite precise, like Zoe is above, about the places they feel comfortable in and those they are determined to avoid, even if it means going the long way round. Students were also quite clear about the desirable areas of the city, characterized by the amount of green space, the type of housing, feelings of familiarity, and a sense of community. Open space, green space, and unoccupied land hold a very high value in England, of course, and students' comments certainly reflected this ideology as well as their middle-class upbringings and general inexperience in strange cities. With a couple of exceptions, none of the students was living in a place they identified as desirable, and while their definitions of desirable varied depending on students' background or future plans, students unfailingly pointed out the same areas as being "very nice, very posh."

Elaine identifies a specific area of Leeds, Adel, "'cause it's rich with big houses; that's the majority of the north really," and when asked to identify what she meant by desirable, Elaine answered, "Mine's materialistic I suppose, big house, nice car, everything that you can visually see in the neighborhood . . . big houses, nice cars and a kind of suburban life, middle England [laughs]." Anna names Beckett Park as an area where she feels "quite happy walking around; it's quite green and tidy and everyone's got their green wheelie-bins out, and people wash their cars on Saturday mornings [laughs]."

The type of housing is one of the most obvious indicators of desirability. Students most often mentioned detached or large semidetached houses with walls and cul-de-sacs. And as Mitchell explains it, houses need gardens to be desirable:

> *I think the houses in this area are still back-to-back houses, but they've made real front gardens and are set back off the road, so they appear to be more desirable . . . whereas if you're living in the back-to-backs in Hyde Park or Burley, your front door is right on the pavement.*

Without a driveway as well, according to Mitchell, your car (your stuff) belongs to "the actual street."

These definitions of desirable hinge on green space, so Woodhouse, where Mitchell is living now, doesn't qualify: "I think the area of Meanwood and Weetwood's quite desirable. . . . [There are] sports pitches up there, the university sports pitches so when you're traveling by bus to that area you can see the big houses and posh cars and lots of grounds." But perhaps the biggest "hinge" is that of ethnic identification. In talking about an area near where he does his weekly shopping, Mitchell says: "If you go a bit past [the Sainsbury's in Moor Allerton], you can see slightly posh houses, and that's the Jewish cluster so I suppose that's an ethnic area as well." This part of the transcript with Mitchell is worth quoting at some length.

I: How do you know that [that it's a Jewish cluster]?

M: 'Cause I'm Jewish so.

I: Okay.

M: I've been there; it's quite well publicized that that's a Jewish area of Leeds and northwest Leeds, . . . and obviously they perceive Jewish people as having a bit more, a bit more wealth.

I: Have you learned in your social geography classes that people tend to congregate, in particular areas?

M: Yeah, we learned about clusters, positive and negative segregation. We learned about people clustering because they felt they have to live together because of discrimination they'd get if they lived in separate areas. Also people want to live together because, if they have to go to mosque five times a day . . . then they can walk to the mosque and they can walk together. That's the problems and the sort of themes you get in a social geography class.

I: I'm just now noticing that there are synagogues marked on the map.

M: Yeah, I think there are two synagogues in the vicinity of the Ring Road, and there's also a lot of golf courses around here, so you can just look on a map and see that that's quite a posh area.

Liam wants to mark the whole of "outside Leeds" as desirable because of the "masses" of green space. Outside of the Ring Road is "the beginning of the great green expanses," he says. Anna also notes that the area around Bodington Hall is desirable because "there's lots of country side, the playing fields were wide open green spaces, and to get into university . . . [11] it was a simple direct route, there and back, very safe, very familiar." Anna particularly liked living there because you could "choose the city, but it wasn't in your face," and she mentions the comforting presence of a police station nearby. For Anna, "the further out you get the better it gets. . . . Out towards Adel behind Bodington Hall all of these houses—they're all old-fashioned, high-walled houses but not threateningly so, very sort of private residences that you feel quite safe walking around."

Along with the desirable suburbs, however, several students noted how happy they would be living downtown, in the new posh flats being constructed along the canal and near the heart of the city center. Sheila talks about this area "where Granary Wharf is [and all of the] gentrification":

> *That's definitely desirable 'cause they're high priced sort of homes and desirable for going out at night to posh restaurants around there, and there's nice walks down there. [This area is] desirable for a yuppie kind of life, young people I suppose, not families.*

When asked "Twenty-somethings?" she answers, "Yeah! People like me when they graduate hopefully." Mitchell, who already has a job in the city center for the following year, also mentions this part of town as desirable:

> *I've thought about living in the city center 'cause they've got quite modern flats. And because I'm still quite young, I'd like to be near the hustle and bustle of town and that's where I'll be working; I think there's quite a lot of young people are living in like modern flats in town because they like to be close to work and they like to be close to going out [at night] as well.*

Finally, desirable places to live are those that have a sense of community, which Liam defines as the presence of "a social center, the local pub, and the chip shop." It's also important to community that those who run the shop be "very friendly people and tend to know everyone in the area." Liam also notes all the kids that run around, enhancing further a positive neighborhood feeling. Liam also notes that there is a green area to this community, but unfortunately, it's "where the joyriders come and dump their cars."

For Zoe, desirable is what she is accustomed to or familiar terrain: "To be honest though, everything up to here from Woodhouse is desirable because I live there." Anna says something similar: "Because it's familiar, then it's desirable in my mind, anyway. Don't know if that's necessarily right, but if I know [a place], then I feel more comfortable. All the pubs and stuff that are along there are similar to pubs that I have back home." Zoe admits that if she were more established with a "permanent job and I could afford to live where I wanted to, I wouldn't live in Woodhouse because it's a student area . . . a happening place but I wouldn't want to live [laughs] in a street full of students if I'm about forty." She names Alwoodley as a "really posh" place, but she wouldn't want to live there now because there wouldn't be other students surrounding her. Elaine is also quick to point out that she suspects her notions of desirable places will change as she gets older. For now, however, desirable means a vibrant area (Zoe's term) or a hustley-bustley place: Anna likes Kirkstall because of the cinema, "which is always a bit hustley-bustley anyway so you feel quite, you know, happy there as well."

As with the no-go category, places designated as desirable tend to have messy boundaries and a slippery status. For example, Mitchell tries to find desirability somewhere in the betweens: "A nice area to live would be just near the university but away from student houses. I suppose if you see an area as being half desirable but very convenient, in a good location, then it becomes even more desirable." Anna, too, sees the city center as neither/nor: "All around the city center, I wouldn't say it was no-go, but I wouldn't say it was desirable. It is no-go if you're in a certain situation, like it's late at night or you're by yourself." Liam's comments about the city center also illustrate how a place can have more than one status or designation, or that perceptions of it can vary according to time of day or past experiences. While Liam and most of the others definitely mark the city center (downtown) as quite a desirable area they feel comfortable in, Liam also identifies the rail station as "a bit unsavory":

L: Round the station actually—behind the station, yeah I'm going to mark the station, just sort of behind it, 'cause I know it's quite a no-go area—

I: Okay, and do you think that because you've been there?

L: That's being there at night and seeing the people that hang around there at night. There's a lot of . . . undesirable people walking around there when I've been there at night coming back from a club or whatever, and it's just a bit unsavory . . . and again that's specifically around the station area.

These students' desires, in general, influenced their judgments about what areas around Leeds were desirable: how did they see themselves as university graduates, as older members of middle England? There were definitely areas of Leeds where these students felt threatened or uncomfortable, but they also felt extremely empowered in the familiar areas of "student land" as well as in the green, large-garden neighborhoods of their imagined futures.

These mental maps of Leeds illustrate that movement through the spatial world hinges upon contested places, geographies of exclusion, and (sometimes invisible) markers of boundaries. The images we carry around in our heads, even those that come from the reports of others, affect our willingness to explore or our choices of residential areas. Even if people move through certain areas or neighborhoods without fear of physical harm, they may feel uncomfortable or they may have minor confrontations about "who belongs there."

Investigating the "imageability" (Lynch) of cities or areas contributes much to our understanding of the social production of space and people's experiences in space, and these are the forms of mapping that I want to claim as spatial practices of the everyday that can help us to re-imagine acts of writing as material and visual. In *Writing Women and Space,* Alison Blunt and Gillian Rose claim that mapping "is a distinctive form of spatial representation because it can be interpreted as visual and/or textual. . . . the spatial imagery of mapping can expose tensions between the dynamics of the visual and the written" (10). I would add, however, that mental mapping, where the real and the imagined or the physical and the emotional come together, adds yet another layer to mapping and its representations.

Mapping, then, in all of its overlapping forms, contributes to geographic rhetorics by insisting upon the realandimagined production of space and more complex ways of representing places and spaces. Along with walking—forms of *flanerie*—and dwelling—the subject of the final chapter—mapping forms part of the techne for geographic rhetorics, those that focus on moving through the world, encountering the rub of differences, the fissures and gaps in discourse, the borders and fault lines. Maps work metaphorically, but they also do rhetorical work: they provide information that influences action; they persuade users to try a new route or stick with the old one; and they communicate an image of a place that may or may not hold up. Maps, like all texts, function in the betweens of metaphor and materiality: cartography is a useful and profitable "skill" done with tools, but mental mapping is a swirl of memory and experience related to race, class, gender, sexuality, age, or abilities. A geographical rhetoric, then, would not ignore longitude or latitude but would try to capture the layers of meaning and the *feelings* of residents or visitors or trespassers.[12] Contested places like Hyde Park in Leeds are not easily "mapped," but as rhetoricians and educators, it is our responsibility to understand not only where our students come from but also what forms of fear or reluctance keep students locked in place.

Students' highly charged responses to certain places in Leeds and their reluctance to explore neighborhoods beyond "student land" highlights how difficult it is to move learners to have a meaningful encounter with difference. The next chapter turns to the cultural geography method of "streetwork" to show how walking and mapping can help us to understand the complex ways in which space hides consequences from us and the ways in which one's "sense of place" is constructed. Like forms of mental mapping, streetwork exposes the workings of geographies of exclusion: how the landscape, the built environment, the inhabitants, or the force of their own preconceptions and expectations can make people feel excluded or alienated from certain places. This bodes ill, I argue, for composition's growing enthusiasm for service learning and literacy projects if such project designs do not include an awareness of the sociospatial construction of difference.

Endnotes

1. This episode was broadcast 28 February 2001 on NBC, titled "Big Block of Cheese Day."

2. As Susan Miller wrote to me in an e-mail, at the very beginning of this project, "you have to know which way is *up* to read a map." And she's right: as attractive as mapping is for all kinds of projects, reading or following maps requires a specialized form of literacy.

3. Readers of postmodern theory will recognize the term *cognitive mapping* as Fredric Jameson's. In an essay of the same name, he borrows Kevin Lynch's model from *The Image of the City* and tries to synthesize it with Althusser's formulation of ideology, which

   > *has the great merit of stressing the gap between the local positioning of the individual subject and the totality of class structures in which he or she is situated . . . this ideology, as such, attempts to span or coordinate, to map, by means of conscious and unconscious representations. (353)*

   In attempting to extrapolate Lynch's spatial analysis to class relations and social structure, Jameson also claims that "the incapacity to map socially is as crippling to political experience as the analogous incapacity to map spatially is for urban experience" (353).

4. Leeds is a growing city of over 700,000 residents, and Leeds-Bradford makes up the largest metropolitan area of West Yorkshire. The University of Leeds, just half a mile from the thriving city center, has a student enrollment of 21,000. Because of a serious shortage of on-campus housing, most of these students live off-campus, in the areas of Headingley (where I also lived), Hyde Park, Woodhouse, and Meanwood.

5. For research and context regarding mental maps, I relied upon Gould and White and Wiegand and Stiell. To ensure that my interviews were methodologically sound, I reviewed the work of qualitative researchers in my own field (Gesa Kirsch, Ruth Ray, Jennie Nelson) and took the opportunity to learn from some new ones (Robert Burgess, Sara Delamont, Gill Valentine). I can't really say, however, that I have side-stepped the criticisms Soja levels at mental mapping, but since he doesn't really define thirdspace epistemologies (choosing to "leave the discussion . . . radically open" [*Thirdspace* 82]), researchers have to depend on secondspace methods for understanding how people interact with the sociospatial world.

6. I have edited these passages considerably, with readers in mind, to sharpen the speaker's point or to eliminate what I considered to be distracting wordiness. Single periods mean a full stop. Ellipses mean I have eliminated words, but if ellipses appear in brackets [. . .] that means I have cut out whole lines. I added marks of punctuation, in particular, and eliminated most of the "ums" or other fillers because my purpose here is not discourse analysis as a sociolinguist might perform. Instead, my purpose is to illustrate, through students' own words, contested relationships to place and space.

7. Students recognized, however, that the term *no-go* is quite specific in social geography as places where the police refuse to go (a term that evolved from Northern Ireland—see Keith).

8. Although I'm a bit uncomfortable using the blanket term "Asians," it is the term that students used. More specifically, however, this area is populated by Pakistanis, and Hyde Park does have one of the largest concentrations of ethnic minorities in Leeds—much smaller, however, than areas of Bradford. Widely recognized to have the largest ethnic minority population in the north, and just a few miles from Leeds, Bradford has a 15.60 percent population from minority groups, according to the 1991 census.

9. It's well known among students that Headingley is just a bit more posh than Hyde Park. Zoe notes: "I wouldn't be able to afford to live in Headingley though, because it's sort of popular to live there—the housing is just too expensive. The cheapest you can get is probably about £45 a week which is too much for me."

10. Anna also identifies Chestnut Avenue as particularly Asian, a street that also holds the title, according to Anna, of being the most burgled street in England.

11. Bodington Hall is a large expanse of "green" land, sports pitches and the like, and a huge residential hall—the home of many first-year students. Located four miles from the campus, built in this location because there was simply no room nearer to the city and university, students rely on the bus to get back and forth between the campus and Bodington Hall.

12. I can imagine some readers wondering why I didn't work also with Asians in the neighborhoods of Headingley or Hyde Park. A seven-month stay, in university housing and possible only through university connections, made me feel uncomfortable about asking Asian residents to participate in this study when I'm not sure I could have argued or articulated what's in it for them. If I could have stayed longer, maybe, but I would have had to think very carefully about how to get access as well as make the interaction somehow reciprocal.

41

The 1963 Hip-Hop Machine: Hip-Hop Pedagogy as Composition

JEFF RICE

Jeff Rice directs the Campus Writing Program at University of Missouri-Columbia and wrote The Rhetoric of Cool. *In his article "The 1963 Hip-Hop Machine: Hip-Hop Pedagogy as Composition" originally published in* College Composition and Communication, *Rice claims that hip-hop music provides a set of strategies for inventing arguments. This article presents a vision and practice of academic inquiry and writing that incorporates meaning-making activities from popular culture.*

This essay proposes an alternative invention strategy for research-based argumentative writing. By investigating the coincidental usage of the term "whatever" in hip-hop, theory, and composition studies, the essay proposes a whatever-pedagogy identified as "hip-hop pedagogy," a writing practice that models itself after digital sampling's rhetorical strategy of juxtaposition.

I begin with an analogy: teaching research-based argumentation and critique in composition studies is like learning how to perform hip-hop music. My analogy's focus on argumentation does not exclude traditional methods of argumentative pedagogy based on models like Stephen Toulmin's complex hierarchies or the Aristotelian triad of deliberative (offering advice), forensic (taking a side in a debate, often a legal or controversial matter), and epideictic (a speech of praise or blame appealing to an already won-over audience) discourse. Instead, I pose the analogy as a first step towards developing alternative or additional ways to engage composition students with the argumentative essay. In choosing hip-hop as a model for the composition essay, I attempt to draw upon a dominant form of contemporary culture familiar to the majority of students I encounter in my classrooms. Does a relationship between hip-hop and composition pedagogy exist as my analogy proposes? Can there be such a thing as "hip-hop pedagogy" for the composition classroom?

My question begins with Houston Baker's work. In "Hybridity, the Rap Race, and Pedagogy for the 1990s," Baker proposes an English studies-based pedagogy centered around hip-hop. Describing his teaching experience at the college level, Baker finds hip-hop helpful in teaching the canon of literary studies to disinterested students. Baker shares an anecdote about teaching one such course, which involved showing students "how Henry V was a rapper—a cold dissing, def con man, tougher than leather and smoother than ice, an artisan of words" (227). The principle behind Baker's pedagogy is to provide students with familiar situations and language that allow for complex textual readings, situations that allow students to identify with the figures of American and European literature.

Baker's lesson compels me to explore my initial interest in hip-hop as a composition pedagogy. What I want to add to Baker's pedagogy, however, is an examination of the way hip-hop constructs discourse, the way it produces rhetorical meaning through its complex method of digital sampling, and how such a rhetoric functions within the scope of argumentation. Baker defines sampling as

> taking a portion (phrase, riff, percussive vamp, etc.) of a known or unknown record (or a video game squawk, a touch-tone telephone medley, a verbal tag from Malcolm X or Martin Luther King) and combining it in the overall mix (The "sample" was called a "cut" in the earliest days). (221)

Sampling is the hip-hop process of saving snippets of prerecorded music and sound into a computer memory. These sounds become cut from their original source and pasted into a new composition. In hip-hop, the "take *whatever* you find and use it" principle acts as the dominant force in sampling. Whatever is available to composers (samplers) often includes TV shows, political speeches, past musical recordings of a variety of genres, or any sound at all. Through the complex juxtaposition of these isolated sounds, samplers construct new forms of meaning. Some of the most complex and intriguing examples of the "whatever process" in digital sampling can be found in Public Enemy's *It Takes a Nation of Millions to Hold Us Back,* Digable Planets' *Reachin' (A New Refutation of Time and Space),* Grandmaster Flash's "The Adventures of Grandmaster Flash on the Wheels of Steel," and the Beastie Boys' *Paul's Boutique.* "High Plains Drifter" from *Paul's*

Boutique, for instance, juxtaposes the unlikely samples of The Eagle's "Those Shoes," The Fatback Band's "Put Your Love in My Tender Care," and The Ramones's "Suzie Is a Headbanger" with scattered cultural references to Hunter S. Thompson's *Fear and Loathing in Las Vegas,* Steve McQueen, *The Andy Griffith Show,* and off-track betting. What emerges from this mix is a writing both provocative and compelling. A song like "High Plains Drifter" reveals that ideas take shape out of the restless culture surrounding writings; in other words, discourse emerges from the cultural odds and ends we assemble. Hip-hop teaches that cultural research and awareness produce composite forms of writing.

The "whatever" principle of sampling extends into general discourse. *Whatever* is best understood as a popular, everyday term used heavily by youth culture when an experience or reaction can't be named. The response, "whatever," evokes not so much a lack of response but either a sense that something has eluded the meaning of the response or of defiance, dismissal, and opposition. The term carries over into hip-hop culture in methodology (sampling) and attitude, where *whatever* informs lyrical composition. As in rap star Redman's "Whateva Man," *whatever* means something indefinable, obscure, out of reach:

> *You ready to get down?*
> *Whateva man.*

"Whatever" as motivating principle within the sampling composition process overlaps Roland Barthes's efforts to understand alternative meanings in photographs. In *Camera Lucida,* Barthes settles on a dichotomy of image meanings—the informational content of the image and the elusive meaning, the detail that draws a viewer into the image on a personal level. Labeling these reading practices *studium* and *punctum* respectively, Barthes constructs an alternative reading practice in which an isolated detail of the image drives its reading. One image Barthes directs attention to is a 1963 Richard Avedon photograph, *William Casby, Born a Slave.* For Barthes, this image shocks; it strikes him with a sense of defiance. Barthes writes, "the essence of slavery is here laid bare: the mask is the meaning, insofar as it is absolutely pure" (34). Barthes's choice of Avedon's photograph stems from an unnamed detail within the image that provokes his interest. Working with this image, Barthes claims that the logic of photography as we currently know it, the referent of the image relating back to a real-life thing, no longer aids critical analysis. In electronic culture, something else remains after we have deducted and named an image's referent, something beyond initial meaning, something elusive. This something is the punctum. By shifting attention to the punctum, Barthes constructs an alternative critique of photography and its relationship to personal experience. Barthes's rationale involves finding the punctum, an isolation of "that accident which pricks me" (27) and which is "the anything *whatever,* the sophisticated acme of value" (34, emphasis added). In its English translation, Barthes' punctum transforms into whatever.

For Barthes, the whatever offers more than just indefinable reaction. Barthes's punctum (or whatever) initiates an attempt to develop an alternative critical practice. The whatever challenges conventional reading practices by cutting a detail from its original source and recontextualizing it within a different setting. Barthes's purpose is to use the detail as a way to critique cultural practices. The detail he extracts from *William Casby, Born a Slave* leads to a general critique of photography. "[The detail] would tell me what constituted that thread which drew me toward Photography" (73). The juxtaposition of Barthes's isolation of the detail with hip-hop's isolation of disparate sounds returns me to my earlier proposition for writing pedagogy. In contemporary digital culture, elusive meanings abound as the emerging, electronic tools of expression rapidly alter discourse in general. Print culture's linear, nonassociative methods of reasoning break down in an electronic realm where cutting and pasting guide communication. Gregory Ulmer makes a similar point in his definition of an emerging post-criticism, a collagist writing practice that models itself after poststructuralist writings and the avant-garde.

> *In criticism, as in literature, collage takes the form of citation, but citation carried to an extreme (in post-criticism), collage being the "limit-case" of citation, and grammatology being the theory of writing as citation. (Ulmer 89)*

For critique, Ulmer proposes a sampling practice of cut-and-paste citation. Ulmer samples Jacques Derrida, Michel Serres, and John Cage to construct his theory of critique as collage. In composition, Geoffrey Sirc extends such thinking as he considers the relationship between popular music (the punks) and composition studies in the mid-1970s. Sirc's project revolves around the idea of the temporal moment as heuristic. "Contemporary scholars of composition studies," Sirc writes, "might have a difficult time believing that CCC 1977–1979 happened at the same time as the Sex Pistols" ("Never Mind" 13). Sirc demonstrates the meaning of this overlap through a temporal juxtaposition of the Sex Pistols with composition studies; he utilizes punk music to reread composition's history and contemporary status.

> *I'd like now to replay sounds from that silenced era; reread the almost erased palimpsest of Punk, on which our field's official history has been overwritten; poke around in a cultural parallelism—popular music and composition theory. ("Never Mind" 10)*

Following Sirc's work with punk music and Ulmer's definition of critique as sample, I introduce the model of digital sampling and hip-hop in order to rethink the argumentative essay. This model asks: how does one account for the ways isolated details prompt analytical gestures? Can one construct critique from a series of unrelated details? Can there be such a thing as a "whatever writing practice?"

The "Whatever Classroom"

In the university classroom, the phrase "whatever" often marks an indifferent or oppositional student reaction to course demand. Patricia Harkin notes that when a student is confronted with a contradiction, "she is less likely to contemplate the cognitive dissonance as a spur to invention and more likely simply to say 'whatever'" (Harkin 496). For Harkin, *whatever* creates "a problem for invention" within the student-research paper (Harkin 497). The typical student reply to instructor demand for analytical expansion, "whatever," challenges instructors to push students for more detailed responses. The university classroom often expects such responses to come in the form of the college essay, a paper-based interface inherited from the Ciceronian breakdown of invention (exposition, narrative, evidence, refutation of opposing opinions, and conclusion). Harkin rejects the whatever response as antithetical to any heuristic basis for student work. Instead of motivating students, Harkin argues, to take a word from their everyday language (whatever) and convert it into an invention strategy, a way to write, instructors should confront the whatever in order to overcome its classroom presence. Missing, then, from Harkin's reading of student responses is how the whatever can become a guide for contemporary student research. In his exploration of a nonbinary discourse (the third sophistic), Victor Vitanza challenges Harkin to consider *whatever* as heuristic.

> *Harkin has her greatest insight in her blindness: reinventing by way of "whatever." Yes! Whatever beings intuit that the principles of identify, non-contradiction, and excluded-middle (all the principles of negation informing reinvention) are the very principles that exclude, that disallow the thing with all its properties, that disallow radical singularities, themselves as such, in community. ("Seeing in Third" 173)*

Vitanza directs Harkin to his essay "From Heuristic to Aleatory Procedures; or, Toward 'Writing the Accident,'" which outlines a whatever-based invention strategy for rhetoric. This strategy allows chance and randomness a prominent role in discursive constructions. My interest is in expanding Vitanza's critique by generating such a practice for the writing classroom and by using sampling as the model for such a practice. The coincidental overlap of Barthes's and hip-hop's usage of the whatever leads me to look to both for instructions on how to create this unnamed way of writing. For Barthes, the whatever (or punctum) is the isolated detail recontextualized. In digital sampling, the whatever offers an alternative research methodology for composition—the accumulation and appropriation of citations recontextualized into a new work. While not all applications of sampling are the same, overall, sampling allows me to expand Baker's interest in hip-hop by offering it as a model for a whatever-centered pedagogy. Such a pedagogy, I propose, might redefine student relationships to the various genres and demands of academic writing: the argumentative essay, the research paper, and the critical analysis paper. In order to explain what such a pedagogy entails, I want to demonstrate a whatever method of writing that students can use for engaging in these areas. Because both hip-hop and Barthes isolate moments from their original context, to create my demonstration of this method, I will use their work as a justification for proceeding. I, likewise, will isolate several moments, and I will do so by specifically drawing upon the date 1963.

The rationale for choosing 1963 as an organizing principle stems from Barthes's temporal choice of the Avedon photograph. In addition, the year 1963 maintains importance to writing and cultural study for a number of reasons. Eric Havelock's observation that 1963 produced an increased awareness in grammatology (the science and history of writing)[1] found the year to be a turning point in the study of how writing shapes culture. In composition studies, the 1963 Los Angeles meeting of the field's most important yearly event, the Conference of College Composition and

Communication (CCCC), led to what several composition theorists have labeled the beginning of contemporary writing instruction.[2] Cultural studies can also be traced to the time period surrounding 1963: the 1964 founding of the Center for Contemporary Cultural Studies at Birmingham, England (the origin of contemporary cultural studies), as well as Raymond Williams's 1962 *Communications,* in which he argued that the analysis of mass media include "the institutions and forms in which ideas, information, and attitudes are transmitted and received" (17). Hip-hop belongs to one such popular cultural institution of mass media, popular music. Following Williams's advice, I ask if this particular institution can serve the interests of writing and, more specifically, cultural study.

I also focus on 1963 by way of Cecil Williams and Allan Stevenson's 1963 composition handbook, *A Research Manual.* The authors suggest that, when doing research, students examining a text for the first time "sample some passages to see what experience, penetration, and logic the writer seems to be endowed with. Sampling will also help you determine whether a work is more on the periphery of a particular study than at the center" (Williams and Stevenson 30). The isolation of Williams and Stevenson's text, juxtaposed with these other 1963 temporal moments, instructs me to sample in order to do research. Therefore, my explanation of hip-hop pedagogy emerges from a series of sampled 1963 moments.[3] My purpose, then, is to demonstrate how composition students can research and form arguments through sampling.

Borrowing from the language of hip-hop, throughout the rest of this essay these samples are interspersed with cuts and breaks, mixes, and playbacks. The fragmented sections I work from follow a whatever logic; read in isolation, their meanings are elusive, possibly evoking the student-inspired response, "whatever." Moreover, they come from *whatever* I have discovered occurring in 1963. When viewed together, they offer the model for hip-hop pedagogy; in other words, I perform hip-hop pedagogy as a way of explaining how it functions. As I cut and paste these moments together, I hope to begin the process of hip-hop pedagogy as argumentation and cultural critique.[4]

Hip-Hop Pedagogy

The cut: Gordon Parks

Gordon Parks's 1963 photograph of Malcolm X, entitled *Malcolm X, Harlem,* exhibits the civil rights leader holding up a newspaper whose bold headline reads: "Seven Unarmed Negroes Shot in Cold Blood by Los Angeles Police." The photograph draws attention to two important issues for the post-World War II era: civil rights and information technology. In Parks's photograph, the two items juxtapose, revealing the subtle ways both inform one another. Parks's photo is a reminder of Gwendolyn Brooks's 1963 poem "Negro Hero": "But let us speak only of my success and the pictures in the Caucasian dailies" (Brooks 19). In 1963, print media, for the most part, belongs to a mostly white, dominant discourse, Directed by white boards of directors, major newspapers, for the most part, tended to treat civil rights issues from the perspective of white, not black, America. Unequal levels of production ownership tainted any reporting regarding key civil rights issues. Familiar today in the long-standing debate of the digital divide, access to information production and distribution proved elusive to an African American populace attempting to voice its opinions and frustrations. Writing in 1963, African American journalist Simeon Booker questioned overall African American access to the communication industry.

> *For too long, Negroes have known and grown to accept news managing of their affairs, attitudes and selection of leaders by most of the communications industry. And for too long, the industry has not recognized Negroes as even a part of the community, locally or nationally, except as an undersirable part. (143)*

Booker's complaint rewrites the Parks image. The degree of being "unarmed" as the headline indicates means more than gun power. The weapon power implicit here resides in information production. To be "shot" in cold blood means to be struck with both a weapon and to be captured within the boundaries of photography; one "shoots" an image. In this case, an African American photographer (Parks) attempts to capture the complexity of Malcolm X's action. In 1963 newspaper photographys, the photograph seems to ask, who shoots whom? Who controls the power of the image and its display? Does Malcolm X remain in power by holding the image? Is this a black-owned or white-owned paper? What is the relationship between information technology and how such technology is controlled?

Paste: Leonard Freed

In Leonard Freed's 1963 photograph *New York City*, an African American man also holds up a newspaper; the headline reads, "We Must Have Justice." Behind him, New York's commercial district comes alive with billboards advertising soda fountains and hot dogs. Around him, people make their way in and out of shops. The demand for justice ties racism to economics. The insertion of one African American man in a crowd of white shoppers is an effort to foreground these connections. The task, though, defies simplicity. Like Charles Mingus's "Freedom," a track not included on his 1963 record *Mingus, Mingus, Mingus* but later added to subsequent printings, African American representations in the arts sustain a continued discourse of social justice that often yields to frustration.

> *Freedom for your daddy*
> *Freedom for your mamma*
> *Freedom for your brothers and sisters*
> *But no freedom for me. (Mingus)*

Mingus's recording, like Parks's photograph, exhibits a disenchantment with the NAACP's slogan "Free by '63," whose purpose was to mark "the Centennial celebration of the signing of the Emancipation Proclamation" (Booker 29). Pasted together, both moments offer a joint critique of an early '60s civil rights rhetoric that centralizes the elusive meanings of freedom in American democracy. Who is free? Who receives justice? These works ask. Lacking a name for a culture whose attention fixates more on commercial consumption than on social justice, moments like Freed's photo and Mingus's music suggest an elusive "whatever" as response.

Cut: Romare Bearden

African American artist Romare Bearden's 1963 Prevalence of Ritual Series approaches such elusiveness through collage and nostalgia. In the works comprising the series, Bearden, the one-time realist painter, "had come back to the subject matter he started out with—Black American life as he remembered it in the South of his childhood in North Carolina, and in the North of his coming of age in Pittsburgh and Harlem and later in life the Caribbean island of St. Martin" (Conwill 8). For Bearden, the rituals of religion and popular culture provided iconic markers of African American practices, practices that could be nostalgically represented within collage. Notably, Bearden's nostalgia for 1920s and 1930s black culture drew inspiration from the Civil Rights movement of 1963, particularly Martin Luther King. Jr.'s March on Washington and "I Have a Dream" speech. Works like *Cotton, The Dove,* and *Jazz* are cut and pasted displays of an African American presence no longer in existence; the nostalgia for the past (and all of its racial struggles) contrasts with the fight against contemporary, institutionalized racism and the exertion to join the developing information-driven economy.

Bearden's collages of the Old South, the Cotton Club, and inner city poverty of the 1920s and 30s appear out of place in contrast to the works' temporal civil rights movement. And yet, this sense of nostalgia marks a moment of temporal cultural critique defined by nostalgia. Bearden's lesson for a hip-hop pedagogy involves utilizing the past in new ways. *The Dove* (1964), for instance, pastes an assortment of cut-up African American faces and bodies over a Harlem stoop. They seem to be nowhere, yet everywhere at once. The markers of African American presence are felt in the images of cigarettes dangling out of empty spaces, masked faces, and solitary hands leaning idly out of windows. While *The Dove* treats African American inner-city life nostalgically (the communal feeling of living in a close area), it also offers the beginnings of a critical gesture intent on questioning the elusive meaning (Where do these people go? What do they do? Why are they idle? What has caused this?). Bearden's collage argues that an impoverished black underclass can search for meaning in carefully composed, visual juxtapositions when no other resolution seems apparent.

Paste: Mo Greens Please

The usage of juxtaposition for critical purposes also appears via the 1963 cover art of Blue Note Records. Blue Note, one of the most prolific producers of jazz in the post-war period, produced a number of record covers in 1963, distinct in their style: Freddie Roach's *Mo Greens Please,* Donald Byrd's *A New Perspective,* Jackie McLean's *One Step Beyond,* Hank Mobley's *No Room for Squares,* Blue Mitchell's *Step Lightly,* and Horace Silver's *Silver's Serenade.* Marked by geometric shapes and patterns, tilted angles, and sharp recolorations and shadings, these record covers, all designed by Reid Miles, revealed a new aesthetic for jazz and marketing, what Felix Cromey calls "an abstract design hinting at innovations, cool strides for cool notes, the symbolic implications of typeface and tones" (Marsh, Cromey, Callingham 7).

In particular, cover art like that of Roach's *Mo Greens Please* used information technology (the record) to emphasize African American pride, even if in somewhat stereotypical ways. *Mo Greens Please* features an African American man purchasing soul food at either a roadside cart or take-out window of a small restaurant. Soul food serves as a prominent iconic display of African American eating habits. Covers like Roach's stressed black pride and power (choices in what African Americans eat as opposed to what white-dominated advertising tells its audience to eat), topics that would eventually govern the themes of hip-hop albums recorded in the '80s and '90s by such groups as Public Enemy, A Tribe Called Quest, Digable Planets, and The Roots.

The design innovations Reid brought to Blue Note's record covers also situate the innovative move within African American musical production to sample themes related to both the immediate African American experience as well as generalized issues of self-reliance, civil rights, and equality. Blue Note's designs and sound fused with the emerging 1960s soul music produced in Detroit and Memphis, fashioning a new level of self-expression as critique. In jazz, this merger led to the formation of "soul jazz" or hard-bop, a movement critic Amiri Baraka felt relevant to the formation of a new African American identity in which political and social detachment (what Baraka called "cool") give way to a new system of value (soul). In his 1963 definition of the move from cool to soul, Baraka claims

> *The step from cool to soul is a form of social aggression. It is an attempt to place upon a meaningless social order, an order which would give value to terms of existence that were once considered not only valueless but shameful. Cool meant nonparticipation; soul means a "new" establishment. It is an attempt to reverse the social roles within the society by redefining the canons of value. (Blues People 219)*

The inclusion of soul into the composition process redirects canonical understandings of not only reading (or listening) practices but writing itself. A new sound demands a new writing form. The most sampled of all soul artists is James Brown, who as Mark Anthony Neal comments, introduced rhythms to "a younger, politically motivated, culturally assured audience raised on the music and production techniques of the Motown and Stax recording companies" (33). This political audience, Baraka's new establishment, forms the basis of contemporary hip-hop culture.

Paste: James Brown

In 1963, James Brown released *Live at the Apollo Vol. I*. Recorded the previous year at the famous Apollo theater in Harlem, Brown's album became the first soul record to significantly chart on the white-dominated Billboard sales charts. Brown's entrance into the segregated music divisions of popular music (rhythm and blues for African Americans, pop music for whites) marked the new establishment Baraka describes, the entrance of black music into the homes of white America. Live at the Apollo also created an iconic identification of African American cultural production through the crossover celebrity, one that would quickly identify black musical production with social concerns and values. Baraka writes:

> *James Brown's form and content identify an entire group of people in America. However these may be transmuted and reused, reappear in other areas, in other musics for different purposes in the society, the initial energy and image are about a specific grouping of people, Black People. (Black Music 185)*

With Brown, cultural transformation manifests by way of song writing. The early love songs on *Live at The Apollo* eventually become manifestos for black empowerment when juxtaposed with Brown's late-'60s work. *Live at The Apollo's* "Please, Please, Please" and "Try Me" read in the light of '60s Black Power become entreaties for equal rights and self-awareness. They become the building blocks of later hits like "Say It Loud—I'm Black and I'm Proud Pt. 1," "Soul Power," and "I Don't Want Nobody to Give Me Nothing (Open Up the Door I'll Get It Myself)." Brown's concerns with social power echo James Baldwin's 1963 *The Fire Next Time* in which he writes, "The only thing white people have that black people need, or should want, is power—and one holds power forever" (Baldwin 95–96). Brown's music is an early reminder of hip-hop's political beginnings, its attempts to decode power relations and ideology through an aggressive back beat configured by cut-and-pasted sound selections. Brown's interest in Black Power re-emerges in Ice-T's "Power," Salt N Pepa's "Solo Power (Syncopated Soul)," and Public Enemy's "Fight the Power." Public Enemy's song remains one of the best examples of hip-hop's interest in unequal power relations. Sampling Brown's "Funky President" and "Funky Drummer," the "I" of Bob Marley's "I Shot the Sheriff," and numerous other sources, Public Enemy shifts musical power from mainstream studio production to the compact digital sampler.

Brown, like many of the artists of Blue Note records, appealed to Djs experimenting with sampling practices in the 1970s, '80s, and '90s. Both Brown and Blue Note's artists addressed conflicts confronting various levels of social class. In addition, they provided a means for a future confrontation with discourse itself, supplying contemporary hip-hop with the basis of a new method of composition: empowerment through sampling.

Playback: The Writing Machine

In order to convert this material into a composition, I sample these cut-and-pasted moments into a hypothetical writing machine, a pedagogical digital sampler. The model for a pedagogical digital sampler comes from Suzanne McElfresh's definition of the electronic version:

> *A recording device that captures sound as digital information, which is then saved in computer memory instead of on magnetic tape, the sampler made it possible to create intricate soundscapes with virtually any source material, including already recorded music and live instruments. (170)*

The pedagogical sampler, with a computer or without a computer, allows cultural criticism to save isolated moments and then juxtapose them as a final product. The student writer looks at the various distinct moments she has collected and figures out how these moments together produce knowledge. Just as DJs often search for breaks and cuts in the music that reveal patterns, so, too, does the student writer look for a pattern as a way to unite these moments into a new alternative argument and critique.

My sampler shifts back and forth through the selections I have fed into it. The pattern I hear includes the ways information technology informs power relations at the levels of race and class. This issue is raised through image (Parks and Freed), sound (Blue Note and James Brown), and method (Bearden). The argument I perform here, therefore, emerges from the juxtaposition of all three areas.

Print literacy advocates the linear argument as the most appropriate way to establish critique. In the contemporary classroom, critique often follows Toulmin's model of argumentation as outlined in the widely adopted *Uses of Argument*. Toulmin's breakdown of the structure of the argument can be summed up as follows:

> *There must be an initial stage at which the charge or claim is clearly stated, a subsequent phase in which evidence is set out or testimony given in support of the charge or claim, leading on to the final stage at which a verdict is given, and the sentence or other judicial act issuing from the verdict is pronounced. (Toulmin 16)*

In the mix of the hip-hop pedagogy, sampling finds Toulmin's work in need of an update. Toulmin's dependence on the "charge" or "claim" as the principal force of argumentation appears out of place within the mix, in which the claim emerges as the result of whatever is played back in juxtaposition. In order to update argumentation for the electronic sphere, hip-hop pedagogy takes its cue from Leronne Bennett's 1963 reading of King's civil rights plan entitled "Project 'C'." Bennett writes:

> *Project "C" was the code name for a proposed series of demonstrations in Birmingham. And what did the "C" stand for? It was a shorthand symbol for a chillingly blunt concept: CONFRONTATION. A confrontation between Negroes and whites—not in the courts but on the steps of city hall, not at the conference table but in the streets, not by ones and twos but by hundreds and thousands. (4)*

Within my mix, the sampled passage from Bennett involves confronting the ways argumentation is formed in writing. Transformed from its 1960s racial purpose, Project "C" becomes a question of confronting the nature of Toulmin's "claim" in the mix. The desire to compose through confrontation appears as well in King's canonized 1963 "Letter from Birmingham Jail": "The purpose of our direct-action program is to create a situation so crisis-packed that it will inevitably open the door to negotiation" (King 767). King asked that his methods of confronting the dominant order be considered extremist. "The question is not whether we will be extremists, but what kind of extremists we will be" (King 773). In its conception of argumentation as confrontation, hip-hop pedagogy borrows King's extremism and joins it to another temporal extremist, William S. Burroughs, whose cut-up method proposed an extreme way of challenging institutionalized discourse: cutting up texts, speeches, slogans, etc., and pasting them back together in provocative ways. Burroughs argued for a confrontation with so-called "reality," the dominant ideology propagated in media formations and often taken for granted as natural. Writing in the time period surrounding 1963, Burroughs wrote that submission to reality without question was analogous to drug addiction:

> *The scanning pattern we accept as "reality" has been imposed by the controlling power on this planet, a power primarily oriented towards total control—In order to retain control they have moved to monopolize and deactivate the hallucinogen drugs by effecting noxious alternations on a molecular level. (53)*

If hip-hop pedagogy seeks to confront these types of power relations, it must alter the ways discourse is formed by student writers (and, hopefully, instructors as well). In this way, hip-hop pedagogy performs an extremist act by arguing that the "reality" of academic writing (the linear structure of thesis, support, conclusion) is in fact an ideological formation that can and should be challenged through the sample. Hip-hop pedagogy, therefore, borrows the student confrontational response to the traditional writing assignment by saying out loud, "whatever."

The Mix

In the mix (the writing I am performing), Allen Kaprow's 1962 Happening *Words* (originally performed at the Simolin Gallery in New York) is the space where my composition finally takes place. Falling within my 1963 series of samples, *Words* collected quotations from a variety of sources (comic books, political slogans, published writings) and hung them from the ceiling and the walls of an enclosed room. Viewers were encouraged to either add to the hanging and posted collections or rearrange the display. In the background, turntables played recordings of Kaprow's voice. The various selections and participant input created a collective-based space in which discourse surrounds viewers/readers rather than being concentrated on a single page. *Words* brought together the output of various media forms as collection. In this sense, communicating means collecting. *Words* also maintains a link to hip-hop; the expression "word" functions as a be-all answer to whatever-type questions, a way to deal with allusive meanings when no answer is forthcoming.

Words, then, serves as an early form of hip-hop pedagogy. Kaprow's collage of text, sound, and image set up a confrontation with the dominant art institution's preference for gallery space and museum shows. The "word" confrontation acts to motivate the sampling process, to push writers to engage with not only the language they use to construct discourse but also the mediums in which the discourse is conveyed. To think of the classroom and the academic essay as two mediums in need of confrontation is to create an analogy with Tricia Rose's definition of rap music. "Rap music is a contemporary stage for the theater of the powerless" (Rose 101). In this sense, students who are powerless (powerless to choose their own forms for writing, powerless to adapt the discourses they are most familiar with such as music, television, or film) become empowered at some level to reshape their relationship to literature, sports, music, politics, art, etc., through the sample. "Powerful, alternative formal possibilities are now key genres of public discourse," Geoffrey Sirc claims, "and kids understand them, and Composition Studies could care less" ("Virtual Urbanism" 14). Or to sample Public Enemy as a voice for the contemporary writing student: "Power and equality / and we're out to get it." ("Party").

Teaching the Whatever: Hip-Hop Pedagogy

I leave this composition as a mix to be played back by different students of contemporary culture, through different isolated moments, through a different whatever. My choice of 1963 acts merely as a model for further exploration; samples do not have to be temporal; they may come from specific spaces of public discourse, contemporary issues, or even physical spaces. And while many of the samples in my composition independently maintain a connection to African American culture, their thematic similarities don't override the disparate concerns of each piece (Mingus and Bearden work in distinctive, separate ways, for instance). For this demonstration, the commonality serves the specific purpose to identify the practice's potential. Student writing benefits from choosing contrasting samples and allowing the dissimilarities of the material to function as heuristic.

However the composition course poses the assignment (as temporal, spatial, or some other form), students gain insight into the writing process at levels they had not yet considered. Taking my performance of 1963 as one such example, the student engaged with a similar temporal project researches the year's moments in a variety of disciplines (film, politics, science, music, television, sports, etc.) and thus gains insight into the process of research. The student finds a common pattern or element that binds these moments and then understands how to form a claim out of research and investigation. The student juxtaposes these moments in one of a variety of ways and thus learns about organization. And through the process of juxtaposing the samples, the student locates her own position within the various cultural, ideological, economic, racial, gendered, etc., discussions consistently taking place around her. The student as sampler creates an argument.[5]

The ultimate test for such a project is to recognize that this process doesn't have to be done only with hip-hop music. The lesson of sampling can be extrapolated from this example in order to form various alternative methods of critique drawing from a variety of isolated details in order to allow pedagogy room for further development. The writing classroom, then, would shift critique from the standardized methodology inherited from figures like Toulmin and, instead, adopt the logic of hip-hop's composition innovators, figures like Grand Master Flash or the group Public Enemy. Doing so allows students to resist the imposed linear methods of critique in favor of practices already working within digital culture. Doing so repeats Digable Planets' message of whatever as resistance, repositioning the student writer's resistance (whatever) to the writing assignment in a productive manner:

> For this is the season of our self savior
> Like Ché Guevara, the guerilla
> Sparks the revolution black tactics, whatever. ("Agent 7")

One can speculate as to what extent this type of writing promotes not only a critical practice for how it synthesizes unlike material in order to construct an argument but also for how it registers our specific involvements in consumer culture. Because this practice models itself after a consumer product (popular music), we must also recognize that the cultural awareness sampling as critical practice brings to light is not a given in itself. The potential for critical understanding always contrasts with the potential for student cynicism (we know how the practice resists dominant thinking, but we still accept the dominant anyway), what Victor Vitanza has called a "false coconsciousness" often prevalent in cultural-studies-influenced classrooms ("The Wasteland Grows" 700). Hip-hop pedagogy is not meant as a given substitute for dominant thinking but, rather, as an alternative practice whose own application must be problematized even while students engage with it. Thus, I propose hip-hop pedagogy as the place to begin such questioning regarding our ability to resist dominant modes of thinking, to engage with consumerism while working against it, to spark the resistance, whatever.

Acknowledgments

I thank Geoffrey Sirc and Victor Vitanza for helpful comments and suggestions on earlier versions of this essay.

Endnotes

1. Because of space limitations, I mark these two observations with footnotes. See *The Muse Learns to Write* for Eric Havelock's observation of the near simultaneous publications on writing by Marshall McLuhan, Jack Goody and Ian Watt, and Claude Levi Strauss.

2. See Stephen North *The Making of Knowledge in Composition: Portrait of an Emerging Field,* Lester Faigley *Fragments of Rationality,* and Geoffrey Sirc's "English Composition As a Happening II, Part One."

3. Geoffrey Sirc has pointed out to me that Fluxus founder George Maciunas engaged with temporal dates for composing in the mid-1970s. His Biography Boxes contained "objects relating to the year of one's birth, perhaps a newspaper from the day one was born, things that were invented that year, etc" (Hendricks 322). See also Larry Miller's "Interview with George Maciunas" in *The Fluxus Reader,* edited by Ken Friedman. Maciunas states that 1963 was the first year he began making related boxes.

4. In addition to Victor Vitanza's response to Patricia Harkin, he also treats the whatever as the focus of an emerging identity. His work on this version of the whatever can be viewed online at <http://www.uta.edu/english/V/test/interface/v.1x.html> and <http://www.uta.edu/english/V/test:/agamben/>. While there exist distinct differences in the way we both use the term, Vitanza's work has greatly influenced my use of *whatever.*

5. Examples of student work that have performed temporal juxtapositions can be viewed online at <http://web.nwe.ufl.edu/~jrice/1629/2> and <http://web.nwe.ufl.edu/~jrice/1685/2>.

Works Cited

Baker, Houston. "Hybridity, the Rap Race, and Pedagogy for the 1990s." *Black Music Research Journal* 11 (2) Fall 1991.

Baldwin, James. *The Fire Next Time.* New York: The Modern Library, 1963.

Baraka, Amiri. *Black Music.* New York: W. Morrow, 1967.

———. *Blues People: Negro Music in White America.* New York: William Morrow and Co., 1963.

Barthes, Roland. *Camera Lucida.* New York: Hill and Wang, 1981.

Beastie Boys. *Paul's Boutique.* Capitol Records, 1989.

Bennett, Leronne, Jr. *The Black Mood and Other Essays.* New York: Barnes & Noble, 1964 (1963).

Booker, Simeon. *Black Man's America*. Englewood Cliffs, NJ: Prentice-Hall, 1964.

Brooks, Gwendolyn. "Negro Hero." *Selected Poems*. New York: Harper and Row, 1963.

Burroughs, William S. *The Nova Express*. New York: Grove, 1992 (1964).

Conwill, Kinshasha Holman. "Introduction." *Memory and Metaphor: The Art of Romare Bearden 1940–1987*. New York: Oxford UP. 1981.

Digable Planets. "Agent 7 Creamy Spy Theme: Dial 7 (Axioms of Creamy Spies)" EMD/Pendulum, 1994.

———. "Cool Like Dat." *Reachin' (A New Refutation of Time and Space)*. EMD/Pendulum, 1993.

Eshun, Kodowo. *More Brilliant Than the Sun*: Adventures in Sonic Fiction. London: Quartet, 1999.

Harkin, Patricia. "Rhetorics, Poetics, and Cultures As an Articulation Project." *JAC: A Journal of Composition Theory* 17.3 (1997): 494–97.

Hendricks, Jon. *Fluxus Codex*. New York: Harry N. Abrams, Inc., 1998.

Grandmaster Flash. "The Adventures of Grandmaster Flash on Wheels of Steel." *Grandmaster Flash Greatest Mixes*. Bangon, 1998.

King, Martin Luther, Jr. "Letter from Birmingham Jail." *The Little, Brown Reader*. Ed. Marcia Stubbs and Sylvan Barnet. New York: Harper Collins, 1996, 763–78.

McElfresh, Suzanne. "DJs Vs. Samplers." *The Vibe History of Hip-Hop*. Ed. Alan Light. New York: Three Rivers P, 1999.

Marsh, Graham, Felix Cromey. and Glyn Callingham. *Blue Note: The Album Cover Art*. San Francisco, CA: Chronicle Books, 1991.

Mingus, Charles. "Freedom." *Mingus, Mingus, Mingus*. Impulse! 1963.

Neal, Mark Anthony. *What the Music Said: Black Popular Music and Black Public Culture*. New York: Routledge, 1999.

Public Enemy. "Can I Get a Witness!" *It Takes a Nation of Millions to Hold Us Back*. UNI/DEFJAM, 1988.

———. "Party for Your Right to Fight." *It Takes a Nation of Millions to Hold Us Back*. UNI/DEFJAM, 1988.

Redman. "Whateva Man." *Muddy Waters*. UNI/DefJam, 1996.

Rose, Tricia. *Black Noise: Black Music and Black Culture in Contemporary America*. Hanover: Wesleyan UP, 1994.

Sirc, Geoffrey. "Never Mind the Tagmemics, Where's the Sex Pistols?" CCC 48.1 (Feb.) 1997.

———. "Virtual Urbanism." *Computers and Composition* 18(1) 2001: 11–19.

Toulmin. Stephen. *Uses of Argument*. Cambridge; Cambridge UP, 1958.

Ulmer, Gregory. "The Object of Post-Criticism." *The Anti-Aesthetic: Essays on Postmodern Culture*. Ed. Hal Foster. Seattle, WA: Bay Press, 1983.

Vitanza, Victor J. "From Heuristic to Aleatory Procedures; Or, Toward 'Writing the Accident'." *Inventing a Discipline: Rhetoric Scholarship in Honor of Richard E. Young.* Ed. Maureen Daly Goggin. Urbana, IL: NCTE, 2000.

———. "Seeing in Third Sophistic Ways." *Rhetoric and Composition As Intellectual Work.* Ed. Gary Olson. Carbondale: Southern Illinois UP, 2002.

———. " 'The Wasteland Grows': Or, What is 'Cultural Studies for Composition' and Why Must We Always Speak Good of It? ParaResponse to Julie Drew." *JAC: A Journal of Composition Theory* 19 (1999): 699–703.

Williams, Cecil B., and Allan Stevenson. *A Research Manual.* New York: Harper and Row, 1963.

Williams, Raymond. *Communications.* London: Chatto and Windus, 1966 (1962).

42

The Veil

MARJANE SATRAPI

This first chapter from Marjane Satrapi's graphic memoir Persepolis: The Story of a Childhood *introduces her attempts as a child to wrestle with widespread social change resulting from the 1979 Islamic Revolution in Iran. An author and illustrator of autobiographical and children's books, Satrapi's work refuses simple categorization of Iranians as religious fanatics and terrorists. In "The Veil," Satrapi demonstrates how she and her family fight for social justice and women's rights while also negotiating responses to and within conservative Islam and Iranian traditions.*

The Veil

THIS IS ME WHEN I WAS 10 YEARS OLD. THIS WAS IN 1980.

AND THIS IS A CLASS PHOTO. I'M SITTING ON THE FAR LEFT SO YOU DON'T SEE ME. FROM LEFT TO RIGHT: GOLNAZ, MAHSHID, NARINE, MINNA.

IN 1979 A REVOLUTION TOOK PLACE. IT WAS LATER CALLED "THE ISLAMIC REVOLUTION".

THEN CAME 1980: THE YEAR IT BECAME OBLIGATORY TO WEAR THE VEIL AT SCHOOL.

WEAR THIS!

WE DIDN'T REALLY LIKE TO WEAR THE VEIL, ESPECIALLY SINCE WE DIDN'T UNDERSTAND WHY WE HAD TO.

IT'S TOO HOT OUT!

EXECUTION IN THE NAME OF FREEDOM.

GIVE ME MY VEIL BACK!

YOU'LL HAVE TO LICK MY FEET!

OOH! I'M THE MONSTER OF DARKNESS.

GIDDYAP!

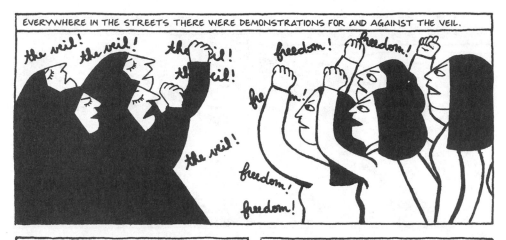

The Veil

I REALLY DIDN'T KNOW WHAT TO THINK ABOUT THE VEIL. DEEP DOWN I WAS VERY RELIGIOUS BUT AS A FAMILY WE WERE VERY MODERN AND AVANT-GARDE.

I WAS BORN WITH RELIGION.

AT THE AGE OF SIX I WAS ALREADY SURE I WAS THE LAST PROPHET. THIS WAS A FEW YEARS BEFORE THE REVOLUTION.

O' Celestial light!

BEFORE ME THERE HAD BEEN A FEW OTHERS.

I AM THE LAST PROPHET.

A WOMAN?

I WANTED TO BE A PROPHET...

BECAUSE OUR MAID DID NOT EAT WITH US.

BECAUSE MY FATHER HAD A CADILLAC.

AND, ABOVE ALL, BECAUSE MY GRANDMOTHER'S KNEES ALWAYS ACHED.

COME HERE MARJI! HELP ME TO STAND UP.

DON'T WORRY, SOON YOU WON'T HAVE ANY MORE PAIN. YOU'LL SEE.

LIKE ALL MY PREDECESSORS I HAD MY HOLY BOOK.

THE FIRST THREE RULES CAME FROM ZARATHUSTRA. HE WAS THE FIRST PROPHET IN MY COUNTRY BEFORE THE ARAB INVASION.

YOU MUST BASE EVERYTHING ON THESE THREE RULES: BEHAVE WELL, SPEAK WELL, ACT WELL.

I ALSO WANTED US TO CELEBRATE THE TRADITIONAL ZARATHUSTRIAN HOLIDAYS. LIKE THE FIRE CEREMONY,

BEFORE THE PERSIAN NEW YEAR, NOROUZ, ON MARCH 21ST, THE FIRST DAY OF SPRING.

ONLY MY GRANDMOTHER KNEW ABOUT MY BOOK.

RULE NUMBER SIX: EVERY-BODY SHOULD HAVE A CAR.

RULE NUMBER SEVEN: ALL MAIDS SHOULD EAT AT THE TABLE WITH THE OTHERS.

RULE NUMBER EIGHT: NO OLD PER-SON SHOULD HAVE TO SUFFER.

IN THAT CASE, I'LL BE YOUR FIRST DISCIPLE.

REALLY?

BUT TELL ME HOW YOU'LL ARRANGE FOR OLD PEOPLE NOT TO SUFFER?

IT WILL SIMPLY BE FORBIDDEN.

EVERY NIGHT I HAD A BIG DISCUSSION WITH GOD.

GOD, GIVE ME SOME MORE TIME. I AM NOT QUITE READY YET.

YES YOU ARE, CELESTIAL LIGHT, YOU ARE MY CHOICE, MY LAST AND MY BEST CHOICE.

EXCEPT FOR MY GRANDMOTHER I WAS OBVIOUSLY THE ONLY ONE WHO BELIEVED IN MYSELF.

WHAT DO YOU WANT TO BE WHEN YOU GROW UP?

I'LL BE A PROPHET.

HAHA! HAHA! HAHA!

SHE'S CRAZY.

MY PARENTS WERE CALLED IN BY THE TEACHER.

YOUR CHILD IS DISTURBED. SHE WANTS TO BECOME A PROPHET.

WHAT ABOUT IT?

DOESN'T THIS WORRY YOU?

NO! NOT AT ALL!

43

Introduction to Geographies of Exclusion

DAVID SIBLEY

Professor David Sibley works in the School of Geography at University of Leeds. In this introduction to Geographies of Exclusion, *Sibley provides examples of interactions between groups in public spaces that illustrate how some populations are actively and systematically excluded from participation in normatively middle class spaces. This piece urges readings of physical spaces as sites steeped in exercises of power with exclusionary effects.*

The human landscape can be read as a landscape of exclusion. This was clear to Engels in his observations on the industrial city, to Raymond Williams in his account of the landscapes of landed capital in eighteenth-century England in *The Country and the City,* and to Lewis Mumford, writing about Baroque cities in *The City in History.* Because power is expressed in the monopolization of space and the relegation of weaker groups in society to less desirable environments, any text on the social geography of advanced capitalism should be concerned with the question of exclusion. My purpose in writing this book, however, is not to provide a comprehensive account of exclusionary processes. There is already a substantial literature on the capitalist city which is, to some extent, concerned with exclusion, insofar as it is concerned with problems of access to urban resources, particularly housing, and associated spatial outcomes.[1] I would also leave off my agenda those programmes of exclusion which are starkly expressed in spatial terms and connect with clearly articulated ideologies, such as apartheid in South Africa and the 'race' policies of Nazi Germany, although I would not wish to suggest that these cases of oppression could not be further illuminated by geographical analysis.[2]

While this may seem like a perverse avoidance of central theoretical issues and crucial social and political problems, my intention in this book is to foreground the more opaque instances of exclusion, opaque, that is, from a mainstream or majority perspective, the ones which do not make the news or are taken for granted as part of the routine of daily life. These exclusionary practices are important because they are less noticed and so the ways in which control is exercised in society are concealed. One cue for my analysis comes from Paul Rabinow,[3] who has suggested that 'we need to anthropologize the West'. Rabinow argues that we need to 'show how exotic [the West's] granted as universal (this includes epistemology and economics); [and] make them seem as historically peculiar as possible'. To me this implies that we need to recognize as problems those aspects of life of which you might be unaware, particularly if you happen to be white, adult, male, and middle class, but which contribute to the oppression of others. Human geography, in particular, should be concerned with raising consciousness of the domination of space in its critique of the hegemonic culture. This has been the objective of Marxist analysis in human geography, but as a totalizing discourse Marxism has inevitably been insensitive to difference, almost as insensitive as the dominant capitalist culture which is the subject of Marxist critique. To get beyond the myths which secure capitalist hegemony, to expose oppressive practices, it is necessary to examine the assumptions about inclusion and exclusion which are implicit in the design of spaces and places. The simple questions we should be asking are: who are places for, whom do they exclude, and how are these prohibitions maintained in practice? Apart from examining legal systems and the practices of social control agencies, explanations of exclusion require an account of barriers, prohibitions and constraints on activities from the point of view of the excluded. I would agree with Jane Flax, however, that there is no single oppressive reality, no single structure obscured by the images of the dominant culture, to uncover. She suggests that

> *Perhaps reality can have 'a' structure only from the falsely universalizing perspective of the dominant group. That is, only to the extent that one person or group can dominate the whole will reality appear to be governed by one set of rules or to be constituted by one privileged set of social relations.*

One part of the problem, then, is to identify forms of socio-spatial exclusion as they are experienced and articulated by the subject groups. These groups, however, may be seen as both dominant and subordinate, depending on the way in which they are categorized. Both men and women may experience exclusion as members of an oppressed minority group, for example, but men may be dominant in their relationship with women in a minority culture.[5] These different realities can be difficult to recognize, and the observer must appreciate that his or her own understanding of the socio-spatial worlds of others will inevitably be limited by his or her own background and perspectives. However, I still feel that it is possible, and certainly desirable, to represent other people's experience of socio-spatial exclusion while acknowledging that the question of positionality is one that has to be addressed.[6]

For the moment, rather than pursuing this argument in the abstract, I will comment on a few cases of exclusion which signal the specific kinds of socio-spatial issues which I will be considering in this book. The first concerns what is now a widely discussed problem, namely, the function of indoor shopping centres as social space.[7] These centres have become a significant mode of retail service provision in the developed capitalist economies, projected by both commercial and civic interests as progressive, and providing an improved environment for consumption and leisure for all the family. In the more extravagant developments, a fantasy world of imagined places is created, effectively removing consumption from associations with need. As Shields has observed in an account of the West Edmonton Mall in Canada, the model for several very large retailing developments in North America and Europe:

> *It fragments conventional geographical space and historical time with its wild combination of interior settings; evoking disparate times and places while it seeks to impose its own stable order on the ensemble. At the turn of a corner, one is in a simulated 'New Orleans'. Another corner—'Paris'.*

In comparable British developments, including the Meadowhall Shopping Centre, near Sheffield, which similarly recreates the romance of Paris and Florence under one roof, and the Metro Centre in Gateshead, their exoticism has stimulated a new form of holiday experience. For some, a coach trip to the shopping centre has become a substitute for a day by the sea, in Blackpool, Scarborough or Skegness. Such places clearly do provide an attractive alternative to a traditional shopping street, polluted by vehicle exhausts and exposed to the weather (and they may be rather more appealing than a decaying seaside resort). Thus, a British television documentary on the Metro Centre in Gateshead focused in a positive way on the characteristic features of international consumption style and the consumers, all apparently white, middle-class nuclear families, the kind of public which populates architects' sketches. The documentary had a rather different sub-text, however. Out of sight in the control room, employees of the private security firm which polices the centre had their eyes fixed on closed-circuit television screens. They were looking for 'undesirables', mostly groups of teenage boys who did not fit the family image projected by the company. When they were located, security guards evicted them, not just from the building but from the precinct. Such actions point to the fact that shopping centres like this one constitute a kind of ambiguous, seemingly public but actually private space. There are implicit rules of inclusion and exclusion in a built form that contribute to the structuring of society and space in a way which some will find oppressive and others appealing. 'Being in the tightly policed, semi-private interior of a mall is quite different from being "on the street". "No loitering", as the signs in the mall say. Certain types of comportment are expected'.[8] In the shopping centre management's response to the presence of adolescents, maybe not consuming very much, in a place dedicated to consumption by the family, there is a connection between the function and design of the space as determined by commercial interests and design professionals, architects and planners, and the construction of one group of the population as 'deviant', out of place, and threatening the projected image of the development. Again, Shields notes that the shopping mall introduces 'an unheard of degree of surveillance, with almost Orwellian overtones, into daily life', and, in this controlled environment, teenagers who have few other places in which to congregate are one of the principal groups targeted by the security guards. Their presence necessarily constitutes deviance.[9] Comparing this with my own experience as a teenager in the 1950s, sitting for hours over a cup of coffee in an ABC café in a north London suburb, undisturbed by staff, it appears that the boundaries between the consuming and non-consuming public are strengthening, with non-consumption being constructed as a form of deviance at the same time as spaces of consumption eliminate public spaces in city centres.

This view gains some empirical support in a number of studies of teenage subcultures. For example, in a Home Office study of 'downtown drinkers' in the planned shopping precinct in Coventry,[10] the writer reported that:

> *Unruly groups of young people were seen as a problem by approximately two out of three interviewees. As with litter, the problem is not just a local matter. Throughout the country, shopping centres often serve as convenient places for youth subcultures to meet—places to which there may be a lack of obvious alternatives. On the other hand, the mere sight of such groups, however rarely they actually infringe any laws, can be alarming to others. This is a delicate issue. [Attempts] to exclude youth groups from shopping centres are likely to bring further problems, and may also be quite unjust. Nevertheless, in Coventry, perception of unruly groups of young people as a common problem was significantly associated with the fear of crime. This link was stronger than that between perceptions of litter and fear of crime but not as powerful as that between perceptions of public drinkers and fear of crime [my italics].*

This quotation, like the television documentary on the shopping centre, suggests that it is not adolescent males as a social category, or even 'unruly' groups of young people, *per se,* who are seen as threatening; rather, it is their presence in spaces which comprise part of 'normal family space' which renders them discrepant and threatening. Exclusion may be an unintended consequence of commerical development. Adolescents will be acutely aware of discrimination against them, while their exclusion is much less likely to impinge on the consciousness of conforming adults.

In the interaction of people and the built environment, it is a truism that space is contested but relatively trivial conflicts can provide clues about power relations and the role of space in social control. This is demonstrated in a second example, dredged from memory, which concerns an incident in Philadelphia in the late 1960s. At this time, hippies were still a threatening species in Philadelphia, the category 'hippy' embracing just about any man with long hair or woman wearing beads. Rittenhouse Square, in the city centre, was popular with slightly non-conforming people at the weekend; in it was a low wall which was a convenient place to sit. One warm Sunday afternoon, there were a lot of people sitting on the wall, some playing acoustic guitars, but mostly just chatting and enjoying the sunshine. At some point, a park guard started to order people off the wall on the grounds that it was *not* a place to sit. The wall, he asserted, was there to separate the path from the grass. It was definitely not to sit on. Almost everyone acquiesced. This might have been because the park guard, who, like many agents of social control in the United States, was equipped with a revolver and a night-stick, appeared intimidating. It could also be the case that this group of middle-class American youth, having been brought up in conformist communities, were accustomed to accepting authority despite their trappings of non-conformity.

There are two aspects of this incident which are of more general significance. The first concerns ambiguity. To the park guard, the function of the wall was unambiguous. It was simply a boundary between one kind of space and another and, apparently, he could not conceive of alternative interpretations. His job was to police the wall, to ensure its sanctity and prevent its violation. It may be reading too much into the incident, but his behaviour appeared to fit a pattern noted in a number of studies of the authoritarian personality, following Adorno's early study of the psychology of authoritarianism.[11] Shils suggested that authoritarians were distrustful and suspicious, that they had *on intolerance of ambiguity,* and, thus, differentiated clearly between those on the outside, the 'other', and the relevant in-group.[12] Similarly, Rokeach[13] suggested that authoritarian individuals '[protected] inner weaknesses by a ready acceptance of the views of higher authorities and by forming unambiguous judgements which rigidly separate, into distinct categories, objects of approval and those of disapproval'.

The issue is not just about an unsuspecting park guard overloaded with theoretical meaning. Apart from the park guard's own perception of non-conformity, the social status of Rittenhouse Square also contributed to the representation of its hippy-ish occupants as conspicuously deviant. The square was surrounded by solid apartment buildings occupied by affluent middle-aged and elderly residents who saw the hippies as polluting 'their' space. In fact, the park guard admitted to me that he had been told to clear the square of young people because their presence offended the residents. The arbitrary use of power by the guard thus reflected a more fundamental aspect of power relations. The square as a contested public space exposed the conflictual nature of social relations and the design of the square itself assumed symbolic importance in this conflict. It should not be seen just as an arena where this particular power game was played, however, but as one instance of the interaction of space and people which forms part of the routines for the reproduction of power relations in an advanced capitalist society.[14]

The policing of Rittenhouse Square, a rather unsubtle example of social control, might be compared with many instances of exclusion where boundaries are drawn discretely between dominant and subordinate groups. Martin Walker notes the spread of the private pool club in the United States, an institution, like the whites-only golf club, which continues 'the discrete and self-deceiving way of modern American apartheid. It is now justified as a way to avoid the crowds, crime and drugs of the municipal pools, these being code words which are used to signify black people.'[15] Elsewhere, Mike Davis has captured the helplessness of the poor and homeless in the large North American city, faced with exclusionary developments by corporate capital.[16] Talking to a black, homeless man in downtown Los Angeles, Davis comments: 'In front of us, tens of thousands of poor people, homeless people; at back opulence, affluence, Bunker Hill, the new L.A.' He then asks: 'Could you walk up there?' and the man replies: 'If they were to catch me in that building, they would have so much security on my ass, I would probably be in jail in five minutes.' Again exclusion is felt acutely, but the homeless are rendered invisible to the affluent downtown workers by the spatial separations of city centre development which keep the underclass at a distance.

These examples give some indication of the concerns of this book, exclusions in social space which may be unnoticed features of urban life. It is the fact that exclusions take place routinely, without most people noticing, which is a particularly important aspect of the problem. In an attempt to make these practices more transparent what I try to do in the first part of the text is to define attitudes to others which inform exclusionary practices and to set the control problem in the broader context of the cultures of modern societies. I then try to show how the processes of control are manifested in the exclusion of those people who are judged to be deviant, imperfect or marginal. A study of exclusion, however, is necessarily concerned with inclusion, with the 'normal' as much as the 'deviant', the 'same' as well as the 'other', and with the credentials required to gain entry to the dominant groups in society. Thus, I focus on processes of boundary erection by groups in society who consider themselves to be normal or mainstream. The curious practices of this majority, the oddness of the ordinary which is examined microscopically by authors and playwrights from Jane Austen to Mike Leigh, have been neglected in social geography, and one of the purposes of this book is to rectify this omission.

My treatment of space and society is concerned particularly with symbol, ritual and myth, taking cues from social anthropology and psychoanalysis, subjects which have not been overly concerned with space but which provide many useful analogues for spatial problems. I would argue that many social problems can be profitably spatialized, but, at the same time, a human geography which attempts to assume a distinct identity within social science is necessarily impoverished. For example, it seems to me that the concern of social anthropology with representation, imagery and alternative world-views should also be central to human geography, hence 'geographies' in the title of the book. To uncover these diverse geographies, reflecting varied experiences and interpretations of space and place, involves drawing on a wide range of ideas located elsewhere in the social sciences and the humanities. A post-disciplinary perspective on social and spatial problems is preferable to viewing the world from within conventional subject boundaries.

In Part I, I first attempt to build up pictures of the rejecting and the rejected and then travel along several theoretical avenues in order to identify exclusionary processes affecting both groups and individuals. In addition to theories of socio-spatial structuring, this section makes reference to psychoanalytic theories of the self, which assumed greater importance as the writing progressed. This was partly because I was trying to familiarize myself with this literature while working on the text but also because some ideas from psychoanalysis seemed to connect with what were, for me, more familiar arguments about boundary formation developed in social anthropology and human geography. I would not claim that this account achieves any real synthesis, but it does suggest some connections between individual and group behaviour, and between environment and behaviour, which might be integral elements of the problem.

These theoretical arguments connect with instances of exclusion at different spatial scales, starting with the home and moving out to the nation-state and questions of geopolitics. Exclusion in the home, in the locality and at the national level are not discrete issues. A number of reciprocal relationships are examined and there is, inevitably, considerable cross-referencing in this part of the book. While there are common strands to the argument here, the problems considered are very different, ranging from conflicts within families and homes to international relations.

In Part II, I get away from the usual subjects of geographical analysis to consider academics as subjects, but what I claim in this section is that we can use the same arguments to explain the exclusion of knowledge as to explain the exclusion of discrepant others. I suggest that the production of knowledge involves both the exclusion of knowledge which is deemed dangerous and the exclusion of some categories of intellectual. The processes of social segregation observable in the modern city, for example, are mirrored in the segregation of knowledge producers. The defence of social space has its counterpart in the defence of regions of knowledge. This means that what constitutes knowledge, that is; those ideas which gain currency through books and periodicals, is conditioned by power relations which determine the boundaries of 'knowledge' and exclude dangerous or threatening ideas and authors. It follows that any prescriptions for a better integrated and more egalitarian society must also include proposals for change in the way academic knowledge is produced.

I do not attempt in this book to give an account of exclusion in advanced capitalist societies which covers all salient forms of difference. There would be a long list of these, including exclusion based on race, gender, sexuality, age, and mental and physical disability. What I hope to do, however, is to clarify some of the spatial and social boundary processes which separate some groups and individuals from society and render deviant those who are different. At the same time, I suggest that social scientists need to look more closely at their own practices and develop critiques of their work which parallel their analyses of the marginalized and oppressed.

Endnotes

1. Thus, much of David Harvey's work could be read as a (class-based) geography of exclusion. His essay 'Class structure and residential differentiation' (in *The Urban Experience,* Basil Blackwell, Oxford, 1989, pp. 109–124) is specifically concerned with closure and exclusion as they operate in the property market. In a similar theoretical vein, we could note Blair Badcock's *Unfairly Structured Cities,* Basil Blackwell, Oxford, 1984. Weberian closure theory is also concerned with exclusion—through the erection of barriers to entry into more privileged groups. Closure theory has been given a spatial dimension, particularly in Christopher Husband's work on racism. See his 'East End racism, 1900–1980', *The London Journal,* 8, 1982, 3–26.

2. Rössler's study of the connection between central place theory and the concept of *lebensraum* in Nazi Germany demonstrates that there is considerable scope for the kind of research on fascist and other authoritarian regimes which explores ideology, spatial theories and spatial practices (Mechtild Rössler, 'Applied geography and area research in Nazi society: central place theory and planning, 1933 to 1945', *Environment and Planning D: Society and Space,* 7 (4), 1989, 363–400).

3. Paul Rabinow, 'Representations are social facts: modernity and post-modernity in anthropology', in James Clifford and George Marcus (eds), *Writing Culture,* University of California Press, Berkeley, 1986, 234–261. This echoes Robert Park's recommendation in his 1925 essay on the city:

   Anthropology, the science of man, has been mainly concerned up to the present with the study of primitive peoples. But civilized man is quite as interesting an object of investigation and, at the same time, his life is more open to observation and study. Urban life and culture are more varied, subtle and complicated, but the fundamental motives in both instances are the same. The same patient methods of observation which anthropologists like Boas and Lowie have expended on the study of the life and manners of the North American Indian might be even more fruitfully employed in the investigation of the customs, beliefs, social practices and general conceptions of life prevalent in Little Italy or the lower North Side in Chicago or in recording the more sophisticated folkways of the inhabitants of Greenwich Village and the neighborhood of Washington Square, New York.

   (*Robert Park, The City, University of Chicago Press, Chicago, 1925, p. 2*)

4. Cited by Linda Nicholson (Linda Nicholson (ed.), *Feminism/Postmodernism,* Routledge, London, 1990, p. 6).

5. In patriarchal Gypsy communities, for example, women suffer double exclusion, as women and as members of a marginalized minority.

6. However, agonizing over position leads to authors denying the possibility of writing with any authority about anybody other than their own social group, which may be quite narrowly defined. Given appropriate methods of investigation, I feel that some generalization about those with different world-views is possible and desirable, although there is always a risk of distortion and misrepresentation which can only be guarded against by repeated engagement with other groups.

7. Rob Shields's 1989 essay is one of the more thoughtful studies of shopping centres, but David Harvey also makes some relevant comments on the blurring of public and private space in the new arenas of consumption. See Rob Shields, 'Social spatialization and the built environment: the West Edmonton Mall', *Environment and Planning D: Society and Space,* 7, 1989, 147–164, and David Harvey, 'Postmodern morality plays', *Antipode,* 24, 1992, 300–326.

8. Shields, op. cit.

9. 'With a thorough application of surveillance technology, the shopping centre can become a panoptican mall', echoing Jeremy Bentham's design for a model prison. See Mike Davis, *City of Quartz,* Verso Press, London, 1990,

pp. 240–244, on 'the mall-as-panoptican-prison' as it has been realized in inner-city Los Angeles.

10. M. Ramsay, *Downtown Drinkers: The perceptions and fears of the public in a city centre*, Crime Prevention Unit, Paper 19, Home Office, London, 1989.

11. Theodor Adorno, *et al.*, *The Authoritarian Personality*, Norton, New York, 1982.

12. Edward Shils, 'Authoritarianism: "right" and "left"', in R. Christie and M. Jahoda (eds), *Studies in the Scope and Method of the Authoritarian Personality*, Free Press, Glencoe, 1954.

13. Michael Rokeach, *The Open and Closed Mind*, Basic Books, New York, 1960.

14. David Harvey makes similar points about social relations in Tompkins Square Park, New York City, where 'On a good day, we could celebrate the scene within the park as a superb example of urban tolerance for difference', but 'on a bad day . . . so-called forces of law and order battle to evict the homeless, erect barriers between violently clashing factions. The park then becomes a locus of exploitation and oppression' (1992, op. cit.).

15. Martin Walker, *Guardian*, 26 May 1990.

16. *Rear Window*, Channel 4 TV, London, 1991. As Davis puts it, rather floridly: 'The Downtown hyperstructure—like some Buckminster Fuller post-Holocaust fantasy—is programmed to ensure a seamless continuum of middle-class work, consumption and recreation, without unwonted exposure to Downtown's working-class street environments' (op. cit., 1990, p. 231).

44

Broken Sentences: Women in Prison Tell Their Stories Straight

ANNA DEAVERE SMITH

This magazine article originally appeared in a 1996 issue of The New Yorker.
*Here Smith presents stories of imprisoned women and a corrections officer
that reveal the violence many women encounter both before and during their
incarceration as well as the complex ways in which they present themselves.
This article addresses how research, such as interviews, and its modes of
delivery can complicate previous beliefs or assumptions. Anna Deavere Smith
teaches performance at the Tisch School of the Arts at New York University.*

FIFTH GRADE: A few weeks before my tenth birthday. Segregated school in Baltimore. My bedroom, where I studied. An O.K. place with a nice window that looked out over a graveyard, which was scary, but we played in the snow there, and I liked the sound of the trains that went by just beside it. My mother was pregnant, with what I prayed on my knees every night would be a girl. I had two brothers. They were disobedient, or so I thought. I was obedient. Or so I thought. But I was headed toward breaking the law. The laws of grammar. I can't imagine where this tendency came from. I had a very respectable mother. An educator. And my aunts and uncles and everyone else were respectable, too. My father? Well, come to think of it . . . He called tomatoes potatoes "just to make us think." He was a black version of Ionesco.

SENTENCES. Grammatical incarceration. My mother began to express a disapproval toward me which I hadn't experienced before. She had an uncompromising disdain for run-on sentences, and for incomplete ones. In school, too, there was a very serious tone about breaking the rules of grammar. And the same serious tone would be used a few years hence about ending up pregnant. In the Baltimore I knew, there was no discussion of drugs, or any apparent threat of them. If there had been, I'm sure the same serious tone would have been used.

THERE was a sudden release of pressure. A few of us were placed in the sixth grade before Christmas. We'd skipped a grade. I was relieved of a fear of failure that was increasing with every book report. The more I had to say, the more improper my grammar became. Thank God the test I had to take to skip the fifth grade had no writing. Just circle the proper answer. Just learn the rules and follow them. Now I had some peace. I did have to write in complete sentences, but I felt it would all be O.K. I could fake it. Nonetheless, I experienced a loss, and I associate the introduction of the perfect sentence with the end of my girlhood.

Truth be told, we all break the laws of grammar. We all have the potential to speak in broken, collaged, colluded, jumbled, run-on sentences. Truth be told, the sentence is sometimes no more and no less than a mask. I have been looking for sentences with enough breath to let the subtext live, in fact, where words don't kill the "truth."

What better place to find the broken sentences of my birthplace than a prison— a women's prison outside my home town? The Maryland Correctional Institution for Women, in Jessup, Maryland, detains many women from Baltimore and surrounding areas, like the Eastern Shore (which was referred to as "the country" when we were kids). There I listened to stories that account for life styles that I barely knew existed in my sheltered Baltimore life. Each time I heard the name of a street, autobiographical images were evoked, of walks with my grandmother, of rides with my father, or of simple journeys to do errands, or to go to another church, or to see a play at a school where my mother taught, sometimes in strange areas of town. Some of those streets never felt familiar or safe, but my father's car or my grandmother's gait made them safe. The stories I heard in the prison told me something about the subtext, the underbelly, of those streets. Times have changed here, in particular for women.

There are about four times more women at the Maryland Correctional Institution than there were twenty years ago, and the overwhelming majority are colored. On the first trip to the prison, I went to, of all things, a Girl Scout meeting. The Girl Scouts bring the daughters of inmates on a bus to the prison on some Saturdays. The mothers meet first as a group, and talk about "issue" having to do with mothering in these restrictive circumstances. There are two whites. The others were black. They ranged in age from their early twenties to mid-thirties. The mothers were coiffed and manicured, and dressed in "casual wear"— jeans, sportswear, etc. (Only the "new admits" wear uniforms—pink jump-suits—and none of them would be allowed in the Girl Scouts, which is a "program" and a privilege to be earned.)

Even in a Girl Scout meeting, there are very specific rules that must be followed. One girl and her mother were dismissed when the girl wore oversized boots to the meeting, which she exchanged with the mother's shoes so that the mother could wear the boots back to her wing. Everyone is suspect. A daughter, like her mother before her, could be a "mule" for drugs or other contraband. Certainly, among adults, contraband is brought into the prison in a variety of creative ways. Drugs come packed in balloons, which are carried in a visitor's mouth and "passed" in a kiss. Perhaps the balloon is swallowed, and the recipient waits until she is able to defecate it out of her system, at which time she can distribute the drugs in the population. One woman told me that she had a friend who died when a balloon she swallowed "burst," and "exploded in her heart."

The members of the Girl Scouts are particularly careful to follow every procedure properly, because they so value the time with their daughters. A child, therefore, cannot bring a gift of any kind to her mother.

I present some of their stories here, excerpted, from tape-recorded interviews. If a word has been added for clarity, parentheses are used.

Serious/Wicked Women
Sherri Rideout

The Visiting Room: The room has several long institutional tables, and there are vending machines against two walls.

Sherri Rideout is tall, with pressed hair that swoops up to the side. She is, by her own definition, a compulsive thief. She comes back and forth to prison a lot. She is thirty-three. Her demeanor is pleasant and open, and she has a very apparent sense of humor. When I asked her to say something into the microphone to test the machine, she yelled, "I love ya!"

Now, I take this place seriously
even the last time when I left here
it wasn't as strict.
I left this place in '93
And two years later
My God.
This is serious here.
This is serious times.
The most serious part about it is
they have a lot a new officers
that more so are young
very young
and the younger generation to me
they can't tolerate a lot of things that
    older people can.
They just cuff you
put you over
and you goin' on lock.
Unh unh.
I'm getting too old.
I'm thirty-three.
My children are getting old.
They need me.
The women, the women in this place
    some of them are so evil and wicked.
Some of these women

You got people that's
took someone else's life
that's chopped their baby and fed it to
    their husband
all kinds of ludicrous things
that has taken place.
And you know
they can get in here and portray
to be this and that
but I'm thinking
well my God
if you did that to your own child
what would you do to me?
To kill your child
and to do all these things?
Unh unh.
Now, there's one girl here
that committed a violent offense
and she got eighteen years for this offense
and she
when her roommate
went to sleep
she took something and shoved it up
    her vagina
It's just, it's some wicked women here.
It really is.

Christmas
Vera Banton

Vera is in prison for murder. By her account, while protecting herself from Sam, her boyfriend, who was coming at her with a steak knife and threatening to kill her, she grabbed the knife, "tousled" with him, and the knife accidentally went into his chest. She got eighteen years. She told me that when she first met Sam he told her he was an angel, and she believed him, but as he abused her she saw he was the devil. "The devil," she told me, "come as an angel, too. He was in Heaven at one time. And he also walks this earth as an angel."

Vera told me that her Christmas package had come from her family, "but there was something wrong in it," so it was sent back. She said she had decided to praise the Lord until she was "all fulled up," instead of getting angry.

This is the most painful time of the
    year for me
cause I'm in prison
I'm in this environment
Away from my family
I have four kids
out there
that I have been away now for three
    years
and I miss
putting up a Christmas tree,
wrapping gifts,
going to the mall buying the gifts,
and just seeing they face,
when they open 'em up,
cookin' the dinner,
sittin' at the table,
we all saying our grace,
we all eat together,

we all go visit Grandma,
go over to Auntie house,
and just being with my kids,
I miss that.
I don't feel like Christmas!
And it's sad
because I have to go back in
past the Christmas tree
past the decorations
and go in the little room and lock in
and it hurts
'cause I didn't do those decorations
I didn't put that Christmas tree up
I didn't have my kids
running around
"Mommy"
now that I have grandkids out there
I'm not able to be with them.
Christmas.

A Mirror to Her Mouth
Paulette Jenkins

It was about 6 P.M. when I met Paulette Jenkins. It was dark outside. The visiting room was quiet. A stream of officers had just gone home. She is black, simply presented, with her hair pulled back, wearing a T-shirt. Most of her sentences end with an upward inflection, as if she knows but is still looking for something, looking for a possibility.

They were still afraid.
They were still confused.
He would beat them.
They were not his children.
I had three children before it was all
     over with
but at the time we all started out it was
     just
me
and my daughter
and then
I had another baby
by my husband
and I left my husband
and went with this man.
It was like jumping out of the pan and
     right into the fire?
And he would beat my children,
out of his own insecurities
or his own jealousness.
He beat my daughter
and he beat my son.
My daughter was nine
and my son was six.
The beatings escalated
and I began to cover it up.
This went on for
five,
seven years
and my daughter had got a beatin' and
     he had scald her foot.
I lied to Social Service and I told them
"This didn't happen. He didn't do it."
You know—
"It was an accident."
I had came home from work and she was
     there with her feet all blistered up
and she told me he made her stand in
     the bathtub with hot water.
It was the fact,
that I didn't believe her
and even if I did believe her—

it was the fact
I hesitated.
I refused to do anything about it.
That was the fact.
It didn't take the blisters down.
It didn't change the fact that I lied to
     Social Service.
I denied all help and assistance.
I pushed my family away, when the
     abuse got so intense
that I wouldn't go visit.
I ran out of excuses!
Of how we got black eyes.
And busted lips and bruises.
And he beat me, too.
But
it didn't change the fact,
that
It was a nightmare for my children.
It was a nightmare.
And I failed them.
Dramatically.
Because I allowed it to continue.
On.
And on.
And on.

That night that she got killed—
we had went out,
And to subside my fear of being petrified
I was shootin' drugs all day long—
and was still able to cook a dinner.
You know.
(*Louder, and more emphatic.*)
Still was able to keep the house clean.
Wash clothes.
Hang 'em on the line.
And be blasted!
Heroin,
marijuana,
alcohol.
Y'know.

And then I started writing prescriptions.
Y'know.
And I thought he was gonna get better.
And I thought I could fix this man!
And the intensity just grew,
and grew,
and grew,
until one night we came home . . .
from getting drugs,
and he
got angry with Myeshia,
and he started beating her,
he would use a belt,
'cause he had this warped
perverted thing,
that Myeshia
was having sex with her little brother
or that they were fondlin' each other.
And he beat her
and he put her in the bathtub
and I was in the bedroom.
But
before
all this happened,
four months before she died,
I thought I could really fix this man
and so I had a baby by him!
Insane?!
Thinking if I give him his own kid,
he'll leave mine alone.
But it didn't work—
I wound up with three children—
and it was a boy
four months old when I came to jail.
So,
the night that Myeshia died
I stayed in the bedroom with the baby.
And every time he would hit her
she would fall,
and she would hit her head on the tub.
I could hear it!
And it happened continuously,
repeatedly.
(*She whispers.*)
And I dared not to move.
I didn't move.
I didn't even go see what was happening.
I just set there and listened.
And then later—
he set her in the hallway
and told her to set there.

And she set there for 'bout
four or five hours
and then he told her to get up
(*She starts to cry, her voice is very soft*)
and when she got up
she said she couldn't see
(*She cries*)
her face was bruised
(*She is whispering*)
and she had a black eye.
All around her head was just swollen.
Her head looked like it was two sizes
of its own size.
I told him to let her go to sleep,
and he let her go to sleep.
(*She is whispering.*)
The next morning
she was dead.
He went and checked on her
for school.
And he got very excited.
He said,
"She won't breathe."
I knew immediately that she was dead.
(*She is crying.*)
So I went in
I didn't want to accept the fact that she
    was dead.
So I went and took a mirror to her
    mouth.
There was no—thing
coming out of her mouth,
nothing.
He said,
"We cannot let nobody know about
    this.
So you got to help me."
So I agreed.
I agreed.
(*She is crying.*)
We waited that whole day.
She stayed in that room that whole day.
With no medical attention.
I didn't dare tell anyone.
'Cause I had been keeping it a secret
    for years and years.
And this just seemed like secondhand
    to me.
To keep a secret.
That night,
we went to the mall

and we told the
security guards in the mall
that she had been missing
that we had, like, lost her.
You know, we fabricated the story
and I went along with it.
And we told them
what she had on.
That night.
We got her dressed.
In—the—exact—same—thing,
that we told the police that she had on.
And we got the baby.
And my other son.
And we drove
like out to
I-95,
I was so petrified
and so numb
All I could look,
was in the rearview mirror
and he just laid her on the shoulder
of the highway.
My own child

I let that happen to.
The six-year-old,
he
was scared.
He was scared.
It was like livin' in a haunted house
for years and years.
She got killed on the fourth of March,
and no later than the sixth
they had found her and it was over
    with.
We had told the media that she was
    missing
'cause he was like—
"Well, why don't you just go on and
    tell'em that she's missing?"
I confessed to everything
I plead guilty.
I took twenty-five on a plea bargain.
He took
sixty on a plea bargain.
Myeshia's birthday was December
    the 6th.
She would have been nineteen.

A Sam Shepardesque "Fool for Love" Kind of Story
Sherri Rideout

And one time—
And he used to gamble—
Compulsive.
He was a compulsive gambler
and I was a compulsive thief—
And
Tell you what!
My baby
was in the baby crib
'bout two months old
and he had a gun in the baby thing
and I didn't know it was in the baby
    thing
and he came home
running
Dumped the baby over!
This is how crazy this man was!
Could have hurt the baby!
And took the gun out and ran out the
    door.
I been through something!

I been through something with that
    man.
And then one time
me and him was in a motel room?
And he accused me of talking to some
    guy?
And he said that he was gon kill me
I said "Go 'head!
Go—'head—and—kill—me!
Go 'head!
I ain't no good anyway!
I ain't no good!
You wanna kill something that ain't no
    good!
Go 'head and kill it!"
Then he didn't kill me.
Then.
We was at this other motel one time.
And it was snow on the ground.
It was snow on the ground.
We was in the motel room.

He talkin' about he seen me talking to
this guy.
He know the guy want me and all this
crazy stuff.
He told me,
"Come on
This is it!
This is it!
You gon die tonight."
He said, "I'm gon take me a shower
and after that you gon die."
I was strip naked in the motel room.
I ran out the motel room
butterball naked in the snow
with nothing on
to get away from this man.
He had a gun in there!
(*She is laughing.*)
He had a gun!
Oh, man!

Coming to jail
coming in these rooms
and telling people
about what
all he used to do to me
and how I used to let him get away
with it,
how he would be with all these women
and they said,
"Stop letting him run free in your own
head!"
And how he still was
trying to say things
and scare me in some ways.
Eight years
me and this man was together
'cause 15, 16, 17, 18, 19, 20, 21, 22,
23, 24
Nine years.

Integration

The broad part of the prison population is called "population." Those women who accumulate a certain number of "tickets" for disobeying rules are placed on "segregation." Claudia McClain and Tyboria Stones have both been confined to segregation for substantial periods of time.

Tyboria Stones

Tyboria is twenty-six and was charged with raping a woman. She says she didn't do it. ("Why would I want to go out and do something to an old woman like that? When I have a woman?") She is stocky and muscular, with hair trimmed very close on the sides, short and curly on top.

I was in a single room.
They said nobody couldn't be my
    roommate
and the officers making a big thing of it
saying we're gonna put a little boy in
    your room
we ain't puttin' a fem in your room.
A fem
a straight woman.
You know they talking
about a little
boy. . . .
They call us
little boys
'cause we dress like men.
Our hair be like men.

We wear men cologne.
And I think that's wrong.
Saying,
"Don't nobody wanta be Tyboria's
    roommate,"
you know . . .
They don't know nothing about it. . . .
And I had that
I don't care attitude
just keep getting tickets
and getting tickets
and it was like a lot of officers kept
    bothering me
officer throwing piss un'neath my door.
The officers don't want me in population.

Ping-Pong Table

Tyboria came with a history of violence from inside institutions as well as out on the street. She described a run-in with a warden at another facility.

The warden . . .
hit me upside the head,
'cause I wouldn't take off a stocking cap.
And I hit him back
and
I threw him on the Ping-Pong table
in the rec area
and I started chokin' him
punchin' him back

and we got to fightin'
and the backups came in and put shack-
    les on me
and cuffs
and he came in the isolation room
and tried to choke me
and they left me in there for two days
    with the
shackles on and the cuffs on from behind.

When I Was About Six or Seven

I asked her where she thinks her violence comes from.

I don't know why I was into a lot of
    violence
I don't know.
'Cause um
I have a nice mother.
I have a real respectful mother.

Q: What about your father?

My father was a very violent person.
My mother was telling me
he always stayed in jail
for assault and batteries.

He shot this woman
he shot her in her stuff
in her vagina
'cause he found her in bed
with another man.
He had left my mother.
It happened when I was about six or
seven.

Claudia McClain

Claudia came to the interview with a sense of purpose, sitting behind the micro-phone in a formal manner. She is twenty-one years old, and she looks tough, like a bullet. Her head is shaved nearly bald. From a distance she looks like a boy. This is by design.

On the streets, she lived, as she said, "on the edges." She was a drug dealer. She is in prison for shooting Diko, a friend who sold drugs for her, when they were both teenagers. By her account, he had thirteen hundred dollars of hers and refused to give it back. She says Diko drew out his gun and pulled the trigger, but nothing came out. In response, she shot him six times, twice in his head and "the rest" in his upper body.

I mean,
I don't care if Warden Carter reads
    about this—
I mean right is right
and wrong is wrong.
Segregation inmates . . .
You get handcuffed
and locked in a cage.
Like you're really an animal.
Since he (*Warden Carter*)
has been here
you get three showers (*a week*).
Now,
what if a woman is menustratin?
Three showers?
What is that?
And then if a shower happens to fall
    on a day of a holiday
you can't come and take a shower
You don't get rec and showers on a
    holiday.
They have so many holidays
while I was in segregation.
Holidays that didn't speak in the calendar.
If they walk in today and don't feel like
showerin' you

'cause today is Wednesday
and shower day
they say it's a holiday.
And you look on your calendar or holler
    out the window
'cause you see the general population
on a working schedule
and you ask them is it a holiday.
And they say no.
The officer say

it doesn't matter
I say it's a holiday.

It makes you feel unclean.
'Cause
small as the sink
is you not gonna get clean.
Just a little strip a water comes
it comes like this.

(She demonstrates an arc, slowly, with her hand, making eye contact with me. Her look is stern.)

Just Playin'

We got to arguin'
me and Diko
so he brought out a gun on me
and said,
"I ain't givin' you shit."
All I seen was a gun and I seen my life
    flash before me

but each day as I think more and more
    about the situation
you know I'm sayin?
Although he pulled the trigger
and nothing came out
maybe he knew it was blanks in there.
Maybe he was just playin'.

No Longer Lovers

I asked her who called the police on her.

Someone living upstairs on the third
    floor.
This female I used to socialize with
intimately
sexually.
We was no longer lovers though.
One day I come in
and seen her throw something
and my instincts was to see what it was
it was a spike (*a needle*)
and I don't subject myself to that.

I do not involve myself in drugs
I mean usin'.
I don't do drugs.
I don't do alcohol.
So.
I left.

Q: And she didn't like that.

CLAUDIA: I guess not.

Pretty Teeth

(She sits closer to the microphone and increases her volume.)

This is on the record!
We had one girl
she has abscesses and

infections in her mouth.
And this other girl here
she just caught hepatitis.

And you know hepatitis could go away
or you could live with that
for the rest of your life.

But see I have pretty teeth
so I don't have to worry.

    (*She smiles, baring her teeth. They
are quite pretty.*)

The Tour of Segregation
Lieutenant Somerville-Jones

*The Lieutenant is an attractive black woman who "loves her job." She has been
at M.C.I.W. for nine years. Our first stop is the segregation wing. The officer on
duty is a large black woman with small black glasses. Her uniform is not clean. She
is wearing a small black knit ski cap. She is the keeper of the hall. The women are
locked into rooms with brown doors that are controlled electronically. There is a
small, thick glass window on each door. There is a slot the size of a small food tray
a little below waist high. If the slot is opened, the women talk can through it.
Otherwise, they communicate by yelling at the top of their lungs or screaming to
each other through the vents. The rooms have a toilet, a bed, and very little else.
The officer seems in good spirits, and so does Lieutenant Somerville-Jones. As the
women realize that she has entered, they start to scream. They all have requests.
One needs a cigarette, one needs to see the doctor, another has a grievance about
an officer, etc. I was surprised at how quickly the entire wing realized Lieutenant
was there. And I was stunned when they realized she had a visitor.*

    *Lt. S.-J. and I stoop down to the slot in order to talk. The woman we talk to
is sitting with her face at the slot. She is light-skinned black woman. She begins to
talk as if she had a very important role in a play or pageant.*

I wan tell you . . .
What I want to say is

That things here
Bein' here at this institution
There's a lot of things
that's not supposed to be done!
Far as like
the way we are being treated here—
like animals!
We get treated like animals!
As for the uh
the hygienes
your hygienes . . .
I been on lock

for two years and ten
months
in segregation . . .
These—officers—
they—egg—us—on
they—lie—on—us . . .
And you don't get showers every day
  here
you get showers three times a week
on segregation.

Within These Fences
Terri

*Terri is the only white woman I interviewed. She preferred not to use her real
name. She is composed and well spoken, has sparkling blue eyes, and is immacu-
lately groomed. She has a life sentence.*

Every single morning
when I go to work,
you can see this fire in the sky,
and I think of my grandmother and my
    grandfather.
And also the birds!
When I hear the birds chirping
I think of my grandmother
who I always thought was an angel.

She would always feed the birds
from her balcony
throwing bread crumbs
so there are things
within these fences
that remind
me of good memories
and loved ones from the past.

Hoppers

You know the housing unit I live on is
    the pits
A
Wing
You have all the
maximum security inmates
and it's where you have all the ticket
    maxes
people that constantly stay in trouble
that are on and off of lock.
So they have all the misfits
and outcasts
that they can't control
They're just loud
They're obnoxious
and just downright disgusting
They're hoppers.
They're buck wild.
Sometimes I have to laugh at 'em.
There are people who have been here
    a long time
that have a lot of time
they aren't troublesome people
they don't get into trouble
they don't look for trouble
they don't follow trouble
and they stay out of trouble

I don't think it's fair that they keep
    them on A Wing
with all the misfits
and the ticket maxes
and all the trouble
I mean we
have to be here
and we're gonna be here for a while
for now we have to be here
and we have to make the best of a bad
    situation
I'm trying to live
as normal a life
as I can possibly live
by getting up every morning
and going to work
and just
and coming in and gettin' your shower
and maybe going to dinner and going
    to school
and then in hopes
of quiet time for an hour
and then getting up and doing it all
    over again
and I just think it's so unfair
that I have to be in an environment
    like that.

Officer on Duty

Warden Carter told me that in 1939, when the prison was built, it was racially segregated, and there "was a handful—maybe twenty" women. The officers were called matrons. There were no security fences until the late sixties.

Lt. S.-J. and I walked around the grounds (called the campus). It was snow-covered and looked exactly like a college, with red brick buildings spaced apart. She yelled out to another officer who had agreed to go pick up her mother, since she'd be staying late with me. That's exactly the Baltimore I remember, a community where folks did favors for one another all the time. Inside these fences, however, a favor for the inmates was loaded. And a favor between officers and inmates could be a disaster. Lt. S.-J. had a kind of confidence about her relationship with the women. I asked her what the crux of it was. "They know I'm fair," she said.

I learned from her that it is often unclear how long a "life sentence" actually is.

Six Numbers
Lt. Somerville-Jones

I can't
judge somebody else
that's what I had to learn
about working in a prison.
I had a problem dealing with the crimes
    that these people had committed.
I was bothered by child murderers.
But I had to do some soul-searching.
Our job is not to judge anybody.
No one can ever say what they won't do.
Because you don't know what a person
    goes through.
Everyone here has six numbers.
There's no big crime
and there's no little crime.
There's no black crime.
There's no white crime.
Not everybody in here is a criminal.
You have people here who have done
    some horrendous things
and they deserve to be here.
But
let's say
last night
when the weather was real bad.
And you go up here to 175.
And you look left and right.
You don't see anything.

You pull out.
You hit a car.
And you kill a little old lady.
You're coming to jail for vehicular
    manslaughter.
So does that make you a criminal?
You have a lot of tragedies here.
I mean
to me
all of'em is tragedies
especially
the teen-agers.
I mean
high-school kids
who had lives
and now they have six numbers.
I'm a Baptist.
I believe in God
and I pray
I pray for the girls every night
on my knees.
Yes I do.
I ask Him to bless everybody
and
let So-and-So get through this time.
And what I want to know is,
how long is life? ◆

45

Black English/Ebonics: What It Be Like?

An introduction to some of the social complexities of language, "Black English/Ebonics" from The Real Ebonics Debate: Power, Language, and the Education of African American Children *addresses a few linguistic patterns and rhetorical strategies in Ebonics or African American English. In this article, Geneva Smitherman, Director of the African American Language and Literacy Program at Michigan State University, demonstrates how language practices of marginalized groups and the political debates that surround those practices constitute rich sites for intellectual inquiry.*

> *I looked at my hands, they looked new*
> *I looked at my feet, and they did too*
> *I got a new way of walkin, and a new way*
>   *of talkin.*

> *Traditional Black Gospel Song*

The month after the Oakland school board passed its resolution, the term *Ebonics* turned twenty-four years old. Yeah, dass right, the name is over two decades old. It was coined by a group of Black scholars as a new way of talkin bout the language of African slave descendants. Like the message of that old Gospel tune, "Ebonics" was about transformation, about intellectuals among the Talented Tenth striking a blow for the linguistic liberation of our people. The

547

guru in this group of scholars at that "Language and the Urban Child" conference, convened in St. Louis, Missouri, in January 1973, was the brilliant clinical psychologist, Dr. Robert L. Williams, now Professor Emeritus, Washington University. In the book of conference proceedings Williams published in 1975, he captures the thinking of that historical moment:

> *A significant incident occurred at the conference. The black conferees were so critical of the work on the subject done by white researchers, many of whom also happened to be present, that they decided to caucus among themselves and define black language from a black perspective. It was in this caucus that the term* Ebonics *was created. [The term refers to] linguistic and paralinguistic features which on a concentric continuum represent the communicative competence of the West African, Caribbean, and United States slave descendant of African origin. It includes the various idioms, patois, argots, ideolects, and social dialects of black people, especially those who have been forced to adapt to colonial circumstances. (1975, Preface, Introduction)*

For this group of scholars, the conceptual framework of "Ebonics" represented an avenue for decolonization of the African-American mind, a way to begin repairing the psycholinguistically maimed psyche of Blacks in America. As Paulo Freire (1985) would put it twelve years later, "language variations (female language, ethnic language, dialects) are intimately interconnected with, coincide with, and express identity. They help defend one's sense of identity and they are absolutely necessary in the process of struggling for liberation" (p. 186). Ebonics reaffirms the inter-relatedness of language and culture and links Africans in America with Africans around the globe.

Ebonics: neither "broken" English, nor "sloppy" speech, nor merely "slang," nor some bizarre lingo spoken only by baggy-pants-wearing Black kids. Rather, the variety of Ebonics spoken in the United States (hereafter USEB) is rooted in the Black American Oral Tradition and represents a synthesis of African (primarily West African) and European (primarily English) linguistic-cultural traditions. The linguistic shape of the words in USEB can readily be identified as Standard English, that is, the Language of Wider Communication here in the United States (hereafter LWC), but these words do not always have the same meaning in USEB as in LWC. Further, there are many words of direct African origin—for example, *okay, gorilla, cola, jazz*—that are now part of LWC (often without props to us African slave descendants). However, what gives Black Language (un-huh, dat ain no typo, I meant "language") its distinctiveness is the nuanced meanings of these English words, the pronunciations, the ways in which the words are combined to form grammatical statements, and the communicative practices of the USEB-speaking community. In short, USEB may be thought of as the Africanization of American English.

Patterns of Ebonics

In the next section, I discuss the following patterns of USEB: (1) aspectual be; (2) stressed *been*; (3) multiple negation; (4) adjacency/context in possessives; (5) postvocalic /r/ deletion; (6) copula absence; (7) camouflaged and other unique lexical forms.

Consider this statement, which comes from some Black women just kickin it in the beauty shop (gloss: conversational chit-chat at a hair salon): "The Brotha be lookin good; that's what got the Sista nose open!" In this statement, *Brotha* is USEB for an African-American man, *lookin good* refers to his style, his attractive appearance (not necessarily the same thing as physical beauty in USEB), *Sista* is USEB for an African-American woman, and her passionate love for the Brotha is conveyed by the phrase *nose open* (in USEB, the kind of passionate love that makes you vulnerable to exploitation). *Sista nose* is standard USEB grammar for denoting possession, indicated by adjacency/context (that is, rather than the LWC /'s, s'/). The use of *be* means that the quality of *lookin good* is not limited to the present moment but reflects the Brotha's past, present, and future essence. As in the case of Efik and other Niger-Congo languages, USEB has an aspectual verb system, conveyed by the use of the English verb *be* to denote iterativity (that is, a recurring or habitual state-of-affairs; contrast *He be lookin good* with *He lookin good,* which refers to the present moment only—not the kind of *lookin good* that opens the nose!). Note further that many Black writers and Rap artists employ the spellings "Brotha" and "Sista." Now, they ain just tryin to be cute. These orthographic representations are used to convey a phonological pattern derived from the influence of West African languages, many of which do not have an /r/ sound. Also in these language communities, kinship terms may be used when referring to African people, whether biologically related or not.

Of course there is overlap between USEB and colloquial, everyday American English—for example, use of "ain't," ending sentences with prepositions, double negatives. However, there are critical distinctions that separate linguistically competent USEB speakers from the wannabes. For example, the colloquial speaker says *gonna* or *goin to* for the LWC form *going to.* But the USEB speaker uses the nasalized vowel form, producing a sound close to, but not identical with, LWC *gone,* thus: "What she go (n) do now?," that is, in LWC, "What is she going to do now?" Another example is in negation patterns. While those obsessed with the "national mania for correctness" often rail against colloquial speakers' double negatives, USEB is distinctive not only for its negative inversion, but also for its *multiple* negatives, that is, three or more negatives formed from combinations of indefinite pronouns and/or adjectives. Check out this exclamation of complex negative inversion from a devout church-goer: "Don't nobody don't know God can't tell me nothin!.," that is, in LWC, "A person who doesn't believe in God and isn't saved has no credibility with me."

As mentioned above, USEB words may look like mainstream American English, but the usage and meaning are different. This is the source of a good deal of miscommunication and misunderstanding between USEB and LWC speakers. In response to the question, "Is she married?," the USEB speaker may answer "She been married." If the speaker pronounces *been* without stress, it means the woman in question was once married but is now divorced. If the speaker pronounces *been* with stress, it means she married a long time ago and is still married. Another example is the use of LWC words that are "camouflaged" (Spears, 1982). For example, in the USEB statement, "She come tellin me I'n [didn't] know what I was talkin bout," the verb *come* does not denote motion as in LWC. Rather the meaning of *come* in this context is one of indignation, that is, in LWC, "She had the audacity to tell me that I didn't know what I was talking about. How dare she!" Yet another kind of cross communication example comes from semantic inversion. Due to crossover and the popular appeal of Michael Jackson, most people are aware that *bad* in USEB translates to *good* in LWC; however, lexical items that haven't enjoyed such a high degree of crossover are problematic in these crosscultural exchanges. For example, consider the following form of address common among many Black males; "Yo, Dog!" *Dog* is a linguistic symbol of male bonding, most likely derived from the African-American fraternity tradition of referring to pledges as *dogs*. *Yo, Dog!* was used by a Brotha on lock down (gloss: imprisoned) to address his European-American male psychiatrist as an expression of camaraderie. Turns out, though, that this white psychiatrist was not yet down (gloss: hip, understanding of the Black Cultural framework). He misinterpreted the Brotha's greeting and made an issue of the "insult."

The above are only some of the patterns in the grammatical, phonological, and semantic systems of USEB. To explore the full 360 degrees of USEB, we need to move on to styles of speaking. In fact, it is the area of communicative practices— rhetorical strategies and modes of discourse—that cuts across gender, generation, and class in the African-American community. USEB speech acts may be classified as follows: (1) Call-Response; (2) Tonal Semantics; (3) Narrativizing; (4) Proverb Use/Proverbializing; (5) Signification/Signifyin; (6) The Dozens/Snappin/Joanin. Discussion of two of these discourse modes follows.

Signification or, more commonly, *signifyin,* which can be rendered with or without the phonological and morphosyntactical patterns of USEB, is a form of ritualized insult in which a speaker puts down, talks about, needles—signifies on— other speakers. In this communicative practice, the speaker deploys exaggeration, irony, and indirection as a way of saying something on two different levels at once. It is often used to send a message of social critique, a bit of social commentary on the actions or statements of someone who is in need of a wake-up call. When signifyin is done with verbal dexterity, it avoids the creation of social distance between speaker and audience because the rich humor makes you laugh to keep from crying. Like Malcolm X who once began a speech with these words: "Mr. Moderator, Brother Lomax, Brothas and Sistas, friends and enemies." Now, you don't usually begin a speech by addressing your enemies. Thus, Malcolm's signifyin statement let his audience know that he knew inimical forces were in their midst. Or like one of the deacons at this Traditional Black Church, where the preacher would never deal with the problems and issues folk were facing on a daily basis. Rather, he was always preachin bout the pearly gates and how great thangs was gon be at dat home up in the sky. So one day this deacon said to the preacher, "Reb, you know, I got a home in Heaven, but I ain't homesick!"

Signifyin is engaged in by all age groups and by both males and females in the Black community. It has the following characteristics: (1) indirection, circumlocution; (2) metaphorical-imagistic (images rooted in the everyday real world); (3) humorous, ironic; (4) rhythmic fluency; (5) teachy, but not preachy; (6) directed at person(s) present in the speech situation (signifiers do not talk behind your back); (7) punning, play on words; (8) introduction of the semantically or logically unexpected.

Types of Signification

There are two types of Signification. One type is leveled at a person's mother (and occasionally at other relatives). Traditionally, this first type was referred to as "The Dozens"/"playin The Dozens." The second type of signifyin is aimed at a person, action, or thing, either just for fun or for corrective criticism. Today, the two types of Signification are being conflated under a more general form of discourse, referred to as "snappin."

To fully appreciate the skill and complexity of Signification, we shall analyze in some detail a conversational excerpt involving two Sistas in a group of several at a wedding shower:

LINDA: Girl, what up with that head? [Referring to her friend's hairstyle.]

BETTY: Ask yo momma. [Laughter from all the Sistas on this conversational set.]

LINDA: Oh, so you going there, huh? Well, I *DID* ask my momma. And she said, "Cain't you see that Betty look like her momma spit her out?" [Laughter from all, including Betty.]

Betty and Linda signify on each other. Instead of answering Linda's question directly, Betty decides to inform Linda that the condition of her hairstyle is none of Linda's business by responding with "Ask yo momma." The usual expectation in a conversation is that a speaker's question will be answered honestly and sincerely; thus Betty's unexpected indirection produces laughter from the listeners.

Speech act theory indicates that communication succeeds or fails as a result of the illocutionary (that is, intended) and perlocutionary (that is, received) effects of a message. The surface meaning of "yo momma" for those outside the USEB speech community is simply "your mother/mom." However, within the Black speech community, the utterance immediately signals that an insult has been hurled. The intended and received meaning of *yo momma* is invective; the game of ritual insult begins with participants creating the most appropriate, humorous, spontaneous, creative, exaggerated/untrue retorts that they can come up with.

The source of the retort "Ask yo momma" probably stems from family patterns in which mothers are consulted ("asked") about all kinds of things, great or small. Fathers may even respond to their children's questions or requests by saying "Ask your mother." In USEB, the speaker does not intend the direct meaning, "You should go and ask your mother about this situation." Rather, given the conversational context, the speaker is indirectly saying "Let the game of The Dozens begin." Linda clearly recognizes the entry into this game as indicated by her response, "Oh, so you going there, huh?" Unskilled players, lacking a spontaneous, apposite, humorous retort, would have let the conversation end at this point. However, Linda shows adeptness in playing the game. She regroups momentarily ("Oh, so you going there, huh?") and fires back skillfully. In fact, she "caps" (gloss: wins) this exchange with a more clever retort. Although Betty's use of the intragroup expression, *ask yo momma,* is humorous and sets up a challenge, it is formulaic, simplistic, and stylized. In this instance, it cannot, and does not, beat:

"Well, I *DID* ask my momma. And she said, 'Cain't you see that Betty look like her momma spit her out?'" (Troutman-Robinson and Smitherman, 1997).

Although Rev. Jesse Jackson and Sista Maya Angelou came out in the national news and dissed the Oakland school board's resolution, they are well versed in USEB. Twenty years ago, in my first major work on USEB, *Talkin and Testifyin,* I quoted both at length and lauded them as linguistic role models, who are adept at capitalizing on the forms of Black Language to convey profound political messages. Like Jesse who is down wit Signification: "Pimp, punk, prostitute, preacher, Ph.D.—all the P's, you still in slavery!" Thus he conveys the message that all members of the African-American community, regardless of their social status, are marginalized and disempowered, by virtue of U.S. historically institutionalized racism and skin color bias. (Jesse also uses copula absence here—"you still in slavery"—which has not been found in any of the dialects of British English that came over on the *Mayflower,* but which is used widely in the languages of West Africa.)

The Dozens

As mentioned above, The Dozens is one of several significant speech acts in USEB. This ritualized game of insult has analogues in West African communicative practices (see Smitherman, 1995, and the several reference cited there). Also referred to as "snappin" by many members of the Hip Hop Nation, The Dozens is like "Yo momma so dumb she thought a quarterback was a refund!"

Sista Maya Angelou is so bad she don't play The Dozens, she play The Thirteens! She uses this USEB discourse mode to critique the actions of Blacks and whites. Here how she do it:

> *(The Thirteens Black):*
>
> *Your Momma took to shouting*
>
> *Your Poppa's gone to war,*
>
> *Your sister's in the streets*
>
> *Your brother's in the bar,*
>
> *The thirteens. Right On . . .*
>
> *And you, you make me sorry*
>
> *You out here by yourself,*
>
> *I'd call you something dirty,*
>
> *But there just ain't nothing left,*
>
> *cept*
>
> *The thirteens. Right On . . .*
>
> *(The Thirteens White):*
>
> *Your daughter wears a jock strap,*
>
> *Your son he wears a bra*

Your brother jonesed your cousin

in the back seat of the car.

The thirteens. Right On . . .

Your money thinks you're something

But if I'd learned to curse,

I'd tell you what your name is

But there just ain't nothing worse

than

The thirteens. Right On.

(Angelou, 1971)

African-French psychiatrist Frantz Fanon (1967) taught that "every dialect, every language, is a way of thinking. To speak means to assume a culture." To speak Ebonics is to assume the cultural legacy of U.S. slave descendants of African origin. To speak Ebonics is to assert the power of this tradition in the quest to resolve the unfinished business of being African in America. While years of massive research (done in the 1960s and early 1970s) on the language of this group (mostly by white scholars) did indeed debunk cognitive-linguistic deficiency theory, in its place arose social inadequacy theory. Although the language was shown to be systematic and rule-governed, since it is not accepted by the white mainstream, difference became deficit all over again, and in the process, Africans in America suffered further dislocation. To speak (of/on/about) Ebonics, to consciously employ this terminology and conceptual framework, as those Black scholars did back in 1973, and as the Oakland school board has done a generation later, is to be bout the business of relocating African Americans to subject position. Large and in charge, as the Hip Hoppers say, Ebonics, then and now, symbolizes a new way of talkin the walk about language and liberatory education for African Americans.

References

Angelou, M. (1971). *Just Give Me a Cool Drink of Water 'fore I Die*. New York: Random House.

Fanon, F. (1967). The Negro and Language. In *Black Skin, White Masks*. New York: Grove Press.

Freire, P. (1985). *The Politics of Education: Culture, Power, and Liberation* (D. Macedo, Trans.). Massachusetts: Bergin & Garvey Publishers, now an imprint of Greenwood Publishing Group, Westport, CT.

Smitherman, G. (1977, 1986). *Talkin and Testifyin: The Language of Black America*. Detroit: Wayne State University Press.

Smitherman, G. (1995). Introduction. In J. Percelay, S. Dweck, and M. Ivey, *Double Snaps*. New York: William Morrow.

Spears, A. K. (1982). The Black English Semi-Auxiliary Come. *Language 58*(4), 850–872.

Troutman-Robinson, D., & Smitherman, G. (1997). Discourse as Social Interaction. In T. A. van Dijk (Ed.), *Discourse, Ethnicity, Culture, and Racism.* (pp. 144–180). London: Sage Publications.

Williams, R. L. (Ed.). (1975). *Ebonics: The True Language of Black Folks.* St. Louis: Institute of Black Studies.

46

Regarding the Torture of Others

SUSAN SONTAG

Author of multiple books and an expert on photography, Susan Sontag originally published "Regarding the Torture of Others" in a 2004 issue of The New York Times Magazine. *This feature article shows how images of American soldiers torturing Iraqi prisoners provide evidence of the abuses that inevitably happen in war and how they implicate the U.S. leadership and citizenry in the torture depicted. This essay argues for recognizing the ethical responsibilities that come from critical encounters with images.*

I.

For a long time—at least six decades—photographs have laid down the tracks of how important conflicts are judged and remembered. The Western memory museum is now mostly a visual one. Photographs have an insuperable power to determine what we recall of events, and it now seems probable that the defining association of people everywhere with the war that the United States launched pre-emptively in Iraq last year will be photographs of the torture of Iraqi prisoners by Americans in the most infamous of Saddam Hussein's prisons, Abu Ghraib.

The Bush administration and its defenders have chiefly sought to limit a public-relations disaster—the dissemination of the photographs—rather than deal

*An Iraqi detainee at Abu Ghraib: The horror of what
is shown in the photographs cannot be separated from
the horror that the photographs were taken.*

with the complex crimes of leadership and of policy revealed by the pictures. There was, first of all, the displacement of the reality onto the photographs themselves. The administration's initial response was to say that the president was shocked and disgusted by the photographs—as if the fault or horror lay in the images, not in what they depict. There was also the avoidance of the word "torture." The prisoners had possibly been the objects of "abuse," eventually of "humiliation"—that was the most to be admitted. "My impression is that what has been charged thus far is abuse, which I believe technically is different from torture," Secretary of Defense Donald Rumsfeld said at a press conference. "And therefore I'm not going to address the 'torture' word."

Words alter, words add, words subtract. It was the strenuous avoidance of the word "genocide" while some 800,000 Tutsis in Rwanda were being slaughtered, over a few weeks' time, by their Hutu neighbors 10 years ago that indicated the American government had no intention of doing anything. To refuse to call what took place in Abu Ghraib—and what has taken place elsewhere in Iraq and in Afghanistan and at Guantánamo Bay—by its true name, torture, is as outrageous as the refusal to call the Rwandan genocide a genocide. Here is one of the definitions of torture contained in a convention to which the United States is a signatory: *"any act by which severe pain or suffering, whether physical or mental, is intentionally inflicted on a person for such purposes as obtaining from him or a third person information or a confession."* (The definition comes from the 1984 Convention Against Torture and Other Cruel, Inhuman or Degrading Treatment or Punishment. Similar definitions have existed for some time in customary law and in treaties, starting with Article 3—common to the four Geneva conventions of 1949—and many recent human rights conventions.) The 1984 convention declares, *"No exceptional circumstances whatsoever, whether a state of war or a threat of war, internal political instability or any other public emergency, may be invoked as a justification of torture."* And all covenants on torture specify that it includes treatment intended to humiliate the victim, like leaving prisoners naked in cells and corridors.

Whatever actions this administration undertakes to limit the damage of the widening revelations of the torture of prisoners in Abu Ghraib and elsewhere—trials, courts-martial, dishonorable discharges, resignation of senior military figures and responsible administration officials and substantial compensation to the victims—it is probable that the "torture" word will continue to be banned. To acknowledge that Americans torture their prisoners would contradict everything this administration has invited the public to believe about the virtue of American intentions and America's right, flowing from that virtue, to undertake unilateral action on the world stage.

Even when the president was finally compelled, as the damage to America's reputation everywhere in the world widened and deepened, to use the "sorry" word, the focus of regret still seemed the damage to America's claim to moral superiority. Yes, President Bush said in Washington on May 6, standing alongside King Abdullah II of Jordan, he was "sorry for the humiliation suffered by the Iraqi prisoners and the humiliation suffered by their families." But, he went on, he was "equally sorry that people seeing these pictures didn't understand the true nature and heart of America."

To have the American effort in Iraq summed up by these images must seem, to those who saw some justification in a war that did overthrow one of the monster tyrants of modern times, "unfair." A war, an occupation, is inevitably a huge tapestry of actions. What makes some actions representative and others not? The issue is not whether the torture was done by individuals (i.e., "not by everybody")—but whether it was systematic. Authorized. Condoned. All acts are done by individuals. The issue is not whether a majority or a minority of Americans performs such acts but whether the nature of the policies prosecuted by this administration and the hierarchies deployed to carry them out makes such acts likely.

II.

Considered in this light, the photographs are us. That is, they are representative of the fundamental corruptions of any foreign occupation together with the Bush administration's distinctive policies. The Belgians in the Congo, the French in Algeria, practiced torture and sexual humiliation on despised recalcitrant natives. Add to this generic corruption the mystifying, near-total unpreparedness of the American rulers of Iraq to deal with the complex realities of the country after its "liberation." And add to that the overarching, distinctive doctrines of the Bush administration, namely that the United States has embarked on an endless war and that those detained in this war are, if the president so decides, "unlawful combatants"—a policy enunciated by Donald Rumsfeld for Taliban and Qaeda prisoners as early as January 2002—and thus, as Rumsfeld said, "technically" they "do not have any rights under the Geneva Convention," and you have a perfect recipe for the cruelties and crimes committed against the thousands incarcerated without charges or access to lawyers in American-run prisons that have been set up since the attacks of Sept. 11, 2001.

So, then, is the real issue not the photographs themselves but what the photographs reveal to have happened to "suspects" in American custody? No: the horror of what is shown in the photographs cannot be separated from the horror that the photographs were taken—with the perpetrators posing, gloating, over their helpless captives. German soldiers in the Second World War took photographs of the atrocities they were committing in Poland and Russia, but snapshots in which the executioners placed themselves among their victims are exceedingly rare, as may be seen in a book just published, "Photographing the Holocaust," by Janina Struk. If there is something comparable to what these pictures show it would be some of the photographs of black victims of lynching taken between the 1880's and 1930's, which show Americans grinning beneath the naked mutilated body of a black man or woman hanging behind them from a tree. The lynching photographs were souvenirs of a collective action whose participants felt perfectly justified in what they had done. So are the pictures from Abu Ghraib.

The lynching pictures were in the nature of photographs as trophies—taken by a photographer in order to be collected, stored in albums, displayed. The pictures taken by American soldiers in Abu Ghraib, however, reflect a shift in the use made of pictures—less objects to be saved than messages to be disseminated, circulated. A digital camera is a common possession among soldiers. Where once photographing war was the province of photojournalists, now the soldiers themselves are all photographers—recording their war, their fun, their observations of what they find picturesque, their atrocities—and swapping images among themselves and e-mailing them around the globe.

There is more and more recording of what people do, by themselves. At least or especially in America, Andy Warhol's ideal of filming real events in real time—life isn't edited, why should its record be edited?—has become a norm for countless Webcasts, in which people record their day, each in his or her own reality show. Here I am—waking and yawning and stretching, brushing my teeth, making breakfast, getting the kids off to school. People record all aspects of their lives, store them in computer files and send the files around. Family life goes with the recording of family life—even when, or especially when, the family is in the throes of crisis and disgrace. Surely the dedicated, incessant home-videoing of one another, in conversation and monologue, over many years was the most astonishing mate-

At left, most of the pictures, like this one of simulated sex, seem part of a larger confluence of torture and pornography. On the right, showing the pictures uncropped gives a different and in some instances more appalling view.

rial in "Capturing the Friedmans," the recent documentary by Andrew Jarecki about a Long Island family embroiled in pedophilia charges.

An erotic life is, for more and more people, that whither can be captured in digital photographs and on video. And perhaps the torture is more attractive, as something to record, when it has a sexual component. It is surely revealing, as more Abu Ghraib photographs enter public view, that torture photographs are interleaved with pornographic images of American soldiers having sex with one another. In fact, most of the torture photographs have a sexual theme, as in those showing the coercing of prisoners to perform, or simulate, sexual acts among themselves. One exception, already canonical, is the photograph of the man made to stand on a box, hooded and sprouting wires, reportedly told he would be electrocuted if he fell off. Yet pictures of prisoners bound in painful positions, or made to stand with outstretched arms, are infrequent. That they count as torture cannot be doubted. You have only to look at the terror on the victim's face, although such "stress" fell within the Pentagon's limits of the acceptable. But most of the pictures seem part of a larger confluence of torture and pornography: a young woman leading a naked man around on a leash is classic dominatrix imagery. And you wonder how much of the sexual tortures inflicted on the inmates of Abu Ghraib was inspired by the vast repertory of pornographic imagery available on the Internet—and which ordinary people, by sending out Webcasts of themselves, try to emulate.

III.

To live is to be photographed, to have a record of one's life, and therefore to go on with one's life oblivious, or claiming to be oblivious, to the camera's nonstop attentions. But to live is also to pose. To act is to share in the community of actions recorded as images. The expression of satisfaction at the acts of torture being inflicted on helpless, trussed, naked victims is only part of the story. There is the

What formerly was segregated as pornography, as the exercise of extreme sadomasochistic longings, is being normalized, by some, as high-spirited play or venting.

deep satisfaction of being photographed, to which one is now more inclined to respond not with a stiff, direct gaze (as in former times) but with glee. The events are in part designed to be photographed. The grin is a grin for the camera. There would be something missing if, after stacking the naked men, you couldn't take a picture of them.

Looking at these photographs, you ask yourself, How can someone grin at the sufferings and humiliation of another human being? Set guard dogs at the genitals and legs of cowering naked prisoners? Force shackled, hooded prisoners to masturbate or simulate oral sex with one another? And you feel naïve for asking, since the answer is, self-evidently, People do these things to other people. Rape and pain inflicted on the genitals are among the most common forms of torture. Not just in Nazi concentration camps and in Abu Ghraib when it was run by Saddam Hussein. Americans, too, have done and do them when they are told, or made to feel, that those over whom they have absolute power deserve to be humiliated, tormented. They do them when they are led to believe that the people they are torturing belong to an inferior race or religion. For the meaning of these pictures is not just that these acts were performed, but that their perpetrators apparently had no sense that there was anything wrong in what the pictures show.

Even more appalling, since the pictures were meant to be circulated and seen by many people: it was all fun. And this idea of fun is, alas, more and more—contrary to what President Bush is telling the world—part of "the true nature and heart of America." It is hard to measure the increasing acceptance of brutality in American life, but its evidence is everywhere, starting with the video games of killing that are a principal entertainment of boys—can the video game "Interrogating the Terrorists" really be far behind?—and on to the violence that has become endemic in the group rites of youth on an exuberant kick. Violent crime is down, yet the easy delight taken in violence seems to have grown. From the harsh torments inflicted on incoming students in many American suburban high schools—depicted in Richard Linklater's 1993 film, "Dazed and Confused"—to the hazing rituals of physical brutality and sexual humiliation in college fraternities and on sports teams, America has become a country in which the fantasies and the practice of violence are seen as good entertainment, fun.

What formerly was segregated as pornography, as the exercise of extreme sado-masochistic longings—as in Pier Paolo Pasolini's last, near-unwatchable film, "Salò" (1975), depicting orgies of torture in the Fascist redoubt in northern Italy at the end of the Mussolini era—is now being normalized, by some, as high-spirited play or venting. To "stack naked men" is like a college fraternity prank, said a caller to Rush Limbaugh and the many millions of Americans who listen to his radio show. Had the caller, one wonders, seen the photographs? No matter. The observation—or is it the fantasy?—was on the mark. What may still be capable of shocking some Americans was Limbaugh's response: "Exactly!" he exclaimed. "Exactly my point. This is no different than what happens at the Skull and Bones initiation, and we're going to ruin people's lives over it, and we're going to hamper our military effort, and then we are going to really hammer them because they had a good time." "They" are the American soldiers, the torturers. And Limbaugh went on: "You know, these people are being fired at every day. I'm talking about people having a good time, these people. You ever heard of emotional release?"

Shock and awe were what our military promised the Iraqis. And shock and the awful are what these photographs announce to the world that the Americans have delivered: a pattern of criminal behavior in open contempt of international humanitarian conventions. Soldiers now pose, thumbs up, before the atrocities they commit, and send off the pictures to their buddies. Secrets of private life that, formerly, you would have given nearly anything to conceal, you now clamor to be invited on a television show to reveal. What is illustrated by these photographs is as much the culture of shamelessness as the reigning admiration for unapologetic brutality.

IV.

The notion that apologies or professions of "disgust" by the president and the secretary of defense are a sufficient response is an insult to one's historical and moral sense. The torture of prisoners is not an aberration. It is a direct consequence of the with-us-or-against-us doctrines of world struggle with which the Bush administration has sought to change, change radically, the international stance of the United States and to recast many domestic institutions and prerogatives. The Bush administration has committed the country to a pseudo-religious doctrine of war, endless war—for "the war on terror" is nothing less than that. Endless war is taken to justify endless incarcerations. Those held in the extralegal American penal empire are "detainees"; "prisoners," a newly obsolete word, might suggest that they have the rights accorded by international law and the laws of all civilized countries. This endless "global war on terrorism"—into which both the quite justified invasion of Afghanistan and the unwinnable folly in Iraq have been folded by Pentagon decree—inevitably leads to the demonizing and dehumanizing of anyone declared by the Bush administration to be a possible terrorist: a definition that is not up for debate and is, in fact, usually made in secret.

The charges against most of the people detained in the prisons in Iraq and Afghanistan being non-existent—the Red Cross reports that 70 to 90 percent of those being held seem to have committed no crime other than simply being in the wrong place at the wrong time, caught up in some sweep of "suspects"—the principal justification for holding them is "interrogation." Interrogation about what? About anything. Whatever the detainee might know. If interrogation is the point of detaining prisoners indefinitely, then physical coercion, humiliation and torture become inevitable.

Remember: we are not talking about that rarest of cases, the "ticking time bomb" situation, which is sometimes used as a limiting case that justifies torture of prisoners who have knowledge of an imminent attack. This is general or nonspecific information-gathering, authorized by American military and civilian administrators to learn more of a shadowy empire of evildoers about whom Americans know virtually nothing, in countries about which they are singularly ignorant: in principle, any information at all might be useful. An interrogation that produced no information (whatever information might consist of) would count as a failure. All the more justification for preparing prisoners to talk. Softening them up, stressing them out—these are the euphemisms for the bestial practices in American prisons where suspected terrorists are being held. Unfortunately, as Staff Sgt. Ivan (Chip) Frederick noted in his diary, a prisoner can get too stressed out and die.

The picture of a man in a body bag with ice on his chest may well be of the man Frederick was describing.

The pictures will not go away. That is the nature of the digital world in which we live. Indeed, it seems they were necessary to get our leaders to acknowledge that they had a problem on their hands. After all, the conclusions of reports compiled by the International Committee of the Red Cross, and other reports by journalists and protests by humanitarian organizations about the atrocious punishments inflicted on "detainees" and "suspected terrorists" in prisons run by the American military, first in Afghanistan and later in Iraq, have been circulating for more than a year. It seems doubtful that such reports were read by President Bush or Vice President Dick Cheney or Condoleezza Rice or Rumsfeld. Apparently it took the photographs to get their attention, when it became clear they could not be suppressed; it was the photographs that made all this "real" to Bush and his associates. Up to then, there had been only words, which are easier to cover up in our age of infinite digital self-reproduction and self-dissemination, and so much easier to forget.

So now the pictures will continue to "assault" us—as many Americans are bound to feel. Will people get used to them? Some Americans are already saying they have seen enough. Not, however, the rest of the world. Endless war: endless stream of photographs. Will editors now debate whether showing more of them, or showing them uncropped (which, with some of the best-known images, like that of a hooded man on a box, gives a different and in some instances more appalling view), would be in "bad taste" or too implicitly political? By "political," read: critical of the Bush administration's imperial project. For there can be no doubt that the photographs damage, as Rumsfeld testified, "the reputation of the honorable men and women of the armed forces who are courageously and responsibly and professionally defending our freedom across the globe." This damage—to our reputation, or image, our success as the lone superpower—is what the Bush administration principally deplores. How the protection of "our freedom"—the freedom of 5 percent of humanity—came to require having American soldiers "across the globe" is hardly debated by our elected officials.

Already the backlash has begun. Americans are being warned against indulging in an orgy of self-condemnation. The continuing publication of the pictures is being taken by many Americans as suggesting that we do not have the right to defend ourselves: after all, they (the terrorists) started it. They—Osama bin Laden? Saddam Hussein? what's the difference?—attacked us first. Senator James Inhofe of Oklahoma, a Republican member of the Senate Armed Services Committee, before which Secretary Rumsfeld testified, avowed that he was sure he was not the only member of the committee "more outraged by the outrage" over the photographs than by what the photographs show. "These prisoners," Senator Inhofe explained, "you know they're not there for traffic violations. If they're in Cellblock 1-A or 1-B, these prisoners, they're murderers, they're terrorists, they're insurgents. Many of them probably have American blood on their hands, and here we're so concerned about the treatment of those individuals." It's the fault of "the media" which are provoking, and will continue to provoke, further violence against Americans around the world. More Americans will die. Because of these photos.

On this photograph, Specialist Charles Graner (shown bottom left)
indicated by the number key who was with him at Abu Ghraib.

There is an answer to this charge, of course. Americans are dying not because of the photographs but because of what the photographs reveal to be happening, happening with the complicity of a chain of command—so Maj. Gen. Antonio Taguba implied, and Pfc. Lynndie England said, and (among others) Senator Lindsey Graham of South Carolina, a Republican, suggested, after he saw the Pentagon's full range of images on May 12. "Some of it has an elaborate nature to it that makes me very suspicious of whether or not others were directing or encouraging," Senator Graham said. Senator Bill Nelson, a Florida Democrat, said that viewing an uncropped version of one photo showing a stack of naked men in a hallway—a version that revealed how many other soldiers were at the scene, some not even paying attention—contradicted the Pentagon's assertion that only rogue soldiers were involved. "Somewhere along the line," Senator Nelson said of the torturers, "they were either told or winked at." An attorney for Specialist Charles Graner Jr., who is in the picture, has had his client identify the men in the uncropped version; according to The Wall Street Journal, Graner said that four of the men were military intelligence and one a civilian contractor working with military intelligence.

V.

But the distinction between photograph and reality—as between spin and policy—can easily evaporate. And that is what the administration wishes to happen. "There are a lot more photographs and videos that exist," Rumsfeld acknowledged in his testimony: "If these are released to the public, obviously, it's going to make matters worse." Worse for the administration and its programs, presumably, not for those who are the actual—and potential?—victims of torture.

The media may self-censor but, as Rumsfeld acknowledged, it's hard to censor soldiers overseas, who don't write letters home, as in the old days, that can be opened by military censors who ink out unacceptable lines. Today's soldiers instead function like tourists, as Rumsfeld put it, "running around with digital cameras and taking these unbelievable photographs and then passing them off, against the law, to the media, to our surprise." The administration's effort to withhold pictures is proceeding along several fronts. Currently, the argument is taking a legalistic turn: now the photographs are classified as evidence in future criminal cases, whose outcome may be prejudiced if they are made public. The Republican chairman of the Senate Armed Services Committee, John Warner of Virginia, after the May 12 slide show of image after image of sexual humiliation and violence against Iraqi prisoners, said he felt "very strongly" that the newer photos "should not be made public. I feel that it could possibly endanger the men and women of the armed forces as they are serving and at great risk."

But the real push to limit the accessibility of the photographs will come from the continuing effort to protect the administration and cover up our misrule in Iraq—to identify "outrage" over the photographs with a campaign to undermine American military might and the purposes it currently serves. Just as it was regarded by many as an implicit criticism of the war to show on television photographs of American soldiers who have been killed in the course of the invasion and occupation of Iraq, it will increasingly be thought unpatriotic to disseminate the new photographs and further tarnish the image of America.

After all, we're at war. Endless war. And war is hell, more so than any of the people who got us into this rotten war seem to have expected. In our digital hall of mirrors, the pictures aren't going to go away. Yes, it seems that one picture is worth a thousand words. And even if our leaders choose not to look at them, there will be thousands more snapshots and videos. Unstoppable.

47

from Ordinary Affects

KATHLEEN STEWART

Kathleen Stewart is an Associate Professor of Anthropology at the University of Texas, Austin, where she holds a joint appointment in the department of Intercultural Studies in Folklore and Ethnomusicology. Ordinary Affects (2007), from which these four chapters are excerpted, is a book about the economic, political, and social forces that shapes lives in the US. Stewart experiments with genre by presenting anthropological insights rendered not in theoretical terms but in short, anecdotal "scenes" that require attention. Though brief, the chapters invite multiple readings in order to engage with Stewart's thinking about "the ordinary" and the—often contradictory—affects that ordinary events trigger.

Running in Ordinary Time

Everyday life is a life lived on the level of surging affects, impacts suffered or barely avoided. It takes everything we have. But it also spawns a series of little somethings dreamed up in the course of things.

It grows wary and excited.

There are all the details of getting the rent money together or of home remodeling, getting messed up and recovering (or not), looking for love (or not), trying to get into something, or trying to get out of something you've gotten yourself into, shopping, hoping, wishing, regretting, and all the tortures of exclusion and inclusion, self and other, right and wrong, here and there.

The ordinary registers intensities—regularly, intermittently, urgently, or as a slight shudder.

We wish for the simple life that winks at us from someone else's beautiful flowerbeds. We flip off other drivers, eye strange or delicious characters on the subway or the street. We scan the headlines, read the luscious novels and sobering memoirs two pages a time before falling asleep at night. We lose hours at a time disappeared into some pleasure or obsession, or flipping hamburgers or filing charts all afternoon to the point of literal senselessness.

Attention is distracted, pulled away from itself. But the constant pulling also makes it wakeful, "at attention." Confused but attuned.

We're busy if we're lucky.

For some, the everyday is a process of going on until something happens, and then back to the going on.

For others, one wrong move is all it takes.

Worries swirl around the bodies in the dark.

People bottom out watching daytime television.

Schedules are thrown up like scaffolding to handle work schedules and soccer practice or a husband quietly drinking himself to death in the living room.

We dream of getting by, getting on track, getting away from it all, getting real, having an edge, beating the system, being ourselves, checking out.

But first we take the hit, or dodge it.

The Politics
of the Ordinary

The politics of ordinary affect can be anything from the split second when police decide to shoot someone because he's black and standing in a dark doorway and has something in his hand, to a moment when someone falls in love with someone else who's just come into view. Obviously, the differences matter. The politics of any surge depends on where it might go. What happens. How it plays itself out and in whose hands.

Ideologies happen. Power snaps into place. Structures grow entrenched. Identities take place. Ways of knowing become habitual at the drop of a hat. But it's ordinary affects that give things the quality of a *some*thing to inhabit and animate. Politics starts in the animated inhabitation of things, not way downstream in the various dreamboats and horror shows that get moving. The first step in thinking about the force of things is the open question of what counts as an event, a movement, an impact, a reason to react. There's a politics to being/feeling connected (or not), to impacts that arc shared (or not), to energies spent worrying or scheming (or not), to affective contagion, and to all the forms of attunement and attachment. There's a politics to ways of watching and waiting for something to happen and to forms of agency—to how the mirage of a straightforward exercise of will is a flag waved in one situation and a vicious, self-defeating deflation in another (as when someone of no means has a get-rich-quick daydream—a daydream to be free at last—that ends them up in jail). There's a politics to difference in itself—the difference of danger, the difference of habit and dull routine, the difference of everything that matters.

Home Is
Where the Heart Is

Home is where the heart is. You can get inside and slam the door. We dream of the big, beautiful sensate commodity-to-live-in, the bathroom done in the textures of old stone and precious metals, a utopia of colorful decor. But the synaesthesia of being at home is always already afloat in the circuits of the prevailing public winds—privatization, sensible accumulation, family values, or some kind or identity or lifestyle or something.

The American dream takes the form of a still life: the little family stands beside the SUV in the driveway, looking up, stock portfolios in hand, everything insured, payments up to date, yards kept trim and tended, fat-free diet under their belts, community watch systems in place. Martha Stewart offers advice on the finishing touches.

But then the little disappearing acts start coming up right in the middle of home's retreat, adding a different charge to things. There are times when it seems as if everything the heart drags home is peppered with a hint of addiction, aloneness, something rotten or worthless.

Horror stories leak in over the airwaves, Seemingly ordinary intimate spaces are revealed to be scenes of hidden corruption, catastrophe, isolation, and crime. There are children on welfare beaten to death in their homes between visits from the social worker; men who burst into their girlfriends' trailers, shooting them and their new lovers in their beds; bodies discovered only after the neighbors hear the dog barking in there for days on end. News of the weird feature stories like the one about the educated, middle-class couple who calmly goes away on vacation, leaving behind a hundred cats—some dead, some alive, wild ones living in the walls.

Odd Moments

At odd moments in the course of the day, you might raise your head in surprise or alarm the uncanny sensation of a half-known influence. The streets are littered with half-written signs of personal/public disasters. The daily sightings of the homeless haunt the: solidity of things with the shock of something awful. They hold up signs while puppies play at their feet: "Hungry," "'Will work for food," "God bless you." The sign hits the senses with a mesmerizing and repellant force. It pleads to be recognized, if only in passing. It gestures toward an ideological center that claims the value of willpower ("Will work for food") and it voices a simple dream of redemption ("God bless you"). But it's too sad. It offers no affect to mime, no scene of common desire, no line of vitality to follow, no intimate secret to plumb, no tips to imbibe for safety or good health.

There is no social recipe in circulation for what to do about homelessness, or even what to do with your eyes when confronted with it face to face.

The eye glances off the graphic lettering of the homeless sign as something to avoid like the plague. But the sign also prompts the surge of affect toward a profound scene.

A dollar bill stuck out of a car window gets a quick surge forward and the heightened, unassimilated, affect of a raw contact. "God bless you."

48

My Five-Paragraph-Theme Theme

ED WHITE

Ed White's essay "My Five-Paragraph-Theme Theme" from College Composition and Communication *offers a humorous critique of formulaic essay structures that stifle critical thinking. By calling attention to the simplistic level of engagement required to work within the traditional five-paragraph essay framework, White urges students and teachers to consider their purposes and structures for writing. Ed White is the author of books such as* Teaching and Assessing Writing: Understanding, Evaluating, and Improving Student Performance.

Since the beginning of time, some college teachers have mocked the five-paragraph theme. But I intend to show that they have been mistaken. There are three reasons why I always write five-paragraph themes. First, it gives me an organizational scheme: an introduction (like this one) setting out three subtopics, three paragraphs for my three subtopics, and a concluding paragraph reminding you what I have said, in case you weren't paying attention. Second, it focuses my topic, so I don't just go on and on when I don't have anything much to say. Three and only three subtopics force me to think in a limited way. And third, it lets me write pretty much the same essay on anything at all. So I do pretty well on essay tests. A lot of teachers actually like the five-paragraph theme as much as I do.

The first reason I always write five-paragraph themes is that it gives me an organizational scheme. It doesn't matter what the subject is, since there are three parts to everything you can think of. If you can't think of more than two, you just have to think harder or come up with something that might fit. An example will often work, like the three causes of the Civil War or abortion or reasons why the ridiculous twenty-one-year-old limit for drinking alcohol should be abolished. A worse problem is when you wind up with more than three subtopics, since sometimes you want to talk about all of them. But you can't. You have to pick the best three. That keeps you from thinking too much, which is a great time saver, especially on an essay test.

The second reason for the five-paragraph theme is that it makes you focus on a single topic. Some people start writing on the usual topic, like TV commercials, and they wind up all over the place, talking about where TV came from or capitalism or health foods or whatever. But with only five paragraphs and one topic you're not tempted to get beyond your original idea, like commercials are a good source of information about products. You give your three examples, and zap! you're done. This is another way the five-paragraph theme keeps you from thinking too much.

The last reason to write this way is the most important. Once you have it down, you can use it for practically anything. Does God exist? Well, you can say yes and give three reasons, or no and give three different reasons. It doesn't really matter. You're sure to get a good grade whatever you pick to put into the formula. And that's the real reason for education, to get those good grades without thinking too much and using up too much time.

So I've given you three reasons why I always write a five-paragraph theme and why I'll keep doing so in college. It gives me an organizational scheme that looks like an essay, it limits my focus to one topic and three subtopics so I don't wander about thinking irrelevant thoughts, and it will be useful for whatever writing I do in any subject. I don't know why some teachers seem to dislike it so much. They must have a different idea about education than I do.

The "student" Ed White is better known as Edward M. White, a visiting professor of English at the University of Arizona and the author or editor of thirteen books on the teaching and assessing of writing. He was one of almost a thousand scorers of the English language and composition Advanced Placement examination in June 2007, reading 280,000 tests written by high school students.

49

Trash and Treasure
The Gleaners and I

JAKE WILSON

From a 2002 issue of Senses of Cinema, *"Trash and Treasure" is a film review by Jake Wilson, a writer living in Melbourne, Australia. Wilson argues for the political and cultural value of Agnès Varda's film,* The Gleaners And I, *as a text that thoughtfully and playfully explores an inquiry. This review engages with aspects of both the content and production of the film to articulate the cultural work it accomplishes.*

Agnès Varda is one of those directors who have never really stopped working, but who tend to get "rediscovered" every so often after a period of relative obscurity. I've seen only a fraction of her complete works, which include many hard-to-access documentaries and shorts as well as features. Still, it's clear that her recent essayistic documentary *The Gleaners And I* (2000) picks up several threads she's followed throughout her career—a concern with traditional crafts and rituals, with the poor and marginalised, and with the everyday minutiae typically excluded from fiction.

The official subject of this film is *gleaning*, the act of gathering remnants of crops from a field after the harvest. As Varda demonstrates, people can be discovered throughout the French countryside gleaning everything from potatoes to grapes, apples to oysters, much as they did hundreds of years ago (though no longer in organised groups). More figuratively, there are also urban gleaners who salvage scraps from bins, appliances from the side of the road, or vegetables from stalls after the markets have closed. And then there's Varda herself, a gleaner of images, driving around France with a digital camera and a tiny crew (at times, she wields a smaller camera herself, permitting an even greater degree of intimacy).

Varda has a (sometimes contested) reputation as a feminist, left-wing artist, and this is very much a political film, though it offers a series of poetic metaphors and concrete encounters in lieu of an explicit, closely reasoned argument. My guess (based mainly on anecdotal evidence) is that the political outlook of *The Gleaners And I* has a lot to do with its popular success—even if Varda herself, who began filming back in 1999, wasn't fully aware how thoroughly she was tapping into the zeitgeist. Without specifically referring to political movements or events, the film embodies a quasi-anarchist ethos now in the air in all sorts of ways—a resistance to consumerism, a suspicion of authority, and a desire to reconnect politics with everyday life.

Obviously gleaning in Varda's sense can be considered a "green" activity, a matter of recycling or conserving items that would otherwise go to waste (several interviewees express outrage that people should allow food to rot while others starve). Yet it probably wouldn't occur to anyone to pigeonhole *The Gleaners And I* as an environmental film, any more than green politics is necessarily focused these days on a single issue. Gleaning, Varda implies, can be understood more broadly as a form of resistance, a way of refusing to be boxed in by conventional expectations; as such, it demands that we re-learn age-old skills as well as supply individual creativity and initiative.

One major way Varda expands the parameters of her subject is by making constant reference to paintings and other artworks, both as illustrations of gleaning's historic past (paintings by Millet and Van Gogh) and as creative examples of gleaning in the present (sculptures, collages and so on made from found materials). Nor is this latter kind of creation restricted to officially accredited artists, as Varda demonstrates through an interview with a man who builds "totem towers" from discarded dolls ("Dolls are my system," he explains). In general, one of the film's most appealing features is its democratic treatment of its interview subjects, who range from gypsies and unemployed young people to a magistrate and a psychotherapist: they're all respected equally, and Varda lets them speak for themselves without passing judgement.

It's odd to see *The Gleaners And I* finally on general release in Australia as a "new" film, a full two years after its completion. As well as certain obvious shifts in the global political climate, the intervening period has seen a major change in the status of digital video, which has become the default choice of many low-budget filmmakers (especially in documentary). Back in 1999, the use of DV was possibly novel enough to seem like a democratic gesture in itself, a way of reducing the distance between Varda and the people she films—not only because video technology is less cumbersome and intimidating, but because the drabness of video tends to demystify the relationship between the filmmaker and his or her raw material. Compared with film, video images are less likely to be perceived as autonomously beautiful in their own right; instead, they often function in a purely kinetic way, as encoded traces of the primary act of camera operation. (This is true of most Dogma movies, and also—intriguingly—the work of the Dardenne brothers, who transfer the strategy from video back to film proper.) Video thus fits well with Varda's explicit concentration on the process of gathering images, and on gleaning as a way of operating within the world rather than transforming it as a whole.

Not that *The Gleaners And I* wholly lacks visual beauty. Its most lyrical shots virtually negate the difference between grasping an object with one's hands and approaching it with the camera, as Varda (or her videographer) pushes up close to a painting, a rain-spattered windscreen, a knobbly potato or human skin. Such moments have the tactile quality of what Laura Marks calls "haptic" imagery[1]—using the camera as a probing instrument rather than the screen as a canvas, dwelling on surface textures rather than offering a totalising three-dimensional perspective.

The film's craft, however, is most visible in its editing, weaving a dense and variegated web of connections with little apparent strain. As a film essayist Varda isn't as brilliantly witty as Chris Marker, but she has a similarly disarming approach—light and whimsical, yet informed by a scrupulous moral and political intelligence. At times, she can seem to succumb to the temptation common to many "diary" filmmakers of making the recording process an end in itself, bestowing a blanket (in)significance on all possible objects by quizzically insisting that one image can be no more valid than another.

Yet a certain recursive poetic logic hints that this loose form should be taken as the ultimate validation of the film's theme. In presenting *The Gleaners And I* as itself a collection of gleanings, Varda proposes something comparable to Ursula le Guin's Carrier Bag Theory of Fiction: narrative not as progress towards a goal but as an open-ended gathering of disparate elements, "necessary elements of a whole which itself cannot be characterised either as conflict or as harmony, since its purpose is neither resolution nor stasis but continuing process."[2] Paradoxically, then, it's precisely the moments in the film that don't seem to "fit" with its subject—like an irrelevant, plangent glimpse of a man looking out across a river—that supply its clearest instances of "gleaning."

In the essay quoted above, Le Guin's argument is specifically feminist, playfully illustrated by a Stone Age parable that presents men as fundamentally hunters, women as gatherers. *The Gleaners And I* doesn't make such heavy weather of the point, but Varda is careful to establish that historically gleaning has been "women's work"—even if the majority of present-day gleaners in the film are male. "Gleaning" as a homely figure for resistance and appropriation certainly has a less than macho ring to it; as a political model it's modest and pragmatic, strengthening our connection to the reality around us rather than offering an escape into some other, transcendent realm. Gleaners are simply people who have learned to value the mundane, trashy and ephemeral, and it's no great shock that in our society these downgraded categories should be associated with women—particularly older women who aren't considered glamorous. Wryly, Varda includes herself under the heading of matter to be salvaged, letting the mini-DV camera roam over her wrinkled hands: "I like filming rot, leftovers, waste."

It says a lot for Varda's poise that she can get away with this kind of gesture without being suspected of self-indulgence or insensitivity. It's only afterwards we might wonder about the gulf between these different types of "gleaning"—ranging from the desperate hunt for food to the playful juxtaposition of images. Varda may be a critically neglected filmmaker, and her work may be economically marginal in relation to the global entertainment industry. But does that give her the right to compare herself to those who are literally starving and homeless? The answer, perhaps, is that we've missed the point if we consider creative achievement and practical survival to be entirely separate. Less fancifully than at first appears, Varda's notion of herself as a "gleaner" suggests the real continuity between superficially different forms of human resourcefulness—both those hailed as art, and those rarely hailed at all.

Endnotes

1. Laura U. Marks, *The Skin Of The Film: Intercultural Cinema, Embodiment, And The Senses*, Durham, Duke University Press, 1999.
2. Ursula K. Le Guin, "The Carrier Bag Theory of Fiction," in *Dancing At The Edge Of The World: Thoughts On Words, Women, Places,* Grove Press, 1989, p. 169.

50

A Boy's Life

*For Matthew Shepard's killers,
what does it take to pass as a man?*

JoAnn Wypijewski

*JoAnn Wypijewski, an independent journalist, uses this article to examine
social dynamics surrounding the 1998 murder of the gay college student
Matthew Shepard. Originally published in a 1999 issue of* Harper's Magazine, *this article considers how a culture of compulsory heterosexuality
and class-based sensibilities are more responsible for, respectively, Shepard's
murder and his memorialization than Shepard's sexuality. Wypijewski illustrates how reading a supposedly exceptional and violent event as implicated
in ordinary social relations yields a provocative analysis.*

> *"When I think of how fragile men are," a dominatrix once said to
> me, "I feel so much pity. All that fear, all that self-mutilation, just to
> be 'men.' When I heard that those guys in Laramie took Matthew
> Shepard's shoes, I was so creeped out. I mean, shoes are so symbolic—
> 'walk a mile in my shoes' and all that, Why did they take his shoes?"*

From the beginning there was something too awfully iconic about the case.
Matthew Shepard—young, small, gay, a college boy in the cowboy town of
Laramie, Wyoming, a kid who, his father says, didn't know how to make a fist
until he was thirteen—lured out of a bar by two "rednecks" ("trailer trash,"

THE ROMANCE OF THE WEST
Photograph by G. Rancinan/Sygma

"drop-outs," every tabloid term has been applied), hijacked to a lonely spot outside of town, strung up like a scarecrow on a buck fence, bludgeoned beyond recognition, and left to die without his shoes, his ring, his wallet, or the $20 inside it. With that mix of real and fanciful detail, it has been called a trophy killing, a hate crime, a sacrifice. Press crews who had never before and have not since lingered over gruesome murders of homosexuals came out in force, reporting their brush with a bigotry so poisonous it could scarcely be imagined. County Attorney Cal Rerucha says death by injection is the just response. At the site where Shepard was murdered, in a field of prairie grass and sagebrush within eyeshot of suburban houses, a cross has been laid out in pink limestone rocks. In crotches of the killing fence, two stones have been placed; one bears the word "love"; the other, "forgive." The poignancy of those messages has been transmitted out and beyond via television; it is somewhat diminished if one knows that the stones were put there by a journalist, whose article about the murder for *Vanity Fair* was called "The Cruci-fixion of Matthew Shepard."

Torture is more easily imagined when masked in iconography but no better understood. Perhaps it all will become clear in October, when one of the accused, Aaron McKinney, goes on trial for kidnapping, aggravated robbery, and capital murder (his companion, Russell Henderson, pled guilty on April 5 and avoided death with two consecutive life terms), but it seems unlikely. "The story" passed into myth even before the trials had been set, and at this point fact, rumor, politics, protective cover, and jailhouse braggadocio are so entangled that the truth may be elusive even to the protagonists.

What is known, though somehow elided, is that in the most literal definition of the word, Matthew Shepard was not crucified. His hands were not outstretched, as has been suggested by all manner of media since October 7, 1998, when the twenty-one-year-old University of Wyoming student was discovered near death, but rather tied behind him as if in handcuffs, lashed to a pole four inches off the ground. His head propped on the lowest fence rail, his legs extending out to the east, he was lying almost flat on his back when Deputy Reggie Fluty of the Albany County Sheriff's Department found him at 6:22 P.M., eighteen hours, it's believed, after he was assaulted. It was Shepard's diminutive aspect—Fluty thought he was thirteen—and the horrid condition of his face and head, mangled by eighteen blows from a three-pound Smith & Wesson .357 magnum, that most compelled her attention.

Shepard had encountered McKinney and Henderson, both also twenty-one, at the Fireside Bar on October 6. They exchanged words that no one heard, then left the bar and got into a truck belonging to McKinney's father. There Shepard was robbed and hit repeatedly. Out by the fence came the fatal beating. Shepard must have been kicked too, because he was bruised between his legs and elsewhere. Amid the blows he cried, "Please don't." He was left alive but unconscious, as McKinney and Henderson headed for an address they'd got out of him. En route they ran into two local punks out puncturing tires, Emiliano Morales and Jeremy Herrera, and started a fight. McKinney cracked Morales's head open with the same gun he'd used on Shepard, coating the weapon with still more blood. Herrera then whacked McKinney's head with a stick. Police arrived, grabbed Henderson (he and McKinney had run in different directions), and found the truck, the gun, Shepard's shoes and credit card. Police wouldn't put the crimes together until later, so Henderson was cited for interference with a peace officer

THE PRESS DESCENDS ON LARAMIE
Photograph by Richard Alan Hannon

and released. Henderson then drove to Cheyenne with his girlfriend, Chasity Pasley, and McKinney's girlfriend, Kristen LeAnn Price (both later charged as accessories after the fact), to dispose of his bloody clothes. McKinney, dazed from the gash in his head, stayed home in bed, and Price hid Shepard's wallet in the dirty diaper of her and McKinney's infant son, Cameron. Six days later, on October 12, Shepard died.

Those are the facts as disclosed by court records and McKinney's confession. (He has pleaded not guilty.) In response, the Equality State—which enfranchised women long before anyplace else, which struck sodomy laws from the books in 1977—has disowned McKinney and Henderson as monsters. So has the rest of the country.

And yet McKinney and Henderson appear to be young men of common prejudices, far more devastatingly human than is comfortable to consider. They acquired the gun a few days before the murder in a trade for $100 in methamphetamine—crank, speed, crystal meth—the drug of choice among white rural youth, cheaper than cocaine and more long-lasting, more relentless in its accelerating effects, more widely used in Wyoming, per capita, than in any state in the country. McKinney, says the friend who traded him for it, desired the gun for its badass beauty—eight-inch barrel, fine tooling, "the Dirty Harry thing." The trade occurred while these three fellows and their girlfriends were on a meth binge. Before it was over they would smoke or snort maybe $2,000 worth of the drug. By the time they met Matthew Shepard, says the friend, who saw them that day, McKinney and Henderson were on the fifth day of that binge. They had not slept, he says, since before October 2, payday, when the partying had begun.

Those unreported facts—to the extent that anything can be factually determined in Laramie these days, with everyone involved in the case under a gag order*—may tell more about the crime, more about the everyday life of hate and

---

The order prohibits lawyers; witnesses; local, state, and federal law-enforcement officers; et al. from discussing the case. McKinney's friend says he was visited by black-suited agents of the Alcohol, Tobacco and Firearms Department shortly after McKinney and Henderson were arrested, and told them this story. Before it passed into his hands, says McKinney's friend, the gun had been stolen, which is consistent with court records. Henderson's grandmother says she noticed nothing unusual about Russell when he visited her on October 5. McKinney's friend and the other drug users, ex-users, or dealers in Laramie spoke with me on condition of anonymity.

hurt and heterosexual culture than all the quasi-religious characterizations of Matthew's passion, death, and resurrection as patron saint of hate-crime legislation. It's just possible that Matthew Shepard didn't die because he was gay; he died because Aaron McKinney and Russell Henderson are straight.

> *"If you're telling your feelings, you're kind a wuss." Brent Jones, a heterosexual who went to high school with McKinney and Henderson, was guiding me through the psychic terrain of a boy's life.*
>
> *"So what do you do when things hurt?"*
>
> *"That's why God created whiskey, don't you think? You get drunker than a pig and hope it drains away—or you go home and cry."*
>
> *"Is that true for most guys, do you think?"*
>
> *"Yeah, pretty much."*
>
> *"So secretly you're all wusses, and you know you're wusses, but you can't let anyone know, even though you all know you know."*
>
> *"You could say that."*
>
> *"Can you talk to girls about this stuff?"*
>
> *"Unless you know this is the one—like, you're going to get married, and then you're in so deep you can't help yourself—but if not, if you think she might break up with you, then no, because she might tell someone, and then it gets around, and then everyone thinks you're a wuss. And you don't want people to think you're a wuss, unless you are a wuss, and then you know you're a wuss, and then it doesn't matter."*

Among the weighty files on the proceedings against McKinney and Henderson in the Albany County Courthouse is a curious reference. The state had charged, as an "aggravating factor" in the murder, that "the defendant[s] knew or should have known that the victim was suffering from a physical or mental disability." The court threw this out; Judge Jeffrey Donnell, who presided over Henderson's case, told me he assumed it referred to Shepard's size (five foot two, 105 pounds) but was legally irrelevant whatever its intent. In a sense, it is sociologically irrelevant as well whether the prosecution regarded Shepard as crippled more by sexuality or size, since by either measure he was, in the vernacular of Laramie's straight youth, a wuss.

Wussitude haunts a boy's every move. It must have haunted Aaron McKinney most of his life. McKinney, too, is a little thing—not as little as Shepard, but at about five foot six, 145 pounds, he doesn't cut a formidable figure. George Markle, who roomed with him after they both dropped out of high school, describes McKinney as having "tiny arms, a tiny, tiny chest, no definition in his body." He affected a gangsta style—droopy jeans, baggy shirt, Raiders jacket, gold chains, gold on all his fingers. He'd ape hip-hop street talk, but "he couldn't get it going if he tried." His nickname was Dopey, both for his oversized ears and for his reputation as a serious drug dealer and user. His shoulder bears a tattoo of the Disney character pouring a giant can of beer on his mother's grave, an appropriation of a common rapper's homage to a fallen brother: "Pour a forty ounce on my homey's grave."

RUSSELL HENDERSON AND AARON McKINNEY
Photograph by Ed Andrieski/AP/World Wide Photos

The prosecution contends that Shepard was lured out of the bar as if on a sexual promise. County public defender Wyatt Skaggs says that neither Henderson nor McKinney ever asserted that they came on to Shepard. And in his confession, McKinney said Shepard "did not hit on or make advances toward" him and Henderson, according to Sheriff's Detective Sgt. Rob De-Bree. Perhaps McKinney said something different when he came home that night and wept in the arms of Kristen Price, or perhaps, presuming homophobia to be an acceptable alibi, she thought she was helping him when she told the press that he and Henderson "just wanted to beat [Shepard] up bad enough to teach him a lesson not to come on to straight people." But once at the Albany County Detention Center, McKinney seemed to take up the pose of fag-basher as a point of pride. At least five prisoners awaiting trial or sentencing have asked their lawyers if the things he's said to them might be leveraged to their own advantage. "Being a verry [sic] drunk homofobick [sic] I flipped out and began to pistol whip the fag with my gun," McKinney wrote in a letter to another inmate's wife. He didn't mean to kill Shepard, he wrote; he was turning to leave him, tied to the fence but still conscious, when Matthew "mouthed off to the point that I became angry enough to strike him more with my gun." Even then, he insists, his attitude toward homosexuals is not particularly venomous and the murder was unintentional.

THE FIRESIDE BAR
Photograph by Richard Alan Hannon

McKinney's mother was a nurse; she died as a result of a botched operation when Aaron was sixteen. Markle says there was a kind of shrine to her in his house, but Aaron rarely spoke of her, and then only superficially and only when he was high: "He was always happy then. Once, on mushrooms, he said that if he would slide backward down a hill, he could see his mom in heaven." According to probate records, McKinney got $98,268.02 in a settlement of the wrongful-death lawsuit his stepfather brought against the doctors and the hospital. "After he got the money, he had a lot of friends," Markle told me. He bought cars and cracked them up, bought drugs and became an instant figure in town. He was engaged at one point—"she got the drugs, he got the sex; I guess it worked out for a while"—until the girl found a more attractive connection. "He wasn't a babe magnet," Brent Jones says. He might make a good first impression—he's funny, I was told, though no one could quite explain how—but he couldn't keep that up. Women were *bitches* and *hos,* just like other men, who might also be called *fag, wuss, queer, sissie, girly man, woman,* the standard straight-boy arsenal, which McKinney employed indiscriminately, says Markle, "about as much as anybody—you know, joking around—he never mentioned anything about hating gays." He talked about marrying Price, who is eighteen, but, according to more than one person who was acquainted with them, he wasn't faithful and didn't seem even to like her much.

He loves his son, I'm told. And what else? Blank. What did he talk about? Blank. What did he fear? Blank. Who is he? None of the boys can really say. Interior life is unexplored territory, even when it's their own. Exterior life, well, "Actually, when he wasn't high he was kind of a geek," says a guy who's done drugs with him since high school. "He wasn't the sharpest tool in the shed. He always wanted to seem bigger, badder, and tougher than anybody," says Jones, a strongly built fellow who first noticed McKinney when the latter hit him from behind. "He usually didn't pick on anyone bigger than him. He could never do it alone, and he couldn't do it toe-to-toe." Markle says nothing much mattered to McKinney in picking a fight, except that if he started to lose, his friends would honor the rule they had among themselves and come in to save him.

A stock media image of McKinney and Henderson in this tragedy has them counting out quarters and dimes with dirty fingers to buy a pitcher of beer at the Fireside. It is meant to indicate their distance from Shepard, who had clean hands and paid for his Heinekens with bills, and to offer some class perspective on the cheap. *They were poor, they were losers, they lived in trailers, for God's sake!* McKinney, as it happens, didn't live in a trailer, though he had when he was younger—a nice double one with his stepfather, until recently program director at KRQU radio. His natural father is a long-haul truck driver whom he was heard to call "Daddy" only a few years ago, and in Aaron's childhood the family lived on Palomino Drive in the Imperial Heights subdivision. As teenagers he and his friends would drink and get high in the field behind it—"quite the hangout," according to Markle—where McKinney had played as a boy and where he would later leave Shepard to die.

Henderson spent most of his childhood in the warmly appointed ranch house where his grandmother runs a day care and to which his late grandfather would repair after work at the post office. At the time of the murder, Russell lived with Pasley, a UW art student, now serving fifteen to twenty-four months, in a trailer court no uglier than most in Laramie and with the same kinds of late-model cars, trucks, and four-wheel-drive vehicles parked outside, the same proportion of people pulling in and out wearing ties or nice coats or everyday workers' clothes, and probably the same type of modest but comfortable interiors as in the ones I visited. No matter, in the monumental condescension of the press, "trailer" always means failure, always connotes "trash," and, however much it's wrapped up in socioculturoeconomico froufrou, always insinuates the same thing: What can you expect from trash?

McKinney and Henderson were workers. At the end of the day they had dirty hands, just like countless working men who head to the bars at quitting time. Dirt is symbolic only if manual labor is, and manual laborers usually find their symbolism elsewhere. The pair had drunk two pitchers of beer at the Library bar before going to the Fireside; no one remembers anything about them at the Library, presumably because they paid in dollars. Maybe they resented a college boy's clean hands and patent-leather loafers and moneyed confidence; they wouldn't have been the only people in town who do, though acquaintances ascribe no such sentiments to them. UW is a state school, the only university in Wyoming. It stands aloof from the town, but no more than usual. Poll a classroom, and about a fifth of the students are from Laramie, and half say their parents are manual workers. Shepard, originally from Casper but schooled abroad because his father is in the oil business, didn't need a job; Pasley, like most students, did. There's nothing unique here about the injuries of class. In a month at Laramie Valley Roofing, McKinney and Henderson each would gross around $1,200, roughly $7.50 an hour.

With rent payments of $370 and $340, respectively, they were like a lot of people in Laramie, where the median household income is $26,000, the average monthly rent is $439, and the average family works two jobs, maybe more.

It's said that McKinney squandered the entire hundred grand from his mother's settlement, and in his application for a public defender he listed $0 in assets. Before moving to his last address, he and his family briefly lived rent-free in a converted indoor stable with no shower, no stove, no refrigerator, and, in some rooms, a cloth ceiling and cloth walls. But everyone I spoke with who was openly familiar with him through drugs was skeptical about the poverty story. To finance his recreation, I was told by the guy tweaking with him in the days before the murder, McKinney would often be fronted an "eight ball" of meth (three grams, an eighth of an ounce, street price about $300; for him, wholesale, sometimes as low as $100), keep two grams for himself, double the amount of the remaining powder by cutting it with vitamin B, sell that, and have $200 and enough crank to keep two people awake for practically a week before he'd even paid a cent. At one point a few years ago, according to a friend now monitored by an ankle bracelet, McKinney was buying an eight ball every few days.

Maybe he miscalculated the costs of his binge in that first week in October. A few days before Shepard would be tied to the fence, McKinney and Henderson walked into the Mini-Mart where George Markle works, and, in an agitated state, McKinney shouted that Markle owed him $4,000 and that he needed it. Years earlier, Aaron had bought George a used Chevy S-10 low-rider truck. First it was called a gift, then a loan, then no one talked about it much, Markle says, and after the friendship broke, he didn't intend to pay anything back. That day in the Mini-Mart, Aaron threatened to kill George. He had threatened him once or twice before within the last few weeks, always with Henderson silently in tow. Markle told his boss, but neither of them thought too much of it. "I'm gonna kill you"—it was just Aaron pretending to be big and bad. It was the way he talked; like when he first came into the Mini-Mart and, seeing George, exclaimed, "Oh, look at that—it's my favorite little bitch, my favorite little whore."

> *"Things are good enough for me to stay for now," Elam Timothy, a writer, gardener, and handyman, was telling me just before we decided what his pseudonym would be. "I have a relationship, I'm out at work and to as many people as I care to be—but I'm not looking through rose-colored glasses. They're demonizing those boys so they don't have to look at themselves. Yes, this could have happened anywhere, but it didn't. Can we please look at it? That whole 'live and let live' myth. In my mind that boils down to one sentence: If I don't tell you I'm a fag, you won't beat the crap out of me."*
>
> *"Have you ever been hurt or threatened here?"*
>
> *"No."*
>
> *"Do you know anyone who has been?"*
>
> *"No, but I don't know many gay men either."*
>
> *"So what is it that's dangerous?"*

"What's scary is just hearing people use the word 'faggot' all the time. It makes me feel like a pig at a weenie roast. Danger isn't palpable, but I keep myself in safe pockets. I wouldn't expect to find safety in the Cowboy [bar], but Coal Creek [coffeehouse], yeah, that's safe."

MCKINNEY'S CONVERTED STABLE APARTMENT
Photograph by Ted Wood

Laramie was founded on sex and the railroad, in that order. Women created the region's first service industry, and soon after the town's establishment, in 1868, it was associated with some thirty saloons, gambling houses, and brothels. Before any of that, it was associated with death. Around 1817, a French Canadian trapper named Jacques LaRamie was working these parts with his mates. As the story goes, he was young and handsome, and in winter decided to take his beaver traps upstream on what is now either the Big or the Little Laramie River. In spring he failed to return, and Indians told his erstwhile companions that he'd been killed by other natives and stuffed under the ice of a beaver pond. His headstone thus became the plains, a mountain range, two rivers, a fort, a county, a railroad terminal, and, ultimately, the city.

From the foothills of the Laramie Range, the high prairie where the city is situated stretches out, scored by steel tracks and pocked by late-model houses defiant of the city's already shaggy boundaries. From the right vantage point those are obscured, and all that's in sight is the plain and, to the west, the Snowy Range and what, against reason, seems like infinity. People may swoon about Wyoming's mountains and river valleys, but the power is all in the wind, which has shaped the plains like a pair of enormous hands playing in a sandbox of soft soil and red clay, massaging the earth into fine overlapping layers and fluid hollows. Such subtlety is merely the profit of aeons. Over spring break a student from the university left his truck out in an open field while the winds blew thirty, forty miles an hour; within two weeks, the windward side of the truck had been sandblasted down to bare metal.

Laramie, a pleasant place of liberal inclination and some 27,000 people, is not a railroad town anymore. Freight lines rush through but are marginal to the city's economy. It's not a sex town either, though in the history-charmed buildings abutting the rail yard along 1st Street shopkeepers will happily show off narrow cubicles in an upstairs flat, or a slotted box in a side door, where nighttime ladies deposited their earnings under the madam's gaze and key, their work organized as on a sharecrop, with ledgered debt always exceeding income. Carol Bowers, an archivist at the university's American Heritage Center, recounts a history in which the town elders seesawed between plans for eradication and regulation, usually recognizing the superior benefits of the latter. (In one nineteenth-century city record, all but $20 out of $240 in fines and fees collected one month came from prostitutes.) So the women were harassed, corralled, controlled by periodic raids, punished for any venture into legitimate civic life by threats to their licenses—but tolerated. "The town didn't want them to go away," Bowers says. "The town wanted them to be invisible."

A hundred years later, sex is almost totally in the closet. Only the truck stops off I-80 are worked, by mobile squads of women or by men, who also work the rest stops. For every other unspoken desire there's The Fort, a rambling warehouse south of town that has survived Cal Rerucha's tireless efforts at suppression. There men, mostly men, stop in (all classes and tendencies, all night on weekends), nervous and chatty—about a practical joke or a bachelor party or the wife—before surveying the aisles, then scuttling to the checkout with a strap-on dildo or a Miss Perfection "port-a-pussy" or a sexual banquet of videos. A tall, lean man of the muscular outdoors type crouches before a display and comes away with the Sauna Action Pump, guaranteed to improve an erection beyond any natural capacity. Now and then one man is followed five minutes later by another, under the red light and into the video booths in back.

In the best of times, sex is playground to the imagination, the place where what is need not be what it seems, where strength and weakness swap clothes, and the thin cry, "This is who I am, this is who I dream of being—don't hurt me" seeks its voice. Laramie happens now to be associated with sex in the worst of times, sex boxed and squared in the unexamined terms of the "natural" course of things or the unexamined terms of "identity." Many in town are irritated by this association and by all the talk of hate since the murder attracted national attention. McKinney and Henderson, it's said, are "not Laramie." Before his death, Shepard was surely "not Laramie" either, if only because he took risks that other gay men in town might not have. Laramie, it's said, is not censorious about sex, homo or hetero—*We're just tight-lipped. We don't go there. We believe "live and let live"*— and it's certainly not hateful, just as most of the country is not, just as, perhaps, even McKinney and Henderson are not. If they all were, everything would be much simpler.

Hatred is like pornography—hard to define, but you know it when you see it. On the morning before Russell Henderson pleaded guilty, the Reverend Fred Phelps of Topeka, Kansas, brought his flock to the county courthouse with signs declaring GOD HATES FAGS, FAG GOD=RECTUM, PHIL 3:19, SAVE THE GERBILS. Phelps cited as his guide for most of this (the Bible has nothing to say about gerbils) such scriptural passages as Leviticus 18:22, "Thou shalt not lie with mankind, as with womankind: it is abomination." I asked if he also subscribes to Moses' suggestion a bit further on in Leviticus 20:13, "If a man also lie with mankind, as he lieth with a woman, . . . they shall surely be put to death." He said he thought all civil law should be based on biblical code, but "it's never going to happen. I'm a pragmatist, a visionary."

"So, if you could, though, you would execute homosexuals?"

"I wouldn't execute them. The government would execute them."

His only audience were police, press, and a ring of angels—counterprotesters dressed in white robes, their great wings sweeping up before his gaudy placards.

The next day the university's student newspaper covered the day's events, running in enlarged type the observation of freshman Kristen Allen that "they have no business using the Bible verses out of context. God hates the sin but loves the sinner." On campus, where Phelps later moved his protest, onlookers expressed disgust at his message and invoked "tolerance."

Before it came to signify the highest state to which straight society could aspire, tolerance was something one had for a bad job or a bad smell or a nightmare relative who visited once a year. In its new guise, tolerance means straight people know of gay men and women, but there is no recognizable gay life, no clubs except a tiny one on campus, no bars or restaurants or bookstores flying the rainbow flag. It means the university might institute a Matthew Shepard Chair in Civil Liberties but has no antidiscrimination policy that applies to homosexuals and no employee benefit policy that extends to domestic partners.* It means the public school curriculum does not say teachers must "avoid planning curriculum promoting perversion, homosexuality, contraception, promiscuity and abortion as healthy lifestyle choices"—the policy in Lincoln County, Wyoming—but it also does not include "homosexuality" among vocabulary terms for sex-ed classes at any grade level and mentions the word only once, for eighth grade, under "Topics to be Discussed . . . particularly as they relate to [sexually transmitted diseases]." It means a father tells his lesbian daughter, "If you have to do this you should do it in the closet," and the mother tells her, "Let's just pretend I don't know, okay?" It means her brother "tries to be as supportive as he can be—and he is—but if a man hit on him, he'd beat the shit out of him. He wouldn't beat up someone for another reason, and he thinks that's an accomplishment—and it is." It means Chasity Pasley's mother won her custody battle over the charge that as a lesbian she was unfit, but her children had to call her partner "Aunt." It means if you're gay and out and attend a company party with your boyfriend, the sense in the room is "We know you're gay and that's okay, but do you have to bring your boyfriend?" It means Fred Dahl, the straight head of UW's Survey Research Center, accepts the university's expression of outrage over Shepard's murder but tells a social work master's candidate named Shannon Bell that her project to poll Wyoming residents on their attitudes toward homosexuality might amount to harassment of straight people, and anyway, "one good rodeo season and Wyoming will be back to normal."

In a graduate-class discussion right after Shepard was found, the high-minded talk was all of tolerance as students challenged a woman who had said she abhorred violence but still . . . homosexuality, it's immoral. Amid the chatter, a cowboy who'd been silent said plainly, "The issue isn't tolerance. We don't need to learn tolerance; we need to learn love."

---

*UW president Philip Dubois told me that the university has such an antidiscrimination policy, but as of July 1999 sexual orientation was still not included as a protected category in the university's official Equal Employment Opportunity/Affirmative Action Statement approved by the trustees. Nor does it appear in the antidiscrimination provisions for student admissions. Only these formal statements of policy have the force of law, says the ACLU's Marv Johnson.

DOWNTOWN LARAMIE
Photograph by Ted Wood

There may be, as the song goes, a thin line between love and hate, but, however many twists it takes, it is life's defining line. And people like Phelps are no more responsible for it than pop music is responsible for the murders at Columbine High School. What keeps that line so strong, like strands of the clothesline used to tie Matthew Shepard's wrists, are all the little things of a culture, mostly unnoticed and unremarked, like the way in which the simplest show of affection is a decision about safety, like the way in which a man entwined with a woman is the stuff of everyday commerce but a man expressing vulnerability is equivalent to a quaint notion of virginity—you save it for marriage.

"Masks are no longer as protective as they used to be," John Scagliotti, the maker of Before (and now After) Stonewall, was telling me. "If you're gay, no longer can you hide, because straight people watch TV, and they see how people hide. And also this has changed straight culture, so all the little things you do might make you question whether you're straight, or straight enough. Your own suspicions are suspicious.

"It gets even more complicated now that all these things that represent maleness are very attractive to both gay and straight men. The

downside of this, in a way, is that straight male bonding, and male bonding in general, especially in rural places, is going to be a very confused thing. Already at gyms, eighteen-year-olds don't take showers anymore—or if they do, they take all their things in with them, like modest little girls. You're confused, you're eighteen, and you really like this guy; he's your best buddy, and you'd rather spend all your time with him than with this girl. And you are straight, but now you're worried too."

The Henderson trial was to have begun on the first Tuesday after Easter. At the Harvest Foursquare full-gospel church that Sunday, people wore name tags and expressed a serene camaraderie. Then they sent the children downstairs to play while the "illustrated sermon"—a dramatization of Christ's Passion and death—took place. It was a stunning performance, beginning with the Jesus character racked with sorrow in the Garden of Gethsemane. The narrator said Jesus suffered like any man. Then he said, departing from the script, "Every time I see an image of a feminine Jesus, it makes my blood boil. Jesus wasn't a weakling. Jesus was a man. If Jesus was here today, he could take on any man in this room." Later, when the Jesus character was tied to a post, flogged by two men—soldiers who took "sensual pleasure" in every fall of the whip, the narrator said—"Jesus didn't cry out for mercy . . . Jesus was a man. Jesus was a man's man." The Jesus character writhed in agony. After he stumbled offstage with the cross, and the only sounds

THE REVEREND FRED PHELPS
Photograph by Kevin Moloney / Liaison Agency

were his moans amid the pounding of nails, the narrator described the tender caress of the hands now ripped by sharp iron. In the congregation, men as well as women were moved to weeping. By the end, they were all singing, swaying, proclaiming their weakness before the Lord.

Time was when "a man's man" could mean only one thing, and in the romance of the West, that meant cowboys. In reality, Laramie is as contradictory as anything liberated from caricature, but in symbolism its outward identity remains hitched to the cowboy. Wild Willie's Cowboy Bar anchors one corner downtown; a few feet away is The Rancher. Farther up the same street is the Ranger Lounge and Motel; down another, the legendary Buckhorn Bar, with its mirror scarred by a bullet hole, its motionless zoo of elk and deer and prong-horned antelope, bobcat and beaver and buffalo, a two-headed foal, a twinset of boar. Around the corner stands the Cowboy Saloon, with its tableau of locomotives and thundering horses, lightning storms and lassos, portraits of grand old men who'd graced the town in history (Buffalo Bill Cody) and in dreams (Clint Eastwood). A wall inside the courthouse bears a silhouette of a bronco buster, whose figure has also appeared on Wyoming license plates since 1936. The university's symbol is the rodeo rider; its sports teams, the Cowboys and Cowgirls; its paper, the *Branding Iron*; its mascot, Pistol Pete; and its recruiting slogan, "It's in our nature."

For the men of Laramie who didn't grow up on a ranch riding horses and roping cattle—that is, most of them—the cowboy cult appears to be as natural as the antlers affixed to a female elk's head hanging on a wall at the Buckhorn. It all seems to fit, until you look closer and realize that this buck is actually Bambi's mother butched up. For those who did grow up to be cowboys, the rituals and vestments may be just as they were for their fathers and grandfathers—like going to the dance hall on a Saturday night, scrubbed and polished and wearing one's best hat and boots—but the meanings have changed, or at least got more complicated. In a different setting, the waves of men kicking it up to "Cotton Eye Joe" at the Cowboy Saloon would be high camp, just as the beautiful, guileless cowboy explaining the rodeo to me, undulating in a pantomime of the art of bull riding, could as easily have been auditioning for a spot with The Village People.

Camp still flies under the radar of straight Laramie: heterosexuals didn't wink when the golden anniversary commemorative booklet of the university union featured a sailor flanked by two gamesome cowboys, circa the 1940s, with the caption "Come alongside cowboys . . . let me tell you a sea story . . ." But the rodeo rider doesn't need to *know* he's a gay icon for such things to tinge his identity, any more than he needs to know he's a Western icon. He grows up on a ranch but takes a degree in civil engineering, forsaking the land but not the culture. His children then trade in the heels and pointy toes for something else, or they affect the look but with a suspect authenticity. Their grandfathers' world is still theirs as well, but now only in nostalgia.

The cowboy was not part of Wyoming's conscious image until after he had ceased to exist in the form later to be romanticized. In 1889, the governor's appeals for statehood contained none of the heroic references advertised on the front of the Cowboy Saloon; instead, he imagined Wyoming as a magnet for industrial capital, a dream that would not be fully abandoned by state planners until 1997. As detailed by Frieda Knobloch, a UW professor of American Studies, the state's history in this regard can be read as a continual longing to be what it is not: anticipation that vast oil and mineral reserves would issue forth factory towns like those in the East; then advancement of the Wild West as a tourist attraction just as the enclosure of the open range was complete. Central to the latter project were artists from the East—Frederic Remington, Owen Wister—whose work was financed or seized upon by local promoters. By 1922 the governor was urging citizens to put on "four-gallon hats" for the benefit of Eastern experience-seekers at the state's Frontier Days celebration. In 1939, even as the Department of Commerce and Industry was lobbying investors with forecasts of a manufacturing dawn, its head man was again reminding locals to dress up as cowboys to "give our guests what they want."

Perhaps some in Laramie bridled so at the presence of the national press on the Shepard case not only out of their own defensiveness and justified outrage at reporters' arrogance—jamming the door when Henderson's grandmother declined to comment, blustering over being barred from the courtroom even though they never reserved seats, mistaking cottonwoods for oaks—but also because of some deep vibrations of that old tradition of outside gawking and self-exploitation. A heterosexual lawyer named Tony Lopez chatted with me for a long time but nevertheless let me know, "This is home, and you're an uninvited guest."

Now in front of the small ranches on the edge of Laramie, the third vehicle might be a school bus, which the rancher drives to make $300, $400 a month in the off-season. No small spread survives just on cattle; in fewer than ten years the price of a calf has fallen from well over a dollar to sixty cents a pound. The profit margin for these ranches, never fantastic, according to Brett Moline, the University Agricultural Cooperative Extension educator for Albany County, is now "squeezed so tight one financial mistake can be enough to wipe you out." Most ranch owners are in their late fifties or early sixties; younger ones have either inherited the land or are carrying so much debt from buying that they won't be in business long. Without a lot of money to live on and huge assets all tied up in land, the only way to realize the value of what they have is to sell it—usually to housing developers or to out-of-state gentility, who might pay three times the land's worth to set up what Moline calls their "ranchette."

Wyoming, with 480,000 people, still has the lowest population density in the country, and where there's space there is a kind of freedom. The state has no income tax, no motorcycle-helmet law, no law against openly carrying a gun, no open-container law on the interstates (meaning you can drink without worry unless you're drunk); there's a seat-belt law, but it's not enforced (police take $5 off the fine for another violation—say, speeding—if you're buckled up); until last year children didn't have to go to school before the age of seven and didn't have to stay in school past the eighth grade; unless there's a weapon involved, Laramie police say they prefer wrestling a suspect to the ground to other kinds of force, and in ten years they have killed only one civilian.

"COME ALONGSIDE COWBOYS . . ."

"This is the last frontier," says Laramie police officer Mike Ernst, with a curl in his voice. After the university, the government is the biggest employer, and after the bars, the most striking commercial establishments are bookstores and restaurants and, near UW, the fast-food strip. On the fringes of town rise some enormous houses, and elsewhere some people have no running water or refrigeration, so the soup kitchen substitutes peanut butter for meat in takeaway lunches in summer. Most, though, live in bungalows in town, trailers and suburban houses a bit farther out. Except for Mountain Cement and the sawmills, there's little manufacturing work, mostly only retail and service jobs, maid work at the motels, short-order cooking and rig washing out at the truck stops, telemarketing for the hippie kids, and temp work from construction to computers, but none of that pays more than $8 an hour.

McKinney and Henderson were roofers. Construction has a short season in Wyoming, intensifying even normally intense work. An eight-hour day can stretch into ten or twelve hours of fitting a shingle, banging a hammer, fitting and banging and banging bent over, on a grade, on your knees—bang, bang, bang. "I hurt a lot every day. I'm only twenty-one," Brent Jones told me. "My back shouldn't hurt." Jones works for a competing roofing company. "It's not bad if you use a nail gun, but if you use a hammer—eight hours of that and you can't even turn a doorknob . . . You just work through the pain. Sometimes you take a bunch of Advil. You go to bed at night and just pray that when you wake up you don't hurt so much."

Sometimes you drink—"booze, the cause of an answer to all of life's problems," in Jones's crisp phrase. Drinking is a pleasure in its own way in Laramie and a curse in all of the usual ways. Officer Ernst said that if alcohol somehow disappeared, Laramie wouldn't need three quarters of its police force. *The Boomerang's* daily police blotter is dominated by DUI and "domestic disturbance" calls, and not by coincidence. News of murder is rare, but it's ugly. In the year before Matthew Shepard was killed, fifteen-year-old Daphne Sulk was found naked in the snow, dead from seventeen stab wounds; eight-year-old Kristin Lamb, while away visiting her grandparents in the town of Powell, was kidnapped, raped, and thrown into the garbage in a duffel bag. No one calls those hate crimes. Just as six years ago no one called it a hate crime when the body of a gay UW professor, Steve Heyman, was found dumped by the side of a road in Colorado. Law enforcement and university administrators alike simply forgot that murder. After hearing of Shepard's beating, State Senator Craig Thomas declared, "It's the most violent, barbaric thing I've ever heard of happening in Wyoming."

ON THE FRINGES OF LARAMIE
Photograph by Ted Wood

There are 14,869 women in Albany County, according to the 1990 census, and 1,059 extra men. Stefani Farris at the SAFE Project, a haven and advocacy center for people who've been abused or sexually assaulted, said she thought "people in this town would be spinning if they knew how many times women were beaten by a husband or boyfriend." The state recorded 163 incidents of domestic violence in the county in 1997, nine rapes, and ninety-nine aggravated assaults. In its 1997–98 report, though, SAFE records 3,958 phone calls, almost all from women, reporting battering, stalking, sexual assault, and other physical or emotional hurts, almost all committed by men. It notes 1,569 face-to-face sessions; 1,118 individuals served; 164 individuals sheltered for 2,225 total days. SAFE can't spend much time analyzing perpetrators, Farris explained. "When you see that women are being battered, their children are being abused, their pets are being killed, you see a woman who comes in and we've seen three other women before come in who were in the same situation with the same guy—it's hard to have any sympathy for what the man went through."

The court remands some batterers to the ADAM Program at the Southeast Wyoming Mental Health Center for reeducation, but the project's director, Ed Majors, says that all he can deal with is behavior. "I can't find a dime for services, [so] the deep issues are still not addressed. If you eat chocolate and use Clearasil, you're still going to have problems."

Such as?

"When it's fear or hurt, which is typically the primary emotion at work, when you can't say, 'I'm scared shitless,' most hurt and fear will come out in the only vehicle men are allowed. It comes out crooked. It looks like anger, it's expressed as anger, but it isn't."

> *"Here's a joke for you," an amiable guy offered: "What do you get when you play a country song backward? You get your car back, you get your dog back, you get your house back, you get your wife back . . .*
>
> *"Here's another one: You can have sex with a sheep in Wyoming, just don't tie the shepherd to the fence . . . Oh, God, now you're gonna think I'm an inbred redneck asshole."*

There was no trial for Russell Henderson in the end, so what drama his story could arouse had to be fit into one early-April hearing. According to his testimony, Henderson had disagreed when McKinney suggested robbing Shepard, but when they all left the bar, McKinney said drive, and he drove. McKinney said go past Wal-Mart, and he proceeded; stop the car, and he stopped; get the rope, and he got it; tie his hands, and he tied them. Henderson never hit Shepard, he said. "I told him [McKinney] to stop hitting him, that I think he's had enough." McKinney, in this account, then hit Henderson, who retreated into the truck. Finally, again McKinney said drive, and Henderson drove.

Henderson offered nothing more. How is it that Shepard left the bar with them? Why did they beat him? Why were they going to 7th Street—supposedly to rob Shepard's house—when he lived on 12th? Why did they fight with Morales and Herrera? When Henderson and Pasley and Price drove to Cheyenne to throw away the bloody clothes, why didn't they take McKinney and little Cameron with them and keep on going? Such questions have to wait for McKinney.

At the hearing Henderson looked like a man numb from combat as Cal Rerucha and Wyatt Skaggs—men whose names appear on court documents involving Henderson since childhood—went through the legal motions, as Judy Shepard told the court of Matthew's sweetness and ambition, of his mounting achievements, of the horror of his last days, and the depth of her loss; as Henderson's grandmother, Lucy Thompson, the woman who raised him, told of his own sweetness and disappointments, of his expectations for his GEDs, of the inexplicability of his actions and the breadth of her grief. When Russell told the Shepards, "There is not a moment that goes by that I don't see what happened that night," he spoke as one does of a bad dream half-remembered, hopeless to resurrect the rest. When Mrs. Shepard told him, "At times, I don't think you're worthy of an acknowledgement of your existence," he did not flinch. In a proceeding marked by sobs and tears suppressed, the only figure who flinched less was Mr. Shepard.

Henderson was transferred to the Wyoming State Penitentiary: The word around town, originating with a prison guard, was that the inmates had held an auction, or perhaps it was a lottery, for his services and those of McKinney. Prosecutor Rerucha says he expects the only time Henderson will leave the pen is as a corpse for burial. Only death would have been a harsher sentence. The tumbrels are rolling for McKinney.

It should be easier for the state to cast McKinney's trial as a contest between good and evil: to caricature Shepard as a child-saint, because to think of him as a man evokes a sexual experience no one wants to know; and to caricature McKinney as a devil-man, because to think of him as Laramie's, or anyone's, child sits harder on the conscience. In this respect, Henderson's was the more difficult case, because from the beginning he emerged as that stock character in the country's rerun violent drama—a quiet boy, kept to himself, "the most American kid you can get," in the words of his landlord.

Judy Shepard told *Vanity Fair*, "I believe there are people who have no souls," and others have told me they believe some people are just "born bad," but Russell Henderson was born like any child of a young mother in bad trouble—premature, sickly, poisoned by the alcohol in her blood. Cindy Dixon was nineteen when she had Russell, and, as Wyatt Skaggs remembers, "she was the sweetest, most considerate, loving person when she wasn't drinking; when she was drinking, she was abusive, obnoxious, every single adjective you could think of for an intoxicated person." On January 3, 1999, at forty, she was found dead in the snow about eight and a half miles from town. Early reports had her somehow losing her way after leaving the bars on foot, in light clothing, on a night so frigid and blustery that Elam Timothy and his boyfriend turned back while driving on the road where she'd be found. The death was later determined a homicide: Dixon was bruised, her underwear torn, there was evidence of semen; and now a Florida man, Dennis Menefee, is on trial for her murder. Somehow the fact that Russell lost a mother—and Mrs. Thompson, a daughter—through another murder, a sex crime, never counted for much in all the stories about Laramie.

"I don't like my place in this town," Henderson said to an old girlfriend, Shaundra Arcuby, not long before Shepard's murder. "Part of it," she said, "had to do with his mom and what people said about her. The thing about this town is that who you are is kind of set in stone. It's not that easy to remake yourself."

Shaundra fell in love with Russell when they both were in high school (he a sophomore, she a senior) and worked at Taco Bell. She was confused about an old boyfriend, who was bullying her to get back with him. "Do what makes you happy," Russell said. "That was the winning point with me," she recalled. "Someone's giving me an ultimatum and someone's telling me to be happy—there was no

INSIDE THE FIRESIDE BAR
Photograph by Chris Anderson/Aurora

question what I'd choose." They'd hang out, watch movies; he always came to the door, spoke to her mom. He made her tapes—Pearl Jam, The Violent Femmes. They went to her prom; friends thought they'd get married. Then she dumped him: "I was the first female in my family to graduate high school and not be pregnant," she said. "I just couldn't think of marriage. It scared me, so I ran away." Not long after, she'd get married, disastrously, and then divorce.

Most of the guys who knew McKinney in high school didn't know Henderson— "he was a little too good." He collected comic books and baseball cards, loved scouting, even beyond making Eagle Scout. He pumped gas, fiddled with an old Corvair. He played soccer—the "fag sport," as it's known. He had fantasies of being a doctor but was headed for Wyoming Technical Institute for mechanics until he was told, days before he was to celebrate high school graduation, that he wouldn't get a diploma because he'd missed a paper. He was prayerful in the Mormon tradition. About homosexuality, Lucy Thompson says, he believed "everyone has a right to their own free agency." Until he was fifteen he helped Lucy with the dialysis machine that kept his beloved grandfather alive, and watched as his life drained away. Bill Thompson never let on how he suffered. Neither did Russell. "He never ever talked about the hurt that was inside him," Lucy told me. "He'd say, 'That's okay, Grandma; don't worry, Grandma.' " She told the court, "When my husband and his grandfather passed away, so did a part of Russell."

Brent Jones remembers Henderson as "kind of an asshole," less of a troublemaker than McKinney but "his elevator didn't go to the top floor either." He had some juvie trouble. A judge once told Cindy Dixon she'd have to choose between Russell and her boyfriend. She was not in good shape that day and said, "Oh, that's easy," with an approving gesture toward the boyfriend.

It's said that over the past forty years Lucy Thompson has raised half the kids in Laramie. She is a woman of profound serenity. Russell was in his grandparents' care from his birth to the age of five, when they thought he should be in the nuclear family. Cindy was married then, with two little girls. Three and a half years later the Thompsons again got custody. In the intervening period, Russell took a physical and emotional battering from his mother's partners. Years of police reports follow Cindy's own familiarity with violence. Once Russell told his grandparents about a harrowing beating he had watched his mother endure. Why didn't he call them? "When that happens, I just freeze, and when I do something about it, I just get retaliation," Lucy remembers him saying.

The standard description of Henderson is that "he was a follower." At work, though, he was the leader, says Joe Lemus of Laramie Valley Roofing. Both boys are nice, friendly people. Sure, they'd talk *fag, wuss, sissy,* Lemus says. "In grade school, you call people *fat, stupid.* When you get older, this is just what you say; it's like calling someone a *retard.*" Everybody does it, even college kids (one of whom scratched KILL THEM under the title of the UW library's copy of *How to Make the World a Better Place for Gays and Lesbians*), even the straight-boy cub reporter at *The Boomerang* who helped cover the case before becoming an intern at *Rolling Stone.* According to police accounts, when McKinney and Henderson came upon Morales and Herrera, it was Henderson who called them "fucking bitches." "Why the fuck are you calling us bitches?" Morales answered, and McKinney hit him from behind. Police Commander David O'Malley testified that in questioning Henderson about the fight, Officer Flint Waters said if police found someone with a bullet they'd have more to talk to him about: "Mr. Henderson laughed and said, 'I guarantee that you wouldn't find anybody with a bullet in them.'"

Lemus says that in the period leading up to the murder Henderson was downhearted; Chasity had cheated on him. McKinney was excited; he'd just bought a gun. They were working between eight and eleven hours a day. Henderson had recently turned twenty-one and was eager to go to a bar. It was new for him, though I'm told he was not a stranger to drink and had his own sources for crank as well. When he was younger, a doctor had told him that because of the circumstances of his birth, alcohol (and presumably drugs) could affect him very badly. His grandfather asked Russell if he understood what that meant. "Deeper than you think," he answered, gesturing to his mother's photograph.

> *"Certain things make sense only if you're out of your mind," a knowing woman told me. "On meth, you would know what you were doing, but in that moment it doesn't matter. We used to have the rankest, most foul sex when we were on dope. Men don't get erections too well on speed, so already that's bad, but then there's the two-hour blow job, because when you start something, you just have to finish, only you can't finish because he won't get an erection and he won't have an orgasm, and you'd really like to stop, but you just can't."*

Maybe Wyatt Skaggs is right when he says "drugs were not involved in this case," or maybe he's just being lawyerly. Rumors abound about what set that night in motion—love triangles, revenge, a mob-style debt collection. Reality is usually less baroque. Matthew Shepard smoked pot and had at least tried methamphetamine; McKinney dealt drugs and used them with Henderson; they all had a mutual acquaintance who regularly carries a police scanner, whose feigned ignorance about drugs could be matched only by an extraterrestrial, and whom every drug user I met recognizes as a link in the trade. Those things are not rumors but maybe just coincidence. And maybe Skaggs is more right when he adds, "That's not to say [meth] couldn't have been used sometime before; you don't need to take it that night to feel the effects." McKinney and Henderson never were tested for drugs, but then police say that one of the beauties of meth for the user is that there's no sure test for it.

History is one long quest for relief through chemicals, more powerful substitutes for endorphins, released when you cry so hard you run out of tears. But it is difficult to imagine a more unappetizing recipe for relief than methamphetamine. It is made from ephedrine or pseudoephedrine, extracted from over-the-counter cold and asthma medicines, then cooked up with any of a variety of agents—lye, battery acid, iodine, lantern fuel, antifreeze. A former user says it tastes like fake crab "sea legs" marinated in cat piss, but its medicinal benefits, especially for its large constituency of construction workers, is that "nothing hurts anymore; you're wide awake; you seem to accomplish what you set out to accomplish. Only later do you understand that you've been up for two days"—and that, depending on how much you smoke or snort or shoot, euphoria morphs into hallucination, which morphs into paranoia, which morphs into God knows what.

According to the state's Methamphetamine Initiative, Wyoming's eighth-graders use meth at a higher rate than twelfth-graders nationwide, and among juvenile offenders in its correctional institutions in 1997 at least 50 percent had a history of meth use. Albany County is not one of the state's top three target zones, but drug sources in Laramie volunteer that meth is everywhere. Maybe McKinney is lying and maybe he's not when he says Shepard "mouthed off," prompting him to the fatal frenzy of violence, but one crank-head told me that he once almost wasted someone just for saying hi—"You're so paranoid, you think, 'Why is he saying hi? Does he know something? Is he a cop?' " And maybe all the meth users I met were lying or wrong or putting me on in saying they immediately took the murder for a meth crime because it was all too stupid and, except for one heinous detail, all too recognizable.

None of this is a defense for what happened, but it all complicates the singular picture of hate crime. Why did they kill him? "That was the meth talking," I was told. But why did they pick on him to begin with? "Because he was a fag." So why do you think they didn't kill him because he was gay? "They were regular guys, and then they beat up the Mexicans." And, anyway, "what kind of a man beats the shit out of a wussy guy?"

Ask around for impressions of Matthew Shepard and you find as many characters as there are speakers: a charming boy, always smiling and happy; a suicidal depressive who mixed street drugs and alcohol with Effexor and Klonopin; a good listener who treated everyone with respect; "a pompous, arrogant little dick" who condescended to those who served him; a bright kid who wanted to change the world; a kid you'd swear was mentally defective; a generous person; a flasher of

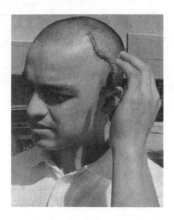

EMILIANO MORALES
Photograph by Ed Andrieski/
AP/World Wide Photos

money; a good tipper; a lousy tipper; a sexual seeker; a naif; a man freaked by his HIV status or at peace with it; a "counterphobic" who courted risk rather than live in fear; a boy who, his father said, "liked to compete against himself," entering races he couldn't win and swimming contests he'd finish "dead last by the length of the pool" just to prove he could do it; a boy never quite sure of his father's approval; a gay man; a faggot; a human being. Any one of those Matthew Shepards could have been set up for death; the only constant is that he'd still be dead, and McKinney and Henderson would still be responsible. Gay men are killed horribly everywhere in this country, more than thirty just since Shepard—one of them, in Richmond, Virginia, beheaded. Gay and straight, male and female, some 40,000 individuals have been murdered since Shepard; the only constant is that they are dead, and that most of their killers are straight and most of them are men.

Among those who advocate hate-crime laws, it's always the sexuality of the victim that's front and center, not the sexuality of the criminal or the everyday, undifferentiated violence he took to extremity. Among the tolerance peddlers, it's always the "lifestyle" of the gay guy, never the "lifestyle" of the straight guy or the culture of compulsory heterosexuality. Even among those who argue that the victim's sexuality is irrelevant—that Shepard died just because a robbery went bad or just because McKinney and Henderson were crazy on crank—the suggestion is that the crime is somehow less awful once homophobia is removed, and what is brewing inside the boys bears less attention. "The news has already taken this up and blew it totally out of proportion because it involved a homosexual," McKinney's father told the press. Eighteen blows with a .357 magnum—murder happens.

A few years ago during an exercise at Laramie High School, students were asked to list the five best things about being a boy or a girl. The boys' list noted no breasts, no period, no pregnancy, and one other scourge of femininity that the guidance counselor who told me this story had been too stunned to remember. I was at the school, flipping through yearbooks, noticing that the class of '96, Henderson's class, had identified its number two "pet peeve" as "skinny wimps who complain about jocks." The previous day, Dylan Klebold and Eric Harris had killed their classmates in Littleton, Colorado, 140 miles away. Through that crime ran a thread from every high-profile school shooting over the past two years. Springfield, Pearl, Paducah, Jonesboro, Conyers—every one of those boy murderers or would-be murderers had been taunted as a wuss, a fag, a loser, or had been rejected by a girl, or was lonely and withdrawn, or had written harrowing stories of mayhem and slaying. Two of them had killed their pets. All of it, like the meanness of the jocks some of them despised, was regarded as just boy play—Oh, Fluffy's in the trash can? Boys will be boys. And by the logic of the culture, it was just boy play, like McKinney's brawling, like Henderson's admonition out by the fence, "I think he's had enough." Only when it turned to murder did it register, and for that there's punishment, prison, the death penalty, more violence.

For any of these boys—for any boy, for that matter—what does it take to pass as a man? At Henderson's hearing, Judy Shepard memorialized the number of languages Matthew spoke, the friends he'd had and books he'd read, the countries he'd traveled, the promise life held. As she spoke the courtroom heaved with her agony. But in the story writ large, it's almost as if Matthew's death counted for more than it might have if he had been just

THE FENCE
Photograph by Reuters / Gary Caskey / Archive Photos

a wuss, a fag, her son; if he had been found in a ramble, with his pants down, with a trick (as have so many murdered gay men, whose cases have never been exploited by presidents to win points or by big, polite gay groups to raise dollars); if he had been killed simply because he was tiny and weak; if anything about the murder or its aftermath had forced a consideration of sex and freedom, instead of only tolerance and hate.

Since Shepard's death, the talk is all of hate-crime laws. But as Rita Addessa of the Lesbian and Gay Task Force in Philadelphia, who nevertheless supports such laws, admits, they "will have no impact whatsoever on addressing the causes of anti-gay violence." They matter only to the dead or the maimed, for even if Wyoming were to become the twenty-third state with a hate-crime law including anti-gay violence, and even if a federal law were to pass, the little Matt and Matty Shepards of America would still grow up learning their place, because for them in all but eleven states discrimination is legal, and everywhere equality under the law is a myth. It's said that hate-crime laws symbolize a society's values. If that is true, it means gay people are recognized only in suffering, and straight people are off the hook. It means Shepard may stand for every homosexual, but McKinney and Henderson stand just for themselves. It means nothing for life and, because its only practical function is to stiffen penalties, everything for death.

In her interview with *Vanity Fair*, Judy Shepard said she thought that her son would probably approve of the death penalty if he could know this case, if it had been his friend and not himself beaten at the fence. And in her conclusion at the hearing, she told Henderson, "My hopes for you are simple. I hope you never experience a day or night without feeling the terror, the humiliation, the helplessness, the hopelessness my son felt that night." Not just that night. As a gay man in America, Shepard must have sensed all of those things just around the corner, and not just in violence, not just in blood. Looking back on Henderson's biography, and on McKinney's, I wonder if, in different measure, they aren't already too well acquainted with such things; if perhaps the injuries of terror and humiliation aren't already too well spread around in this season of punishment and revenge.

> *"If a guy at a bar made some kind of overture to you, what would you do?"*
>
> *"It depends on who's around. If I'm with a girl, I'd be worried about what she thinks, because, as I said, everything a man does is in some*

way connected to a woman, whether he wants to admit it or not. Do I look queer? Will she tell other girls?

"*If my friends were around and they'd laugh and shit, I might have to threaten him.*

"*If I'm alone and he just wants to buy me a beer, then okay, I'm straight, you're gay—hey, you can buy me a beer.*" ■